T0318882

THE ROUTLEDGE COMPANION TO THE HISTORY OF RETAILING

Retail history is a rich, cross-disciplinary field that demonstrates the centrality of retailing to many aspects of human experience, from the provisioning of everyday goods to the shaping of urban environments; from earning a living to the construction of identity. Over the last few decades, interest in the history of retail has increased greatly, spanning centuries, extending to all areas of the globe and drawing on a range of disciplinary perspectives.

By offering an up-to-date, comprehensive thematic, spatial and chronological coverage of the history of retailing, this Companion goes beyond traditional narratives that are too simplistic and Euro-centric and offers a vibrant survey of this field.

It is divided into four broad sections: 1) Contexts, 2) Spaces and places, 3) People, processes and practices and 4) Geographical variations. Chapters are written in an analytical and synthetic manner, accessible to the general reader as well as challenging for specialists, and with an international perspective.

This volume is an important resource to a wide range of readers, including marketing and management specialists, historians, geographers, economists, sociologists and urban planners.

Jon Stobart is Professor of History at Manchester Metropolitan University. His research ranges across a wide variety of topics relating to retailing and consumption in England during the long eighteenth century.

Vicki Howard is a Lecturer at the University of Essex and author of *From Main Street to Mall: The Rise and Fall of the American Department Store*, which won the Hagley Prize in Business History.

They are co-editors of the Taylor & Francis journal, *History of Retailing and Consumption*.

ROUTLEDGE COMPANIONS IN BUSINESS, MANAGEMENT AND ACCOUNTING

Routledge Companions in Business, Management and Accounting are prestige reference works providing an overview of a whole subject area or sub-discipline. These books survey the state of the discipline including emerging and cutting edge areas. Providing a comprehensive, up to date, definitive work of reference, Routledge Companions can be cited as an authoritative source on the subject.

A key aspect of these Routledge Companions is their international scope and relevance. Edited by an array of highly regarded scholars, these volumes also benefit from teams of contributors which reflect an international range of perspectives.

Individually, Routledge Companions in Business, Management and Accounting provide an impactful one-stop-shop resource for each theme covered. Collectively, they represent a comprehensive learning and research resource for researchers, postgraduate students and practitioners.

Published titles in this series include:

THE ROUTLEDGE COMPANION TO MANAGEMENT BUYOUTS
Edited by Mike Wright, Kevin Amess, Nick Bacon and Donald Siegel

THE ROUTLEDGE COMPANION TO CO-OPETITION STRATEGIES
Edited by Anne-Sophie Fernandez, Paul Chiambaretto. Frédéric Le Roy and Wojciech Czakon

THE ROUTLEDGE COMPANION TO REWARD MANAGEMENT
Edited by Stephen J. Perkins

THE ROUTLEDGE COMPANION TO ACCOUNTING IN CHINA
Edited by Haiyan Zhou

THE ROUTLEDGE COMPANION TO CRITICAL MARKETING
Edited by Mark Tadajewski, Matthew Higgins, Janice Denegri Knott and Rohit Varman

THE ROUTLEDGE COMPANION TO THE HISTORY OF RETAILING
Edited by Jon Stobart and Vicki Howard

For more information about this series, please visit: www.routledge.com/Routledge-Companions-in-Business-Management-and-Accounting/book-series/RCBMA

THE ROUTLEDGE COMPANION TO THE HISTORY OF RETAILING

Edited by Jon Stobart and Vicki Howard

LONDON AND NEW YORK

First published 2019
by Routledge

2 Park Square, Milton Park, Abingdon, Oxfordshire OX14 4RN
52 Vanderbilt Avenue, New York, NY 10017

Routledge is an imprint of the Taylor & Francis Group, an informa business

First issued in paperback 2020

British Library Cataloguing-in-Publication Data
A catalogue record for this book is available from the British Library

Library of Congress Cataloging-in-Publication Data
Names: Stobart, Jon, 1966– editor. | Howard, Vicki, 1965– editor.
Title: The Routledge companion to the history of retailing / edited by Jon Stobart and Vicki Howard.
Description: Abingdon, Oxon ; New York, NY : Routledge, 2019. |
Series: Routledge companions in business, management and accounting |
Includes bibliographical references and index. |
Identifiers: LCCN 2018023990 (print) | LCCN 2018025760 (ebook) |
ISBN 9781315560854 | ISBN 9781138675087 (hardback)
Subjects: LCSH: Retail trade—History.
Classification: LCC HF5429 (ebook) | LCC HF5429 .R68 2019 (print) |
DDC 381/.109—dc23
LC record available at https://lccn.loc.gov/2018023990

ISBN: 978-1-138-67508-7 (hbk)
ISBN: 978-0-367-65607-2 (pbk)

Typeset in Bembo
by Apex CoVantage, LLC

CONTENTS

FIGURES

TABLES

CONTRIBUTORS

Bruno Blondé is Professor at the History Department of the University of Antwerp, where in 2003 he founded the Centre for Urban History. His major research interests include the history of transportation, economic growth sand social inequality, material culture, retail and consumption in the Low Countries (fifteenth–nineteenth century). With Ilja Van Damme, he is writing a new synthesis on the material culture of Antwerp.

Christopher Dyer is Emeritus Professor of History at the University of Leicester, and he previously taught at the Universities of Edinburgh and Birmingham. He has been President of the Society for Medieval Archaeology and Editor of the *Economic History Review*. His books include *Making a Living in the Middle Ages* (Yale University Press), *An Age of Transition?* (Oxford University Press) and *A Country Merchant. Trading and Farming at the End of the Middle Ages* (Oxford University Press).

Fiona Ellis-Chadwick is Senior Lecturer in Retail Management at Loughborough University. She had a successful commercial career in retail management before becoming an academic. She has worked on projects in digital marketing; online retail management and the digital high street and is published in the *Journal of Business Research, European Journal of Marketing, International Journal of Retail Distribution and Management, Internet Research* and *Journal of Retailing and Consumer Services*.

Sarah Elvins is Associate Professor of History at the University of Manitoba, where she teaches courses in American history. She is the author of *Sales and Celebrations: Retailing and Regional Identity in Western New York State, 1920–1940* and articles about the history of Depression scrip and cross-border shopping. Her research explores consumption, retailing, food and culture in the modern United States.

Omar Foda is a historian of the modern Middle East. He has published in *Arab Media and Society*, the *International Journal of Middle East Studies*, *Social Sciences and Missions* and in several volumes, including *The Birth of the Arab Citizen and the Changing of the Middle East*. Currently the Middle East and North Africa Librarian at George Washington University, he is working on his monograph *Grand Plans in Glass Bottles: Making, Drinking, and Selling Beer in a Changing Egypt 1880–Present.*

Laurence Fontaine is Senior Researcher in the CNRS attached to the Center Maurice Halbwachs (CNRS-ENS-EHESS). She was professor at the History and Civilisation department of the European University Institute (Florence-Italy) from 1995 to 2003. Her most recent publications include *Alternative Exchanges: Second-Hand Circulations from the Sixteenth Century to The Present,* L. Fontaine (ed.), Berghahn, Oxford, 2008; *The Moral Economy. Poverty, Credit and Thrust in Early Modern Europe*, Cambridge University Press 2014 [Gallimard: 2008] and *Le Marché. Histoire et usage d'une conquête sociale*, Paris Gallimard, 2014.

Rika Fujioka is Professor of Macro-marketing at Kansai University. She was an associate of the Oxford Institute of Retail Management and held visiting positions at University of Oxford and Erasmus University. Her recent publications include: 'European luxury big business and emerging Asian markets, 1960–2010', *Business History* (2015, edited with Pierre-Yves Donzé), *Comparative Responses to Globalization: Experiences of British and Japanese Enterprises,* (Palgrave Macmillan, 2013, edited with Maki Umemura) and *Global Luxury: Organizational Change and Emerging Markets since the 1970s*, (Palgrave Macmillan, 2018, edited with Pierre-Yves Donze).

Sergi Garriga is an architect and researcher in the theory and history of architecture. He has been awarded a scholarship to develop his doctoral thesis at the Polytechnic University of Catalonia on the contemporary renovation of the Barcelona markets. His subjects of interest have been developed around the changing relationships between architecture, the urban form and its historical contexts.

Manel Guàrdia is Professor of Urban History at the Vallès Higher Technical School of Architecture of the Polytechnic University of Catalonia. His most recent books include: M. Guàrdia, J.L. Oyón, *Memòria del mercat del Born*, El Born CCM, Barcelona, 2017; M. Guàrdia, J.L. Oyón (eds), *Making Cities through Market Halls. Europe, 19th and 20th Centuries*, MUHBA, Barcelona, 2015; and J.L. Oyón, *La ciudad en el joven Reclus. Hacia la fusión naturaleza-ciudad*, Ediciones del Viaducto, Barcelona 2018.

Stephen Halebsky is Associate Professor in the department of Sociology and Anthropology at State University of New York, Cortland. He is the author of *Small Towns and Big Business: Challenging Wal-Mart Superstores* (Lexington Books, 2009) as well as articles on the politics of retail development, the effect of chain stores on their local economies and the modern corporation. He received his Ph.D. from the University of Wisconsin.

Mary Hilson is Professor of History at Aarhus University. Her publications include: *The International Co-operative Alliance and the Consumer Co-operative Movement in Northern Europe, c. 1860–1940* (Manchester University Press, 2018); *Co-operatives and the Social Question: The Co-operative Movement in Northern and Eastern Europe 1880–1950*, edited with Pirjo Markkola and Ann-Catrin Östman (Welsh Academic Press, 2012) and *A Global History of Consumer Co-operation since 1850* with Silke Neunsinger and Greg Patmore (Brill, 2017).

Marjorie L. Hilton is Associate Professor of History at Murray State University in Murray, Kentucky (USA). The author of *Selling to the Masses: Retailing in Russia, 1880–1930* (2012), she has also published articles on Soviet advertising and gendered cinematic representations of the ideological rivalry between capitalism and communism in the 1930s. She is currently researching the re-opening of the State Department Store (GUM), following Stalin's death in 1953.

Vicki Howard is Visiting Fellow in the history department at the University of Essex. She is the author of two monographs published by University of Pennsylvania Press: *Brides, Inc. American Weddings and the Business of Tradition* (2006) and *From Main Street to Mall: The Rise and Fall of the American Department Store* (2015), winner of the Hagley Prize in Business History. She is currently editing the *Cultural History of Shopping, 1920–present* forthcoming with Bloomsbury and is co-editor of the Routledge journal, *History of Retailing and Consumption.*

David Delbert Kruger is Agricultural and Business Research Librarian at the University of Wyoming in Laramie, Wyoming. He has published two award-winning articles on the history of J. C. Penney stores in the United States as well as a recent book *J. C. Penney: The Man, the Store, and American Agriculture* through the University of Oklahoma Press.

Bettina Liverant is Adjunct Assistant Professor in the Department of History at the University of Calgary, Canada. Liverant has a degree in architecture as well as a Ph.D. in Canadian intellectual history. She has written extensively on Canadian consumer society, on corporate philanthropy and on architecture for both academic and general audiences. Her most recent publication is *Buying Happiness: The Emergence of Consumer Consciousness in English Canada* (University of British Columbia Press, 2018).

Richard Longstreth is Professor of American Studies, Emeritus, at George Washington University, where he taught from 1983 to 2018. He is author of many works, including *Looking Beyond the Icons: Midcentury Architecture, Landscape and Urbanism* (University of Virginia Press, 2015) and *The American Department Store Transformed, 1920–1960* (Yale University Press, 2010) His *City Center to Regional Mall* (1997) and *The Drive-In, the Supermarket, and the Transformation of Commercial Space* (MIT Press, 1999) won four national awards in the fields of architectural history, urban history and historic preservation.

Harada Masami completed the doctoral programme in commercial science from Doshisha University, in 1988. He became an associate professor of the Faculty of Economics at Fukui Prefectural University in 1992 and became a professor of the Faculty and the Graduate School at Fukui Prefectural University in 1996. He took his doctorate in Economics at Kyoto University in 1993. He has been a representative of the Market History Society (Sijo-shi Kenkyu-kai) and a director of Socio-Economic History Society (Shakai-Keizashi Gakkai) since 2015.

Douglas McCalla is University Professor Emeritus, Department of History, the University of Guelph, where he formerly held the Canada Research Chair in Rural History. His books include *Consumers in the Bush: Shopping in Rural Upper Canada* (McGill-Queen's University Press, 2015) and *Planting the Province: The Economic History of Upper Canada, 1784–1870* (University of Toronto Press, 1993). His articles include the memoir, 'A World Through Commerce: Explorations in Upper Canada (and Beyond)' (*Canadian Historical Review*, 97: 2 [June 2016], 244–71).

Dale Miller is Adjunct Senior Lecturer in the Department of Marketing, Griffith University. Dr. Miller's research on branding and retailing appears in the *Journal of Historical Research in*

Marketing, Journal of Retailing and Consumer Services, the International Journal of Retail & Distribution Management, Journal of Business Research, European Journal of Marketing and *Journal of Brand Management*. She is joint winner of the 2013 Stanley Hollander Best Paper Award at the 2013 CHARM Conference, Copenhagen.

Ian Mitchell is Honorary Research Fellow at the Centre for Historical Research, University of Wolverhampton, UK. After graduating from Oxford University, he worked for two government departments, and then as a Church of England minister. On his retirement from full-time ministry, he returned to his long-standing interest in the history of retailing and consumption in England in the period 1700–1850. His book, *Tradition and Innovation in English Retailing, 1700–1850: Narratives of Consumption* was published by Ashgate in 2014.

Silke Neunsinger is Associate Professor in economic history and Director of Research at the Labour Movement Archives and Library in Stockholm. She has recently edited a number of volumes, amongst them together with Dirk Hoerder and Elise van Nederveen Meerkerk, *Towards a Global History of Domestic and Caregiving Workers* (Brill, 2015); together with Mary Hilson and Iben Vyff, *Labour Unions and Politics under the North Star. The Nordic Countries 1700–2000* (Berghahn, 2017) and together with Mary Hilson and Greg Patmore, *A Global History of Consumer Co-operation since 1850* (Brill, 2017).

Daniel Opler is Associate Professor and Chair of History at the College of Mount Saint Vincent in the Bronx, New York. His primary research interests include the overlap of class, gender and radical politics in twentieth-century New York City. His book, *For All White-Collar Workers: The Possibilities of Radicalism in New York City's Department Store Unions, 1934–1953*, was published by Ohio State University Press in 2007. He is currently working on a study of radicalism and American composers in 1930s America.

José Luis Oyón is Professor of Urban History at the Vallès Higher Technical School of Architecture of the Polytechnic University of Catalonia. His most recent books include: M. Guàrdia, J.L. Oyón, *Memòria del mercat del Born*, El Born CCM, Barcelona, 2017; M. Guàrdia, J.L. Oyón (eds), *Making Cities through Market Halls. Europe, 19th and 20th Centuries*, MUHBA, Barcelona, 2015; and J.L. Oyón, *La ciudad en el joven Reclus. Hacia la fusión naturaleza-ciudad*, Ediciones del Viaducto, Barcelona 2018.

Greg Patmore is Professor Emeritus of Business and Labour History and Chair of the Business and Labour History Group and the Co-operative Research Group in the University of Sydney Business School. He is currently researching the history of Australian co-operatives, and the history of the Berkeley Consumer Co-operative. His publications include: *A Global History of Co-operative Business* (2018, with Nikola Balnave), *Worker Voice: Employee Representation in the Workplace in Australia, Canada, Germany, the UK, and the US, 1914–1939* (2016) and *Australian Labour History* (1991).

Patrick Hyder Patterson is Associate Professor in the Department of History at the University of California, San Diego. His research centres on the history of twentieth-century Eastern Europe and the Balkans, with major emphases on everyday life and consumer culture and on the interplay of Islam, Christianity and secular society. He is author of *Bought and Sold: Living and Losing the Good Life in Socialist Yugoslavia* (Cornell University Press, 2011) and numerous articles on consumer society in Eastern Europe.

Sara Pennell is Senior Lecturer in early modern British history and Programme Leader for the undergraduate History programmes at the University of Greenwich. Her most recent book, *The Birth of the English Kitchen, 1600–1850* (Bloomsbury, 2016), combines these concerns. At the moment, she is working on two very different projects: a biography of a seventeenth-century woman writer of domestic manuals; and a cultural history of domestic mobility in England.

Martin Purvis is Senior Lecturer in Geography at the University of Leeds. He has a long-standing interest in the history and geography of retailing in Britain and continental Europe. Martin's research initially explored the nineteenth-century origins and development of consumers' co-operation. More recently he has published on retailing in interwar Britain, including aspects of the managerial practice of Marks and Spencer. Martin's current research focuses on retailing during the years of depression, war and austerity from the 1930s to the 1950s.

Nitin Sanghavi is Professor of Retail Marketing and Strategy at Manchester Business School. He has held senior positions in major retail and retail-related organisations in the UK and overseas and founded the MBS Retail Centre. His publications include: 'Employing Social Networking Media as a Marketing Tool in Large Emerging Markets: The Case of India', *Proceedings of* 14th International Conference of the Society for Global Business & Economic Development (2016).

Susan Spellman is Associate Professor of History at Miami University. Her research focuses on American business and capitalism in the late nineteenth and early twentieth centuries. She is the author of *Cornering the Market: Independent Grocers and Innovation in American Small Business* (Oxford University Press, 2016). She received the 2005 Russel B. Nye Award for the Outstanding Article published in the *Journal of Popular Culture.*

Howard R. Stanger is Professor in the Department of Management at Canisius College and holds an affiliated appointment in History. His research has focused on marketing, employee relations and corporate culture in the United States. He has written about employers' associations in the commercial printing industry and labour relations in the newspaper and digital media industries. Stanger holds degrees from Queens College (CUNY), Rutgers University and Ohio State University.

Jon Stobart is Professor of History at Manchester Metropolitan University. His research ranges across a wide variety of topics relating to retailing and consumption in England during the long eighteenth century. These include the grocery trade, village shops, the sale of second-hand goods, and country houses as sites of consumption. His most recent books are two edited collections: *A Taste for Luxury in Early Modern Europe* (Bloomsbury, 2016 – with Johanna Ilmakunnas) and *Travel and the British Country House* (Manchester University Press, 2016). He is currently working on a project which explores comfort in the eighteenth-century country house.

Ilja Van Damme is Professor in Urban History at the University of Antwerp. He is the current academic director of the Centre for Urban History (CSG), and board member of the Urban Studies Institute (USI) of the University of Antwerp. His research interests relate to the late 18th- and 19th-century city as lived and spatial environment. He recently co-edited *Cities and Creativity from the Renaissance to the Present* (Routledge: London, 2017).

Martín Monsalve Zanatti is Associate Professor at Universidad del Pacífico and President of the Universidad del Pacifico Press. His most recent publications include: *Regional Elites in Peru in a Context of Fiscal Boom: Arequipa, Cusco, Piura y San Martín, 2000–2013* (co-author with Paula Muñoz et al.) and Evolution of the Peruvian large family business, 1896–2012 in Paloma Fernández Pérez and Andrea Lluch (editors), *Evolution of Family Business: Continuity and Change in Latin America and Spain.*

1

INTRODUCTION

Global perspectives on retailing

I. Introduction

The digital age has severed retail's historic ties to geography and place. Shoppers have turned to their smart phones and computers to purchase everyday items like food and clothing as well as luxury goods and personal services. Internet commerce is now a global challenge to the so-called brick-and-mortar retailer. On both sides of the Atlantic, historic retail firms have gone under, whilst many others are struggling to compete in the new environment. By many accounts, the High Street is in crisis in the United Kingdom, indicated by declining footfall of shoppers in central business districts and by store closures. Concerns over the displacement of the High Street economy in the UK have spurred numerous studies and hopeful plans for redevelopment (Portas, 2011; Wrigley, 2015). In the United States, a country with much more retail space per person than Europe, "dead malls" have become a well-known phenomenon (Europe's Retail Market, 2017). Although a global trend, e-commerce has diffused across national markets in varying degrees: in the United States, it hovered between 9% and 10% of total retail sales in 2017; Great Britain saw online sales hit 16.5% of total retail sales in January 2018, yet China dwarfed this, accounting for 40% of total e-commerce spending globally. Every nation has experienced growth and disruption in this sector, signalling another retail revolution is upon us (Statistical Bulletin, 2018; Quarterly Retail, 2018). While the future is not foreseeable, it is safe to say that recent trends are unprecedented in their global reach. Industry observers have described a "retail apocalypse", seeing the end of traditional face-to-face modes of selling in a physical setting. The rise of e-commerce, which is less labour intensive by nature, has negatively affected retail employment opportunities as well. Amazon might employ more than half a million people, but these are lean numbers in relation to the firm's value. Currently the world's third most valuable company, its market capitalisation stands at more than $702 billion at the beginning of 2018 and its founder, Jeff Bezos, is the richest person in the world (Carr, 2018).

This revolutionary commercial landscape calls for a reconsideration of the general history of retailing. Retail has never been static, as the chapters in this volume amply demonstrate, and lessons for the present can be learned from the past. Just to take the United States as an example, current concerns over retail monopoly and the effect of bigness on small business enterprise can be seen to have a long history. Nineteenth-century American department stores were the Walmarts of their era, posing a threat to single-line merchants who were unable to complete with their low prices. Mail order firms like Sears and Montgomery Ward reached rural markets as never before with their general merchandise catalogues and subsidised distribution, undercutting small retailers in the same manner as Amazon. Chain stores undersold independents which instigated a successful movement in the interwar period to tax and regulate away their economies of scale. After World War II, American branch department stores in the suburbs began to undercut downtown sales, damaging urban centres. And, by the late twentieth century, discounters and big-box stores overtook them all. In the past, such retail developments were geographically confined: their effects limited to local, regional, and in some cases national markets. Place shaped the identity, practice and success of retail firms throughout most of its history. In the computer era, however, this is less the case. But, although the Internet age has collapsed time and space, allowing unprecedented market access for a diverse range of entrepreneurs and firms, the chapters in this volume demonstrate how different national contexts continue to play an important role in shaping retail traditions and practices.

Despite recent threats to the survival of traditional retailing, the industry is still a vital part of the early twenty-first century economy. In the UK, the retail sector as a whole contributed just over 11% of total economic output in 2016 and was the largest private sector employer (The Retail Industry, 2017). Wholesaling and retail combined were the second largest employer in the EU, after manufacturing, constituting 13% of the labour force (Retail and Wholesale, 2014). And across the Atlantic, retail employed roughly 16 million people in the United States at the beginning of 2018 and contributed $2.6 trillion to the nation's GDP (Current Employment, 2018; Economic Impact, 2018). Brick and mortar retailing remains a central feature of the commercial landscape, the physical place where everyday business is conducted and the ordinary experience of life goes on. Whether located on UK High Streets, American Main Streets, in open-air street markets or in privately developed shopping complexes and malls, it provides the public space that creates communities.

And it has done so for a long time. Indeed, we might argue that retail history tracks the evolution of human societies and their economic activity, which makes it surprising that scholarship has often been quite narrowly defined. Previous histories of retailing have followed national lines or tracked the evolution of different retail formats, such as public markets, shopping malls, or department stores. In this *Companion to the History of Retailing*, the authors draw on their disciplinary specialties, but were tasked to bridge national divides wherever possible. As a result, some key influences and processes are revealed. Western retailing practices, for instance, shaped business enterprise and shopping experiences the world over, but local and regional differences are also shown to have persisted or in some cases, created interesting hybrid forms. A longer perspective has also shaped the picture of change over time, with strong continuities being identified and new periodisations suggested. Previous scholarly works have focused on the consumer revolution or the rise of modern mass retailing, but what comes from our longer chronological view and global perspective is a messier, more interesting history.

II. Approaches

Retail history is a rich, cross-disciplinary field that demonstrates the centrality of retailing to many aspects of human experience, from the provisioning of everyday goods to the shaping of urban environments; from earning a living to the construction of identity. This diversity is reflected in the broad range of disciplines that contribute to retail history, including economics, business, labour, architectural and social and cultural history, historical geography, marketing and management studies and urban planning. This diversity is a real strength, making the study of retail history a vibrant and constantly changing field of enquiry: each discipline brings its owns perspectives and concerns, asking a different set of questions, and each writes retail history in a different way. Diverse sources are drawn on to reconstruct the spaces, dynamics and practices of retailing: architectural historians might use plans, designs and the extant fabric of the city, whereas economists utilise statistics of sales, wages and the like, and business historians draw on the records of individual companies. These different sources reflect different methodologies: the quantification and model building of economists, for example, or the case studies and "thick descriptions" of social historians.

Such diversity is underscored by the different approaches and timeframes considered by historians in different countries. To caricature: American scholars tend to focus on the emergence of big business in the nineteenth and twentieth centuries, whereas those in Europe also examine medieval and early modern retailing, and are more concerned with a diversity of retail forms (Strasser, 1989; Leach, 1993). More subtly, definitions of key institutions (such as department stores) can vary, as can the relative importance of issues such as race or the role of central and local government in retail regulation (Benson, 1986; Howard, 2015; Monod, 1996). This disciplinary and national diversity is readily apparent in this volume, bringing to it a range of voices and perspectives that illustrate the varied ways in which retail history is studied and written. For instance, the discussion of itinerant tradesmen, written by the French social historian, Laurence Fontaine, is very different in style from Nitin Sanghavi's account of the retail history of India, which reflects the perspective and priorities of business management. Yet both, and all the other contributions to this volume, offer rich and varied insights in the many facets of retail history. Indeed, this diversity enriches our understanding of retail history in its many forms.

Uniting these different perspectives and approaches is a broad consensus around the overall narrative of retail development, a consensus that has both temporal and spatial dimensions. Starting from the ancient world, the focus is largely on markets and fairs, which were increasingly formalised and regulated. Social and spatial gaps in provision were met by an array of itinerant retailers who were especially significant in serving the needs of rural populations less able to access urban markets (Holleran, 2012; Stabel, 2001; Fontaine, 1996; Calaresu and van den Heuvel, 2016). Yet shops were always present alongside the market, often operated by craftsmen who made as well as sold their wares; these fixed shops became increasingly important, eventually dominating retail provision, especially for durable goods and non-perishable foods – a process traced by Dyer in this volume (see also Keene, 1990; Welch, 2005; Carlin, 2007). In part because of gild regulations in many European cities and in part because of the growing array of goods available, retail provision diversified and specialised, a process that often involved the separation of production from retailing. In colonial America, import merchants sold goods through several distribution chains, including their own stores located at their warehouses in port cities and through networks of smaller merchants in the hinterland (Matson, 1998). Across Europe, the eighteenth century witnessed a proliferation of shops that were much more geared towards actively selling their wares, as Blondé and Van Damme outline in this volume. This process continued into the nineteenth century with the emergence of 'modern' retailing in the form of department stores and chain stores, which ushered in a new set of retail practices (Leach, 1993; Levinson, 2011; Spellman, 2016). The spatial focus here switches to America, where the development of mass retailing is seen as being most rapid and thorough (see the chapters by Elvins, Kruger and Liverant). Through the late nineteenth and early twentieth centuries, retailing grew further in scale and in its impact on both cities and citizens (Howard, 2015; Isenberg, 2004; Longstreth, 1997) with US practices being copied across the world (see the chapters by Miller, Howard and Stobart, and Purvis). As the twentieth century progressed, new forms of retailing took hold, including self-service and supermarkets; growing personal mobility drove a process of suburbanisation and a consequent decline in city centres – a trend first seen in the USA and accelerated in recent years by the emergence and growth of online shopping, as discussed here by Hyder, Halebsky, Stanger and Ellis-Chadwick.

Variations on this basic narrative reflect local differences in timing, emphasis and extent, but there is broad agreement on the sequence of change. Whether this amounts to evolution or revolution is, in part, a matter of perspective, although there is a growing scepticism about notions of a single retail revolution, as we discuss below. What remains clear, however, is the way in which retailing offers a window onto other key social, economic and cultural changes, including the emergence of a consumer society, the vibrancy of the economy (ides of consumer confidence and retail sales), the vitality of towns and urban institutions and relationships of power, such as race, gender and class.

III. Key themes

Given the variety of disciplinary perspectives, it is unsurprising that there are many different themes within retail history. Naturally, these have changed over the course of time, one of the most notable shifts in the last few decades being a move away from supply side to demand-side viewpoints, a move which reflects the emergence of the consumer as the key economic actor in the 1980s era of Thatcherism and Reaganomics (Koehn, 2001; Jacobs, 2005). This not only illustrates very clearly how retail history, like any aspect of history, is at least partly a product of the time in which it is written. Trying to step back from the detail of myriad approaches can be difficult, but doing so allows us to identify three broad groups of themes: economic, spatial and socio-cultural.

The idea of modernity and the process of modernisation form a perennial focus, especially for economic and business historians (Hollander, 1960; Chandler, 1977; Benson and Shaw, 1992). At their worst, such approaches can be teleological: seeing all changes in retailing as part of an inevitable and inexorable march to the present day, often in a series of stages which involve new forms of retailing replacing more traditional formats. Thus, markets decline in the face of fixed shops; traditional specialist retailers are replaced by department stores and multiples, and suburban shopping malls replace the High Street/downtown. Conversely, other studies find harbingers of modernity in the early modern world: fixed prices, perhaps, or active marketing (e.g. Walsh, 1999; Stobart, 2013). Despite a growing distrust of such approaches and the simple readings of modernity on which they are often based (see Cox, 2000; Mitchell, 2014; Blonde and Van Damme, 2010), there remains a focus on key transformative formats and practices – department stores, advertising, "scientific" management and new technologies – and on measuring shifts in productivity and profitability (Belisle, 2011; Elvins, 2004; Howard, 2015; Lichtenstein, 2009 Longstreth, 2010; Scott and Walker, 2012; Spellman, 2016). Whilst simple notions of retail revolution have long since lost their traction, the key measures and building blocks of this transformation remain important parts of retail history – see, for example, the chapters by Elvins and Purvis. At the same time, the idea that any transformation was all encompassing has been largely abandoned, not least because of growing evidence that 'traditional' retail formats thrived into the 'modern' era: open markets, itinerants, village shops and second-hand exchange, as seen in the chapters by Guardia et al., Fontaine, McCalla and Pennell.

Running in parallel with ideas of modernisation is the question of the role of retailing in creating or nurturing a consumer society – an issue discussed in detail by Blondé and Van Damme. The publication of McKendrick's seminal analysis in 1982 created a tidal wave of studies that attempted to discover how changes in retailing and consumption were connected, and determine the direction of causality (e.g. Blaszczyk, 2000; Coquery, 2011; Stobart, 2010). Some have challenged the periodisation, finding evidence of a productive symbiosis in earlier times (Peck, 2005; Welch, 2005) or arguing that both sets of changes belong more properly in the age of mass retailing and mass consumption (Leach, 1993). Others have argued that consumer transformation took place in an essentially traditional retail context (Blonde and Van Damme, 2010). Retail credit is seen by some as being central to modern consumerism; store cards and credit cards gave easy access to personal credit in the late twentieth century, building on the freedom provided earlier in the century by hire purchase agreements which brought a wide range of consumer durables within the reach of ordinary householders (Calder, 1999; Hyman, 2011)). Yet credit has always been central to the selling and buying of goods and to the relationship between retailers and consumers. It is apparent that the link between supply- and demand-side changes remains a key focus for historical enquiry, with the conclusions reached often reflecting the location and social group being examined, and the perspective of the researcher.

Debates about retail and consumer revolution often assume that both shopkeepers and their customers were entirely free agents, able to determine the course of history through their personal agency. Yet retailing has always been subject to government regulation (Cohen, 2003; Esperdy, 2008; Jacobs, 2005; Monod, 1996). As Dyer demonstrates in his chapter, medieval markets were closely controlled by civic and manorial authorities concerned with open and fair trading, and Guardia et al show that state involvement in markets has continued into the present era. Gilds played a large role in shaping retailing in many European cities into the eighteenth century and sometimes beyond, while civic authorities were increasingly active in asserting planning control and devising improvement schemes that involved radically remodelling retail streets – a process which reached its apogee in the comprehensive redevelopment schemes of postwar Europe (Howell, 2010; Morrison, 2003; Gosseye, 2015). National, state and local governments also stepped in, regulating prices, wages and hours of operation and sometimes using retail as a political tool for social and economic modernisation – see the chapters by Harada and Foda.

Globalisation is another thread that ties the various histories of retail together. One perspective on this focuses on the growing power of retailers to shape production. This is perhaps most obviously seen in the influence of late twentieth-century supermarkets to influence price and product specification of a wide range of agricultural products, but there is a long tradition of retailers involving themselves directly in the supply chain – from co-operatives to department stores (Lichtenstein, 2009; Spellman, 2016). A second perspective highlights the spread of Western-style retailing throughout the world. However, as many of the chapters in section 4 of this volume attest, this influence was not always monolithic or one-directional. Non-Western and socialist societies developed department stores and shopping malls, for instance, but their meaning and even the shopping practices they encouraged were somewhat distinct from their American and European origins – see the chapters by Miller, Foda and Hilton. And Western models might be hybridised and exported to other parts of the world, as Fujioka demonstrates was the case with Japanese department stores.

The relationship between retailing and the city forms a second broad theme, linking retail history to urban and architectural history, and historical geography – as highlighted in particular in Longstreth's chapter. Despite the growing industrial specialisation of urban economies, especially from the eighteenth century, retailing continued to dominate town and city centres; understanding its geography and its impact has therefore been a key topic of enquiry. For historians of ancient and medieval cities, this has often meant focusing on market buildings and market squares; for more recent periods, attention switches to shops and the high street, and subsequently to precincts, malls and shopping centres (Stabel, 2001; Coquery, 2011; Furnee and Lesger, 2014; Howard, 2015; Longstreth, 1997, 2010). This sequence can be traced through the chapters by Dyer, Mitchell and Howard and Stobart which draw out the shifting functional and geographical locus of urban retailing over the *longue durée*. Mapping the changing location of retail infrastructure or the concentrations of specialist retail trades provides a window onto a range of broader processes and relationships, from business location strategies and the economics of clustering, to the daily pathways of urban dwellers and the persistence of local and regional identities (Hardwick, 2004; Elvins, 2004). Retail is seen as playing a key role in shaping the layout of the city, and more especially its built environment: the style, scale and orientation of buildings were determined in part by imperatives of selling. This is most obvious in department stores and malls, but is also apparent in market halls and corner shops (Morrison, 2003; Longsreth, 1997, 2010; Guardia and Oyon, 2015). Buildings carry messages about the retail company, for example through monumentalism and house architectural styles; together they help to define the identity of the city, although a key concern in recent years has been with the growing sameness of high streets and city centres, as highlighted in Mitchell's chapter.

The link between retailing and the city centre has been weakened by the progressive decentralisation and suburbanisation of shops. Originally, retail location was determined by accessibility on foot; mass transport systems, especially trams and omnibuses, provided a strong impetus for shops to locate along the route and particularly around terminals. All these meant that city centre locations were favoured. However, this was first challenged and then broken, from the 1950s in the USA and slightly later in Europe, by the rise of the motorcar and the personal mobility that this offered. Residential decentralisation in the United States following World War II spurred development of new shopping complexes outside of traditional city centres (Longstreth, 1997, 2010). American car culture increasingly dominated the commercial landscape with the appearance of new competitors in the shape of discounters and big-box retailing, built on low-cost land outside of city centres. These shifts have created fundamental changes in the urban fabric: downtown in many American cities in particular now has little to do with retail. Restaurants, bars, cafés, cinemas and other leisure-oriented businesses have populated downtowns, replacing the types of businesses that serve everyday needs, such as grocery and hardware stores. While many lament the death of downtown in America, historians have emphasised the continual evolution of retail formats and their meaning (Howard, 2015; Isenberg, 2004; Spellman, 2016). Over the last decade or so, focusing on grassroots movements and local efforts, some have emphasised survival and transformation, rather than destruction and decline (Isenberg, 2004).

Historians are also interested in retail space at a finer scale, within malls, arcades and even within shops themselves. Some of this concerns the ways in which store layout influenced consumer behaviour, as seen in analyses of the infrastructure for display that increasingly characterised eighteenth-century shops and the heightening of such practices in nineteenth-century department stores (Walsh, 1999; Stobart et al., 2007; Whitaker, 2011; Howard, 2015). It is also apparent in the construction and layout of supermarkets, malls and shopping centres – see the chapters by Hyder, Halebsky and Howard and Stobart. In all these retail environments, space was produced and manipulated by retailers to mould people's interactions with goods and their perceptions of the retailer, with the ultimate aim of increasing sales. However, more recently, there has been growing interest in the ways in which retail space has been constructed and sometimes subverted by the spatial practices of shoppers: high streets and arcades were used as promenades and by flaneurs, department stores formed distinctly female spaces, and malls were colonised by the young and old as places to hang out or stay warm and dry. Moreover, retail venues, operating as a quasi-public privatised space, have been sites of political resistance. Sociologists, for example, have examined the various ways that different groups, such as women and the politically oppressed, have deployed such spaces for their own purposes (Srivastava, 2015).

As this suggests, retail history is increasingly being explored through a social or cultural lens. This includes using traditional categories such as gender, class and race, and increasingly in terms of identity construction and counter cultures. Class has often been examined in terms of labour relations. On the one hand, this has involved juxtaposing powerful merchant princes and penny capitalists, as Spellman does in her chapter (see also Benson, 1992). This can be seen as part of a broader historical tradition that explores economic and social change through the actions of great heroic figures, be they manufacturers, social reformers or retailers. It is most prominent in histories of department stores, but also characterises the histories of chain stores and even supermarkets (Briggs, 1956; Moss and Turton, 1989; Mathias, 1967; Buenger, 1998). On the other hand, there is the relationship between the shop owner and their workers, which could sometimes be highly antagonistic. The former often fought attempts at statutory control of working hours, whilst also pushing for resale price maintenance, which meant that goods cost more to the consumer (Scott and Walker, 2018). The latter, meanwhile, are often portrayed as being deskilled as retailing 'modernised' through adopting new management practices, fixed prices, open display and self-service – a trend that continues through to today, with zero-hours contracts and automated check-outs (see the chapters by Purvis and Opler). Class was also important in terms of the status of customers, where they shopped, how they interacted with salespeople and what they purchased sometimes being determined by and then serving to cement their social standing (Abelson, 1989; Benson, 1986; Miller, 1981). In this context, co-operative stores has been portrayed as empowering the working classes by assuring good quality and fair prices, an aspect developed by Hilson et al in their chapter. In contrast, second-hand was increasingly seen as the recourse of the poor, but this was, as Pennell demonstrates, time and sector specific: before the eighteenth century, second-hand was important for all sectors of society and recent years have seen the growth of "vintage" shops (see also Stobart and Van Damme, 2010). Department stores, meanwhile, are celebrated a democratising luxury, although different stores catered to different social groups (especially when we look beyond the Western world (Whitaker, 2006).

In the USA, race was also important in shaping peoples experience of retailing. The Jim Crow practices of Southern retailers and boycotts of segregated store facilities and discriminatory labour practices have been well-documented by historians of the civil rights movement. Business historians have evaluated the response of managers to boycotts and legislative pressure, and have also documented the contributions of black-owned business to retail history (Chambers, 2008; Dyer, 2013; Weems, 1998; Wright, 2013). The broader subject of racialised consumption and racial discrimination in the commercial sector has recently attracted the attention of scholars across a wide disciplinary spectrum (Bay and Fabian, 2015). Race has been less of an issue in the history of European retailing, although the growing number and variety of small shops owned by immigrants from former colonies and the more recent growth of shops selling east European foods demand fuller attention – as Van Damme notes in his chapter.

A more general and widely shared concern in the more recent historiography is with gender and especially women's relationship with retailing and shopping. As with class, attention has focused on issues of oppression and inequality versus empowerment and liberation. Shopkeepers have long included women as well as men, and the shopkeeper's wife was often crucial in running the family business (Van den Heuvel, 2013; Barker, 2017). However, there has always been a tendency for women to trade in lower status and less remunerative retail trades, sometimes at the margins of legality. The rise of big retail businesses is sometimes seen as offering greater opportunities for female shop assistants, although their opportunities for advancement through the tiers of management were restricted in Europe, at least before World War II (Lancaster, 1995). In the United States, department stores provided more opportunities for women to rise up the ladder as buyers and middle managers, though with the arrival of big discounters after World War II a more male-dominated climate prevailed (Howard, 2015). Poor working conditions and the danger of sexual exploitation were apparent in the early modern era and continued into the twentieth century. As a key female occupation, retail work has attracted attention from women's and labour historians (Benson, 1986; Opler, 2007). Although the unionisation of retail workers has also lagged behind that of industrial workers in the United States, women played key roles in the history of union organising, a position that created sometimes antagonist relationships with customers (Opler, 2007). Analyses of women as customers paint a more positive picture. Shops and shopping formed an arena in which they could engage in the public sphere, although the liberating spaces of department stores were balanced by the dangers of social heterogeneity which it brought with it (Lancaster, 1995; Benson, 1986). Social historians have documented the tensions within an emergent culture of consumption, visible within retail institutions such as the department store. Concerns about gender and class in Victorian America, for example, came together within the shoplifter-kleptomaniac identity given to middle-class white women (Abelson, 1989), although recent work has questioned this association – as discussed in the chapter by Blondé and Van Damme.

IV. Volume overview

The world's retail history is too rich and vast to receive full coverage within one volume, no matter how broad its remit and ambition. Recognising that it is impossible to cover every conceivable topic, retail format and location, we have sought wide-ranging coverage that is both thematically and geographically inclusive. To this end, our *Companion to the History of Retailing* is divided into four broad sections: [1] Contexts, trends and relationships, [2] Spaces and places, [3] People, processes and practices and [4] Geographical variations. Thematic chapters in the first three sections focus mostly on Europe/UK and North America, reflecting the strength of scholarly literature in this area. The geographical scope of the chapters in section 4 provides an opportunity to move beyond the European/UK/North American perspective of the volume and much of the literature. Here, we get a clearer picture of variations in retail histories across the globe although some notable global players are sadly absent. It is our hope that future studies will address areas we were not able to investigate.

Spanning the medieval world to the present, the history of retail is marked by both change and continuity. The distribution of goods and services might seem a universal activity, but as the scholars here demonstrate, everyday market exchanges are the product of diverse historical contexts, trends and relationships. Thematic chapters in this section attempt to address the historical contingency of retail phenomenon by placing such activity within its broader economic, political, technological and environmental contexts. Examining the chronological breadth of retail activity from the medieval and early modern periods and into the modern era allows the subject's connection to broader trends to emerge. Globalisation, urbanisation, industrialisation, the emergence of consumerism and the rise of bureaucratic and state controls shaped retail activity in vastly different ways over time as our authors demonstrate. Chapters reveal social relationships forged by economic exchange undergoing immense change in the modern era, first with the consumer revolution and the rise of mass markets, then with the more recent upheavals of the internet age. At the same time, several of our authors warn against seeing retail history as a succession of revolutions, with many values and practices continuing from one era into the next.

The chapters in section 2 also examine retail activity in all its diversity and distinctiveness, but a focus on building and organisational typologies highlights many interesting similarities of retail form across the globe. Architectural formats are shown to have evolved slowly over time, for instance from open-air markets and market stalls to purpose-built market halls and from village and high street shops to the large-scale enterprises that emerged in the late nineteenth century. Chapters draw attention to the shared social and cultural experience of the spaces and places where people shopped. As our authors show, retail spaces and places exerted tremendous cultural and social power over more than simply shopping or consumer behaviour. Indeed, department stores, shopping malls and big-box stores like Walmart helped constitute the very meaning of consumer society, providing the spaces where modern identities took shape. Other retail modes influenced the most fundamental of human activities – eating. The rise of supermarkets not only transformed food provisioning and eating habits, but was also connected to new agricultural and technological regimes. Retail change influenced the shape of cities and their commercial districts. By detailing the evolution of retail spaces and places, these chapters contribute to an understanding of these broader historical changes across national boundaries.

Section 3 turns to the human actors who comprise all retail enterprise. Here, chapters document the wide variety of people, processes and practices behind the retail industry, from the level of individual enterprise to big business. That retail history can be told from the bottom up or the top down is reflected in this section, which includes contributions on itinerants and peddlers and on shop workers, as well as managers and merchant princes. In addition, this section reflects the variety of retail processes or organisational modes within the distribution chain. The focus here is on large-scale organisational structures – multiples, mail order firms and co-operatives – and the ways in which their economic practices were suffused with social and cultural implications, most overtly in the case of co-operative societies with their conscious social and political agendas. Smaller-scale retailers receive perhaps less attention than they merit, which in part reflects their relative neglect in the literature: obscured by the bright lights of the high street and mall, and the growing dominance of big business. Overall, the section overviews the evolution of business and labour practices within a consumer-oriented society.

National boundaries, shaped by law, custom and geography, determine economic practices. The final section seeks to illuminate the shared structures and diverse practices of different regions and nations across the world. Chapters cover the retail history of the USA and Canada, Western Europe, Eastern Europe, Australia and New Zealand, Latin America, the Middle East, Japan and India. Additional chapters on individual countries would have helped clarify national differences, for example between countries in Mediterranean and northern Europe or different states in India; but limits of space and a desire to provide a coherent overview of geographical variations meant that we focus on global regions rather than dig down into local specificities. The authors draw on their historical specialties to situate retail practices within their national contexts, but also seek to highlight connections across borders. In many cases, different countries shared markets, language, and political cultures and it made sense to treat them together. Two notable absences within the volume – China and Africa – have extremely long and diverse retail histories and need to be addressed by further study.

Through its various sections and chapters, this volume aims to provide both an overview of the history of retailing and an entrée to its many and varied elements. It is unlikely that the reader will tackle the whole book or even read through an entire section, although both would, we feel, be rewarding exercises. Each chapter is thus written in a way that allows it to be read on its own, to provide an overview of the history of itinerants or supermarkets, for example, or the development of retailing in the Middle East or Japan. In whatever way the reader chooses to approach this volume, it offers rich insights into retail history and its links to wider economic, social, cultural and urban histories.

References

Abelson, E.S. (1989), *When ladies go a-thieving: Middle-class shoplifters in the Victorian department store* (New York: Oxford University Press).

Barker, H. (2017), *Family and business during the industrial revolution* (Oxford: Oxford University Press).

Bay, M. and Fabian, A. (2015), *Race and retail: Consumption across the color line* (New Brunswick, NJ: Rutgers University Press).

Belisle, D. (2011), *Retail nation: Department stores and the making of modern Canada* (Vancouver: University of British Columbia Press).

Benson, J. (1992), *The penny capitalists: Study of nineteenth century working class entrepreneurs* (New Brunswick, NJ: Rutgers University Press).

Benson, J. and Shaw, G. (eds.) (1992), *The evolution of retail systems, c.1800–1914* (Leicester: Leicester University Press).

Benson, S.P. (1986), *Counter cultures: Saleswomen, managers, and customers in American department stores 1890–1940* (Urbana, IL: University of Illinois Press).

Blaszczyk, R.L. (2000), *Imaging consumers: Design and innovation from Wedgwood to Corning* (Baltimore, MD: Johns Hopkins University Press).

Blondé, B. and Van Damme, I. (2010), 'Retail growth and consumer changes in a declining urban economy, Antwerp (1650–1750)', *The Economic History Review*, 63 (3), pp. 638–663.

Briggs, A. (1956), *Friends of the people: The centenary history of Lewis's* (London: B.T. Batsford, First Edition).

Buenger, V. and Beunger, W.L. (1998), *Texas merchant: Marvin Leonard & Fort Worth* (College Station, TX: Texas A&M University Press).

Calaresu, M. and van den Heuvel, D.W.A.G. (eds.) (2016), *Food hawkers. Selling in the streets from antiquity to the present* (London: Routledge).

Calder, L. (1999), *Financing the American dream* (Princeton, NJ: Princeton University Press).

Carlin, M. (2007), 'Shops and shopping in the thirteenth century: Three texts', in L.D. Armstrong, I. Elbl and M.M. Elbl (eds.) *Money, markets and trade in late medieval Europe: Essays in honour of John H.A. Munro* (Leiden/Boston, MA: Brill) 491–537.

Chambers, J. (2008), *Madison Avenue and the color line: African Americans in the advertising industry* (Philadelphia, PA: University of Pennsylvania Press).

Chandler, A. (1977), *The visible hand: The managerial revolution in American business* (Cambridge, MA: Belknap Press).

Cohen, L. (2003), *A consumers' republic: The politics of mass consumption in postwar America* (New York: Knopf).

Coquery, N. (2011), *Tenir boutique a Pa'ris au XVIIIe siècle: Luxe et Demi-Luxe* (Paris: Comité des travaux historiques et scientifiques – CTHS).

Cox, N. (2000), *The complete tradesman: A study of retailing, 1550–1820* (New York: Routledge).

Dyer, S. (2013), 'Progress plaza: Leon Sullivan, Zion investment associations, and black power in a Philadelphia shopping center', in M. Ezra (ed.) *The economic civil rights movement: African Americans and the struggle for economic power* (New York: Routledge).

Elvins, S. (2004), *Sales and celebrations: Retailing and regional identity in Western New York State, 1920–1940* (Athens, OH: Ohio University Press).

Esperdy, G. (2008), *Modernizing main street: Architecture and consumer culture in the new deal* (Chicago: University of Chicago Press).

Fontaine, L. (1996), *History of pedlars in Europe* (translated by Vicki Wittaker, Cambridge: Polity Press).

Furnee, J.-H. and Lesger, C. (eds.) (2014), *The landscape of consumption: Shopping streets and cultures in Western Europe, 1600–1900* (Basingstoke: Palgrave MacMillan).

Gosseye, J. (2015), 'Milton Keynes' centre: The apotheosis of the British post-war consensus or the apostle of neo-liberalism?', *History of Retailing and Consumption* 1 (3), pp. 209–229.

Guàrdia, M. and Oyón, J.L. (eds.) (2015), *Making cities through markets halls, 19th and 20th centuries* (Barcelona: Museo d'Història de Barcelona).

Hardwick, M.J. (2004), *Mall maker: Victor Gruen, architect of an American dream* (Philadelphia, PA: University of Pennsylvania Press).

Hollander, S.C. (1960), 'The wheel of retailing', *Journal of Marketing* 25, pp. 37–42.

Holleran, C. (2012), *Shopping in ancient Rome* (Oxford: Oxford University Press).

Howard, V. (2015), *From Main Street to mall: The rise and fall of the American department store* (Philadelphia, PA: University of Pennsylvania Press).

Howell, M.C. (2010), *Commerce before capitalism in Europe, 1300–1600* (Cambridge: Cambridge University Press).

Hyman, L. (2011), *Debtor nation: The history of America in Red Ink* (Princeton, NJ: Princeton University Press).

Isenberg, A. (2004), *Downtown America: A history of the place and the people who made it* (Chicago: University of Chicago Press).

Jacobs, M. (2005), *Pocketbook politics: Economic citizenship in twentieth-century America* (Princeton, NJ: Princeton University Press).

Keene, D. (1990), 'Shops and shopping in medieval London', in L. Grant (ed.) *Medieval art, architecture and archaeology in London* (London: Routledge), 29–46.

Koehn, N.F. (2001), *Brand new: How entrepreneurs earned consumers' trust from Wedgwood to Dell* (Boston, MA: Harvard Business School Press).

Lancaster, B. (1995), *The department store: A social history* (Leicester: Leicester University Press).

Leach, W. (1993), *Land of desire: Merchants, power, and the rise of a New American culture* (New York: Vintage Books).

Levinson, M. (2011), *The great A&P and the struggle for small business in America* (New York: Hill and Wang).

Lichtenstein, N. (2009), *The retail revolution: How Wal-Mart created a brave new world of business* (New York: Metropolitan Books).

Longstreth, R. (1997), *City center to regional mall: Architecture, the automobile, and retailing in Los Angeles, 1920–1950* (Cambridge, MA: MIT Press).

Longstreth, R. (2010), *The American department store transformed, 1920–1960* (New Haven, CT: Yale University Press).

Mathias, P. (1967), *Retailing revolution: A history of multiple retailing in the food trades* (London: Longmans).

Matson, C. (1998), *Merchants & empire: Trading in colonial New York* (Baltimore, MD).

Miller, M.B. (1981), *The Bon Marché: Bourgeois culture and the department store, 1869–1920* (Princeton, NJ: Princeton University Press).

Mitchell, I. (2014), *Tradition and innovation in English retailing, 1700 to 1850: Narratives of consumption* (New York: Routledge).

Monod, D. (1996), *Store wars: Shopkeepers and the culture of mass marketing, 1890–1939* (Toronto: University of Toronto Press).

Morrison, K. (2003), *English shops and shopping* (New Haven, CT: Yale University Press).

Moss, M. and Turton, A. (1989), *A legend in retailing: House of Fraser* (London: Weidenfeld & Nicolson).

Opler, D. (2007), *For all white-collar workers: The possibilities of radicalism in New York City's department store unions, 1934–1953* (Columbus, OH: Ohio State University Press).

Peck, L. (2005), *Consuming splendor: Society and culture in seventeenth-century England* (Cambridge: Cambridge University Press).

Scott, P. and Walker, J. (2012), 'The British "failure" that never was? The "productivity gap" in large-scale interwar retailing: Evidence From the department store sector', *Economic History Review*, 65, pp. 277–303.

Scott, P. and Walker, J. (2018), 'Retailing under resale price maintenance: Economies of scale and scope, and firm strategic response, in the inter-war British retail pharmacy sector', *Business History*, 60 (6), pp. 807–832.

Spellman, S.V. (2016), *Cornering the market: Independent grocers and innovation in American small business* (New York: Oxford University Press).

Srivastava, S. (2015), *Entangled urbanism: Slum, gated community, and shopping mall in Delhi and Gurgaon* (Delhi: Oxford University Press India; UK edition).

Stabel, P. (2001), 'Markets in the cities of the late medieval low countries: Retail, commercial exchange and socio-cultural display', in S. Cavaciocchi (ed.) *Fiere e mercati nella integrazione delle economie europee, secc. XIII–XVIII* (Florence: Le Monnier), 797–817.

Stobart, J. (2010), 'A history of shopping: The missing link between retail and consumer revolutions', *Journal of Historical Research in Marketing* 2 (3), pp. 342–349.

Stobart, J. (2013), *Sugar and spice: Grocers and groceries in provincial England, 1650–1830* (Oxford: Oxford University Press).

Stobart, J., Hann, A. and Morgan, V. (2007), *Spaces of consumption: Leisure and shopping in the English Town, c.1660–1830* (London: Routledge).

Stobart, J. and Van Damme, I. (eds.) (2010), *Modernity and the second-hand trade: European consumption cultures and practices, 1700–1900* (Basingstoke: Palgrave Macmillan).

Strasser, S. (1989), *Satisfaction guaranteed: The making of the American mass market* (Washington, DC: Smithsonian Institution Press).

van den Heuvel, D. (2013), 'Guilds, gender policies and economic opportunities for women in early modern Dutch towns', in D. Simonton and A. Montenach (eds) *Female agency in the urban economy: Gender in European towns, 1640–1830* (London: Routledge), 116–133.

Walsh, C. (1999), 'The newness of the department store: A view from the eighteenth century', in G. Crossick and S. Jaumain (eds) *Cathedrals of consumption* (London: Ashgate Publishing), 46–71.

Weems, R.E. (1998), *Desegregating the dollar: African-American consumerism in the twentieth century* (New York: New York University Press).

Welch, E. (2005), *Shopping in the renaissance: Consumer cultures in Italy, 1400–1600* (New Haven, CT: Yale University Press).

Whitaker, J. (2006), *Service and style: How the American department store fashioned the middle class* (New York: St. Martin's Press).

Whitaker, J. (2011), *The department store: History, design, display* (London: Thames & Hudson).

Wright, G. (2013), *Sharing the prize: The economics of the civil rights revolution in the American South* (Cambridge, MA: Harvard University Press).

Contemporary industry statistics, reports cited

Carr, F. (2018), Amazon Is Now More Valuable Than Microsoft and Only Two Other Companies Are Worth More. *Fortune*. 15th February 2018. Available at: http://fortune.com/2018/02/15/amazon-microsoft-third-most-valuable-company/ (Accessed February 21, 2018).

Current Employment Statistics: Table B-1. Employees on Nonfarm Payrolls by Industry Sector and Selected Industry Detail. *Economic Research, Federal Reserve of St. Louis*, January 2018. Available at: https://fred.stlouisfed.org/release/tables?rid=50&eid=4881&snid=5205 (Accessed February 21, 2018).

The Economic Impact of the Retail Industry. *National Retail Federation*. Available at: https://nrf.com/resources/retail-library/the-economic-impact-of-the-us-retail-industry (Accessed February 21, 2018).

Europe's Retail Market Is Ahead of the Curve in Dealing With Global Structural Change. *JLL Report*, October 25, 2017. Available at: www.jll.eu/emea/en-gb/news/768/europe-us-retail-market-different-ahead-of-curve-new-report-jll (Accessed February 21, 2018).

The Portas Review: An Independent Review into the Future of Our High Streets. December 2011. Available at: www.gov.uk/government/uploads/system/uploads/attachment_data/file/6292/2081646.pdf (Accessed February 20, 2018).

Quarterly Retail E-Commerce Sales. *U.S. Census Bureau News*, U.S. Department of Commerce, Washington, DC, February 16, 2018. Available at: www.census.gov/retail/mrts/www/data/pdf/ec_current.pdf (Accessed February 20, 2018).

The Retail Industry: Statistics and Policy. *Briefing Paper*, Number 06186, October 9, 2017, House of Commons Library, p. 4.

Reynolds, J. and Cuthbertson, R. (2014), *Retail and wholesale: Key sectors for the European economy* (Oxford: Oxford Institute of Retail Management, Said Business School, University of Oxford), p. 7.

Statistical Bulletin, Great Britain: January 2018. *Office for National Statistics*. Available at: www.ons.gov.uk/businessindustryandtrade/retailindustry/bulletins/retailsales/january2018 (Accessed February 20, 2018).

Wrigley, N. and Lambiri, D. (2015), *British high streets: From crisis to recovery* (Southampton: University of Southampton, ESRC). Available at: http://thegreatbritishhighstreet.co.uk/pdf/GBHS-British-High-Streets-Crisis-to-Recovery.pdf (Accessed February 20, 2018).

PART I

Contexts, trends and relationships

2

RETAILING IN THE MEDIEVAL AND EARLY MODERN WORLDS

Christopher Dyer

Introduction: traditional views of retailing in the past

Commerce before the industrial revolution, and particularly before 1500, was once seen as dominated by great merchants typically from such ports as Venice and Antwerp carrying bulky and valuable cargoes over long distances. The traded goods would be for the benefit of the wealthy elite: the rulers, aristocrats, higher clergy, and the patricians of the larger cities. Spices and silks from the east, fine wines from south-west France or the Mediterranean, high-quality cloth made in Ghent and Ypres, and the metal work of south Germany including armour, were the expensive commodities which the courts of Europe required (Spufford, 2002). They would be bought from the merchants by the officials of the grand households. Some producers of prestigious artefacts, such as the painters, sculptors and goldsmiths, would often be employed or commissioned directly by their wealthy patrons. This type of trade was seen as originating around the year 1000 when the emerging urban economy was driven by the demands of aristocrats for luxuries which were traded from afar or manufactured in the towns. Towns expanded as aristocrats increased their spending in the twelfth and thirteenth centuries, and faltered when the elites suffered losses of income.

In this view of pre-industrial society, the great majority of the population, mainly living from agriculture with a smattering of artisans, were expected to subsist on a few essentials, with a mainly cereal diet. A high proportion of people, it was thought, practised self-sufficiency by growing their own food and gathering from the commons. As much as possible they made their own clothing and agricultural implements. The peasantry are depicted as achieving only low levels of productivity in their farming, which prevented them from setting aside more than a small surplus, and much of that would have been swallowed up by lords and rulers demanding rents and taxes. The mass of the population existed insecurely because of periodic harvest failures. The production and consumption of food took priority, and left little to spare for manufactures such as cloth or utensils. The limited number of exchanges was conducted in weekly markets and annual fairs, at which tolls were collected for the benefit of rulers and lords. The majority of the population found it difficult to accumulate much cash, and exchange often took the form of lending and bartering among neighbours.

Change came about through fluctuations in the human population, which grew up to c.1300, perhaps to unsustainable levels, and then declined after famines and plagues into the fifteenth century. Recovery in numbers lay behind the economic revival in the sixteenth century, but yet more crises in the seventeenth, including a devastating war in central Europe, ushered in a new episode of uncertainty.

Studies of towns have tended to concentrate on their government, above all by the wealthy merchants and administrators who were anxious to protect the towns' privileges. The majority of the population were taxed and policed in such a way that profit and enterprise were discouraged. From the thirteenth century one of the major industries in the towns of Flanders, Brabant and northern France, clothmaking, was controlled by entrepreneurs who supplied the craftsmen with their materials, and supervised each separate stage of manufacture such as spinning, weaving, fulling, dyeing and finishing. The guilds formed by these artisans, when they were permitted, tended to concentrate on protecting the narrow interests of their members.

The historians' picture of gross inequality, widespread poverty, and low levels of production can be connected to the contemporary moral climate. The catholic church (in effect the only church before the 1520s) endorsed versions of austerity and voluntary deprivation, from the specialised life of poverty professed by the friars, to the universal practice of fasting in Lent and on days of abstinence throughout the year. Merchants who bought cheap and sold dear were regarded with suspicion, and commercial practices such as charging interest on loans were forbidden in the strongest terms. The secular authorities in seeking to control the market and protect the consumer made life difficult for middlemen, and imposed price and quality regulations. Buying goods was apparently surrounded by risks: it was a necessity, and could serve a useful function, but offered few pleasures.

Recent approaches to the history of retailing

The once prevalent view of a bleak pre-industrial past is supported by evidence and has some validity as an interpretation. However, it serves the purpose of those who believe in the overwhelming importance of the industrial revolution to highlight the misery and deprivation experienced before 1700. The exaggeration of backwardness makes the advances of modern civilisation seem all the more beneficial. In revising and modifying the general picture, historians have shown, particularly in the last twenty years, that pre-industrial retail trade was not a trivial or fringe activity, but a central feature of society.

Recent research finds that most trade was regional and local, but not narrowly confined to close neighbours. For example, Cologne in Germany's Rhine valley had a vital relationship with its surrounding district extending as far as 40km to 70km from the city (Eiden and Irsliger, 2000). The city's 40,000 inhabitants (in the period 1340–1750) bought foodstuffs, firewood and timber that had been produced or collected in nearby farms and villages, and in return sold to country people leather goods, textiles and metal utensils made in the city. As well as dealing in relatively low value everyday goods produced in the region, such as grain, Cologne's wider hinterland kept its specialised industry in metal utensils supplied with raw materials, such as iron bars for the city's forges. The citizens' demands for sea fish, wine and large quantities of livestock were satisfied by traders operating at a considerable distance. Smaller towns around Cologne, such as Julich and Neuss, interacted closely with their rural surroundings and would not have had the large city's wide connections.

The character of the trading and retail system can be assessed by noting the number of towns and trading places, the proportion of people living in them and the occupations that they pursued. Towns and markets had proliferated in the twelfth and thirteenth centuries, and most towns persisted in spite of economic troubles after the Black Death into the sixteenth and seventeenth centuries. Counting small towns as well as large, the total in 1600 in Sweden was forty-nine, and in Austria eighty-six. The Hesse region in Germany had as many as 138 in the early modern period, and England around 700 (Clark, ed., 1995, pp. 80, 90, 190; Epstein, ed., 2001, p. 32). These figures include not just large towns with populations in excess of 2000, but also market towns with a few hundred inhabitants. Country markets are not included, only those places with a concentration of permanent residents pursuing variety of non-agricultural occupations. The best way of assessing the contribution of towns to the whole society is to calculate the 'urban ratio', that is the proportion of the population living in towns. When this is done at various times between 1350 and 1700, including small towns, the figure is often in the region of 20%, rising to 30% and more in the Low Countries and northern Italy (Clark, ed., 1995, p. 186). In England the figures in 1377–81 and 1522–5 fell below 20% in the more underdeveloped counties, but rose above 25% in Suffolk, in a region noted for its commerce and industry. Towns usually lacked the agricultural resources to support their inhabitants, and instead the townspeople gained a living from intense engagement with trade and manufacture.

As towns grew the transport infrastructure was being developed, above all with the replacement of fords and ferries with bridges, which often included causeways which allowed convenient access to travellers across low lying meadows (Harrison, 2004). Roads were rerouted and improved, and wharfs and waterfronts were built alongside rivers. New channels for waterways were dug, often for the convenience of a monastery, but also for general use (Blair, ed., 2007). Attempts were made to protect road users from crime, such as clearing vegetation from road sides where thieves might lurk, and by arresting and punishing highway robbers. Inns were founded in towns on road junctions, and even out in the country, where travellers and their horses and vehicles could be sheltered securely and provided with food and drink (Hare, 2013). Speedier and more robust horse-drawn carts replaced the clumsy ox wains which had been used in the twelfth century (Langdon, 1986).

The occupations of townspeople leave no doubt about the importance of making relatively cheap goods for a large number of ordinary customers, some of them living in the town, but many from the surrounding countryside. In any English town the food trades figure prominently: bakers, brewers, butchers, fishmongers and cooks. As well as the raw materials for cooking at home customers could buy "ready meals" and "fast food" in the form of pies, pasties, puddings and sauces. Trade in cloth and clothing gave employment to drapers, mercers, tailors, kempsters (dressmakers) cappers and hosiers. People wore and used leather goods, so shoemakers were always prominent, with glovers and saddlers. The list grows with workers in wood, notably coopers and wheelwrights, the metal trades such as smiths and braziers (dealing in copper alloy goods), and the chandlers who made and sold candles. These descriptive labels exaggerate the degree of specialisation, as many townspeople would have a number of sources of income, and would trade in a variety of commodities. Many dealt in at least small quantities of grain, but few people were named as specialist grain traders, and the badgers, bladers or cornmongers tended to be confined to the largest centres. The artisans often kept a shop or stall, selling goods through a window at the front of their house, while making items such as shoes and caps in a workplace at the back. The fishmongers and mercers were buying their stock in bulk from other towns, and selling small quantities to their customers. Some producers would increase their sales by engaging lesser traders to distribute their wares, most commonly the brewers whose ale was sold by gannockers, tipplers and the like, who were often female. When we think of retail trade we naturally focus on shops and market stalls, selling goods set out on a board. However a large numbers of consumers were buying services, for example by hiring carpenters and roofers to do work on houses or barns in the town or surrounding villages. Evidence that townspeople were trading goods or services to customers from nearby villages comes from wills and court records which give the names of those who owed money.

The number of artisans and traders, and the mundane character of their produce, shows that most towns were not mainly engaged in supplying luxuries to wealthy aristocrats. Again using England as an example, even small towns might contain a goldsmith or spicer, but these suppliers of expensive high-grade goods and services were greatly outnumbered by the bakers and shoemakers. A minority of peasants or artisans who had made a good living would occasionally buy a silver spoon or a few ounces of pepper. Elite consumers would not be patronising a spicer, tailor or shoemaker in the nearest market town: they would normally take their custom to high status traders in very large towns or London. Purveyors of the most expensive goods, such as vintners or grocers, are rarely found in small towns but instead congregated in ports such as Southampton, or regional centres like Coventry, or the capital. Concentrating on the evidence from smaller towns, if the links between individual rural buyers and urban sellers are plotted on a map, the retailing hinterland is revealed as extending about 12 km from the town.

The artisans and traders selling goods and services to the mass of consumers attract our attention because of their number, and therefore their collective contribution to the economy as a whole. The rich deserve attention because they represent a sizeable proportion of consumer spending. They negotiated their needs with great merchants, but they can be encountered visiting shops and selecting goods. We find Francesco Castellani, a patrician of Florence, in 1459 buying fish for a dinner with guests, and in 1447 he visited a goldsmith to choose twelve silver forks for a wedding present (these were relative novelties, as spoons and knives were the main eating implements of the later Middle Ages) (Welch, 2005, p. 230). In Venice in the sixteenth century, silk was sold in a specially organised display called a *paragon* at which the customers made a choice in enforced silence (Welch, 2005, pp. 123–125). Such luxury purchases made a major contribution to the retailing landscape of the largest towns, from Florence and Venice to London, Paris and Bruges.

The number, size and occupational structure of towns is not the only evidence of the interaction between retailers and a broad spectrum of the population. Inventories of possessions of ordinary people, or bequests made in wills, mostly of the sixteenth and seventeenth centuries, contain lists of items that could not have been made at home by someone without special skills or contacts with distant markets. Furnishings for example included carpets (that is, table coverings), painted cloths hanging from the walls of principal rooms, bedding, cushions, chairs and chests. In the kitchen would be pots and pans of cast metal, pewter vessels and many other items that would have been bought from suppliers in towns (Overton et al., 2004). This is reinforced by finds from archaeological excavation of rural sites, where cheaper items which are not mentioned in documents include ceramics which would sometimes be made in towns, but more often were the products of a rural industry but distributed through the urban marketing network. By the seventeenth century, superior pots, such as majolica in the Netherlands, were regarded as valuable enough to appear in documents (Baatsen et al., 2016).

Demand for retailers' services

In view of the limited spending power of a high proportion of the population, was there enough demand to enable the retailers to survive? By a paradox shops, market stalls and other retailing outlets were much used by the least affluent section of society, the smallholders, cottagers, labourers and landless wage-earners. They were sometimes paid in grain or with meals, but the cash that they received would have been used to buy food, clothing and other items. Peasants with middling holdings (around 3 to 6 ha of arable) would work part-time for wages if the produce from their land did not suffice for their food needs, so they might have bought from bakers and butchers. Peasants with larger holdings would become customers of retailers if they chose, as some did, to specialise. For example, peasants in fifteenth-century Worcestershire lived in areas unsuitable for growing oats (in the south of the county) or peas (in parts of the north), so they would buy these crops to feed their livestock (Dyer, 2016). Villagers in late medieval Yorkshire, at Wharram Percy, would also purchase preserved sea fish from remote sources. In many villages there were households which specialised in brewing ale or making cheese, and sold their surpluses to their neighbours, or those seeking better quality foods would go to the retailers in a nearby town. There is limited evidence for peasants making their own cloth or utensils at home: instead they bought their textiles, clothing, shoes, spades and larger implements from specialist artisans, or middlemen dealing in manufactures. Rents and taxes did not absorb all of their surplus, which meant that a tenant with 12 ha might have enough money in a normal year to buy a 10m length of cloth or a cart and its gear. Part-time craftsmen worked in many villages, of whom the smiths are best documented from the twelfth century onwards, but might include tailors or shoemakers. Peasants retailed agricultural produce in towns, not just the men who sold bulky loads of grain and wool, but also their wives and daughters contributed to the household economy by selling eggs, poultry, dairy products, vegetables or fruit from baskets (Dyer, 2000, pp. 126–127).

This story of partial self-sufficiency, meaning that country people were at least occasionally engaged in retail trade both as buyers and sellers, does not apply in the towns, where a minority only would have access to land, and everyone depended on the market for the necessities of life. The demand for food, clothing, fuel and other goods from townspeople, working as artisans and traders, labourers and servants ensured that many retailers were kept busy. In regulating trade at Tarascon in Provence in 1370–1400 priority was given by the authorities to grapes, wine, bread, wheat, oats, barley and salt meat, which were the main purchases of the townspeople. The urban government protected general well-being by encouraging the flow of these foodstuffs into the town, and sought to prevent traders taking these basic commodities out of the town in times of shortage (Hebert, 1979, pp. 163–165).

Retail trade was stimulated by a growth in demand in the sixteenth and seventeenth centuries, and this was possible because of an increase in disposable income. The period has been characterised, initially on the basis of the experience of the Netherlands, by the phrase "industrious revolution", but this is now regarded as a more general European phenomenon. It is argued that members of households together maximised their earnings, not in order to survive, but to enable them to buy goods which they desired. Women's work made an important contribution, and that of children, and longer hours were worked so that while daily rates of pay to individuals sometimes declined, annual household earnings rose. Supply and demand moved in a circle, because the efforts of the workers were often devoted to making the consumer goods for which demand was increasing. In England knitted stockings, lace and straw hats were characteristic products of industriousness: they required great quantities of labour, and were sold to a wide spectrum of consumers. English labourers in the seventeenth century spent three-quarters of their earnings on food, but this included some beef and other non-cereal foods, and inventories written after the death of labourers show that during their lives they had bought quantities of textiles, both for clothes and for furnishings such as bed hangings. Most labourers who have left inventories (the upper ranks of their class) owned pewter vessels and chairs (Muldrew, 2011).

In pursuing the question, "was consumption affordable?" historians tend to be drawn into rather speculative calculations of income, based on rates of pay, days in employment, and likely profit from cultivating a number of hectares of land. This mathematical exercise often results in a negative judgement: consumption was not possible. However, this is ignoring the ability of even poor consumers to borrow money, and we have abundant evidence that sellers extended credit to buyers, allowing them to delay payments. In Italy where pawn shops operated more actively than in northern Europe consumers would buy items such as bed linen when the going was favourable, but in hard times would use these goods to raise money (Welch, 2005, pp. 196–203, 231–235). The trade in second-hand goods ought to be brought into the calculation, as it enabled poorer consumers to afford clothing or household utensils.

Investigating the roots of the growth of consumption, which is apparent at least as early as the thirteenth century and which expanded after 1500, requires posing questions about the decision-making and motives of ordinary people who have left little direct record of their thinking. Were they impelled by a competitive spirit, seeking to own more and better goods than their neighbours? Or were they anxious to live in a style which was appropriate to the status group to which they believed that they belonged? We know so much about the bonds of kinship, and networks among neighbours, demonstrated by such organisations as religious fraternities, that we could suppose that groups of people moved along parallel lines, influenced by their fellow townspeople or villagers, but not necessarily in competition (Rosser, 2015). Some historians have seen a desire among the middling sort and lower ranks of society to emulate the lifestyle of the elite. These ordinary people could not rival the magnificence and splendour of the great aristocrats and churchmen, but they could borrow some customs and emblems of affluence such as household textiles or spiced food, in a movement towards the "democratization of luxury", or a desire among townspeople to "live nobly", both phrases applied to changes in the consumption patterns in the Netherlands in the sixteenth and seventeenth centuries. Perhaps these desires could have been generated within non-aristocratic society, without the need to aspire to matching upper-class role models. Ideals of convenience, comfort, enjoyment of colour and pursuit of pleasure could have been regarded positively by those who were acquiring the means to buy goods beyond the reach of their predecessors.

Who made the decisions to spend, and then what specific items to buy? The evidence is not consistent, as the account books and correspondence of upper-class Italians in the fifteenth and sixteenth centuries show the domination of the male head of household. Such individuals were often older than their wives, and society frowned on women going into the market place on their own, so men did not just decide to buy, but went to the shops to make the purchase (see above p. 18). In northern Europe in the same period women were more often seen as partners, who could participate in collective decisions. Women might have their own source of income, through a craft or trade of their own, which increased their capacity for independent judgements about purchases (Howell, 2010, pp. 93–144).

The rise of retailing gives us an insight into one dimension of a society in which individuals were developing self-confidence and a greater degree of independence. Particularly after 1350, when the fall in population gave scarce tenants and workers more bargaining power, the power of lords diminished and families exercised less control over the young. Both before and after the Black Death, evidence for travel, migration, political and religious consciousness tell us that people of all kinds had wide horizons. They knew about the kingdom or lordship in which they lived, and about remote places of importance, such as Rome and Jerusalem. They were also aware of the places where the best bargains could be found, or where, if they were selling goods, the demand was greatest and the prices highest.

The location of retail trade: shops and shoppers

The settings in which retail trade took place varied over time, place and commodity. In the early Middle Ages, people gathered in remote places, and left behind a dense scatter of coins and metal objects apparently mislaid by the traders and their customers. For example at Cottam in east Yorkshire on the site of a farmstead significantly sited on a long-distance trackway more than a hundred metal objects, mostly belt fittings, have been found, together with thirty-five knife blades and twenty-five coins of the eighth and ninth centuries. Such a concentration of objects would not normally be associated with an agricultural settlement (Richards, 2003). In the later Middle Ages fairs were trading occasions which were held annually, often to coincide with a religious festival, and their timing gave them a specialist purpose. Local fairs were held for the sale of livestock in May and June, or cheese and butter at the end of the summer. They were also opportunities for retail trade, such as purchases of wooden household utensils for people living within a few miles. In the thirteenth century a network of international fairs across Europe, such as the fairs of Champagne, or those held at St Ives (Huntingdonshire) or Stourbridge near Cambridge in England, had become opportunities for merchants to meet and conduct wholesale transactions. Cloth often figured prominently among the goods that changed hands, but almost any high value commodity traded over distances, such as furs and wax from the Baltic, spices from Asia and Mediterranean dried fruits and nuts could be on offer at the temporary booths erected on the fairground. Royal courts bought bales of cloth, and bishops and rich monasteries acquired their spices and preserved fish at fairs. These rich consumers could acquire goods in the large quantities that they needed, and at reasonable prices. In some countries fairs gradually lost importance as more deals were struck in cities in merchants' houses or in public buildings where traders congregated. At the French city of Reims, the drapers sold cloth from the ground floor of their houses in the city centre, and customers wanting linen would find it being sold in a mercery where the linen merchants gathered (Desportes, 1979, pp. 371–375). The need for fairs revived in the fifteenth and sixteenth centuries when states and cities developed new networks focused on fairs such as those held at Geneva and Medina del Campo in Spain (Epstein, 2000, pp. 73–88).

Retail trade was focused on towns in the period 850–1320, both in weekly markets and shops which opened daily. A typical set of market privileges in Scotland was issued by the king for Dumbarton in 1221, establishing the market day as Wednesday, and exempting the burgesses of Dumbarton from paying tolls on their transactions anywhere in the Scottish kingdom. In addition, all those bringing merchandise to buy and sell in the market "shall have my peace", that is come under royal protection (Ballard and Tait, ed., 1923, pp. 246, 254, 271).

Towns required extended space for market places. These often consisted of wide main streets, which could accommodate rows of market stalls and still allow room for traffic. Alternatively a larger rectangular or triangular space was created, with ample room for stalls and other structures. If they were being planned after the town centres had filled with dense housing and churches, as at Florence and Bologna, buildings were cleared away, though sometimes market places were sited on the edge of the town. In south-western France the early market places (in the eleventh and twelfth centuries) lay within the walls of the castle, where the traders could be protected, but also dominated and exploited by the lord. This limited space was abandoned and the market was typically held near a church, or even in the churchyard in the thirteenth century, which would be in a more central and convenient place. In the Hundred Years War the market moved back into the security of the castle, but with the return of peace in the mid fifteenth century migrated once more into the town (Petrowiste, 2004, pp. 176–194).

The typical English urban market place contained many stalls, ideally consisting of trestles, boards and awnings which could be dismantled and stored until the following week, but some stallholders turned their temporary booths into permanent structures with upper stories, or rows of stalls were built by the authorities. A monumental stone cross would occupy a prominent place, and its steps would be appropriated on market day by groups of traders who could not aspire to open a stall, such as women selling butter from baskets. An official building would serve as a toll booth, and be provided with a hall for courts to meet. Here a pillory would stand as a deterrent for those offending against the rules on weights and measures or product quality. Part of the toll booth or town hall, or a purpose-built market hall would serve as a covered market, where traders would be better protected from rain. Specific groups of traders might be assigned buildings, such as the shambles for the butchers. In English and French towns would be a drapery and mercery for the sale of cloth, and Flemish towns such as Ypres had cloth halls. Even without these designated spaces for trade, occupational groups tended to occupy the same streets, like the linen sellers of seventeenth-century Amsterdam who set up their shops in Niewendijk (Lesger, 2011). In the market place at the small town of Newmarket in Cambridgeshire separate groups of stalls were assigned (at least in name) to the mercers, drapers, ropers, cheesemongers and shoemakers (Davis, 2012, p. 280).

A great quantity of trade passed through the larger urban market places, but they usually were held for one day in the week, while the permanent shops opened most days. They were often located on the ground floor of houses fronting on to streets, though some occupied wooden structures leaning against buildings, including churches. The "shoprows" are often found in or near market places, with a dozen or so lock-up shops in a terrace. Selds were similar structure, not unlike small-scale shopping malls, in which customers walked along a covered passageway with small shops on either side. The size of this type of shop was very small, often less than 2 metres wide. Some consisted of a board, chest or hutch like the fishmonger's stall in Reims which measured 8 feet by 4 feet (Desportes, 1979, p. 373). Modern tourists can gain a sense of the high density of retail spaces in a prime city centre location by walking across the Ponte Vecchio in Florence. The larger shops displaying a merchant's wares would be built to impress, like the draper's premises in Toulouse where a large vaulted room of four bays with brick arches occupied the street frontage of a merchant's house (Wolff, 1954, p. 515). In less prestigious retail outlets goods could be displayed in a window, or on a "stall board" jutting out into the street and covered with an awning. A customer visiting a shoemaker's house would be shown at the front of the shop an array of goods by a salesperson, often the artisan's wife, but would also be able to see in the background the craftsman at work. The shop would be equipped with a counter and a chest or chests for storing stock. At the end of the day the shop would be "shut" by lifting or removing the stall board and locking the shutters across the window (Clark, 2000). A less common type of retail premises can be found in towns with stone-built undercrofts with access to the street. In these basement rooms in Southampton for example wine would be sold, but other goods could also have been available for purchase (Figure 2.1).

Shops were numerous and concentrated in particular streets, demonstrating the importance of the retail sector. In Chester the space for shops was greatly increased by building on the frontage of the main streets rows of shops along a walkway on the first floor, in addition to those conventionally available at street level. Oxford had 147 shops listed in the survey of 1279 (and there were probably more); and in 1417, 118 shops were located along the High Street of Winchester. These were dwarfed by the retailing capacity of London, with 4000 shops in Cheapside (the main shopping street, the Oxford Street of its day) in about 1300 (Keene, 1990). The flow of trade through these shops, stalls and chests should not be underestimated. Around 1300 in Cheapside tenants of shop premises were willing to pay an annual rent above £1, even as high as £4, at a time when a labourer was paid not much more than £1 per annum. The quality and quantity of shops varied from one street to another, and the most prized location was a corner shop where two busy streets met, preferably near the market place.

Other points of sale could be found in the towns, such as the hawkers and huxters selling from baskets in the street or going from door to door. Outside the town markets were held in the countryside, and while some were quite small and inactive, others had stalls and shambles, and generated a revenue in tolls which suggests quite a high volume of trade. Shops could still

Figure 2.1 Early sixteenth-century shop, Lavenham in Suffolk, England

Source: Courtesy of Abby Antrobus.

be encountered in villages, especially those with a market or acting as a place where trade was focused, such as the Huntingdonshire village of Yaxley in the fourteenth century, a port on the system of inland waterways in the fenland. In seventeenth-century Cheshire a scatter of village shops identified as mercers, drapers and grocers are revealed by lists of their stock to have carried a great variety of merchandise, which was supplied by traders active in nearby towns (Stobart, 2016, pp. 89–102). Some of these shops were located in villages which were not particularly large or important. In both town and country bargains were often struck in inns, though these could belong in the category of wholesale rather than retail trade.

Country dwellers bought from peddlers or chapmen. They were often based near a town, and having obtained their packs of assorted goods from urban suppliers, walked or less often took a pack horse from village to village. They gained a bad reputation, especially during episodes of moral panic about vagrants, but their customers welcomed the opportunity to buy haberdashery, pins, gloves, kerchiefs, beads and combs (Davis, 2007). Their numbers grew in the seventeenth century, and when they were licensed in 1697, 2,559 were listed in England. They sold a great miscellany of goods, but a very prominent element were textiles, that is linen and cotton rather than woollens, and haberdashery, and so were providing country wives with the materials for making clothes at home. The combined value of their annual sales in the late seventeenth century could have exceeded £100,000, which amounts to a significant proportion of the country's commercial exchanges (Spufford, 1984).

The regulation of retail sales, both in markets or shops, were designed to maintain order, as those in authority wished their markets to be peaceful and well-conducted. Shops were distrusted on a number of grounds, mainly because it was believed that honesty was most likely if transactions were conducted in an open public market. In Paris from the late twelfth century, second-hand clothes dealers were regarded with suspicion, as the trade was believed to have links with thieves who were disposing of stolen property (Geremek, 1987, pp. 263–269). Middlemen also attracted criticism, as it was feared that they forced up prices. Legislation forbade forestalling, that is intercepting goods on their way to market in order to sell them at a higher price. Regrating was also outlawed, as this meant acquiring produce, especially foodstuffs, in order to sell at a higher price. Cooks and innkeepers were distrusted as they bought meat and fish, cooked them as ingredients in meals, and made a profit from the diners. The authorities dreamt of an ideal of honest producers, of fruit and vegetables for example, travelling to market to sell direct to the consumers. In the real world a network of middlemen handled goods of all kind: even in the apparently simple world of horticulture leekmongers and garlicmongers bought up sacks of vegetables and passed them on to retailers. We now see this as an aspect of efficient distribution, and regard middlemen as playing a necessary role in keeping commodities flowing along the complex commercial chain (Davis, 2012).

The authorities in towns were especially concerned to protect consumers from exploitation by food traders, which led them to restrict price rises and therefore to impose limits on the profit margins of brewers and butchers. Bakers in England were especially closely regulated, by the assize of bread which laid down the weight of loaves which were sold for fixed prices of 1d., a halfpenny and a farthing. In a bad harvest year, as the price of grain rose, the weight of the loaf was reduced according to a sliding scale. The consumers were getting less bread for their money, but at least the bakers were not making excessive profits, and the rules were known to the public and regarded as fair. Similar measures were adopted on the continent, as is shown by the fining of 30 traders at Ypres in Flanders in 1267–8 for selling loaves that were either small or of low quality (van Uytven, 2001, pp. 90–91).

The town governments ensured that weights and measures were checked, and in some markets the price of grain was set by the town authorities. Trading days were regulated, and shops were not supposed to open on specified religious holidays. Trade began at an agreed time, with the ringing of a bell. Often the early part of the day was reserved for domestic consumers, to prevent merchants buying the grain or bread and selling at an extra profit. Residues at the end of the day, such as unsold fish, were reserved for the poor. Credit was subject to intervention by the local courts, and in particular customers could be compelled to pay their debts. In general such strong measures were not used frequently, because the trading system depended on trust and a sense of mutual obligation.

Market places lay at the heart of the town, and the markets were the focus of the commercial economy, both for the major traders such as drapers and the mass of consumers buying necessities. The market place also occupied a central position in the civic consciousness of the townspeople, as it was the site of the town halls and other civic buildings. In Italian cities the *podesta* and the captain of the people might have their palaces there, and in both southern and north European cities a high bell tower with a clock symbolised the inhabitants' sense of identity. Here townspeople gathered to attend meetings and celebrations, to hear proclamations and to witness judicial punishments. The town's militia would assemble in the market place in times of troubles, and rebels would gather in the same place (Bocchi, 2015).

All of this suggests a cohesive system designed to promote the common good. As is often the case apparently benevolent motives are found to be combined with self-interest. The authorities had to be seen to protecting the consumer, or otherwise they feared disturbances, and occasionally food riots erupted in years of shortage, when crowds broke open granaries and mills and sold the grain at a "fair" price. In years without extreme shortages a well-regulated food market gave the wage-earning section of the population no excuse to ask for higher wages. An example of market rules with mixed motives can be found at Liege in the Middle Ages. In this town with many consumers, 20,000 in 1500, many of whom were wage-earners, markets were to be held in daylight, that is under public scrutiny, and townspeople were given priority in their purchases. However, the bishop of Liege and the canons of the cathedral, who had large landed estates, were given monopolies at certain times for their profit. The consumer protection measures were frequently announced, but there is little evidence for their enforcement (Wilkin, 2015).

Much of the governance of marketing, and our evidence for actual sales, suggests a relatively straightforward relationship between towns and the surrounding countryside. Towns and markets were widely spaced, often at least 20 km apart, and hinterlands based on convenience of travel defined the area from which country people went to market to sell their produce and make purchases. Only in some places and periods was such a relationship compulsory, for example when the state gave a town a monopoly on trade, or when, as in Italy, rural producers were compelled to sell their grain in the market of a town that ruled over the surrounding countryside. Normally the rural population had a choice between markets and towns, which competed for trade. They might sell their produce in a local market town, which would then sell it on to a larger place, as happened when wine grown in southwestern France was ultimately gathered at Bordeaux for export. Traders in a large town dealing in a specialist imported commodity, like the dye needed by rural cloth makers, would distribute it through the smaller market towns. A striking example of the connection between large towns practising an international trade and local consumptions comes from the marriage contracts of peasants living around Vic in Catalonia in c.1300. These documents might specify that a young woman's trousseau would include a dress made from cloth from towns in northern France and Flanders, such as Bruges, Chalons or Ypres. These textiles would have been sold by retailers in towns like Vic, but their ultimate origin in a famous textile centre was not forgotten (To Figueras, 2016).

Changes in retail trade in the long term

The economic and social history of Europe is reflected in changes in retail trade. Little detailed evidence survives for shopkeeping in the generation of towns that grew in the ninth, tenth and eleventh centuries. An English riddle refers to a garlic seller, allowing us to glimpse a street hawker at work. The archaeology of the period offers evidence for trade between town producers and rural consumers in the form of small metal dress fittings and brooches made by urban artisans but found in the countryside (ten Harkel, 2013).

The great expansion of towns and markets in the twelfth and thirteenth centuries, which was associated with thousands of new shops, stalls and other places for sale, embedded marketing into social relations throughout much of Europe. In the period 1350–1500, when the population declined and the overall volume of trade was reduced, towns shrank in size, but so did the villages, so the proportion of the population living in towns did not change a great deal. Plenty of shops remained in business, and industry continued to supply demand, for cloth for example. A French commentator on the period remarks on the increased range of commodities, the extension in the range of social groups who were able to participate in consumption, and the development of fashion (Petrowiste, 2018). Although the numbers of consumers everywhere was reduced, incomes of individuals were rising as holdings of land grew in size and wages tended to increase. Those active in industry had to respond to shifts in demand, such as the potters who made vessels for drinking, both cups and jugs, as individual consumption of alcoholic drinks rose.

In the sixteenth and seventeenth centuries, population growth resumed, production in the countryside increased and prices rose. A number of sections of society, such as better-off peasants, did well in this environment, and although real wages fell, the "industrious revolution" enabled the households of smallholders to increase their earnings. Calculations of English GDP and consumption per head suggest that after some wavering after 1520, both increased decisively in the late seventeenth century (Broadberry et al., 2015, pp. 206, 207). In the Netherlands, in its Golden Age, households acquired "turned" furniture (that is parts of chairs and other items were finished on a lathe) and a more varied range of textiles and household goods were acquired.

The facilities for trade changed. Shops became grander and more important features of the city landscape. In Madrid in the late sixteenth century, at the centre of a unified state and a great empire, the Plaza Mayor was planned as an imposing centrepiece of the city. The central square was used as a food market, and bread and meat were sold from specially designed buildings, but the colonnades of the main structure contained shops selling luxury goods to a wealthy clientele (Escobar, 2007). London by the end of the seventeenth century had grown to become one of the largest cities in Europe, and was developing as an imperial centre with trade links across the Atlantic, and to the Far East and Muscovy. Its shopping facilities grew in size and sophistication with the building of arcades (as we would call them) or galleries, of which one of the most celebrated was the New Exchange, opened in 1609. These shopping venues were built as investments by aristocrats with spare land in central London, in the case of the New Exchange by the earl of Salisbury who owned the site on the Strand. Within the building large numbers of small, specialist shops, selling high-quality goods, were built in line beside a walkway, along which the customers could inspect the wares and negotiate purchases. They were assured that their fellow shoppers were exclusive and well-behaved because a beadle monitored those passing through the door. There was a good chance that visitors would meet friends and associates, so the galleries served a social as well as a commercial function (Walsh, 2003).

In reviewing the economic importance of retail trade there is a tendency to see shops and their wares as secondary symptoms of growth. This view presumes that production was the prime mover in the economy, from which consumption followed. Yet the cumulative total of retail trade could play an important role in forming the great chain of interactions that made up an economy, and consumer demand could act as a general stimulant. Analysing demand from the perspective of the purchaser leads us to explain their motives in terms of competition or emulation, but we should take note of feedback from the retailer. Shopkeepers tempted customers, offered attractive items, set standards of consumption, informed customers about products, including novelties and encouraged them to indulge their ambitions. Tailors in particular persuaded their customers to adopt new fabrics and styles.

The culture of retail

Sales in shops and markets served a useful purpose, in that households satisfied their needs, and shopkeepers made a profit, but retail trade was not entirely functional. Markets and fairs were public occasions which often included an element of display and even entertainment. The opening of fairs could involve some ceremony. The fair usually coincided with a saint's day, perhaps a local saint who was commemorated with processions and religious services. Flemish authorities in the sixteenth century who wished to promote their market would hire musicians and organise displays of flowers (Stabel, 1997). Entertainers wishing to make money would attend markets and fairs on their own initiative and give displays of juggling or music, and a dancing bear might be exhibited. Attendance by local sellers and buyers at markets would change seasonally, with increased activity before or soon after the great feasts of Christmas, Easter and Whitsun. Those attending would drink, and some stalls would tempt buyers into making frivolous or trivial purchases – of playing cards, ribbons, children's toys, pots decorated with comical faces, or in the seventeenth century, chapbooks. Contemporary literature celebrates the pleasures of the fair. A Welsh poet of the fourteenth century imagined events at a fair at Rhosyr (Newborough on Anglesey), where young men wore goat skins and horns (symbolic of lechery), and well-dressed people attended, including a young woman who rejected the poet's advances. He had been drinking wine (Fulton, 2012).

For Italian painters of the sixteenth century the displays of goods at markets carried meanings beyond the simple temptation to purchase. The artists depicted market stalls, as a metaphor for abundance, well-being and happiness. Fruit and vegetable stalls with their mass of colourful produce hinted at sensuality and fecundity. Attractive women were shown in attendance, and there were hints of sinful conduct (Welch, 2005, pp. 65–68). Throughout Europe women played an important role in the management of stalls and shops. The wives of the artisans promoted sales by standing outside the shop in the street to lure customers, and then used their feminine wiles (as contemporaries alleged) to persuade them to buy. They would presumably have adopted a different approach with the high proportion (in northern Europe) of female shoppers.

Sales were promoted in ways that resonate with modern practices. Goods were not branded, but there were close associations between particular places and their distinctive products. In England, Thaxted knives, Kendal cloth and Banbury cheese all attracted instant recognition among fifteenth-century consumers. Clothes, hats and head coverings, shoes, jewellery and metal dress accessories all changed style quite rapidly, and some cities such as London and Paris led the way and were much imitated. Fashion consciousness was widespread, and peasant clothes reflected new styles. Advertising through the medium of print appears in the late seventeenth century, with a leading role being taken by patent medicines.

A visit to shops could have been an opportunity for people to meet, converse and conduct business. Galleries such as the New Exchange in London became an important part of the social scene for the elite, as Pepys's diary shows in the 1660s. But shops always lay on the edge of respectability, offering opportunities for customers to flirt with the shop girls, and the New Exchange eventually gained a reputation as a centre for prostitution.

Conclusion

Any discussion of retail trade leads historians along an optimistic route that gives an impression of the early onset of modernity, and tempts us to overestimate the affluence that was possible in a pre-industrial economy. The moralists of the time condemned the frivolity and waste arising from following fashion. Critics with some justice warned that buying excessively expensive and often trivial goods was self-indulgent and exposed all those involved to moral dangers. The traders cheated, and the customers had suspect motives as they were tempted by the sins of pride, avarice, envy, gluttony and lechery. Sumptuary laws were passed in order to maintain social distinctions based on the quality of clothing, or to limit perceived damage to the economy from expensive foreign imports.

Those who emphasise the limitations of the pre-industrial economy, whose views were expressed at the beginning of this chapter, have a point when they say that surpluses were insufficient to generate a very large retail sector. In particular there were regions with sparse populations and poor communications, such as Norway, where towns were few and small, and the rural population could not afford to buy consumer goods in quantity. In the more developed areas wealth was very unevenly distributed, and some groups such as unskilled labourers around 1300 had very limited spending power. Throughout the whole period a substratum labelled as "poor", estimated sometimes at 5% of the population, were excluded from the world of retail, except for buying basic supplies of food. If their clothes resembled those of their neighbours, it would have been the result of charitable gifts, or purchases of second-hand garments. Retailing did not expand continuously, though it seems in the late seventeenth century to have embarked on a long-term upward movement. Before that there were many short-term ups and downs, including slumps lasting decades, affecting England in the middle years of the fifteenth century, and the Low Countries towards the end of the same century. In years when harvests were deficient, consumer spending would have been reduced, and trade was also highly seasonal, with more activity in the period after the harvest and at Christmas than in Lent or early summer.

Retailing was born and grew up in the medieval and early modern periods, but its childhood was uncertain and insecure.

References

Baatsen, I., Blonde, B., De Groot, J. and Sturtewagen, I. (2016), 'Thuis in de stad: dynamieken van de materiele cutuur', in A.L. van Bruaene, B. Blonde and M. Boone (eds.) *Gouden eeuwen: Stad en samenleving in de Lage Landen, 1100–1600* (Ghent: Academia Press) 251–286.

Ballard, A. and Tait, J. (ed.) (1923), *British borough charters 1216–1307* (Cambridge: Cambridge University Press).

Blair, J. (ed.) (2007), *Waterways and canal-building in medieval England* (Oxford: Oxford University Press).

Bocchi, F. (2015), 'The topography of power in the towns of medieval Italy', in A. Simms and H. Clarke (eds.) *Lords and towns in medieval Europe: The European historic towns atlas project* (Farnham: Ashgate) 65–86.

Broadberry, S., Campbell, B., Klein, A., Overton, M. and van Leeuwen, B. (2015), *British economic growth 1270–1870* (Cambridge: Cambridge University Press).

Clark, D. (2000), "The shop within': An analysis of the architectural evidence for medieval shops', *Architectural History*, 43, pp. 58–87.

Clark, P. (ed.) (1995), *Small towns in early modern Europe* (Cambridge: Cambridge University Press).

Davis, J. (2007), ''Men as march with fote packes': Pedlars and freedom of movement in late medieval England', in P. Hordern (ed.) *Freedom of movement in the middle ages* (Donington: Shaun Tyas) 137–156.

Davis, J. (2012), *Medieval market morality: Life, law and ethics in the English marketplace, 1200–1500* (Cambridge: Cambridge University Press).

Desportes, P. (1979), *Reims et les Remois aux XIIIe et XIVe siecles* (Paris: Picard).

Dyer, C. (2000), 'Gardens and orchards in medieval England', in C. Dyer (ed.) *Everyday life in medieval England* (London: Hambledon Press) 113–131.

Dyer, C. (2016), 'Peasant farming in late medieval England: Evidence from the tithe estimations by Worcester cathedral priory', in M. Kowaleski, J. Langdon and P. Schofield (eds.) *Peasants and lords in the medieval English economy: Essays in honour of Bruce M.S. Campbell* (Turnhout: Brepols) 83–109.

Eiden, H. and Irsliger, F. (2000), 'Environs and hinterland: Cologne and Nuremberg in the later middle ages', in J. Galloway (ed.) *Trade, urban hinterlands and market integration c.1300–1600* (London: Centre for Metropolitan History, Working Paper Series, No. 3) 43–58.

Epstein, S. (2000), *Freedom and growth: The rise of states and markets in Europe, 1300–1700* (London: Routledge).

Epstein, S. (ed.) (2001), *Town and country in Europe, 1300–1800* (Cambridge: Cambridge University Press).

Escobar, J. (2007), *The Plaza Major and the shaping of baroque Madrid* (Cambridge: Cambridge University Press).

Fulton, H. (2012), 'Fairs, feast-days and carnival in medieval Wales: Some poetic evidence', in H. Fulton (ed.) *Urban culture in medieval Wales* (Cardiff: University of Wales Press) 223–252.

Geremek, B. (1987), *The margins of society in late medieval Paris* (Cambridge: Cambridge University Press).

Hare, J. (2013), 'Inns, innkeepers and the society of later medieval England, 1350–1600', *Journal of Medieval History*, 39, pp. 477–497.

Harrison, D. (2004), *The bridges of medieval England: Transport and society 400–1800* (Oxford: Oxford University Press).

Hebert, M. (1979), *Tarascon au XIVe siècle: Histoire d'une communaute urbaine provencale* (Aix-en-Provence: Edisud).

Howell, M. (2010), *Commerce before capitalism in Europe, 1300–1600* (Cambridge: Cambridge University Press).

Keene, D. (1990), 'Shops and shopping in medieval London', in L. Grant (ed.) *Medieval art, architecture and archaeology in London* (Leeds: British Archaeological Association) 29–46.

Langdon, J. (1986), *Horse, oxen and technological innovation: The use of draught animals in English farming from 1066 to 1500* (Cambridge: Cambridge University Press).

Lesger, C. (2011), 'Patterns of retail location and urban form in Amsterdam in the mid eighteenth century', *Urban History*, 38, pp. 24–47.

Muldrew, C. (2011), *Food, energy and the creation of industriousness: Work and material culture in agrarian England, 1550–1780* (Cambridge: Cambridge University Press).

Overton, M., Whittle, J., Dean, D. and Hann, A. (2004), *Production and consumption in English households, 1600–1750* (London: Routledge).

Petrowiste, J. (2004), *A la foire d'Empoigne: Foires et marches en Aunis et Saintonge au moyen age (vers 1000–vers 1500)* (Toulouse: Le Mirail).

Petrowiste, J. (2018), 'Consommateurs et marches locaux a la fin du moyen age: un etat de la question', in M. Lafuente Gomez and J. Petrowiste (eds.) *Faire son marche au moyen age: Le consommateur et le marche en Mediterraneee occidentale* (Madrid: Casa de Velazquez).

Richards, J. (2003), 'The Anglian and Anglo-Scandinavian sites at Cottam, East Yorkshire', in T. Pestell and K. Ulmschneider (eds.) *Markets in early medieval Europe* (Macclesfield: Windgather) 155–166.

Rosser, G. (2015), *The art of solidarity in the middle ages. Guilds in England, 1250–1550* (Oxford: Oxford University Press).

Spufford, M. (1984), *The great reclothing of rural England: Petty chapmen and their wares in the seventeenth century* (London: Hambledon Press).

Spufford, P. (2002), *Power and profit: The merchant in medieval Europe* (London: Thames and Hudson).

Stabel, P. (1997), *Dwarfs among giants: The Flemish urban network in the late middle ages* (Leuven/Apeldoorn: Garant).

Stobart, J. (2016), 'The village shop, 1660–1760: Innovation and tradition', in R. Jones and C. Dyer (eds.) *Farmers, consumers, innovators: The world of Joan Thirsk* (Hatfield: University of Hertfordshire Press) 89–102.

ten Harkel, L. (2013), 'Of towns and trinkets: Metalworking and metal dress accessories in Viking age Lincoln', in D. Hadley and L. ten Harkel (eds.) *Everyday life in Viking-age towns: Social approaches to towns in England and Ireland, c.800–1100* (Oxford: Oxbow) 172–192.

To Figueras, L. (2016), 'Wedding trousseaus and cloth consumption in Catalonia around 1300', *Economic History Review*, 69 (2), pp. 522–547.

Van Uytven, R. (2001), *Production and consumption in the Low Countries, 13th–16th centuries* (Aldershot: Ashgate).

Walsh, C. (2003), 'Social meaning and social space in the shopping galleries of early modern London', in J. Benson and L. Ugolini (eds.) *A nation of shopkeepers: Five centuries of British retailing* (London: I.B. Tauris) 52–79.

Welch, E. (2005), *Shopping in the Renaissance: Consumer cultures in Italy 1400–1600* (New Haven, CT/London: Yale University Press).

Wilkin, A. (2015), 'Time constraint on market activity and the balance of power in medieval Liege', *Continuity and Change*, 30, pp. 315–340.

Wolff, P. (1954), *Commerces et Marchands de Toulouse (vers 1350–vers 1450)* (Paris: Librairie Pion).

3

FROM CONSUMER REVOLUTION TO MASS MARKET

Bruno Blondé and Ilja Van Damme

Introduction

Questioning the 'consumer variable' in history goes straight to the heart of most important debates in recent retail historiography. Once causality in retail change was thought to be rather straightforward: the distributive trades were seen as an appendage of the supply side system, responding sensitively to production change and growth. Small-scale production equaled buying directly from producers' shops or via periodic markets and peripatetic salesmen; whereas ensuing industrialisation and mass production were followed by an equally 'revolutionary' and large-scale retail transformation (Jefferys 1954). Since the twin curves of demography and living standards were thought to bump inevitably against certain structural ceilings, any active role of consumer demand in engendering retail change was in any case reckoned to be small and unsustainable before the nineteenth century.

Only from the end of the 1970s did historians start to study the agency of consumer demand in earnest (Bianchi 1998). Unfortunately, the horizon and terms of these initial consumer debates were very much a continuation of normative, Cold War intellectual skirmishes. In direct opposition to the older, influential conceptualisations of the *Frankfurther Schule* and radical sociologists of the 1950s and '60s – in which shrewd salesmen and an ever more persuasive advertising machinery were accused of creating a hollow, materialistic society of one-dimensional, civically unengaged citizens – the consumer now entered the ring as champion of free choice. The (neo-)liberal political-economic context of Thatcherism and Reaganomics goes a long way in explaining why the consumer, and the act of consumption itself, was suddenly given a crucial empowering, even liberating role (Slater 1997, 33–62; Trentmann 2006, 1–27). If society were to be imagined as a marketplace, then the real puppeteers could never have been the capitalist suppliers and advertisers of goods and services, but the end-users of these commodities whose individual consumer preferences and decisions eventually guided collective investments, historical change and the progress of the nations.

In this "consumer democracy" vision of history, the locations and activities of shopping and retailing were discovered anew as important sites of cultural experience and meaning, rather than places and moments that fulfilled the basic utilitarian functions of distribution and provisioning. The notion that such a thing as consumer culture was less of an oxymoron than was once thought, gained precedence in concomitant postmodern theorising. After all: in a world where complex signs and meanings, and the continuous appropriation and aestheticisation of everyday practices, is believed to take precedence over simple needs and wants, core societal values and identities become entangled with or negotiated through consumption and the world of goods (Slater and Tonkiss 2001, 6–35). Inspired by such postmodern beliefs about the self and society, the historical reappraisal of material culture, the study of fashion cycles and the history of shopping were only one aspect of a growing body of literature devoted to the active role of demand-side issues. The real challenge for historians, however, became finding the source of everything that followed: answering the gnarling, almost existential questions of how and why we became a world of consumers, and where and when to locate the birthplace of our equally celebrated and condemned consumer society.

Looking back with hindsight on almost forty years of debate over the active role of the demand-side in (retail) history, it is apparent that our collective attachment to origins – our urge for finding a consumer (r)evolution of some sort – has not only been historically misleading but also an intellectual *cul-de-sac*. Speaking of the birth of a consumer society leads to historical tunnel vision: it was an unfortunate metaphor, as Frank Trentmann recently stressed, because 'unlike a baby, consumption was not set on a natural, almost universal path of growth and development' (Trentmann 2016, 10). When our demand-side perspectives continue to broaden in time as well as in space – taking in, for instance, the consumer variable in Renaissance Italy (fourteenth-seventeenth centuries), Ming China (1368–1644), or for that matter Mogul India (1526–1857) and Tokugawa Japan (1603–1868) – the diversity and complexity in material culture, tastes and lifestyles in world history urges us to become more nuanced and modest in our grand narratives. But even more important is nurturing a post-colonial awareness and sensitivity for our own historical discourses and situatedness – a point still curiously absent in most textbooks on consumption and retail history alike. To be sure, an origins perspective blinds us intellectually: it obscures the fact that consumer revolution narratives are fundamentally enmeshed with core western values and persistent western narratives of modernity, progress and superiority.

To illustrate and substantiate this central historiographical claim, we will focus in the rest of our chapter on two consumer (r)evolutions and specifically their impact on retailing and shopping. This will be done for two periods of almost axiomatic importance in the history of North-Western Europe – the region against which other European and non-European regions continue to be weighed in consumer debates, and this despite our recent turn to the global. Firstly, we will delve into The Enlightenment (c.1670–1830), which cemented our typical core Western values and narratives of assigning freedom and liberation to consumer choice. By demoralising private consumer wants and stimulating material desires, North-West European societies – England and the Low Countries especially – were set on a track towards further commercialisation, industriousness and eventual industrialisation. The demand-side, and especially the consequent cultural constructions around consumption and the role of the consumer in society, played a crucial role in explaining why present-day nations like England, Belgium and The Netherlands figure prominently in historical debates on the birth of a consumer society. However, despite a growing propensity or willingness to consume among the (urban) layers of North-Western Europe and the concommittant development of retail circuits, our reappraisal of recent literature and research will be of a more nuanced and less superlative kind: social inequalities, rooted in an *ancien-régime* political-economy, remained very large and debates have often focused more on newness in consumer habits and behaviour, rather than considering continuities and path-dependencies.

Secondly, we turn to the *Fin-de-Siècle* World (c.1870–1914), a period that again became crucially linked to core Western notions and assumptions that people should not only have the freedom, but also the means and possibilities to consume. Late-nineteenth-century North-Western

Europe undertook a feverish technological journey towards mass production of standardised consumer goods. These were distributed, among others, through large-scale, mass retail innovations, such as chain stores and department stores, which experienced their real breakthrough in this period. Western imperialism and accompanying rapid globalisation were integral to this move towards the consumer masses, not only for opening up consumer markets abroad, but also for importing cheap energy and raw materials (especially grain) to North-Western Europe (Moore 2015). By freeing the increasingly dominant industrial wage labourer – albeit still partially and imperfectly – from the high costs of paying for food, industrial nations like England and Belgium were set on the path to become true mass consumer societies. Not only were cities and the number of urban consumers growing, people in general had more financial leeway to indulge in consumer wants and desires above basic needs at the start of the Interbellum. Gaining access to more and diverse consumer products, and crucially being "entitled" to consume, became integral to the rise of another retail innovation, the co-operatives. Meanwhile, widespread social and political mobilisation around consumer interests gradually paved the way for North-West European welfare states.

In the light of this historical change, it is again small wonder that demand-side issues, and their connections with retailing, figure dominantly in historical discourses on the late-nineteenth-century. However, we will end on a sobering note, warning against all too triumphalist perspectives that link consumption to conquering and liberating Western consumer modernity. We do well to remember that this period started and ended with bloodshed, warfare and influential social unrest, such as the 1870 Paris Commune and the Russian Revolution in 1917. In a period where, on both sides of the Atlantic, the so-called robber barons were becoming increasingly wealthy on the basis of their returns on capital and the exploitation of natural resources, the returns for labour were – despite growing labour productivity – still very small and not well protected by laws and collective labour agreements. The Fordist mode of turning labourers *en groupe* into mass consumers would only become a fully realised, albeit unstable, political project after WWII.

An enlightened 'consumer revolution'?

On 12 May 1740, Jan Teding van Berkhout, son of a prominent Delft family, wrote a letter home from Paris. Whilst there, Jan Teding had commissioned beautiful summer clothes from one of the most famous Parisian *couturiers*. Writing to his brother, however, he admitted that he would, most likely, not be in position to wear these garments upon his return in Holland because they were 'trop beau pour oser les porter en Hollande' (Verhoeven 2009, 271–272). This nicely illustrates the major importance of Paris as a fashion making metropolis in the late seventeenth and eighteenth century (Coquery 2011). While Louis XIV failed on the battlefield, the French fashion paradigm conquered Europe – albeit, as this anecdote demonstrates, not without appropriation. It also indicates how, even in the absence of stringent sumptuary legislation, consumer practices in the Low Countries were still regulated by forces of social control and moral restraint. In the bourgeois society of the Netherlands, a careful management of conspicuous consumption was needed to avoid any over-ostentation. As such, this anecdote emphasises the very idea of the Netherlands as the cradle of a new, bourgeois consumer model, one that eventually paved the way towards our new consumer society: 'It was in north-west of Europe, in the Netherlands and Britain, that a more dynamic, innovative culture of consumption came to take hold in the seventeenth and eighteenth centuries' (Trentmann 2016, 53). In both of these countries, economic growth and urbanisation paved the way for a new consumer model adapted to the needs and mentalities of an urbanised society with strong middling sort of people, rather than courtly and socially skewed societies. The following paragraphs will build on that claim, highlighting and discussing the changing mental and moral mindset of consumption in the late early modern period; the related changes in European material culture and the propensity to consume, and the links between this feverish consumer culture and changing retail structures and practices.

In the early eighteenth century, Bernard Mandeville wrote his provocative *Fable of the Bees* in which he argued that the pursuit of luxury, obviously a private vice, was highly beneficial to public welfare (De Vries 2003). Mandeville, a Dutchman who migrated to England, wrote in marked contrast to a long-standing European tradition of the critique of luxury, which itself continued through the eighteenth century. It was one of the seminal texts that fueled the famous eighteenth-century luxury debate. On both sides of the English Channel, awareness among intellectuals grew that, on an aggregate level, the individual appetite to consume – a vice – was a powerful source of improvement and economic growth. Later in the eighteenth century David Hume, among others, refined Mandeville's framework by connecting luxury to refinement and civilisation. Increasingly, as the luxury debate of the eighteenth century progressed, private wants were considered (either positively or negatively) as a major stimulus of industriousness and civilisation (Berg 2005, 21–45). The new luxury discourse did little but offer the theoretical sanctioning of an already modified practice. It was not without antecedents, moreover. In Renaissance Italy, another major cradle of a refined and feverish consumer culture, splendour and magnificence were positively appropriated as reflecting virtue (Guerzoni 1999; Welch 2002), even though the moral regime of pre-modern Italy still had little in common with a modern consumerist attitude (Allerston 2007). Yet, it also coincided with a major transformation in European luxury culture. Italy in particular has been credited with a profound refurbishment of the home. The material renaissance was urban, favoured design above the intrinsic value of things and was fueled by an ever-expanding world of goods that required appropriate urban behaviour (Goldthwaite 1987, 1993; Welch 2005).

The lively luxury debate of the Enlightenment did not come as a coincidence, therefore, but went hand in hand with a world of goods that fundamentally transformed: one that was marked by novelty, variety and availability. Generally speaking, Europeans at the end of the eighteenth century were surrounded by an empire of things. Their material culture was more varied, comfortable, colourful and pleasurable. According to Jan de Vries, industrious revolution was not only marked by an intensification of the allocation of household time to the production and consumption of market-mediated goods and services, it also implied the transition from an 'old luxury' to a 'new luxury' model (De Vries 2008). The former was geared towards leisure and the conspicuous consumption of elites in society; luxury consumption was morally suspect, since it always bore the risk of endangering vested social hierarchies. In contrast, new luxury was not necessarily preoccupied with social distinction per se, but appealed to a larger set of values, such as comfort and pleasure. The new luxuries required taste and civilisation; they were also cheaper and so accessible to larger groups in society than were the ostentatious old luxuries. In his search for the origins of this new luxury model, Jan de Vries arrived in the Netherlands where the bourgeois model of consumption described above blossomed in the seventeenth century (Blondé and Ryckbosch 2015). This new model would come to full force in eighteenth-century England, where Neil McKendrick and others identified the birth of a consumer society (McKendrick 1982b): a beneficial love triangle of social equity, economic growth and consumption, facilitated by the political and moral liberty to consume freely. Historians no longer believe in a pre-industrial consumer revolution, let alone the birth of a consumer society in eighteenth-century England; but the very idea that the pre-industrial era somewhere witnessed a critical transition towards a new consumer model never lost its appeal (Berg 2004, 85). What exactly defines the essential features of the "new luxury" model is not easy to pinpoint, though novelty, variety and the speed of change (fashion sensitivity) clearly distinguished the late eighteenth-century consumer basket from its antecedents. It did so with a series of new goods (such as hot drinks, tobacco, toys and trinkets) as well as important changes in the design and value construction of the world of goods (Trentmann 2016, 53; Blondé 2002).

The material culture changes that came along with this 'new luxury' pattern, were first mapped for the Netherlands and England (De Vries 1975; Weatherill 1988; Shammas 1990; Overton 2004); but they were not confined to these rapidly growing economies. Increasingly, economic historians find evidence from all over Europe attesting a broad and widely shared consumer transition in both expanding and stagnating economies (Wijsenbeek-Olthuis 1987; Blondé and Van Damme 2010). Jan de Vries hypothesised about the origins of an industrious revolution, and especially a transformation in the allocation of household resources to the market economy, to reconcile the evidence of an apparent material affluence with low real incomes and modest economic growth. Other scholars argue that product changes and productivity gains account for a relative fall in the price of industrial products and a consequent increase in the consumption of consumer durables, even in countries where income and wages lagged behind (Malanima and Pinchera 2012). Generally speaking, even with less money, eighteenth-century town and countryside dwellers could afford and consciously enjoy more things, very often of a so called populuxe nature (Fairchilds 1993). In short, the transition towards a new material culture was not confined to the core regions of the Atlantic economy; rather, it applied to Europe in general. Moreover, it did not require economic growth, which also casts doubt on the Adam Smith's argument for the beneficial interplay between the desires of men and economic improvement.

This remarkable proliferation of the empire of things went hand in hand with the expansion of retailing and retail modernisation, as was suggested by the extensive treatment of advertisements and new commercial techniques such as the use of showrooms, trade cards and the like in McKendrick's seminal work (McKendrick 1982a). Indeed, the commercial landscape of early modern Europe was rapidly evolving in the centuries prior to the industrial revolution. Although figures are extremely hard to compare, almost everywhere shops grew in number, both in absolute and relative terms. This was paralleled with a growing diversity of specialised shops serving a varied clientele (Mui and Mui 1989; Van Aert and Van Damme 2005; van den Heuvel and Ogilvie 2013; Mitchell 2014). For sure, fixed shops were already a common feature in medieval towns and they were successful and complementary to markets, as is demonstrated by the obligation for sixteenth-century Venetian shopkeepers to shut doors and take stalls in the square during the Sensa Fair (Welch 2006, 43). Yet, as Fernand Braudel noticed in the 1970s, the real take off of fixed retail outlets happened in the early seventeenth century (Braudel 1979, 2:52–53). Ever since, with varying degrees and intensities, one witnessed a more or less general growth of retail outlets everywhere in Europe; a phenomenon that intensified in the period after 1650 and paralleled the rise in the wide array of new consumer goods and colonial groceries that became available at that time. This growth was not confined to England where Mui and Mui recorded a shop density of about one shop for every fifty-nine inhabitants in 1759, while the London ratio stood at 1:30 (Mui and Mui 1989, 37–41). Even in the Southern Low Countries, an area deprived of strong economic growth in the late seventeenth century, the number of retailers expanded from 1:26 by 1690 to 1:16 in 1773 (Van Aert and Van Damme 2005, 149–150). Overall the growth in the number and variety of shops is generally recognised as part and parcel, if not the backbone, of an early modern "retail revolution". Indeed, generally associated with the advent of the department store and its economies of scale, fixed prices and price ticketing, early modernists were quick to discover modern retailing practices before the advent of the industrial society already (Stobart and Hann 2004).

A large share of this expansion of the retail sector in the eighteenth century was closely intertwined with rapidly changing consumer habits and preferences in the late early modern period (Blondé and Van Damme 2010). The changes in consumer and material culture we briefly touched upon earlier help to explain the rapid growth of the commercial sector in various ways. First and foremost, the attested retail densification was intimately connected with the growing importance of imported goods in the consumption bundle. Colonial groceries such as sugar, coffee, tea, chocolate and spices impacted enormously on the early modern consumer and the world economy. They also affected the retailing scene, reinforcing vested trades and trade patterns (Stobart 2013). In many countries these newly imported products were sold by members of the retailer's guilds or integrated into the supply of general stores. In no time tobacco, coffee and tea conquered households of all social ranks, profoundly reconfiguring consumer patterns. While in the mid-seventeenth century only a handful of tobacco sellers were recorded in Amsterdam, by the mid-eighteenth century a little army of at least 233 tobacco shops serviced the daily needs of Amsterdam citizens at various selling points across the urban map (Lesger 2013). In Antwerp as well, a substantial part of the growth of retail businesses can be accounted for by the increase of imported groceries, but small-town mercers shared in the prospects of these new consumer habits as well. The volume of tobacco sold in the small town of Maastricht, for instance, almost doubled in thirty years' time, from about 31,000 kilograms in 1730–34 to 56750 kilograms in 1757–62. Coffee and tea followed this trend, albeit at a slightly more modest rate of growth. Unsurprisingly, these colonial groceries were dispatched to countryside consumers as well (Steegen 2006, 267). Hence, the need to supply imported groceries to consumers reinforced the weight of shops in society. Whether this was to the detriment of local suppliers such as beer brewers is harder to figure out, but it seems highly likely.

Not only did the retail sector grow as a result of the inclusion of new products, the changing material culture also impacted enormously (Blondé, Van Aert, and Van Damme 2014). The eighteenth century was characterised by the gradual replacement of expensive, durable products possessing a high secondary market value and a potential for resale and reuse, by cheaper, less durable and more fashion sensitive products (Blondé 2002; Stobart and Van Damme 2010). Cheaper textiles (such as printed cottons) came to replace more expensive woollens; tapestries and gilt leather wall hangings made way for textile and paper wall hangings, and silver and pewter lost in importance relative to porcelain (Shammas 1994). On the daily scene, these transitions fundamentally altered the relationship between people's material culture stock and the flow of their consumption. They also necessitated more frequent shop contacts, a result of the declining durability of goods and a growing fashion sensitivity. Across the urban hierarchy, consumers were increasingly subjected to metropolitan fashion and the fashion cycle was moving faster as the century progressed (Berg 2006). Consumers eager to find their way through the increasing consumer choice and the volatility of fashion cycles, had to rely upon the advice of commercial middlemen, such as upholsterers and shopkeepers to steer their consumer choices (Sargentson 1998; Craske 1999; Edwards 2005; Blondé and Van Damme 2010). The latter did everything to offer a pleasurable shopping environment, an arena of polite shopping, to their consumers. Daniel Defoe, for instance, complained how, in London there 'never was such painting and gilding, such sashing and looking-glasses among shopkeepers as there is now' (quoted in Stobart and Hann 2005, 178). Undoubtedly, the majority of shops across North-Western Europe were still sparsely furnished, with a major emphasis on the mere displaying of the variety of the goods for sale. While metropolitan retail outlets were pulling in shoppers with attractive sales environments and novel commercial techniques, most provincial and village shops were simply furnished and relied upon rather 'traditional' sales techniques (Stobart 2007). However, elaborate metropolitan models were not without influence in provincial towns and the commercial vocabulary of trade cards and advertisements, with a major emphasis on the variety of goods, prices, qualities as well as the novelty of goods both betraying and enhancing a growing consumer fever (Coquery 2004).

Such transformations also affected the balance of power in the retail landscape. As long as furniture, silverware, clothing represented an important asset (with an high intrinsic value), it could always be used as an alternative currency allowing people to barter or pawn (Lemire 2005). As material culture increasingly shifted from intrinsic value to design, taste and extrinsic attributes, the resale value of used objects was detrimentally affected. Secondary markets were and remained firmly rooted in pre-industrial societies where they played a strategic role in redistributing used goods across the map and the social hierarchy (Allerston 2007; Fontaine 2008; Stobart and Van Damme 2010). They also contributed to spreading the eighteenth-century fashion imperative among different social groups. Overall, however, secondary markets declined in turnover and social esteem compared to the retail circuits that specialised in producing and selling novelties (Allerston 1996; Blondé and Van Damme 2009). Eventually, the social depreciation of reselling resulted in a geographically and socially segmented low-end market for used goods next to a high-end market for valuable antiquities in the nineteenth century (Van Damme 2015a). That said, the expanding world of the shopkeeper did not prevent traditional circuits from contributing to the new consumer climate as well, as is amply shown by the role played by peddlers in spreading consumer innovations (Fontaine 1996; Deceulaer 2006). In short, while alternative uses and exchanges did not disappear, it was shops that profited most from the expansion of semi-luxuries in the age of Enlightenment. Even producers were obliged to enlarge the variety of goods on offer by including products made by others and elsewhere into their product array (De Munck 2010; Coquery 2011).

The number of shops and the frequency of shop visits grew as a result of new material culture and changing consumer patterns in the eighteenth century. However, this happened in the context of overall economic stability (Van Zanden 2001). How can this paradox be explained? The answer seems to be twofold. On the one hand, the growing number of shops did not necessarily imply an equally growing prosperity for shopkeepers. While much of the retail revolution narrative is inspired by the spectacular growth of retail densities in eighteenth-century society, part of this growth was offset by lower incomes earned by many shopkeepers. Several popular new products – such as hot beverages, tobacco, haberdasheries, cottons and fashion shops – required smaller amounts of capital from aspiring shopkeepers and, as a result, attracted salesmen and women of relatively modest means. The new luxury goods recruited more and more participants, but most buying and selling practices still depended upon very traditional ways of connecting with clients. In the absence of real productivity gains in retailing itself, the importance of their *direct* contribution to a sustained increase in per capita incomes, and hence to economic growth, must be questioned. Both the lower capital intensity and the cheaper location of several new luxuries can be credited with having facilitated the entrance onto the retail market of more modest players that also appealed to a more modest social clientele (Coquery 2011, 286–300).

Even though the aggregate income growth of the retail sector was much more modest than employment growth, overall per capita expenditure on shopping still seems to have risen in the eighteenth century: 'Households reoriented their consumer behaviour to make heavy use of shops despite their high cost, not because of major supply side reductions in the transactions cost of retailing' (De Vries 2008, 170). What the economic historian could frame as a transaction cost problem seems to have been perceived and experienced rather as an enjoyable cultural phenomenon. Moreover, it was a phenomenon that trained or even conditioned consumers in becoming the sort of material pleasure seekers that underpin modern consumer economies. Both in the metropolis and the provincial town, a pleasurable shopping environment and culture became part and parcel of polite society (Borsay 1989; Walsh 1995, 2003; Stobart, Hann, and Morgan 2007). In fact, shopping achieved its particular linguistic significance in this period. Elite customers of the *Au magasin de Paris*, an Antwerp fashion shop, frequented its luxury premises on a very regular basis, most of the time to buy a handful of haberdasheries or services while expending modest sums of money only. It is clear from this that the need to spend more money and time on the act of buying – the need for more frequent shop visits that went hand in hand with the more fashionable and less durable consumer culture – was turned into a valuable and pleasurably pastime: a real culture of shopping.

This shopping and consumer culture, however, did not come as a revolution; it had already matured for centuries. From at least the end of the Middle Ages, changing sensibilities in shopping behaviour began to influence retail practices (Keene 2006). In line with Renaissance notions of the personal and public display of taste and affluence, luxury consumption was gradually un-attached from its religious and moral overtones. The daily world of shopping for necessities continued to colour the world of buying and selling, but its practices were enriched by an urban, civilised lifestyle aimed at aesthetic refinement, knowledge of taste and being *à la mode*. Shopping as a public performance of collectively shared norms and values, and as a polite pastime, became intrinsically linked to being urban and urbane (Blondé and Van Damme 2013). Economically speaking, the practices that were fostered by this shopping culture developed along very traditional paths of the retailing business. What mattered was variety and choice, trust, knowledge, proximity, advice and the provision of credit (Mitchell 2014; Van Damme 2015b). In sum, the best model into which we might fit the rapidly changing world of retailing in early modern Europe is a cultural one and a traditional one as well – a model that has little to do with an imagined economic revolution.

Towards mass consumption and retailing in the *fin-de-siècle* world

On 14 April 1910, the new department store *Grand Magasins Leonhard Tietz* had its grand opening in the Rue Neuve, one of the major shopping streets in *belle-époque* Brussels. The newspaper reporting on this major social event was overwhelmed by the enormous quantity and variety of goods, offered in a luxurious and splendid, bright setting, which the journalist described as kind of "Noah's Ark" of material culture (Arnout 2015, 37–41). Journalistic reports such as this were the rule rather than the exception for the time: whether in London, Paris, Brussels, New York or Chicago, contemporaries in Europe and North America were impressed by the sheer architectural monumentality of these retail structures that so heavily contrasted with the more modest and mundane shops with which they entered into competition. Increasingly equipped with restrooms, restaurants and cafés, department stores not only offered goods for sale, but crucially also provided tactile entertainment: a genuine, modern and leisurely shopping experience (see the chapter by Elvins in this volume).

There are many reasons why department stores figure so prominently in consumer and retail historiographies of the turn-of-the-century world (Crossick and Jaumain 1999; Howard 2015). Department stores – some of which had inauspiciously and gradually evolved from drapery shops – became icons of a late nineteenth-century consumer revolution, the shock waves of which were soon to be felt all over the world. From their very beginnings, these cathedrals of consumption echoed Western modernity: they became the perfect foil for contemporary and later commentators to project both awe and anxieties about Western civilisation (see the chapter by Fujioka in this volume). In Europe, early urban theorists like Walter Benjamin and Georg Simmel saw them as embodiments of modern Western culture, centred around urban shopping and a tantalising, sensory spectacle of objects; the economist Werner Sombart equated them with modern Western capitalism (Slater and Tonkiss 2001; Trentmann 2016). With the benefit of hindsight, however, it seems fair to say that department stores were more important as an idea or imagining of Western progress and superiority than as forces that fundamentally revolutionised the retail landscape. At the end of the 1930s, for instance, they still monopolised only a tiny fraction of retailing in Britain (no more than 5.5% of total retail sales). This was not significantly different in many other Western and non-Western countries where department stores had been heralded as shining symbols of modernisation (Haupt 2012, 272; Harada's chapter in this volume). The real question then becomes why it was that department stores encapsulated and warped Western imaginations. Using department stores as a starting point, we question how to reinterpret retailing and its connection with the consumer variable in a period that figures so prominently in consumer and retail historiography. It focuses anew on how our shared consumer and retail knowledge have become fundamentally enmeshed with persistent, western narratives of modernity and with core western values, and concludes that any triumphalism about this period is misplaced and unwarranted.

When reconsidering consumer and retail evolutions at the end of the nineteenth-century, it is essential to adopt a broader contextual perspective. Department stores should never be isolated from the environment in which they emerged: they were an integral aspect of urbanisation in a feverish period of city building, starting in the middle of the nineteenth century, that had radically broken open the pre-industrial urban landscape of North-Western Europe. Beginning in Paris under the influential guidance of Baron G.E. Haussmann, new, apartment-filled *boulevards* and shopping *avenues* began to emerge in capital cities such as Vienna, Brussels and Berlin, and in many expanding metropolitan centres in America. Private, commercial enterprise was integral and, in many ways, essential to such endeavours, since it drove up property values and promised future owners and urban municipalities a healthy return on investments by transforming the most congested and unsanitary inner-city neighbourhoods. Especially after the 1870s, when a global economic downturn hit financial markets, wealthy investors and local politicians followed each other into urban renewal and channelled massive public and private capital into the beautification of the public domain and the modernisation of the accompanying hotel, café/restaurant, and retail sectors. Promoting Western cities as shining stars of a fashionable and rapidly modernising leisure and consumption landscape became integral to attracting a growing group of visitors and wealthy, suburbanising citizens alike (Wagenaar 2001; Howard 2015).

Department stores clearly profited from and contributed to this urban "boosterism": some of the technological and architectural marvel and expertise that accompanied the planning and engineering of urban renewal rubbed off on the outsides and insides of department stores. Built out of iron and sometimes with spectacular glass facades, connected to electric lightning, gas and water pipes, modern sewage systems, and equipped with new escalators, these buildings were themselves seen as an exhibition of what Western "superiority" and industrial progress were able to accomplish at the turn of the century. Moreover, just as the impressive arcades and covered market hall buildings, which for similar reasons underwent an upsurge from the last quarter of the nineteenth-century, department stores materialised a radical symbolic break with the past. From a physical point of view, such a break with the filth and ugliness of days gone by was quite genuine, and Romantic observers woefully lamented the destruction of picturesque streets and structures that had to make room for modern city-making. Outside North-Western Europe as well, in cities as diverse as Shanghai, Cairo, Istanbul, Buenos Aires and Mexico City, *Haussmannisation* and the arrival of Paris- and US-styled department stores, not only signalled the foreign penetration of Western capital and imperialistic efforts, but was also seen quite literally as a physical *tabula rasa* over a "horrendous" and "barbarous" non-Western past (Hazel Hahn 2015).

Figure 3.1 Exterior of La Maison Tietz, a grand department store in *fin-de-siècle* Antwerp, Belgium

Source: Courtesy of Collection Janssens.

Figure 3.2 Interior of La Maison Tietz, Antwerp, Belgium

Source: Courtesy of Collection Janssens.

However, from the point of view of an already long-running consumer and retail continuity in North-Western European cities, the department store-myth – the idea of it being connected to Western progress and modernisation – begins to crumble when placed in proper retail perspective. Department stores were not only applauded for their architectural and technological prowess, but also for allegedly opening up the market for an unparalleled cornucopia of material plenty and desires: haberdashery, furniture, clothing, glass, china – they were all organised in different sections of the department store. In reality, however, this was not mass consumption, since most of the products that department stores sold were rather highly priced and aimed at an upper market clientele. True, the sheer diversity and variety of goods on offer could never be matched by the type of much smaller eighteenth-century fashion shops and *à la mode magazins* described above. Yet, these fashion shops had promoted themselves by stressing diversity and variety of supply, and effectively offered cheaper semi-luxuries to a much wider segment of people than before – very similar to what department stores were doing a century later (Walsh 1999).

It can also be seriously questioned if department stores were really as liberating for urban consumers as often has been claimed. In particular, their importance in the life of shopping women – providing a civilised safe haven from the vulgarity of the street and marketplace – has been much exaggerated. Emile Zola, most famously, focused in *Au Bonheur des Dames* (1883) on the inner psyche of a young, fragile country girl from Normandy, Denise Baudu, who becomes completely intoxicated and seduced by the machinery of a Parisian department store. The topos lingered on and became stock material for typical masculine anxieties and phantasies about women (Tiersten 2001, 15–54). If Zola's text could at least be interpreted as a socially heartfelt critique of the working conditions in department stores, others had a harder time keeping in check their male, erotic imaginations around consuming women, with a sex scene in the bedding department of a Swedish store being the questionable climax of *Det stora varuhuset* (1926) by Sigfrid Siwertz (Trentmann 2016, 216). In the real world, shopping women in North-Western European cities had been a common and unremarkable sight for centuries; much of the late nineteenth-century moral panic around kleptomaniac or insatiable, spend-crazy female shoppers should in fact be read in reverse. Far from being an adequate description of the urban world, they tell us more how the puritan and curtailed Victorian mind filtered department stores and female shopping in the imagination. They can be placed in the same category as other conservative or well-meant paternalistic reactions against the "New Woman", who was gradually emancipating herself in the social, economic and political male-dominated arenas of society (Rappaport 2001).

The point where contemporaries and generations of historians did get it right about department stores is in their use of relative innovative marketing and business techniques. Department stores deployed efficient and cost-cutting business strategies, in part by acting as wholesalers or by directly contracting producers, while in the meantime also importing some of the bad working conditions that had been pioneered in the industrial sector: long hours, low wages, authoritarian rule and organisation, etc. Goods were ticketed, prices fixed, keen prices advertised, end of season sales promoted and a choice offered between paying ready money for lower prices or via more expensive forms of product instalment credit. Lower profit margins per item sold were compensated by higher turnover which also facilitated a more direct interplay with fashion cycles and warranted large advertising budgets bent on luring as many customers as possible into the stores (Alexander and Akehurst 1998; Howard, 2015 – see also the chapter by Elvins in this volume).

In many of these retail innovations, however, the department store was not a stand-alone in the consumer landscape of the nineteenth-century city (Lesger and Furnée 2014). The breakthrough of the department store was built on a whole range of earlier retail innovations pioneered in shops and previous large-scale retail formats such as the sixteenth-century *panden*, seventeenth-century shopping galleries and early nineteenth-century *bazaars* (Vermeylen 2003, 19–28; Walsh 2003, 52–79; Stobart 2014, 26–27). More importantly, other emerging late-nineteenth-century retail formats – most conspicuously the retail chain and co-operative – used similar business innovations, arguably to much wider effect. Retail chains and co-operatives certainly started to attract and reach bigger segments of society than the *belle-époque* department store (Alexander, Shaw, and Hodson 2003).

However, with the advent of the retail chain and co-operative, urban consumer landscapes did not change overnight. Almost everywhere the number of shopkeepers followed urban population growth (bakeries, for instance, are a good case in point) and even old retail circuits, such as the peddlers, successfully defended their position in the changing consumer and retail market of the *fin-de-siècle* world. Street vending as well as open-air markets proved extremely resilient in fulfilling the basic needs and wants of the masses (Stobart and Van Damme 2016; Calaresu and Van den Heuvel 2016). Yet, both the retail chain and the co-operative, much more as the department store, can be seen as formats linked to burgeoning mass market aspirations and profound social transformations in the urban field. With the increase of urban population, working-class demand for cheap food and standardised goods (shoes, clothing, etc.) was on the rise. Often growing organically out of small food shops, grocers, chemists, and shops attending to, for instance, the sale of cheaply manufactured *prêt-à-porter*, the retail chain or multiple retailer, tried to find a rational solution to what had become a growing problem in the expanding North-Western European cities around 1870, namely provisioning for basic, day-to-day needs at much lower prices than before (Stobart 2008, 138–143). Moreover, with the final breakthrough of industrial modes of production, consumer trust had to be earned for selling mass-produced items, including hitherto unknown items such as meat extracts, margarine, conserves, canned food and so on.

Figure 3.3 A typical narrow street near the centre of Antwerp, Belgium, c.1893. On the right, street sellers have arranged merchandise on the pavement in large reed baskets

Source: Courtesy of Collection Janssens.

Although retail chains were not solely, nor even firstly devoted to selling food, distributing cheap food and manufactured foodstuffs became central to the political economy of industrialising Europe and North America, since this would cut directly into the high cost of living for the expanding and still badly paid labour force (Atkins and Oddy 2008). When, due to agricultural mechanisation and innovations in rail transport and steam shipping, cheap grain – and soon afterwards fruit, vegetables and frozen meat – began to pour into European ports from the 1870s onwards, the multiple retailer followed suit by branching out their operations on both the local and supra-local levels (see the chapter by Kruger in this volume). Soon, retail chains, addressing their customers with recognisable shop architecture, brands and names (Sainsbury's is a long-lived example in Britain), operated complex networks of logistics and distribution which allowed for unprecedented retail coverage, economies of scale, and in the end cheaper prices and a trustworthy retail format for everybody. Co-operatives started developing and multiplying along similar lines, sometimes producing their own food to secure quality and trustworthiness of sale in an industrialising product market. They differed, however, from the more commercially oriented multiple retailers by being built on dominant political-ideological concerns about the material improvement of the labouring classes. Customers had to become a member of the co-operative and commercial profits of the retail operation could eventually be used for schemes of social and

Figure 3.4 A traditional shop selling dried fish displayed on the shop front and on trestles in the street; next door, a more modern looking tobacconist has neatly arranged his merchandise behind a glazed window. Antwerp, Belgium, c.1893

Source: Courtesy of Collection Janssens.

moral betterment (Furlough and Strikwerda 1999; see also the chapter by Hilson et al. in this volume).

By focusing on the co-operative movement, among others, the *fin-de-siècle* world has rightly been recognised for putting consumer rights and the entitlement to consume high on the social and political agenda. The idea that better-paid labourers could be made into consumers became integral to the Fordist mode of production; as was the Taylorian idea that a more structured and better organised working schedule could both improve labour productivity and create leisure time for the employed (Tomka 2013, 192–262). For most North-West European and North American countries, however, the actual implementation and legal realisation of these ideas would only come after the horrors of the World Wars and the setbacks of the Great Depression, which made social restructuring mandatory. In Belgium, for instance, new social laws were being issued in the last two decades of the nineteenth century under pressure of, among others, the rising Socialist Party, but these only remedied the most grievous ills of the industrial labour model (abolishment of child labour and required schooling, wage protection by abolishing truck systems, and so on). Of arguably greater importance in placing the consumer in the centre of the political arena in this period were the growing consumer movements taking the form of both concerned 'leagues' of housewives and full-blown urban protest and social mobilisation around essential consumer goods and services, like gas and water (Chatriot, Chessel, and Hilton 2004; Taylor and Trentmann 2011). In their attention for public safety and health, however, the initiatives of concerned consumer-citizens stayed very much in tune with typical turn-of-the-century bourgeois prerogatives and sensibilities. Mass mobilisation around improvements in the purchasing power of the labouring classes was in general not part of the agenda.

All in all, the rise of new retail formats at the end of the nineteenth century did not revolutionise the retail world. Retailers proved to be innovative in adapting to larger changes in the *fin-de-siècle* world; from the perspective of the urban consumer, however, not that much fundamentally changed. Although the building of new department stores, and to a lesser extent the new arcades and market halls, was accompanied by physical destruction and uprooting of existing streets and neighbourhoods, these core symbols of nineteenth-century consumerism should not, in the end, be understood as having invented urban shopping as a leisurely and civilised pastime; they merely coloured its flamboyant, *belle-époque* outlook. Catering for rising urban consumer demand had a big impact on the activities of especially multiple retailing and the co-operative movement, yet here as well claims about the advent of an age of mass consumerism should be nuanced. Despite unquestionable improvements in the living standards of the expanding middle classes, North-Western Europe and North America around 1900 remained highly socially polarised and divided between labour and capital. Mass markets did not come with an impressive treats-for-all consumer party before wartime: avoiding hunger and making hard choices around proper clothing and the home was the best most labouring people could aspire for.

Conclusion

While major narratives about Western retail and consumer revolutions were severely attacked in the past decades, they continue to govern our interpretations of late early modern and nineteenth-century transformations in buying and selling practices. And while, quite often, the connections between the changing worlds of retailing and consumption are intuitively presupposed – as is exemplified for instance in the abundant literature on advertising – studies that really interconnect changes in consumption and distribution are few. By focusing upon two periods of critical transformation in material culture of North-Western Europe, consumption and retailing, this chapter explored the possibilities of bringing together these research traditions. Other regions and periods might readily serve this purpose as well, although they remain underrepresented and under-theorised in overall historiography.

Recent research has done a good job in downplaying the revolutionary character of consumer and retail changes. After all, economic growth was slow and even supposedly modern late nineteenth-century retailing took place in the context of a socially skewed society, targeting urban elites and the middle classes, rather than the mass market consumer. Hence, it probably does not come as a surprise that linear stage models, in which the rise of the department stores was seen as the logical and necessary outcome of economic modernisation and urbanisation, were quickly abandoned. Throughout the eighteenth and nineteenth centuries different commercial circuits coexisted, competed but also complemented each other. Shopkeepers, as is clear by now, were not only victims of the competition of department stores: to a certain extent they also benefited by intercepting customers frequenting these same department stores. And while street vending was considered an obsolete and ill-trusted model, it continued to play its role well into the nineteenth and even twentieth centuries. The same argument can be made about basic open-air markets, which often proved to be more attractive and successful as the newly constructed, but sometimes cumbersome covered market buildings. Without necessarily downplaying the cultural and societal impact of these eye-catching nineteenth-century retail innovations and enterprises, at the start of the twentieth century, the lion's share of buying and selling across Europe developed in rather common, "traditional" retail outlets, often using well-known, day-to-day retailing methods.

However, by stressing deep-historical lines of continuity and downplaying triumphant Western modernisation theses, it would be easy to miss one crucial and very important long-term transformation. Strikingly enough, both in the early modern period and the nineteenth century alike, shopping and retailing were clearly on the rise, and their development was determined to a large extent by consumer and material culture changes that necessitated more frequent shopping activities, preferably in an enjoyable and civilised (urban) context. Despite clear and obvious innovations in doing retail business, common traditional sales qualities – such as the personal and informative relationship between buyer and seller – continued to dominate. In fact, on an aggregate level, a large part of the retail growth and diversification happened *despite* the absence of significant productivity gains in retailing practices. People spent more time and money on shopping, without necessarily enriching the individual shopkeeper. In the nineteenth century as well, supply side cost reductions in the production and transport of goods ultimately turned the retailing moment into a challenging economic bottleneck. Remarkably enough, however, shopping was not considered an increasing social cost, but instead became framed as a civilised and pleasurable part of an urban, bourgeois lifestyle. Indeed, the early modern consumer changes, such as the growing fashion sensitivity of the material culture, necessitated more frequent shop visits. Yet, the need to go out for shopping (and spend more money on the act of shopping) was captured and appropriated by turning it into an enjoyable and pleasurable pastime and leisure activity. Hence, shopping activities were increasingly part of an evolving bourgeois mindset through the deployment of a genteel shopping environment and vocabulary. The arcades, covered market halls and department stores – as iconic cathedrals of consumption – were the elaborated outcome of a process that set in well before the industrial revolution took off. In the metropolitan environment, at least, the retail revolution was foremost a cultural revolution – albeit in the first place one for the well-to-do and bourgeois.

References

Alexander, A., Shaw, G. and Hodson, D. (2003), 'Regional variations in the development of multiple retailing in England, 1890–1939', in J. Benson and L. Ugolini (eds.) *A nation of shopkeepers: Five centuries of British retailing* (London: I.B. Tauris) 127–154.

Alexander, N. and Akehurst, G. (1998), 'Introduction: The emergence of modern retailing, 1750–1950', *Business History*, 40, pp. 1–15.

Allerston, P. (1996), 'Le marché d'occasion à Venise aux XVIe–XVIIe siècles', in J. Bottin and N. Pellegrin (eds.) *Echanges et cultures textiles dans l'Europe préindustrielle* (Lille: Revue du Nord) 15–29.

Allerston, P. (2007), 'Consuming problems: Worldly goods in Renaissance Venice', in M. O'Malley and E. Welch (eds.) *The material Renaissance* (Manchester: Manchester University Press) 11–46.

Arnout, A. (2015), 'Sights/sites of splendor: The shopping landscape in nineteenth-century Brussels', Unpublished PhD, University of Antwerp.

Atkins, P. and Oddy, D.J. (eds.) (2008), *Food and the city in Europe since 1800* (Aldershot: Ashgate).

Berg, M. (2004), 'In pursuit of luxury: Global history and British consumer goods in the eighteenth century', *Past and Present*, 182, pp. 85–142.

Berg, M. (2005), *Luxury and pleasure in eighteenth-century Britain* (Oxford: Oxford University Press).

Berg, M. (2006), 'French fancy and cool Brittania: The fashion markets of early modern Europe', *Journal for the Study of British Cultures*, 13 (1), pp. 21–46.

Bianchi, M. (ed.) (1998), *The active consumer: Novelty and surprise in consumer choice* (London/New York: Routledge).

Blondé, B. (2002), 'Tableware and changing consumer patterns. Dynamics of material culture in Antwerp, 17th–18th centuries', in J. Veeckman (ed.) *Majolica and glass from Italy to Antwerp and beyond: The transfer of technology in the 16th–early 17th century* (Antwerp: Stad Antwerpen) 295–311.

Blondé, B. and Ryckbosch, W. (2015), 'In "splendid isolation": A comparative perspective on the historiographies of the "material renaissance" and the "consumer revolution"', *History of Retailing and Consumption*, 1 (2), pp. 105–124.

Blondé, B., Van Aert, L. and Van Damme, I. (2014), 'According to the latest and most elegant fashion: Retailing textiles and changes in supply and demand in seventeenth- and eighteenth-century Antwerp', in J. Stobart and B. Blondé (eds.) *Selling textiles in the long eighteenth century: Comparative perspectives from Western Europe* (London: Palgrave Macmillan) 138–159.

Blondé, B. and Van Damme, I. (2009), 'Fashioning old and new or moulding the material culture of Europe (late seventeenth-nineteenth centuries)', in B. Blondé, N. Coquery, J. Stobart and I. Van Damme (eds.) *Fashioning old and new: Changing consumer preferences in Europe (seventeenth–nineteenth centuries)* (Turnhout: Brepols) 1–13.

Blondé, B. and Van Damme, I. (2010), 'Retail growth and consumer changes in a declining urban economy, Antwerp (1650–1750)', *The Economic History Review*, 63 (3), pp. 638–663.

Blondé, B. and Van Damme, I. (2013), 'Early modern Europe: 1500–1800', in P. Clark (ed.) *The Oxford handbook of cities in world history* (Oxford: Oxford University Press) 240–257.

Borsay, P. (1989), *The English urban renaissance: Culture and society in the provincial town 1660–1770* (Oxford: Clarendon Press).

Braudel, F. (1979), *Civilisation matérielle, économie et capitalisme, XVe–XVIIIe siècle*, 3 Vols. (Paris: Colin).

Calaresu, M. and Van den Heuvel, D. (2016), 'Introduction: Food hawkers from representation to reality', in M. Calaresu and D. Van den Heuvel (eds.) *Food hawkers: Selling in the street from antiquity to the present* (London/New York: Routledge) 1–18.

Chatriot, A., Chessel, E. and Hilton, M. (eds.) (2004), *Au nom du consommateur: Consommation et politique en Europe et aux Etats-Unis au XXe siècle* (Paris: La Découverte).

Coquery, N. (2004), 'The language of success: Marketing and distributing semi-luxury goods in eighteenth-century Paris', *Journal of Design History*, 17, pp. 71–89.

Coquery, N. (2011), *Tenir boutique à Paris au XVIIIe siècle: Luxe et demi-luxe* (Paris: Editions du comité des travaux historiques et scientifiques).

Craske, M. (1999), 'Plan and control: Design and the competition spirit in early and mid-eighteenth century England', *Journal of Design History*, 12, pp. 187–216.

Crossick, G. and Jaumain, S. (1999), 'The world of the department store: Distribution, culture and social change', in G. Crossick and S. Jaumain (eds.) *Cathedrals of consumption: The European department store, 1850–1939* (Aldershot: Ashgate) 1–45.

Deceulaer, H. (2006), 'Dealing with diversity: Peddlers in the Southern Netherlands in the eighteenth century', in B. Blondé, P. Stabel, J. Stobart and I. Van Damme (eds.) *Buyers and sellers: Retail circuits and practices in medieval and early modern Europe* (Turnhout: Brepols) 171–198.

De Munck, B. (2010), 'One counter and your own account: Redefining illicit labour in early modern Antwerp', *Urban History*, 37 (1), pp. 26–44.

De Vries, J. (1975), 'Peasant demand patterns and economic development: Friesland 1550–1750', in W.N. Parker and E.L. Jones (eds.) *European peasants and their markets: essays in agrarian economic history* (Princeton, NJ: Princeton University Press) 205–259.

De Vries, J. (2003), 'Luxury in the Dutch golden age in theory and practice', in M. Berg and E. Eger (eds.) *Luxury in the eighteenth century: Debates, desires and delectable goods* (Basingstoke: Palgrave Macmillan) 41–56.

De Vries, J. (2008), *The industrious revolution: Consumer behavior and the household economy, 1650 to the present* (Cambridge: Cambridge University Press).

Edwards, D. (2005), 'The upholsterer and the retailing of domestic furnishings 1600–1800', in B. Blondé, E. Briot, N. Coquery and L. Van Aert (eds.) *Retailers and consumer changes in early modern Europe: England, France, Italy and the Low Countries* (Tours: Presses Universitaires François-Rabelais) 53–69.

Fairchilds, C. (1993), 'The production and marketing of populuxe goods in eighteenth-century Paris', in J. Brewer and R. Porter (eds.) *Consumption and the world of goods* (London: Routledge) 228–248.

Fontaine, L. (1996), *History of pedlars in Europe* (Oxford: Polity Press).

Fontaine, L. (ed.) (2008), *Alternative exchanges: Second-hand circulations from the sixteenth century to the present* (New York/Oxford: Berghan Books).

Furlough, E. and Strikwerda, C. (eds.) (1999), *Consumers against capitalism? Consumer co-operation in Europe: North-America and Japan, 1840–1990* (Oxford: Rowman & Littlefield Publishers).

Goldthwaite, R. (1987), 'The empire of things: Consumer demand in Renaissance Italy', in F.W. Kent and P. Simons (eds.) *Art and society in Renaissance Italy* (Oxford: Oxford University Press) 153–175.

Goldthwaite, R. (1993), *Wealth and the demand for art in Italy, 1300–1600* (Baltimore, MD: Johns Hopkins University Press).

Guerzoni, G. (1999), 'Liberalitas, magnificentia, splendour: The classic origins of Italian Renaissance lifestyles', *History of Political Economy*, 31 (5), pp. 332–378.

Haupt, H.-G. (2012), 'Small shops and department stores', in F. Trentmann (ed.) *The Oxford handbook of the history of consumption* (Oxford: Oxford University Press) 267–285.

Hazel Hahn, H. (2015), 'Consumer culture and advertising', in M. Sale (ed.) *The fin-de-siècle world* (Abingdon/New York: Routledge) 392–408.

Howard, V. (2015), *From main street to mall: The rise and fall of the American department store* (Philadelphia, PA: University of Pennsylvania Press).

Jefferys, J. (1954), *Retail trading in Britain, 1850–1950* (Cambridge: Cambridge University Press).

Keene, D. (2006), 'Sites of desire: Shops, selds and wardrobes in London and other English cities, 1100–1550', in B. Blondé, P. Stabel, J. Stobart and I. Van Damme (eds.) *Buyers and sellers: Retail circuits and practices in medieval and early modern Europe* (Turnhout: Brepols) 125–153.

Lemire, B. (2005), 'Shifting currency: The culture and economy of second-hand trade in England, c. 1600–1850', in A. Palmer and H. Clark (eds.) *Old clothes, new looks: Second hand fashion* (Oxford: Berg) 29–48.

Lesger, C. (2013), *Het winkellandschap van Amsterdam: Stedelijke structuur en winkelbedrijf in de vroegmoderne en moderne tijd, 1550–2000* (Hilversum: Verloren).

Lesger, C. and Furnée, J.H. (2014), 'Shopping streets and cultures from a long-term and transnational perspective', in C. Lesger and J.H. Hein Furnée (eds.) *The landscape of consumption: Shopping streets and cultures in Western Europe, 1600–1900* (Houndmills: Palgrave Macmillan) 1–15.

Malanima, P. and Pinchera, V. (2012), 'A puzzling relationship: Consumptions and incomes in early modern Europe', *Histoire & Mesure*, 27 (2), pp. 197–222.

McKendrick, N. (1982a), 'George Packwood and the commercialization of shaving: The art of eighteenth-century advertising or "the way to get money and be happy"', in N. McKendrick, J. Brewer and J.H. Plumb (eds.) *The birth of a consumer society: The commercialisation of eighteenth-century England* (London: Europa Publications) 146–196.

McKendrick, N. (1982b), 'The consumer revolution of eighteenth-century England', in N. McKendrick, J. Brewer and J.H. Plumb (eds.) *The birth of a consumer society: The commercialization of eighteenth-century England* (London: Europa Publications) 3–36.

Mitchell, I. (2014), *Tradition and innovation in English retailing, 1700 to 1850: Narratives of consumption* (Farnham: Ashgate).

Moore, J.W. (2015), *Capitalism in the web of life: Ecology and the accumulation of capital* (London: Verso).

Mui, H.C. and Mui, L.H. (1989), *Shops and shopkeeping in eighteenth-century England* (Kingston: McGill-Queen's University Press).

Overton, M. (ed.) (2004), *Production and consumption in English Households, 1600–1750* (London: Routledge).

Rappaport, E. (2001), *Shopping for pleasure: Women in the making of London's West End* (Princeton, NJ/Oxford: Princeton University Press).

Sargentson, C. (1998), 'The manufacture and marketing of luxury goods: The marchands merciers of late 17th- and 18th-century Paris', in R. Fox and A. Turner (eds.) *Luxury trades and consumerism in Ancien Régime Paris: Studies in the history of the skilled workforce* (Aldershot: Ashgate) 99–138.

Shammas, C. (1990), *The pre-industrial consumer in England and America* (Oxford: Clarendon Press).

Shammas, C. (1994), 'The decline of textile prices in England and British America prior to industrialisation', *Economic History Review*, 48, pp. 483–507.

Slater, D. (1997), *Consumer culture and modernity* (Cambridge: Polity Press).

Slater, D. and Tonkiss, F. (2001), *Market society: Markets and modern social theory* (Cambridge: Polity Press).

Steegen, E. (2006), *Kleinhandel en stedelijke ontwikkeling: Het kramersambacht te Maastricht in de vroegmoderne tijd* (Hilversum: Verloren).

Stobart, J. (2007), 'Accomodating the shop: The commercial use of domestic space in English provincial towns, c.1660–1740', *Cittá & Storia*, 2, pp. 351–363.

Stobart, J. (2008), *Spend, spend, spend: A history of shopping* (Stroud: Tempus).

Stobart, J. (2013), *Sugar and spice: Grocers and groceries in Provincial England, 1650–1830* (Oxford: Oxford University Press).

Stobart, J. (2014), 'The shopping streets of Provincial England, 1650–1840', in C. Lesger and J.H. Hein Furnée (eds.) *The landscape of consumption: Shopping streets and cultures in Western Europe, 1600–1900* (Houndmills: Palgrave Macmillan) 16–36.

Stobart, J. and Hann, H. (2004), 'Retailing revolution in the eighteenth century? Evidence from North-West England', *Business History*, 46, pp. 171–194.

Stobart, J. and Hann, A. (2005), 'Sites of consumption: The display of goods in provincial shops in eighteenth-century England', *Cultural and Social History*, 2, pp. 165–188.

Stobart, J., Hann, A. and Morgan, V. (2007), *Spaces of consumption: Leisure and shopping in the English town, c.1680–1830* (London/New York: Routledge).

Stobart, J. and Van Damme, I. (eds.) (2010), *Modernity and the second-hand trade: European consumption cultures and practices, 1700–1900* (London: Palgrave Macmillan).

Stobart, J. and Van Damme, I. (2016), 'Introduction: Markets in modernization: Transformations in urban market space and practice, c. 1800–c. 1970', *Urban History*, 43 (3), pp. 358–371.

Taylor, V. and Trentmann, F. (2011), 'Liquid politics: Water and the politics of everyday life in the modern city', *Past & Present*, 211, pp. 199–241.

Tiersten, L. (2001), *Marianne in the market: Envisioning consumer society in Fin-de-Siècle France* (Berkeley, CA/Los Angeles, CA/London: University of California Press).

Tomka, B. (2013), *A social history of twentieth-century Europe* (London/New York: Routledge).

Trentmann, F. (2006), 'Knowing consumers – histories, identities, practices: An introduction', in F. Trentmann (ed.) *The making of the consumer: Knowledge, power and identity in the modern world* (Oxford/New York: Berg) 1–27.

Trentmann, F. (2016), *Empire of things: How we became a world of consumers, from the fifteenth century to the twenty-first* (London: Allen Lane).

Van Aert, L. and Van Damme, I. (2005), 'Retail dynamics of a city in crisis: The mercer guild in pre-industrial Antwerp (c.1648–c.1748)', in B. Blondé and N. Coquery (eds.) *Retailers and consumer changes in early modern Europe: England, France, Italy and the Low Countries* (Tours: Presses Universitaires François-Rabelais) 139–167.

Van Damme, I. (2015a), 'Recycling the wreckage of history: On the rise of an "antiquarian consumer culture" in the Southern Netherlands', in A. Fennetaux, A. Junqua and S. Vasset (eds.) *The afterlife of used things: Recycling in the long eighteenth century* (London/New York: Routledge) 47–48.

Van Damme, I. (2015b), 'From a "knowledgable" salesman towards a "recognizable" product? Questioning branding strategies before industrialization (Antwerp, seventeenth to nineteenth centuries)', in B. De Munck and D. Lyna (eds.) *Concepts of value in European material culture, 1500–1900* (Farnham: Ashgate) 75–102.

Van den Heuvel, D. and Ogilvie, S. (2013), 'Retail development in the consumer revolution: The Netherlands, c.1670–c.1815', *Explorations in Economic History*, 50, pp. 69–87.

Van Zanden, J.L. (2001), 'Early modern economic growth: A survey of the European economy, 1500–1800', in M. Prak (ed.) *Early modern capitalism: Economic and social change in Europe, 1400–1800* (London/New York: Routledge) 69–87.

Verhoeven, G. (2009), *Anders reizen? Evoluties in vroegmoderne reiservaringen van Hollandse en Brabantse elites (1600–1750)* (Hilversum: Verloren).

Vermeylen, F. (2003), *Painting for the market: Commercialization of art in Antwerp's golden age* (Turnhout: Brepols).

Wagenaar, M. (2001), *Stedebouw en burgerlijke vrijheid. De contrasterende carrières van zes Europese hoofdsteden* (Bussum: Thoth).

Walsh, C. (1995), 'Shop design and the display of goods in eighteenth-century London', *Journal of Design History*, 8, pp. 157–176.

Walsh, C. (1999), 'The newness of the department store: A view from the eighteenth century', in G. Crossick and S. Jaumain (eds.) *Cathedrals of consumption: The European department store, 1850–*1939 (Aldershot: Ashgate) 46–71.

Walsh, C. (2003), 'Social meaning and social space in the shopping galleries of early modern London', in J. Benson and L. Ugolini (eds.) *A nation of shopkeepers: Five centuries of British retailing* (London: I.B. Tauris) 52–79.

Weatherill, L. (1988), *Consumer behaviour and material culture in Britain 1660–1760* (London: Routledge).

Welch, E. (2002), 'Magnificence and the private display: Pontano's "De Splendore" and the Domestic Arts', *Journal of Design History*, 15, pp. 211–227.

Welch, E. (2005), *Shopping in the Renaissance: Consumer cultures in Italy, 1400–1600* (New Haven, CT/London: Yale University Press).

Welch, E. (2006), 'The fairs of early modern Italy', in B. Blondé, P. Stabel, J. Stobart and I. Van Damme (eds.) *Buyers and sellers: Retail circuits and practices in medieval and early modern Europe* (Turnhout: Brepols) 31–50.

Wijsenbeek-Olthuis, Th. (1987), *Achter de gevels van Delft: Bezit en bestaan van rijk en arm in een periode van achteruitgang (1700–1800)* (Hilversum: Verloren).

4

RETAIL DEVELOPMENT AND URBAN FORM IN THE UNITED STATES DURING THE NINETEENTH AND TWENTIETH CENTURIES

Richard Longstreth

Introduction

A succession of sweeping changes has occurred in the form and location of facilities for retail distribution in the United States between the late eighteenth and early twenty-first centuries. By the 1850s, districts primarily devoted to retail activities and buildings expressly tailored to those functions had emerged in cities and towns throughout settled areas of the nation. These commercial districts were key defining components of urban form, identity and life. Concentrated shopping areas were also a major force in the overall trend towards centralisation, which began to affect the American landscape in earnest after the Revolution continued as the dominant pattern of settlement well into the twentieth century. At the same time, the particulars of retail development were in a constant state of flux, with frequent changes made in the form, scale, materials, size and character of retail architecture. The location of retail districts was also subject to shifts, albeit at a more gradual pace.

The rate of change accelerated during the twentieth century, not just in the design of facilities, but also in their locations within the urban matrix. Retail decentralisation became well-established during the 1920s and gained momentum over the next two decades. By the 1950s, this tendency became dominant. Decentralisation sometimes assumed forms similar to those that characterised downtown, with miniature satellite retail centres. However, new forms of development began to be established early on with lone-wolf stores and shopping centres. These fundamentally new kinds of outlets were foremost tailored to motorists; driving distance became a major determinant of location; and ever-increasing amounts of land were allocated to parking space. Both kinds of development contributed to the emergence of the regional shopping mall during the 1950s and, with it, an unprecedented level of planning in an effort to create new metropolitan centres that functioned as equivalents to downtown. By the 1960s, increasing concerted initiatives were launched to rejuvenate the city centre, adapting lessons learned from the regional mall. There have also been an array of specialised developments, ranging from new festival market places to preserved main streets, as well as mixed-use projects that have brought a new residential market to the urban core.

Emergence of retail districts, 1785–1840

The development of an architecture in the United States purposefully configured to accommodate retail functions was a direct outgrowth of the large-scale rise of cities as the major instruments for manufacturing, financial transactions and the distribution of goods and services – a phenomenon that did not coalesce until after independence. Cities existed prior to the revolution, most notably Philadelphia, which was among the largest population centres in the British Empire in 1770. But limits of trade and the amassing of capital precluded the emergence of much in the way of a specialised commercial infrastructure (Figure 4.1).

Figure 4.1 Commercial buildings, 100 block of Chestnut Street, Philadelphia, mostly late eighteenth and early nineteenth centuries. The rapid growth of major cities after the Revolution led to the emergence of centralised commercial districts. Located along what was becoming a primary retail street by the 1840s, this group of buildings was a typical mix of houses converted wholly or in part to business purposes and a scattering of only slightly larger purpose-built commercial edifices. Owing to this block's location near the waterfront, warehouses occupy the lots further to the east (right).

Source: Quarter plate daguerrotype by William Young McAllister, 1842. Library of Congress, Prints & Photographs Division (LC-USZ62-128556).

Even in Philadelphia, outlets for selling were generally mixed with spaces for warehousing, production and living. Political and economic independence began to alter the situation. The process was greatly accelerated by the rise of large-scale manufacturing that occurred in the decades that followed. Concentrated populations were essential for most, if not all, enterprises of mass production. Such places were no less essential for the financial and other services that enabled such work. Finally, cities fostered consumption on a scale that made the mass-manufacturing of goods profitable. As a result city building occurred in the US with an intensity unimaginable in the colonial period. Established seaports expanded exponentially; major new coastal centres such as Baltimore and Savannah emerged; and an array of new cities grew along the Great Lakes (including Buffalo, Cleveland and Detroit) and major rivers (including Pittsburgh, Cincinnati, Louisville and St Louis). For every settlement that grew into a major centre, myriad others were founded in the hopes of achieving a comparable scale. Cities in embryo were the primary agents of transforming the vast frontier of the new republic.

Within this framework, the design of buildings primarily to accommodate retail functions developed slowly and in incremental stages. Houses that had been fully converted to revenue-generating functions comprised a significant portion of commercial buildings during the early nineteenth century. Many purpose-built examples retained the basic form of their colonial predecessors, which were dwellings with at least part of the main floor allocated to selling wares. In a large city such as Philadelphia or New York, these buildings were typically 3.5 stories tall and 20–25 feet wide. One major change occurred at street level, where large shop windows or a more-or-less open front framed by granite piers and lintels, allowing for extensive display of goods and for easy access to the premises. A then-novel practice of what was termed window shopping began as early as the 1830s and would become a basic staple of urban life over the decades that followed. Inside new stores, the main floor was primarily devoted to selling, while upper levels accommodated support functions, including storage, and, perhaps, one or more additional commercial tenants. Addressing the needs to purvey specialised, manufactured goods, as opposed to the traditional range of artisan wares produced on the premises, and the growing desire among merchants to live away from ever more crowded, noisy, and unsanitary commercial districts contributed to the shift. Steadily rising land values in such places also entailed the need for quarters to generate as much revenue as possible.

During the early nineteenth century, too, retail and wholesale functions became increasingly segregated in their own, respective districts. Stores that catered to the urban elite took quarters in proximity to one another on blocks of what became the premier shopping street, such as certain blocks of Broadway in New York or Market and Chestnut streets in Philadelphia. The clustering of retail operations was in many cases fostered by the presence of a public market, which since colonial times had been the principal way of providing sizable communities with a regular supply of fresh food. Subject to municipal regulations, these public complexes attracted an array of other merchants to situate nearby. The most common form was an open-air shed, which provided basic shelter from the elements while affording ample circulation for both air and people. Market sheds could extend for several blocks, aligned in a linear fashion, with a head house accommodating various government or other civic functions. The 1841 Public Market in Charleston, South Carolina, is a primary remaining example from the antebellum period. Well before then, Faneuil Hall (popularly known as Quincy) Market (1823–26) pioneered the concept in the United States of fully enclosing food vendors' stalls so that the sale of food was completely separated from the street. The project was not only of unprecedented size, it was part of a major expansion plan that included two massive flanking ranges of buildings that housed stores and other commercial functions – all resting on newly filled land that extended Boston's burgeoning city centre.

If the public market was a standard fixture for settlements of some significance, the commercial arcade, another early attempt to cluster compatible outlets, proved a short-lived phenomenon. Inspired directly from examples of recent vintage in England, these buildings were intended to provide a safe and respectable haven for women shoppers to peruse a range of select shops away from the dirt, noise, and crowds of the street. In most cases they connected two thoroughfares, and thus provided a natural shortcut for perambulating consumers. Typically the speculative investors who initiated the project screened prospective tenants to ensure a mix that would appeal only to the well-heeled. The largest example was in Philadelphia (1824–26), which was intended to create a new retail centre, but failed to connect Chestnut with another major street. It also failed to attract a critical mass of merchants and proved a financial disaster. But even better situated arcades of the period, such as the one that remains in Providence, Rhode Island (1827–28) fared little better. For all its promise, the commercial arcade had an inconsequential impact on retail development through the mid-nineteenth century.

Maturation of retail districts, 1840–1890

The basic pattern of narrow-fronted specialty stores forming a dense cluster of retail activity that developed during the early nineteenth century did not appreciably change in the decades that followed. Such places often grew in extent. Sometimes shopping districts moved along an established axis, as they did westward on Philadelphia's Chestnut Street. Occasionally circumstances fostered the creation of a new primary shopping thoroughfare, as occurred in Chicago with the emergence of State Street after the Great Fire of 1871. If the overall pattern remained constant dramatic increases occurred in size and scale beginning in the 1840s. four-, five-, even six-story buildings became the standard in the largest cities as a response to soaring land values in prime commercial areas. The increase in height often fostered enlarging the footprint. A large commercial building, with stores at ground level and offices or other functions above, could extend at least several times the street frontage common to work of earlier decades. The height of the principal story increased to as much as 15 feet and the average height of upper stories grew as well so a building of five floors from 1850 could be twice as tall as one of 3.5 stories from two decades earlier. Finally changes occurred in the character of store buildings, reflecting the rise in a taste for ornamental embellishment generally. As a result the chaste façade treatment common to Neoclassical architecture gave way of elaborate decorative treatments, where carved stone and frequently cast iron were used to create palatial allusions. When store buildings of the 1820s and 1830s lay close to successors of two decades later, the contrast was pronounced indeed (Figure 4.2).

The mid-nineteenth century also gave rise to a new building type, the palatial dry goods emporium. First developed by Alexander T. Stewart for the store (1845–46) that bore his name on Broadway just above City Hall Park in New York, this retail outlet exuded luxury on a scale more associated with aristocratic European gathering places than with elite shops in the United States. The array and presentation of merchandise was as extravagant as the architecture. Yet despite all the sumptuous surroundings, the huge scale of the building was geared to high volume sales, and thus its clientele was of necessity broader than the well-to-do patrons of elite specialty stores. Stewart's "Marble Palace" proved a pathbreaking success. Four years after it opened the store was substantially enlarged and aggrandisements continued even though Stewart opened a huge second store farther north on Broadway in 1862 and substantially expanded it seven years later. Stewart's became a model for Lord & Taylor (1867–70), Abraham & Straus in Brooklyn (1860s–1870s) and the transformation of R.H. Macy during the 1870s and 1880s. Marshall Field pursued this path following the great Chicago fire of 1871 when he commissioned a

Figure 4.2 Astor stores and other commercial buildings, Broadway, New York, ca. 1850s and before. During the mid-nineteenth century, large urban centres expanded into new territory, where the landscape consisted primarily of purpose-built commercial buildings. New York pioneered in building sizable dry goods houses such as the Astor stores, which dominated their immediate areas. Neighbouring buildings were more modest in dimension and scale, but, at least in New York, often rose to five stories.

Source: Albumen print, stereograph by George Stacy, 1860. Library of Congress, Prints & Photographs Division (LC-DIG-stereo-1s04894).

huge emporium on State Street. As the idea spread so the spectrum of merchandise grew to encompass a broad range of goods targeted to affluent and middle-class consumers alike – a shift that often led such emporia to be referred to as department stores rather than simply dry goods houses. By 1890 such establishments existed in many cities across the United States. The department store was in fact becoming a principal defining component of a city and a major force in the distribution of goods, challenging the role of specialty stores and making inroads on the dominance of wholesaling in the distribution of goods (Figure 4.3).

The ongoing growth of retail districts, with department stores now the key destinations, was predicated on an ever-growing network of public transportations line, employing horse-cars, cable cars, and by the end of the period, electric streetcars. These private-sector ventures enabled large numbers of households with disposable income to reside increasing farther afield from the urban core while still accessing its services with relative ease. Like spokes in a wheel, car lines emanated from one or a few key points downtown – places that were considered optimal for retail development. As a result the shopping districts of the Gilded Age remained fairly compact, seldom extending more than half a dozen blocks – enough space to accommodate a density of outlets, yet sufficiently small to encourage perambulation from one block to another.

A parallel trend towards giantism occurred in the development of public markets during the second half of the nineteenth century. Enormous central markets were created in strategic locations in Washington, DC (1872–75) and a number of other cities. Campaigns to build complexes that entailed both retail and wholesale operations and could extend for several city blocks were undertaken to stimulate high volume turnover among swelling urban populations and the ability of railroads to transport large amounts of fresh food expeditiously to a single location.

Figure 4.3 Marshall Field & Company department store, 1902–14, D. H. Burnham & Company, architects (on left) and other commercial buildings, State Street, Chicago. The scale of commercial development sharply increased once again during the late nineteenth and early twentieth centuries with the advent of multi-story, steel-frame buildings. Though home to a spectrum of business activities, State Street had become Chicago's premier retail corridor, and indeed one of the greatest concentrations of stores in the United States. Most prominent in prestige, as well as in size, was Marshall Field's mammoth pile, portions of which were still under construction when this photograph was taken. Further south on the same side of State Street can be seen two rivals, Mandel Brothers and Carson Pirie Scott.

Source: Photograph by Detroit Publishing Company, 1907. Library of Congress, Prints & Photographs Division (LC-DIG-det-4a25229).

Coalescence of the downtown retail centre, 1890–1930

At the end of the nineteenth and during the first three decades of the twentieth centuries the centralisation process that began nearly 100 years earlier culminated, giving retail functions in the urban core hegemony. Not only did the urban population continue to swell, inter-urban rail service helped turn major cities into regional hubs for shoppers. Widespread use of the telephone by the 1920s, and increasingly sophisticated delivery systems, enabled many patrons to secure goods without making a trip downtown. To serve this burgeoning clientele stores of every description lay in proximity to one another and to rail lines. Most stores remained concentrated along a single corridor such as Washington Street in Boston, Market Street in Philadelphia, Euclid Avenue in Cleveland, State Street in Chicago and Broadway in Los Angeles; or formed dense clusters, as occurred in Detroit and San Francisco. Among large cities, only New York, by virtue of its immense in-town consumer population, deviated from this pattern, with primary centres scattered along the Ladies Mile (Sixth Avenue), Herald Square and, later, Fifth Avenue.

Department stores anchored these districts by the late nineteenth century, when the idea of a giant, multi-story emporium that had originated decades earlier became a widespread trend coast to coast. Pioneering department stores in their respective communities such as J.L. Hudson in Detroit and Jordan March in Boston were joined by many others in cities of all sizes, purveying a wide range of merchandise and services. By the early twentieth century, retailing had eclipsed wholesaling in prestige and often in profits, fueled by the ever-swelling ranks of middle-class consumers, who could purchase most of the goods they desired under one roof.

A new standard for the department store was set in the 1900s with the phased rebuilding of facilities for Marshall Field's in Chicago and John Wanamaker in Philadelphia, both of them encompassing entire city blocks and rising twelve stories above the street. The buildings offered magisterial, even palatial, settings that manifested their respective companies' prestige and role as an authority on consumer goods. They also provided centres for entertainment, relaxation and cultural stimulation, with dining facilities, lounges, auditoria, exhibition galleries and even concert halls. The great department store became a defining element of American urbanism, a yardstick by which cities of all sizes measured their progress and potential.

The trend to build ever-larger, more-encompassing stores reached a feverish pitch during the 1920s. In city after city, establishments that had been relatively modest in scope, focusing on apparel and other dry goods, for example, broadened to include hardware, furniture, musical instruments, radios, sporting equipment, luggage, silverware, china, books and paintings and prints, and an array of services from fur storage to upholstery. Major cities could boast a half-dozen or more such emporia. An unstated, but widely recognised hierarchy existed among them, ranging from the most fashion-oriented and prestigious to those best known for the bargains they offered. This competition and diversification offered consumers a wide range of choices. People of moderate means could occasionally splurge at a leading store such as Marshall Field's, while the well-to-do might hunt for savings at lower-priced emporia such as Lit Brothers in Philadelphia or the Fair Store in Chicago. Smaller cities had fewer department stores, but the differences were primarily ones of scale rather than the basic patterns of design and operation.

If they dominated the trade, the grand emporia hardly enjoyed a monopoly on retail functions. Specialty stores, while deeply affected by their giant competitors, remained viable components of the downtown retail mix, and some rebounded to become significant draws in their own right by the 1920s. During that decade, many furniture stores such as Barker Brothers in Los Angeles expanded to the point where they offered a greater selection than department stores and did so in new buildings that were almost as large. Women's apparel stores also enjoyed resurgence, both with companies that catered to a large middle-income market and others that purveyed high-end fashions. In the latter category, major, departmentalised outlets such as San Francisco's I. Magnin, Dallas's Neiman-Marcus or New York's Saks Fifth Avenue became closely associated in the public mind with the big department stores themselves.

Most department stores were locally owned. However, national chain stores also became a significant presence in urban centres during the 1920s as part of the larger phenomenon of national branding and the creation of national markets. The largest of these were variety stores, such as F.W. Woolworth, but many others specialised in clothing, shoes, pharmaceuticals and other frequently purchased goods. Most such establishments stocked low-priced merchandise targeted to moderate-income households. Their proliferation adversely affected some of the lower-end department stores, but the chain phenomenon as a whole, with its fast growth and high profit margins, became a source of nervousness even among owners of prestigious department stores.

The effect of retail growth during the first three decades of the twentieth century was a substantial increase in downtown density, with larger and often taller store buildings. In some cases, too, the business district made conspicuous territorial increases, as it did along both Broadway and Seventh Street in Los Angles and Euclid Avenue in Cleveland. In a few instances, this extension took the form of new, perceptually discrete nodes such as North Michigan Avenue in Chicago or Union Square in San Francisco.

The increase in commercial density during the 1920s unfolded in tension with the rapid ascendancy of motor vehicles. On one hand, trucking allowed for more efficient distribution of goods. On the other hand, automobiles soon clogged downtown streets. The structure of the urban core in general and the concentration of retail outlets in particular had been possible because of the network of streetcar lines (and high-speed rail transit lines in New York and Chicago) that converged on the city centre. The desirability of a given downtown location for retail purposes was predicated on its proximity to the most important of these public transit routes. Increasing use of automobiles, especially among affluent female shoppers, became a substantial problem by mid-decade both because of traffic congestion and a scarcity of parking. In cities from Syracuse to Los Angeles, planners, politicians and downtown commercial interests began to see the traffic problem as a crisis of major proportions. Efforts directed at traffic regulation and initiatives to create offstreet parking facilities abounded in cities nationwide, but the problem was never resolved until consumer trips to the urban core began to decline markedly in the 1960s and 1970s.

Development of outlying retail nodes, 1900–1940

Establishments purveying basic goods and services for nearby residents could be found in outlying sections of cities throughout the nineteenth century, but it generally was not until the latter decades of that century that they began to form nodal centres and not until the 1920s that the largest of such places began to compete with downtown. The increasing lateral spread of the residential districts that fueled this development was enabled by horsecar and, especially, electric streetcar lines that allowed an easy commute to the urban core. Major stops along those lines often gave rise to the most concentrated outlying commercial development, with typically one- and two-story "taxpayer" buildings forming a strip of several blocks. The decentralisation of many industrial functions and, with them, blue-collar households, likewise spurred new commercial nodes for people with neither time nor money to go far afield to shop. After World War I, a new intensity of growth occurred in outlying centres. In Chicago, for example, some of the largest-scale developments arose in middle-class districts such as Englewood and Uptown, boasting multi-story office buildings, major department stores, and immense movie palaces. Similar developments could be found in some prosperous working-class areas, such as along Chicago's Milwaukee Avenue and Milwaukee's Mitchell Avenue. Chain stores such as Woolworth's became an increasing presence in outlying centres of many sizes, proliferating during the 1920s and again in the years before the attack on Pearl Harbor.

Increasing reliance on automobiles for middle-class consumers spurred arterial development where stores could be sited specifically to attract the motorist. Among the most celebrated projects of this sort took place along Los Angeles's Wilshire Boulevard, where two prominent nodes began to emerge during the late 1920s and boomed after the mid-1930s. Both sported high-end branches of downtown-based stores catering to a well-heeled clientele. Lacking streetcar lines, Wilshire was conducive to smooth traffic flow, which was further facilitated by back-lot parking areas that served many of the stores. Known as the Miracle Mile, the westernmost of these developments also departed from precedent by anticipating residential growth rather than following it.

The prestigious branch stores found along the Wilshire corridor were indicative of a broader, if not yet widespread, trend among leading downtown retailers, some of whom began to erect outlets in high-end suburban centres around Boston, New York, Philadelphia and Chicago, among other cities. The Depression ended such expansion, but it resumed on a more modest scale with economic recovery and became a major thrust in retail development after World War II. By 1940, then, the biggest cities boasted a range of miniature "downtowns", some decidedly urban in form, others noticeably less so – a galaxy of nodes that were beginning to compete with the retail core for a significant range of the consumer public.

Departures from the urban norm, 1920–1940

If the Wilshire Boulevard projects embodied pathbreaking adaptation of urban form to accommodate motorists, many other developments of the interwar decades represented more radical departures. When Sears Roebuck entered the retail field in 1925, it located most of its full-fledged department stores along major thoroughfares. However, it selected sites that were isolated from existing retail clusters of any size yet proximate to blue-collar residential areas, enabling easy access by motorists of moderate means. The inexpensive land chosen allowed architects to design laterally organised stores rather than the traditional multi-storied ones and to allocate at least half the property to offstreet parking.

For well-heeled patrons, Kansas City developer J.C. Nichols built the Country Club Plaza (begun 1922), which became the key conceptual basis for later shopping centres. Eventually occupying over a dozen blocks with more than two hundred stores and services, the complex boasted wide streets; scattered, offstreet parking; and buildings of no higher than two stories. Nichols's company owned and managed all the property, carefully selecting tenants so that each would complement the others. No less important, key stores were strategically placed to diffuse pedestrian and vehicular traffic, thus boosting the number of prime locations. Control was also exercised over hours of operation, signs, and window displays. Holidays were celebrated with street embellishments and special events. Nichols envisioned the Plaza not as competition with downtown stores, but to function as a high-end enclave catering to the fashionable residential tracts he was developing nearby. In configuration and appearance, the Plaza was the antithesis of the urban norm, exuding the intimate charm of an idealised, pre-industrial town, albeit one overtly tailored to the automobile.

Smaller versions of the Country Club Plaza sprouted up in a number of posh suburbs, including Cleveland's Shaker Heights and Dallas's Highland Park. However, the Plaza model (single ownership and management; planned tenant mix targeted to a specific market) was most widely applied to another commercial type, known as the neighbourhood shopping centre. These projects generally encompassed no more than twenty tenants purveying basic goods and services gathered into a single, linear building. A major prototype for such projects was the Park and Shop in Washington, DC (1930), which also employed the then unorthodox arrangement of stores facing a front car lot. This arrangement became popular in Washington during the 1930s and proliferated nationwide during the post-World War II era. The building's configuration was adapted from a southern California phenomenon, known as the drive-in market, which began in the mid-1920s and became a ubiquitous fixture in the regional landscape within a few years.

Another novel aspect of the drive-in was having a spectrum of food products sold under one roof in a setting that catered to motorists. This latter concept was subsequently adapted for the supermarket. Led by the Los Angeles-based Ralphs Grocery Company, the supermarket revolutionised the nature of retail space, allowing customers to select goods on their own and pay for all of them at a single checkout area. With small profit margins, the supermarket concept was predicated on rapid inventory turnover and volume sales, which, in turn, requited ample facilities for unloading goods from delivery trucks and for loading purchases into customers' automobiles. Capacious docking and parking areas thus formed an integral component of Ralphs stores beginning in 1929. Supermarkets could be found in many cities a decade later, although few matched the size or the dramatic atmosphere of Ralphs stores until after World War II, when the type became the primary vehicle of food distribution nationally. The spatial demands of a large supermarket resulted in many being built as stand-alone projects, close to, but somewhat apart from, retail nodes. By the late 1930s, however, some supermarkets became catalysts for adjacent commercial development in peripheral locations where open land remained abundant. Either way, the supermarket stood as a landmark amid the burgeoning suburban commercial strip.

Decentralisation boom, 1945–1970

The post-World War II period saw the most radical and widespread changes in American urban structure, to which retail development was a major contributor. A huge, new, and mobile mass market comprised of both white- and prosperous blue-collar households, coupled with an acute housing shortage and ever-intensifying decentralisation of jobs spawned an unprecedented boom in residential construction well beyond established urban areas. This epic population shift led to a proliferation of new retail developments, many of them drawing from the innovations of the interwar decades. Branches of leading downtown stores could be found in these peripheral areas coast to coast by the mid-1950s. While many businesses, including supermarket companies, opted for stand-alone buildings along major arteries, the benefits of a group of retail outlets in a complex managed as a unified operation became ever more apparent. While it had remained somewhat of a novelty before World War II, the shopping centre became a staple of retail growth thereafter. Neighbourhood shopping centres grew to be commonplace along major commercial arteries, and larger complexes, anchored by a variety store and/or a junior department store chain unit such as J.C. Penney, proliferated by the early 1950s. Many shopping centres were built by the developers of large, adjacent housing tracts, but many others were created independently to draw from a multitude of new residential areas. The growing dependence on automobiles for transportation led to ever more space devoted to parking, with three or four times the square footage occupied by stores consumed by asphalt. The traditional configuration of buildings set at the front property line and abutting one another gave way to a sprawling arterial landscape in which open space predominated. Such widespread accommodation of motor vehicles created a wholly new spatial order.

The scattering of retail outlets also prompted efforts to create new, very large complexes that would in effect re-centralise shopping into a few satellite nodes, each approximately equivalent in function to downtown. Major department store companies were the primary agents of change in this realm. A large branch department store did not always work well in isolation. By grouping it with forty or fifty other stores, all carefully selected to complement rather than compete with the "parent" establishment, department store executives believed they could regain the hegemony they had until recently enjoyed from their downtown operations alone. Pioneering developments completed prior to the Korean War included Northgate (1948–50) in Seattle, Shopper's World (1948–51) west of Boston (both built by Allied Stores), Lakewood Center (1950–52) in Los Angeles County (May Company) and Stonestown (1950–52) in San Francisco (Emporium Capwell). With the return of peace came a flurry of sequels undertaken by numerous leading retailers, including J.L. Hudson in Detroit, R.H. Macy in New York and San Francisco, Marshall Field's in Chicago and the Dayton Company in Minneapolis. These regional shopping centres, as they were known, revolutionised retail practices and the retail landscape over the next quarter century.

Regional shopping centres not only were much larger than any previous outlying retail development, they contained a spectrum of stores that allowed consumers to purchase most goods and services they used all in a single complex, in effect becoming a surrogate for the great downtown department stores themselves. These new loci of trade also assumed a configuration that was fundamentally different from other retail facilities, including most smaller shopping centres. Instead of fronting the street or a parking lot, stores were clustered along one or more pedestrianways, with parking encircling the compound. The thinking behind this layout was to minimise walking distance from car to stores and to place shoppers in a novel and appealing environment where they would be inclined to meander, stay for longer periods, and patronise more stores than they may have initially intended. Embellishment of the mall through landscaping, fountains, sculpture, and other features gave each regional centre a clear identity, while having stores line both sides of these spaces trimmed the distance from end to end to half of what would be using a conventional shopping centre layout (Figure 4.4).

The design of regional malls underwent ongoing modifications between the mid-1950s and the mid-1970s. Beginning with the Dayton Company's Southdale (1953–56) outside Minneapolis, pedestrian spaces were fully enclosed, providing shelter from adverse weather and relief from climatic extremes. Southdale was also a pioneer in having two department store anchors, and during the 1960s, regional centres with three or even four department stores became the new industry standard. Gerald Hines's Galleria (1969–71) in the Post Oak district of Houston introduced the atrium configuration, with several tiers of shopping floors topped by a glazed roof. This variation of the great nineteenth-century shopping arcades of Europe soon became a hallmark of the most ambitious regional centres. While department stores remained at the core of these complexes, real estate developers began to make such work a specialty during the mid-1950s, emerging as the driving force in both conceptualisation and realisation. One of the leaders, James Rouse, played a major role in advancing enclosed malls, while at the Galleria, Hines consummated the idea of the regional mall as an integral part of a large-scale, mixed-use commercial centre.

Department store executives and real estate developers alike sought to locate their regional malls so as to preclude competition nearby, in some cases buying up large parcels of surrounding land for residential, office, and/or institutional development. In many cases the regional mall remained somewhat isolated rather than serving as a catalyst for new business growth on a large scale. Yet elsewhere, competing centres were erected nearby, and in a number of cases, the regional mall eventually became part of a large node of commerce. Finally, a few regional malls spurred major new, multi-functional business centres, as occurred at Tyson's Corner, southwest of Washington, DC, and Buckhead, north of Atlanta.

Figure 4.4 Cross County Center, Central Park Avenue and Cross County Parkway, Yonkers, New York, 1947–52, Sol G. Atlas, developer, Lathrop Douglass, architect. View of pedestrian mall, looking south towards Gimbel Brothers department store, added to complex 1953–55. Cross County Center was a pioneering development of a new kind of retail centre during the post-World War II years. What became known as the regional shopping mall was intended to compete with the traditional urban core in the array and quality of goods and services to be found there. Unlike downtowns, the complex was under single ownership and operated by a single management. Its configuration, with stores facing one or more pedestrianways – all surrounded by acres of surface parking, was an equally radical departure from convention.

Source: Photograph by Gottscho-Schleisner, 1959. Library of Congress, Prints & Photographs Division (LC-G613-73745).

Decline and renewal of downtown retail districts, 1930–1985

While retail activity dispersed with metropolitan growth, central cities continued to provide important shopping options through the mid-twentieth century. Stores in the urban core were hard hit by the Depression, and growth in this sector never again reached the levels it had earlier in the century. Constructing new stores was the exception rather than the rule once the economy started to recover. The postwar years, on the other hand, held promise of a full rebound. Huge department stores and ambitious additions to existing ones were built in some major urban centres, including those of Houston, Kansas City, Boston, Pittsburgh and Atlanta, as well as in many smaller ones. Chain companies also embarked on big downtown expansion campaigns. Led by F.W. Woolworth, variety stores opened new, multi-story plants carrying a far greater breadth of merchandise than in previous decades, in effect competing with the lower-end department stores. Junior department stores, most notably J.C. Penney, also enlarged their holdings to emerge as rivals to the traditional downtown establishments. Many chain companies specialising in apparel for both men and women opened new plants as well. In a number of small-to-medium-sized cities – Savannah, Georgia; Richmond, Virginia; and Rochester, New York, for example – chains became primary agents in the renewal of downtown shopping districts into the 1960s, boasting some of the most modern as well as some of the largest emporia.

For every new store constructed after 1930, dozens of others undertook remodelling, often more than once. Updating retail facilities had long been a common practice, but many remodelings of the 1930s and postwar years encompassed sweeping changes indoors and out, creating what seemed like an entirely new facility. Facades were re-sheathed, while sales areas were transformed by innovations in lighting and display as well as dramatic new decorative schemes. Air conditioning use increased during the 1930s and became widespread by the 1950s. This development, combined with new forms of artificial illumination, obviated the longstanding need for natural light. Aside from street-front display windows, stores were now optimally sealed boxes, with centralised selling spaces surrounded by storage, a change that markedly affected exterior treatment and the character of the shopping area as a whole. The remodelling boom assumed new proportions after World War II, when changes made as little as a decade earlier gave way to new designs. By the mid-1950s, retailers increasingly made use of thin, lightweight metal veneers that could be affixed to existing fronts, greatly reducing construction costs and furthering the tendency to make vintage buildings appear brand new. By the 1960s, downtown commercial districts bore scant resemblance to their state in 1930 or even 1950, despite the fact that wholly new buildings remained relatively few. The primary exceptions to this shift were many of the grand department stores, which kept exterior remodelling to a minimum while frequently modernising their interiors.

As early as the mid-1950s, many advocates of downtown commerce charged that sprucing up individual buildings and orchestrating business promotional campaigns were insufficient if the core was to compete successfully with outlying retail centres. One solution that attracted widespread interest was to create a pedestrian way along the main retail street, echoing the still new phenomenon of the regional mall. The idea actually first surfaced during World War II, but no such plan was implemented until municipal officials cleared the way for a redevelopment of downtown Kalamazoo, Michigan, in 1958. The architect, Victor Gruen, who was by then a leading figure in the design of regional malls, argued that a street mall, in itself, could not transform the urban core. Rather, the mall should be part of a downtown circulation plan that included new traffic circulation routes and extensive offstreet parking facilities. He was able to realise much of this more comprehensive approach to revitalisation in Fresno, California, several years later. Many retailers nationwide remained skeptical of such costly projects; however, continuing declines in their downtown businesses made them more amenable to the idea. By the 1970s, street malls and street conversions limiting motorised traffic to public transportation, often without the supporting infrastructural changes Gruen advocated, took root in some major cities such as Boston and Philadelphia; a host of smaller ones, from Raleigh, North Carolina, to Louisville, Kentucky; and in many town centres as well.

More radical interventions in downtown retail districts were seldom condoned by affected merchants and property owners until the 1970s and 1980s when the decline of those districts became pronounced. Ambitious schemes emerged for large new retail facilities, office towers, and parking garages covering several blocks and sometimes including skywalks or enclosed streets. Examples of this approach include The Center in Worcester, Massachusetts (1966–72) or multi-story arcades as at The Gallery in Philadelphia (1974–77) and the St Louis Galleria (1982–85). These interventions ranked among the most decisive and conspicuous changes to the commercial core since the 1920s. Most of the initial efforts to revive a moribund shopping quarter fell short of expectations, and in some cases they have either been substantially altered or demolished. Several projects begun a decade or more later, most notably Circle Centre in Indianapolis (1988–95) and Providence Place in Providence, Rhode Island (1994–1999), that focus on retailing and entertainment have enjoyed greater success.

Another substantial impetus of revitalisation has been the festival marketplace, pioneered by developer James Rouse's Quincy Market in Boston (1976–78). With years of experience in creating regional shopping malls, Rouse adapted lessons in management and marketing to a much smaller-scale operation comprised of dozens of specialty shops and food vendors. Housed in a historic complex and oriented to outdoor pedestrian spaces, the scheme was heralded as a welcome antidote for the vast, enclosed mall. Efforts to replicate the concept have met with mixed results. A major variant, San Diego's Horton Plaza (1977–85), on the other hand, offered a high-density and visually stimulating, open-air environment loosely inspired by old town centres in southern Europe, and was connected to large, new retail and office facilities that has provided a catalyst for greater downtown development.

Retail showdown, 1985–2016

Sweeping changes have occurred in virtually every sphere of retailing over the past three decades, many of which have had a profound effect on urban development. The takeover of most downtown-based department store companies by what has become a small number of major corporations has left shopping districts and shopping centres alike with only one such emporium and, perhaps, a unit of a national chain such as Sears or J.C. Penney. Many regional malls have experienced a decline paralleling that of the urban core decades earlier. A number of these sprawling complexes have been demolished for other configurations of retail outlets or other functions altogether. Some have enjoyed continued success by greatly enlarging their plants or spawning complementary development nearby. At the same time, an array of competing shopping centre forms have emerged, most notably those housing outlet stores and others warehouse-type facilities for electronics, clothing, general merchandise, home supplies, and the like. Discount stores, led by Walmart, have diversified to the point where they supply many people with most of the goods they need. At the other end of the spectrum, developers adopting New Urbanist design principles have created shopping and entertainment complexes that evoke a nineteenth- or early twentieth-century town centre. Following the New Urbanist precept of developing communities that are primarily oriented to pedestrians, with buildings oriented to the street and arranged in a density common to many communities prior to use of the automobile, a number of new retail centres have been designed as latter-day Main Streets, with a central artery (pedestrian and vehicular) lined by buildings that appear to have been constructed as different projects over time. Most such developments, however, are not integral parts of a tightly knit community, but rather are stand-alone centres surrounded by extensive parking areas. Irrespective of their complexion, retail centres have been even more affected by the rise in online and catalogue purchases. Online and catalogue purchases have begun to cut significantly into sales by many forms of retail outlets.

Yet strands of continuity can be found amid a sea of change. Without significant physical alterations, some downtown retail districts, including those in New York, Chicago, Seattle and San Francisco, remain magnets of trade. Many neighbourhood retail centres survive in sound condition or have been successfully revived. The Main Street commercial corridors of towns nationwide have enjoyed a spirited comeback, sometimes serving their longstanding role as centres of community and in other cases assuming a niche role for outsiders. Specialty emporia of varied kinds – from hardware stores to ones purveying top-of-the-line apparel – remain in demand, as does the corner convenience store. If more people prefer to shop without leaving their homes than ever before, many others enjoy the opportunity to peruse goods firsthand and to enjoy the visual and even social stimulus of the marketplace. The multi-faceted physical world of retailing remains an integral part of life in American communities.

References

Baerwald, T. (1978), 'The emergence of a new "downtown"', *Geographical Review*, 68, pp. 308–318.

Benson, S.P. (1986), *Counter cultures: Saleswomen, managers, and customers in American department stores, 1890–1940* (Urbana, IL: University of Illinois Press).

Cheyne, M. (2010), 'No better way? The Kalamazoo Mall and the legacy of pedestrian malls', *Michigan Historical Review*, 36, pp. 103–128.

Cohen, J.A. (2013), 'Corridors of consumption: Mid-nineteenth century commercial space and the reinvention of downtown', in L. Iarocci (ed.) *Visual merchandising: The image of selling* (Burlington, VT: Ashgate) 158–174.

Cohen, L. (1996), 'From town center to shopping center: The reconfiguration of community marketplaces in postwar America', *American Historical Review*, 101, pp. 1050–1081.

Conzen, M.P. and Kathleen, N.C. (1979), 'Geographical structure in nineteenth-century urban retailing: Milwaukee, 1836–1890', *Journal of Historical Geography*, 5, pp. 45–66.

Davis, H. (2012), *Living over the store: Architecture and local urban life* (London: Routledge).

Deutsch, T. (2010), *Building a housewife's paradise: Gender, politics, and American grocery stores in the twentieth century* (Chapel Hill, NC: University of North Carolina Press).

Ervin, J. (2008–2009), 'San Diego's urban trophy: Horton plaza redevelopment project', *Southern California Quarterly*, 90, pp. 419–453.

Esperdy, G. (2008), *Modernizing main street: Architecture and consumer culture in the new deal* (Chicago: University of Chicago Press).

Fogelson, Robert M. (2001), *Downtown: Its rise and fall, 1880–1950*) New Haven, CT: Yale University Press).

Gardner, D.S. (1984), '"A paradise of fashion": A. T. Stewart's department store, 1862–1975', in J.M. Jensen and S. Davidson (eds.) *A needle, a bobbin, a strike: Women needleworkers in America* (Philadelphia, PA: Temple University Press) 60–80.

Geist, J.F. (1983), *Arcades: The history of a building type* (Cambridge, MA: MIT Press).

Goss, J. (1996), 'Disquiet on the waterfront: Reflections on nostalgia and utopia in the urban archetypes of festival marketplaces', *Urban Geography*, 17, pp. 221–247.

Hardwick, M.J. (2003), *Mall maker: Victor Gruen, architect of an American dream* (Philadelphia, PA: University of Pennsylvania Press).

Harris, N. (1990), *Cultural excursions: Marketing appetites and cultural tastes in modern America* (Chicago: University of Chicago Press).

Hepp, J.H. IV (2003), *The middle-class city: Transforming space and time in Philadelphia, 1876–1926* (Philadelphia, PA: University of Pennsylvania Press).

Howard, V. (2015), *From Main Street to mall: The rise and fall of the American department store* (Philadelphia, PA: University of Pennsylvania Press).

Iarocci, L. (2014), *The urban department store in America, 1850–1930* (Burlington, VT: Ashgate).

Isenberg, A. (2004), *Downtown America: A history of the place and the people who made it* (Chicago: University of Chicago Press).

Jakle, J.A. and Sculle, K.R. (2004), *Lots of parking: Land use in a car culture* (Charlottesville, VA: University of Virginia Press).

Leach, W.R. (1993), *Land of desire: Merchants, power, and the rise of a new American culture* (New York: Random House).

Lindgren, J.M. (2014), *Preserving South Street Seaport: The dream and reality of a New York urban renewal district* (New York: New York University Press).

Logemann, J. (2009), 'Where to shop? The geography of consumption in the twentieth-century Atlantic world', *Bulletin of the German Historical Institute*, 45, pp. 55–68.

Longstreth, R. (1986), 'J.C. Nichols, the country club plaza, and notions of modernity', *Harvard Architecture Review*, 5, pp. 120–135.

Longstreth, R. (1992), 'The neighborhood shopping center in Washington, D.C., 1930–1941', *Journal of the Society of Architectural Historians*, 51, pp. 5–34.

Longstreth, R. (1997), *City center to regional mall: Architecture, the automobile, and retailing in Los Angeles, 1920–1950* (Cambridge, MA: MIT Press).

Longstreth, R. (1997), 'The diffusion of the community shopping center concept during the interwar decades', *Journal of the Society of Architectural Historians*, 56, pp. 268–293.

Longstreth, R. (1999), *The drive-in, the supermarket, and the transformation of commercial space in Los Angeles, 1914–1941* (Cambridge, MA: MIT Press).

Longstreth, R. (2000), *The buildings of Main Street: A guide to American commercial architecture* (1986, reprint ed.) (Woodland Hills, CA: Alta Mira Press).

Longstreth, R. (2006), 'Sears, Roebuck and the remaking of the department store, 1924–42', *Journal of the Society of Architectural Historians*, 65, pp. 238–279.

Longstreth, R. (2007), 'Bringing 'downtown' to the neighborhoods: Wieboldt's, Goldblatt's and the creation of department store chains in Chicago', *Buildings & Landscapes*, 14, pp. 13–49.

Longstreth, R. (2010), *The American department store transformed, 1920–1960* (New Haven, CT: Yale University Press).

Longstreth, R. (2015), 'The continuous transformation of Savannah's Broughton Street', in R. Longstreth (ed.) *Looking beyond the icons: Midcentury architecture, landscape, and urbanism* (Charlottesville, VA: University of Virginia Press).

Mayo, J. (1993), *The American grocery store: The business evolution of an American space* (Westport, CT: Greenwood Press).

Metzger, J.T. (2001), 'The failed promise of a festival marketplace: South street seaport in lower Manhattan', *Planning Perspectives*, 16, pp. 25–46.

Muller, P.O. (1976), *The outer city: Geographical consequences of the urbanization of the United States* (Washington, DC: Association of American Geographers).

Olsen, J.A. (2003), *Better places, better lives: A biography of James Rouse* (Washington, DC: Urban Land Institute).

Quincy, J., Jr. (2003), *Quincy's Market: A Boston landmark* (Boston, MA: Northeastern University Press).

Resseguie, H. (1965), 'Alexander Turney Stewart and the development of the department store, 1823–1876', *Business History Review*, 39, pp. 301–322.

Satterthwaite, A. (2001), *Going shopping: Consumer choices and community consequences* (New Haven, CT: Yale University Press).

Sewell, J. (2011), *Women and the everyday city: Public space in San Francisco, 1890–1915* (Minneapolis, MN: University of Minnesota Press).

Siry, J. (1988), *Carson Pirie Scott: Louis Sullivan and the Chicago department store* (Chicago: University of Chicago Press).

Smiley, D. (2013), *Pedestrian modern: Shopping and American architecture, 1925–1956* (Minneapolis, MN: University of Minnesota Press).

Stamper, J.W. (1991), *Chicago's North Michigan Avenue: Planning and development 1900–1930* (Chicago: University of Chicago Press).

Tangires, H. (2003), *Public markets and civic culture in nineteenth-century America* (Baltimore, MD: Johns Hopkins University Press).

Tangires, H. (2008), *Public markets* (Washington, DC: Library of Congress/New York: W. W. Norton).

Treu, M. (2012), *Signs, streets, and storefronts: A history of architecture and graphics along America's commercial corridors* (Baltimore, MD: Johns Hopkins University Press).

Upton, D. (2008), *Another city: Urban life and urban spaces in the New American Republic* (New Haven, CT: Yale University Press).

Upton, D. (2012), 'Commercial architecture in Philadelphia lithographs', in E. Piola (ed.) *Philadelphia on stone: Commercial lithography in Philadelphia 1828–78* (University Park, PA: Pennsylvania State University Press/Philadelphia, PA: Library Company of Philadelphia) 152–175, 249–253.

Wall, A. (2005), *Victor Gruen: From urban shop to new city* (Barcelona: Actar).

Whitaker, J. (2006), *Service and style: How the American department store fashioned the middle class* (New York: St. Martin's Press).

5

THE FUTURE OF RETAILING*

From physical to digital

Fiona Ellis-Chadwick

Introduction

In 1995, few retailers considered the Internet sufficiently important to the future of their businesses to even register a domain name. Between 2000 and 2005, some traditional high street retail businesses were encouraged to experiment with the Internet as a retail channel to market (Doherty & Ellis-Chadwick, 2010). In contrast, by the end of this 5-year period, Amazon, the US online retailer, had not only established that it could operate its business on a large scale, delivering books across the US and entering European markets with country specific domains (e.g. www.amazon.co.uk), but had also developed an innovative and tax efficient business model that provided a solid foundation for future growth. Meanwhile, the rate of adoption by traditional physical high street retailers continued slowly, with few offering consumers the opportunity to spend online. This lack of progress left the door wide open for online retailers to hone their skills, build extensive online trading platforms and find ways to entice new customers to spend online. History may prove this period of experimentation to be pivotal to the future development of our towns and cities because what happened in the next few years changed how we shop, when we buy and importantly who we buy from. Early predictions of the Internet closing the High Street may yet become a reality as more trade moves online and the number of physical retail outlets continues to decline. More optimistically, the resilience of many retail businesses and the desire of humans to congregate and share their experiences in physical places may prevail and lead to a post-digital era of retailing that benefits from the advantages of the integration of digital and physical.

This chapter takes us on a journey through the development of online retailing from the first commercial sales via the Internet, through the growth of online shopping from consumer and retailers perspectives, to the future implications for high streets in towns and cities around the world.

Building a road to the future: the information superhighway

The Internet emerged from the interweaving of computer and telecommunication technologies and in less than four decades has been transformed from an obscure piece of technology of interest to defence scientists and a few academics into a communications and trading network used by businesses and consumers around the globe. However, it is important to note that the Internet was not designed for commerce. Its military origins demanded that it be robust enough to withstand nuclear attack, which meant that it had to be able to operate without central authority, meaning that computers can be added and removed without disrupting the network's performance. Its key strengths were derived from being able to facilitate global communication (using a multiplicity of interactive communication formats: text, graphic, verbal and audio) and access to a global reservoir of information.

These qualities attracted the attention of computer users around the world. The digital medium added new dimensions to the concept of communication (Palmer, 1995) allowing users to interact on a one-to-one (electronic mail), one-to-many (company Websites) or many-to-many (Internet Relay Chat) basis. The facilities offered meant there were calls for the Internet to become more commercial and not just serve academic and research institutes (Coursey, 1992). With the benefit of hindsight, it is important to reflect on the impact of these fundamental qualities of Internet technology and emergent business models and to consider the extent to which these benefits, once unleashed in the commercial arena, have enabled the creation of a global trading environment that is difficult to govern and control.

In 1989, the Internet was commercially liberated (Zakon, 1994) and trading online took on a new dimension, encouraging many newcomers to get connected, especially business users eager to exploit this new communication medium. In 1991, Berners-Lee et al. (1994) and his colleagues at CERN (European Particle Physics Laboratory) developed the World Wide Web (WWW) based on hypertext to simplify and extend access to networked computing around the globe (Nelson, 1991). The WWW was predicted to become the predominant method of accessing the Internet (Krol, 1994) and part of its success is attributed to the graphical browsers that gave WWW users easier access to audio, graphic, video and text documents on computers around the world. For retailing, the graphical user interface of the World Wide Web made it easier for everyone with a computer to get online. Whilst there were still technical requirements involved, once connected users could search for content, join online service provider platforms and begin to engage with a whole new range of online activities.

CompuServe, was the first major commercial online service provider in the USA, pre-dating the WWW; it offered a gateway to get online and provided chat, forums gaming, and other consumer facing services (Wikipedia, 2018). In the UK, CompuServe led the way for major retail brands to get online, including W.H. Smiths (selling books and CDs), Tesco (flowers and wine), Virgin (music videos and computer games). Great Universal Stores started selling sportswear ranges and had a great advantage over other retailers as they had a sophisticated and well-established delivery network through its catalogue home shopping business (Cope, 1995).

In 1993, Bob McCool and Marc Andreessen, wrote the client application Mosaic (the first Web browser), which made the WWW accessible to a range of new users by removing the need for the technical expertise previously required (McGarty & Haywood, 1995; Verity, 1995). The capabilities of Web browsers improved and Mosaic was superseded by the new Netscape browser, which was distributed at no charge to Internet users around the globe at a time when it was relatively unknown for a company to give away its main product. However, whilst Mosaic, Netscape and others have long since been superseded by Google Chrome, the radical new business model of giving product freely arguably paved the way for emerging digital brands to exploit the future potential of digital markets.

The web, web browsers and search engines (all made freely available to anyone with a dial up Internet connection) were fundamental to the growth of online retailing and shopping. By 1995, the information superhighway was starting to attract global attention from businesses and shoppers alike and, as demand grew and the numbers of Internet users expanded exponentially year-on-year (Ovum Reports, 1996), so too did the number of commercial websites offering a range of information-based and interactive services (Pyle, 1996).

More serious attempts to trade online began to emerge towards the end of the 1990s when innovative, technically savvy companies responded to the opportunities and challenges posed by the Internet to develop sophisticated websites to serve customers in their homes. Many multiple retailers developed their own independent websites, selling goods ranging from books and computers to the full range of groceries. Often these sites were grouped together to form electronic malls. Barclay Square was a UK example, which made the claim to be 'a prime site for large multiples, medium sized retail chains and smaller independents and specialist shops, in fact anyone who wants an upmarket and rapidly growing retail location' (Barclay, 1995). These electronic malls attempted to follow the format of physical malls by grouping together an assortment of retailers in one virtual location. This strategy was not particularly successful as real-world advantages to the consumer of single destination shopping were lost in the virtual world (Classe, 1996). Other specialty malls that grouped suppliers offering goods from a single product class began to emerge, but they too failed to achieve significant success, as this time it was the retailers that derived little advantage from making it easy to allow consumers to comparison shop. So, the most successful websites seemed to be those developed by individual retailers. Blackwell's Bookshops was the first UK retailer to announce profitable online trading with their global online bookshop, but this type of evidence was limited and online retail business performance was generally disappointing (Economist, 1997; Poon & Swatman, 1999).

Going into the new millennium, new entrants to the online market place were capturing global attention. Amazon.com, trading exclusively via the Internet with operational support from a large warehouse in Seattle, offered customers continuous access to a wide assortment of books and associated products, and speculation increased about the Internet's ability to rapidly promote such businesses to a position of dominance in global retail markets by using a virtual retail space free from restrictions of time and space (Jones & Biasiotto, 1999).

Retailers in the UK perhaps felt less inclined to be concerned about these new entrants as the cost of access for the average UK consumer adopting the Internet was higher than in the US. However, about this time, British Telecom introduced new pricing tariffs offering discounts to customers based on total expenditure across a range of services. This change altered the charging structure for operators using lo-call numbers, such as 0345. According to the telecommunications regulatory body OFTEL this change gave service providers the opportunity to develop longer-term relationships with their customers through the offer of the new tariff low-cost calls (OFTEL, 1998). Dixons plc seized on this opportunity and began offering free Internet access to their customers and Dixons Freeserve soon claimed to be the UK's largest Internet service provider with over 1.5 million users (Nuttall, 1999). Many other organisations launched similar offers (e.g. Tesco, Barclays Bank, British Telecom, Games Workshop), providing users with free email addresses, Web space and a bundle of other free offers. In this way many retailers diluted their efforts by offering Internet services rather than concentrating on building their capacity to sell online. Many retailers appeared to be attempting to derive competitive advantage by creating Web portals whereby the main aim, according to Watson (1998, p. 14) was to 'get the suckers under the tent and keep them there'. This perhaps suggests that retailers were attempting to emulate off-line business models and more traditional strategic thinking to guide their online activities, developing websites that attempted to keep customers inside their websites in much the same way as they are encouraged to remain within a physical retail store. This inward-looking approach gave free reign to online retailers that enjoyed trading in an environment with very limited competition.

The increased level of activity online grabbed the interest of academics who started to explore the likely impacts that this exciting, new digital technology would have on retailing in the future. For example, Burke (1997) questioned the extent to which the virtual world would change the principles of retailing and asked whether it would ultimately displace existing retail formats or serve as a natural complement to current marketing practices. Similarly, Malone et al. (1987) raised the possibility that manufacturers would target their consumers directly and, in so doing, simply cut the retailer, as the "middle man", out of the equation. It was argued that this form of 'Pirating the Value Chain' (Ghosh, 1998, p. 126) might change the balance of power within electronic channels of retail sectors. Other commentators went beyond raising questions about the Internet's likely impact on retailing to make fairly specific predictions. Many commentators were extremely optimistic about how quickly and enthusiastically the consumer would adopt this new channel. Pavitt (1997) believed that 'by the year 2005 it [the Internet] would capture between 8% and 30% of the UK retail market', whilst, over a similar time frame, 'high street stores face an estimated loss of 20% of their business to electronic shopping' (Angelides, 1997).

The reality was very different. Fast forward 10 years to the mid-2010s and it is possible to assess the extent to which the early predictions have proved to be credible. Although the rate of Internet adoption amongst retailers might not have been as rapid as originally envisaged, as Pentina et al. (2009) note, the key question for both marketing scholars and practitioners is no longer whether but when an incumbent retailer should adopt an online channel. The fact that, with the benefit of hindsight, many of the original predictions have proven to be rather optimistic, has not quenched the enthusiasm of Internet watchers for trying to predict the future trajectory of online shopping. Estimates by the IMRG (Interactive Media Retail Group) indicate that in 2005 online sales were about £12 billion and the equivalent total retail sales £245 billion (Figure 5.1), giving online sales figure of just under 5%; by 2020 they predict that online sales will account for approaching 45% of all retail sales.

By 2005, the information superhighway was firmly established as a new route to market. Online retailers were freely growing their capacity to serve an ever-expanding online marketplace whilst long-established high street brands were on the one hand experimenting with how they could entice shoppers to use their online services and on the other sitting on their hands and watching the growth of a phenomenon that projections suggested would put them out of business by 2020.

Consumers learn to navigate and shop the web

While retailers were wrestling with how to get online, deciding which services to offer and working out how to get their goods the last mile to the customer, consumers were getting an education that would empower them as future online shoppers. From the academic perspective, there has been a disproportionate amount of the research into the uptake and adoption of retail websites from the customer perspective. This very significant body of research has sought to understand better the behaviour of potential consumers and in particular the likelihood that they will purchase from retail websites. The bulk of these studies have applied variants of models such as the Theory of Reasoned Action (TRA), the Theory of Planned Behaviour (TPB) or the Technology Acceptance Model (TAM) to provide insights into the factors that influence a consumer's intention to shop online (Celik & Yilmaz, 2011; Crespo & del Bosque, 2010; Dennis et al., 2009; Lin, 2008). A wealth of related, customer-oriented studies has now also been conducted that explore the factors that affect a variety of dependent variables other than intention to shop online. For example, such studies have evaluated how a range of independent variables – such as website design, convenience, usability, reliability and security and service quality – impact

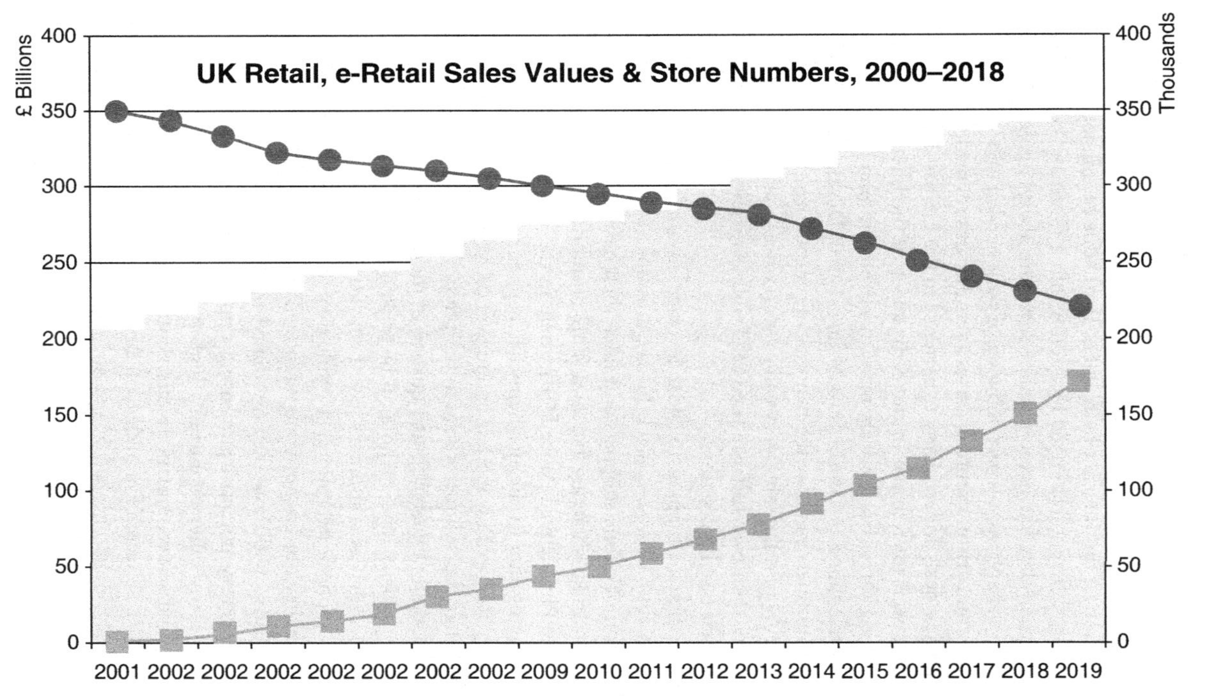

Figure 5.1 Retail profitability: UK retail and e-retail sales values and store numbers, 2000–2018

on an variety of dependent variables, such as customer loyalty, customer retention and overall customer satisfaction (Christodoulides & Michaelidou, 2010; Goode & Harris 2007; Kassim & Asiah Abdullah, 2010; Zhang et al., 2011). From the customer perspective, researchers have also focused on identifying those risk factors that are most likely to deter consumers from shopping online, highlighting issues such as risk of information misuse, distrust of payment systems, need to see product prior to purchase, and risk of failure to gain product benefits (Glover & Benbasat, 2010; Iglesias-Pradas et al., 2013).

Despite the potential barriers, consumer demand for online shopping has been a key factor in driving widespread adoption of the Internet by retailers. Partly due to online retailing offering an experience that is totally different from fixed location retailing (Westland & Au, 1997) shoppers can buy where and when they like because online stores are always open. In the early days, learning how to find the best bargains was part of the set of skills needed to become a competent online shopper. Price and comparison shopping across a number of sites made it easier and more convenient to locate the best deals. Indeed, early experience in the US has shown that more and more consumers used the web for research in the early stages of the buying decision-making process. Rather than buying direct on the web, many subsequently purchased the product in store or by ordering via telephone or fax (Ernst & Young, 1999). Developing this skill set has continued to empower consumers and now the majority of pre-purchase information searching is done online. Typically, 80% of online shoppers will *google* (i.e. use a search engine) to find the products they want to buy, then over half will then read online reviews (product and levels of service) before making their buying decision.

Specific events in the digital shopping calendar leverage advantage by understanding the online shopper's desire to find a bargain. Black Friday, introduced to the UK by Amazon in 2010, grabbed the attention of online shoppers and since then has grown into an event which kick-starts the online Christmas shopping bonanza. This promotional event – the origins of which are attributed to the Philadelphia Police Department in the 1950s, which gave this name to the day after Thanksgiving due to the mayhem that happened as shoppers flocked to the high street sales – is closely followed by another online event: Cyber Monday. These two online promotional events challenge the volume of sales in the physical high street and have begun to affect performance in the highly valuable fourth quarter of the year, which many retailers rely on to secure their positive returns for the whole of the trading year.

During the last two decades, as consumers have been learning how to shop online, their skills have become more sophisticated and as a result their decision-making more complex. This changing consumer behaviour has not gone unnoticed by savvy online retailers, which are becoming increasingly creative with how they use digital media as a continuous communication channel, tapping into every potential purchasing opportunity. In the UK, Germany, the Netherlands, the US and many other countries, a high proportion of customers use multiple channels when making purchase decisions, quite often combining online research with physical store visits (Hart et al., 2017). Research found that, on a typical visit to a town centre, consumers can refer to multiple digital touchpoints before and during their shopping journeys (Hart et al., 2017; Stocchi et al., 2016). Many shoppers are able to encounter multiple digital touchpoints on their journey to making a purchase decision; their path to purchase can mean that they not only encounter all of the traditional (pre-Internet) purchasing cues and search online, but are also able to assimilate a range of new digitally enhanced cues during their shopping journeys (Fulgoni, 2014).

Before we leave the consumers and their learning journey it is important to recognise that not all consumers are the same. We can group variables into two distinct sub-categories: classification variables and character variables. Classification variables are those personal attributes that tend to remain static throughout an individual's lifetime or evolve slowly over time – e.g., age, education, socio-economic groupings. These variables are particularly useful for retailers as they can help to identify particular consumers and target groups. Character variables are less straightforward to understand and identify for marketing purposes as they comprise any attributes of a consumer's perceptions, beliefs and attitudes, which might influence online behaviour – e.g. innovativeness, enjoyment, skills and experience and emotions. Character variables are also more likely to develop, change and be significantly modified over time by online shopping experiences. For example, if a consumer has negative beliefs about, say, privacy and security of online transactions, perhaps due to lack of computer skills, these beliefs are likely to shape negative attitudes towards the Internet and reduce the intention to shop online. Conversely, if a consumer believes the Internet is easy to use, they are more likely to have a positive attitude towards the idea of online shopping and ultimately have an increased intention to shop online. Each stance may be continually reinforced by positive or negative feedback from online shopping experiences (Doherty & Ellis-Chadwick, 2010).

Ultimately, those retail businesses that have ignored or failed to understand how consumers make use of digital channels are at best playing catch up or at worst have gone out of business (Doherty & Ellis-Chadwick, 2009). A very good example of how developing an understanding of consumer needs and wants can boost online performance comes from ASOS. ASOS identified the value of social media and used it to create competitive advantage by pioneering online social shopping, where customers use online social network sites to share product ideas before they buy. ASOS used social media to build a community of "fashionistas" who are prepared to share their views and opinions on what to wear via Facebook, Twitter and Google plus, giving its young shoppers fashion inspiration. With a target audience of over 12 million followers on social media sites, the company has made significant inroads to developing its own community of fashion buyers. ASOS learned how to deploy digital technology in response to online consumer behaviour and used this knowledge to build an online brand that is one of the most successful online fashion retailers the UK. ASOS offers tens of thousands of branded and own-label fashion items to millions of 20-something men and women around the globe; in 2017 its market valuation was greater than Marks & Spencer, the UK's largest seller of clothing. Nick Robertson and Quinten Griffiths created their business idea while watching the US television series Friends. They decided to create a web retail business that would sell items seen by television viewers, hence the name As Seen on Screen (ASOS). They started selling clothing worn by celebrities, but soon the company began developing its own brand. This focus enabled the company to start to build a reputation that was attractive to young fashion buyers. By developing a unique position in the market, which was particularly attractive to generation web (the millennials – eighteen to thirty somethings), and by deploying superior technical capabilities, the brand has grown significantly in the UK and internationally.

During the last 25 years, shoppers have developed new skills that have enabled them to buy in complex trading environments. Whilst there are different shopper profiles and motivations to shop (or not) online, the global spend online is growing and the retailers that are succeeding are those which have spent time developing digital resources and capabilities.

Retailers take tentative steps onto the digital high street

As the story of online retailing unfolds it is becoming more and more apparent that this mode of purchasing is set to continue to grow: consumers are becoming highly adept at shopping online and some retailers very accomplished at meeting and driving consumer demand online. The key questions to consider, therefore, are which retailers are succeeding and what might this mean for the future shape and function of our towns and cities?

Arguably, there have be some significant opportunities missed during that last three decades, which may well have altered the balance of power between off line and online retail brands. Earlier in the chapter, it was suggested that, if retailers missed the opportunity to go online at the first feasible opportunity, then they were likely to go out of business. We can now delve a little deeper into the extent to which being an early adopter of e-commerce increases the likelihood of a physical retailer still being in business in the future and also whether being an early adopter of e-commerce puts a retailer in an advantageous position when it comes to deploying wider range e-commerce functionalities.

Over the last 25 years, the number of high street retail brands in the UK has fallen steadily. Much of this reduction can be explained simply in terms of retailers going out of business, but there has also been some evidence of merger and take-over activity over this period. In terms of their broad levels of Internet activity, the number of retailers that have either done nothing or no more than simply register a domain name has fallen sharply, with the majority of major brands owning their own domains. A longitudinal study by Ellis-Chadwick and Doherty (2018), looking at the uptake of online retailing by leading brands in the UK revealed that the number of retailers actively using the Internet as a sales medium had risen dramatically from just 3% in 1997 to 62% by 2013 (Figure 5.2). This shift in levels of adoption of the Internet as a channel to market has potentially had a profound effect on the growth of online shopping. In 1997, there was a very limited choice of products for an online shopper and limited competition around pricing and service; in other words, the digital retail landscape was quite desolate. However, most well-known high street brands have now developed sophisticated online stores and in doing so significantly increased the opportunity to shop via the Internet. According to Ellis-Chadwick and Doherty (2018), 2013 appears to have been a tipping point in the UK at least: after this year, it became important for retailers to develop a digital presence.

The 'live, but no sales' is an interesting category, as it represents those retailers that had invested in a customer-facing website to provide some combination of product and promotional information and/or direct communication, but had decided not to offer their customers the opportunity to purchase goods and services online. In all three samples this category is prominent and formed the largest single category in 2005, accounting for 27% of the sample. This was just the point in time when Amazon, ASOS and other online retailers were really beginning to grow their online operations and target markets. It is useful, therefore, to dig below the surface and explore the specific types of functionalities that retailers have been offering through their websites and compare these with the provision of online sales. As seen in Figure 5.3, the provision of product information was by far the most commonly adopted piece of functionality to be adopted by retailers on their websites across all three dates, followed fairly closely by the provision of email facilities to allow customers to communicate directly with staff members. It is interesting to note that, whilst the numbers of retailers providing promotional information relating to money offs, discounts, bonus buys, sales etc., rose from 1997 to 2005, it then dropped noticeably by 2013. The most obvious explanation for this is that, because many retailers were by then attempting to target their customers with tailored promotional information, via email or other forms of social media (Ellis-Chadwick & Doherty, 2012), there was less need to post promotional information online. Whilst the facility to order goods and services started from the lowest base, it grew steadily and it now threatens to catch up with the provision of product information in the years to come.

That said, retailers just starting to sell online in 2006 onwards were playing catch up not only with their peers, but also with the online-only retailers. Further analysis revealed that in 1997

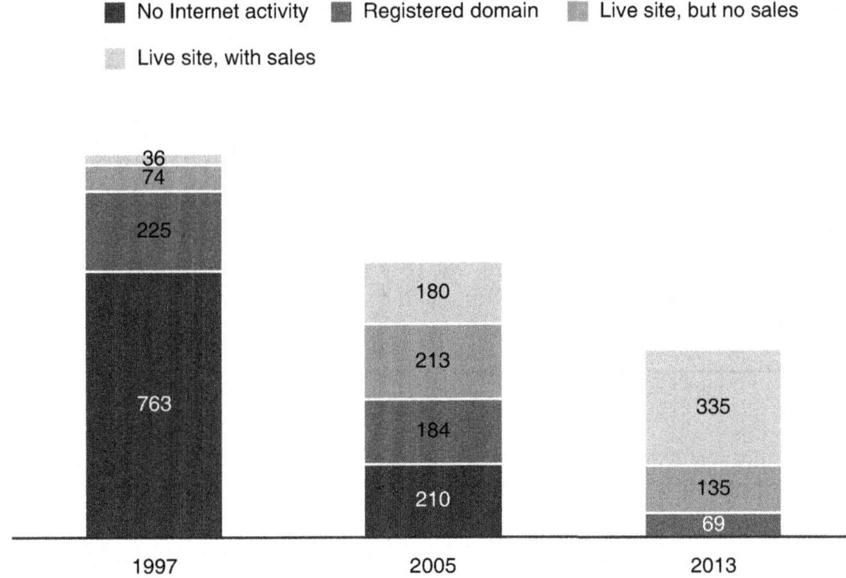

Figure 5.2 The changing face of online retailing

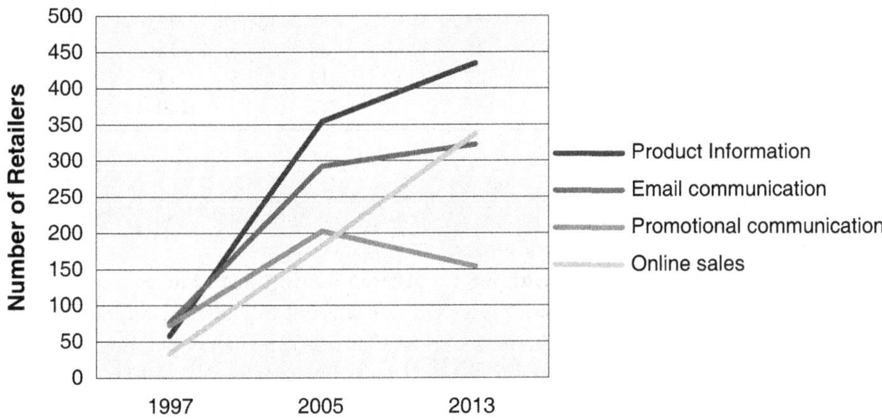

Figure 5.3 The uptake of basic online functionalities

that the vast majority of retailers (763 cases or 69%) had not even registered a domain name, let alone started to develop an active website. Secondly, there was a highly significant association between retail category and the level of Internet activity experienced by the retailers operating in that category. Table 5.1 shows where the actual number of cases in a specific cell (bold number) in the contingency table differs markedly from the number that would be expected (in parentheses) if there had been a uniform uptake across all categories. More specifically, it can be seen that, in 1997, there was a higher than expected chance of a retailer operating in the mail order, home furnishing or leisure and entertainment sectors having already developed an active Internet presence, possibly including sales. In the case of mail order, the reason for this is

Table 5.1 The Adoption of E-commerce by Retail Category (in 1997)

	No Domain		*Not live*		*Live or Sales*		*Totals*
Clothing & Accessories	**161**	(163.3)	**53**	(48.2)	**21**	(23.5)	**235**
Food & Consumables	**54**	(64.6)	**28**	(19.1)	**11**	(9.3)	**93**
Health & Beauty	**80**	(67.4)	**11**	(19.9)	**6**	(9.7)	**97**
Home Furnishings	**92**	(104.9)	**39**	(30.9)	**20**	(15.1)	**151**
Leisure & Entertainment	**102**	(112.6)	**35**	(33.2)	**25**	(16.2)	**162**
Mail Order	**68**	(82.7)	**32**	(24.4)	**19**	(11.9)	**119**
Mixed Offering	**80**	(75.0)	**22**	(22.1)	**6**	(10.8)	**108**
Specialist Retailers	**126**	(92.4)	**5**	(27.3)	**2**	(13.3)	**133**
Grand Total	**763**		**225**		**110**		**1098**

Table 5.2 The Adoption of the Internet by Retail Category (in 2005)

	No Domain		*Not live*		*Live (no sales)*		*Sales*		*Totals*
Clothing & Accessories	**43**	(46.2)	**43**	(40.4)	**43**	(46.8)	**44**	(39.6)	173
Food & Consumables	**24**	(17.3)	**9**	(15.2)	**24**	(17.6)	**8**	(14.9)	65
Health & Beauty	**23**	(20.8)	**27**	(18.2)	**21**	(21.1)	**7**	(17.8)	78
Home Furnishings	**16**	(25.9)	**20**	(22.7)	**39**	(26.3)	**22**	(22.2)	97
Leisure & Entertainment	**22**	(29.6)	**32**	(25.7)	**21**	(29.8)	**35**	(25.2)	110
Mail Order	**21**	(28.0)	**11**	(24.5)	**29**	(28.4)	**44**	(24.0)	105
Mixed Offering	**18**	(19.2)	**15**	(16.8)	**24**	(19.5)	**15**	(16.5)	72
Specialist Retailers	**43**	(23.2)	**27**	(20.3)	**12**	(23.5)	**5**	(19.9)	87
Grand Total	210		184		213		180		787

the operational advantages of existing logistics systems that could handle both distribution and return of goods delivered to the end consumer.

By 2005, the number of retailers without a registered domain had reduced very markedly, whilst the number hosting a live website, either with or without full sales capabilities, had risen very significantly (Table 5.2). Again, the data suggest that it was retailers operating in the mail order or leisure & entertainment sectors that were most likely to have developed a full web presence, whilst specialist retailers and those organisations operating in the health and beauty sector were least likely to have taken the plunge to sell online. Eight years later, in 2013, the vast majority of those retailers still in business (62.2%) were by then offering their customers the opportunity to purchase products directly online, although it was still retailers operating in the mail order or leisure and entertainment sectors that were most likely to have developed a full web presence (Table 5.3).

One of the most significant elements of this study was that it allowed analysis of the relationship between the level of online activity in which retailers were engaged at a particular point in time and their trading status at later times. Unsurprisingly, those retailers that had no discernible activity in 1997 were the least likely to still be trading in 2005, whilst those organisations that had developed an active website, with or without sales, were most likely to still be trading in 2005. Similar trends continued into the following period. There are at least two plausible interpretations to these patterns. First, it could be that retailers who were already struggling to survive did not want the distraction of engaging in a completely new strategy. Alternatively, it could be that

Table 5.3 The Adoption of the Internet by Retail Category (in 2013)

	Domain or Live (no sales)		*Sales*		*Totals*
Clothing & Accessories	**26**	(48.61)	**99**	(79.83)	**125**
Food & Consumables	**24**	(12.59)	**10**	(20.67)	**34**
Health & Beauty	**30**	(20.40)	**22**	(33.50)	**52**
Home Furnishings	**24**	(27.78)	**45**	(45.62)	**69**
Leisure & Entertainment	**15**	(27.34)	**55**	(44.90)	**70**
Mail Order	**20**	(32.12)	**60**	(52.74)	**80**
Mixed Offering	**18**	(16.49)	**27**	(27.09)	**45**
Specialist Retailers	**47**	(18.66)	**17**	(30.65)	**64**
Grand Total	**204**		**335**		**539**

those organisations that were active and early adopters of the Internet either got some direct benefits that helped them survive or saw Internet use as a catalyst for rethinking their strategy, which indirectly helped them survive (Bordonaba-Juste et al., 2012; Lee & Grewal, 2004).

The future of the high street

In 1994, shoppers took the first tentative steps to buy online; since then tens of thousands of physical shops have disappeared from retail centres across the UK and other parts of the world. In response, towns and city planners have worked hard to reconfigure places in order to provide the kind of experiences that shoppers want. But where is all this heading? Will in-store and consumer technology transform retailing forever? Will voice-enabled assistants execute our every wish, with absolute precision removing the need for physical shops altogether? Or will retailers take a turn back in history, going for the total physical experience with high levels of customer service and quality products, enabling them to head the vanguard into the future? Realistically, predictions of the future can be exaggerations of past events, extrapolated into a distance point in time or little more than "finger in the air" musings of an idealist vision of the world we might inhabit. What will happen is probably somewhere in between. This chapter has looked at the growth and impact of online retailing from different perspectives, including consumers and retailers, and sought to address some of the key questions of the digital age.

Is the physical high street about to disappear? This is unlikely. However, retailing is going through significant change, and the places that thrive in the future are going to be those that have attracted and retained the most digitally capable retail brands, which in turn have developed the capacity to trade through multiple channels. Fulgoni (2014) identified priorities for retail businesses wanting to trade online: eliminate silos and create seamless experiences for consumers all the way along the path to purchase; increase opportunities to digitally interact; analyse and measure consumer behaviour at all touchpoints in order to develop deep and insightful understanding in what is driving shoppers' choices and purchase decisions. But these are priorities that may require significant changes to the way a business operates and, in some cases, it is too late to make the necessary changes to be able to compete effectively with those businesses that have spent the last 20 years learning how to operate online. Research suggests that, in the next 5 years, the retailers that survive are going to be those that have developed digital capabilities and resources, that understand their customers in much greater detail than in the past, and are able to provide products and services that are highly differentiated.

Note

* This chapter is dedicated to Professor Neil F. Doherty.

References

Angelides, M.C. (1997), 'Implementing the Internet for business: A global marketing opportunity', *International Journal of Information Management*, 17 (6), pp. 405–419.

Barclay Merchant Services (1995), *Bringing the customers to you: Barclay Square shopping the UK's most exciting retail location* (Barclay Merchant Services).

Berners-Lee, T., Cailliau, R., Luotonen, A., Neilson, H.F. and Secret, A. (1994), 'The world wide web', *Communications of the ACM*, 37 (8), pp. 76–84.

Bordonaba-Juste, V., Lucia-Palacios, L. and Polo-Redondo, Y. (2012), 'Antecedents and consequences of e-business adoption for European retailers', *Internet Research* 22 (5), pp. 532–550.

Burke, R.R. (1997), 'Do you see what I see: The future of virtual shopping', *Journal of the Academy of Marketing Science*, 25 (4), pp. 352–360.

Çelik, H.E. and Yilmaz, V. (2011), 'Extending the technology acceptance model for adoption of e-shopping by consumers in Turkey', *Journal of Electronic Commerce Research*, 12, pp. 152–164.

Christodoulides, G. and Michaelidou, N. (2010), 'Shopping motives as antecedents of e-satisfaction and e-loyalty', *Journal of Marketing Management*, 27 (1–2), pp. 181–197.

Classe, A. (1996), 'Scenes from a mall: Electronic commerce and planning an electronic retail site', *Computer Weekly*, p. 36.

Cope, N. (1995), 'High Street's big names go online', *The Independent.*

Coursey, D. (1992), 'Kapor calls to connect all Americans via the Internet', *InfoWorld*, 14 (21), p. 94.

Crespo, A.H. and del Bosque, I.R. (2010), 'The influence of the commercial features of the Internet on the adoption of e-commerce by consumers', *Electronic Commerce Research and Applications*, 9 (6), pp. 562–575.

Dennis, C., Merrilees, B., Jayawardhena, C. and Tiu Wright, L. (2009), 'E-consumer behaviour', *European Journal of Marketing*, 43 (9/10), pp. 1121–1139.

Doherty, N.F. and Ellis-Chadwick, F.E. (2009), 'Exploring the drivers, scope and perceived success of e-commerce strategies in the UK retail sector', *European Journal of Marketing*, 43 (9/10), pp. 1246–1262.

Doherty, N.F. and Ellis-Chadwick, F.E. (2010), 'Internet retailing: The past, the present and the future', *International Journal of Retail & Distribution Management*, 38 (11/12), pp. 943–965.

Economist (1997), 'In search of the perfect market', 343 (8016), p. 3.

Ellis-Chadwick, F. and Doherty, N.F. (2012), 'Web advertising: The role of e-mail marketing', *Journal of Business Research*, 65 (6), pp. 843–848.

Ellis-Chadwick, F. and Doherty, N.F. (2018), 'Winners and Losers in the race to deliver on-line shopping: A longitudinal analysis', *EIRASS*, Maderia.

Ernst & Young (1999), *The second annual Ernst & Young Internet shopping study* (New York).

Fulgoni, G.M. (2014), '"Omni-channel" retail insights and the consumers path-to purchase: How digital has transformed the way people make purchasing decisions', *Journal of Advertising Research*, 54 (4), pp. 377–380.

Ghosh, S. (1998), 'Making business sense of the Internet', *Harvard Business Review*, pp. 126–135.

Glover, S. and Benbasat, I. (2010), 'A comprehensive model of perceived risk of e-commerce transactions', *International Journal of Electronic Commerce*, 15 (2), pp. 47–78.

Goode, M.M. and Harris, L.C. (2007), 'Online behavioural intentions: An empirical investigation of antecedents and moderators', *European Journal of Marketing*, pp. 512–536.

Hart, C., Ellis-Chadwick, F. and Haji, I. (2017), 'The role of digital in town centre experience', European Association for Education and Research in Commercial Distribution Conference, Dublin.

Iglesias-Pradas, S., Pascual-Miguel, F., Hernández-García, Á. and Chaparro-Peláez, J. (2013), 'Barriers and drivers for non-shoppers in B2C e-commerce: A latent class exploratory analysis', *Computers in Human Behavior*, 29 (2), pp. 314–322.

Jones, K. and Biasiotto, M. (1999), 'Internet retailing: Current hype or future reality?', *The International Journal of Retail Distribution and Consumer Research*, 9 (1), pp. 69–79.

Kassim, N. and Asiah Abdullah, N. (2010), 'The effect of perceived service quality dimensions on customer satisfaction, trust, and loyalty in e-commerce settings: A cross cultural analysis', *Asia Pacific Journal of Marketing and Logistics*, 22 (3), pp. 351–371.

Krol, E. (1994), *The whole Internet: Users guide and catalog* (Brewster, MA: O'Reilly & Associates Inc).

Lee, R.P. and Grewal, R. (2004), 'Strategic responses to new technologies and their impact on firm performance', *Journal of Marketing*, 68, pp. 157–171.
Lin, A., Gregor, S. and Ewing, M. (2008), 'Developing a scale to measure the enjoyment of web experiences', *Journal of Interactive Marketing*, 22 (4), pp. 40–57.
Malone, T.W., Yates, J. and Benjamin, R.I. (1987), 'Electronic markets and electronic hierarchies', *Communications of the ACM*, 30 (6), pp. 484–496.
McGarty, T.P. and Haywood, C. (1995), 'Internet architectural and policy implications for migration from high-end user to the 'new user'', in B. Kahin and J. Keller (eds.) *Public Access to the Internet. Publication of The Harvard Information Infrastructure Project* (Cambridge, MA/London, England: The MIT Press).
Nelson, T.H. (1991), 'As we will think', in J.M. Nyce and P. Kahn (eds.) *From memex to hypertext vannevar bush and the minds's machine* (Boston/New York: Academic Press) 245–260.
Nuttall, R. (1999), 'Dixons floats Freeserve as Granada jeers', *The Express*, p. 12.
Ovum Reports (1996), 'Intranets for business applications: User and supplier opportunities', Ovum Ltd.
OFTEL (1998), Tariffing Issues: Bundling of Inbound and Outbound Services Statement October.
Palmer, M.J. (1995), 'Corporate invitational publishing: Commerce doesn't mean hard sell, and multimedia doesn't mean hype', 16th Proceedings of On-Line Meeting, New York.
Pavitt, D. (1997), 'Retailing and the super highway: The future of the electronic home shopping industry', *International Journal of Retail & Distribution Management*, 25 (1), pp. 38–43.
Pentina, I., Pelton, L.E. and Hasty, R.W. (2009), 'Performance implications of online entry timing by store-based retailers: A longitudinal investigation', *Journal of Retailing*, 85 (2), pp. 177–193.
Poon, S. and Swatman, P.M.C. (1999), 'A longitudinal study of expectations in small business internet commerce', *International Journal of Electronic Commerce*, 3 (3), pp. 21–33.
Pyle, R. (1996), 'Electronic commerce and the Internet', *Communications of the ACM*, 39 (6), pp. 22–24.
Stocchi, L., Hart, C. and Haji, I. (2016), 'Understanding the town centre customer experience', *Journal of Marketing Management*, 32.
Verity, J. (1995), 'The Internet', *Business Week*, (3398), pp. 80–88.
Watson, T. (1998), 'Alternative doorways to the Internet are popping up in the spirit of free-flowing information', *New York Times*.
Westland, C.J. and Au, G. (1997), 'A comparison of shopping experiences across three competing digital retailing interfaces', *International Journal of Electronic Commerce*, 2 (2), pp. 57–69.
Wikipedia (2018), 'CompuServe', Available at: https://en.wikipedia.org/wiki/CompuServe, (Accessed April 18, 2018).
Zakon, R.H. (1994), 'An Internet timeline highlighting some of the key events which helped shape the Internet as we know it today', *Hobbes Internet Timeline*, Available at: http://info.isoc.org/guest/zakon/Internet /history/HIT.html.
Zhang, Y., Fang, Y., Wei, K.K., Ramsey, E., McCole, P. and Chen, H. (2011), 'Repurchase intention in B2C e-commerce – a relationship quality perspective', *Information & Management*, 48 (6), pp. 192–200.

6

BARGAIN HUNT? SELLING SECOND-HAND, c.1600 TO THE PRESENT

Sara Pennell

Introduction

Let us start with an object: a desk bookcase, a rather flamboyant example of japanned style decoration, on a pine carcase dated to around 1700–1720, which is on display in the so-called pre-Revolutionary room in the Metropolitan Museum of Art (New York). It is a good place to start this chapter, because by sheer dint of their longevity, most museum objects have a pre-history of *not* being museum objects, and so are inevitably 'used' goods, travelling through conduits of retailing, gifting and exchange in which the not-brand-new predominate. Indeed, in its prior life, well before it became museum artefact, the desk bookcase was explicitly sold as a piece of second-hand furniture, by one of the modes of retail that looms large in these second-hand circuits. The bookcase was put up for sale by auction (or vendue, as they were called in colonial America), with other household "sundry" goods sometime in the spring of 1754 as a consequence of its owner's alleged suicide in October 1753 (Westerfield, 1920; Gottesman, 1938; Hartigan O'Connor, 2011: 156–159). Sir Danvers Osborne (1715–53) had, but days before he was found strangled, possibly by his own hand and certainly by his own handkerchief, been invested with the powers of governor, with a remit to clear up a city administration riven with corruption. But this is not a chapter about colonial dark deeds: it is the bookcase which had an after-life (much more so than Osborne), being sold onto Osborne's successor (and, in the minds of some, his nemesis), Lieutenant Governor James De Lancey at the vendue. For the subsequent 180-odd years, the desk bookcase remained the possession of the De Lancey-Verplanck family, who finally donated it to the museum in 1939 (details from Metropolitan Museum of Art online catalogue) (Figure 6.1).

Even before Osborne shipped the desk bookcase to New York, it is quite possible that it was already what would pass in modern parlance as "pre-loved". Given its Augustan style and the fact that Osborne was only born in 1715, it is likely to have either been a piece he inherited from his own family, or that Osborne had himself purchased at one of the many household auctions already running in London and advertised in the daily and weekly press or from one of the many retailer-makers, operating as upholders, cabinet makers, sworn appraisers and/ or undertakers; or from an upholsterer like Mr Rickett, whose late eighteenth-century trade card depicts some of the "modern" styles of furniture he dealt in new and second-hand as an 'upholder, cabinetmaker, sworn appraiser and undertaker' (Rickett, u.d.). Today, if ever made

Figure 6.1 Osborne desk bookcase, c.1700–1720

Source: Courtesy of The Metropolitan Museum of Art.

available on the open market, the bookcase desk would be classed as an "antique", subject to a specific sort of marketing and trade which itself was unknown for furniture in the eighteenth century, but which is now inhabited by exclusive dealers and fine art auctioneers who can claim direct ancestry with the early Georgian brokers and jacks-of-all-trade gavel-wielders, one of whom might have sold Osborne his bookcase.

In this chapter, the focus will be on the evolution of some of these modes of selling second-hand that Osborne's desk bookcase might have been subject to, and the conditions which created and sustained the markets for such retailing across four centuries, from part-exchange to specialised dealing to auctioneering. As a historian of material culture across the long eighteenth century, I dwell a little longer on developments from between c.1660–1850, but not only because of that: this is the period upon which much extant scholarship also focuses. By starting with an object which now resides in a museum, I want to unpick the enduring but unwarranted connection between second-hand retailing and those "economies of makeshifts" characteristic of the least well-off and supposedly least market-integrated in societies. For much of the four centuries surveyed here, selling second-hand did not mark one out as a Fagin but rather more as the self-confident provincial auctioneer in George Eliot's *Middlemarch* (1871–2), Borthrop Trumbull; or one of the many dealers and salesmen with capital enough to produce a trade card or advertise in the metropolitan or provincial press. The goods sold by these retailers were not by default shabby or outmoded, either: they could as easily be "elegant", "as new" and "ingenious" goods bookcases to barouches, laundry coppers to Trumbull's 'very recherchy . . . trifles' (Eliot, 1992: 653).

Selling second-hand: historiographies

That markets for second-hand goods existed historically is much acknowledged, but inexplicably understudied. Unsurprisingly perhaps, the enduring appeal of the used has been especially overshadowed within historiographies of consumer, production and commercial revolution of the last five or so centuries, by the lustre of the new. It is the novel, not the pre-loved and familiar, which catches the scholarly light, even though it is abundantly clear that the conditions for mass production and marketing of many such new objects did not exist until the later eighteenth, indeed the nineteenth century (Van Damme and Vermoesen, 2009: 275). Osborne's desk is a (book)case in point: in the English American colonies domestic manufacturing was minimal and discouraged for a good part of the eighteenth century, so as not to jeopardise the market opportunities offered up by trans-Atlantic trade, 'the principal *Cornucopia* of *Great Britain's* wealth', as one mid-eighteenth-century trade commentator gushed (cited Breen, 2004: 86). Even if tastes for such goods were stimulated across a wide social spectrum, whether by the capricious rotations of a fashion cycle, or the siren call of emulation or the wish for comfort, second-hand retailing was essential to satisfying such tastes, in the absence of an unlimited supply of newly manufactured goods.

Ignoring just how ubiquitous second-hand circulation was has also meant that more modern adherence to practices of material waste and inbuilt obsolescence has leached into our expectations of what happened to goods and possessions, once their initial lustre had worn off. This is particularly problematic for the period before 1800, since, as Laurence Fontaine has argued, 'the values extolling the new and the need for replacement to keep pace with fashion were late to gain precedence over those of conservation and tradition' (Fontaine, 2008a: 2). Material stewardship and an abhorrence of waste loomed large in pre-modern societies, and we cannot simply look at pre-modern consumption choices through late twentieth and early twenty-first century lenses. Consuming in the pre-capitalist economy demanded (for all but those at the apex of societies) moderation and decorum, and the promotion of thrift and good housewifery, rather than an out-and-out thirst for the new (McCants, 1995: 194).

What then explains the tendency to bracket second-hand retailing as part of the "informal economy" of any given society, to see it as a marginal rather than central economic practice, a function of need rather than of desire? Some forms of second-hand circulation, such as pre- and post-*mortem* bequests, gifting and barter-exchange, undoubtedly complicate and blur the boundaries of a neoclassical economic understanding of the "market", but that market itself has a dubious historical pedigree. Perhaps more significant has been the scholarly attention paid to clothing and other textiles as circulating material through the licit and illicit conduits used to keep poor households afloat and mouths fed. Areas like Rosemary and Petticoat Lanes in late seventeenth-century London and the markets of Temple and Notre Dame in pre- and post-Revolutionary Paris, where no questions would be asked of clothing and linens bought and offered for resale, and the "brokers" who fenced and found buyers for stolen petticoats, waistcoats and greatcoats, have dominated accounts of second-hand dealing in certain regions (e.g. Lemire, 1991; Roche, 1997; Charpy, 2008; Barahona and Sánchez, 2012).

This is, of course, too extreme. As Ilja Van Damme has argued, to see second-hand retailing as a matter of binary and opposing markets, articulating 'a rigid dichotomy between antique collecting for the rich and economic necessity for the poor', is to overlook much, not least 'the complex consumer motivations of the middling sorts, and the continuous distribution of second-hand goods, that were neither "bad" nor "luxurious"' (Van Damme, 2010: 86). Selling second-hand produced particular forms of retailer, retail spaces and processes, that were neither "informal", if we take that word to mean without regulation or some notion of professional identity, nor marginal to the local or regional economies in which they operated (Deceulaer, 2008). From sixteenth-century "criers" and "uitropers" whose business it was to "cry" or advertise the sales of used goods, to the auctioneers, vendue-masters, brokers and general and specialist dealers whose names are scattered across the pages of eighteenth- to twentieth-century European and American newsprint, trade cards and occupational directories, there were distinct and, at times, highly profitable careers to be had in selling second-hand, just as the environs in which second-hand retailing occurred could be fashionable and exclusive – more Pall Mall than Petticoat Lane.

Osborne's desk bookcase also demonstrates that used goods are not always marginal in a second sense: they do not have to be broken, damaged or worn, but could be "as new". Even out with the specialist markets for used books, artworks and specific types of antiquities such as coins, medals and sculpture which began to develop across Europe in the seventeenth century, the appetite for "neat" used furniture and soft furnishings as well as for coaches, stock-in-trade and tools in good working condition or of "as new" appearance and feel was met by retailers and circuits that dealt mostly if not exclusively in hardly worn or well-maintained and cared-for goods. These supply chains were, in turn, not just fed by picking over the estates of the needy bankrupt or destitute deceased. Goods flowed into these circuits as fashions shifted and people moved, married or "left off trade". Indeed, the costs and logistics of carrying bulky goods over even short distances fed directly into the disposal of household goods as a preliminary to moving house. That is why in 1834 Thomas and Jane Carlyle, having decided to move to London to further Thomas's career as an essayist, planned to rent out their Scottish house and 'to sell off all the furniture but what will equip a very modest house in the Suburbs of London' (*Carlyle Letters Online*, lt-18340225-TC-JAC-01).

Even when sales of goods were necessary because of indebtedness or hard times, those implicated were as likely to be Spanish monarchs, as they were impoverished *madrileños*: the need for hard cash could strike the wealthy no less than the indigent. The fact that goods in the second-hand goods sales in Antwerp and its surroundings studied by Ilja Van Damme sold for prices ranging from fewer than 50 to more than 1,000 guilders, suggests that not only was there a very socio-economically diverse clientele eager to buy such goods, but that such goods came from no less diverse sources (Alvarez, 2007; Van Damme, 2009: 111). Buyers of second-hand goods were indeed socially diverse and discerning, with their purchases intended not just for servants' garrets or impoverished hovels, but for furnishing key rooms in gentry and aristocratic households. Jean Scott Hay (1629–88), countess of Tweeddale's letter, sent from their Scottish seat, Yester Castle to her husband, John Hay (1626–97), the second earl, in London in the 1670s, about sourcing 'a damask bed & if you could get a second-hand one were not soiled and fashionable, you might buy it if it be either a blew or crimson', tells us two things: that such textiles were widely available second-hand in later Stuart London; and that members of the aristocracy had no qualms about buying via this route (Tweeddale Papers, [1674]: fol. 84r). As Jon Stobart and Mark Rothery have shown in recent work on the processes of furnishing, re-arranging and dismantling the country house interior, providing access to select, well-chosen second-hand items for such clientele and also disposing of such goods for them or their descendants, was the remit of highly respectable businessmen, working as upholsterers, furniture dealers and society auctioneers, in the mould of James Christie (1730–1803) and precursors to the superstar *fin-de-siècle* antique dealers-cum-interior designers, like the Duveens of London, Georges Hoentschel at Maison Leys in Paris and the Syphers in New York, serving clients trans-continentally and transatlantically (Sypher, 1992; Herrmann, 2004; Roberts, 2004; Kisluk-Grosheide, Krohn, and Leben, 2013; Stobart and Rothery, 2016).

The concentration in much of the extant literature on second-hand circulation on clothing, and to a lesser extent, household textiles more generally, may also have skewed approaches to other goods and materials in the second-hand sphere. The development of specific forms of second-hand trading in horses, books and manuscripts, and fine art and antiquities gleaned from the Grand Tour, already suggests that we need to be careful in seeing in the modes and mechanisms for selling textiles and clothing second-hand a universal model of second-hand retailing more generally. As the anthropologists Nicky Gregson and Louise Crewe note 'we need to ask in which conditions particular goods might be acquired through the second-hand market, where, how, by whom and for whom' (Gregson and Crewe, 2003: 6). Shifts in fashion and aesthetics, as well as the adaptability of the materials – textiles, especially linens, were not only reusable but recyclable as rags to the paper trade – may have made textiles recirculation faster, with quicker rewards for participants, and without much (or indeed any) capital outlay. After all, clothes and household linens needed but chests to store them, while furniture took up valuable floor space, and coaches yards or stabling.

The specialised conduits for those goods in which producer/production quality, provenance and antiquity or patina were emerging as connoisseurial virtues in the eyes of potential buyers, also had features which were by no means common to *all* forms of second-hand retail. The second-hand selling of books and fine art emerged in key European centres in the late seventeenth century, notably Amsterdam, the Hague and London, with specific formats for selling (the bidding auction rather than the fixed-price sale), and networks for circulation, focused on gentry and elite male-dominated groups, specialist dealers and auctioneers, and the emergence of self-generated value systems for the commodities involved, that depended in part on building and sustaining an informed community of connoisseurs for circulation (Harris, Mandelbrote, and Myers, 2001; di Marchi, 2004; Cowan, 2006).

Finally, we need to think about the geographies covered by extant research, since many scholars have fixed their gazes on continental second-hand trading, rather than extra-European or even global circuits, with sixteenth-century Italian cities, the Low Countries in the seventeenth- and eighteenth centuries and early modern Paris and its environs attracting important studies. The most recent collection of essays on the subject cast its net wider, to include studies of Scandinavia, the colonial South African Cape and imperial British India (Stobart and Van Damme, 2010b; see also Finn, 2010). We nonetheless still lack studies which attempt comparative analyses of how different types of second-hand circuit endured and thrived in some regions but not others; and which explore the legacies of second-hand selling across north America, Africa and the Indian sub-continent (especially given the centrality of second-hand trading and materials recycling in these latter regions today). The roots of the now-global second-hand trade – where decommissioned British railway carriages find a new lease of life on Indian tracks, to use a perhaps extreme example – is just no less a significant part of that tentacular, cross-continental material flow of costly silks, ceramics and comestibles that historians have become increasingly enamoured of tracing in the past decade.

Conduits and occupations in used goods retailing

Peruse any domestic account book from the seventeenth to the nineteenth centuries and you would be wrong to assume that all the goods listed as purchases were new-made. Alongside new items and expenditures on maintenance of existing items – retinning pots, replumping mattresses and mending shoes – there are almost always second-hand purchases. Sometimes these latter entries might hint at the seller (a neighbour, a broker, a shopkeeper) or the locus of purchase (a sale, a shop, the local fair), but, as Fontaine has bewailed, the widespread invisibility of second-hand exchange (for much of early modern Europe at least), where the exchange could be barter, part-exchange or a form of gifting, makes quantifying and qualifying the types and locations of, and values assigned to such exchange like connecting a particularly random, widely scattered set of dots (Fontaine, 2008a: 11). Thanks to particular archival survivals, in this section some of these dots will be brought into sharper focus.

Guilds and state operations

Some of this survival is down to the ways in which the form of corporate governance and nature of economic controls meant that the conduits for second-hand retail were formal components of highly regulated commodity markets. Specialised trade guilds to oversee and control retail practices in a wide range of used goods operated in Italian city-states like Venice and Florence; across early modern Spain, in cities like Barcelona and Madrid, Low Countries' villages (for example Erdemobogen, in modern Belgium) and mercantile entrepots (Antwerp; Bruges). These corporate organisations and the spaces in which they operated, were either government-run or held state/crown monopolies: Stockholm's city Auction House was established in 1674 and its monopoly confirmed by the crown in 1772 (Lilja, Murhem, and Ulvaeng, 2009). In sixteenth- and seventeenth-century Spain, the royal court itself was both organiser of and subject to auction sales of their collections, to enable the extensive *post mortem* testaments of dead monarchs to be carried out (Alvarez, 2007).

The useful archival paper trails left by these institutions enable historians to map the economic value of second-hand trading in such markets, as well as the variety of goods traded in this way, the customer bases involved, and the shape of and challenges to such trade over time. They record the apprenticing and training of officers with expertise in appraising, crying and directing sales developed cadres of specialists, and with political and economic influence to boot; the leading members of Antwerp's *Oudekleerkopers* [literally, "old clothing buyers"], controlled the city's Friday Market, with its zones for different types of second-hand good, and also leased the majority of real estate around it (Van Damme, 2009). There are also records of the policing and licensing activities that empowered these bodies to manage the quality of goods being sold by their members and proscribe or limit the sale of such goods by non-members, as well as control the profile of their membership.

By contrast, England's archives afford very little evidence of either regulation or geographical zoning of particular types of second-hand trading beyond the City of London, and beyond the fifteenth century, until the passing of the 1777 Auction Duty Act (Ohashi, 2007; Staples, 2015: 298). Although second-hand clothing and other textiles were traded by "fripperers" in the fourteenth and fifteenth centuries, and the City of London appointed an "outroper" or official crier, to "cry" sales of goods, there is however little other evidence until the late seventeenth century of how such sales were run, whether they involved new or used (or both) commodities, and what sort of goods were sold via them (although we know wine and shipping was being sold by auction in the fifteenth century). The Upholders' Company, the notional occupational "home" of upholsterers, was in decline by the end of the seventeenth century, with only a modest bureaucratic reach: a poor cousin to the *Oudekleerkopers* or the Venetian *arte degli strazzaruoli* (Allerston, 1996: 20; Staples, 2010).

Intermingled commerce

In a striking phrase, Manuel Charpy argues that, in pre-1900 Europe, the second-hand simply 'melted into all other aspects of economic life' (Charpy, 2008: 147). In some locales, there were restrictions on who could sell "new" goods and who could sell second-hand, as in eighteenth-century Antwerp and Stockholm, and early nineteenth-century America. Elsewhere, however, it was very common for artisans retailing their own wares and specialist shopkeepers selling more generally, to hold a small stock of used items alongside new goods (Allerston, 1996: 4). The 1667 inventory of the widow of a Norwich (England) pewterer, Anne Beart, contained a listing of 'one old copper' alongside the pewter, iron and other domestic metalwares in the shop stock valuation, while in early eighteenth-century Oxford, a visit to John Airey, tinsmith's workshop would have furnished a 'second-hand grate' (Beart, 1667; Airey, 1715). By the eighteenth century, this intermingling of old and new was advertised quite clearly on the trade cards of a broad spectrum of makers and retailers, like the clock- and watchmaker Thomas Denton of Abingdon (England), advertising exchange of "old for new" alongside the options of buying new or second-hand on his mid-eighteenth-century trade card (Figure 6.2).

Beart and Airey probably came by their second-hand stock through two routes: buying in "left-off" or used goods, or from customers part-exchanging old wares for new. In communities and markets where specie was in short supply or retained for its own value, and where second-hand goods could be useful supplementary shop stock, part-exchange was an accustomed form of retail transaction, and not just for metalwares. Thomas Mort, a sixty-something bachelor, living in north-west England in the early eighteenth century, recorded his "exchanging" on many types of good alongside pewter and kitchen metalwares, from shoes with his cobbler to books with his bookseller (Mort, 1703–25). Although Clive Edwards has suggested (for furniture) that this was to benefit clients, those on both sides of the counter could profit from this exchange, with artisans gleaning materials and parts to reuse in repairs and to recycle into new goods (Edwards, 2009: 48; Stobart, 2009, 140–141). When Jane Carlyle wanted to buy a second-hand sofa for Cheyne Row in 1843, she baulked at the dealer's original price of £4 10 shillings. By supplying her own cushions and giving him 'the old green curtains... [which] were become beastly and what was better superfluous', she managed to reduce the price down

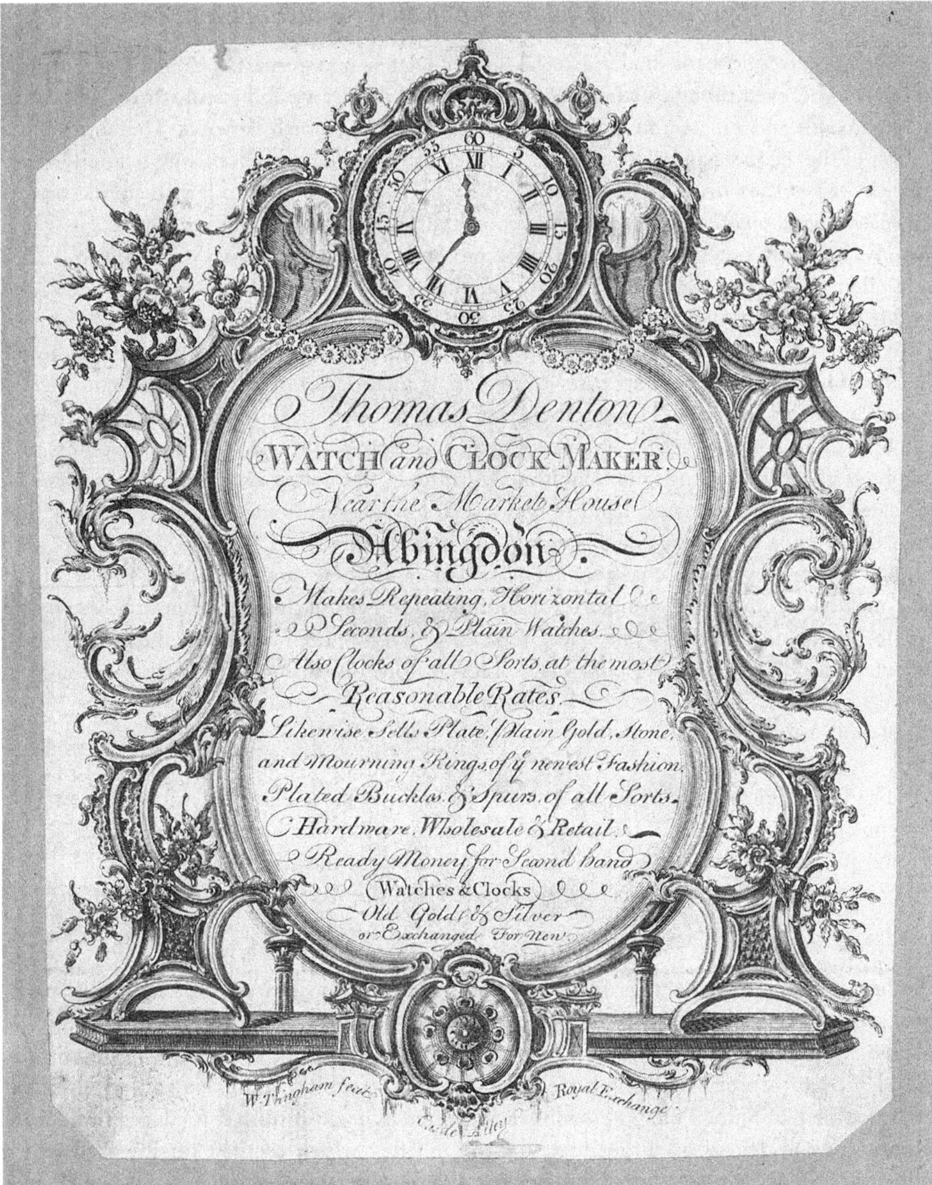

Figure 6.2 Trade card of Thomas Denton of Abingdon, clockmaker [no date]

Source: Courtesy of The Lewis Walpole Library, Yale University.

to just one pound. Although we do not know the dealer's reckoning about this exchange, it was presumably worth his while; Henry Mayhew's account, in *London Labour and the London Poor*, of what second-hand curtains could be turned to by industrious hands suggests that the 'beastly' fabric probably became the cover for someone else's second-hand sofa (*Carlyle Letters Online*: t-18430827-JWC-TC-01; Mayhew, 1968: II, 14).

Specialists: upholders, upholsterers, auctioneers

The specialist second-hand trader, like his maker-retailer counterpart, cannot be tied to just one stereotype, even though such stereotypes prevailed in literary and visual satires right across the eighteenth and nineteenth centuries, across Europe and north America. The anti-semitic portrait of the second-hand clothes dealer or fence was a well-worn idiom long before Dickens came to write *Oliver Twist* in 1837–9, or Mayhew his lengthy section on Jewish clothes dealers in *London Labour and the London Poor*. But those who sold clothes "plain" and "rich", new and second-hand, were not always marginal characters and certainly not always Jewish. Instead, they were often sufficiently well-set-up to have an address at which to advertise their services; and confident enough of their reputations to advertise as "honest" traders (Figure 6.3).

To be an effective middleman in the (legitimate) dealing of used goods, be they clothes or chests of drawers, substantial expertise – in materials, methods of manufacture, current prices – was the entrée to the trade. This surely helps explain the frequency (in England at least), with which retailing artisans such as upholders (who traditionally supplied and sold bedding) and upholsterers (soft furnishings and upholstered furniture), were often also, or became exclusively, associated with selling second-hand domestic textiles and furnishings. Such trades were also often called upon to appraise such items when householders died, because such goods were amongst the most valuable chattels, after plate and cash. These complementary aspects of the trade melded together in the career of one John Taylor, who started out as an upholsterer and "house-broker" in Cow-foot Hill, New York City in 1768, then moved in the same year to "Newfoundland" in the city, to pursue upholstery, before advertising his expertise and business acumen as 'cabinet-maker, upholsterer and auctioneer' in 1772, adding that his pedigree in this line of work was substantial:

> The buying and selling of all the above recited articles has been his sole study for seventeen years, viz. eight of them under his father, and nine for himself; and farther is at this juncture a sworn exchange broker and appraisor, of the City of London.
>
> (New York Gazette and the Weekly Mercury, *4 June 1770: see also Gottesman, 1938: 139–140*)

The link between undertaking, upholstery and appraising, in particular, speaks to a complicated web of supply, from the mourning textiles and hatchments accompanying death, to the valuation and then, often, buying in, of estate goods: all trapping seen to good effect in the mid-eighteenth-century trade card of Charles Grange and Son, upholders and appraisers 'at the Royal Bed' in Snow Hill, who confidently offered 'funerals furnish'd' (Grange, u.d.). There was also a small degree of authority vested in (and fees which accrued to) so-called sworn appraisers, who swore under oath to undertake the inventory and valuation of goods and chattels at death for the purposes of probate. Licensing increased this sense of distinction: the exclusive licence granted to vendue-masters in Charleston (South Carolina) and calls for such licensing in early eighteenth-century Philadelphia suggests that even in these frontier states, auctioneers were expected to be men of standing (Hart, u.d.: 14). In England, even though the 1777 Auction Duty Act did not automatically separate out auctioneering as a distinct profession, the licensing requirement did increasingly serve to distinguish the auctioneer from the general second-hand trader (Ohashi, 2013: 193).

Although selling by auction is an ancient practice, used throughout the Roman empire for new commodities, captured war booty and indeed captive people, of all the specialist modes of selling second-hand, the rise of the auction as a European conduit for selling second-hand from

Figure 6.3 Thomas Mayhew, "Petticoat Lane"

Source: Courtesy of Wellcome Images.

at least the sixteenth century onwards is perhaps the most notable (Morcillo, 2013). Auctioneering was not only a specialist type of dealing but also of *selling*, in which prices were not set but agreed *during* the selling process, in concert and competition with other potential buyers. This distinguished the auction from what (in England) were usually termed "open" or "hand" sales in which goods were ready-priced, and bargains struck between seller and buyer without competition. Thus, the London newspaper, the *Daily Post* of Monday 28 May 1733 contains one sale notice of the stock-in-trade of a cabinetmaker, 'the lowest price being fix'd', followed by several for household sales explicitly to be conducted 'by Auction' (*Daily Post*, 1733: 2).

Despite the long history of the auction, it is clear that across the seventeenth century it became a more widely adopted mode of selling, especially in regions like the Low Countries and (probably influenced by Dutch migrants and by trading connections) England, and, their respective colonies, especially the Dutch African Cape and the American eastern seaboard colonies from the Carolinas to New England. While the origins of the high-value end of this trade – in artworks and antiquarian books – has been the focus of attention by art historians and economic historians alike, the experience of the auction was by no means limited to the elites who sought Dutch masters or old Roman coins (Cowan, 2006: 26; Warren and Turpin, 2007). The inhabitants of the villages of Alost/Aalst (north-west of Brussels) and Troutbeck in the English Lake District, and colonial port towns like Charleston and Kingston (Jamaica), knew how to buy at auction, just as well as any genteel *habitué* of Christie's Great Rooms on Pall Mall (Van Damme and Vermoesen, 2009; Pennell, 2010).

Indeed, auctioning goods was a mode of selling that specifically suited non-urban environments where other retail opportunities might be a day's horse- or carriage-ride away, since it needed no fixed premises. As Edward Bird's 1812 painting, 'The country auction' (oil on panel, 1812, private collection, currently on loan to the Henry E. Huntington Library and Art Gallery, San Marino, CA), suggests, with its auctioneer set up under the shade of a large tree amidst a throng of keen village bidders, his lots scattered around him, it could be done outside, with a barrel or furniture lot as a makeshift rostrum, or in the house of the deceased or bankrupt owner, or wherever the goods to be sold might be. The auctioneer starting out needed no great capital to launch himself, other than the knowledge of prices and an awareness of the markets to be served: hence the symbiosis with the upholstery and upholding trades. As R. Campbell, writing in 1747, noted of sworn appraisers, whom he explicitly associated with dealing in "old goods", 'the trade is learned by experience' and 'requires a universal knowledge in the nature of all household Utensils' (Campbell, 1747: 175).

It should already be clear that different market conditions and settings made for different types of auctioneering. As Emma Hart's research into the colonial American vendue suggests, the exigencies of trans-Atlantic trading relations and wartime disruptions between the 1760s and 1820s meant that the auction sale was the *primum mobile* of much eastern seaboard trade in both new and second-hand commodities. A Briton or Dutchman attending an American vendue might have found much that was familiar, but while auctioneering in London, Amsterdam and Paris was already a respectable profession by 1800, in pre- and post-Revolutionary Charleston, New York and Philadelphia the vendue was a "sell 'em fast, sell 'em low" phenomenon that threatened to undermine the colonies' and the Republic's precarious economy (Hart, u.d.; Hartigan O'Connor, 2011). In rural England and especially Scotland, where the country roup or household sale was as much a social as it was a selling occasion, such sales mixed disposal of real with chattel estate, and domestic with agricultural livestock, equipment and harvested crops; it was only in the later nineteenth century that estate auctioneers specialising in land sales and some agricultural goods emerged as distinct from chattel auctioneers (Walton, 1984; Pennell, 2010).

At the margins? Brokers, general dealers, marine stores and street sellers

If the fast-talking, dapper auctioneer might sit at one (respectable) end of the spectrum of second-hand retailers, the "general dealer" in a small-shop or street-seller out of doors, occupied the other, more down-at-heel end. The shabby general dealers – epitomised by Dickens and by Mayhew in mid-Victorian London, is well-known not just via literary portraits, but also because of the archival traces they left through their appearances in legal records, as accessories or defendants in cases of theft and fencing stolen goods, the targets of institutional regulations to prohibit marginal trading, or in satirical or romanticised genre depictions of street-selling. Looking beyond the exceptional situations in which these second-hand traders found themselves immortalised in the archives, however, and we see a trade perfectly suited to the socio-economic ecologies of larger towns and cities, places where hard cash was often in the shortest supply. This was also not just buying and selling fuelled by textiles and clothing alone, even though they were often amongst the most frequently "dealt" goods. Using part-exchange, barter and credit, dealers provided routes by which almost all types of household and personal goods, as well as tools and stock became fungible currency: old clothes were exchanged for new (or nearly new) ceramics, broken ceramics for new spoons, and handkerchiefs for gin. In an Old Bailey theft case from 1742, Robert Delany and George Campbell were indicted for stealing a variety of shoes, gloves and other clothing, that were alleged to have come into the hands of one of their wives, 'an earthenware woman', who took them as exchange for her wares (Old Bailey Online, 1742).

Material circulations such as these are inevitably characterised as shady because they often took place in the street, on doorsteps or in pubs. Yet we cannot know how many such transactions took place that were not based on dishonestly procured goods: probably a great many, as T.H. Breen suggests, oiling the 'enterprises ... of marginal although honest men and women' (Breen, 2004: 104). Street-selling second-hand goods was also a highly organised and complex mode of retailing. Henry Mayhew's magisterial account of the varieties of and distinctions between who sold what second-hand and where on London's streets, points to it being highly segmented and specialised – brush-sellers, telescope dealers and old metal men – and also seasonal; sellers might move between a "shop" premises and the street to maximise selling opportunities as the seasons and supplies allowed. Mayhew also records the precise commercial grasp many such sellers had of the products they sold, the people they could sell to, the (slim) profits to be made and when best to make them (Mayhew, 1968: II 5–47). Recent work on "survival strategies" amongst the poor have stressed the flexible and fluid use of material goods in this way, as resources to hold onto, or to lend, pledge or exchange, as and when economic security shaded into precarity. But surely such transactions and behaviours were only possible because of a pre-existent robust market in used goods and materials. To be sure, these traders were themselves often only a few steps from pauperism, as Joseph Samuel acknowledged, when called on to give evidence in an Old Bailey case of arson in 1790: '[I am] a general dealer, when I can find nothing else' (Old Bailey Online, 1790). Nonetheless, this was not marginal but mainstream commercial activity and an essential cog in the operation of many western economies late into the nineteenth century, and in developing economies today (Carbonell, 2000; Fontaine, 2014: 14, 16).

Spaces and strategies of second-hand selling

Second-hand retailing is not easily tied down to one type of space: a Charleston vendue house on the newly built late eighteenth-century Vendue Range, a London street or Venetian square, the country seat of an English aristocratic family or beneath a tree outside an English cottage – all could be sites for second-hand buying and selling, and all are far removed from the stereotypical dealer's backstreet shop (Hart, u.d.; Welch, 2005: 194–197; MacArthur and Stobart, 2010: 185–192). Few of these sites could claim clientele in common, but certain types of second-hand selling – general household auctions in particular – could bring together miscellaneous potential buyers, from other dealers looking to replenish stock, to those with an eye to what has been labelled "clever" consuming: buying goods that were 'nearly fashionable' at competitive prices (Stobart, 2006: 235).

A successful second-hand transaction needed the right conditions to happen, and this was nowhere more true than in the emergence of the auction *house* as a specific site to cultivate brisk bidding up of the lots. Successful eighteenth-century London auctioneers like Aaron Lambe (d. 1777) and James Christie moved on (and up) from *in situ* estate sales to being proprietors of their own establishments, usually moving westward across London. Although Lambe was the first auctioneer to set up shop in Pall Mall, Christie's Great Rooms, established there in 1766–8, featured as a specifically fashionable place of resort, in Regency London. The design, with a soaring clerestory, was (as Christie himself noted in an advertorial of 1768), intended through its 'repose of light . . . magnitude and desirable situation' to show off the artworks and furniture coming under the hammer to the best advantage, and to provide for the comfort and convenience of the auction-goers who came to socialise as well as possibly buy (Wall, 1997: 4–6). These features are certainly made much of in Thomas Rowlandson's and Augustus Pugin's early nineteenth-century aquatint of the space (Ackermann, 1808–10: volume 1).

But the preparation of the audience began well before auction-goers took up their seats on the day of sale. Auctioneers used all of the techniques available to an expanding commercial network to whet the appetites of potential buyers. They advertised through newspapers in major centres and via street criers and placards in smaller towns and the countryside; they printed catalogues for free collection at sites like local inns and booksellers; and they purchased tobacco, beer and wine to loosen inhibitions and purse strings on the day of sale (or used an inn or coffee house as the venue, with refreshments on tap). Pre-sale viewing gave potential purchasers the chance to examine and evaluate the lots, as well as decide upon the price one might bid to, while catalogues disseminated the details of what was on offer well beyond the immediate locality. For important country house or city sales, these catalogues found their way over county and state boundaries, and may even have made it overseas (MacArthur and Stobart, 2010: 178–182; Pennell, 2010: 42–44).

Aesthetics and the pursuit of shopping as a practice of politeness surely fed into other forms of second-hand buying, too. Shopkeepers no doubt worked hard to make saleable second-hand wares appealing, through cleaning, small repairs and presentation. In 1703, the father of clergyman Thomas Brockbank voiced what was probably a widely held belief, cautioning that his son should beware buying from dealers or sales what "may seem new", because appearances at the sale might be deceptive, and the goods rather more worn than at first glance suggested (Trappes-Lomax, 1930: 258). The use of terms such as "hardly worn" and "as new" in advertisements for those selling second-hand goods, or in descriptions of auction lots, offered up items that would pass as new purchases, but at temptingly proportionate prices, just as using descriptors such as "fine" and "genteel" flattered readers that they too might be just the sort of new, discriminating owner for whom these items were intended (MacArthur and Stobart, 2010: 183–184).

Beyond the auction, *how* second-hand retailers presented goods to appeal to potential buyers is not easy to recover, outside of the modes of print advertising already encountered: trade cards and newspaper advertisements. These formats nonetheless tell us that those advertising felt comfortable with conveying the availability of old alongside new; and were prepared to offer incentives to potential sellers of such goods. Samuel Foyster, operating 'at the Indian Queen', in the well-known second-hand textiles district around Monmouth Street and Seven Dials (London) made a point of specifying that he bought and sold 'all manner of rich and plain second hand Cloathes, pistols, swords & watches' on his trade card, as well as offering to pay the messenger who brought any such items to him for valuation (Foyster, mid-eighteenth century).

Foyster's offer, and others like it, speak to the competitiveness of the Georgian market in which he operated. Those with goods to sell or exchange in a crowded metropolis like sixteenth-century Venice or eighteenth-century London had many options for their business, and no doubt sought out those retailers offering up added extras like free collection, or home visits for valuations. Across the eighteenth century, these incentives put pressure on established sellers to change their practices; the Antwerp *Oudekleerkopers* extended their activities beyond the bounds of the Friday Market in the late eighteenth century, in order to compete with the rising number of non-guild sales being organised beyond the city walls, suggesting that for those in the hinterlands of Antwerp, locally organised sales were as productive (and well-stocked) as those held centrally (Van Damme, 2009: 111–112). From the perspective of the buyer, quality, cleanliness and convenience were the desirable attributes of second-hand wares which retailers needed to place front and centre in their strategies for both securing stock *and* selling it. Auctioneers and dealers who could regularly offer up good quality furniture and textiles from respectable bug-free households (an increasingly visible concern by the end of the eighteenth century) on a regular basis at accessible venues, won out over those who could not (Pennell, 2014).

Separating the 'valued from the valueless'? Changing chronologies and practices

So, at what point did selling "second-hand" become more about junk disposal and charitable ridding, than about "clever" consumption? The enduring association of second-hand retailing with the soiled and sub-standard took root in what were clearly changing market conditions in much of Europe and post-revolutionary America from the late eighteenth century onwards. This was a period of apparent bifurcation in the markets for second-hand goods, in which specialist dealing in fine and decorative arts, fuelled by wealthy private collectors like the Rothschilds and Rockefellers, and public museums like the Victoria and Albert and Metropolitan, laboured to conceal the used nature of the goods dealt in a connoisseurial fog of patina and "taste" (Stobart and Van Damme, 2010a: 4–5; Van Damme, 2010). Dealing in 'cast-offs and rubbish', the stuff of Victorian rag and bottle stores in London and the booty of the Parisian *chiffonier*, was only somewhat less romanticised in paintings like Edouard Manet's 1869 *Le Chiffonier* (oil on canvas: the Norton Simon Foundation, Pasadena, F. 1968.09.P), although such lives were hard-won from the detritus, dust and even worse.

Several factors drove this change. First, we must acknowledge the shifting sands of consumer choice and material innovation. The advent of so-called "semi-durable" materials such as ceramics and cottons meant that the resale values of goods made from them depreciated more quickly, while the 'lure of the new' finally muted strictures that had traditionally counselled material stewardship and reuse as moral virtues (Van Damme, 2009: 116). This was an age in which rising industrial production across Europe was as yet unfettered by environmental or ecological concerns, and as yet untarnished by concerns about the health effects of new materials, new manufacturing techniques or novel, fashion-driven behaviours.

However, while the decline in the appeal of some categories of second-hand good – notably household textiles and clothing – is clear in the text of advertisements for household sales as well as in accounts of the grubby, shabby milieu of the old clothes dealers and street sellers, the reasons behind this decline cannot be applied to *all* second-hand objects. Concerns about hygiene and the transmission of diseases via clothing, bedding and curtains certainly curtailed second-hand dealing at the more respectable end of this market, but such concerns were less crucial within the market for second-hand furniture, for example. Although they too describe this market as one also undergoing "polarization", Clive Edwards and Margaret Ponsonby note that within the furniture trade in mid-Victorian England, patina and the solid construction of some older furniture were highly valued and marked it out for discerning middling buyers, in contrast to the shoddy or shiny furnishings of 'fateful newness' favoured by the less well-off and (more pointedly) the less well-educated in aesthetic matters (Edwards and Ponsonby, 2010: 99–102, 104–105). Indeed, even amongst the poor clientele of London's Petticoat Lane, good quality second-hand items (if affordable) were purchased over new shoddy ware; to deceive such buyers, not just cheap new furniture, but also musical instruments and metalwares were "duffed" to make them seem "second-hand", a strange inversion of the previous century's preference for used goods to seem "as new". Middling and even poor consumers were still in the market for solid second-hand goods, both for necessary purchases like bedsteads, tables and metal kitchenwares (the second-hand market for which did not dwindle until World War I in Europe and the collection of metals for wartime *matériel*); and for "curios" and collectibles, to furnish their parlour mantelshelves (Westgarth, 2013).

Rather than "bifurcation" and "polarization" of second-hand circuits across the nineteenth century and into the twentieth, we might instead be looking at temporary disruption and segmentation within some types of second-hand commodity and retailing organisation; and changes of scale of operation in others. As Henry Mayhew observed in London, what had found a ready market some years earlier (glass and crockery, small woodenwares such as knife boxes and tea caddies), could no longer make money because of the ready availability of cheap new products; other goods (stuffed birds, small telescopes), were simply no longer desirable. By contrast, used clothes and textiles constituted such a large proportion of the second-hand trade at the time that two used clothes exchanges were set up in Spitalfields in the late 1840s; and a substantial export trade-in used clothes and textiles to Ireland and the continent (especially the Netherlands) transacted. The specific regional variation in what one might find in what Mayhew called 'marine stores', general dealers' shops, suggests that even amongst poor labouring communities, the second-hand offer was highly attuned to the demands of the local market (Mayhew, 1968: II: 25–28).

As yet, few scholars have written about the period between the middle of the nineteenth century and the mid-twentieth century, from which point on social scientists and anthropologists have turned their attention to contemporary practices of buying and selling second-hand, and environmental historians have started to take stock of past resource uses and abuses. But this is perhaps the most crucial period of change in how second-hand goods were sourced, marketed and retailed, an age in which the novelty of the shiny spectacle of the department store as purveyor of novel marvels to the middle classes, and the cheap and cheerful aesthetic of the retail bazaar for the less well-off, surely wore off. Since at least the end of World War I, during the economic downturns of the 1920s and 1930s, anxieties fuelled by periods of recession-driven austerity as well as engagement with newly debated notions of environmental and civic responsibility, particularly around the disposal of waste, reshaped attitudes to consuming the already used (e.g. Strasser, 1999; Gregson and Crewe, 2003; Cooper, 2010).

It was in this period too, that the moral indigestibility of untrammelled consumption began to be offset by attempts to channel disposal and sales of second-hand goods towards what Jennifer le Zotte has called 'philanthropic capitalism' (Le Zotte, 2013). Church jumble sales and charity bazaars raised money as a source of welfare for local communities or sometimes for more distant or elevated ends (supporting missionaries or the victims of natural disasters), and became a model for later, more permanent forms of charitable second-hand collection and retail (Richmond, 2010). In *fin-de-siècle* America, Goodwill stores grew out of a Methodist campaign in Boston in 1902 to provide employment and resources to the poor and needy through the mending and distribution of used goods collected from wealthier householders. In Britain, the modern charity shop, the twentieth-century successor to Victorian ventures like the Salvation Army's clothes collections for the poor, first opened its doors in 1947–8, when Oxfam used a storefront in Oxford to dispose of excess donations gathered for sending to postwar Greece. These collection and retail institutions dominated the Anglo-American second-hand trade in non-luxury clothing, furniture and books, amongst many other items, until the advent of the two online sites which have come to dominate second-hand trading in the twenty-first century, eBay and Craigslist, both founded in 1995. In Britain alone, charity shops still account for over £270 million in revenue to the charities they support, while a 2014 report on the involvement of British households in charities identified purchasing from a charity shop as the most frequent type of engagement with a charitable organisation (Charity Retail Association, u.d.; Glennie and Whillans-Welldrake, 2014: 15).

New commodities in the twentieth century also created opportunities for furthering specialist second-hand trading and information circuits around second-hand goods. The rising ownership of cars in interwar America and post-1945 Europe brought with it opportunities for a second-hand market that shared some features of pre-modern practices (part-exchange, the selling of old alongside new stock in car showrooms), but which also created specialist retailers and new cultural stereotypes. Second-hand car sales outstripped new-car sales in America as early as 1927, providing the stimulus for sales outside of the networks run by the big car companies such as Ford and Packard (Gelber, 2008). It also fuelled a new archetype of the disingenuous dealer, in the cultural trope of the used car salesman (used on a Democratic campaign poster to such devastating effect to question the ethical standing of the Republican candidate, Richard Nixon, in the 1960 American presidential election).

Cars, like coaches before them, also enabled owners to be sellers themselves, cutting out the dealer-middleman altogether. This type of person-to-person transaction was not entirely new, of course, but it developed quickly in this period, fuelled not only by improved transportation and mail networks, but also by the lengthening classified columns of provincial news organs across nineteenth-and twentieth-century Britain and America, and new specialist classified periodicals. The British weekly paper, *Exchange and Mart*, launched by lawyer-turned-publisher Edward Cox in 1868, grew out of a segment of the upmarket mid-Victorian women's magazine, *The Queen*, which gave column space for readers to advertise goods that they had for sale or exchange. The paper, to which modern online person-to-person market places for second-hand goods such as Gumtree, Craigslist and eBay, owe their *modus operandi*, continued in hard and then electronic formats for over a century, finally closing in 2005 (Brake and Demoor, 2009: 149–150).

Conclusion

Certainly the marketplace for second-hand goods *looks* very different now to that of the seventeenth, eighteenth or nineteenth centuries, and we have the advent of the Internet and social media to thank for that. But while environmental concerns and recalibration of the second-hand as "retro", "vintage" and (my favourite American euphemism) "gently used" have made buying such goods ethically and aesthetically valid for generations whose parents and grandparents before them would have shunned them, many methods of selling and distributing second-hand goods have deep roots in the past four centuries, from the thrill of winning with that last-minute bid on eBay, to the eagle-eyed hunt at the car boot sale and *marchés aux puces*. The Victorian rag and bottle storeman would claim the house clearance "man and van" as his direct descendant, while the charity shop is but a cleaner version of the marine store, albeit with an admittedly different economic agenda. The second-hand trade in goods and materials and its diversified wholesale and retail conduits, from artworks to worn-through clothing waste, has never ceased to be economically and culturally central across the developed and developing world – understanding the complexity and evolution of its histories, never more important.

References

Ackermann, R. (1808–10), *The microcosm of London*, 3 Vols (London: T. Bensley).

Airey, J. (1715), Oxford archives, MS Wills Oxon., 160/2/8, John Airey, probate inventory taken 28 October 1715.

Allerston, P.A. (1996), 'The market in second-hand clothes and furnishings in Venice, 1500–1650', Unpublished European University Institute PhD.

Alvarez, M. (2007), 'The *Almoneda*: The second-hand art market in Spain', in J. Warren and A. Turpin (eds.) *Auctions, agents and dealers: The mechanisms of the art market, 1660–1830* (Oxford: Beazley Archive/ Archaeopress), 33–40.

Barahona, V.L. and Sánchez, J.N. (2012), 'Dressing the poor: The provision of clothing among the lower classes in eighteenth-century Madrid', *Textile History*, 43 (1), pp. 23–42.

Beart, A. (1667), Norfolk RO, DN/INV 52a/42, Anne Beart, probate inventory taken 31 January 1666/7.

Blondé, B., Coquery, N., Stobart, J. and Van Damme, I. (eds.) (2009), *Fashioning old and new: Changing consumer patterns in Western Europe (1650–1900)* (Turnhout: Brepols).

Brake, L. and Demoor, M. (eds.) (2009), *Dictionary of nineteenth-century journalism in great Britain and Ireland* (Ghent: Academia Press).

Breen, T.H. (2004), *The marketplace of revolution: How consumer politics shaped American independence* (Oxford: Oxford University Press).

Campbell, R. (1747), *The London tradesman: Being a compendious view of all the trades, professions, arts, both liberal and mechanic, now practised in the cities of London and Westminster* (London: T. Gardner).

Carbonell, M. (2000), 'Using microcredit and restructuring households: Two complementary survival strategies in late eighteenth century Barcelona', in L. Fontaine and J. Schlumbohm (eds.) *Household strategies for survival, 1600–2000: Fission, faction and cooperation, International Review of Social History. Supplement, 8* (Cambridge: Cambridge University Press) 71–92.

Carlyle Letters Online (2007–16), B.E. Kinser (ed.) *The Carlyle Letters Online* [CLO], Duke University Press, Available at: http://carlyleletters.dukeupress.edu (Accessed 15 August 2017).

Charity Retail Association (u.d.), Available at: www.charityretail.org.uk/charity-shops/ (Accessed 11 August 2017).

Charpy, M. (2008), 'The scope and structure of the nineteenth-century second-hand trade in the Parisian clothes market', in L. Fontaine (ed.), *Alternative exchanges: Second-hand circulations from the sixteenth century to the present, International Studies in Social History, 10* (New York/Oxford: Berghahn Books), 127–155.

Cooper, T. (2010), *Longer-lasting products: Alternatives to the throwaway society* (Farnham: Gower).

Cowan, B. (2006), 'Art and connoisseurship in the auction market of later seventeenth-century London', in N. di Marchi and H.J. van Miegroet (eds.) *Mapping markets for paintings in Europe, 1450–1750, Studies in European Urban History 6* (Turnhout: Brepols) 263–284.

Daily Post (1733), *Daily Post*, 28 May 1733, issue 4274.

Deceulaer, H. (2008b), 'Second-hand dealers in the early modern low countries: Institutions, markets and practices', in L. Fontaine (ed.), *Alternative exchanges: Second-hand circulations from the sixteenth century to the present, International Studies in Social History, 10* (New York/Oxford: Berghahn Books), 13–42.

di Marchi, N. (2004), 'Auctioning paintings in late seventeenth-century London: Rules, prices and segmentation in an emergent market', in V. Ginsburgh (ed.) *Economics of art and culture: Invited Papers of the 12th International Conference of Cultural Economics International* (Amsterdam: Elsevier) 97–128.

Edwards, C. (2009), 'Perspectives on the retailing and acquisition of new and old furniture in England, 1700–1850', in B. Blondé, N. Coquery, J. Stobart and I. Van Damme (eds.) *Fashioning old and new: Changing consumer patterns in Western Europe (1650–1900)* (Turnhout: Brepols), 43–59.

Edwards, C. and Ponsonby, M. (2010b), 'The polarization of the second-hand market for furniture in the nineteenth century', in J. Stobart and I. Van Damme (eds), *Modernity and the second-hand trade: European consumption cultures and practices, 1700–1900* (Basingstoke: Palgrave Macmillan), 93–110.

Eliot, G. (1871–2/1992), *Middlemarch: A study of provincial life* (Harmondsworth: Penguin).

Finn, M. (2010), 'Frictions of empire: Colonial Bombay's probate and property networks in the 1780s', *Annales*, 65 (5), pp. 1175–1204.

Fontaine, L. (2008a), 'Introduction', in L. Fontaine (ed.), *Alternative exchanges: Second-hand circulations from the sixteenth century to the present, International Studies in Social History, 10* (New York/Oxford: Berghahn Books): 1–12.

Fontaine, L. (ed.) (2008b), *Alternative exchanges: Second-hand circulations from the sixteenth century to the present, International Studies in Social History, 10* (New York/Oxford: Berghahn Books).

Fontaine, L. (2014), *The moral economy: Poverty, credit, and trust in early modern Europe* (Cambridge: Cambridge University Press).

Foyster, mid-18th-century. Printed trade card. Lewis Walpole Library, 66 726T675 Quarto (Yale University, Farmington, CT).

Gelber, S. (2008), *Horse-trading in the age of cars: Men in the marketplace* (Baltimore, MD: Johns Hopkins University Press).

Glennie, A. and Whillans-Welldrake, A. (2014), *Charity street: The value of charity to British households* (London: Institute for Public Policy Research).

Grange, C. and Son (u.d.), Printed trade card. British Museum, Prints & Drawings, Heal, 125.39.

Gregson, N. and Crewe, L. (2003), *Second-hand cultures* (Oxford: Berg).

Harris, M., Mandelbrote, G. and Myers, R. (eds.) (2001), *Under the hammer: Book auctions since the seventeenth century* (London: British Library).

Hart, E. (u.d.), 'An empire of goods? Auctions and market cultures in the English-speaking world, 1730–85', Unpublished paper, Available at: www.academia.edu/5966108/_An_Empire_of_Goods_Auction_and_Market_Cultures_in_the_English-Speaking_World_1730-1785_?auto=download (accessed 21 July 2017).

Hartigan O'Connor, E. (2011), *The ties that buy: Women and commerce in revolutionary America* (Philadelphia, PA: University of Pennsylvania).

Herrmann, F. (2004), 'Christie, James (1730–1803)', in *Oxford Dictionary of National Biography* (Oxford: Oxford University Press), Available at: www.oxforddnb.com.huntington.idm.oclc.org/view/article/5362 (accessed 18 May 2017).

Kisluk-Grosheide, D., Krohn, D.L. and Leben, U. (eds.) (2013), *Salvaging the past: Georges Hoentschel and French decorative arts at the Metropolitan Museum of art* (New Haven, CT/London: Yale University Press).

Le Zotte, J. (2013), '"Not charity, but a chance": Philanthropic capitalism and the rise of American thrift stores, 1894–1930', *The New England Quarterly*, 86 (2), pp. 169–195.

Lemire, B. (1991), 'Peddling fashion: Salesmen, pawnbrokers, tailors, thieves and the second-hand clothes trade in England, c. 1700–1800', *Textile History*, 22, pp. 67–82.

Lilja, K., Murhem, S. and Ulvaeng, G. (2009), 'The indispensable market: Auctions in Sweden in the eighteenth and nineteenth centuries', in B. Blondé, N. Coquery, J. Stobart and I. Van Damme (eds.), 185–209.

MacArthur, R. and Stobart, J. (2010), 'Going for a song? Country house sales in Georgian England', in J. Stobart and I. Van Damme (2010b), 175–195.

Mayhew, H. (1851/1968), *London labour and the London poor*, 4 Vols (London: Dover Publications).

McCants, A. (1995), 'Meeting needs and suppressing desires: Consumer choice models and historical data', *Journal of Interdisciplinary History*, 26, pp. 191–208.

Morcillo, M.G. (2013), 'Auctions', in R.S. Bagnal et al. (eds.) *The encyclopaedia of ancient history* (Malden, MA: Wiley-Blackwell), 937–938.

Mort, T. (1703–25), Henry E. Huntington Library, San Marino, HM72811, account book of Thomas Mort (c.1648–1725).

Ohashi, S. (2007), 'The Auction Duty Act of 1777: The beginning of institutionalisation of auctions in Britain', in J. Warren and A. Turpin (eds.) *Auctions, agents and dealers: The mechanisms of the art market, 1660–1830* (Oxford: Beazley Archive/Archaeopress), 21–31.

Ohashi, S. (2013), 'Auctioneers in provincial towns in England and Wales at the end of the eighteenth century', *Shi'en: The Journal of Historical Studies*, Rikkyo University, pp. 174–198.

Old Bailey Online (1742), *Old Bailey Proceedings Online* (www.oldbaileyonline.org, version 7.2, 26 May 2017), September 1742, trial of Robert Delany, George Campbell & Patience Forrester (t17421208-23).

Old Bailey Online (1790), *Old Bailey Proceedings Online* (www.oldbaileyonline.org, version 7.2, 27 May 2017), October 1790, trial of Edward Lowe and William Jobbins (t17901027-17).

Pennell, S. (2010), 'All but the kitchen sink: Household sales and the circulation of second-hand goods in early modern England', in J. Stobart and I. Van Damme (eds), *Modernity and the second-hand trade: European consumption cultures and practices, 1700–1900* (Basingstoke: Palgrave Macmillan), 37–56.

Pennell, S. (2014), 'Making the bed in later Stuart and Georgian England', in B. Blondé and J. Stobart (eds.) *Selling textiles in the long eighteenth century: Comparative perspectives from western Europe* (Basingstoke: Palgrave Macmillan) 30–45.

Richmond, V. (2010), 'The English church jumble sale: Parochial charity in the modern age', in J. Stobart and I. Van Damme (eds), *Modernity and the second-hand trade: European consumption cultures and practices, 1700–1900* (Basingstoke: Palgrave Macmillan), 242–258.

Rickett (u.d. but late 18th century), Printed trade card. British Museum, Prints and Drawings, Heal, 125.95.

Roberts, W. (2004), 'Duveen, Sir Joseph Joel (1843–1908)', rev. Helen Davies, *Oxford Dictionary of National Biography*. Oxford: Oxford University Press, Available at: www.oxforddnb.com.huntington.idm.oclc.org/view/article/32946 (Accessed 15 August 2017).

Roche, D. (1997), *The culture of clothing: Dress and fashion in Ancien Regime France* (Cambridge: Cambridge University Press).

Staples, K. (2010), 'Fripperers and the used clothing trade in late medieval London', *Medieval Clothing and Textiles*, 6, pp. 151–171.

Staples, K. (2015), 'The significance of the second-hand trade in Europe, 1200–1600', *History Compass*, 13 (6), pp. 297–309.

Stobart, J. (2006), 'Clothes, cabinets and carriages: Second-hand dealing in eighteenth-century England', in B. Blondé, P. Stabel, J. Stobart and I. Van Damme (eds.) *Buyers and sellers: Retail circuits and practices in medieval and early modern Europe* (Turnhout: Brepols) 225–244.

Stobart, J. (2009), 'In and out of fashion? Advertising novel and second-hand goods in Georgian England', in B. Blondé, N. Coquery, Stobart and Van Damme (eds.), *Fashioning old and new: Changing consumer patterns in Western Europe (1650–1900)* (Turnhout: Brepols), 133–144.

Stobart, J. and Van Damme, I. (2010a), 'Introduction', in J. Stobart and I. Van Damme (eds.), *Modernity and the second-hand trade: European consumption cultures and practices, 1700–1900* (Basingstoke: Palgrave Macmillan), 1–14.

Stobart, J. and Van Damme, I. (eds.) (2010b), *Modernity and the second-hand trade: European consumption cultures and practices, 1700–1900* (Basingstoke: Palgrave Macmillan).

Stobart, J. and Rothery, M. (2016), *Consumption and the country house* (Oxford: Oxford University Press).

Strasser, S. (1999), *Waste and want: A social history of trash* (New York: Metropolitan Books).

Susswein Gottesman, R. (1938), *The arts and crafts in New York 1726–1776: Advertisements and news items from New York City newspapers* (New York: J. J. Little and Ives Company).

Syphor, R (1992), 'Syphor and co.: A pioneer antique dealer in New York', *Furniture History*, 28, pp. 168–170.

Trappes-Lomax, R. (ed.) (1930), *The diary and letter book of the Rev. Thomas Brockbank, 1671–1709* (Manchester: The Chetham Society), p. 89.

Tweeddale Papers (1674), National Library of Scotland, Tweeddale Papers, MS 14402, fols 83r-86v: Letter from Jean Scott Hay, countess of Tweeddale to John Hay, 2nd earl of Tweeddale, from [Yester?]: 28 February [1674].

Van Damme, I. (2009), 'The lure of the new: Urban retailing in the surroundings of Antwerp (late seventeenth-early eighteenth centuries)', in B. Blondé, N. Coquery, J. Stobart and I. Van Damme (eds.), *Fashioning old and new: Changing consumer patterns in Western Europe (1650–1900)* (Turnhout: Brepols), 97–120.

Van Damme, I. (2010), 'Second-hand dealing in Bruges and the rise of an "antiquarian culture", c.1750–1870', in J. Stobart and I. Van Damme (eds.), *Modernity and the second-hand trade: European consumption cultures and practices, 1700–1900* (Basingstoke: Palgrave Macmillan), 73–92.

Van Damme, I. and Vermoesen, R. (2009), 'Second-hand consumption as a way of life: Public auctions in the surroundings of Alost in the late eighteenth century', *Continuity and Change*, 24 (2), pp. 275–305.

Wall, C. (1997), 'The English auction: Narratives of dismantlings', *Eighteenth-Century Studies*, 31 (1), pp. 1–25.

Walton, J.K. (1984), 'The rise of agricultural auctioneering in eighteenth- and nineteenth-century Britain', *Journal of Historical Geography*, 10 (1), pp. 15–36.

Warren, J. and Turpin, A. (eds.) (2007), *Auctions, agents and dealers: The mechanisms of the art market, 1660–1830* (Oxford: Beazley Archive/Archaeopress).

Welch, E.S. (2005), *Shopping in the renaissance: Consumer cultures in Italy, 1400–1600* (London/New Haven, CT: Yale University Press).

Westerfield, R.B. (1920), 'Early history of American auctions: A chapter in commercial history', *Transactions of the Connecticut Academy of Arts and Sciences*, 23, 159–210.

Westgarth, M. (2013), *The emergence of the antique and curiosity dealer in Britain 1815–1850: The commodification of historical objects* (Farnham: Ashgate).

PART II

Spaces and places

7
MARKETS AND MARKET HALLS

Manel Guàrdia, José Luis Oyón and Sergi Garriga

Introduction

In medieval and pre-modern cities, markets were the central nodes of the social metabolism, the link to the rural hinterland and the fundamental mechanism of food supply. Underpinned by ancient privileges, they were at the heart of 'economic forces'. They were also well-regulated spaces, subject to inspection, to ensure tax revenues and proper exchanges. According to Braudel – quoting Adam Smith – 'intermittent or continuous, these elementary markets between the countryside and the city, by their number and their continuous repetition, represent the biggest of all known exchanges' (Braudel, 1979: 9–10). It's not surprising that so many historians have seen the market as the city's driving force, its *raison d'être*.

Retail historians have been interested in the renewal of markets in Western cities. This is a process that began in the late eighteenth century as a transitional period. Covered markets were built as an intermediate step in the sequence of successive substitutions of old forms of commerce by other increasingly more efficient ones and by more modern forms of consumption, as today's peripheral shopping centres. From this perspective, urban markets have been seen as an anachronism doomed to disappear (Stobart and Van Damme, 2016: 363). Nevertheless, their extraordinary resilience and often their resurgence in recent decades as outdoor markets or as market halls, proves their history has not come to a complete close. The city food market as an elementary expression of retailing has been and continues to be present in all cultures. Its forms have changed according to historical and geographical contexts, the dimensions and layout of the city, its ties to outlying rural areas, and the model of urban food supply. Conditioned by commercial policies and regulations, city food markets generally continue to form part of the urban retailing mix. For this reason, they provide a good observatory of retailing history and its evolution over time.

From the traditional market to the market hall as a facility

Markets have been the driving force behind the configuration of European cities. The rebirth of the medieval city was formerly attributed to mercantile activity and long-distance trade (Pirenne, 1952). Today, however, it is thought that modest trade carried out in markets by local farmers boosted the long-cycle growth of medieval Europe (Bois, 1989; Guerreau, 1990; Verhulst, 1991). Large-scale trade and the birth of capitalism came into effect at a later date.

Markets often contributed to shaping the urban morphology of the medieval and pre-modern city. Originally held weekly, markets became a daily affair in larger centres. Classical analyses of the morphological evolution of European cities clearly confirm the degree to which these commercial activities formed the backbone of the urban space (Ganshof, 1943; Lavedan and Hugueney, 1974; Conzen 1960 and 1962: 383–414; Carter, 1983). Municipal governments, firmly established since the thirteenth century, focused primarily on assuring good urban provisioning. They reorganised the markets that outgrew their traditional premises, distributing the various products on streets and squares, while endowing some of these spaces with covered depots: granaries or *halles* for the storage of grain, or covered pavilions for butchers and fishmongers, some of which were large-scale buildings such as the fifteenth-century Ghent Meat Market (Pevsner, 1976: chap. 15; Kostof, 1992: 92–102). Market and city hall were so closely bound that they could come to form a single body. In the large municipal edifices of Flemish or Italian cities, a ground floor with arcades was left completely open to the market square space. This was where the most perishable articles were stored, such as butter, eggs and poultry, while municipal employees collected the sales fees. The upper floor was used as a city council meeting hall (as was the case of the Halles of Bruges, twelfth-fifteenth centuries, the Palazzo del Broletto in several of Lombardy's towns and cities and the Palazzo della Regione in Padua). The numerous and more modest market houses of some British market-cities, which continued to be built until the middle of the nineteenth century, followed the same pattern (Schmiechen and Carls, 1999).

The combination of limited urban growth and institutional continuity from the end of the Middle Ages to the eighteenth century contributed in most cities to a long period of stability in urban structures and, consequently, in food market systems (Calabi, 2004). Subsequently, the agricultural revolution and improvements in regional transport and in international trade and the correlative population explosion increased the demand for food and for many other manufactured products such as clothing, kitchen utensils and other household items sold in markets. All this meant greater congestion and overcrowding in market streets and squares: more people, more stalls, more vehicles and more animals packed the public space. The traditional outdoor market became a source of great tension, especially in England and France.

Urban markets and their surroundings attracted peddlers, petty thieves and crowds of revellers. By the eighteenth century, there was a new enlightened perception of public space that looked unfavourably upon traditional open-air markets, characterised by blasphemy, taverns and the non-payment of municipal sales taxes. The market was viewed as 'a place of disorder and chaos and a magnet for the worst elements in society', a focal point of ungovernable street culture (Schmiechen and Carls, 1999: 10–19).

Old outdoor markets also stood at the heart of social tensions, mainly involving subsistence riots (Rudé, 1970). These riots, associated with agricultural crises and with the 'moral economy' of the poor, were sometimes tolerated by municipal magistrates as an indirect way of preventing dishonest business practices and of lowering food prices (Thompson, 1971; Wells, 1987). Indeed, many of the first European market halls emerged after political uprisings associated with protests against the high cost of food.

In the closing decades of eighteenth century in the UK, we find the first examples of markets separated from the street. This represents the first major conceptual step towards the invention of the covered market as an architectural form. This period was characterised by great typological diversity. After 1750, new markets continued to be built for mixed uses in the long-established shed form, however, they began to incorporate some original designs such as arcades or circular shapes. After 1800, the pioneering enclosed market prevailed. From the latter half of the eighteenth century in the United States, long sheds that were open and extendable became very popular thanks to the influence of British markets and as a result of their location in the communal space, in the middle of wide streets. The most famous example was the Philadelphia High Street Market built in 1785. Long markets with mixed use, with council offices on the ground floor, were less common, although their size and urban personality surpassed those of all the markets hitherto built in the former British colonies (Tangires, 2003 30–347).

Thus, markets were enclosed in order to free streets and squares from the invasion of buyers and sellers, and to get obstacles out of the way and out of sight, in accordance with an enlightened ideal of 'transparency'. Stalls were neatly set out, circulation was facilitated and hygiene was assured, all for the purpose of stricter controls and inspections (Foucault, 1977: 17 and ff.; Bentham, 1995: 29–95).

The abolition of feudal rights led to stricter controls of markets on behalf of municipal bodies who wanted to ensure 'urban order', tax collection and in particular provisioning, subject to recurrent crises. In the case of France, the disentailment of assets belonging to the Church and the émigré nobility gave new markets the opportunity to occupy confiscated plots of land. The end of feudal privileges, and the availability of urban land after the triumph of the Revolution, paved the way for the Napoleonic reorganisation of the Parisian market system, following more 'rational' and 'informed' bourgeois models of respectability and order.

The idea of providing Paris with a coherent homogeneous system of market halls arose in 1808 during the Napoleonic Empire. Frochot, the Prefect of the Seine, declared:

> It is essential that public markets begin to provide solid shelter to stallholders, customers and purveyors in a regular fashion, that they be greater in number, larger and healthier . . . and be established as far away as possible from private houses.,

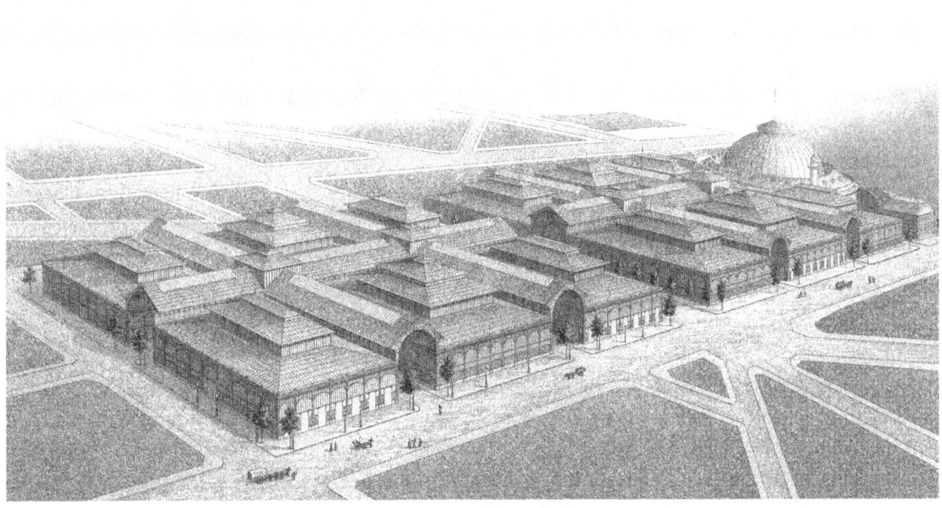

Figure 7.1 Birds-eye view of Les Halles, París

Source: Félix Narjoux, *Paris. Monuments élevés par la Ville, 1850–1880*, volume II, Paris, 1883, engraving IV.

Five large free-standing market halls were built (Saint-Honoré, Saint-Martin, Saint-Germain, Saint-Jean and Les Carmes) as was the wonderful cast-iron dome of the wheat market, the Halle au Blé, erected between 1802 and 1811 (Lemoine, 1980: chap. 4, 42). As early as 1813, the civil engineer responsible for public works in Paris, Bruyère, had presented the Minister for Home Affairs with his *Collection des marchés de Paris avec projets* with the overall plan for the city's markets. It included 127 drawings of markets, among them his Grande Halle design. In 1823 he specifically devoted the fourth volume of his Parisian publication *Recueil* to the subject of markets (Bruyère, 1813).

The centralised organisation of the French State, under the supervision of the Conseil des Bâtiments Civils, also favoured the adoption of a homogeneous system for managing and assigning land uses and of a programmed method for assessing needs and for distributing and building spaces that signalled institutional and technical modernity. This gave rise to the so-called "city of facilities" (Foucault, 1977; Teyssot, 1977a; Lepetit, 1988: 255–265) and between 1801 and 1851 the Conseil des Bâtiments Civils revised 253 projects for new markets, enlargements and repairs across the whole country. Market buildings, grain exchanges and slaughterhouses were registered as facilities alongside prefectures, hospitals, state-run schools, law establishments, prisons, police stations, theatres, concert halls and museums.

The great age of market halls

New criteria, such as order and functional rationalisation, were expressed in the new facilities and were manifested in the market halls' internal organisation: 'the sales cell, geometrically identical for all . . . the space of circulation, which must be as consistent and operative as possible, the sales area and the general layout, that responds to the desire to classify and control' (Lemoine, 1980: 32). The idea was also to ensure that markets had improved hygienic conditions and higher levels of respectability: the market thereby became a facility and a school for manners, an ideal that pervaded Europe throughout the century (Schmiechen and Carls, 1999: 47; Thompson, 1997).

New British market halls were even more innovative than French ones. As from 1820, large market buildings were designed to be totally covered and enclosed structures in the form of semi-detached elongated naves, while smaller markets had single naves. The fact that they were completely closed to the outside, their height and the lightness and transparency of their structures – achieved through the use of iron and glass – entailed a genuine typological reinvention of markets. The first monumental example of the new type was Saint John's Market, built in Liverpool in 1822. The introduction of iron pillars preceded the use of this material by Charles Fowler in London's Covent Garden Market (1828–1830) and in the famous Hungerford Fish Market in 1835 (Stamp, 1986). The iron structure would not become the standard for retail markets in other British cities until ten years later when it first appeared at Birkenhead Market, designed by the civil engineers Fox and Henderson. At that time, it was the largest metal structure in the world.

The nineteenth century was indeed the golden age of British markets, particularly in the period of intensive construction between 1821 and 1890, dominated by the new type of large free-standing and completely covered market (Schmiechen and Carls, 1999). Almost two-thirds of all these structures were erected during this 70-year period, including some of the most original from a construction standpoint. By 1850, the United Kingdom was the first European country to welcome this new type of structure, which soon became consolidated. A significant feature characterising British markets was the complete dissociation between the buildings' interior metal structures and their façades. These were huge frameworks with their own styles, initially Neoclassical and later increasingly eclectic.

In the rest of Europe, the renewal and spread of new market models advanced at a fast pace. Solutions varied considerably across the continent and within each country propagation was not uniform. In Great Britain, the dissemination of new market halls had hardly any effect on Scotland or the east of England. The case of London is even more surprising. The world's most dynamic and innovative city lacked a system of covered retail markets. The biggest metropolis on earth depended exclusively on itinerant vending for its provisioning. Between 1850 and 1939, London's street markets grew significantly, with both rapidly increasing numbers of facilities and a steady increase in the number of stalls overall (Kelley, 2016). Its main market halls became wholesale markets, like Covent Garden, Billingsgate or Smithfield (Schmiechen, 2015). The great renewal of British markets was galvanised by industrial cities in the north and west, areas of great urban and industrial growth. City councils usually built a large, single market in a central location (sometimes replacing the old pre-industrial open-air market). While the metal-structured interior was light and unencumbered – allowing for an orderly display of products and the circulation of shoppers – the exterior was grand and monumental.

In the United States, in the first half of the nineteenth century, public markets were considered essential to the economic survival of a growing urban population. The new country's municipal councils provided public space and broader streets for the markets, constructed market buildings, established specific rules of commercial conduct and appointed civil servants to enforce those rules and to supervise the markets' correct functioning. Most of the markets were simple free-standing sheds in the middle of a street or a square, as was common since the colonial period. Sometimes, however, they were very costly structures as in the case of Boston's sumptuous Faneuil Hall, built between 1823 and 1826 (Tangires, 2003). In order to supply the biggest US city, New York, in the first half of the nineteenth century, a large system of markets was developed which polarised a considerable part of food retailing. In the 1830s the city, which had just over 200,000 inhabitants, boasted thirteen market halls dotted across the urban space (Baics, 2012, 2016).

Back in Europe, before 1850 there was already an initial dissemination of French-influenced covered models. This was the case in the Savoy region, where Turin endowed itself with a considerable set of market halls of Neoclassical tradition. In Spain, the Encarnación Market in Seville, the Central de Abastos Market in Cádiz, the San Ildefonso Market in Madrid and the Santa Caterina Market in Barcelona also adopted the Napoleonic French model. The disentailment of religious properties in 1836 was a key moment, making land available to the councils of these cities to build the new structures. In Belgium, the Madeleine Market in Brussels and the markets in other cities such as Antwerp, Ghent or Mechelen were more innovative, introducing metal structures in the middle of the century. In Germany, a covered market was built in Hamburg in around 1850 with a partly metal structure.

Within this context, the construction of Baltard's Les Halles in Paris in the early days of the Second Empire entailed a radical change in the architecture of European markets. Les Halles in Paris became the epicentre of the great cycle of dissemination of covered iron markets. After a great debate in 1853, the architectural solutions put forward favoured lightness and transparency and these proved to be an instant success. Each of the ten cubic pavilions of metal and glass boasted a large central area that organised the space. The glass face and the light ceramic finish of the façades revealed the rhythm of the structure's metal pillars and became a model of constructional simplicity and elegance that lent itself to mass dissemination due to its industrialised nature (Lemoine, 1986: 166).

The decisive public intervention in Paris would not only translate into the imposing central markets of Les Halles but also into a complete system of thirty-two neighbourhood markets that applied the same construction criteria. What is more, several hundred others were built in France's leading provincial cities. Although the repetition of this model was criticised by French architects, the industrial replication of building elements and the ease of assembly favoured its national dissemination and even its export to such places as Romania, Algeria and South American countries. French technical experts and iron building contractors erected markets in Bucharest, while the burgeoning cities of South America were also centres of dissemination of the new French-made iron markets (Leun, 2016: 29; Lortie, 1995). If we turn to the monographs and articles published in technical journals, we find that the markets built in French cities received a greater number of references, and Les Halles was certainly the most prominent of them all, followed closely by British markets (Baltard and Callet, 1863; Baltard, 1873; Osthoff and Schmitt, 1909; Risch, 1867; Hennicke, 1881; Guàrdia and Oyón, 2015).

The dissemination of the model

The intensity of the dissemination process also highlights the singularities of the various national and local contexts. In Germany, after early experiences of iron markets in Hamburg and Munich, the Stuttgart Market was opened in 1865, that of Frankfurt in 1879 and between 1885 and 1908 many other German cities endowed themselves with markets. In 1909 a total of forty markets in twenty-one cities were mentioned (Osthoff and Schmitt, 1909). Each city usually had a single market, although some cities like Strasbourg, Cologne and Dresden built two or more markets – a central one and one or at most two neighbourhood markets. The case of Berlin, which built a large and well-coordinated system of markets as of 1886, is exceptional (Lohmeier, 1999; Paflik-Huber, 2015). In Vienna, discussion on the renewal of the markets began in the 1850s, but no covered iron markets were completed there until 1865 (Haiko, 2015).

Market halls in Scandinavian cities were built rather late. Initiatives in Denmark began at an earlier date but only a few halls materialised and they were not very successful (Toftgaard, 2016). In the mid-1870s, works began on the market at the port of Bergen and the Fiskehallen in Gothenburg. Most of the markets there, however, like the nine market buildings erected in Stockholm (1882–1914) or the Dock Market in Helsinki, did not go into operation until the following decade (Omilanowska, 2015; Nordin, 2009). Helsinki had built four market halls just before the outbreak of WWI. Warsaw had a central market and three neighbourhood markets. Gdansk had several markets as well. In Wroclaw, in the German orbit, two market halls were built, one of them in 1908, with an innovative structure of parabolic arches made of reinforced concrete. Many other cities joined this wave of new markets: Vilnius, Riga, Katowice, Chorzow, Kiev, Odessa, Sofia, Ploesti, Ljubljana, Turku, Tampere and Oulu (Omilanowska, 2015). In 1869, Bucharest celebrated its recently acquired status as a capital with its first market project, the Halele Centrale, built by a French company. Zurich's Fleischmarkethalle opened that same year.

In the Russian Empire and in Balkan Europe, the introduction of new iron market halls run parallel to a process of renewal and expansion of the commercial structures of Oriental tradition. Saint Petersburg, the most westernised of Russian cities, began to erect its first iron markets at a very early date, in 1863. Moscow, however, which opened the Nikiforov Market in 1877, built the big *torgovie riadi* following the local tradition over the course of the nineteenth century. The *torgovie riadi* were also predominant in other large cities in the Russian Empire like Odessa. The Russian case shows how the centralisation of decisions prevented many initiatives and how important the degree of municipal autonomy and decision-making power was.

Figure 7.2 Interior view of the market hall in Wroclaw (Breslau), Poland, with concrete arches, 1906–1908

Source: Author's own photograph.

In Italy, the first important iron markets – such as the three markets of Turin and the first two markets of Milan – were built in the 1860s (De Pieri, 2015). The original market system of Florence began to operate between 1869 and 1876. In Spain, Madrid's two markets – the Cebada Market and the Mostense Market which opened in 1875 – were built with imported French materials. In most cities, however, and especially in the most industrial ones like Barcelona, markets were designed by local experts and built by local industries. Some ninety iron markets have been documented between 1870 and 1920 (Castañer, 2015). As in other countries of Latin Europe, cities, both large and small, continued to build markets during the first third of the twentieth century. There are many examples of this: the Colón Market (1914–1916) and the Central Market (1914–1929) in Valencia, the Salamanca Market in Málaga (1923–1925), the market in Alicante (1914–1921), La Ribera Market (1929) in Bilbao, and the Olavide Market (1931) in Madrid, as well as many more in towns, such as the market in Sabadell (1927–1930) or the one in Sant Feliu de Guíxols (1928–1930) in Catalonia.

The centre-periphery dissemination of typological and technological solutions may at first seem to be an imitation phenomenon. However, the construction and proper upkeep of public markets also depended on the level of consolidation of a food market on a national level, transport networks, the development of new forms of distribution, the strength and diversity of regional agricultural production, the degree of involvement of municipal authorities in the building and governance of markets, and on the pattern of urban development adopted in each city. The new market halls had the role of increasing the transparency of exchanges and of containing the prices of perishable seasonal foods from local, regional and national areas.

In the United Kingdom, the towns most influenced by the phenomenon of market halls were industrial cities, areas of great urban and industrial growth that generated a huge demand for food for the working classes and which had an intensive agricultural and livestock output based on meat, dairy products and vegetables. Half a century later, the map of cities with markets in Spain resembled that of Britain: all the country's most industrialised cities and regions built covered markets (Catalonia, the Basque Country and Asturias) as it was also the case of the urban centres of intensive farming areas (Valencia and Murcia). In both cases, the construction of the railway network was a driving force that brought new horizons to small market towns, hitherto confined to local supply areas. On a regional level, the railway played a very selective role in Britain: some markets saw how their field of influence greatly increased when they became railway junctions (Schmiechen and Carls, 1999: 158–159, 163–166) while the sphere of influence of other smaller markets remained as it had been since the pre-industrial era. In each city across England, the fate of the market varied depending on its type of management – municipal or private – and the efficiency of said management. According to some comparative studies, the way in which each city was governed appears to be decisive not only with respect to the fate of its markets but also in terms of the evolution of the particular food retail mix of the whole city (Mitchell, 2011).

The period of great expansion of markets in many continental European cities in the closing decades of the nineteenth century coincided with the onset of the decline in pioneering countries, such as the United Kingdom, the United States or France. This decline was especially notable in the UK. Between 1910 and 1920, no new markets were built and very few were erected up to 1950. New urban developments were increasingly dispersed and difficult for markets to supply. The distances to and from markets in these suburban areas, dotted with detached and semi-detached houses, grew greatly and the area that could be served on foot was too large to make such a service profitable. These low density urban sprawls were much more suited to popular grocery stores or to shopping parades, just as had been the case in many North-American cities since the mid-nineteenth century (Schmiechen and Carls, 1999: 95,

101, 185–187). This kind of urban growth, however, was just one more factor contributing to the decline of markets. Other fundamental factors gradually undermined the municipal markets. The public market system in these countries flourished when the economic structure of the production and consumption of food was highly local or regional. When the railway transport network and new tinning and freezing systems of some fresh foods placed many national agricultural products on the market, only an interventionist public ownership and management of markets could maintain, in the long run, the distribution of foods in stalls in the face of the steadily growing competition of grocery businesses in cities and, later, of the national commercialisation chains and co-operatives.

The case of the United States shows that the more liberalising policies actually progressed to the detriment of the market halls. After the first half of the nineteenth century, in which public markets underwent great development, local and state governments opted for the liberalisation of fresh food commerce. Many cities, for example, had allowed butchers to run their own establishments outside public markets. Large-scale corporate privileges were granted to merchants and investors who wished to manage big food stores, which were often equipped with the latest innovations in building, lighting, refrigeration and ventilation. Moreover, the railway allowed wholesale commission agents to establish direct ties with producers outside the framework of the markets (Tangires, 2003 201–205). The privatisation movement flourished in a period of great economic and urban growth and of debilitation and even corruption of the local authorities. The competition of big private stores and grocery stores in residential neighbourhoods meant that municipal markets reached crisis point.

In the case of the United Kingdom, reduced public intervention, more open and liberalised exchanges and the scale and dynamic nature of the economy were also essential. We can observe an early predominance of wholesale intermediaries that were directly or indirectly connected with big co-operatives or the thriving food distribution chains that sold products such as imported meat and fish and, increasingly, fruit, vegetables (potatoes in particular), eggs and dairy products. In 1914, the co-operatives and the food distribution chains accounted for one-fifth of the total food sales, and by the end of World War II, they were making one-third of the total sales (Schmiechen and Carls, 1999: chap. 19, 128; Benson and Shaw, 1992: 200; Scola, 1975, 1992; Hodson, 1999).

In France, in the late nineteenth century, we also observe a weakening of the market halls due to the decline of traditional agriculture and to new forms of commercialisation of agricultural products with the intervention of wholesalers and co-operatives. The decline of the markets was accentuated by the war of 1914–1918 and diminishing public budgets that affected their proper upkeep and renewal. Outdoor markets, which had never disappeared, did not call for major investments or facilities and they adapted themselves more flexibly to needs. Around 1890, Julien Guadet commented that in Paris, while some old markets held under tarpaulins continued to function, many of the new and costly market halls had to close down (Bailly and Laurent, 1998: 45).

Focusing exclusively on market halls gives a distorted view of market systems. In fact, many European urban centres never came to have market halls, or these often coexisted with open-air markets of long-standing tradition. Some big cities like Amsterdam or Rotterdam continued to function with outdoor markets alone, in stark contrast to neighbouring Belgium. London depended primarily on kerb markets and on itinerant vendors, while its principal markets became big wholesale centres. Open-air markets are a phenomenon that never disappeared, their continued existence and recurrent resurgence are historical constants, as Nordin showed in his brilliant study of this type of market in Stockholm and other European cities (Nordin, 2009).

Wholesale markets and new commercial formats

The progressive increase of wholesaling contributed decisively to the specialisation of crops and, at the same time, to the progressive erosion of neighbourhood market halls. While in smaller towns local farmers continued to sell directly to consumers at local markets, the expansion of big cities made this direct relationship more difficult. The new scale of business, the railway network and, subsequently, refrigeration facilitated the intervention of intermediaries. As it emerged, wholesaling widened its radius of supply and facilitated the growing import of some foods that had been obtained locally until then. These activities required large market halls. Although wholesaling was distributed among the various markets, a large central market, or central markets for the various products (fruit and vegetables, fish, meat, flowers) usually predominated. The presence of multiple products at these large markets assured greater transparency and a fluid regulation of prices thanks to supply and demand. As intermediaries and wholesalers had more resources, they went about displacing producers and retailers from the leading markets. This was the case of Covent Garden and Les Halles. The fact is, however, that even around 1910 it was common in Europe for wholesaling to co-exist with retailing in the central markets (King, 1913). In Vienna, the new meat market of 1898–1899 was expanded with the Viktualienhalle in 1904–1906, which had wholesale and retail stalls as well as space for farmers.

Nonetheless, exclusively wholesale markets started to become the norm in leading urban centres. In Rome, where the wholesale fruit and vegetable market – having been located in various different open spaces in the city – had been the subject of debate for decades, a municipal government formed by Republicans and Socialists approved the project for the new central markets in 1910. These markets were connected with the Rome-Ostia railway and had a section devoted to fruit and vegetables and another section for fish, lamb, chicken, eggs and other foodstuffs (Stemperini, 2009). They formed part of a policy aimed to establish tight municipal control of distribution and to allow the setting of food prices. The farmer's lobby often exerted pressure in a demand for markets in proper conditions, as may be seen in the case of Rome. In Barcelona, the farmers' management association was the foremost advocate of organising the wholesaling of fruit and vegetables in order to increase the transparency of exchanges and to favour the establishment of prices with a view to curbing the intermediaries' high margins to the benefit of producers and consumers. This reasoning was common in the press of the period as may be seen, for example, in the case of the Budapest market, which published a daily bulletin giving the wholesale price of the various articles and a weekly bulletin giving the retail prices (King, 1913: 109). In Barcelona, it was only the severe subsistence crisis – caused by WWI inflation and the postwar period – that led El Born Market, the first cast-iron market built in 1876, to be provisionally turned into a wholesale fruit and vegetable market in 1921 (Guàrdia and Oyón, 2017). In Madrid, a modern central fruit and vegetable market with a concrete structure, served by the railway, opened in 1935.

In the early twentieth century, the regulation of the growing wholesale business became a widespread process. Germany was the pioneer of a new generation of concrete wholesale markets, which were usually located in places accessible by railway, river transport and road, with loading docks to facilitate the handling, processing and distribution of agricultural products, and sometimes with refrigerated spaces for storing fresh products. These were called "terminal markets" because accessibility and connection to transport infrastructures were more important than central locations near big urban retail markets. Both in Germany and the United States, road transport and loading docks for lorries gradually became the norm in the interwar period. In Germany, concrete structures were developed to achieve greater spans and increasingly light-filled covered spaces. The foremost examples were Frankfurt's huge concrete wholesale market, which opened in 1928, and the Leipzig Wholesale Market, which opened one year later. The wholesale markets did not confine themselves to supplying their own populations but rather they became large redistribution centres serving a broader territory. Moreover, their growth diminished the importance of retail markets and especially neighbourhood markets as they served the city's entire food commerce fabric. In 1913, Willy Levin, a magistrate in Frankfurt – a city of global fame since the end of the nineteenth century thanks to the Social Democratic governance of its mayor Franz Adickes in such fields as planning, housing and transport – placed his confidence in the trend towards the centralisation of markets in large cities, their capacity to regulate prices by bringing together producers and wholesalers, and the trend of food retailing 'to leave the market halls for the stores'. At the same time, the neighbourhood or district market halls declined and municipal involvement in this respect was not worth the trouble (Levin, 1913: 159).

At the beginning of the twentieth century in the United States, after a long period of complete deregulation and at a point when public markets were most compromised, a phase of firm public intervention was paradoxically initiated. In 1894, reform groups had organised the National Municipal League, whose agenda included the renewal of the markets. Just as happened in the same period for Japan (Harada, 2016), the European markets were studied in depth and even became the subject of a set of consular reports published in 1910 (Tangires, 2015; Guàrdia and Oyón, 2015).

In 1913, the Department of Agriculture (USDA) formed a federal Markets Office in order to establish a model of a market system with more economical and more efficient food commercialisation facilities for the interested cities. This was the necessary response to the country's new economic era, as was stated in an article from that same year:

> Hitherto the United States has occupied a position of unique advantage. We have had such abundant resources that, after taking care of our wants, we have been able to supply the markets of the Old World with enormous quantities of foodstuffs. This abundance has relieved us of the necessity of economical distribution in the home territory. Within the last ten years there has been a remarkable change in conditions. Our cultivated land has increased thirty percent while consumption has increased sixty percent. Three million more men are earning enough to enable them to buy meat, but there has been a heavy decrease of meat producing cattle on American farms. Municipalities are therefore confronted with the duty of meeting these changed conditions. The most effective means of solving the problem lies in the organization of publicly controlled markets that will afford economical facilities for distribution.
>
> *(Black, 1913)*

The aim was to adapt to needs, urban changes and intense population movements. The USDA promoted three basic types of markets: two types of retail markets and terminal markets. First came the market halls, built following hygienic and functional criteria for consolidated urban centres. Secondly, there would be kerb markets, that is, open-air farmers' markets, which would be appropriate for smaller centres because they did not demand major initial investments, they were easy to set up, they were highly flexible and they were very popular during WWI. In many cases they were set up on vacant lots, allowing an aisle to be formed between two rows of vans or lorries parked with their rear ends facing shoppers. The most innovative type, however, was unquestionably that of the terminal markets. As in Germany, the goal was primarily to assure good municipal control and economic rationalisation by means of public wholesale terminal markets, accessible by rail, river or sea, and if possible, conditioned for quick inspection and loading and unloading. They were equipped with spacious halls containing sections for each of the products, which were connected by freight lifts with refrigerated basements. The most notable cases were those proposed for New York, Los Angeles and Chicago.

Although this process ran out of steam in the 1920s, the policies put forward to contain food prices and reduce agricultural surpluses specific to the Great Depression increased interest in municipal markets. Criticism of municipal intervention and praise of free enterprise were not lacking. In a context of tough competition, 'market managers had to adopt more effective business techniques if the public markets were to survive' (Mayo, 1991: 54). Moreover, as US cities became more suburban, the centrally located urban plots where the old public markets stood came to be increasingly coveted. Even though the public markets were profitable, their profit margins were smaller than those of other businesses that aspired to these central locations. Likewise, between 1914 and 1945, new food commerce formats in the United States were intensely developed, ranging from the first self-service grocery stores to big supermarket chains that can supply large quantities of foods at low prices. The market halls unavoidably lost price competitiveness, failing to achieve one of their goals within the overall field of food commercialisation. The growing importance of big food companies also entailed a transition from the bulk sale of products to the sale of packaged articles and the responsibility of quality assurance fell on the brand rather than on the sales establishment. The rise of national corporations that specialised in food processing took advantage of the mass-distribution possibilities provided by the railroad network and refrigeration technology and led to the decline of public markets. When the national distribution of perishable foods became possible with refrigerated rail car, the corporate system of food distribution 'increasingly replaced more localized public markets' (Mayo, 1991: 55).

The idea of the public market as an answer to the need for food retailing came to be displaced by chain grocery stores and subsequently by supermarkets. This was a fundamental displacement in the political economy of food retailing. The rise and fall of public markets reflects the transition of the American political economy from a local mercantilism to a corporatism of national scope. The evolution undergone by the public markets in the United States would have a big influence on Europe and on the rest of the world in the last half of the twentieth century.

The persistence of an "anachronism"

Between 1945 and 1973, a period characterised by 'increasingly global agrobusiness corporations and their role creating agrofood complexes', supermarkets and big food distribution chains had a huge effect on public markets (Bernstein, 2015; Friedman and McMichael, 1989). First they prevailed in the United States, afterwards in Northern Europe and then progressively in other European and extra-European countries. Although this was not confined to a mere transfer process and the forms and intensities of the adoption of supermarkets varied considerably in each context, they were generally instruments of price containment in national economic policies. Accordingly, public markets came to play an increasingly residual role. Even so, this did not prevent the building of a new generation of markets in countries in the Soviet orbit – with a more controlled economy – or in Spain, which had been left out of the Marshall Plan and maintained a strongly autarchic and interventionist economy. The scarcity and deficiency of food in Spain's long post-civil war period made the markets policy in Madrid and Barcelona an aspect of central importance. Between 1939 and 1943, Madrid went from having ten to fourteen markets. Despite attempts made by Spain's technocratic governments to renew the economy at the end of the 1950s, obsolete commercial distribution practices and tariff policies ruined the attempts to introduce the American supermarket model. As a result, they were forced to trust in the public market policy with the goal of containing food prices. Between 1939 and 1977, twenty-six new markets were built or rebuilt in Barcelona, bringing the total number to over forty (Fava, Guàrdia and Oyón, 2016; Miller, 2015). In the context of the post-WWII economic boom in Europe, these processes were seen as anomalies and the old markets were seen as residual elements that were doomed to disappear.

Despite the unquestionable erosion of market hall systems during this period, markets in their various forms have shown a considerable resilience. Of the thirty-four market halls that Paris possessed in 1870, only sixteen were still standing in 1961 (Pinol and Garden, 2009: 156–157). Nevertheless, the French capital had fifty-eight outdoor markets that operated two or three days a week and served the most popular neighbourhoods in the south and east of the city. On studying sixteen Western European countries in 1992, Nordin found only 3,100 market halls in operation (Nordin, 1992). Compared with this, the outdoor markets and fairs that open a few days each week or each year were easier to set up, more flexible and eighteen times more numerous. Some recent studies on leading cities in Europe's four Latin countries highlight a growing trend in which market halls are replaced by outdoor markets, with peripheral areas being supplied by this type of market. Turin, for example, still maintains today a network of neighbourhood markets, which is as strong as that of Barcelona's market halls but with the difference that they are mainly outdoor markets (Coppo and Osello, 2006). In the United States

Figure 7.3 Clientele areas of Barcelona's zonal municipal market halls, 2011

as well, at the beginning of the 1970s, some voices defended farmers' markets as fully functional "anachronisms" (Pyle, 1971). They were more expensive than supermarkets but they had proven themselves capable of meeting consumers' demands for fresh products and quality produce from the surrounding rural area. This revived the traditional contact between producers and shoppers, a contact that had never actually disappeared in many European cities, especially those in the South, with a thriving agriculture, intensively producing fruit and vegetables (Nordin, 2009). Markets can not only compete with the quality of their products, they also offer an especially attractive shopping experience which the new commercial formats often try to imitate without much success. For this reason, as opposed to simplified evolutionary views, it should be recalled that markets, in their different forms, have never ceased to operate, although they have adopted very diverse forms in various contexts.

The theory of the two circuits of urban economy formulated by Milton Santos in the 1970s with respect to developing world metropolises evidenced the fact that the process of modernisation of activities was accompanied by a paradoxical increase in poverty, giving rise to apparently contradictory results (Santos, 1979; Sposito, 1996; Marina, 2012). These cities functioned like a comprehensive system formed by interdependent complementary subsystems in a state of balance. This reality may be read in the morphology of these big cities and it explains the frequent coexistence of traditional markets and modern commercial formats, just as may be seen in such cities as Bangkok, Mumbai or Manila, or in African cities like Dakar, Kinshasa or Dar es Salaam, which maintain centrally located markets full of vitality (Beeckmans and Bigon, 2016). The subsequent globalisation process has confirmed that it was not a residual effect of modernisation but rather a trait that is destined to endure. Even in such global cities as New York, London or Tokyo, one may observe the clear expansion of informal work, and it is not surprising that the enormous vitality of traditional markets may also be seen in the most dynamic cities like Seoul or Singapore (Sassen, 1991). All in all, outdoor markets can no longer be considered to be mere anachronisms but rather fully modern elements of the urban retailing mix.

The case of Lima is paradigmatic. As opposed to many other big cities in South America, Lima maintains today, together with over one thousand open-air market sites, several hundred covered and semi-covered markets that are evenly distributed across its sprawling territory (Leung, 2016). These are over five times more numerous than the seventy-two supermarkets, which serve the wealthiest areas, and supply the city's very extensive working-class areas, representing over 70% of basic foodstuff purchases. Likewise, although a very different case, it is surprising to observe the enduring vitality of Hong Kong's "wet markets" in contrast to the weakness of supermarkets in the sale of fresh foods:

> given the well-developed economy of Hong Kong, one would have expected supermarkets to dominate fresh food retailing and wet markets to be in retreat. But consumers' shopping and consumption culture, the effectiveness of wet markets in handling consumers' needs, and the appropriateness of the simple technology used by wet markets are at the basis of this dominance.
>
> *(Goldman, Rider and Ramaswami, 1999; Blake, 2013)*

As from the 1970s, to this underlying resilience was added a clear movement of resistance to the expansive hegemonic food model governed by the processes of capital accumulation, which bases its principles on long-distance transport and on preservation techniques. The defence of 'proximity and seasonality/sensitivity to place and time, healthy food and environmentally sound agriculture' has led to a growing advocacy for farmers' markets in the United States and to the promotion of regional agriculture assuring the supply of fresh local products while providing support for farmers (Bernstein, 2015). Since 1976, the Council on the Environment of New York has organised and managed outdoor farmers' markets, and since 1994 the USDA has published the annual National Directory of Farmers' Markets. The increase has been quite significant, with the number of farmers' markets rising from 1,775 in 1994 to 8,476 to date. Although their market share is unquestionably small, the growth of the farmers' markets clearly indicates a reaction that is also unmistakably manifested in Europe, usually with a more identity-based nuance relating to the various areas' claims to their own food tradition. This has been expressed in Italy and France through campaigns against the growing success of fast food. Especially significant among the resistance movements is the Slow Food alternative, which has not ceased to grow since the 1980s and which defends the need to preserve each ecoregion's own cuisine and crops. The defence of the Mediterranean diet is based in part on similar principles. Its promotion as World Heritage is doubtless the result of growing social activism and the coordinated initiative of various institutions. That said, it also highlights its status as a threatened heritage asset in need of protection (García-Fuentes, Guàrdia and Oyón, 2014).

It is not by chance that countries advocating traditional food are precisely those which have not only accumulated and maintained a richer gastronomic culture but also a commercial fabric of fresh products which is less dependent on supermarkets and on big distribution chains. It may appear paradoxical, but a clear correlation has been observed between the resilience of small food commerce establishments and the strength of fresh food wholesale markets in such countries. It is hard to separate cultural factors in food consumption from the evolution of the structure and development of the food distribution sector, up to the point that 'the structure of the food retail and catering sectors . . . is the leading driver in modelling the structure of the food wholesale industry' (Cadilhon, Fearne, Hughes and Moustier, 2003). The consolidation of well-stocked fresh food wholesale markets is a fundamental support for small-scale commerce, whereas it is superfluous for big distribution chains or hypermarkets.

It is an undeniable fact that progressive commercial liberalisation and capital accumulation processes have not ceased to promote, in recent decades, the globalisation of food commerce throughout the world. A simple exploration on the Internet, however, reveals the great number of new market halls that have been built in recent times, or renewed market halls, both inside and outside of Europe. In many cases these structures feature very striking architectures, as one finds in the recent Rotterdam Market or the new Ghent Market Hall. In the case of Barcelona, after the crisis of the 1970s, the renewal of the city's forty neighbourhood market halls, which were in full operation, appeared to be a good strategy for recovering the fabric of a highly deteriorated food commerce. These market halls were the tools for containing the effects of hypermarkets, which were beginning to proliferate in urban peripheries.

An even greater abundance of uncovered markets of diverse characteristics are found in most cities. It should not be forgotten, either, that in a world in which inequalities are growing itinerant commerce continues to be an overwhelming reality, a phenomenon that is hard to organise and regulate in many countries. As opposed to what could have been believed some years ago, markets should not be considered anachronisms doomed to disappear, but rather one more expression of the overall retail sphere which, in its various forms, appears, disappears or adapts itself according to the economic, social and cultural conditioning factors in each place and each time in history, to meet specific demands of consumers. As Fernand Braudel said many years ago:

> If this elementary market has survived unchanged down the ages, it is surely because in its robust simplicity it is unbeatable – because of the freshness of the perishable goods it brings straight from local gardens and fields and because of its low prices.
>
> *(Braudel, 1979: 9–10)*

References

Baics, G. (2012), 'Is access to food a public good? Meat provisioning in early New York City, 1790–1820', *Journal of Urban History*, XX (X), pp. 1–26.

Baics, G. (2016), *Feeding Gotham, the political economy and geography of food in New York, 1790–1860* (Princeton, NJ: Princeton University Press).

Bailly, G.-H. and Laurent, Ph. (1998), *La France des Halles & Marchés* (Toulouse: Privat).

Baltard, V. and Callet, F. (1863), *Monographie des Halles de Paris* (Paris: A. Morel).

Baltard, V. (1873), *Complément à la monographie des Halles centrales de Paris, comprenant un parallèle entre divers édifices du même ordre* (Paris: Ducher).

Beeckmans, L. and Bigon, L. (2016), 'The making of the central markets of Dakar and Kinshasa: From colonial origins to the post-colonial period', *Urban History*, 43, p. 3.

Benson, J. and Shaw, G. (eds.) (1992), *The Evolution of Retail Systems, c. 1800–1914* (London/New York: Leicester University Press).

Bentham, J. (1995), 'The Panopticon', in M. Bozovic (ed.) *The panopticon writings* (London: Verso) 29–95.

Bernstein, H. (2015), 'Food regimes and food regime analysis: A selective survey', Land Grabbing, Conflict and Agrarian-Environmental Transformations: Perspectives from East and Southeast Asia, International Academic Conference, 5–6 June, Chiang Mai University.

Black, E. (1913), 'Communal benefits from the public control of terminal markets', *The Annals of the American Academy of Political and Social Science, "The Cost of Living"*, 48, pp. 149–153.

Blake, M.K. (2013), 'Ordinary food spaces in a global city: Hong Kong', *Streetnotes*, 21 (1), pp. 1–12.

Bois, G. (1989), *La mutation de l'an mil: Lournand, village mâconnais, de l'antiquité au féodalisme* (Paris: Fayard).

Braudel, F. (1979), *Civilisation matérielle, économie et capitalisme XVe–XVIIIe siècle, 2: Les Jeux de l'Echange* (Paris: Colin).

Bruyère, L. (1813), *Collection des marchés de Paris avec projets* (Paris: École Nationale des Ponts et Chaussées, Manuscript, Fol. 486, 127 prints).

Cadilhon, J.J., Fearne, A.P., Hughes, D.R. and Moustier, P. (2003), "Wholesale markets and food distribution in Europe: New strategies for old functions", January. Available at: www.researchgate.net/publication/242172462_Wholesale_Markets_and_Food_Distribution_in_Europe_New_Strategies_for_Old_Functions.

Calabi, D. (2004), *The market and the city: Square, street and architecture in early modern Europe* (Hampshire: Ashgate).

Carter, H. (1983), *An introduction to urban historical geography* (London: Arnold).

Castañer, E. (2015), 'Iron markets in Spain', in M. Guàrdia and J.L. Oyón (eds.) *Making cities through markets halls* (Barcelona: Museu d'Història de Barcelona) 401–431.

Conzen, M.R.G. (1960), 'Alnwick, Northumberland: A study in town-plan analysis', *Transactions and Papers (Institute of British Geographers Publication)*, 27 (London: George Philip).

Conzen, M.R.G. (1962), 'The plan analysis of an English city centre', in K. Norborg (ed.), *Proceedings of the IGU Symposium in urban geography* (Lund: Gleerup-Lund) 383–414.

Coppo, D. and Osello, A. (eds.) (2006), *Il disegno di luoghi e mercati di Torino* (Torino: Celid).

De Pieri, F. (2015), 'Covered markets in liberal Italy: A comparison between four cities', in M. Guàrdia and J.L. Oyón (eds.) *Making cities through markets halls* (Barcelona: Museu d'Història de Barcelona) 195–230.

Fava, N., Guàrdia, M. and Oyón, J.L. (2015), 'The Barcelona market system', in M. Guàrdia and J.L. Oyón (eds.) *Making cities through markets halls* (Barcelona: Museu d'Història de Barcelona) 261–296.

Fava, N., Guàrdia, M. and Oyón, J.L. (2016), 'Barcelona food retailing and public markets, 1876–1936', *Urban History*, 43 (3), pp. 454–475.

Foucault, M. (1977), 'L'œil du pouvoir. Entretien avec Michel Foucault', preface to Jeremy Bentham, *Le Panoptique* (Paris: Pierre Belfond).

Friedman, H. and McMichael, P. (1989), 'Agriculture and the state system: The rise and decline of national agricultures, 1870 to the present', *Sociologica Ruralis*, 29 (2), pp. 93–117.

Ganshof, F.L. (1943), *Étude sur le développement des villes entre Loire au moyen âge* (Paris/Brussels: Presses Universitaires de France).

Garcia-Fuentes, J.-M., Guàrdia, M. and Oyón, J.L. (2014), 'Reinventing edible identities: Catalan cuisine and Barcelona's market halls', in R.L. Brulotte and M.A. Di Giovine (eds.) *Edible identities: Food as cultural heritage* (Farnham: Ashgate).

Goldman, A., Krider, R. and Ramaswami, S. (1999), 'The persistent competitive advantage of traditional food retailers in Asia: Wet markets' continued dominance in Hong Kong', *Journal of Macromarketing*, 19 (2), pp. 126–139.

Guàrdia, M. and Oyón, J.L. (2015), 'Introduction: European markets as makers of cities', in M. Guàrdia and J.L. Oyón (eds.) *Making cities through markets halls, 19th and 20th centuries* (Barcelona: Museu d'Història de Barcelona) 11–71.

Guàrdia, M. and Oyón, J.L. (2017), *Memòria del mercat del Born* (Barcelona: El Born Centre de Cultura I Memòria), pp. 68–102

Guerreau, A. (1990), 'Lournand au Xe siècle: histoire et fiction', *Le Moyen Age*, 96, pp. 519–537.

Haiko, P. (2015), 'Covered markets in Vienna', in M. Guàrdia and J.L. Oyón (eds.) *Making cities through markets halls* (Barcelona: Museu d'Història de Barcelona) 167–194.

Harada, M. (2016), 'Japanese modern municipal retail and wholesale markets in comparison with European markets', *Urban History*, 43 (3), pp. 476–492.

Hennicke, J. (1881), *Mitteilungen über Markthallen in Deutschland, England, Frankreich, Belgien und Italien* (Berlin: Ernst & Korn).

Hodson D. (1999), "The municipal store': Adaptation and development in the retail markets of nineteenth-century urban Lancashire', in N. Alexander and G. Akehurst (eds.) *The emergence of modern retailing. 1750–1950* (London: Frank Cass).

Kelley, V. (2016), 'The streets for the people: London's street markets 1850–1939', *Urban History*, 43, p. 3.

King, C.L. (1913), 'Municipal markets: Reducing the cost of food distribution', *The Annals of the American Academy of Political Science*, 50, pp. 102–117.

Kostof, S. (1992), *The city assembled* (New York/London: Thames and Hudson).

Lavedan, P. and Hugueney, J. (1974), *L'urbanisme au moyen âge* (Geneva: Droz).

Lemoine, B. (1980), *Les Halles de Paris. L'histoire d'un lieu, les péripéties d'une reconstruction, la succession des projets, l'architecture des monuments, l'enjeu d'une 'cité'* (Paris: L'Equerre).

Lemoine, B. (1986), *L'architecture du fer: France XIXe siècle* (Seyssel: Champ Vallon).

Lepetit, B. (1988), *Les villes dans la France moderne (1740–1840)* (Paris: Albin Michel).

Leung J. (2016), 'Abastecer o ser abastecido: La influencia de los mercados tradicionales de sobre el tejido urbano de Lima', M.A. Dissertation, ETSAB-UPC, Barcelona.

Levin, D. (1913), 'Wholesale terminal markets in Germany and their effect on food costs and conservation', in C.L. King (eds.) *"Municipal markets: Reducing the cost of food distribution", The Annals of the American Academy of Political Science*, 50, pp. 153–165, 159.

Lohmeier, A. (1999), '*Bürgerliche Gesellschaft* and consumer interests: The Berlin public market hall reform, 1867–1891', *Business History Review*, 73, pp. 91–113.

Lortie, A. (1995), *Paris s'exporte: Architecture modèle ou modèles d'architecture* (Paris: Éditions de l'Arsenal-Picard).

Marina, R.M. (2012), 'A teoria dos dois circuitos da economia urbana de Milton Santos: de seu surgimento à sua atualização', *Revista Geográfica Venezolana*, 53 (1), pp. 147–164.

Mayo, J.M. (1991), 'The American public market', *Journal of Architectural Education*, 45, pp. 41–57.

Foucault, M., et al. (eds.) (1978), *Les machines à guérir: Aux origines de l'hôpital moderne* (Liège/Brussels: Pierre Mardaga).

Miller, M. (2015), *Feeding Barcelona, 1714–1975: Public market halls, social networks and consumer culture* (Baton Rouge: Louisiana State University Press).

Mitchell, I. (2011), 'Supplying the masses: Retailing and town governance in Macclesfield, Stockport and Birkenhead, 1780–1860', *Urban History*, 38 (2), pp. 256–275.

Nordin, Ch. (1992), 'The hidden dimension: European mobile trade: Statistical estimates and an attempt to classify various forms of market halls and mobile trade', in D.L. Huff (ed.) *International dimensions of commercial systems* (Austin, TX: University of Texas) 186–215.

Nordin, Ch. (2009), Oordning-torghandel i Stockholm, 1540–1918 (Lund: Sekel) (French resumé: *Les leçons du passé: Géographie historique des marchés de Stockholm, 1540–1918*, pp. 298–306).

Omilanowska, M. (2015), 'Market halls in Scandinavia, Russia and Central and Eastern Europe', in M. Guàrdia and J.L. Oyón (eds.) *Making cities through markets halls* (Barcelona: Museu d'Història de Barcelona) 410–413.

Osthoff, G. and Schmitt, E. (1909), 'Markthallen und Marktplätze', in *Handbuch der Architektur: Gebäude für die Zwecke der Landwirtschaft und der Lebensmittelversorgung* (Leipzig: Alfred Kröner), Vol. IV, 3rd edition, 295–429.

Paflik-Huber, H. (2015), 'Covered markets in Germany: From iron markets to central concrete markets', in M. Guàrdia and J.L. Oyón (eds.) *Making cities through markets halls, op. cit.* (Barcelona: Museu d'Història de Barcelona) 327–362.

Pevsner, N. (1976), *A history of building types* (Princeton, NJ: Princeton University Press).

Pinol, J.-L. and Garden, M. (2009), *Atlas des Parisiens: De la révolution à nos jours* (Paris: Parigramme).

Pirenne, H. (1925, 1952), *Medieval cities: Their origins and the revival of trade* (Princeton, NJ: Princeton University Press).

Pyle, J. (1971), 'Farmers' markets in the United States: Functional anachronisms', *Geographical Review*, LXI (2), pp. 167–197.

Risch, Th. (1867), *Bericht über Markthallen in Deutschland, Belgien, Frankreich, England und Italien* (Berlin: Selbstverlage des Magistrats/Wolf Peiser).

Rudé, G. (1970), *Paris and London in the 18th century: Studies in Popular Protest* (London: W. Collins & Sons).

Santos, M. (1979), *O espaço dividido* (Rio de Janeiro: Francisco Alves).

Sassen, S. (1991), *The global city: New York, London, Tokyo* (Princeton, NJ: Princeton University Press).

Schmiechen, J. (2015), 'London and the British public market: Urban food, architectural form and cultural language', in M. Guàrdia and J.L. Oyón (eds.) *Making cities through markets halls* (Barcelona: Museu d'Història de Barcelona) 73–102.

Schmiechen, J. and Carls, K. (1999), *The British market hall: A social and architectural history* (New Haven, CT/London: Yale University Press).

Scola, R. (1975), 'Food markets and shops in Manchester 1770 –1870', *Journal of Historical Geography*, 1 (2), pp. 153–168.

Scola, R. (1992), *Feeding the Victorian city: The food supply of Manchester 1770–1870* (Manchester/New York: Manchester University Press).

Sposito, E.S. (1996), 'Teoria dos dois circuitos da economia urbana nos países desenvolvidos: seu esquecimento ou sua superação?', in *O mundo do cidadão – um cidadão do mundo*, Homenagem ao Prof. Milton Santos (São Paulo: Universidade de São Paulo).

Stamp, G. (1986), 'The Hungerford market', *AA-Files*, 11, pp. 58–70.

Stemperini, G. (2009), *La politica annonaria del comune di Roma tra Ottocento e anni trenta del Novecento. La questione dei mercati all'ingrosso* (Roma: Croma-Università degli Studio Roma Tre).

Stobart, J. and Van Damme, I. (2016), 'Markets in modernization: Transformations in urban market space and practice, *c.* 1800–1970', Introduction to *Urban History* special issue, 43 (3), pp. 358–371.

Tangires, H. (2003), *Public markets and civic culture in nineteenth-century America* (Baltimore, MD/London: John Hopkins University Press).

Tangires, H. (2015), 'Lessons from Europe: Public market reform in the United States during the Progressive Era, 1894–1922', in M. Guàrdia and J.L. Oyón (eds.) *Making cities through markets halls, 19th and 20th centuries* (Barcelona: Museu d´Història de Barcelona) 431–461.

Teyssot, G. (1977a), 'Città-servizi. La produzione dei 'bâtiments civils' in Francia (1795–1848)', *Casabella*, 424, pp. 56–65.

Teyssot, G. (1977b), 'Heterotopia e storia degli spazi', in G. Teyssot (ed.) *Il dispositivo Foucault* (Venice: CLUVA).

Thompson, E.P. (1971), 'The moral economy of the English crowd in the eighteenth century', *Past and Present*, 50, pp. 76–136.

Thompson, V.E. (1997), 'Urban renovation, moral regeneration: Domesticating the halles in second empire Paris', *French Historical Studies*, 20, pp. 87–109.

Toftgaard, J. (2016), 'Marketplaces and central spaces: Markets and the rise of competing spatial ideals in Danish city centres, *c.* 1850–1900', *Urban History*, 43 (3), pp. 372–390.

Verhulst, A. (1991), 'The decline of slavery and the economic expansion of the Early Middle Ages', *Past and Present*, 133, pp. 195–203.

Wells, R. (1987), 'Counting riots in eighteenth-century England', *Bulletin for the Society of the Study of Labour History*, 37.

8
HIGH STREET/MAIN STREET

Ian Mitchell

Introduction

There is no "High Street" in the centre of the large English city of Leeds. Neither is there in the smaller city of Chester, a place long important as a retail centre out of proportion to its size. In Manchester, High Street was and is a relatively insignificant street just outside the main shopping area while in Scotland's capital, Edinburgh, it is Princes Street not High Street that is the city's principal shopping street. By contrast, in the small Oxfordshire town of Burford the "High Street" remains a very photogenic collection of independent shops which could easily be regarded as typical of the English high street. Yet this may not be the case. Without trying to impose a definition on high street (or main street in the American context), it is clearly not limited to a street of that name. But neither is it simply any collection of shops in a town or village. One defining characteristic in larger towns might be that it is located in the central business district of the place in question. It should also contain a mix of different types of shops: different in terms of both the types of goods offered for sale and ownership and management structures. A typical high street/main street will provide shops that meet consumers' needs for everyday essentials, for fashion items and consumer durables. At least from the mid-nineteenth century onwards it will also include department stores, chain stores and independent shops. It will not be a street specialising in one type of trade; nor will it be a collection of basic shops grouped around a market place. However, from at least the late seventeenth century, if not earlier, it will be the principal shopping street of the town or city.

This chapter takes a broadly chronological view of the evolution of high street/main street in Europe and in the United States of America. It begins by considering its origins in the development of shopping in the medieval and early modern period. It then looks at the period between 1700 and 1850 when the high street became a place of display and leisure. This was the beginning of the era of shop widow browsing and was the age of the *flaneur*. Section 3 considers the era of the classic high street/main street when the mix of large stores and independent shops dominated shopping and drew consumers into the downtown areas of both American and European cities. The final section discusses current issues around the decline or possible demise of high street as shopping moves away from urban centres into out-of-town shopping malls or into the virtual world of the Internet. Is there any future for high street/main street?

Origins and early development to 1700

Although shops and shopping streets were clearly important in classical antiquity, this chapter takes the later medieval period in Italy and north-west Europe as its starting point. This is partly because of the availability of source material, but mainly because it is then possible to trace fairly continuous change and development without a significant break in the story in the late antiquity/early-medieval period. Shopping streets were well-established in Italian cities by at least the late fourteenth century or early fifteenth. The best shops were generally located along major thoroughfares or around key bridges (Blondé et al., 2006). In Siena the *Strada Romana* was effectively a shop front for the city's luxury industries, and many palaces built in the fifteenth century incorporated shops (Nevola, 2006). There was an attempt in 1452 to move the butchers from the centre of the city so that best locations would be occupied by the more prestigious trades. In Naples there was a clustering of luxury trades such as mercers, cotton sellers, goldsmiths and armourers in the principal central streets. The same was true of Venice, particularly around the *Rialto* and the streets of the mercers and drapers. As in Siena, shops were often included in the ground floors of palaces and let out to provide rental income (Welch, 2005, pp. 99, 134–135)). In England, London Bridge was important, and Cheapside even more so, boasting around 400 shops as early as 1300 (Morrison, 2003, p. 19).

From the thirteenth century onwards in England, rows of shops were erected on a speculative basis by religious bodies, colleges and wealthy merchants. Others were simply carved out of existing house space. Either way, such early shops were not necessarily very impressive. Many were small, perhaps a mere five feet wide by 12 to 18 feet deep. They may have occupied the front of the service wing of a house; or have been lock-ups which had no means of communication with the main house. Most were open-fronted and stall like with much selling taking place through the window opening, although more valuable goods were probably sold from inside the shop. Somewhat later, goods were displayed and sold on large solid bulks of wood which projected beneath the shop window opening (Morrison, 2003, pp. 21–27). Italian shops were similar, often rented from institutions and rarely glazed: curtains were used to provide shelter from heat and dust. But they could be very well-stocked with valuable items. Venetian shops were used to display the wealth of the city and could seem like warehouses to those who visited. The internal space provided locations for gossip and gambling as well as trading. Although many high-class medieval shops specialised in particular types of goods, others were very much general stores: a fifteenth century Prato cheesemonger sold sewing materials, glassware, ironware and a wide range of foodstuffs as well as cheese (Welch, 2005, pp. 150–151).

Street shops have always had to compete with other outlets. In the medieval period many shops were located in or near the market place and the distinction between shop and stall was sometimes rather blurred. In England, selds were also an important part of the retail mix. These were large, hall-like buildings set back from the street and which could accommodate a large number of traders – perhaps not unlike the nineteenth century market halls. Selds were found particularly in London but also in Winchester and Chester (Keene, 2006). From the late sixteenth century onwards, purpose-built shopping galleries were of particular importance in London. There were two floors of small shops in the Royal Exchange which was completed in 1567. Around a quarter of these were occupied by haberdashers and one-tenth by mercers. By the end of the century there was a waiting list for shops. The New Exchange which opened in the Strand in 1609 was sometimes called England's *Rialto*. Shops were larger than in the Royal Exchange, and goods on sale included such luxuries as porcelain, glass, imported oriental items and high-quality textiles. Galleries were places to be seen and to socialise; they were public places, but also controlled spaces and protected consumers from the dirt and noise of the street (Baer, 2007; Peck, 2005, pp. 47–52). The gallery rather than the street was the fashionable place to shop in seventeenth century London.

Across the North Sea, shopping streets were becoming increasingly important in the Low Countries. Although Antwerp was experiencing economic decline from at least the mid-seventeenth century, its retail sector continued to grow and to flourish, implying that retailing was more influenced by shifts in taste and consumer behaviour than by the city's wealth. During the seventeenth century, retailers selling everyday essentials such as food tended to move away from expensive central locations while specialist and luxury retailers congregated in the centre of the city and on arterial roads. Similar types of shops often still clustered together and luxury goods continued to be sold at fairs. Although shopping streets were becoming more sophisticated, Antwerp was not perceived as a fashionable shopping centre and much selling continued to take place through open doors and windows (Blondé and van Damme, 2010; van Damme and van Aert, 2014). By the end of the seventeenth century, Amsterdam was the most planned and organised large urban space in Europe, but even so its retail landscape lagged behind that of Paris or London. Many shops still resembled stalls, though by at least the seventeenth century there were some specialist shopping streets such as Warmoesstraat where metalware and fabrics were to be found. (Lesger, 2014).

The second half of the seventeenth century saw significant changes to the retail landscape in England. Shopping galleries were becoming less fashionable and the most fashion-conscious retailers in London were increasingly to be found not in the traditional shopping streets of the City but in the newly fashionable West End, including Covent Garden, the Strand and the area around St James (Morrison, 2003, pp. 33–34). There were also indications of changes to come, including increased regulation of market trading and the beginnings of the sort of urban improvement that would try to move markets and street trading away from the most fashionable streets. Changes such as these tended to privilege fixed shop retailing, often with intimate selling spaces, at the expense of other forms of retailing (Walsh, 2014). The fashionable high street with its mix of different types of shops and with opportunities for window shopping and sociability was beginning to be a part of the townscape of larger provincial English towns. As Celia Fiennes noted around the turn of the century, in Newcastle-upon-Tyne, 'their shops are good and are of distinct trades, not selling many kinds of things in one shop as is the custom in most country towns and cittys'. She also commented on the fashionable walks and public gardens (Morris, 1984).

The high street and polite shopping 1700–1850

Urban improvement was a key feature of eighteenth century provincial England. As well as the construction of some imposing public buildings, the laying out of squares and the building of fashionable terraces of houses for the growing middle classes, there was a perceived need to integrate separate buildings into an harmonious streetscape and to improve the quantity and quality of the space within it. Ideally streets were to be wide, straight and open with obstructions cleared away. Better paving, lighting and cleansing were also desired and often achieved (Borsay, 1989). Shopping and leisure were increasingly intertwined and so streets had to be the backdrop for encounters and performances that reflected the prevailing attitudes of polite society. By the middle of the eighteenth century, most respectable English towns had some form of public oil lighting in their streets, thus permitting their use after dark for socialising and shopping. Many shops were also lit at night, adding to the illumination of the street and facilitating window shopping. Many shopkeepers improved the appearance of their shops in order to project a positive image;

others were ordered to remove bulk windows and other projections that obstructed footways (Stobart et al., 2007, pp. 86–97).

Most British towns had their well-identified principal shopping streets. These could range from the very glamorous to the more ordinary provincial high street. In early nineteenth century London there were two main series of shopping streets stretching from east to west: Mile End, through Cornhill to The Strand; and Shoreditch to Oxford Street. The creation of Regent Street in the 1810s with its palace-like shops and broad windows set a new standard for retail elegance (Adburgham, 1981, pp. 5–12). Elsewhere, Castle Street, Dale Street and Bold Street emerged as the principal shopping streets of Liverpool, with Foregate Street in Worcester, Eastgate and Bridge Street Rows in Chester, Milsom Street in Bath, and Highgait (later High Street) in Dundee having the same role. Even in the small Cheshire town of Nantwich it was possible to pick out Hospital Street and High Street as the most fashionable streets (Stobart et al., 2007). Local inhabitants would of course be familiar with these streets, but in the late eighteenth century and early nineteenth information about shopping streets was increasingly widely available. Initially this might have taken the form of urban maps and prospects, and then towards the end of the eighteenth century trade directories providing addresses for the principal retailers in many provincial towns, and in some cases for a much wider range of traders (Mitchell, 2014, pp. 38–39).

The nature of some of this information suggests that shopping streets were being perceived, alongside public buildings, as tourist attractions. This was not only true of Britain. Eighteenth century travellers' accounts of Paris almost invariably mentioned shops and described the most important shopping areas of the city. By the later eighteenth century, Parisian shops had acquired the status of tourist places and key shopping streets were described in guide books. Individual shops were also described giving travellers information about where to obtain the best luxury goods (Walsh, 2000; Coquery, 2011). In England, William West's *History of Warwickshire*, published in 1830, took the reader on a tour of Birmingham, tracing out six circuits each centred on the Royal Hotel at the top of Colmore Row. West pointed out shops as well as public buildings, and took the stroller inside many of them, emphasising the way in which Birmingham's status was based on commerce and industry. New Street's 'well stocked shops, in articles of taste, of luxury, and of general consumption' were singled out for particular attention (Stobart et al., 2007, p. 103). Chester's principal streets were illustrated by George Batenham in the 1810s. Shops, both fashionable ones with bow windows and more traditional ones with simple boards, are depicted, but the one street surprisingly ignored by Batenham was the south side of Eastgate Street and its row which was where the city's best shops were located (Batenham, 1816).

The appearance of individual shops was also changing in this period. The shop front was very important as it needed to lure passers-by off the street and into the shop. Glass was probably being used by London's most fashionable retailers from about the mid-seventeenth century onwards, but open fronts could still be found in the early eighteenth century. By 1750, Cheapside was lined by shops with glass windows, modest frames and hanging signs. The latter were replaced in the 1760s by fascias with the shopkeeper's name and some indication of his or her business on them. Bow fronts were generally popular as they made displays more conspicuous and admitted more light. Their size might, however, be limited as in Bath to minimise obstructions on the pavement. Plate glass was available from the late eighteenth century but was very expensive while Argand lamps improved illumination inside shops. Bow fronts remained common until the mid-nineteenth century when sheet glass made large panes in shopfronts possible, thus enhancing window displays (Morrison, 2003, pp. 41–47). Going inside the shop, the potential customer might be confronted by a counter, drawers and possibly some glazed display cabinets. He or she might be able to wander through a series of showrooms. Chairs, tables and looking glasses created a congenial setting and gave an impression of politeness and reliability. Some customers might penetrate the more intimate areas of the shop to be entertained by the shopkeeper, and perhaps be offered advice about fashion or the latest novelties (Hann and Stobart, 2005).

Yet it would be misleading to suggest that the high street of the eighteenth century and early nineteenth was all about fashion and politeness. It was very often contested space. Shopping streets were still often close to the traditional market place with its dirt, noise and smells, especially if there was a fish market as part of it. The market place might also be an area where traditional pastimes continued to take place and where people who did not form part of polite society gathered. Bull-baiting and performing bears could be found in the heart of provincial towns well into the nineteenth century, including "polite" locations like Chester. Street traders and hawkers could be a disruptive influence impacting on the respectability of shopping streets (Stobart et al., 2007, pp. 105–109). Nor was the much desired regularity of the streetscape necessarily achieved in practice. The Batenham etchings of Chester streets reveal a row of butchers' stalls in Bridge Street directly below some the city's most fashionable shops. In Northgate Street a row of respectable looking glazed shops, including gunsmith, linen draper and grocer terminates in an old-fashioned open-fronted butcher's business (Batenham, 1816). Chester was unusual because of its rows: covered passageways with shops at the rear running above the street level shops. Row level shops were generally more prestigious than those at street level. Those shopping there were certainly protected from the filth of the street; but the rows must have been relatively dark before the advent of modern street lighting and window shopping may have been quite difficult (Figure 8.1).

Paris and London were undoubtedly the leading retail centres in Europe in this period. Paris, in particular, had a reputation for the very best luxury shops. The *Rue St Honoré* and its

Figure 8.1 Northgate Street, Chester, c.1810

Source: T. Hughes, *Ancient Chester: A Series of Illustrations of This Old City*, London, 1880.

environs emerged in the eighteenth century as the principal area for retailing silks, fine furnishings and fashionable dress. Some Parisian mercers stocked English goods and shop design was similar to that of the best London shops (Sargentson, 1996). Not all Paris shopping streets were elegant: many were narrow, muddy, smelly and lacked pavements. Arcades and bazaars, providing offstreet shopping, were important in the first half of the nineteenth century (Gillet, 2014). There was gradual change in the Low Countries. In Antwerp, shopping for pleasure was not unknown but was not on the same scale as in Paris or London, while daily necessities were increasingly bought from shops rather than markets (van Damme and Van Aert, 2014). Brussels was becoming a significant shopping centre in the second quarter of the nineteenth century, with the best streets for consumer goods being those around the *Grand Place*; as in Paris arcades were important (Arnout, 2014). Amsterdam also saw the emergence of a central shopping hub during the eighteenth century with Nieuwendijk as the most important shopping street while luxury goods, fashion items, art objects and booths were found in Warmoesstraat, Kalverstraat and Dam Square. Shops selling comparison goods dominated the main arterial routes into the city. Shops were getting larger and displaying goods more effectively, but in 1800 still did not really bear comparison with the best London shops (Lesger, 2011, 2014). The economy of The Hague was based on consumption rather than production and its central thoroughfares were well-established as the places to shop and to be seen by the mid-eighteenth century (Furnée, 2014). Germany tended to lag behind other Western European countries, with markets and fairs remaining more important and shopping streets relatively undeveloped until well into the nineteenth century (Homburg, 2014).

By 1850 there were recognisable high streets in towns and cities throughout Western Europe. They were places where a wide range of goods could be bought, ranging from items for everyday consumption, through more specialised foods found, for example in Italian warehouses in England, to a growing range of consumer and household goods and to imported luxuries like high-quality textiles. Most shops were small, though large emporia, warehouses for shoes and clothing and even shops divided into several departments were becoming increasingly common in the first half of the nineteenth century. The high street was also a place to be seen, to socialise and to enjoy shopping, or window shopping, as a leisure pursuit. High street shops continued to face competition from markets, and the building of large market halls from the 1820s onwards probably intensified this, not only for basic consumables but also for a growing range of consumer goods. There was also continued competition from street traders and, in some places, from more novel forms of retail outlets such as covered arcades and bazaars. Two key components of the classic high street, the department store and the multiple store, were yet to make their appearance.

The classic high street/main street 1850–1970

High street (with or without capital letters) was rarely a single street, but more often a cluster of shopping streets in the centre of a town or city and still in the late nineteenth century frequently near the market place. For example in the medium sized English industrial town of Chesterfield, the area around the traditional open market was home in the 1890s to grocers, drapers, clothes sellers, shoemakers, ironmongers, glass and china dealers, jewellers and watchmakers among other retailers. The local co-operative society was also present, as were two of the early multiple stores: the Singer Sewing Machine Company, whose first shop had been in Glasgow in 1856, and Boots the Chemists. A branch of Liptons, the grocers and provision dealers, opened soon afterwards. There was nothing special about Chesterfield and similar retail provision could be found in many other places. Nor was the high street confined to urban areas. The small

Derbyshire mining village of Stonebroom, where prior to 1860 there were only a handful of houses, boasted over twenty shops along its high street in 1893. These included three grocers, a confectioner, a fishmonger, two shoe dealers, two drapers, an ironmonger, a chemist, and a glass and china dealer (Kelly, 1893). In Stornaway on the Isle of Lewis, the Woolworths store which opened in the town's high the street (The Narrows) in 1935 became the focal point for islanders' social and commercial life (Morrison, 2015, p. 96). The general high street was a standard feature of places large and small (Figure 8.2).

There was nothing static about the high street in Britain or elsewhere. Individual streets could undergo significant change, often in association with street improvements; and in some places the location of the central shopping area could move over time. The redevelopment of Deansgate in Manchester offers a good example of the former. By the late 1860s, the city authorities were determined to widen the street, which had long been one of the city's principal shopping streets but which had not really kept up with the times. Shopkeepers along Deansgate were, however, less than enthusiastic about the local authority's plans, particularly when they involved compulsory purchase and demolition of property. The owners of Kendal Milne, the city's leading drapery and home furnishing store, were strongly opposed to the widening of the street, but were eventually compelled to come to an agreement with the Council and accept a significant amount of compensation which was used to finance the building of a spacious and spectacular new store. Another property owner made a deal with the Council that enabled him to build an arcade. The Council's plans for modernisation prevailed and Manchester got the

Figure 8.2 High Street, Chesterfield, England

Source: Author's own photograph.

wide shopping street it needed; but with the reluctant acquiescence rather than whole-hearted support of some large retailers (Bertramsen, 2003). In Bradford, the Council's plans for street improvement also required the co-operation of one of the town's largest retailers: the draper and house furnisher Brown Muff. In this instance the shopkeepers were more enthusiastic. Brown Muff got a coveted island site for their new store and the town got its wider streets (Bradford Observer 29 April 1871). In Glasgow, Sauchiehall Street was developed as part of the city's westward expansion in the early nineteenth century and although originally mainly residential had become one of the city's finest and most prestigious shopping streets by the early twentieth century and home to several upmarket department stores (Jones, 2010). Probably the most grandiose street improvement scheme in Europe was, of course, Haussmann's bulldozing of old Paris and replacing narrow streets with wide boulevards. These became the stage set for fashionable Parisian department stores (Trentmann, 2016; Miller, 1981).

Large glazed windows and internal illumination made high street shops a real spectacle in the second half of the nineteenth century. Particularly around Christmas time, newspapers were frequently ecstatic in their descriptions of shop window displays. The high street would have been a crowded, noisy and at times a slightly dangerous place. The outward appearance of shops continued to change. In England, there were some cast iron shopfronts in the mid-nineteenth century, for example in South King Street, Manchester. There was also a fashion for lettering advertising the business to spread all over the shop front. In the early twentieth century entrance lobbies were favoured because they increased the display area; and in some cases shop entrances were set back from the building line and the intervening space occupied by showcases. After World War I, there was a reaction against some of the more elaborate styles with retailers favouring cleaner lines, geometric shapes and minimal decoration (Morrison, 2003, pp. 51–59). The art deco style Woolworth's in Dumbarton typified the updating of traditional high streets, although such striking modern storefronts did not necessarily blend in with neighbouring historic buildings (Morrison, 2015, p. 100). More recently there has been a loss of individuality, particularly as multiple stores have used shopfronts to project a corporate image, leading to the accusation that high streets appear simply to be cloned.

Although it has generally been true that there has been much continuity, often over several centuries, with regard to the location of the high street, there have been exceptions to this. The West End continued to be London's principal fashionable shopping area, but the later nineteenth century saw the emergence of other areas such as Kensington and Bayswater as well as the proliferation of high streets in London suburbs (Adburgham, 1981). It was hard in some towns to decide which the best locations were, and in a sense therefore where the high street was, particularly if these did not seem fixed. For example, in Hanley, one of the constituent towns of Stoke-on-Trent, the area around the Market Square was the centre of its shopping district in the second half of the nineteenth century; by the 1930s this had become the northern boundary of the central shopping area with Piccadilly and Parliament Row further south becoming more significant. Recently, there has been a shift back to the Market Square area. One result of this was that the town's department stores became locked into the area near the Market Square and effectively formed the north-western boundary of the central shopping district (Stobart, 2001). Derby's central shopping area has been moving southwards for at least the last century and a half and is now over half a kilometre south of its earliest location at the northern tip of the town centre around Iron Gate and Sadler Gate. This southward drift was completed in the twenty-first century with the opening of a large shopping mall at the southern end of St Peter's Street.

Two northern industrial English cities illustrate different ways in which the high street developed in the second half of the nineteenth century. In Leeds, the traditional principal shopping area around Boar Lane, Briggate and Vicar Lane was transformed between 1870 and 1914 from a slightly old-fashioned, and in places slightly unsavoury, district into one of the most fashionable shopping locations in provincial England. This was achieved thanks both to a fairly pro-active local authority prepared to initiate and invest in street improvements and in a reconstructed and grandiose market hall; and to the availability of potential additional retail space in the heart of the city. In the last quarter of the nineteenth century ancient courtyards behind Briggate were transformed into shopping arcades populated by relatively small but fashionable shops. These arcades, coupled with Kirkgate market hall may to some extent have fulfilled a similar role to that of the earlier department stores in allowing shoppers to search for and buy a wide range of goods in an enclosed space. The city was not at the forefront of those places in which large department stores were beginning to emerge in the late nineteenth century, although it was well supplied with such stores a little later in the twentieth century. By 1909 Leeds' retailers were happy to promote their city as 'the shopping centre of the north' (Burt and Grady, 1992; Grady, 1980).

Sheffield, just under 50 kilometres to the south of Leeds, had a less clearly defined shopping centre in the late nineteenth century and early twentieth. There were some large and fashionable shops, but these could still be in close proximity to small workshops where metal working and cutlery manufacture were being carried on. This meant that there was a relatively high proportion of non-retail businesses in the central area. On the other hand, the city had at least three substantial early department stores – or at least large stores on their way to becoming department stores: Cockaynes established in 1829; Walsh's founded in 1875 by John Walsh, a former Cockayne's buyer and who built a spectacular new store in the 1890s with cast iron columns and huge plate glass windows; and Coles located on a corner site which became a favourite meeting place for Sheffield's inhabitants. These three stores, located quite close to each other, became the anchor point for the city's central shopping area in the early twentieth century and essentially defined that area. In Sheffield, large independent retailers rather that the local authority were the driving force in shaping the character of the central shopping area (Hey, 2010; Dallman, 2002).

Transport links were important in the shaping and reshaping of the high street. The coming of the railways enabled consumers to travel further and possibly to patronise larger centres at the expense of smaller ones. In the second half of the nineteenth century Chambers of Trade, largely composed of shopkeepers, lobbied railway companies for cheap fares from outlying villages and smaller towns to the towns where they were located. Municipal tramways were also significant in enabling many more people to travel cheaply into the centre of town. The Bradford Chamber of Trade was in constant contact with the town's Transport Department to ensure that shopkeepers were not disadvantaged by changes to the tram network. In 1903 it protested strongly against the withdrawal of the tram service from Heaton and Saltaire to Rawson Square because of the impact on retailers in many of the main shopping streets in the town. The service appears not to have been re-instated even though the Chamber of Trade presented a petition with 3,000 signatures (Bradford, 1903).

In many other parts of Europe and the wider world, high street/main street consolidated its position as the key urban shopping area in the period after 1850. There were of course significant national differences. The wide boulevards of Paris lined with department stores and fashionable boutiques were not really replicated elsewhere. Department stores certainly represented a challenge to more traditional shops, but to the extent that they stimulated consumer demand they may have benefitted those smaller shops that were prepared to adapt in the face of competition. Thus a high street with a mixture of shop types became the norm. This seems to have been true in Besançon in France (Gillet, 2014). In Brussels, the north-south axis became more important after about 1850 with Rue Neuve emerging as the main fashionable shopping street.

Arcades were important and successful; attempts to decentralise markets into purpose-built market halls less so (Arnout, 2014). New shopping streets were laid out in The Hague in the second half of the nineteenth century, with pavements and with more impressive shop architecture. By the end of the century the principal shopping streets were the place to be seen with the daily afternoon promenade a key feature (Furnée, 2014). Display windows were important in German shopping streets from the middle of the century, permitting window shopping but also separating the buyer from the merchandise and perhaps creating an air of mystery about the products (Spiekermann, 2000).

Market and street traders continued to compete with shop retailers in most countries and in some cases this had an impact on the nature of the high street. For example, in mid-nineteenth century Denmark, markets were favoured as the hub of urban food provisioning. This did not suit the growing number of upmarket shopkeepers who were concerned about the plebeian atmosphere of markets located close to the gradually emerging fashionable shopping streets. Shopkeepers prevailed in this case and markets were relocated to outlying districts allowing the high street to become a polite space (Toftgaard, 2016). In Barcelona, dispersed market halls remained the focus for much food shopping well into the twentieth century. Arterial routes out of the city were the main locations for high street shops; the most central thoroughfares had no food shops (Fava et al., 2016). Japan's retailing sector had long been dominated by itinerant traders, although the late nineteenth century saw an increase in fixed shops and the first department store was opened in 1904. The development of shopping streets was encouraged by the government in the Meiji period with Ginza Street in Tokyo laid out in the 1870s and soon becoming the most famous shopping street in the country (Hirano, 1999).

Main Street, USA

By the late nineteenth century, 'although not every [American] town had a skyscraper or an opera house, they all had a Main Street' (Isenberg, 2004, p. 7). For a period of a little less than one hundred years from the mid-nineteenth century, downtown was the dominant shopping area in cities and towns across the nation. Downtown was arguably a uniquely American phenomenon: the place to work, shop and do business; but not to live. This geographical separation of residential and business was taken further in the United States than in European cities where separation was achieved vertically: living above the shop. But main street was not just about shopping and commerce. It was also the embodiment of an urban and cultural ideal, the bastion of community-minded and small-scale enterprise. It was the beating heart of thousands of small towns, a place for interaction and negotiation of difference. Postcards depicting main street projected an image of a managed, simplified and beautified retail corridor. Reality did not always match up to the image A typical small town main street would include a grocery store, a clothing store, a drugstore, and a gasoline station. Almost all were small, independently owned stores with annual sales of under $12,000 by the 1920s. There could be a depressing sameness about small town main street, and buildings were often undistinguished (Esperdy, 2008; Isenberg, 2004).

In larger cities, downtown was generally a small area: about one-third of a square mile in late-nineteenth-century Boston. It was also noisy, dirty and very congested. It was said that women shoppers in Boston had to hold paper boxes above their heads to prevent them from being crushed. The location of main street was quite unstable in many cities. In New York, for example, the most fashionable area shifted from Broadway to Fifth Avenue in the late nineteenth century and early twentieth; in Seattle it moved northwards; in Philadelphia westwards. Nor did downtown grow much in size, at least horizontally (Figure 8.3). Instead it grew vertically with ever taller department stores of twenty stories or more. Although uncomfortable at times, this

Figure 8.3 Main Street, Buffalo, c.1905

Source: Author's own postcard.

highly concentrated business and retail area had advantages both for shoppers and businesses. Consumers could combine work and shopping in a single journey, could find all they wanted on main street and could compare quality and prices; shops benefitted because a shopper who intended to purchase from one or two shops would almost certainly browse or buy in several more simply because they were so close together (Fogelson, 2001).

The success of main street depended on good access, and the presence of department stores. Rapid mass transport, particularly steam and elevated railways, was essential. By 1890, there were 32,000 streetcars in America operating on 6,000 miles of line; Philadelphia alone had 277 miles of street railways, over five times as many miles per head as Paris. But there were limits as to how far surface transport could cope with increasing demand and from the late 1890s the emphasis was on building subways (Fogelson, 2001, pp. 45, 61–63). Department stores can be dated to the last third of the nineteenth century. In the 1860s, A.T. Stewart in New York created a new kind of shopping environment for the female market where it was possible to browse without buying and where shopping became a major source of urban leisure. Later in the century stores like Marshall Field's in Chicago were palaces of consumption offering a portal to luxury goods, services and amenities. Department stores were the anchors of main street and downtown; if a store moved, the central retail district tended to follow (Howard, 2015).

By the 1920s, there were signs that main street was in trouble. Several factors contributed to this. People were increasingly using cars rather than mass transit to reach downtown even though this added to traffic congestion and parking places were in short supply. Main street businesses responded by trying to persuade the authorities to make it easier to access downtown by car. But if it was easier to get in, it was also easier to get out and shop in peripheral districts (Fogelson, 2001). Chain stores, which were becoming increasingly dominant in American retailing, tended to prefer to locate in outlying districts; and some department stores, such as Marshall Field, were opening suburban branches. Retail trade was growing more quickly in the periphery than in the centre. Main street retailers were also perhaps partly to blame. Their focus was very much on female shoppers, particularly respectable middle class housewives who were responsible for much consumer spending. The Afro-American market was almost completely ignored. It was wrongly assumed that Afro-Americans were only interested in bargain basements and had little sense of style; they were generally expected to keep a low profile and use segregated facilities. At the end of the nineteenth century black-owned businesses were well integrated into downtown but over the following twenty or so years many were pushed to the fringe or to sites near black residential districts. Black main streets emerged such as Auburn Avenue in Atlanta (Isenberg, 2004). Even before the depression hit, between 10% and 15% of main street businesses failed each year, and between 30% and 60% of new main street businesses failed in their first year. The depression made matters worse: by 1933 the same number of stores as in 1929 competed for half as much business (Esperdy, 2008).

In the early 1930s main street shops often looked outdated, while empty business units blighted the whole area. But main street was not going to be allowed to die. Instead it would be given a makeover, and would be actively promoted. Starting from the assumption that first impressions were very important, the modernisation of main street focused on the storefront. In a 10-year period from the mid-1930s, $5 billion dollars was spent by financial institutions, property owners and retailers on store modernisation, most notably on new facades. As part of the New Deal, low-interest federally insured loans were made available; architects and builders were persuaded that their local main street offered profitable work; and retailers were told that the increased profits from modernisation meant that the work would soon pay for itself. The late nineteenth-century downtown district of Gainesville, Georgia was flattened by a tornado in 1936; 2 years later main street had been rebuilt with uniform building lines and harmonised facades and signage but without loss of storefront individuality. Westlaco in Texas was given a makeover in Spanish Mission style, but with modern glass storefronts. In Newark, the Star Electrical Supply Company modernised its turn of the century building by using wraparound light blue glazed terra-cotta for its facade and large sans serif letters for its advertising display. Modern materials such as structural glass, laminated plastic and enamelled steel were widely used and the new storefronts helped disseminate European modernist architecture in America (Esperdy, 2008).

There had been business associations to promote downtown since at least the 1920s in, for example, Buffalo, Detroit and Cleveland. These campaigned for improvements such as better lighting, cleaner streets and reduced congestion. By the 1930s there was growing concern about the need to counter the spectre of decentralisation. The Downtown Property Owners Association of Oakland aimed to stop the movement of retail trade to uptown Oakland. In June 1944. the Downtown Association of Milwaukee sponsored a Downtown Day, using the slogan 'Shop where you can supply all your needs' and encouraging shoppers to take in a restaurant and a show as well. But no amount of modernisation or promotion could buck the long-term trends towards decentralised shopping in outlying business districts. In the admittedly exceptionally decentralised Los Angeles, the downtown share of retail trade fell from 30% in 1929 to 11% in 1948 (Fogelson, 2001).

These trends continued after World War II. Although large retailers tried to remain loyal to downtown, retaining flagship stores on main street, branch stores increasingly showed bigger profits and smaller expenses than those in the centre. From the mid-1950s onwards, department stores in landmark downtown locations were being closed down. But even in the mid-1960s it was far from clear that in smaller towns the main street department store was on its way out. In 1963 towns of fewer than 10,000 people were served by 218 department stores and those of between 10,000 and 24,999 by 764 such stores (Howard, 2015, pp. 144–145). What was increasingly clear, however, was that the fate of main street rested with Afro-American shoppers, not white suburban women. Black shoppers were generous downtown spenders, but were still expected to keep a low profile and shop mainly in bargain basements or other low-end businesses (Isenberg, 2004). There may have been missed opportunities here. There was some renewed investment in the postwar years, but with Americans increasingly moving to the suburbs it was hardly surprising that retail sales were falling in many central business districts. Main street might hold memories; but it was no longer the place to shop except for budget items. The closure of old-established department stores, like G. Fox & Co. in Hartford, Connecticut in 1992, might have been mourned by former customers, but most were elderly (Fogelson, 2001, p. 1). Such stores no longer appealed to a younger generation.

In the early 1970s Cardiff in south Wales and Charlotte in North Carolina were cities of a similar size, around 300,000 population, and a similar retail catchment area. Both had substantial city centre retail areas, especially for comparison goods. By 1990, central Cardiff's gross retail area had increased, though with a shift from convenience retailing to non-food and variety stores; Charlotte's had shrunk dramatically and three major department stores had closed. There had been no attempt by local government in Charlotte to stop the shift out of town whereas in Cardiff the local authority had both opposed major out-of-town retail development and pedestrianised the main shopping area (Guy and Lord, 1993). Much has no doubt changed since, but public policy can have an impact on high street/main street. Even so, as car ownership grew and shoppers became more mobile it was increasingly likely that consumers would desert the main street of smaller towns in favour of big cities; or in due course in favour of out-of-town shopping. Main street might retain its glamour in New York, San Francisco and a handful of other major cities; but in small town America the independent department stores have gone and with them the kudos of main street (Howard, 2015). The rise of the mass discounters; the growth of regional shopping centres and of shopping malls; consumer preference for shopping out-of-town where parking is easier; and the growth of Internet shopping have all impacted on downtown and main street. One effect of this is that retail space as a whole (and not just the inside of shops) is increasingly privately owned and managed; there is consequential loss of space for free speech and free assembly (Cohen, 2004, pp. 277–278).

High street/main street in crisis 1970 to present day

Montague Burton opened his first shop in Chesterfield in 1904. Since then there has been a Burton's menswear shop in the centre of Chesterfield, as in many other towns and cities, until June 2016. Its art deco shop in the town's High Street now (2017) stands empty, the business having relocated to an out-of-town Tesco supermarket. Burtons was just one of the shops that would have been found in any self-respecting high street in Britain in the last three-quarters of the twentieth century. Also to be found there would probably have been at least one department store (more in large cities); several multiple stores specialising in menswear, women's clothing and household goods; and variety stores like Marks and Spencer, Boots and Woolworths. These big names attracted consumers to high street; but because they were the ones that could best afford high rents, they tended to push smaller independent stores to the periphery of the town. High streets lost their individual character and every town began to look the same (Stobart, 2008). But even the big chains were not immune from change. The fate of Burtons in Chesterfield is just one illustration of the crisis that many commentators perceive to have faced the high street in the last two decades or so. Is the British high street about to share the fate of small town American main street, or will it conform more closely to the European experience?

In a survey of the state of retailing in the European Union in the early twenty-first century, Stewart Howe argued that in the 1980s Britain was essentially alone in Europe in its 'virtual abandonment of any retail planning' (Howe, 2003, p. 206). While generalisations are dangerous given the wide variations in retailing across the European Union, there are arguably a number of reasons to suspect that the high street in continental Europe may be in a less parlous state than in the UK or US. First, and particularly in southern European countries like Spain, Italy and Greece, there is still a strong tradition of small, independent and often family businesses. Secondly, Britain has been unusual in Europe in that town centre redevelopment has often included a significant element of retailing, particularly in the form large shopping malls such as the Arndale Centre in Manchester or Highcross in Leicester. Branches of multiple and department stores which once dominated the high street are now located in such malls. In much of the rest of Europe, new retail developments have tended to be out-of-town. These clearly impact on city centre retailing, but arguably less so than urban malls. Thirdly, government in many European Union countries, including France and Germany, has been more pro-active in trying to prevent socially adverse retail development and in protecting smaller shops. In France, government policy may even have been partially responsible for the revival of city centre department stores. The European high street faces the same challenges from out-of-town centres and the Internet but is likely to be more resilient than American main street was, or the British high street appeared to be in the last few decades (Howe, 2003; Walker, 1996).

The scale of the problem in the UK was apparent from market research conducted in the mid-1990s. This identified an over-supply of poor quality town centre retail space while the demand for out-of-town space was high and growing. Shoppers were attracted to out-of-town retail parks because of their convenience; and to city centres because of the wide choice of shops. High streets in small towns had little to offer and their customer base was essentially older and poorer people (Mintel, 1995). Matters were even worse by the time Mary Portas was asked in 2011 by the British Prime Minister to conduct an independent review into the state of the high street. Her findings were bleak: town centre vacancy rates had doubled over the previous 2 years and total consumer spend away from the high street was over 50%. She summarised her findings as follows: 'Although some high streets are thriving, most have a fight on their hands. Many are now sickly, others are on the critical list and some are now dead. We cannot and should not attempt to save every high street' (Portas, 2011).

Identifying the causes of the crisis in the high street was relatively straightforward. Some were to do with the relationship between local authorities, landlords and retailers; but most were to do with fundamental changes in consumer behaviour and the changing nature of the retail sector. Much of this mirrored the American experience. In particular, almost universal car ownership privileged out-of-town retail parks and shopping malls over town centre and high street shopping. There was easier parking and everything was on one site. High street pedestrianisation was perhaps a mixed blessing: good if you were young and active; less so if you were one of the older consumers with declining mobility who had remained loyal to the town centre but now had to park on the periphery and walk to the high street shops. Shopping outlets offering branded goods at discounted prices impacted on the high street: why shop at Marks and Spencer in town if you can buy the same goods at a motorway junction outlet with ample parking and many other shops to browse? Similarly, supermarket diversification into clothing and household goods had its effect: why journey into town for basic clothing if you can buy an equivalent item while doing the grocery shopping? Finally, the Internet is having a growing impact on traditional shopping. This may, however, affect malls, outlets and supermarkets as much as the high street. Indeed the high street, with its promise of individual attention and service, may be better faced to meet the challenge of the Internet than are some of the newer forms of retailing.

There are no easy answers. Portas offers a range of recommendations addressed to local authorities, community groups, property owners and retailers themselves. A slightly better understanding of retail history than some recent commentators have displayed might suggest the following. First, not every high street and every shop can be saved. There has always been considerable fluidity both in where the high street was located and which shops comprised it. Some changes cannot be resisted. Second, every town is different. There is no 'one size fits all' solution. It is important to be aware of the socio-economic nature of the town and of its retail history. It is not only that the promotion of artisan and craft shops which may work well in, say, a spa town will be less successful in an ex-steelmaking community; it is also that big cities have their own histories: Sheffield is not Leeds. Third, as Portas rightly recognises, the high street of the future will not simply be about shopping; it may also again be a place where people live and engage in a range of cultural and social activities. If this is right, the demise of the high street has been greatly exaggerated.

Conclusions

High street has been at the heart of European retailing for at least the last 500 years. It has never been static and has varied significantly over time and from nation to nation. But a central urban shopping area has been the essential place for shoppers to go since the Middle Ages until the last decade or so. Main street fulfilled the same purpose in the United States for a much shorter period but was hugely influential in the creation of a distinct American form of consumer culture. High street/main street is not dead, but is in an almost critical condition in many parts of the western world. There are some renewed signs of life and its demise would have some devastating consequences. Simply shifting where people shop is both inevitable and not that significant. But shifting the context within which people shop is important. High street/ main street has always been public space and contested space: people used it to do things the authorities disapproved of, but the populace enjoyed. The privatisation of retail space, typified by shopping malls and outlets, but also by shopping areas incorporating shopping streets like Liverpool 1, threatens this. High street matters, both as a shopping environment and as public space for public protest.

References

Adburgham, A. (1981), *Shops and shopping 1800–1914: Where, and in what manner the well-dressed Englishwoman bought her clothes* (London: Allen & Unwin).

Arnout, A. (2014), 'Something old, something borrowed, something new: The Brussels shopping townscape, 1830–1914', in J.H. Furnée and Clé Lesger (eds.) *The landscape of consumption: Shopping streets and cultures in Western Europe, 1600–1900* (Basingstoke: Palgrave Macmillan) 157–183.

Baer, W.C. (2007), 'Early retailing: London's shopping exchanges, 1550–1700', *Business History*, 49/1, pp. 29–51.

Batenham, G. (1816), *Panoramic delineations of the four principal streets of the city of Chester* (Chester: John Fletcher).

Bertramsen, H. (2003), 'Remoulding commercial space: Municipal improvements and the department store in Late-Victorian Manchester', in J. Benson and L. Ugolini (eds.) *A nation of shopkeepers: Five centuries of British retailing* (London: I.B. Tauris) 206–225.

Blondé, B., Stabel, P., Stobart, J. and van Damme, I. (eds.) (2006), *Buyers and sellers: Retail circuits and practices in medieval and early modern Europe* (Turnhout: Brepols).

Blondé, B. and van Damme, I. (2010), 'Retail growth and consumer changes in a declining urban economy: Antwerp (1650–1750)', *Economic History Review*, 63/3, pp. 638–663.

Borsay, P. (1989), *The English urban renaissance: Culture and society in the provincial town 1660–1770* (Oxford: Oxford University Press).

Bradford Chamber of Trade (1903), 'Minute Book 1903', Unpublished Manuscript, Bradford Chamber of Trade, West Yorkshire Archive Service, 56D85/1/1.

Bradford Street Improvements, *Bradford Observer* (1871), 29 April.

Burt, S. and Grady, K. (1992), *Kirkgate Market: An illustrated history* (Leeds: The Authors).

Cohen, L. (2004), *A consumers' republic: The politics of mass consumption in postwar America* (New York: Vintage).

Coquery, N. (2011), 'Promenade et shopping', in C. Lois and L. Turcot (eds.) *La Promenade au Tournaut des xviii et xix Siecles* (Bruxellres: Etudes sur le 18 siecle), 61–75.

Dallman, P. (2002), *The story of Sheffield's high street from the 16th century to modern times* (Sheffield: ALD).

Esperdy, G. (2008), *Modernizing main street: Architecture and consumer culture in the new deal* (Chicago/London: University of Chicago Press).

Fava, A., Guardia, M. and Oyon, J.L. (2016), 'Barcelona food retailing and public markets, 1876–1936', *Urban History*, 43/3, pp. 454–475.

Fogelson, R. (2001), *Downtown: Its rise and fall, 1880–1950* (New Haven, CT/London: Yale University Press).

Furnée, J.H. (2014), '"Our living museums of Nouveautés": Visual and social pleasures in Th Hague's shopping streets, 1650–1900', in J.H. Furnée and Clé Lesger (eds.) *The landscape of consumption: Shopping streets and cultures in Western Europe, 1600–1900* (Basingstoke: Palgrave Macmillan) 208–231.

Gillet, M. (2014), 'Innovation and tradition in the shopping landscape of Paris and a provincial city, 1800–1900', in J.H. Furnée and Clé Lesger (eds.) *The landscape of consumption: Shopping streets and cultures in Western Europe, 1600–1900* (Basingstoke: Palgrave Macmillan) 184–207.

Grady, K. (1980), 'Commercial, marketing and retailing amenities, 1700–1914', in D. Fraser (ed.) *A history of modern Leeds* (Manchester: Manchester University Press) 177–199.

Guy, C. and Lord, J. (1993), 'Transformation and the city centre', in R.D.F. Bromley and C.J. Thomas (eds.) *Retail change: Contemporary issues* (London: UCL Press) 88–108.

Hann, A. and Stobart, J. (2005), 'Sites of consumption: The display of goods in provincial shops in eighteenth-century England', *Cultural and Social History*, 2/2, pp. 165–187.

Hey, D. (2010), *A history of Sheffield* (Lancaster: Carnegie).

Hirano, T. (1999), 'Retailing in urban Japan, 1868–1945', *Urban History*, 26/3, pp. 373–392.

Homburg, H. (2014), 'German landscapes of consumption, 1750–1850: Perspectives of German and Foreign travellers', in J.H. Furnée and Clé Lesger (eds.) *The landscape of consumption: Shopping streets and cultures in Western Europe, 1600–1900* (Basingstoke: Palgrave Macmillan) 125–156.

Howard, V. (2015), *From Main Street to mall: The rise and fall of the American department store* (Philadelphia, PA: University of Pennsylvania Press).

Howe, S. (ed.) (2003), *Retailing in the European union: Structure, competition and performance* (London: Routledge).

Isenberg, A. (2004), *Downtown America: A history of the place and the people who made it* (Chicago: University of Chicago Press).

Jones, C. (2010), 'Sauchiehall Street,' Available at: www.glasgowhistory.com/sauchiehall-street.html.

Keene, D. (2006), 'Sites of desire: Shops, selds and wardrobes in London and other English cities, 1100–1550', in Blondé et al. (eds), *Buyers and sellers*, 125–153.

Kelly (1893), *Kelly's directory of Derbyshire* (London: Kelly and Co.).

Lesger, C. (2011), 'Patterns of retail location and urban form in Amsterdam in the mid-eighteenth century', *Urban History*, 38/1, pp. 24–47.

Lesger, C. (2014), 'Urban planning, urban improvement and the retail landscape in Amsterdam, 1600–1850', in J.H. Furnée and Clé Lesger (eds.) *The landscape of consumption: Shopping streets and cultures in Western Europe, 1600–1900* (Basingstoke: Palgrave Macmillan) 104–124.

Miller, M. (1981), *The Bon Marché: Bourgeois culture and the department store, 1869–1920* (London: Allen & Unwin).

Mintel Marketing Intelligence (1995), *Survival of the High Street* (London: Mintel International Group Ltd.).

Mitchell, I. (2014), *Tradition and innovation in English retailing, 1700–1850: Narratives of consumption* (Farnham: Ashgate).

Morris, C. (ed.) (1984), *Illustrated journeys of Celia Fiennes* (London: Macdonald & Co.).

Morrison, K. (2003), *English shops and shopping: An architectural history* (New Haven, CT/London: Yale University Press).

Morrison, K. (2015), *Woolworth's: 100 years on the high street* (Swindon: Historic England).

Nevola, F. (2006), '"Piu honorati et suntuosi ala Republica": Botteghe and luxury retail along Siena's Strada Romana', in Blondé et al., *Buyers and Sellers*.

Peck, L. (2005), *Consuming splendour: Society and culture in seventeenth-century England* (Cambridge: Cambridge University Press).
Portas, M. (2011), *The Portas review*, Available at: www.gov.uk/government/publications/the-portas-review-the-future-of-our-high-streets.
Sargentson, C. (1996), *Merchants and luxury markets: The marchands merciers of eighteenth-century Paris* (London: V and A Museum).
Spiekermann, U. (2000), 'Display windows and window display in German cities of the nineteenth century: Towards the history of a commercial breakthrough', in C. Wischermann and E. Shore (eds.) *Advertising and the European city: Historical perspectives* (Aldershot: Ashgate) 139–171.
Stobart, J. (2001), 'City centre retailing in the late nineteenth- and early twentieth-century Stoke-on-Trent: Structures and processes', in J. Benson and L. Ugolini (eds.) *A nation of shopkeepers: Five centuries of British retailing* (London: I.B. Tauris) 155–178.
Stobart, J. (2008), *Spend, spend, spend: A history of shopping* (Stroud: Tempus).
Stobart, J., Hann, A. and Morgan, V. (2007), *Spaces of consumption: Leisure and shopping in the English town, c. 1680–1830* (London: Routledge).
Toftgaard, J. (2016), 'Marketplaces and central spaces: Markets and the rise of competing spatial ideals in Danish city centres, c. 1850–1900', *Urban History*, 43/3, pp. 372–390.
Trentmann, F. (2016), *Empire of things: How we became a world of consumers, from the fifteenth century to the twenty-first* (London: Allen Lane).
van Damme, I. and van Aert, L. (2014), 'Antwerp goes shopping! Continuity and change in retail space and shopping interactions from the sixteenth to the nineteenth century', in J.H. Furnée and Clé Lesger (eds.) *The landscape of consumption: Shopping streets and cultures in Western Europe, 1600–1900* (Basingstoke: Palgrave Macmillan) 78–103.
Walker, G. (1996), 'Retailing development: In town or out of town', in C. Greed (ed.) *Investigating town planning: Changing perspectives and agenda* (Harlow: Addison Wesley Longman) 155–180.
Walsh, C. (2000), 'Shopping et Tourisme: L'Attrait des Boutiques Parisiennes au xviii Siecle', in N. Coquery et al. (eds), *La Boutique et la Ville* (Tours: Université François Rabelais) 223–237.
Walsh, C. (2014), 'Stalls, bulks, shops and long-term change in seventeenth- and eighteenth-century England', in J.H. Furnée and Clé Lesger (eds.) *The landscape of consumption: Shopping streets and cultures in Western Europe, 1600–1900* (Basingstoke: Palgrave Macmillan) 37–56.
Welch, E. (2005), *Shopping in the Renaissance: Consumer cultures in Italy 1400–1600* (New Haven, CT/London: Yale University Press).

9
HISTORY OF THE DEPARTMENT STORE

Sarah Elvins

In the mid to late nineteenth century, department stores in Europe and North America assumed a cultural prominence that was dazzling to observers at the time and has tantalised scholars of retailing in the years since. These "cathedrals of consumption" enticed shoppers in London and Paris and inspired Emile Zola to set a novel in the exotic and dreamlike space of the department store. In Manhattan, Henry James saw with alarm the new "towers of glass" of stores that dwarfed other structures in the city (Leach, 1993, p. 39). In large and small centres, they came to dominate downtown spaces, and culturally and economically took on positions of prominence. Despite the sense of some observers that these new forms of retailing had sprung up like gleaming mushrooms overnight, as Claire Walsh (1999) has noted, department stores had roots that stretched back to the eighteenth century (p. 46). While the subjects of some popular histories vie for the status of "first department store", it is impossible to name a single year or a single institution as the definitive start of this new form of merchandising. Instead, it is more useful to see department stores as evolving from a few lines of previous retail business: dry goods merchants and general merchants. These businesses expanded, often in piecemeal fashion, into what we now would recognise as a department store. This transition did not occur immediately, and even observers at the time did not always fully comprehend the innovative nature of these changes. The term "department store" itself was not in wide usage until the 1880s and 1890s, but the changes in retailing which it would eventually denote were spreading rapidly around the globe.

In England, pioneers like Harding, Howell & Co., located in St. James's in London, catered to fashionable women by offering not only the traditional line of millinery but furs, fans, perfumes, haberdashery, jewellery and clocks all in one large house. Ackerman's *Repository* (1809) described the store in 1809 as so extensive that 'there is no article of female attire or decoration, but what may be here procured in the first style of elegance and fashion'. The store stocked a dizzying array of items from every manufacturing town "in the kingdom" and across Europe. Paris became home to the *grands magasins*, most famously the Bon Marché, which opened in 1852 and expanded greatly over subsequent decades. France's reputation as an international fashion capital was borne out in the glittering merchandise cases and window displays where shoppers could peruse the latest clothing and accessories. In New York, A.T. Stewart expanded a small dry goods emporium by adding new lines of merchandise like carpets, furniture, draperies and other home accessories (Howard, 2015, p. 13). Stewart was also one of the first retailers in the world to erect a specially designed building of multiple levels to house his store (Resseguie, 1965, p. 304). Philadelphia's John Wanamaker established the Grand Depot at the abandoned freight depot of the Pennsylvania Railroad and added specialised lines including the first toy department in 1880.

The many "departments" of these retailers were thus one feature which set them apart from other shops specialising in single lines of merchandise. Under one roof, customers could now view traditional dry goods including linens, notions and haberdashery. Macy's of New York enlarged existing lines of fancy goods and costume jewellery and eventually departed even further from the dry goods trade by offering house furnishings, kitchen utensils, baby carriages, woodenware, bird cages and a wide variety of other goods in over thirty departments by 1877 (Hower, 1967, p. 162). The store expanded into neighbouring buildings and rebuilt so that by 1880 it occupied the end of a city block on Sixth Avenue between 13th and 14th Streets, with a new iron face and an elaborate ventilation system to pump fresh air throughout the store (Hower, 1967, p. 167). John Wanamaker's Philadelphia "store of a thousand surprises" boasted stained-glass skylights and gas chandeliers, and over 1,400 stools positioned in front of the sales counters for the convenience of tired shoppers (Hendrickson, 1979, p. 78). When Wanamaker opened a new store in 1911, it was palatial in size, with twelve floors above ground plus a basement and subbasement. Timothy Eaton's in Toronto called itself "Canada's Greatest Store", and by 1897 had over 326,000 square feet of retail space, selling everything from groceries to furniture. In Mexico City, when Centro Mercantil held its opening celebration in 1899, visitors marvelled over the sheer size of the store, with four stories of glass and colour stretching more than a city block (Bunker, 2012, p. 88). Even in smaller communities, department stores often dwarfed the competition, taking up entire city blocks and offering an array of goods not seen in small shops or country stores (Whitaker, 2006, p. 78).

Beyond the multiplying departments of goods, these retailers were distinguished by new merchandising policies. Their adoption of set pricing and rapid stock turn revolutionised business practices. By the middle of the nineteenth century, it is thought that major American retailers including Lord & Taylor, A.T. Stewart and Macy's had adopted the one-price policy (Hower, 1967, p. 94). Customers did not have to haggle with the proprietor to ensure that they got the best deal on an item; now all patrons would be charged the same price, whether rich or poor, friend or stranger. For proprietors of large-scale stores, set pricing was necessary, as individual clerks could not be allowed to make final decisions about the price of individual items. For consumers, the ability to freely enter a store, inspect the merchandise and easily learn its price without interference before making a decision was liberating. Related to the one-price policy was the new willingness of stores to accept the return of any merchandise which consumers declared unsatisfactory. Finally, purchases were facilitated by new credit opportunities. Some stores were unwilling to forgo their cash only policies: at Eaton's in Toronto, customers could place charges against a deposit account where they would contribute cash balances prior to shopping. The deposit account system at Macy's paid interest of 4% with an annual Christmas bonus of 2% on net purchases for the year (Santink, 1990, p. 225). Eventually these deposit accounts evolved into the practice of dry goods houses offering "charge privileges" to their best customers; credit was expanded to middle-class people so that by the early twentieth century customers were able to open charge accounts in every large retailer in New York (Leach, 1993, p. 124). In France, Georges Dufayel helped to normalise instalment buying, allowing customers to put 20% of the standard purchase price down for household goods, with the rest to be paid in weekly instalments (Williams, 1982, p. 93). Easier access to credit encouraged people to buy more, and to buy more often. Charge accounts further encouraged patron's loyalty to one store over another. For working and middle-class patrons, it allowed dreams to become reality and aspirations of wealth and luxury to be expressed through consumption.

Over time, the business practices of the stores became more and more standardised, with larger retailers taking on new roles not only in distribution but in manufacturing and wholesaling. The Bon Marché in Paris drew on a network of small workshops and artisans to acquire lingerie, shirts and ready-to-wear items (Miller, 1981, p. 57). Eaton's built factories as it expanded, so that by 1910 it was both producing and selling much of the consumer goods sold in Western Canada (Belisle, 2011, p. 30). More commonly, stores entered into agreements with wholesalers and manufacturers, sometimes striking exclusive deals with large orders which allowed them to dictate costs and furnish their own "private label" store lines in clothing, notions and fancy goods. Managers carefully monitored stock and held periodic clearance sales to get rid of overstocked items. Eventually these clearance sales would come to mark the yearly retail calendar, so shoppers would expect white sales of linens in January and the discounting of seasonal merchandise at other times of the year. Filene's of Boston moved unsold goods to its famous bargain basement, where tables piled high with discounted goods enticed shoppers and freed up the upper selling floors for new, full-priced merchandise. Advertising in local newspapers became a major way for retailers to tell consumers about new items. R.H. Macy of New York experimented with the layout of his newspaper ads, using white space and patterns to catch the eye (Hower, 1967, p. 57). Department store advertising became a major source of revenue for urban newspapers. Stores routinely purchased full pages of ad space, touting the arrival of new lines, announcing upcoming sales and occasionally including personal messages to the community from the store's owner.

The department store's large display windows were also a vital part of its advertising strategy. The fanciful displays behind plate glass became a draw for shoppers and spectators passing by, transforming the visual iconography of the city (Figure 9.1).

The store became an exciting new architectural form in downtown areas. Louis Sullivan's design for the Schlesinger and Mayer store in Chicago (later Carson Pirie Scott) reduced the walls of the structure to a bare skeleton of glass and steel, bringing light into the interior and maximising the size of the windows. Schlesinger and Mayer directly linked their windows to other promotional efforts, using the distinct ornamental motifs surrounding the show windows on State Street in their print advertising (Siry, 1988, p. 133). Initially some stores drew curtains in front of the displays on Sundays to prevent passers-by from being tempted by material goods on the Sabbath, but that practice largely was discontinued by the early twentieth century (although Marshall Field's famously carried on this practice well into the 1930s). Window dressers competed for the attention of passers-by with elaborate geometric displays of handkerchiefs and toiletries, often in white or a single colour. Crowds gathered to examine merchandise artfully presented on mannequins with coordinated backgrounds and dramatic lighting. At Christmas, snow-filled scenes of villages and children playing drew crowds to bask in the light of the display window (Figure 9.2).

L. Frank Baum, author of *The Wizard of Oz*, used his creative talents initially to design fanciful "illusion windows" for dry goods stores, and edited a trade publication for window dressers. William Leach (1993) argues that the windows allowed shoppers to gaze upon goods without smelling or touching them, enticing viewers and highlighting the refinement of department stores in contrast with open-air markets or immigrant bazaars (p. 62).

The atmosphere within the store was carefully cultivated to please the eye and encourage crowds to give in to the temptations of goods. Paris's Bon Marché was a stunning spectacle of light and colour, with high ceilings and walls festooned with ribbons, Oriental rugs and fine fabrics. Small items like cosmetics and jewellery were carefully arrayed in mirrored and lighted cases. Larger items might be given space in a model showroom, like the ones in Gimbel Brothers of New York, where customers could see how furniture would look in a sample

Figure 9.1 Wanamaker's department store bridal window display, John Wanamaker Collection, Historical Society of Pennsylvania

home, complete with draperies, lighting and rugs. Wanamaker's "House Palatial" was an actual two-story home in the store's rotunda. Exotic décor, from "Arabian Nights"-themed displays to Japanese gardens and Parisian street scenes, could help to transport crowds to far-off lands and turn mundane items like notions or shirtwaists into tickets to another world. Instead of the humble country store that dominated country life during the eighteenth century, the department store became synonymous with urbanity and sophistication. In not only large centres like Paris, London and New York, but smaller cities and towns across Europe and North America, department stores signified a connection to larger national and international trends in fashion, style and manners. The crowds who bustled through the doors of the department store were drawn by the beautiful surroundings, the many departments of merchandise, and the promise of a glimpse of something more exotic and exciting – the fulfilment of needs that shoppers might not even have identified yet.

In the services it provided, as well, the department store bore striking differences from other contemporary merchants. From the moment patrons entered the store, they could entertain the fantasy of being waited on by willing servants. For middle-class consumers, the level of service offered in department stores was a swift departure from the typical interaction with the clerks of a general store or small merchant. Uniformed doormen welcomed customers at the entrances, and in some cases young men were available to whisk one's carriage (and later motorcar) away to a nearby parking area. A fleet of female clerks showed merchandise to the consumer, bringing pairs of gloves or stockings out from behind glass cases for customers to peruse. In departments

Figure 9.2 Wanamaker's New York store rotunda interior with Christmas decor, John Wanamaker Collection, Historical Society of Pennsylvania

like women's clothing, customers could enjoy personal attention and advice from shop girls, who accompanied them into the changing room and helped to select garments to try. Elaborate pneumatic tube systems that twisted through the different levels of the stores like arteries whisked cash and receipts from the departments to unseen central offices. Customers could arrange the delivery of the items that they purchased, and check parcels and coats so that they could more comfortably amble through the store aisles.

The selling floors were the main attraction for shoppers, but the other services provided by department stores added to the sense of indulgence and escape. Luxurious facilities – from powder rooms where female shoppers could rest and recuperate, to writing desks and light-filled atriums – encouraged shoppers to linger within the store. Medical clinics, public library branches and post offices allowed shoppers to combine browsing for goods with other errands.

Restaurants added another dimension to the experience, and could become a destination of their own for groups of women to meet and socialise. Tea rooms acted as a sort of feminine counterpart to male urban spaces like the saloon or men's club. Their tasteful décor and menu of refined dishes hid the fact that they were designed to serve large numbers of patrons as efficiently as possible. Marshall Field's elegant tea room was expanded to fill the entire seventh floor of the store by 1902, serving 2,000 people a day on linen tablecloths and fine silver (Satterthwaite, 2001, p. 43). One of the Siegel stores in Manhattan, Simpson, Crawford, and Simpson, created a dining room that was intended to compare with exclusive metropolitan restaurants. Louis Sullivan designed a French café in the Schlesinger and Mayer store in Chicago with elaborate ornamental designs (Siry, 1988, p. 217). These amenities added to the sense that the store was a world apart, a place of indulgence and relaxation where customers could meet for a meal to socialise, before ambling through the selling floors together.

Stores were also sites of theatre, sometimes in a literal sense. Shoppers paraded themselves in their finery, and shop girls applied cosmetics with the skill of thespians taking the stage. Product demonstrations might feature a woman on a stage showing just how to use a new feature of a sewing machine. Store aisles were often the first in the community to be illuminated with new technologies like electric lights. Beyond the spectacle of shopping, the department stores hosted performances for the local community. Most stores featured auditoriums for a variety of performances – in the early twentieth century, live music in the form of piano recitals, string quartets, and choral performances were regular features on the store's calendar. In Philadelphia, Wanamaker's Grand Court was the site of a live performance of the Philadelphia Orchestra, in front of an audience of 15,000 people (Whitaker, 2006, p. 134).

The Wanamaker great organ was built for the Louisiana Purchase Exposition, and purchased by the store in 1911. It became a store tradition to have daily organ concerts at 10:00 a.m., noon, and 5:30 p.m. (Hendrickson, 1979, p. 79). The A. Hamburger store in Los Angeles boasted a 1,000 seat auditorium. Stores in smaller centres acted as cultural arbiters, bringing the latest fashions, trends and educational exhibits to the community. In 1929, Wolf & Dessauer department store in Fort Wayne, Indiana, held a modern art exhibit in their auditorium, complete with a lecture on modernism by the director of a local art school. The store's advertising manager boasted of a window display featuring modern objects, and tie-ins to merchandise like furniture, draperies, fabrics, rugs and lamps that were 'exquisite in line – scorning all unnecessary ornamentation – beautifully proportioned' (*Dry Goods Merchants Trade Journal*, 1929, p. 31). Merchants offered opportunities to meet celebrities like film and sports stars, get autographs from authors, and hear recording artists. Rochester, New York, patrons had the chance to meet bandleader Guy Lombardo at Sibley, Lindsay & Curr's, while shoppers in nearby Buffalo bought copies of baseball player Walter Johnson's board game and shook his hand at Hengerer's Toyland (Elvins, 2004, p. 150).

The combination of large scale and new style proved irresistible to urban consumers. These new palaces of consumption transformed urban space in Europe and North America, and redrew the boundaries of commercial districts, encouraging members of the general public, particularly women, to venture in to the business district. Shopping became a tourist attraction of its own, with Chicago's Ladies' Mile, London's West End and New York's Fifth Avenue drawing consumers from surrounding suburbs and indeed around the world. Shopping became a leisure

Figure 9.3 Line drawing of the centre of Wanamaker's store, John Wanamaker Collection, Historical Society of Pennsylvania

pursuit in itself, as consumers derived pleasure from perusing sparkling displays and wandering the aisles of the store. Department store shopping was highly gendered. As Erika Rappaport (2000) describes, London's West End was filled with bustling crowds of "fashionable ladies", wealthy upper and middle class women who spent their time outside of their homes 'discussing, looking at, touching, buying, and rejecting commodities' (p. 5). The feminised space of the store and its respectability gave middle- and upper-class matrons a destination in the downtown that they had never enjoyed previously.

Where men could retreat to the saloon, club, or sporting venue, the department store now offered a public space for women to congregate without chaperones. The well-appointed tea rooms, lounge areas and communications centres facilitated meetings between women. Marshall Field's famous proclamation to his staff, "Give the lady what she wants", reflected not only his attention to customer satisfaction but his acknowledgement that women were his primary clientele. In London, Selfridge's rooftop restaurant was a favourite meeting place for the middle-class members of the suffragette group the Women's Social and Political Union. As the group became more militant, it held demonstrations in which women with hammers smashed shop windows along Oxford Street. Activists explained that shopkeepers should support the vote for women, their most important customers. Those who did not lobby the government to recognise the rights of women as full citizens, not merely consumers, would face punishment. Because Harry Selfridge supported female suffrage, his store was largely spared (Chapman, 2014, pp. 241, 244). After women in the United States were granted the franchise, campaigns to get out the vote organised by the League of Women Voters were carefully coordinated with local department stores, with information booths in prime selling spaces and messages about voting incorporated in newspaper ads and windows (Gidlow, 2004, p. 176).

The liberation enjoyed by women who could step out into urban spaces unchaperoned was tempered by the stereotype of the female shopper as easily seduced and lacking in self-control. Women's so-called "natural" role as consumers had a dark side: the medical diagnosis of kleptomania played on notions of women as irrational and at the mercy of their hormonal and emotional impulses (Abelson, 1989). Newspapers filled with stories of middle-class matrons caught stealing trifles like lipstick and stockings. Often these women could easily afford the items, and typically the store and the women's husbands would come to an agreement to settle the matter quietly without requiring the police to press charges. Clerks and store owners tried various strategies to cut down on shoplifting, including the hiring of store detectives who posed as shoppers and kept an eye out for suspicious behaviour; a more widespread consequence of the discussion of kleptomania was the reinforcement of the image of the store as an exotic space filled with temptations for irrational female shoppers. Even women who were not accused of shoplifting were portrayed in advertisements and contemporary cultural representations as being unable to resist the allure of the store, spending time and money that they did not possess because of the pull of shiny displays and fascinating new fashions.

The initial success of the department store was often credited to its ability to cater to the masses. Indeed, members of the working class were able to freely enter stores, and some merchants consciously cultivated a clientele that skewed lower, by emphasising low prices and high stock turnover. Newly arrived immigrants to east coast cities like Boston, New York and Philadelphia experienced the department store as a force of Americanisation, and observed the displays in shop windows and the piles of goods as a means of learning how to fit into their host society. But it would be a mistake to assume that class distinctions disappeared in the aisles of the store. In larger cities, there were often several department stores that catered to specific segments of the population, with elite stores that served the "carriage trade", big stores for the middle class, and bargain stores for the working class. The Fair, in Chicago, aimed to provide "Everything for Everybody", and welcomed a wide range of patrons, while Marshall Field's was known for pursuit of a more affluent and limited clientele. Paris's Grands Magasins Dufayel catered to workers in the northern Goutte d'Or neighbourhood of the city, introducing them to a vast range of merchandise and even providing an in-store cinema (Wemp, 2011). Some stores managed to divide the carriage trade from the shawl trade within the same store – by separating stock by price, merchants like Filene's could welcome upper-class matrons looking for designer gowns on the upper floor ushering working-class housewives to the bargain basement (Benson, 1988, p. 90).

Culturally, as the department store as a retailing type matured, it increasingly became identified with the middle class. Elite stores reached out to a wider clientele, and more popular-priced stores began to offer services more typical of upper-class stores. In Paris, the fashions and home décor of the department store helped to form a distinct bourgeois sensibility – the continually changing new styles of linens, fashions, and other marketable goods encouraged the sense for the middle classes that consumption was a modern means of self-expression and fulfilment. Notions of class were also highly racialised. Canada's Eaton's stores were slightly more downmarket, capturing urban bourgeois as well as working-class and rural consumers, but the store's advertising promoted a type of consumer citizenship based on a primarily white, middle-class vision of Canada. Indigenous and black customers faced condescension and poor treatment (Belisle, 2011, pp. 81, 105). In the United States, it is worth underscoring that the experience of department store shopping was a generally white phenomenon. Throughout the Southern US, black patrons were by either custom or law denied the levels of service enjoyed by white customers. Southern stores segregated black patrons in fitting areas and restrooms (Howard, 2015, p. 160). In both the north and south, black workers were routinely relegated to lower-paying jobs that did not involve their interaction with the public. For all of the rhetoric of department stores promoting "one price for all" and the democratisation of luxury, some groups of consumers remained outside of its imagined clientele.

The experience of shopping in the store helped to reinforce the sense of class distinction among white, middle-class patrons. Indeed, this was part of the store's appeal for many. Middle class women who by the early twentieth century might be less likely to be able to afford "help" around the household could revel in being pampered at the department store. Waited on while trying on dresses, coiffed in the salon, served tea and dainties on fine china in the tea salon and saluted by uniformed doormen, middle-class patrons were able to exert a new level of authority within the store. The customer experience, too, evolved into a very distinct set of practices, with its own rules and expectations. Instead of merchants dictating what goods their customers should buy, customers were permitted access to merchandise in ways that they had never experienced previously. They could touch, smell, try on and compare a range of items instead of being at the mercy of a clerk to select an item from behind a glass case or stockroom door. After World War I, stores became more concerned with acquiring stock that met consumer desires, rather than assuming that customers would eventually buy any items on display, as long as the price was right (Whitaker, 2006, p. 38).

For female employees, the store offered new possibilities and opportunities, in particular. Instead of the monotonous, cramped or dirty conditions facing those in sweated trades or textile mills, shop girls could enjoy the ambiance of the store and in some cases come to personify the glamour and fashionability of the institution. In the 1927 silent movie "IT", film star Clara Bow is able to showcase her vivacious personality while selling lingerie on the first floor of a large department store. Her position allows her to interact with members of the public as well as other shop girls. She and her co-workers happily gossip about customers and the attractive owner of the store, and in their hairstyles and use of cosmetics embody the freedom and sexual experimentation of the flapper. Women worked behind counters but also found some opportunities for advancement within the store ranks, with a tiny minority managing to advance to positions as head of stock, assistant buyer or full-fledged buyer in women's clothing and lingerie departments, where it was assumed that their intimate knowledge of female likes and dislikes would give them a competitive edge. Shop girls too experimented with the power relations involved in their interactions with customers. As Susan Porter Benson (1988) has ably demonstrated, managers came to recognise the central role of salespeople in shaping the experience of the customer, in both positive and negative ways (p. 115). A skillful clerk could guide customers and suggest certain items, cultivate personal relationships with clients and encourage their loyalty to the store; a rude or uncooperative clerk could lose sales and ruin a store's image.

Systems of employee paternalism rewarded those who saw themselves as part of the store family, while those who broke the rules faced sharp discipline. Employee newsletters, picnics, sporting clubs, and group outings encouraged sociability within departments. Store owners picked up on the rhetoric of family, describing themselves as proud fathers and suggesting that workers were part of a co-operative effort to serve the community and make the business a success. Perks for employees encouraged company loyalty. Filene's implemented profit-sharing and employee discount plans as early as 1903, and created a credit union which became a model for dozens of other department store credit unions in America (Hendrickson, 1979, p. 132). The veneer of paternalism attempted to gloss over divisions between employees and management. Workers might be thought of as family members, but if they pushed for more rights or more control over their working conditions, they could be quickly written off as disobedient and ungrateful children. In Britain, female shop assistants could be fined for a range of unbusinesslike behaviour, including gossiping, standing in groups, reading the newspaper, or failing to address a customer by the correct name. Stores were active in discouraging unionisation. In Canada, striking or joining a union were grounds for dismissal, and during the six-week Winnipeg General Strike of 1919, Eaton's threatened to close the store for a year if the strikers won. Afterwards, it fired workers who had participated in the strike (Belisle, 2011, pp. 188–189). Moreover, female workers in department stores found that their wages were consistently lower than for clerical workers and other branches of white-collar work. Despite the fact that store employment was a steady, year-round phenomenon, the pay received by workers did not reflect the fact that they were required to dress in a manner befitting their role as store representatives. Even an employee discount of 10% or 20% could not compensate for the requirement of dresses or other attire deemed sufficiently formal and respectable for interaction with the public.

Although consumers largely accepted department stores as appealing new additions to the retailing landscape, they were viewed with suspicion by older retailers – the Bon Marché was part of 'the commercial bulldozer crushing [Paris's] small shops and shopkeepers' (Satterthwaite, 2001, p. 31). In France, critics decried the anonymity of the larger store, which some feared could lead female shoppers into morally questionable behaviour, as they were manipulated by clerks or thrown into compromising positions with strange men (Tiersten, 2001, p. 28). The fact that department stores were prominent in bringing ready-to-wear clothing to a much larger public led to outcry from traditional tailors and dressmakers, who bemoaned the poor quality of non-bespoke fashions. The threat of competition led small shopkeepers to denounce the "Department Store Octopus" and to vilify Marshall Field and John Wanamaker. Many protested the ability of large stores to cut prices on one line while making up the difference because of the vast array of other goods offered. Yet there was little that smaller merchants could do to fight the emergence of department stores. Various US state legislatures experimented with new licensing fees that would require separate licenses for each individual line of goods carried in a store, but these initiatives were largely defeated, and by 1900 the momentum behind the anti-department store movement shifted, with most small-town merchants instead focusing on chain stores as their biggest threat (Howard, 2015, p. 34).

Competition between stores ensured that any time a new innovation was adopted by one retailer, others would soon imitate and adopt a similar practice. The flow of information and personnel between stores could be within communities or indeed span nations and continents. Harry Gordon Selfridge was integral to the growth of Marshall Field's in Chicago, and then took his expertise to London, where he opened the marvellous Beaux Arts-style palace Selfridge's on Oxford Street. A buyer from Eaton's in Toronto visited the Siegel Cooper store in Chicago and observed its successful grocery department, and the following year the Canadian store had a full grocery line (Santink, 1990, p. 168). Retailers carefully monitored the advertising and display areas of their rivals, attuned to discounts and ready to follow any initiative that seemed promising. In New York, the rivalry between Macy's and Gimbels was legendary, but Don Herold (1932) of the trade magazine *The Merchandise Manager* described how both big stores and 'little hole-in-the-wall emporiums watch Macy's like hawks', often with mixed success as they tried to adopt policies that might work in Manhattan but would flounder elsewhere. 'Store business', Herold argued, 'relies, more than almost any other business, on side glances' at the competition (p. 34). Stores at times hired sets of eyes to spy on their rivals: many employed comparison shoppers (usually women) who pretended to be customers, and paid close attention to merchandise displays, levels of service and amenities in stores, reporting back to their employers in the hope of giving a competitive advantage.

Department stores were innovators in distribution. Stores long offered home delivery of goods as a form of customer service. But even customers who were unable to visit the store in person could still make purchases using mail order. In Canada, the Timothy Eaton company had its flagship store in Toronto but sent mail-order parcels across the country, bringing the fashions and conveniences of the city to rural customers from coast to coast. Some merchants, like Sears Roebuck, moved from catalogue sales into building brick-and-mortar stores. Richard Sears built his business by catering to rural consumers, selling everything from farm implements to tombstones. The initial Sears stores were located in working-class neighbourhoods, but by the 1920s the chain was opening large stores in urban areas and retail sales were overshadowing catalogue sales. Montgomery Ward also expanded from selling through its famous "Wish Book" catalogue to open hundreds of stores in the 1920s, including a flagship store on Michigan Avenue in Chicago. For Montgomery Ward and Sears, the catalogue could act as a supplement to the physical store, reinforcing the brand's prominence and offering even more items than could be shown in actual retail displays, including farm machinery or even prefabricated homes. These newer types of stores were technically branches of chain organisations, but this distinction might not have been so clear to customers at the time. Within the retail industry, observers noted that the chains were able to use their buying clout to ensure great deals with manufacturers. In a smaller community, a chain branch of a more downmarket chain (or "junior department store") like J.C. Penney or Woolworth might be the closest thing to a department store that most residents would encounter. These branches did not have glamourous amenities as did stores like Macy's in Manhattan, but they still sold a range of goods in different departments, and were likely among the largest retail structures in their particular towns. To further complicate matters, some successful independent stores were able to expand into small, regional chain operations.

Just as the department store itself marked a new stage in the evolution of retailing, the form itself continued to change, adopting new business practices and forms. Trade magazines like the *Dry Goods Merchants Trade Journal* allowed stores to compare their strategies in merchandising, display, stock turnover and bookkeeping. Articles featured not only large, internationally known merchants like Macy's of New York, but also stores in smaller cities and towns that had developed new methods of efficient and modern storekeeping. The efforts of merchants in Marshalltown, Iowa, to co-ordinate Christmas decorations and sales contests made the front page of the *Journal* in 1924. A survey that asked owners of twenty-eight stores how much they invested in fixtures featured department stores in Minnesota, Connecticut, South Dakota and Illinois (*Dry Goods Merchants Trade Journal*, 1927, p. 49). When chain retailers became more of a competitive threat, some independent department stores organised into buying groups, to gain the benefits of large-scale buying while still remaining independent in daily operations. As early as 1916, a group of five stores including New York's Lord & Taylor, Newark's Hane & Co, and Buffalo's J. N. Adam's came together to form Associated Dry Goods. The Midwest was home to the Central States Department Stores, a group buying affiliation of twenty stores located in Illinois, Wisconsin, Minnesota, Indiana, and Iowa which was consciously formed as a response to the threat of chain stores and mail-order competition (Elvins, 2004).

Department stores' relationship to branded goods shifted over time. Consumers during the early twentieth century were inundated with the message that brand names signified quality and style. Although house brands remained important to department store's bottom lines, particularly in less glamourous departments like household linens, consumers searching for style could look for and find the labels of nationally recognised brands in the aisles of the department store, from Jantzen swimsuits to Monet costume jewellery to Coty lipsticks. Retailers coordinated their marketing with manufacturers, who could blanket the country with advertising campaigns in the pages of mass market magazines and newspapers, and might provide display materials or in some case even pay the salaries of sales help in specific departments. This practice became increasingly common during the 1920s and would be well entrenched by the 1960s (Whitaker, 2006 p. 216). Some stores attempted to raise the profile of their own private-label items by creating new private brands, like Sears' Kenmore appliance line or Marshall Field's Frango Mints, but generally consumers preferred national brands (Howard, 2015, p. 81). The development of group buying may have further accelerated this trend: the large orders required to supply not a single store but a group of twenty or thirty necessitated doing business with large manufacturers. The additional perks of assistance in display, promotion and in magazine and newspaper advertising made branded goods increasingly alluring for retailers.

Department stores reached their zenith in the early twentieth century, when they were economically and culturally the most dominant form of retailing. Across Europe, North and South America, stores were innovators in their communities, bringing the latest merchandise to local consumers and continuing to modernise and expand their operations. Department stores were crucial to community development and civic celebration: think of the annual Santa Claus parades which wound through the downtowns of countless communities, coordinated by local stores. Eaton's of Canada began holding parades in Toronto in 1905 and by the 1920s the practice had spread to Winnipeg, Montreal, Edmonton and Calgary (Penfold, 2016, p. 46). On Thanksgiving Day in 1924, adults and children crowded the sidewalks of New York to catch a glimpse of Macy's employees in costume, along with floats, clowns, bears, donkeys and other attractions as they passed by. Police estimated about 10,000 excited spectators were gathered on 34th Street at 7th Avenue to witness the arrival of Santa and the unveiling of the store's Christmas window, showing the "Fairy Frolics of Wondertown" (*New York Times*, 1924). Beyond events like parades, retailers were leaders in design in their communities, bringing new technologies and attention to visual display to their communities. Some were early adopters of modernist architecture, as was the case with the Schocken Department Stores, designed by Erich Mendelsohn in Stuttgart and Nuremburg during the late 1920s, which were arresting curvilinear structures of glass and steel.

The economic disruptions of the Great Depression understandably slowed the expansion of department stores. As stores grappled with plummeting sales and stagnant local economic conditions, many cut back on services and amenities in an effort to contain costs. Some held elaborate sales in an effort to win back consumers. Others used their advertising to try to explain to the public how essential it was for consumers to resume "normal buying", which would help to create new jobs and keep the wheels of the economy turning (Elvins, 2004, p. 120). Used to acting as civic leaders in good times, retailers experimented with ways to restore consumer confidence and drum up sales. In Rochester, New York, Sibley, Lindsay & Curr used its forty-five show windows and other display areas to stage a massive "Made in Rochester" exposition, featuring one hundred local businesses in an effort to draw in local shoppers and express the store's commitment to the area. Others, like Strawbridge and Clothier in New York, forged ahead with store expansions and remodelling not only to help with local unemployment but also because building costs were the lowest they had been in a decade (Longstreth, 2010, p. 34). Interiors were modernised, with new technologies like escalators (or "electric stairways" to the uninitiated), air conditioning and fluorescent lighting.

As the severity of the crisis became clear, many department stores became even more earnest in their imitation of chain store and discount store operations. Writing in a trade journal, H. L. Post (1934) argued that the "Independent Retailer Not Need to Surrender", but instead should try to cater to lower-middle and middle class groups. During the "whoopee era" of the 1920s, Post argued, too many department stores were caught up in selling luxuries to the upper classes, and lost sight of the average customer. Chain stores had swooped in to capture these patrons, using a limited number of fast-selling items, standardised merchandise and open displays that required less sales staff. The answer for many was to imitate the chains. The American trend towards consolidation which had begun in the 1920s continued throughout the 1930s and 1940s. Department store corporations like Allied, May, and Federated Department Stores aggressively acquired new stores and centralised their operations, particularly in purchasing and merchandising. In Britain, department stores were more able to hold their own against chain stores and actually increase their share of retail sales over the interwar years (Scott and Walker, 2010, p. 1126).

The outbreak of war created new challenges. Stores showed their wartime patriotism in displays of flags and bunting and lists of names of servicemen. They used their powers of marketing and persuasion to help the war effort. The treasury relied on retailers to sell bonds, giving them monthly quotas (Howard, 2015, p. 116). During World War II, Filene's in Boston sold more than $51 million in war bonds (Satterthwaite, 2001, p. 83). Stores dealt with shortages in goods and had to cooperate with official policies on rationing. In the United States, the Office of Price Administration imposed price controls, and stores scrambled to comply with rules that required them to post ceiling prices for specific items (Howard, 2015, p. 125–128). The imposition of the General Maximum Price Regulation set limits on the prices for nearly 6,000 commodities, interfering with the ability of stores to stock and price items as they chose. Paradoxically, these palaces of consumption were now required to spread a message of conservation, encouraging women to sew at home, recycle and reuse materials, and saving fuel to be used for military purposes. There were some new opportunities for new business, including bridal services that could plan quick weddings in various price brackets, complete with flowers, jewellery, music and bridal gowns (Howard, 2015, p. 121).

The postwar return to consumption was facilitated by government policies that encouraged private spending and the financing of homes for returning veterans in America. The growth of new subdivisions filled with ranch houses promised a new era of affluence, and a new emphasis on the suburbs rather than the urban centre. The early history of the department store was synonymous with downtown: these stores were geographically and culturally located in the centre of urban life. But as early as the 1920s we can see hints of changes in the spatial orientation of retailing. Some stores invested in new, planned shopping centres outside of the city centre. J.C. Nichols opened the Club Plaza to cater to an affluent suburb of Kansas City, Missouri (Satterthwaite, 2001, p. 47). As suburbanisation transformed American cities, drawing white middle-class families out of the downtown, department stores gambled with various strategies to retain their clientele. Some reinvested in the core, attempting to create city-center malls and build new parking facilities. More commonly, stores opened branches to act as anchors for the new malls springing up beside new subdivisions outside of the city. As Lizabeth Cohen (2003) has noted, during the late 1950s there was a rapid proliferation of shopping centres: 940 were built by 1957, and that number would double by 1960 and again by 1963 so that by 1976 there were 17,520 scattered across the United States (p. 258).

Department store companies were key in initiating the development of regional shopping centres. In Seattle, the president of the Bon Marché department store worked with the architect John Graham to create Northgate Shopping City, a mall which was highly successful and became a model for others in the industry. Even when department stores did not spearhead a project, their key role as anchor tenants helped to shape the size and scope of new developments (Longstreth, 1997, p. 310). The design of the new stores opening in the malls was different from those of the downtown. By orienting all stores inward towards each other in an enclosed space, shoppers were encouraged to think of the mall as a single entity, rather than an array of individual shops. This meant a new way of viewing store competition: where in the past retailers had been wary of being located too close to the competition, now two department stores would commonly be located on opposite ends of a single mall, creating more of a draw for customers and enhancing each other's business. Selling areas in branch stores tended to be spread out horizontally, typically on two or three levels, instead of the elevator-assisted, multi-story downtown store. Architects and designers devoted more attention to the interiors of branches, as the exterior was no longer located on a busy urban street with foot traffic, but in the middle of a parking lot. Some might have ground-floor display windows, but most had modern, spare, and unadorned exteriors, in contrast to the lavish and ornate Beaux Arts or Art Deco styles of many metropolitan stores. Parking was a crucial element of the mall's success. Planners calculated how to move a high volume of cars to and from shopping centres, and provided thousands of parking spots so shoppers coming from nearby areas would have ample room to park their cars.

The shift to the suburban mall had social consequences. By the 1960s, the pattern of "white flight" had increased racial and class segregation in American urban spaces. Department stores and mall developers carefully plotted the location of their projects, hoping to make it as enticing as possible for affluent suburban housewives to come and shop. Other groups were excluded. Lack of transportation, discriminatory real estate and hiring practices and low pay meant that African Americans were less likely to be able to purchase homes in suburban areas, and thus were largely absent from malls as either patrons or employees (Cohen, 2003, p. 288).

Suburban stores were more likely to hire part-time workers, often middle-class women who resided nearby. By changing store layouts to encourage more customer self-service, stores aimed to keep labour costs down, and reduced the number of full-time staff. As a result, suburban stores appeared homogenous, with virtually no visible minorities or members of the working class working or shopping. White consumers often took for granted how these spaces had been designed for their convenience. Black civil rights groups during the 1950s and 1960s worked to eliminate racial barriers to their participation in public life, including their ability to sit at lunch counters and work as sales staff in the department store, by instigating sit-ins and boycotts of retailers with less progressive policies. Activists succeeded in changing store rules that segregated public areas and restricted black hiring, but the geographic separation of city and suburb, of black and white, proved a more formidable obstacle to overcome.

The 1970s and 1980s were a period of consolidation and increased global competition for department stores. By this point one could no longer really speak of independent retailers, in the sense of the locally based and often family-run outfits which had been so common during the late nineteenth century. Most stores in the United States were either explicitly chain branches of national brands like Sears or J.C. Penney, or were part of national outfits like Federated Department Stores, Robinson-May or Carter Hawley Hale. A series of acquisitions and bankruptcies spelled the end to many longstanding stores, including Miller & Rhoads of Richmond, which was acquired by Allied Stores, sold off when Allied was acquired by investor Robert Campeau, mismanaged by a real estate developer, and closed in 1990 (Howard, 2015, p. 200). The decline of smaller, independent stores was reflected in popular culture in Britain: the BBC sitcom "Are You Being Served" followed the antics of the bored sales staff at the once prosperous, now dingy and declining Grace Brothers flagship store. Episodes featured the efforts of the store's management to slow plummeting sales by making the clerks wear ridiculous costumes, or to cut costs by turning off heating in the building.

A more precarious global economy during the 1990s and early 2000s further contributed to the decline of the department store. Bargain-conscious consumers turned away from the high-service and presumably higher-priced world of the large mall or downtown department store. Even upscale buyers proudly shopped at discount chains like Kmart and Target. Filene's famous basement changed from a separate floor within the store, to a chain of its own, housing marked down and discontinued items. Newer chains that specialised in bargain apparel like T.J. Maxx and Marshall's emerged in strip malls or discount malls, and outlet stores for designers and manufacturers like London Fog, Brooks Brothers and Coach enticed shoppers with the promise of "direct from the factory" prices (ironically, as most of the items were actually produced in Southeast Asia) (Satterthwaite, 2001, p. 182). Stores that specialised in one type of merchandise like toys, electronics or linens became known as "category killers" as they drew sales away from product lines that had long been features of the department store. Toys 'R' Us and Best Buy were typical of the chains able to present low prices and tremendous selection to consumers for one particular line of goods. Traditional department stores attempted to keep up with this frenzy for bargains by offering deep discounts and store promotions, and in the process lost much of their appeal. Gone were the knowledgeable sales staff, the beautiful displays, the elaborate dining areas, and the trusted house brands once associated with particular stores. Instead, racks of discounted clothing cluttered once-elegant showrooms, and little was invested in updating the design of stores.

Today the department store is a relic of another age. Those that survive in many markets seem only a shadow of the "big stores" of the early twentieth century. Some are able to trade on their connection with particular metropolises. In New York, tourists flock to Bloomingdale's, carrying purchases in "Big Brown Bags" as they hit other historic landmarks in Manhattan. The Christmas windows at Barney's and displays at Macy's still warrant occasional mention in the press. Harrods of London has managed to turn a visit to its Food Hall into a tourist experience listed on travel websites and tour guides. The shopping experience within most department stores today, however, is more generic. Most heavily rely on easily recognisable brands of cosmetics and apparel, combined with occasional private-label items. The level of service is very limited – the sales staff are often reduced to a lone person in an entire department ringing up sales, rather than the fleet of eager clerks who had assisted consumers in the early twentieth century. Amenities like bridal registries, if offered at all, tend to be do-it-yourself affairs online rather than a chance for shoppers to rely on the expertise of trained staff in selecting appropriate items for their homes. In smaller cities, the only evidence left of department stores is often an abandoned shell of a building dotting a declining Main Street. While some developers have managed to turn these retail relics into loft apartments in cities like Denver and Columbus, in other communities it has been a challenge to find other uses for these large retail spaces. Attempts at expanding or rebranding have had mixed results. In 1999, Sears purchased Eaton's of Canada and attempted to give the chain a makeover, renaming it eatons and launching a new, more upscale direction for the store. Less than 2 years later, it conceded defeat and the once venerable national institution closed its doors. Marshall Field's was acquired by the retailing division of British-American Tobacco, then passed through a number of other companies before eventually being purchased by Federated Department Stores.

Traditional department stores have even started to disappear from the suburban mall, as new retail behemoths like Walmart and big-box stores began to dominate the landscape. The bare-bones décor and requirement that customers find and carry many items without any sort of sales assistance allows retailers like Costco, Price Club and Sam's Club to keep prices down. These warehouse stores cultivate a downmarket aesthetic, yet they sell many items that in previous years would have been mainstays of department stores, including jewellery, cookware, apparel, high-end electronics, or appliances. This has created a scenario where affluent urban and suburban shoppers patronise Costco but express nostalgia for the service and atmosphere of the grand old stores. Online shopping has also made it increasingly difficult for department stores to compete. Where once department stores could boast that they carried every possible item a customer could want, in the age of amazon.com, choosy customers often decide to comparison shop or order specific items online without having to make the trip to a physical store. J.C. Penney had some success in the early 2000s by encouraging online shopping, becoming one of the first retailers to allow shoppers to place orders on the Internet and pick up and return items at stores. This slowed but did not stop the chain's decline, as it continued to lay off workers and close stores for the next decade.

Consumers in the twenty-first century seem to be seeking a different kind of retail experience. Gone are the days when women would spend a day at the store, socialising and perusing the aisles of merchandise in the big store. Time-pressed modern shoppers order online and bargain hunt; they don't walk downtown, and they are even showing less interest in patronising the large shopping malls that were built in the 1970s and 1980s, with their acres of concrete parking lots and thousands of square feet of selling space. The tendency of chain organisations to promote a more homogenised and generic style of retailing has further alienated more affluent consumers who patronise specialty stores or seek out unique, custom-made items. That is not to say that the public does not mourn the loss of the department store. Residents of Chicago protested when Federated decided to rename all Marshall Field's stores Macy's, some ceremoniously cutting their store credit cards in two. On September 8, 2006, Federated renamed over 400 regional stores, relegating long time brands like Boston's Filene's, Houson's Foley's and L.A.'s Robinson-May to the dustbin of history (Danto, 2006). In the Canadian city of Winnipeg, the traditional Christmas window displays that delighted visitors to Eaton's downtown are now preserved in the local children's museum, so that future generations can experience this holiday tradition. Websites and coffee-table books devoted to the history of local department stores sell well at area bookstores, and local residents think fondly of their formative shopping experiences in the big stores, recalling shopping trips to view store windows or meals in the store tea room. Shoppers remember how at Godchaux's store in Baton Rouge, Louisiana, clerks greeted customers by name and children received a nickel to buy a Coke (Sternberg and Shelledy, 2009). Residents of Marinette, Wisconsin think fondly of Lauerman Brothers and their famous frosted malt cones (Leannah, 2013). Customers lament the loss of regional and specific identity, as distinctive local stores become more standardised as part of larger chains (Howard, 2015, p. 216). More typically, the stores simply fade away. In 2016, Macy's announced that it was closing 100 stores, nearly 15% of its total number, conceding that the land underneath some of the branches was worth more than the stores themselves (Olen, 2016). The profitability of the department store has waned, and the old formulas which had led it its success – hand-on service, large scale and boundless selection – now seem anachronistic. But these grand old institutions linger on in memory, a testament to the tremendous cultural and economic power they once wielded.

References

Abelson, E. (1989), *When ladies go a-thieving: Middle-class shoplifters in the Victorian department store* (New York: Oxford University Press).

Ackermann's Repository of Arts, Literature, Commerce, Manufactures, Fashions and Politics (1809), *Harding, Howell, & Co.'s Grand Fashionable Magazine*, No. 89, Pall Mall (Plate 12: Vol. 1, No. 3, March).

Belisle, D. (2011), *Retail nation: Department stores and the making of modern Canada* (Vancouver: University of British Columbia Press).

Benson, S.P. (1988), *Counter cultures: Saleswomen, managers, and customers in American department stores, 1890–1940* (Urbana, IL: University of Illinois Press).

Bunker, S.B. (2012), *Creating Mexican consumer culture in the age of Porfirio Diaz* (Albuquerque: University of New Mexico Press).

Chapman, J. (2014), 'The argument of the broken pane', *Media History*, 21 (3), pp. 238–251.

Cohen, L. (2003), *A consumers' republic: The politics of mass consumption in postwar America* (New York: Alfred A. Knopf).

Danto, G. (2006), 'Letter from Chicago – in Memoriam: Marshall Field's', *Brandweek*, September 25, p. 40.

Dry Goods Merchants Trade Journal (1927), 'How much should you spend for fixtures?', February, pp. 49–50, 56.

Dry Goods Merchants Trade Journal (1929), 'Introducing modern art to the community', April, pp. 31–32.

Elvins, S. (2004), *Sales and celebrations: Retailing and regional identity in Western New York State, 1920–1940* (Athens, OH: Ohio University Press).

Gidlow, L. (2004), *The big vote: Gender, consumer culture, and the politics of exclusion, 1890s–1920s* (Baltimore, MD: Johns Hopkins University Press).

Hendrickson, R. (1979), *The grand emporiums: The illustrated history of America's great department stores* (New York: Stein and Day).

Herold, D. (1932), 'The Macy complex', *The Merchandise Manager*, 3 (1), p. 34.

Howard, V. (2015), *From Main Street to mall: The rise and fall of the American department store* (Philadelphia, PA: University of Pennsylvania Press).

Hower, R. (1967), *History of Macy's of New York* (Cambridge, MA: Harvard University Press).

Leach, W. (1993), *Land of desire: Merchants, power, and the rise of a new American culture* (New York: Pantheon Books).

Leannah, M. (2013), *Something for everyone: Memories of Lauerman Brothers department store* (Madison, WI: Wisconsin Historical Society).

Longstreth, R. (1997), *City center to regional mall: Architecture, the automobile, and retailing in Los Angeles, 1920–1950* (Cambridge, MA: MIT Press).

Longstreth, R. (2010), *The American department store transformed, 1920–1960* (New Haven, CT: Yale University Press).

Miller, M.B. (1981), *The Bon Marché: Bourgeois culture and the department store, 1869–1920* (Princeton, NJ: Princeton University Press).

New York Times (1924), 'Greet Santa Claus as "king of kiddies" – Crowds cheer him in parade and witness coronation in Macy's new store', November 28, p. 15.

Olen, H. (2016), Macy's is closing 100 stores: Where did all of its customers go? [online] *Slate*. Available at: www.slate.com/blogs/moneybox/2016/08/11/macy_s_is_closing_ 100_department_ stores_ where_did_its_customers_go.html (Accessed November 13, 2016).

Penfold, S. (2016), *A mile of make-believe: A history of the Eaton's Santa Claus parade* (Toronto: University of Toronto Press).

Post, H. (1934), 'The independent need not surrender', *Dry Goods Merchants Trade Journal* February, p. 21.

Rappaport, E. (2000), *Shopping for pleasure: Women in the making of London's West end* (Princeton, NJ: Princeton University Press).

Resseguie, H. (1965), 'Alexander Turney Stewart and the development of the department store, 1823–1876', *Business History Review*, 39 (3).

Santink, J. (1990), *Timothy Eaton and the rise of his department store* (Toronto: University of Toronto Press).

Satterthwaite, A. (2001), *Going shopping: Consumer choices and community consequences* (New Haven, CT: Yale University Press).

Scott, P. and Walker, J. (2010), 'Advertising, promotion, and the competitive advantage of interwar British department stores', *The Economic History Review*, 63 (4), pp. 1105–1128.

Siry, J. (1988), *Carson Pirie Scott: Louis Sullivan and the Chicago department store* (Chicago: University of Chicago Press).

Sternberg, H. and Shelledy, J. (2009), *We were merchants: The Sternberg family and the story of Goudchaux's and Maison Blanche department stores* (Baton Rouge, LA: Louisiana State University Press).

Tiersten, L. (2001), *Marianne in the market: Envisioning consumer society in fin-de-siècle France* (Berkeley, CA: University of California Press).

Walsh, C. (1999), 'The newness of the department store: A view from the eighteenth century', In G. Crossick and S. Jaumain (eds.) *Cathedrals of consumption: The European department store, 1850–1939* (Burlington, VT: Ashgate) 46–71.

Wemp, B. (2011), 'Social space, technology, and consumer culture at the Grands Magasins Dufayel', *Historical Reflections*, 37 (1), pp. 1–16.

Whitaker, J. (2006), *Service and style: How the American department store fashioned the middle class* (New York: St. Martin's Press).

Williams, R. (1982), *Dream worlds: Mass consumption in late nineteenth-century France* (Berkeley, CA: University of California Press).

10

THE SUPERMARKET AS A GLOBAL HISTORICAL DEVELOPMENT

Structures, capital and values

Patrick Hyder Patterson

Supermarkets sell abundance. Built to maximise purchases by guiding customers through a carefully programmed experience of pleasure and ease, stocked with the expansive range of goods needed to make the ideal of one-stop shopping a reality, and managed with a dogged pursuit of efficiency, consistency, and certainty, the big-footprint contemporary supermarket holds out to its customers an equally big promise: satisfaction guaranteed, all under one roof, every time. As such, it represents something novel and remarkable in retailing history, and one of the most potent, effective, and significant sales methods ever developed. The consequences have been profound. Through its rise to prominence during the twentieth century, the supermarket has reordered the commodity chains of food supply from start to finish, restructuring retail markets with its characteristic insistence on the logics of uniformity, competition and economies of scale. In the process, the supermarket system and its array of associated techniques and systems have emerged in the developed world as the leading model for modern, rational, technology-driven grocery sales, often extinguishing older business practices.

The analysis provided here presents an interpretation of the historical trajectory of the supermarket, emphasising those elements most critical to an integrative understanding of the conceptual aspects of the supermarket model, and those not limited to particular cases. As a *model technology*, the supermarket emerged as a distinctive, preferred form for the retail distribution of food and grocery items, a type marked throughout its history by claims of impressive advantages for both sellers and shoppers, and one that was heavily dependent on supporting technologies and, at the same time, a driver of new technological innovations. As a potent *extension of modern urbanism*, the supermarket form represents one of the most influential expressions of the patterns of modern urban and suburban development, with important connections to the spread of motor vehicles and roadways. As a distinctive *structure for enterprise organization and function*, the supermarket model made the grocery trade big business, turning it into a modern industry and driving it towards highly consolidated operations in the hands of centralised firms that were managed by professionals and owned by large corporate entities commanding massive capital. As an original *instrument of capitalist business*, the supermarket has routinely figured in scholarly and critical studies as an intrinsically capitalist tool, though such judgements lose some force in light of the relatively successful transfer of the model to the retail environments of communist societies. As a compelling and attractive *transnational paradigm for development*, the supermarket form has spread far beyond its origins in the United States and proven a genuinely global model, gaining sizeable market share in economically advanced societies and, increasingly, in developing countries as well, albeit with considerable modification and local adaptation in the process. As both a *mirror and engine of culture*, the supermarket has shaped and carried the values of a transnational culture of modern retailing rooted in abundance, variety, satisfaction, competition, individuality and choice. And finally, as an *important formative factor in the economic, social, business, labour, and cultural history* of the recent past, supermarket retailing continues to be understudied in many ways, although it has proven a durable and resilient form that remains positioned as a dominant model and seems likely to do some for some time, notwithstanding continuing pressures, obstacles and competitive threats.

As we seek to develop an integrative account along these lines, it should be noted at the outset that the boundaries of the category "supermarket" have long been imprecise. Part of the problem here is that the term itself arose as, in essence, a form of advertising, meant more to showcase the advantages of new stores and a novel sales method than to delineate a distinctive type with taxonomical rigour. The power of the label proved remarkably attractive and enduring: as the signifier of what has become an enormously popular business form, the supermarket designation is one that promotionally minded retailers have often applied to their own stores in an imitative way, regardless of whether or not those outlets actually satisfied the customary definitional criteria of any particular place and period.

Not surprisingly, those criteria have been divergent, fluid and variable. In recent years, for example, the Food Marketing Institute, the leading trade association for supermarket and grocery retailing activities in the US, has defined a "traditional supermarket" as one with a complete assortment of produce, meats, and grocery items, normally stocking from 15,000 to 60,000 distinct products, with no more than 15% of sales deriving from the non-food general merchandise and health and beauty care categories, and registering at least $2 million in retail transactions each year (Food Marketing Institute, 2018). Historically, however, there have been many other definitions. This longstanding looseness in nomenclature means that many "supermarkets" are, in fact, better thought of as something different, especially when these venues are small and offer only a limited product assortment. Complicating this problem, the quest for innovation, promotional advantage, and higher earnings has led to new store designs that transcend the classic supermarket to offer, as it were, The Next Big Thing. Accordingly, not every shop that calls itself a supermarket (or is called that by customers) comes anywhere close to the classic supermarket form, while true, full-scale supermarket operations are also to be found within expanded or hybridised store variants that have discarded or otherwise sought to move beyond the "supermarket" label. Considered in world-historical perspective, the definition of the supermarket has thus been fuzzy at best: subject to dispute and to divergent interpretations, rooted in the self-understandings (and commercial motives) of enterprise managers and entrepreneurs, shaded inevitably by local particularities and circumstances and evolving over time.

Consequently, and with an eye to the value of a broader comparative viewpoint, the analysis here adopts a broad and pragmatic understanding of the category, one that acknowledges the distinctiveness of the supermarket model and its related technologies and management processes in their paradigmatic (indeed, now "traditional") iterations, while at the same time recognising that the classic supermarket form has been, for almost the entire course of its historical development, supplemented and in some instances supplanted by other types including smaller-scale superettes and mini-marts, large-format warehouse stores and wholesale clubs, and enormous hypermarkets and supercenters that combine a full range of grocery sales and services with a similarly broad offering of non-grocery items.

Satisfaction by design: the supermarket as a model technology

Historical scholarship on the development of supermarkets remains, on the whole, underdeveloped and incomplete, particularly with regard to the global and comparative dimensions of the supermarket phenomenon. The origins of the genre, however, are well-documented in a variety of useful works on the rise of self-service grocery sales and, perhaps most notably, on the impact of pioneering institutions and entrepreneurs such as Michael Cullen of the King Kullen stores in the early 1930s, the programmed flow of the famous Piggly Wiggly chain built by Clarence Saunders in the late 1910s and 1920s, and the energetic promotion of the self-service system by industry groups, including the publishers of the influential trade journal *Progressive Grocer* (Zimmerman, 1955; McAusland 1980; Tedlow, 1990; Tolbert, 2009; Cochoy, 2016). These roots in the self-service method, with its emphasis on continual technical refinement and relentless rationalisation, signal some of the most important conceptual dimensions of this retail form: from almost the very beginning, those responsible for the design and management of supermarkets have routinely approached them *as a model technology* – a distinctive physical form, coupled with a similarly distinctive set of operational systems, understood by its creators and enthusiasts as the pinnacle of technical progress and the consummate achievement of the science of selling. Moreover, while the supermarket has always been a technology-*dependent* form, relying on a host of supporting tools and practices, it has also been a technology-*promoting* form, spurring and in some cases dictating the development of further technological innovations as the new style of shopping led to new demands and expectations on the part of both consumers and retailers.

The most immediately noticeable feature of the supermarket as a distinctive technological form is the coupling of self-service for most (not all) goods on offer with the elaborate and extensive material infrastructure and vast sales-floor area of the store.

Business purposes are paramount here: as James Mayo (1993) notes, 'the history of the grocery store is the history of economic competition over space' (p. 235), and constant pressures for reconfiguration and enhancement mean that 'the design remains in place as long as it is economically competitive' (p. xvii). What the customer encounters in a classic supermarket is, first and foremost, a space noteworthy for its sheer size and scale, for the enormous variety of items offered, and for the unmediated, hands-on contact with those products that a trip through the supermarket affords. Less apparent to non-specialists and to the consuming public is the carefully crafted layout of the supermarket form, one designed to create a customer experience that is planned and managed from start to finish – and therefore, the technology promises, reliably productive of higher sales volume. Control of movement through the store, signage and logical positioning to ease customers' self-service routines, staging of sensory stimuli, engagement with products on display, exposure to in-store advertising, presentation of opportunities for unanticipated "impulse" purchases: all of these, and more, have been organised and executed with an attention to detail that is frequently invisible to shoppers themselves but nonetheless painstaking, employing models and methods continually refined through what soon developed into a huge technical-operational management literature for retailing specialists (e.g., Brand, 1963). Obviously or not, the supermarket is *programmed* shopping.

In its origins, this systems-minded programming mirrored the preferences and passions of the broader commercial and industrial culture. For the United States and Europe, the mid-twentieth century was an age fascinated by the power of technology to transform human experience. In

Figure 10.1 Interior of an Albertson supermarket. Modernity, rationality, technology, abundance: a typical postwar American supermarket in the Albertsons chain. Seattle, Washington, USA. February 1955.

Source: Seattle Municipal Archives, photographer unknown (public domain).

that environment, the thoroughgoing connection of supermarket operations to technological advances – and indeed, the prevailing understanding among retail specialists that the new store model was a technological advance in its own right – rapidly made the supermarket the grocery-sales method that drew the most attention as the shape of things to come. Mechanised, standardised, rationalised, and optimised, it became a symbol of achievement and modernity for retailing, popular with customers and celebrated among businesspeople for its scientific advantages and technical superiority over old-fashioned methods (e.g., Zimmerman, 1937).

Just as retailing specialists pursued the planning, design, and layout of supermarkets as, at their core, matters of technology, the stores themselves were dependent on a wide range of supporting technologies, without which they could not function properly (Keh, 1998). Making purchases on the scale that the supermarket offered posed technical problems for customers from the moment they arrived at the giant stores: the old hand-held baskets and bags into which customers once packed the paid-for items handed to them by store clerks in traditional over-the-counter outlets now had to be replaced by a technology that would be suitable for self-service use by the dozens or even hundreds of shoppers that could be inside a store at any moment and, at the same time, large enough to carry greatly increased volumes. Baskets provided by the markets themselves did and still do remain available even in the most "modern" of stores, but the supermarket model shifted customer habits in an entirely new direction, encouraging them to load up with more items than could be comfortably carried by hand and spurring the development of a new device to solve the new problem, the shopping cart (Grandclément, 2009; Cochoy, 2016; pp. 166–198).

A less obvious technological dynamic proved important here as well: for enterprises, their workers, and their customers, the supermarket model also functions as a critical technology of time management. Big stores of this kind, and especially big chains of such outlets, require considerable investments of company resources simply to guide the flow of employee labour in order to ensure reliable service and presentation in stores that are – if the model is to live up to its promise – always full, with nothing missing from the shelves. Just as employees' time is carefully organised, shoppers' time is also valuable, with store operations calculated to strike the proper balance between, on the one hand, the need to ensure that the supermarket experience feels quick and convenient for customers and, on the other, the desire to keep them in the store aisles longer to raise sales.

As supermarkets rose to prominence, technology was everywhere, almost from the very beginning: refrigerators and freezers to prevent spoilage, spray misters to keep produce fresh and appealing, lighting to enhance the visual appeal of products, music to create a pleasant atmosphere, customised in-store advertising displays and specialised shelving and free-standing gondolas to put the right items in front of the right eyes in the right place, at the right time. The end of the shopper's circuit brought an encounter with new technologies of theft prevention and cash control: checkout lanes staffed by specialised cashiers who, in the new division of labour that self-service contemplated, did little other than handle money, logging each transition using yet another technology critical to the success of supermarkets, the cash register. Meanwhile, behind the scenes and away from the eyes of shoppers on the carefully staged sales floor, the service areas of the store likewise bore the marks of a pervasive reliance on technology, from the loading docks where enormous volumes of freight were continually received and processed, to the massive storerooms and cooling units where products were held for quick deployment on store shelves, to modern food-preparation facilities where fish and meat, baked goods, delicatessen items, and prepared foods were readied for sale. Eventually, the efficiency and data-handling demands of supermarket sales would drive innovations in the technology of the checkout lane, with further refinements of the cash register that had played a major role in the 'deskilling of clerks into cashiers' (Palm, 2017; p. 49), the widespread implementation of the Uniform Product Code and related scanning and inventory-management methods (Morton, 1994), and later on, the introduction of self-checkout technologies that eliminated cashiers entirely.

The supermarket's thoroughgoing dependence on technology has not been confined to what happens in the stores themselves. It has imposed a corresponding set of technological requirements extending all the way through the countless supply routes that end on supermarket shelves and in display cases. Where supermarkets predominate, each node and link in these commodity chains – local and regional delivery vehicles, warehouses, wholesale distribution centres, food processing and small-goods manufacturing plants, long-distance transportation and farms – has been shaped and conformed to the needs of supermarket-style sales, with their insistence on uniformity, reliability, constant quality, continuous replenishment, uninterrupted supply and an enormous range of product choice. Accordingly, the supermarket system's demand that both quality and quantities be consistent led to the proliferation of standardised items produced using technological processes to ensure the needed certainty.

Similarly, the increasing popularity of the densely stocked, highly regularised supermarket format stimulated parallel developments in packaging. These changes arose in part from the concrete material requirements of the grocery trade (product preservation, convenience in handling, easy fit in store displays), but they were also a response to promotional considerations that took on greater significance when a given product could likely command only a few inches of display space on shelves jammed with competing options. To be most effective, packaging now had to serve as a means of advertising and brand distinction: everything that faced the shopper was expected not only to inform, but also to attract, appeal, inspire, persuade and sell.

Often enough, a grocery item that came packaged was one that had been manufactured or processed, and self-service supermarket sales helped drive a shift away from raw, unprocessed and bulk merchandise, generating widespread demand for factory-made articles and the technologies needed to supply them. Heavy reliance on coolers and freezers, a critical part of in-store infrastructure, meant that refrigeration technology had to be implemented back throughout the supply chain, necessitating extensive networks of refrigerated shipping, trucking and warehouses. Agricultural output responded, too. The new store model placed a high value on products that could survive their long journeys from farms to shopping carts unblemished and arrive at least seemingly fresh, with the consistent supermarket look and feel that both store owners and customers came to expect. To meet that need, growers and ranchers reoriented their production around factory-based food processing, turning to genetic science to originate new breeds and varieties that might better serve the new demands of the market. As examples like these suggest, the evolution of the supermarket has generated pervasive pressures for the introduction of new technological solutions throughout the production and distribution networks that it engages. The model retailing technology so eagerly promoted and celebrated by its early advocates now finds itself embedded in, and continually reinforcing, a far broader systemic technological dependency.

Driving forces: the supermarket as an extension of modern urbanism

Grounded in the complex network of technologies and technically oriented management methods just described, the supermarket appears as a paradigmatic expression of the distinctive patterns of urban and suburban development that have characterised late modern industrial and post-industrial societies. The relationship here is reciprocal: modern urbanism's comparatively concentrated configurations of housing and businesses render the mass-scale supermarket form economically viable, while the availability of supermarket shopping helps to make cities and towns appealing and "liveable".

In the United States, the expansion of the supermarket system appears closely linked with a specific variant of modern urbanism resulting from the rapid rise in ownership of private automobiles. By the latter half of the twentieth century, cars and supermarkets had become, along with single-family homes, emblems of the Good Life and the American Dream. The connection with driving was no mere coincidence: for the United States, the automobile was the essential convenience technology that made the supermarket a truly countrywide phenomenon, bringing shoppers to the big stores they seemed to love so much. Nowhere was America's car culture in its early decades stronger than in Southern California, and what started there as limited moves by local innovators later prompted much broader changes. The auto-driven refinements and elaborations of the supermarket model undertaken in the Los Angeles area from the 1930s through the 1950s soon influenced national trends, and what had been specific practices devised for grocery sales ended up reshaping other retailing forms such as drugstores and variety stores (Longstreth, 1999). America became the quintessential supermarket society, and cars were a big part of what made that happen.

But while it is true that supermarket retailing was at once a prime cause and prime beneficiary of the profound transformations that Chester H. Liebs (1995) calls 'the shift of commerce from city to highway' in the United States (p. vi), it is important to recognise that even as supermarkets spread along new roads and highways, they did not vanish from American cities. Indeed, the supermarket model has managed to survive – and make room for the automobile – in urban centres. Big store footprints grew even bigger with the incorporation of adjacent parking lots, while in some cases developers have invested in expensive garage infrastructure to accommodate drivers, all intended to incorporate the ease of auto-oriented suburban, exurban and small-town supermarket shopping into the fabric of larger, denser cities.

It would be a mistake, however, to approach the supermarket model as entirely an epiphenomenon of automobilism. Widespread reliance on personal cars is by no means an indispensable condition for the proliferation of the supermarket form. Quite to the contrary, the large-scale, full-assortment supermarket has proved sustainable in many areas where either suitable concentrations of high-density housing or reliable, convenient networks of urban public transportation, or some combination of the two, can ensure that stores have the customer counts and purchasing volumes needed to support a model premised on massive in-store inventories and high throughput. To some extent this has occurred even in American city centres, but it is especially true of developed urban areas outside the United States, where town dwellers enjoy more sophisticated mass-transit systems and where the supermarket model has managed to take root and survive, albeit in modified forms tailored to local customs and conditions.

At least as important as the personal automobile, though far less salient for shoppers, has been another critical aspect of motoring technology and modern urban development: the extensive network of roads and delivery vehicles needed to ensure that stores stay stocked with a wide variety of goods and to guarantee the regular refreshment of perishable items.

The supermarket method cannot be understood without a recognition of its fundamental dependency on high-quality roads and transportation networks. Railways and seagoing freighters can do some of the long-distance shipping work, but distribution from local and regional depots must rely extensively on large fleets of wheeled vehicles in continuous circulation. Cars may not be a requisite for success, but supermarkets have not functioned and will not function without reliable trucking. At the same time, this dependence on road-transportation networks meant that supermarket operators were among the most important sources of trucking demand, giving them enormous market power over not only transportation providers but also over the makers of the products they moved (Hamilton, 2008).

No analysis of the relationship between supermarkets and modern urbanism would be complete without a recognition of the connections between one of the most conspicuous failures of contemporary food distribution systems and the distinctive demands of the capital-intensive, high volume, low-margin supermarket model. Patterns of land use that have accelerated suburban sprawl away from urban cores (or more precisely, away from those parts of cities that have stirred misgivings about "blighted" zones and prompted white flight) have resulted in the emergence of so-called "food deserts", areas where substantial portions of the population lack access to a wide range of grocery options, especially healthier foods like the fresh

Figure 10.2 Montgomery, Alabama. Produce truck making deliveries at a supermarket, March 1943. The unnoticed infrastructure of the supermarket form: urban sites and transportation networks.

Source: Library of Congress, photographer John Vachon (public domain).

produce routinely stocked in supermarkets. The problem has been most serious and best studied in the United States, but it has appeared in other developed countries as well, notably in Britain, where in recent decades a burgeoning automobile culture has in some ways mirrored patterns seen in America, diminishing the availability of supermarkets in city centres (Shaw, 2014). Linked as it is with the broader tendency to shift shopping to the urban periphery, the widespread adoption of the "progressive" supermarket model thus has not guaranteed progress for all consumers.

Progressive grocers: the supermarket as an enterprise structure

Progress or not, the changes have been enormous. Writing in 1958, one management specialist weighed in on the transformation that by then had become so apparent in the business of food distribution, noting that 'twenty years ago the "supermarket industry" was

Figure 10.3 New brands and new uses in a new capitalist era: A department store from communist Czechoslovakia's state-owned PRIOR chain, now repurposed for use as a shopping mall, with a large ground floor supermarket operated by the Austrian Billa chain, a subsidiary of Germany's REWE Group. Note the multi-modal access: the store complex is sited directly adjacent to the Prague Metro's Prosek station, with automobile parking and bus stops in front and many large socialist-era apartment blocks in the surrounding area. August 2017.

Source: Author photograph.

non-existent' (Lawrence, 1991; p. 8). In short order, however, an industry had indeed materialised. The supermarket model altered the commercial landscape not just for shoppers but for enterprises as well, and grocery retailing was well on the way towards the patterns that have since typified the supermarket business for both the stores themselves and their suppliers: ownership has become increasingly corporatised, management highly professionalised, and operations unmistakably industrialised. At the same time, supermarket proprietors and managers have sought to carefully optimise the scale of their firms using methods grounded in the new principles of scientific management. And usually, "optimal" has meant big – sometimes very big.

The key factors highlighted in the foregoing discussion – the importance of technology, the reliance on sufficiently dense population clusters that can furnish adequate consumer markets, the overriding concern for cost-cutting and efficiency, the magnitude of economies of scale – have meant that ongoing optimisation presses supermarket operations towards the concentration of capital and management resources. And that pressure has favoured the consolidation of supermarket holdings in chains of considerable size. In many ways, the history of supermarkets is a history of increasing scale: the pursuit of economic efficiency drove the evolution of the big store, and the big store made the establishment of the big chains all the more profitable and all the more logical.

This tendency has, not surprisingly, spelled trouble for small, independent store owners. In the United States, market share had by the mid-1960s shifted with astonishing speed towards highly centralised firms, with one analyst then noting that 'the fact that the ten largest chains sell almost 30% of all the food purchased at retail and that the three largest chains account for almost half the business done by all food chains is giving some substance to the hue and cry arising across the land that "there out to be a law"' (Markin, 1964/1965; p. 36). As that observation suggests, competitive pressures from the chains sparked fierce resistance. Even before the self-service and supermarket revolutions, small proprietors fearful of price cutting and consolidation fought back. Many joined what ultimately became a 'century-old battle between independent merchants and large retailers' (Levinson, 2011; p. 22), a conflict that continues in various ways to this day and one that did, especially early on, result in some victories for the smaller firms, even in the more free-wheeling American environment.

The struggle prompted a variety of notable competitive adaptations, as seen, for example, in the independent outlets banded together under the brand IGA (Independent Grocers Alliance). Part of the longer history of independent resistance, this network predated by a few years the emergence of the supermarket form. With time, it developed into a noteworthy mechanism for pushback against what the group calls "cookie-cutter chains", now operating, in most American states and more than thirty countries, almost five thousand "Hometown Proud" supermarkets, a designation meant to evoke the independents' local, community-oriented virtues (IGA, 2018). But despite certain successes that cushioned at least some independent owners, there were lots of failures, too. Often, and especially in the more laissez faire legal environment of United States, the competitive advantages of the big chains proved difficult if not impossible to withstand (Markin, 1968; Yee, 2003; Levinson, 2011).

The supermarket is a global phenomenon (or perhaps more aptly, one in the process of ongoing globalisation), and it is critical to acknowledge that not all the world has taken the anti-protectionist posture that has long encouraged so much enterprise consolidation in the United States, or the course towards deregulation that has marked more recent British history, with similar effects. Especially in continental Europe, frameworks of government policy have helped loosen the hold of big chains, shielding independent supermarkets, smaller firms and indeed smaller stores (Logemann, 2012). Europe has also seen some noteworthy departure from the otherwise well-traveled path towards ownership by publicly traded corporations. As Andrew Seth and Geoffrey Randall (2011) note, a number of the most significant supermarket firms there operate with a commitment to "behind-the-scenes family control", while 'the question "Who needs shareholders anyway, and what can they tell me about running my business?" has never been very far away in the continental European retail markets' (p. 130). Nevertheless, such companies remain large, powerful, chains with highly concentrated capital assets and massive economies of scale at their disposal. They are no less manifestations of "big business" for their lack of accountability to stockholders, and in that respect they still confirm the broader trend towards consolidated and centralised enterprise structures driven by the cost-cutting logics of the supermarket form itself.

Purchasing power: the supermarket as an instrument of capitalism

Critical to both the enterprise structures just described and to the supermarket form as an inherently technology-dependent model is the evident need for substantial, indeed often massive, investment. With their large-scale, heavy reliance on expensive infrastructure and extensive transportation networks and far-flung commodity chains, supermarket operations and the enterprises that support them simply cannot go forward in the absence of big capital holdings, and in practice this capital has often been heavily concentrated in firms controlling many stores. Capital counts.

And because big capital counts for so much, capitalism itself has routinely figured as an essential element in efforts to tell the supermarket story. The practical bonds between supermarket operations and the structures of modern capitalist business have yielded a widely shared conceptual construct: scholars have commonly treated the form as something characteristically and indeed even intrinsically capitalist. It is easy enough to see how this conclusion might arise without any serious reservations from the cases most often studied. For there is no denying the very capitalist origins of the supermarket model in the very capitalist United States, and there is a certain apparent naturalness to interpretations of the supermarket as an extension of the market logics of capitalist efficiency and profit-seeking. Along these lines, for example, Victoria de Grazia (2005) observes that the history of Italy's Supermarkets Italiani/Esselunga chain appears in many ways to be 'the story of a purposeful, consumer-oriented globalizing capitalism', one that 'tells of a forceful entrepreneur working with an expert staff to forge a new social alliance between foreign capitalism and local consumer interests by endorsing a high-volume, low per-unit-cost operation' (p. 379). In the same vein, Tracey Deutsch (2010) notes that supermarkets became 'vehicles for establishing the superiority of America and, more broadly, of capitalism itself' in the rhetoric of their backers in business and government circles, who insisted that 'because supermarkets lowered food prices, celebrated freedom of choice, and made customers feel they were being treated equally, they reduced the appeal of communism and showcased the real value of American capitalism and free enterprise' (p. 192). Deutsch is therefore pointing to something quite important about the way grocery retailing has functioned in the United States when she concludes that supermarkets and similar store forms are sites where 'capitalism is embedded, undermined, reinforced, and indeed constituted and made meaningful through social relations at the point of purchase' (p. 229).

Those adopting a more normative, explicitly critical stance, as in the case of various observers writing from the perspectives of anthropology, sociology and cultural studies, have frequently gone even further, seeing the supermarket not just as another manifestation of capitalist business practice, but as a tool of capitalism. If celebratory accounts from industry boosters typically assume that the interests of shoppers and supermarket owners "automatically coincide", as Rachel Bowlby notes (1997), such critiques habitually posit the opposite: 'the more the capitalists benefit, the less the customers do' (p. 94). Accordingly, the supermarket functions, in one such critical reading, as 'the dominant contemporary symbol of capitalist penetration into the food system' (Mann, 2014, pp. 19, 26). Proceeding along similar lines to identify the supermarket as 'the highest temple of the modern food system' (p. 216), Raj Patel (2007) treats the big grocery chains as thoroughly and hopelessly entrenched in that system, one that follows the 'cardinal rule of market capitalism: "buy cheap, sell dear"' (p. 10). Seeking some remedy, Patel endorses community-oriented, cooperatively managed challengers to the supermarket model and to the corporatised food structures that supply it, arguing that 'what's at stake isn't only the dominion of the supermarket, but the stability of an entire matrix of living, working and consumption, one that shapes not only our choices but . . . our very selves' (p. 252). Viewed from such vantage points, capitalism is crushingly coercive. The supermarket *is* capitalism.

That common assumption, however, has thus far not been subjected to much in the way of serious and sustained analytical scrutiny. There has been, to be sure, some pushback against totalising views that treat the supermarket as a place where, naturally and invariably, capitalism works its dangerous magic. Kim Humphery's study (1998) of the cultural impact of the supermarket in Australia, for example, endeavours to articulate a revised yet still critical analytical stance that is neither blithely celebratory of the consumption experience in developed capitalist societies nor constrained by an unwavering, simplistic hostility towards contemporary retailing as the creature and servant of big capital and its self-interested culture (pp. 209–210). He thus cautions against reductionist interpretations that see supermarkets as inherently, and more or less inescapably, the devices of capitalist power (pp. 16–17). But notwithstanding some reservations like these, the tendency towards a straightforward linkage of the supermarket model with the purposes and market logics of capitalist economics continues to prevail. Capitalism, in the dominant view, is intrinsic to the supermarket, part of the essential nature of this retail form.

A careful comparative study of a broader range of historical cases, however, should elicit some reservations about pushing that diagnosis too far. No matter how unshakeable the capitalist global economy may seem from the standpoint of the early decades of the new millennium, a longer world-historical view reminds us that there were alternatives to that economy – and potent, entrenched, durable ones – during the consolidation of the retail systems and practices that came to typify the developed West in the latter part of the twentieth century. Communism offered other options. Yet despite its capitalist beginnings, the supermarket was enthusiastically embraced by members of the political, planning, and trade establishment in a number of communist-led societies. Ultimately, the form proved perhaps surprisingly adaptable to commercial settings grounded in Marxist principles and thus in the state or collective ownership and control of the means of production. And at least in the most prosperous and consumer-oriented communist countries, supermarkets functioned reasonably well given the constraints of the broader economic system (Patterson, 2009). For our conceptualisation of the relationship between the supermarket model and the private ownership and control of business and investment assets, the implications are clear: the supermarket model requires large-scale capital. But it does not require capitalism. Considered in global terms, the supermarket form is therefore best understood as an instrument shaped and wielded with great effect by capitalist owners, but not invariably or intrinsically a tool that does the work of capitalism.

The distribution of choice: the supermarket as a transnational model

The quickest and most dynamic importations of the supermarket model occurred, understandably enough, in other highly developed capitalist countries. Proximity to and frequent contacts with the US, certain parallels in urban design and land use, and a comparative lack of war-related displacement and destabilisation helped make the Canadian marketplace one of the earliest sites of supermarket expansion. But the spread of the supermarket would soon involve something much more than efforts to replicate the achievements of successful next-door neighbours. After World War II, the appeal of the model proved very far-reaching, and the transnational networks of business expertise, information and know-how, investment, and ownership that propagated the supermarket form would become, with time, genuinely global.

Europe in particular offered tempting new markets for supermarket operators. The United Kingdom is perhaps the best-studied case, and retailers there were comparatively early and eager promoters of the model (Shaw, Kurth & Alexander, 2004; Alexander, 2008; Shaw, Bailey, Alexander, Nell & Hamlett, 2012; Bailey & Alexander, 2017). The burgeoning English-language professional literature that had resulted from the enthusiastic embrace of the supermarket in North America was, naturally, readily available to British commercial specialists, easing the flow of ideas and contacts. In business, networks matter, and in mass-scale retailing in the latter half of the twentieth century, influential network leaders in Britain, as in a number of other countries, grew excited about the promise of the supermarket. Fairly quickly, the UK saw the coalescence of 'something akin to a self-service retailing "community of practice" emerging from the activities of key stakeholders connected with the retail trades', with impetus coming from advocates and analysts in the business press, from government officials charged with regulating and promoting commerce, from retail firms and entrepreneurs who saw opportunities as supermarket pioneers, and from industries specialising in the design and furnishings of retail outlets who stood to profit from a big new modernising shift. (Alexander, Shaw & Curth, 2005; p. 807). There were bumps in the road, to be sure, with energetic competitive opposition and some regulatory obstacles, as seen in the early phases of the American case. But the new store form was, in fairly short order, on the path to becoming an essential feature in UK grocery retailing, with the country's largest chain Tesco ultimately becoming Europe's biggest grocery enterprise and, since the 1990s, a major driver of the ongoing expansion of supermarkets and supermarket-style shopping venues into developing countries and other new markets.

On the European continent, patterns of diffusion varied significantly depending on national and local conditions. Seen from the standpoint of the first two decades of the twenty-first century, the supermarket and its close variants appear as dominant forms in European retailing, with recent decades witnessing the maturation and diversification of the business. As the supermarket model has taken root firmly, a more favourable legal and regulatory climate for cross-border expansion within Europe has seen the consolidation of several very large national and international chains operating both traditional supermarkets and other stores that, whether bigger or smaller, incorporate key aspects of the supermarket model. These giant firms are headquartered in a number of European countries, including France (e.g., Carrefour, Auchan, E. Leclerc), the Netherlands (Ahold Delhaize), and Germany (REWE, Edeka, Aldi, Lidl), with many managing a variety of store types under multiple brand names and maintaining a substantial European and global presence well beyond their institutional bases and countries of origin (Mouncer, 2017).

Yet as impressive as the supermarket industry may be in Europe today, the historical trajectory of supermarket expansion there was anything but uniform. The "diverging itineraries" seen across European countries – a pattern found in the history of self-service stores more generally – were the product of multiple, complex, interacting factors, and the results on the ground were remarkably mixed, with the market penetration of the form by 1972, as measured in supermarkets per million residents, marked by wide variations: Denmark with sixty-five supermarkets per million; Belgium with sixty-two; the UK, fifty-eight; Switzerland, fifty-five; the Netherlands, forty-seven; West Germany, forty-six; France, forty; and Italy registering only eleven stores per million (Van den Eeckhout, 2012; p. 78; citing Lescent-Giles, 2005, p. 199). More than is commonly recognised, the law loomed large: in a number of European countries, there were big difficulties, especially early on, in overcoming regulatory barriers and the policy-shaping power of entrenched local market incumbents. There is likewise no doubt that the cold economics of competition figured enormously, but culture mattered too, sometimes speeding, sometimes hindering the uptake of the supermarket model.

Although the United States and its big, captivating, sometimes spectacular stores held an undeniable appeal for many, especially the entrepreneurial advocates of the supermarket form, there were also recurring worries about American influence and, accordingly, unease about and resistance to the proliferation of the new sales methods. This raises the issue of "Americanization", a term that, for all its importance and power, is often deployed too broadly, and with too little rigour. For historians' core concerns with causes, effects, and the agents and sources of change, it is best reserved for instances in which we can demonstrate either (1) a strong case: identifiable, discrete transfers from the United States to other societies (with or without intermediaries) of elements of culture, behaviour, thought, or practice that clearly and indisputably originated in the US, and their adoption in the societies receiving such transfers; or (2) where specific transfers from the US cannot be proven, a weaker but still sufficient case: the adoption by other societies of elements of culture, behaviour, thought, or practice that are so distinctively associated with the US as to be convincingly if not indisputably "American". The supermarket is, without a doubt, so strongly associated with its origins and success in the US as to be fairly considered "American", but its reception in Europe offers, in fact, so many examples of discrete, direct transfers from and through American institutions and actors that even the strong case of Americanisation is, for many European societies, amply proven. Here the label fits.

That said, the mechanics and results of Americanisation were by no means straightforward, unvarying, or predictable. In Italy, Americanisation – real and imagined – proved an especially hot issue. The ongoing contest between leftist and rightist blocs in the immediate postwar decades meant that the supermarket figured as something much more than just a food store in the minds of those concerned with the country's future. Businessmen, investors, companies and ideas from the US were at the forefront of the effort to popularise the supermarket form, and American influence and the power of capitalist big business were major concerns for Italians. 'Amid the Cold War climate', as Emanuela Scarpellini (2012) notes, 'this often turned the opening of a supermarket into a *cause politique*' (p. 60). Italy did ultimately see the penetration of the supermarket model and the rise of a number of large chain-style enterprises, but early efforts there were remarkable for their slow pace and for the difficulties that entrepreneurs and managers encountered (De Grazia, 2002; De Grazia, 2005; Scarpellini, 2005; Scarpellini, 2012). For another important case, West Germany, Lydia Langer (2012) concludes that although there is abundant evidence of an 'important push factor' in the form of direct transfers of the self-service and supermarket models from the US, such borrowing was 'not in fact the decisive factor' for the transformation of German grocery sales and the rise of the supermarket, which instead depended more on 'the establishment of a European network promoting the rationalisation of distribution policies' (p. 72). (This finding, of course, raises the question of whether the European network on which the Germans relied might itself fairly be described as the product of Americanisation.) Across Europe, there was rarely if ever anything like a direct, cookie-cutter replication of American practice. Instead, the process was marked by considerable localisation and hybridisation, making for a wide range of outcomes in practice.

There were, moreover, a few notable European laggards. In Spain, for example, a combination of political and economic circumstances connected with the survival of Francoism until 1975 meant that the model would be quite slow to take hold (Ruiz, 2007), though the transformation in later years has been dramatic, moving the country's commercial practices more in line with prevailing European dynamics that have made the supermarket a common feature of the retailing landscape.

The model proved attractive in developed countries beyond Europe and North America as well. In Australia, for example, expansion was rapid and robust, and by the mid-1990s three large chains accounted for three-quarters of the prepackaged grocery items sold in the country (Humphery, 1998; p. 2). Japanese developments attest to both the power and the limits of the supermarket form, as well as to its flexibility in the face of new and different competitive conditions and cultural expectations. After the first experiments with self-service retailing in the late 1950s, a number of innovative Japanese firms and business leaders worked hard over the next several decades to harness the country's economic dynamism through supermarket-style retailing. In the ensuing consumer boom from the 1960s through the 1980s, grocery sales in many Japanese retail outlets started to take on many of the attributes that characterised supermarket retailing elsewhere, with a wide variety of prepackaged and processed foods sold in increasingly large stores. The supermarket-style would not be dislodged from its prominent position even as Japan's economy slid towards stagnation in the 1990s. At the same time, however, urban settlement patterns and distinctive consumer preferences for certain fresh foods and freshly prepared dishes have meant that Japan has also seen a number of departures from the dominance of the traditional supermarket. Many Japanese consumers continued to opt for daily or near-daily shopping trips, encouraging the persistence of small neighbourhood stores, while supermarkets themselves responded to local market conditions by adding special sections catering to the demand for the fresh, daily items that shoppers insisted on. Meanwhile, supermarket-style food sections were often integrated into a distinctive hybrid retailing form (customarily called *super* in Japanese even though many are not, strictly speaking, just supermarkets), one that blends a wide variety of self-service grocery options into much larger stores with the extensive non-food offerings typically found in department stores and discounters (Usui, 2014; pp. 111–153).

Despite its tight connections with the power of capitalist business in Western Europe and the United States, the supermarket model held an undeniable allure for many planners and commercial specialists in socialist societies. Yugoslavia's unorthodox and innovative system of "self-management socialism" under Josip Broz Tito, for example, proved unusually open to the promise of the new grocery sales method. In as clear an instance of a direct Americanising transfer as might be imagined (and, at the same time, an unmistakable use of the supermarket success story for Cold War messaging about the superiority of capitalism), the manager of a socially owned Yugoslav retailing enterprise, wowed by the exhibition of a functional, full-scale exemplar at the Supermarket USA exhibit at the 1957 International Trade Fair in Zagreb, purchased the furnishings and equipment of the entire store, carting them off for installation in a prime location in downtown Belgrade (Hamilton, 2009; Rusinow, 1969). On the heels of that extraordinary episode, Yugoslavia eagerly participated in the "supermarket revolution", with more big stores established in urban centres during the 1960s, and many thereafter (Rusinow, 1969; Patterson, 2009). The model also proved attractive in several other, comparatively prosperous East European countries, with the construction of limited but nonetheless impressive networks of supermarkets and smaller-scale superettes in East Germany, Hungary and Czechoslovakia (Patterson, 2009). Even the Soviet Union, a stronghold of communist orthodoxy and no great wellspring of commercial innovation, finally took steps towards the adoption of the model, opening the country's first supermarket in Leningrad in 1970, with many new stores planned in subsequent years and 239 built by the end of the decade (Skurski, 1983; p. 131). In many cases, these early socialist-era store networks formed the basis for the expansion of Western firms into newly opened East European markets following the collapse of communism and the resultant privatisation of retailing assets (Dries, Reardon & Swinnen, 2004).

Turning our examination now to the developing world, we find further confirmation of the profound influence of the supermarket form as a favoured model for development and modernisation. Suggesting that the phenomenon has truly global dimensions, Reardon and Gulati (2008) describe a "supermarket revolution" occurring in four waves. The first wave, seen in much of South America, East Asia (excluding the People's Republic of China), and South Africa, began in the early 1990s, with supermarkets' share of relevant sector sales in these areas rising from about 10% around 1990 to approximately 50–60% by the middle of the next decade. The second phase, encountered in Mexico, Central America, and many countries of Southeast Asia, started in the middle and later years of the 1990s and saw supermarkets' market share rise from a baseline of 5–10% in 1990 to 30–50% by the mid-2000s. A mix of political and economic factors meant that China, India, and Vietnam would wait to participate in these trends until the

Figure 10.4 SPAR hypermarket entrance, New South China Mall, Dongguan, China. The supermarket as an adaptable transnational model for retail development: a massive grocery/non-grocery hypermarket operated by local owners under the internationally licensed SPAR brand at the New South China Mall, Dongguan, Guangdong Province, China. February 2010.

Sources: Wikimedia Commons, photographer User David290 (public domain); https://commons.wikimedia.org/wiki/File:NewSouthChinaMall-SPAR.jpg

third wave that began in the late 1990s and early 2000s, with market share ranging from 2% to 20% by the middle part of the 2000s. By the latter part of that decade, sales in modern, self-service stores were expanding dramatically in these third-wave countries, increasing 30–50% per year and far outstripping these economies' already remarkable rates of growth in gross domestic product, indicating that major sectoral realignments were underway. Finally, by the latter half of the 2000s, a more recent fourth wave appeared to be building in very poor and comparatively less developed countries including Bangladesh, Cambodia and various West African nations, though these areas were marked by considerably slower growth, with the prospect of 'another one or two decades before supermarket diffusion in the fourth wave areas is appreciable' (Reardon & Gulati, 2008; p. 1; see also Reardon, Timmer, Barrett & Berdegué, 2003; Weatherspoon and Reardon, 2003). The analysis used in delineating these four waves applies a broad definition of supermarkets that includes all "modern retail", thus encompassing not just traditional supermarkets and larger hypermarkets with full-assortment supermarket sections, but also modern convenience stores and neighbourhood stores. Nevertheless, these research findings are strongly suggestive of the timing, pace, geographic variation and extent of the spread of the supermarket model.

For businesses and the consumers they seek to attract, the implications of these changes have been enormous. In at least some parts of Latin America, the "traditional image" of supermarkets as 'niche players for rich consumers in the capital cities of the region' was rendered invalid by the early 2000s, quickly becoming 'a distant memory of the pre-liberalisation period before the 1990s' (Reardon and Berdegué, 2002; p. 517). (Here "supermarket" is defined in narrower terms that include traditional supermarkets, hypermarkets, and other large-format venues such as warehouse stores and membership clubs; p. 319.) The transformations involved here are astonishing for their magnitude and speed. 'In one globalising decade', as Reardon and Berdegué observe with respect to the huge shifts in market share attributable to these "modern" store forms, 'Latin American retailing made the change which took the US retail sector 50 years' (p. 517).

Although historical work can draw usefully from recent empirical findings of researchers in fields like business, management, economics, planning and policy studies, developing a truly global account of the contemporary history of the supermarket will prove difficult. Conditions are shifting, markets and retail strategies are rapidly changing, case studies are patchy, data are fragmentary and interpretations are, as a result, incomplete. Some caution is in order. Readings of the same record are, moreover, sometimes widely divergent in their emphases, in some ways even contradictory. Thus we find one pair of analysts (Reardon & Minten, 2011) concluding that 'supermarkets have taken-off quickly in the "traditional retail setting" of India' (136), a market environment that they find to be essentially comparable in key aspects (urban density and agricultural patterns) to many other Asian settings that have already experienced their own "supermarket revolution", noting that, in the end, 'India seems to differ in just doing it faster, combining lessons from others, creating new solutions' (137). Others interpreting the same conditions, however, stress that 'in India, even in the most advanced urban settings, there are no "true modern shoppers". Nor are there "true modern outlets" since even the Western-style superstores generally have to incorporate some traditional elements' (Dholakia, Dholakia & Chattopadhyay, 2012; p. 252). As variant readings like these suggest, to some extent it remains unclear just what has taken place "on the ground" as the supermarket has extended its reach into new markets. There is obviously much more work to be done. Yet despite such reservations, the available evidence leaves no doubt that, even in these less-studied cases that have only recently started to attract sustained scholarly consideration, the supermarket form has functioned as a profoundly influential transnational and global model, and it continues to do so.

Everyday values: the supermarket as a site of culture

As it has travelled to occupy a worldwide stage, the supermarket model has been recognised by both scholarly and popular observers as among the most potent cultural forces in modern commercial life. Commentaries on supermarket shopping are filled with affirmations of the novel and remarkable cultural power of the form. The account provided by Sharon Zukin (2004), describing developments seen in American society in the latter half of the twentieth century, offers a signal example:

> Shopping in supermarkets changed us as a public. Our geographical mobility – our ability to range much farther from home in quest of goods – empowered us; it made us feel we had a wider choice. But shopping in the most modern stores, which were not only larger but located at a greater distance from home and work, made shopping more tiresome. And though parking lots, shopping carts, and multiple checkout lines . . . made it faster to get in and out of the store, it took longer to escape the

> supermarket's totalizing environment. . . . We were emotionally immobilized by the immense abundance.
>
> (p. 79)

Moving beyond the much-discussed American case, and beyond even any literal connection with what goes on in grocery stores, the supermarket has become a familiar metaphor for more general cultural conditions (Bowlby, 2000), evoking for better or worse the broader human predicament in a modern world shot through with commercialism and filled with choices that call out for our attention, our action, our money, our love.

Generalisations about culture are both useful and treacherous. For what is really at work here is not culture but *cultures* – multiple, fragmentary, overlapping and sometimes competitive and contradictory. This observation certainly holds true for the manifold cultures that arise from and connect with the world of business: the undeniable importance of the supermarket as a cultural phenomenon points promisingly to the value of crafting defensible generalisations, but caution is required. Along these lines, Kim Humphery (1998) offers a useful distinction when he asserts that

> retailers develop *retail forms* and construct *retail cultures*; they do not create smoothly functioning mass consumer cultures, however hard they may try. *Consumer cultures* arise only in the interaction between those who have something to sell and those who look, listen, watch, wander, feel and sometimes buy.
>
> (p. 5)

The same insight applies with full force to the culture, or cultures, of the supermarket. Critically, the supermarket is at once an important arena for market culture (the designation I use to emphasise the efforts and values of businesspeople in the marketplace, including but extending beyond the retail setting) and for consumer culture (a term that shifts the inquiry back towards what shoppers and buyers actually do with the markets and goods they encounter). Occupying in this way a prominent place not just in business and commercial affairs but also in the broader currents of social and private life, the mass-scale, full-assortment, self-service grocery store has come to function as an important setting for and generator of a pattern that I have previously described as an expansive "culture of the supermarket" that was consolidated over the course of the late twentieth century and spread well beyond the developed capitalist societies where it first emerged (Patterson, 2009).

Examining world-historical trends, key comparative cases, and global flows, we find that supermarkets have been (and, for now at least, remain) prime sites and drivers of a still larger pattern, one that may properly be termed *the transnational culture of modern retailing*. Built and maintained not only in supermarkets but in other prominent retail venues as well, the vital assemblage I identify here attempts to capture the most important aspects of both business-built market culture and shopper-supported consumer culture. It exhibits the following key elements:

- *the emphasis of the pleasurable, satisfying qualities of shopping*
- *the promise of spontaneity and discovery*
- *the pursuit of modernity through innovative, up to date, progressive shopping*
- *the promotion of the virtues of novelty and progress*
- *the security of satisfaction guaranteed*
- *the restructuring of shopping sociability towards a more individualised experience*

- *the eclipse of labour and the subordination of production to consumption*
- *the demarcation of a feminine domain of consumption complementing shifting work roles*
- *the elevation of abundance as an end in itself*
- *the embrace of competition*
- *the acknowledgement of the sovereign consumer and the primacy of choice*

As a set of common behaviours and expressive activities grounded in the communication of shared ideas, beliefs, attitudes, preferences and identities – in other words, as a *culture* – these ways of marketing, buying, thinking, feeling and living all combine to make the supermarket experience a powerful marker and multiplier of prevailing priorities, norms and ideals. In a sense rather different from the promises made in advertisements and store promotions, the supermarket really is where everyday values are found.

The customer-retailer interactions that take place in supermarkets routinely serve to reinforce those values, with every element of the pattern set forth above amply attested in the scholarly and trade literature on supermarket operations and supermarket culture. Of course, many messages about modernity, novelty, pleasure, satisfaction and abundance are, by design, immediately apparent to shoppers themselves as part of the in-store experience. Features like

Figure 10.5 Housewife shopping in supermarket (Gisella). The transnational culture of modern retailing: satisfaction, pleasure, progress, abundance, competition, choice and the feminine domain of consumption. A self-service shopper amid the promises of consumer sovereignty in an American supermarket. May 1957.

Source: Library of Congress, photographer Thomas J. O'Halloran (public domain) www.loc.gov/resource/ppmsca.51756/

these surface so frequently and with such force that the claim that these are prime constituents of contemporary retail culture will likely seem uncontroversial. Other important aspects of the prevailing cultural pattern, however, tend to be revealed only through deeper, sustained analysis. The supermarket sells more than meets the eye, and greater care is needed to discern what the retail style works to obscure, as happens with the tendency to render labour invisible and elevate consumption practices above the underlying production relations that make all the purchases possible. When self-service retail methods seek to drive labour costs down by 'employing the customer' throughout the shopper's circuit around the store (Palm 2017; p. 41) as the supermarket model does so consistently, it is not clear that many of those who have ended up doing the labour for themselves actually recognise the scope and impact of the larger dynamics to which they are contributing. Investigations of the gendered dimensions of the supermarket suggest similarly interesting results. Past practice has seen, for example, efforts by a number of store operators to encourage men to embrace grocery shopping, while husbands' control of household budgets has required some caveats about the supermarket as a feminised domain (Cohen, 2003; p. 148). But on the whole, the culture sustained through grocery shopping remains one attuned to the critical importance of women's roles, with American supermarkets by the 1950s established at the forefront of what Tracey Deutsch (2010) calls 'a new gender system', one in which grocery retailers of various types moved towards 'a remarkable convergence' of styles and messaging built around the norms and expectations of comfortably middle-class female shoppers, a system that departed from the more varied cultural palette of past retail cultures to present women instead with 'glamour and convenience – not autonomy or authority' (p. 134; see also Deutsch, 1999). While most shoppers may remain heedless of their participation in such regimes, a lack of conscious awareness does not render the resultant effects any less shared, any less reflective and expressive of values, any less cultural.

Notwithstanding the various reservations voiced by critics about the constraints that they believe the supermarket and related sales methods impose on the welfare and freedom of shoppers, the internationalised culture of modern retailing is one that vigorously asserts the importance of consumer sovereignty and consumer alternatives. It is, ultimately, a culture of *choice*. Evidencing its power and appeal, that culture has arisen in places where choices are harder to come by, including those that do not share the characteristics of fully developed industrial and post-industrial capitalist societies. Indeed, the culture of choice managed to take hold even in communist-led polities where there was no large-scale private ownership of retailing capital and, at least in comparison to the capitalist world, rather limited choices in the stores and on the shelves (Patterson, 2009). Further testimony to the influence of the cultural pattern is the fact that its diffusion has taken place not just spatially, but across retail categories as well, into food and grocery stores that, by virtue of their reduced size and more restricted product assortment, do not really warrant classification as supermarkets. Limited as they are, many of these smaller shops acknowledge and reinforce the power of the transnational cultural ideal as they attempt to capture and communicate the vision of abundant modernity and choice that is regularly on display in the classic supermarket, the model form.

This lane open? The supermarket as history

Supermarkets cannot, of course, function everywhere. As explained above, they are heavily reliant on technology and complex supply networks, dependent on proximity to concentrated urban, suburban, and exurban pools of mobile consumers, and better suited for wealthier developed economies with purchasing power that warrants the major capital investments that the form requires. Such limitations help explain the persistence of a variety of different grocery-sales models alongside the massive, full-selection, chain-operated supermarket form that has thus far attracted the most attention from scholars, observers and business managers. Small and independent stores that fill quite different market niches, or just a part of the market niche of the classic supermarket, persist as an important feature of the grocery retailing landscape (Logemann, 2012). Still, as its global spread goes forward, the supermarket remains a highly favoured retailing model among both business specialists and consumers.

Nevertheless, supermarket operations and the supermarket model itself have been and will likely continue to be subject to pressures, primarily economic but also social and cultural, that can result in considerable modifications. Over the past decades, what is meant by the concept "supermarket" has changed in notable ways and no doubt will do so in the future. The supermarket form is a *flexible* form. But in spite of that adaptability and the obvious success of the supermarket as it nears the end of its first century of practical implementation, there is at least some reason to wonder whether the grand-scale, full-assortment supermarket model is sure to survive as the dominant paradigm for grocery retailing. Is the supermarket in the process of becoming a modernism of the past?

Recent developments have seen the form pressed in new directions. Perhaps most notable are those modifications that have incorporated supermarkets into expanded venues such as hypermarkets, superstores and supercenters (e.g., Walmart), and similar outlets that operate in an even larger format and offer a much wider variety of non-grocery items than is found in the standard supermarket product range. Such businesses, along with warehouse stores and discounters (Costco, Sam's Club) that sell many grocery items without attempting to stock anywhere near the full range that a supermarket must offer to meet customers' expectations, pose significant threats to the profitability of traditional supermarket enterprises (Smith, 2009; pp. 180–181). In addition, market conditions in some highly developed countries have encouraged the emergence of stores that occupy notably narrower niches than classic supermarkets, with a restricted selection of products and marketing that is targeted at limited consumer segments, while still cultivating the evident "feel" of a supermarket and exploiting the form's technological, operational and productivity advantages. Along these lines, for example, we find non-traditional supermarkets (or not-quite-supermarkets) aimed at upscale or health-conscious consumers (e.g., Whole Foods in the US, Bio-Planet in France), food-savvy value-minded customers (Trader Joe's in the US) and discounters (Aldi in Europe and beyond). Outlets like these differ from traditional supermarkets through their option to offer not quite "everything" or a different, niche-inflected version of "everything", yet they remain deeply influenced by the supermarket model and represent in many ways a fairly straightforward revision or extension of that template.

Predictions about the future are rarely the province of historians, or at least of cautious ones. That said, a sensitivity to history can usefully inform assessments of present developments and trends, in turn offering at least a few clues about what may lie in store (literally and figuratively) for the future. And on that point much of the answer may emerge from a return to this essay's earlier emphasis of the driving forces of profit-driven efficiency imperatives and, especially, technology. If the supermarket model is to be superseded, the causes of its decline will most likely be found there. Just as efficiency opportunities are dependent on a constantly shifting set of economic, demographic, technical, legal, environmental and other factors, technology itself is continually in flux – today remarkably so. Supermarket operations have been, as we have seen, quick to adopt technologies for an apparent market edge. But store owners readily modify or even abandon technological solutions when circumstances compel it: witness the ongoing displacement of throwaway bags made of polyethylene and other plastics, an invention that not long ago was treated as an essential convenience technology for supermarket shoppers (lightweight, remarkably durable) and supermarket operators (cheap, compact, self-opening). Today, however, what once seemed the indispensable disposable is under serious pressure as a worrisome source of pollution, an externalised cost increasingly unsustainable in new environmental and regulatory conditions.

Given that the ancillary technologies of the supermarket form continue to emerge and decline as circumstances demand, it is conceivable that similar forces might also weaken the supermarket model itself. Present developments already allow us to imagine a future in which new automated or semi-automated delivery systems, made possible through innovations in energy, transportation, and information technology, may at last oust the supermarket from its dominant position as a vital, large-scale cost saving link between warehouse and customer. Admittedly, early efforts at web-based delivery systems during the dot-com boom of the first decades of the Internet did not prove much of a disruption, and some failures (e.g., the e-commerce grocer Webvan) were spectacular (Kornum & Bjerre, 2005). But there is reason to think that future refinements could pose more of a threat to the supermarket model, as recent speculation about the long-term significance of the acquisition of the Whole Foods chain by Internet shopping behemoth Amazon suggests. Live by the price cut, die by the price cut.

Even so, an essential element of the equation will be the expectation, long cultivated through the supermarket model itself, that more or less "everything" will always be available to grocery shoppers. Competing with supermarkets is not just about costs and ease. It is about the completeness of the assortment on offer. It is, in other words, about *choice*. Any alternative model will have to respond to the multiple strong advantages that the supermarket has provided to shoppers and sellers alike. Consequently, there seems little reason at present to wager that the supermarket form will not survive much longer. It has proven both remarkably persistent and remarkably mutable, and it likely will for some time.

How, then, might historically minded scholars continue to most profitably address the supermarket phenomenon? Developments in the practice of business history in recent years have demonstrated the value of approaches that draw more deeply on concerns with the broader social, cultural, political, and economic dimensions of business and commerce and, in so doing, move away from narrower, more traditional examinations of enterprises and their managers. More studies along these lines could helpfully augment a literature that was in some ways, early on at least, a bit too prone to hagiographic accounts of the great entrepreneurs and the great companies. Labour needs more attention, too. The tendency of supermarkets, and self-service more generally, to render invisible much of the work necessary to put all the abundance on the shelves leaves historians the task of remedying that invisibility. Further emphasis on the lives and labours of supermarket workers should help build a more complicated, revealing and productive picture. Building on impressive extant work, further investigation of the deep connections between supermarkets and gender roles could likely yield interesting results, while the complicated relationship between food shopping, food retailing and issues of race, ethnicity and class presents a terrain with great untapped potential, as does the supermarket industry's engagement with children and with people living in small towns and population centres at the demographic limits of the supermarket model's viability. And while recent decades have brought a welcome attention to the extraordinary importance of consumption practices, there is still plenty to be done to assess how consumers experienced their supermarkets (and the alternatives) and to determine what difference the much-vaunted method of modern shopping has really made.

The supermarket's power as a transnational commercial and cultural model, and its connections with the global economic order and international flows of capital, technology and know-how, suggest the value of further work on the geographic diffusion of the supermarket form. Despite some very interesting contributions on the history of grocery sales beyond the United States in recent years, considerably more work is needed, particularly work on the food distribution systems of poorer developing countries, where the supermarket model may have great appeal but where structural limitations may hinder its spread or require more extensive local adaptations to make the format viable. Along these lines, it would be profitable to consider how supermarkets may or may not function in those few places where Marxist-Leninist governance and socialised ownership of the means of production still prevail (e.g., Cuba), as well as the trajectory of the supermarket model in post-socialist societies (Eastern Europe and the former Soviet Union) and in the rapidly changing business systems of states that have managed to combine elements of capitalism and Leninism (China, Vietnam).

The extensive connections, obvious or not, between supermarket commerce and the underlying political orders that govern business likewise indicate the potential payoffs from new studies that probe more persistently the legal and regulatory frameworks that have shaped supermarket development and operations. On matters as diverse as labour regulation, land use and zoning, opening hours, price setting, and restrictions on permitted product assortment such as Europe's widespread bans on sales of over-the-counter non-prescription medications (Chave, 2014), the success and dominance of supermarkets is dependent on supportive legal regimes, and historical writing should grapple with law and policy more consistently and more carefully.

Similarly, the importance of concentrated capital (typically in the form of big business chains) for the supermarket's characteristic economies of scale points to the value of further examination of divergent management structures. Even if, globally speaking, socialist ownership no longer offers much of an alternative, it certainly did at one time, and there still remain meaningful and significant options for collective ownership and governance. With respect to stores run by co-operative societies, for example, we may learn a great deal about the import of the supermarket model more generally by asking how such operations have been shaped and constrained by the broader patterns established by for profit private chains and by the prevailing culture of modern retailing, with its profound insistence on variety, competition and choice.

Finally, there is a clear need to bring the fields most concerned with the big things that supermarkets do into a much closer conversation – and one that is more explicitly historical. To a notable extent, work undertaken by scholars in business, economics, management, marketing, advertising, planning, design and architecture directs little attention to historical developments and their impact, and along these lines there remain some deficiencies even in sociology, anthropology, cultural studies, and related critical disciplines. By the same token, historians need to dig more deeply into the key findings and governing concerns of those working in these other fields and take them more seriously on their own terms. Much of the history of the supermarket remains to be written, and there are big opportunities both for illuminating, conceptually sophisticated studies of particular cases and for wide-ranging integrative, comparative and interdisciplinary work.

References

Alexander, A. (2008), 'Format development and retail change: Supermarket retailing and the London co-operative society', *Business History*, 50 (4), pp. 489–508.

Alexander, A., Shaw, G. and Curth, L. (2005), 'Promoting retail innovation: Knowledge flows during the emergence of self-service and supermarket retailing in Britain', *Environment and Planning A: Economy and Space*, 37, pp. 805–821.

Bailey, A.R. and Alexander, A. (2017), 'Cadbury and the rise of the supermarket: Innovation in marketing 1953–1975', *Business History*, pp. 1–22. DOI: 10.1080/00076791.2017.1400012.
Bowlby, R. (2000), *Carried away: The invention of modern shopping* (London: Faber and Faber).
Bowlby, R. (1997), 'Supermarket futures', in P. Falk and C. Campbell (eds.) *The shopping experience* (London: Sage).
Brand, E.A. (1963), *Modern supermarket operation* (New York: Fairchild Publications).
Chave, J. (2014), 'The challenges we share with some EU countries: What can we learn?', *The Pharmaceutical Journal*. Supplements, 11th February 2014. Available at: www.pharmaceutical-journal.com/the-challenges-we-share-with-some-eu-countries-what-can-we-learn/11134173.article.
Cochoy, F. (2016), *On the origins of self-service* (Jaciara Topley-Lira, Trans.) (London/New York: Routledge).
Cohen, L. (2003), *A consumers' republic: The politics of mass consumption in postwar America* (New York: Vintage).
De Grazia, V. (2002), 'American supermarkets versus European small shops: Or how transnational capitalism crossed paths with moral economy in Italy during the 1960s', *Trondheim Studies on East European Cultures & Societies*, 7, pp. 2–26.
De Grazia, V. (2005), *Irresistible empire: America's advance through twentieth-century Europe* (Cambridge, MA: Belknap Press of Harvard University Press).
Deutsch, T. (1999), 'From "wild animal stores" to women's sphere: Supermarkets and the politics of mass consumption, 1930–1950', *Business & Economic History*. 28 (2), pp. 143–153.
Deutsch, T. (2010), *Building a housewife's paradise: Gender, politics, and American grocery stores in the twentieth century* (Chapel Hill, NC: University of North Carolina Press).
Dholakia, N., Dholakia, R.R. and Chattopadhyay, A. (2012), 'India's emerging retail systems: Coexistence of tradition and modernity', *Journal of Macromarketing*, 32 (3), pp. 252–265.
Dries, L., Reardon, T. and Swinnen, J.F.M. (2004), 'The rapid rise of supermarkets in Central and Eastern Europe: Implications for the agrifood sector and rural development', *Development Policy Review*, 22 (5), pp. 525–556.
Food Marketing Institute (2018), *Supermarket Facts*, Available at: www.fmi.org/our-research/supermarket-facts (Accessed February 11, 2018).
Grandclément, C. (2009), 'Wheeling one's groceries around the store: The invention of the shopping cart, 1936–1953', in W. Belasco and R. Horowitz (eds.) *Food chains: From farmyard to shopping cart* (Philadelphia, PA: University of Pennsylvania Press) 233–251, notes at 291–294.
Hamilton, S. (2008), *Trucking country: The road to America's Wal-mart economy* (Princeton, NJ: Princeton University Press).
Hamilton, S. (2009), 'Supermarket USA confronts state socialism: Airlifting the technopolitics of industrial food distribution into Cold War Yugoslavia', in R. Oldenziel and K. Zachmann (eds.) *Cold War kitchen: Americanization, technology, and European users* (Cambridge, MA, MIT Press) 137–159.
Humphery, K. (1998), *Shelf life: Supermarkets and the changing cultures of consumption* (Cambridge, MA: Cambridge University Press).
Independent Grocers Alliance (2018), *About IGA*, Available at: www.iga.com/about.aspx (Accessed February 22, 2018)
Keh, H.T. (1998), 'Technological innovations in grocery retailing: Retrospect and prospect', *Technology in Society*, 20 (2), pp. 195–209.
Kornum, N. and Bjerre, M. (eds.) (2005), *Grocery e-commerce: Consumer behaviour and business strategies* (Cheltenham, UK: Edward Elgar).
Langer, L. (2012), 'How West German retailers learned to sell to a mass consumer society: Self-service and supermarkets between "Americanization" and "Europeanization," 1950s–1960s', in R. Jessen and L. Langer (eds.) *Transformations of retailing in Europe after 1945* (Farnham, UK: Ashgate) 72–85.
Lawrence, P.R. (1991 [1958]), *The changing of organizational behavior patterns: A case study of decentralization* (New Brunswick, NJ: Transaction).
Lescent-Giles, I. (2005), 'The rise of supermarkets in twentieth-century Britain and France', in C. Sarasua and P. Scholliers (eds.) *Lands, shops and kitchens: Technology and the food chain in twentieth-century Europe* (Turnhout: Brepols) 188–211.
Levinson, M. (2011), *The great A&P and the struggle for small business in America* (New York: Hill & Wang).
Liebs, C.H. (1995 [1985]), *Main Street to miracle mile: American roadside architecture* (Baltimore, MD: Johns Hopkins University Press).
Logemann, J. (2012), 'Beyond self-service: The limits of "Americanization" in post-war west German retailing in comparative perspective', in R. Jessen and L. Langer (eds.) *Transformations of retailing in Europe after 1945* (Farnham, UK: Ashgate) 87–100.

Longstreth, R. (1999), *The drive-in, the supermarket, and the transformation of commercial space in Los Angeles, 1914–1941* (Cambridge, MA: MIT Press).
Mann, A. (2014), *Global activism in food politics: Power shift* (Basingstoke: Palgrave Macmillan).
Markin, R. (1964–1965), 'The supermarket – a study of size, profits, and concentration', *Journal of Retailing* (Winter), pp. 22–36.
Markin, R. (1968), *The supermarket: An analysis of growth, development, and change* (Revised ed. Pullman) (Washington, DC: Washington State University Press).
Mayo, J.M. (1993), *The American grocery store: The business evolution of an architectural space* (Westport, CT: Greenwood Press).
McAusland, R. (1980), *Supermarkets: 50 years of progress* (Washington, DC: Food Marketing Institute).
Morton, A.Q. (1994), 'Packaging history: The emergence of the uniform product code (UPC) in the United States, 1970–75', *History and Technology, an International Journal*, 11 (1), pp. 101–111.
Mouncer, B. (2017), 'Top 10 biggest supermarket chains in Europe', *Business Chief*, 28th September. Available at: http://europe.businesschief.com/top10/1436/Top-10-biggest-supermarket-chains-in-Europe.
Palm, M. (2017), *Technologies of consumer labor: A history of self-service* (New York: Routledge).
Patel, R. (2007), *Stuffed and starved: The hidden battle for the world food system* (Brooklyn, NY: Melville House).
Patterson, P.H. (2009), 'Making markets Marxist? The east European grocery store from rationing to rationality to rationalizations', in W. Belasco and R. Horowitz (eds.) *Food chains: From farmyard to shopping cart* (Philadelphia, PA: University of Pennsylvania Press) 196–216, notes 285–288.
Reardon, T. and Gulati, A. (2008), 'The supermarket revolution in developing countries: Policies for "competitiveness with inclusiveness"', *International Food Policy Research Institute. IFPRI Policy Brief 2*, June.
Reardon, T. and Berdegué, J.A. (2002), 'The rapid rise of supermarkets in Latin America: Challenges and opportunities for development', *Development Policy Review*, 20 (4), pp. 317–334.
Reardon, T. and Minten, B. (2011), 'Surprised by supermarkets: Diffusion of modern food retail in India', *Journal of Agribusiness in Developing and Emerging Economies*, 1 (2), pp. 134–161.
Reardon, T., Timmer, C.P., Barrett, C.B. and Berdegué, J. (2003), 'The rise of supermarkets in Africa, Asia, and Latin America', *American Journal of Agricultural Economics*, 85 (5), pp. 1140–1146.
Ruiz, J.L.G. (2007), 'Cultural resistance and the gradual emergence of modern marketing and retailing practices in Spain, 1950–1975', *Business History*, 49 (3), pp. 367–384.
Rusinow, D. (1969), 'Yugoslavia's supermarket revolution: The self-service shopping cart as a vehicle of modernization', *American Universities Field Staff Reports, Southeast Europe Series*, 16 (1).
Scarpellini, E. (2004), 'Shopping American style: The arrival of the supermarket in postwar Italy', *Enterprise & Society*, 5 (4), pp. 625–668.
Scarpellini, E. (2012), 'The long way to the supermarket: Entrepreneurial innovation and adaptation in 1950s – 1960s Italy', in R. Jessen and L. Langer (eds.) *Transformations of retailing in Europe after 1945* (Farnham, UK: Ashgate) 55–69.
Seth, A. and Randall, G. (2011), *The grocers: The rise and rise of supermarket chains*, 3rd ed (London: Kogan Page).
Shaw, G., Bailey, A., Alexander, A., Nell, D. and Hamlett, J. (2012), 'The coming of the supermarket: The processes and consequences of transplanting American know-how into Britain', in R. Jessen and L. Langer (eds.) *Transformations of retailing in Europe after 1945* (Farnham, UK: Ashgate) 35–53.
Shaw, G., Kurth, L. and Alexander, A. (2004), 'Selling self-service and the supermarket: The Americanisation of food retailing in Britain, 1945–60', *Business History*, 46 (4), pp. 568–582.
Shaw, H. (2014), *The consuming geographies of food: Diet, food deserts and obesity* (London: Routledge).
Skurski, R. (1983), *Soviet marketing and economic development* (New York: St. Martin's Press).
Smith, A.F. (2009), *Eating history: 30 turning points in the making of American cuisine* (New York: Columbia University Press).
Tedlow, R.S. (1990), *New and improved: The story of mass marketing in America* (New York: Basic Books).
Tolbert, L. (2009), 'The aristocracy of the market basket: Self-service food shopping in the New South', in W. Belasco and R. Horowitz (eds.) *Food chains: From farmyard to shopping cart* (Philadelphia, PA: University of Pennsylvania Press) 179–195, notes at 283–285.
Usui, K. (2014), *Marketing and consumption in modern Japan* (New York: Routledge).
Van den Eeckhout, P. (2012), 'Shopping for food in Western Europe in the nineteenth and twentieth centuries', *Food and History*, 10 (1), pp. 71–82.
Weatherspoon, D.D. and Reardon, T. (2003), 'The rise of supermarkets in Africa: Implications for agrifood systems and the rural poor', *Development Policy Review*, 21 (3), pp. 333–355.

Yee, A. (2003), *Shopping at giant foods: Chinese American supermarkets in Northern California* (Seattle, WA: University of Washington Press).
Zimmerman, M.M. (1937), *Super market: Spectacular exponent of mass distribution* (New York: Super Market Publishing Co).
Zimmerman, M.M. (1955), *The super market: A revolution in distribution* (New York: McGraw-Hill).
Zukin, S. (2004), *Point of purchase: How shopping changed American culture* (New York: Routledge).

11

VILLAGE SHOPS AND COUNTRY STORES[1]

Douglas McCalla

Introduction

'The history of shopping has been written, but not the history of shops', T.S. Willan wrote in a pioneering account of Abraham Dent, an eighteenth-century shopkeeper in Kirkby Stephen, a market town in northwest England with a population of about a thousand (1970, p. 8).

> This may be the result of a persistent belief that people, before the nineteenth century, obtained their goods at fairs and markets or from pedlars. People did buy goods at fairs and markets and from pedlars . . . but shops were more numerous and more important than is commonly realised.

For the historian, one challenge in showing this was 'the paucity of sources. If shopkeepers kept accounts, few of those accounts seem to have survived'. Useful diaries and letters were equally rare. For Dent, however, a variety of documents allowed closer examination of shopkeeping. Working with, then succeeding, his father, Dent sold mercery (textiles and sewing supplies), groceries, stationery and 'a considerable range of goods, which almost defied classification' (p. 11). Few of these goods were local; he 'sold exotic products, the market sold local produce' (p. 12). Concluding, Willan noted (p. 147) that Dent's activities 'drew him into contact with a much wider world extending from Newcastle to London. If more were known about more Abraham Dents, eighteenth-century England might appear less bucolic and less provincial'. On the other hand, he wondered if Dent was representative:

> it would be misleading to regard [him] as typical of the small town shopkeeper of the eighteenth century. Dent was too versatile, he combined too many roles, to be typical. Had he been simply a shopkeeper or a hosier or a wine merchant or a brewer he would have been more typical of the small town business man.

In the years since Willan's study, the problem of detailed records of actual businesses has hardly been solved. More have been identified, especially in North America (e.g., an informed estimate is that there are 'at least 1,000 examples of shopkeeper account books alone for Nova Scotia' [Gwyn 2015, p. 114]), and a few have been intensively used. Historians have also found other paths towards a more comprehensive understanding of early modern retailing, including in village and rural settings. Among them are tax records and directories, which are external to individual businesses, and bankruptcy records and probate inventories, which provide an internal perspective, albeit at a particular moment. The stereotype of a static, routine and timeless provincial world to which Willan referred has not disappeared, but wherever close analysis has been possible, Dent and his shop have proven to be more representative than Willan imagined. Rural retailing was highly competitive; success at it required skill, work, judgement and risk-taking. And because most of the world's people were rural, the market served by such retailers constituted a significant part of the whole marketplace.

The easiest way of defining rural is as a residual after urban is accounted for. 'Dividing cities from non-cities . . . cannot help but be arbitrary', Jan de Vries writes in his analysis of urbanisation (1984, p. 11). When a threshold population of 10,000 is used to define a city, about 10% of Europe's population lived in such places in 1800 (with England and Wales and the Netherlands the most urbanised, at more than 20%). By 1890, the European figure had risen to almost 30%, with England and Wales and Scotland over 50%. In the United States, the urban population was just 5% of the total in 1790 and 35% of an exponentially larger population a century later (*Historical Statistics* 2006, Series Aa36 and Aa46). For the world as a whole, cities of over 10,000 accounted for only about 5% of the population in the early nineteenth century (de Vries 1984, pp. 39, 45–8, 349–350). A place did not have to be this large, of course, to have essentially urban functions; as de Vries recognises (1984, p. 22), 'a serviceable definition of urban population in early modern Europe is the inhabitants of densely housed settlements of at least 2000 or 3000 population'. A lower threshold still is suggested by George Grantham (1989, p. 190), who argues that during the Ancien Régime it was 'the little market towns that in many ways represent the heart of France'. Whatever the threshold, until at least the early nineteenth century, most people almost everywhere lived outside such places, in villages and the countryside. In much of the world, that was still the case far into the twentieth century. And wherever population was growing rapidly, rural numbers could continue to increase alongside urban population; in the United States, for example, the non-urban population grew more than tenfold between 1790 and 1890.

According to a mythology that has proven "remarkably resistant to change" (Cox 2000, p. 14), a majority of rural people lived outside the marketplace. In France, as Philip Hoffman argues (1996, p. 13), 'the consensus about the French countryside . . . begins with a large number of subsistence peasants, who farmed in isolation from markets'. Thus, Fernand Braudel could write (1982, pp. 59–60) of 'the life going on at the level underneath [the market], a modest but independent life of total or near self-sufficiency'. In North America, an influential interpretation held that until the nineteenth century most rural communities lived largely outside markets; even a thoughtful survey that recognises rural shopkeeping can still speak of 'the relatively simple material lives and insular community economies' of rural America prior to the Civil War (Matson 2006, p. 55). In this powerful story, rural people were on one side of a set of dichotomies, with consumption on the other side (see Stobart, Hann and Morgan 2007, pp. 13–14). They were traditional rather than modern, producers rather than consumers, participants in a customary more than a market economy, etc. That left little room for village shops. As an anthropological study of retailing in a small Irish town notes, outside a specialist literature, retailers

> have not captured the historical imagination or historians' interest; and this has been exacerbated by a general and common antipathy towards retailers in western society. . . . [T]here has been an obsessive stereotype of Ireland and of rural western Europe as comprising regions of farmers, farmworkers, or peasants.
>
> *(Gulliver and Silverman 1995, p. 354)*

Among the reasons to question this understanding is evidence that in the early modern era goods produced beyond the immediate locality were clearly reaching ordinary rural people (e.g., North 2016). These increasingly included goods new to western society. Exotic groceries such as tobacco, tea, and sugar and Asian manufactures such as cottons and ceramics were already widely consumed in North-Western Europe by the early eighteenth century; and import volumes tended to grow, despite various efforts to limit them by protective trade restrictions and taxes. In England, the latter helped to promote domestic manufacturing that met an increasing share of the demand for manufactured imports (and that then began to export them, notably to the colonies). Rising volumes did not imply that everyone consumed the new products, but in a mainly rural world the scale of trade makes it unlikely that the entire rural population was excluded from the market. In work and household situations where a substantial proportion of earnings was paid in kind, much consumption was 'hierarchically structured', with choices made by employers and masters (Shammas 1990, p. 203). But however decisions were made, a study of early modern England concludes that

> consumer goods [were] available . . . to a large proportion of the population. The evidence used by many historians to indicate a substantial rise in the use of consumer goods throughout all strata of society is proof of the success of retailers in distributing them.
>
> *(Cox 2000, pp. 227–228)*

On the continent too, it has been argued that 'colonial groceries stimulated growing transport flows and favoured retail outlets and pedlars as the last part of a long chain in the supply of a growing army of consumers of tea, coffee, tobacco, sugar, and fashion' (Blondé and Van Damme 2013, p. 247). The distribution of shops and goods was uneven, but in at least Western Europe only the most isolated areas can have been wholly untouched. For example, evidence from the enforcement of sumptuary laws that aimed to restrict consumption also reveals the attractiveness of new goods and their availability: in a well-documented case from a small southwestern German community, almost 10% of the population was fined for violations in a single year (1713–14). Most were women, charged with wearing forbidden clothing, typically 'small items of silk or calico' (Ogilvie 2010, p. 308). In Britain's American colonies, Lorena Walsh writes (1983, p. 117), 'rural dwellers were ready to participate in their own way in an increasingly sophisticated material culture where artefacts took on a critical role in defining family routines and relationships with the community at large'. And T.H. Breen speaks (2004, p. xvii) of a 'mid-eighteenth-century transformation' there, marked by 'the flood of imports that found its way into even the most humble provincial households'.

The way in which the rural market would be served is a separate question. Acquiring the many goods produced for local consumption need not involve a retail shop selling from a stock. Agricultural produce could be purchased directly from farmers or at the regular markets that had long characterised town and even village economies, and local artisans sold their products either from their workshops or by working at the premises of the buyer (Everitt 1967; Willan 1976, pp. 56–58; Mui and Mui 1989, p. 27). For the growing array of goods not produced locally, rural consumers could buy in larger centres, going there themselves or ordering from suppliers there. Nevertheless, it is clear that in the early modern era shops were a normal part of the economy of a village (defined, for our purposes, as a compact place with a population of less than a thousand – many were substantially smaller). Evidently some shops were modest, perhaps operated part-time, but shops on the scale of Abraham Dent's were found in many villages. How

Figure 11.1 Store at Lang Pioneer Village, Peterborough County, Ontario. North American living history museums commonly include a general store. Although modest in size, these buildings housed large and varied stocks. Villages of any size had more than one such store, and competition was a fundamental element in country retailing.

Source: Photo by Dennis Halstead, courtesy of Lang Pioneer Village, www.langpioneervillage.ca/

they made a profitable space for themselves is the principal focus of this essay. A concluding section briefly addresses the long-term vitality of a form of retailing that thrived as long as villages themselves did so.

The first requisite was the potential of the local market to support permanent retailing, a function of population numbers and density, family incomes, and the character of the local economy. As a study of nineteenth century Europe (relevant a century earlier too) writes, 'viable peasant farming generated the commercialised villages and *bourgs* which were dotted amongst the small farming communities, and whose artisans and shopkeepers served expanding rural markets' (Crossick and Haupt 1995, p. 56). Variety within rural society was reflected in the intensity and complexity of urban hierarchies. In the eighteenth-century, village retailing was more developed in southeast England, the western provinces of the Netherlands and northeastern and Mediterranean France than in other parts of these countries (Cox 2000, pp. 63–65; van den Heuvel and Ogilvie 2013; Lepetit 1994, pp. 354–363). But retailing was anything but absent in other regions. In the north of England, John Styles writes (2007, p. 146), 'There is little doubt that . . . in the eighteenth century the bulk of the fabric used to make garments for ordinary men and women came from retailers of various kinds'. The shops that sold these fabrics could be found in villages as well as towns. A case in point is early modern Cheshire, where 'nowhere was more than five miles or so from the type of fixed shop which might reasonably be expected to carry a range of consumer items' (Stobart 2016, p. 92). Beyond Western Europe, other patterns were possible. Villages could be the largest nodes in the urban hierarchy when a region first opened, as in settlement colonies, or where there were geographic barriers to movement on land, as in mountain valleys and along coasts. In Tokugawa Japan, there was a well-established network of towns and cities, yet much of the country's economic development after 1750 focused at the village level, with corresponding growth in village shops. A heavy weight of regulations, enforced in towns, could not be effectively imposed in the countryside. Hence the complaint of leaders in Mito, a castle town north-east of Edo (Tokyo), that 'Year after year the retail trade in the country districts increases. Saké, dyes, dry goods, toilet articles, lacquerware and everything you can think of are sold in villages. Moreover, recently [village shops] have begun to buy directly from Edo' (Smith 1973, p. 141).

Goods

Although village shops might deal in local products, their distinguishing role was stocking and selling products from outside their immediate region. Like Abraham Dent, they carried a diversified stock, extending far beyond what the descriptors given in directories (e.g., draper, mercer or grocer) suggest. The complexity and range of products (and thus of the demand for them) can be seen in surviving inventories, invoices and shop accounts. If village shops could not hope to match the breadth of stock of the principal shops in larger towns (Baulant 1987, p. 120), they nevertheless stocked hundreds of distinct products, many of which encompassed substantial variations in quality and character. As Nancy Cox writes of retailers in general (2000, p. 59),

> The most cursory study of the contents of their shops shows their importance as distributors of consumer goods. Their shops are stuffed with household items like glass and earthenware, cooking pots and tools, needles and soap; quality fabrics like broad cloth, stuffs and Holland; crape for funerals and ribbon favours for courtship; and exotic imports like sugar, spices and dried fruits, not to mention tea, chocolate and coffee.

Among these products, some clearly were much more important than others. For example, a study of seven village shops in Upper Canada found thousands of transactions in tea, very modest purchases of coffee – and not a single transaction in chocolate (McCalla 2015, pp. 67–83).

Where it is possible to see the specifics of goods, the scope and variety of the merchandise at village shops become clearer. At John Hook's country shop in Virginia, the eleven leading products (presumably by number of transactions) among a total of almost 250 sold in the autumn of 1771, which together accounted for about 40% of his sales, were rum, osnaburg (a multi-purpose, unbleached, long-wearing linen), hats, handkerchiefs, buttons, gun powder, sugar, thread, linen, hose and cotton (Martin 2008, p. 75). Most, perhaps all, of these goods were imported, rum and sugar from the Caribbean colonies and the remainder from Britain (Shammas 1982, pp. 266–267). Many disappeared or were transformed in consumption, and none were durable; as a result, except in inventories of shops themselves, they are rarely individually visible in the probate inventories that have been used to study consumption and living standards in the early modern period (Main 1982, p. 241; de Vries 2008, pp. 150–154; Styles 2007, p. 327). A list like this also fails to catch nuances essential to an appreciation of shops and their place in customers' lives. At a later shop, Hook's stock included 124 distinct types of buttons (Martin 2008, pp. 148, 150). Such products were not only functional, they were, Nancy Cox notes (2015, p. 129), 'important in proclaiming identity'. As Ann Smart Martin writes (2008, p. 84), 'a hat is not merely a hat; it is a particular kind of hat that is desired and available'. Hook's textile imports in early 1772 included twenty-five different linens, more than a thousand yards, at prices ranging from under one shilling to three shillings six pence per yard. Besides their many practical purposes, these and other textiles represented 'goods offering color and drama and romance, the sensuous world of beautiful textiles' (Martin 2008, pp. 78–79).

One reason for Abraham Dent's wide network of connections was the need to acquire such a diversified stock. From his ledger, about 190 different suppliers can be identified, forty-seven of them in 1763 alone (Willan 1970, pp. 28–29); many were nearby, but over two decades he had twenty suppliers in Newcastle and twelve each in London and Manchester. Another example is Thomas Turner, a village shopkeeper in Sussex, who visited twenty-seven suppliers on a three-day visit to London in 1759, 'settling accounts, buying goods, and exchanging bills' (Vaisey 1984, p. xxxvii). Directories suggest the range of their (and his) trades: tobacconist, druggist, "horse-millener", grocer, ironmonger, hosier, warehouseman, hat warehouse, metal button and hardware warehouse, woollen draper, "chinaman", distiller, pewterer, "merchant", cheesemonger, wholesale mercer, oilman, hop factor, hatter, two linen drapers and two haberdashers (Vaisey 1984, pp. 343–346). These were not all of equal importance. Notably, one of the haberdashers acted as Turner's London banker, accepting bills of exchange drawn on the firm; and one of its partners was a regular visitor to Turner's shop and home. The London journey was unusual, as he normally dealt with more distant suppliers (some as far away as Manchester) by correspondence or when their representatives visited him. He did travel extensively to closer locations, including to visit suppliers in Sussex and Kent.

In Britain's trans-Atlantic colonies and in New France, this kind of direct access to suppliers was impossible. The system in which Hook learned his trade in Virginia was created mainly by Glasgow merchants in the mid-eighteenth century in colonies that could supply staple exports such as sugar and tobacco. They sent out or recruited men, often quite young, to operate chains of shops which they supplied from Britain, based on orders from their local partner or shopkeeper-employee. Although most of the country retailer's stock would thus appear to come from the parent firm, it too would have been assembled from many suppliers; for example, one firm recorded 'forty different manufacturers, craftsmen, and merchants' as sources for a single shipment in 1757 (Martin 2008, p. 19). For these British-based firms and networks, intercolonial trades were also coordinated and financed through Britain, even for goods shipped directly. If any goods produced nearby figured in such shops' stocks, they could be purchased from the maker or through a colonial wholesaler.

Country shops not part of this system were supplied by importers in the leading cities, such as Boston, Philadelphia, New York, Baltimore and Montreal. For many goods, nuances of style, quality and price mattered, and personal selection was preferred where distance made that practicable and where the shopkeeper was able to take the time away from the business. (When settlement moved west, the desire to select goods in person was a factor in the emergence of wholesaling inland, as cities developed there [McCalla 1979].) Often country merchants had one main supplier to whom they were closely linked by credit, but it is clear that they also bought from other sources. For example, one Upper Canadian business with shops in two villages on the upper St Lawrence River acquired about two-thirds of its $12,000 in purchases in 1808 from a single Montreal wholesaler but also bought from nine other firms in Montreal and four in its immediate vicinity, three on the American side of the river (McCalla 2015, p. 218). What a buying trip involved is suggested by an 1838 letter to his father in Scotland from Adam Hope, a young emigrant whose shop in a growing village near the Upper Canadian frontier was backed by a leading Glasgow merchant house. He selected many goods from the firm's Montreal branch, but also patronised other importers.

> I will not be able to get through my business before Wednesday, which will be a stay *of two weeks*! . . . Our purchases will amount at least to £3,000 or $12,000 & when you consider the multiplicity of articles required for an Upper Canada Store you will be able to form some idea of the *time* & *Care* required to make a judicious selection & to see that the prices will enable us to compete successfully with our neighbours.
>
> *(Crerar 2007, p. 298)*

'Year in, year out, the range of goods demanded by rural customers remained remarkably stable', Allan Greer writes (1985, p. 156) of Samuel Jacobs' long-lived shop in rural Quebec, which opened in the 1760s. 'Consumer demand was rather inelastic as it was dominated by the real needs of the population, mostly habitants'. It is reasonable to picture rural demand as based on 'real' needs, yet the effort shopkeepers put into buying suggests that needs were not as static as this phrasing implies – a point confirmed by Greer's subsequent detailed discussion of Jacobs' stock and clientele. In the first place, products such as rum, tea and cotton had not always been necessities. In the second, if categories (such as textiles) were constant, variation and changes within them mattered vitally to the shop and its clientele. In the third, rural populations were less homogeneous than this suggests, and their demands were more varied.

Shopping

For many goods, any bourgeois and (in the old world) aristocratic and gentry families in the vicinity were likely to prefer the greater possibilities afforded by urban suppliers. But they might still buy locally, for convenience and in the context of relationships that were both hierarchical and reciprocal, such as between landlord and tenant (Bailey 2013, p. 11). A close analysis of clothing purchases by a family of the English 'rural lesser gentry' finds, for example, that it acquired 'most essential items' locally, notably from a village shop with which it had a very long-term relationship (Bailey 2011, pp. 91–101). Members of such families did not necessarily shop in person, however. They might instead send a message or a servant and have goods delivered (Stobart 2012, p. 267). Families of this status must have been among the most valued customers for shops that attracted their patronage. But no village had many such families. Most customers were farmers, artisans and labourers (and their families) – categories that themselves encompassed substantial variation in wealth and in needs. To attract buyers of all classes, shops had to anticipate their requirements, even as they sought to influence demand by their choice of goods to stock. They also faced competition, as Hope noted, not only from other shops in the village but from shops in other villages in the area (which might be equally accessible for many rural customers), from retailers in nearby towns, and sometimes from pedlars (see Stobart and Bailey 2018).

Thus, shopping involved choosing where to shop as well as what to buy (e.g., Stobart, Hann and Morgan 2007, pp. 46–53). For the former, proximity and the value of time were important considerations. Customers living in or near the village could shop often, if they wished. People living at greater distance might combine shopping with other activities, such as visiting a mill or attending the local market. Credit was also crucial; having an account at a shop was a reason for buying there rather than elsewhere. To Fernand Braudel (1982, p. 73), credit was 'the principal reason for the development of shops'. But that understates the importance of the goods themselves: the only reason for taking on a debt was the desire for the goods it purchased

(Dépatie 2003, p. 176). Some buyers had much larger accounts – and closer ties to the merchant – than others. Where it has been possible to study purchasing in detail, however, it is clear that no families bought all their supplies from a single shop (e.g., Pronovost 1998, p. 190; Craig 2009, p. 121). That suggests the reality of customer choice, as does the turnover in clientele that merchants experienced. 'Beneath the semblance of continuity, domination and changelessness', a study based on the detailed accounts of two shops in a nineteenth-century Newfoundland fishing community shows, 'there was very substantial movement' (Sweeny, Bradley and Hong 1992, p. 14).

For England, Cox and Dannehl write (2007, p. 36), 'No illustrations of eighteenth-century village shops have been found at all'. The shop, they speculate (p. 45), was 'unsettling. . . [and] could thus be written out of economic and social equations. Its presence was neither acknowledged in the travel books and guides nor depicted in the paintings of the rural scene'. There are more images for the nineteenth century, and a general store is essential to many North American representations of historical villages of that era [see Figure 11.1]. They seem small to our eyes, but modest dimensions were the norm for retail shops (even, indeed, on principal streets in leading urban centres [Jenkins 2018, pp. 17–21]). A mid-eighteenth-century merchant on the St Lawrence River below Montreal, for example, began with a store and grain storage space of 20 by 30 feet (Michel 1979, p. 233). John Hook's first shop, whose substantial stock we have already noted, measured 42 by 20 feet, which gave it 'a larger footprint than most others in the region' (Martin 2008, pp. 29–30, 152). The shop itself was 20 by 20 feet, divided by a counter 2 feet 10 inches wide, with a space of 8 feet by 20 feet for customers. As well, the building included a lumber (storage) room and a counting room (office). His later shop, a rare shop building to survive from the eighteenth century, seems no larger (Martin 2008, p. 203). Hook lived nearby; often, in fact, merchants (including Thomas Turner) lived above or behind their shops.

In the early modern era, some shops sold goods through a window on the street. If the practice continued, it implies a social distance between the shopkeeper and those who traded without entering the shop. Customers worthy of credit must have been welcome inside, and the most valued might conduct their business in the merchant's private room (Stobart 2010, p. 344). If most accounts were in the name of a male household head, the actual buyer could be a family member (wife, child, brother, etc.), a servant, an employee or a neighbour. Many buyers (and some suppliers) were women (Innes 1988, pp. 32–33; Mancke 1995). Sometimes a buyer carried explicit written authorisation but in most cases that was not needed; the shopkeeper knew his or her clientele. 'With the counter . . . as the focus for exchange of goods' (Stobart 2016, p. 95), every purchase entailed personal contact with the shopkeeper or a clerk. As the role of credit also indicates, transactions were part of a continuing 'face-to-face, personal' relationship with the merchant (de Vries 2008, p. 175). For the many goods that varied in quality or pattern, selecting, then weighing, measuring, cutting or counting could be time-consuming, especially when a number of products were purchased at the same time, as was often the case. For common goods, such as tobacco and gun shot, merchants could prepare packages of standard quantities in advance.

The conversations during such transactions may help explain a common story, here from an argument about foods but widely found in descriptions of shops of every kind: 'there were no fixed prices and no price ticketing . . . and the final price for any food item was arrived at through a process of haggling' (Walsh 2008, p. 23). There must have been talk of prices, but careful studies of retailing have shown that 'haggling' was not an everyday practice (Stobart 2012, pp. 159–163; Mui and Mui 1989, pp. 223, 239; Willan 1970, p. 13; Craig 2009, p. 121). In support of this argument are the detailed lists of a year's orders or of inventory at three Upper Canadian village shops, which run to at least five hundred distinct entries, each with a specific cost. As we have seen, that number was not unusual. A busy shopkeeper must have had some means of recording this information, not just for personal use but for a clerk or apprentice (if there was one) or the person (often a family member) who looked after the business when the proprietor was absent, a not uncommon situation. Evidence from 750 charge accounts at these and four other village shops in Upper Canada also fails to reveal the variation in retail prices that the story of bargaining requires (McCalla 2015, p. 148).[2] Prices were consistent whether the buyer was the account holder or someone else, even a child, and whether the transaction involved the merchant or a clerk or substitute. Typically, unit prices were also consistent when quantities varied. When prices varied, at a single shop or among shops, the differences can nearly always be attributed to other factors, particularly seasonal and long-term variations that were consistent among customers and quality variations within a category – the kind of differentiation represented by John Hook's 1772 linen imports.

Credit

Ordering goods and managing credit required literacy and numeracy. Essential for business, these skills might also be called upon in community life and in such business-related processes as conducting probate and bankruptcy inventories. For example, Thomas Turner 'was one of the few people in East Hoathly who thoroughly understood financial matters' (Vaisey 1984, p. 340). If many shopkeepers did not meet the accounting standards recommended by contemporary manuals (e.g., Coquery 2008, p. 348), all needed at least to record 'who owed how much to whom' (Craig 2009, p. 125). Without written documentation of a debt, there was no basis for a legal claim to its repayment. The usual basic record was a journal (daybook) in which credit (but rarely cash) transactions were recorded in sequence, generally with the date, the name of the account holder, the identity of the actual buyer, the product and quantity purchased and the unit and total price. The journal might record payments on account, with date and means of payment, or entries in it might simply be crossed out when paid or marked 'settled', without further detail. Payments might instead be recorded elsewhere, most commonly in a ledger. Organised by customer, with information transferred from the journal, typically in summary form with a cross-reference to the original source, it provided an overview of each account and permitted periodic reckoning of the balance due. At this stage, if a debit balance was long-running (say more than twelve months), it was common to begin to charge interest at the standard legal rate and sometimes to expect the debt to be acknowledged formally, in a promissory note. This was all the routine accounting many shopkeepers attempted, particularly if they were sole proprietors. A formal partnership required a further stage, valuing assets (inventory and debts due, with an allowance for bad debts) and liabilities, crediting interest on each party's share of the firm's capital, and calculating profits (or losses) to be allocated among the parties (e.g., Crerar 2007, pp. 344–345).

Clearly a sale did not complete a transaction; it was necessary to secure payment, ultimately in ways that allowed the shop to pay its bills to non-local suppliers and creditors. The shopkeeper had to think carefully about customers' probable ability to pay. If that estimate proved incorrect and the account fell behind, securing payment called for persistence and imagination. Although a debtor who was still nearby could be pursued through the law, that was costly, far from certain of actually securing repayment, and (within such small communities) stressful as well (Vaisey 1984, pp. xxiv, 149). Thus, a gloomy Thomas Turner reflected, 'The long credit that I am obliged to give must greatly hurt my trade' (Vaisey 1984, p. 153). He was not alone. Not even a retailer as prudent as William Stout (a late-seventeenth-century shopkeeper in an English market town) could avoid accumulating bad debts (Craig and Schofield 1967, pp. 24–25). This reality underlies a common understanding that shopkeeping was notably insecure. As Braudel writes (1982, p. 73), 'the shopkeeper was a capitalist in a very small way, [who] lived between those who owed him money and those to whom he owed it. It was a precarious sort of living, and one was always on the verge of disaster'. Actually, because debt was a normal feature of economic life, this kind of insecurity was widely shared. More fearful were extraordinary events that could completely disrupt routine payment processes – a war, commercial or political crisis, or natural disaster. Problems specific to the individual merchant and family were a second unpredictable source of potential disaster – including accidents, illness, or unfortunate outcomes from a business venture (and not only the merchant's own speculations – it was common to post bonds or guarantee transactions for others, particularly within the family). The latter circumstances could likewise affect a customer (and thus the likelihood of being paid) or a major creditor (and thus the possibility of continuing support from that source).

One attraction of credit for many rural buyers was that their incomes were irregular – farmers, labourers and artisans all depended on being paid for their produce or work. In deciding what to buy and from whom, they also had to anticipate how they would eventually pay. This might be in cash (coin and bank notes), forms of payment more prevalent where a sophisticated financial system existed and welcomed by the shopkeeper because they could be used to pay creditors and suppliers. Negotiable instruments such as pay warrants, warehouse receipts or bills of exchange were close substitutes. An option was to sell goods to or work for the shopkeeper, who required local goods and services for everyday living and for the business and who might hire help for the household, the shop, and associated business ventures (such as a mill). Proto-industrial activities could have the same character. In addition to selling non-local goods, some shops took artisans' products and/or farm produce in payment and resold them locally. In principle, transactions in such goods could have been conducted directly between producer and consumer; evidently trades via the shop offered an advantage to the producer and/or the buyer (such as convenience and credit), as well as to the shop. It is also possible that some goods that seem local were not; when rural marketing patterns can be explored in detail, more complex and nuanced patterns of local and non-local exchange appear (e.g., Postel-Vinay and Robin 1992).

Many shops also accepted or actively sought local products that could be sold beyond the immediate region. Thomas Turner, for example, bought rags (sold to paper-makers), wool, butter, hops and horse hair. If necessary, the shopkeeper arranged for processing, at a grist, saw, or woollen mill or another facility (such as a tannery). In staples-oriented locations, buying the principal export product was the original purpose of many shops, such as the ones established by Glasgow merchants in Virginia to secure tobacco. Equally, buying furs was the raison d'être for the posts of trading companies such as the Hudson's Bay Company. Although it was not practicable in the case of furs, customers in other settings had options besides selling to the shopkeeper to whom they owed money.[3] For the principal exports, there were usually a number of active local buyers; and producers could also use the merchant's own network to consign produce for sale on commission in a distant market (e.g., Wermuth 2001, pp. 57–58; Bruegel 2002, p. 93). Such trades benefited the merchant, whose account was credited when the produce was sold, and the consignor, whose shop account was credited with the net proceeds.

Exchanges in which goods and labour were credited to a customer's account are sometimes described as barter or truck. But these labels can be misleading, because transactions were rarely simultaneous (i.e., a direct exchange of one good for another), goods were valued at current prices, and work was credited at standard wage rates. Once it is recognised that most goods and work had market prices, the idea that one commodity was traded for another disappears, as does another idea, that the merchant could dictate the terms of the exchange (Craig 2009, p. 12). Even in the fur trade, easily imagined as based on barter, extending credit was normal, and a pricing system allowed valuing the variety of furs delivered and goods purchased by indigenous traders (Ray and Freeman 1978, pp. 54–55, 186–187). A further element to exchanges through the shop were third-party transactions, in which a credit on one customer's account was charged to another's (e.g., Wermuth 2001, p. 56), a process reflecting wider patterns of local exchange. As a study of late-eighteenth-century rural Pennsylvania notes, 'an extensive web of sales of goods and services among . . . shoemakers, joiners, shopkeepers, and the like bound . . . neighbors together and created an interdependent community' (Clemens and Simler 1988, p. 114).

Management

What proportion of shops routinely employed sales or other staff is not clear, but few if any shopkeepers could do entirely without help, for busy days, heavy work and times when the owner was absent. When the shop was associated with another business establishment, such as a mill or another shop, an owner could not directly oversee everything; much responsibility had to be delegated. If an employee took charge of a shop, long-term success required aligning the shopkeeper's and owner's interests. Keeping the relationship within the family was common. Another approach was to give the shopkeeper a share of the profits, possibly through a formal partnership agreement. Or the owner could rent the shop to someone to operate independently. A successful shop might generate enough revenue to reward two partners who shared work and responsibility; alternatively, having a second responsible figure could make a larger operation possible (Bruegel 2002, p. 165). The durability of such relationships depended on mutual respect, a sense of shared interests (in which family ties were often vital), and the continuing ability of the business to earn a return large enough to support both partners.

Becoming a shopkeeper required skills and capital. Here too family connections were frequently central, including through inheritance, financial backing and access to work experience. In a village shop, a young helper might mainly be paid in knowledge, room and board. In larger mercantile enterprises, the employment relationship could be formalised in an apprenticeship. Either setting could prepare someone for village shopkeeping. Some shops were operated by women, including widows or sisters who continued a family business. Many of them already had experience of daily shop operations, but even if not, they benefited from knowledge acquired from association with it. To minimise capital requirements, a shop could be rented, and credit could supply part of the working capital. Wholesalers were on the watch for promising locations and people, to expand their markets and also to replace clients lost to failure and competitors. Writing in 1840, a leading Upper Canadian wholesaler described this process (albeit with some exaggeration): 'the wonderful success of my operations in Canada may be to a great extent attributed to my . . . system of rearing up a new set of customers for myself who are generally two young Scotchmen associated as partners' (McCalla 1979, p. 38). Some of these men had been clerks in the firm, which helped in judging their potential.

A rapidly expanding rural economy provided many retail opportunities, both in new villages and in the growth of favourably situated existing villages (e.g., Hofstra and Mitchell 1993). In established societies where village structures were more stable, entry into shopkeeping tended to come through an existing shop. The failure or death of a shopkeeper could provide an opportunity to take over an ongoing business or vacant premises. Or an owner wishing to retire or move on might sell his shop. Doing so on credit, however, ran the risk that a buyer might run the business poorly and fail to maintain payments. That was what prompted William Stout's return to retailing some years after he had transferred his shop to an apprentice (Craig and Schofield 1967, p. 25) and Thomas Turner's caution as he considered a possible sale: 'I would part with it on no other terms but by his taking the goods all at prime cost, and all the fixtures, and the money to be paid down' (Vaisey 1984, p. 92). Over the long term, market, demographic and individual factors made for considerable business turnover; few families managed successful transitions through multiple generations. As a study of this issue in a small Irish market town over 150 years discovered, there was a 'relatively high degree of discontinuity amongst retailer families' (Gulliver and Silverman 1995, p. 264). That was not necessarily evidence of failure. Children might be raised to imagine other possibilities or too young to take over on a parent's death; and ambitious shopkeepers could move on to new opportunities, as Stout and Dent did and Turner often imagined. In Upper Canada, Adam Hope moved from village retailer to urban wholesaler. One of his customers, Timothy Eaton, who had emigrated from Ulster in 1854 at the age of twenty after training in a village shop, began with a shop in the small village of Kirkton, later moved to a nearby town, and then in 1869 to Toronto; there, over the next twenty-five years, he would create Canada's leading department store (Santink 1990).

Continuity and change

There was considerable continuity in the goods that shops stocked. Godfrey's Cordial, a patent medicine purchased at several Upper Canadian shops in 1861, had been sold by Thomas Turner in the 1760s. And hats, handkerchiefs, buttons, gun powder, sugar, thread and cotton, among the most-purchased goods at John Hook's shop in Virginia in the 1770s, rank high on a list of the purchases at village shops in Upper Canada in the early and mid-nineteenth century (McCalla 2015, pp. 203–212). (But the ranking of gun powder and shot fell substantially during that period.) Tea and tobacco, two of the three highest ranked goods on the latter list, had long been important to village shops. But rural demand was not timeless and unchanging. For example, osnaburg, second only to rum on the list for Hook's shop, had just nine buyers among the 750 customers whose accounts were the basis of the Upper Canadian study. Demand there for linens of all kinds was modest; cotton was the leading fabric for rural buyers in Upper Canada (and evidently far more widely), purchased in many variations and in large quantities (see Styles 2007, pp. 109–132; Riello 2013). Other goods whose production was transformed by industrialisation in the nineteenth century, such as nails, boots and shoes, also became prominent on the Upper Canadian list. Products like kerosene, paint and matches, new in the mid-nineteenth century, appeared almost immediately in rural shops.

Beginning about the middle of the nineteenth century, the context for village shops, at least in Western society, changed in many ways. The development of new forms of transportation and communication, the growth of banking institutions and more formal channels of rural credit and payment, new technologies (including growing farm mechanisation), continuing industrialisation (including of an increasing share of clothing production), and urbanisation had a variety of implications for village economies. Some rural trades (such as shoemakers, tailors and coopers) faded, as did rural industries that were overtaken by the factory system. Railways afforded easier personal access to larger centres and could bring rural people merchandise purchased through the catalogues that flourished at the beginning of the twentieth century. On the other hand, growing rail networks (even if they bypassed many villages) improved transportation for farm produce, and city growth expanded demand for foods and other primary products. Village shops benefited from changes that brought many new products to stock and to make a shop more attractive (the latter including lighting, larger panes of window glass and eventually refrigeration), a more developed financial system that facilitated payments by customers, and the easier access to suppliers provided by railways and the telegraph (including via the rising importance of travelling sales representatives).

Figure 11.2 Store at Lang Pioneer Village, Peterborough County, Ontario (Interior). The main story line at Lang aims to "tell the pioneer story" and "demonstrate traditional . . . trades", but the interior of its store is set in a later era. The cash register and packaged groceries (such as Salada Tea, a brand launched in 1892) suggest the modernity that was essential to stores' continuing viability.

Source: Photo by Dennis Halstead, courtesy of Lang Pioneer Village, www.langpioneervillage.ca/

The new developments in retailing represented by department and chain stores, co-operative stores, catalogue merchandising, advertising, and branding affected the competitive environment for shopkeepers in many ways, and they rightly worried about competitors' buying power. But the wholesale sector that was crucial to independent retailers proved very resilient, large enterprises had managerial and other overhead costs that an owner-operated shop did not, and shopkeepers were anything but passive in responding to the challenges (Monod 1996, pp. 205–213). Thus, alongside bins, sacks and barrels of bulk groceries and high shelves of textiles, which reflected long-term continuities in demand, early twentieth-century photographs of village shops' signage and interiors reveal up-to-date stocks (packaged and branded groceries, cigarettes, chewing gum, gasoline, etc. – see Figure 11.2). Some shopkeepers also sought agency business, representing manufacturers (of sewing machines, pianos, farm equipment, etc.), insurance and mortgage companies and other outside enterprises (Drummond 1987, p. 276). In most villages, a shop served as the post office, which generated income and drew people to the shop. As well, until the 1920s, when the automobile began to have a substantial impact (at least in North America), little changed in the time constraints governing the lives and work of village and farm families or in transportation at the immediate local level, which relied on walking and on horses.

For many goods, that gave customers strong reasons to value the convenience of a nearby shop (Gal 2016).

Thus, even as the village sector declined in relative importance in the developed world, it was possible for village shops to earn a return attractive enough to sustain their owners (see Crossick and Haupt 1995, pp. 216–218). A Canadian case in point is that there were almost as many country general stores in Ontario in 1930 as there had been in 1871 (Drummond 1987, p. 302). Writing of English retailing in general at the time, Michael Winstanley (1983, p. 217) sums up the continuing resilience of the independent shop:

> Together . . . large-scale retailers were significant in certain trades but elsewhere the private shopkeepers, despite their misgivings, still dominated retailing. . . . The most interesting feature of the distributive trades was not the emergence of such giants but the much larger, and not as observers seemed to think, smaller, number of general and specialist independent shopkeepers.

The 'golden age of general stores', according to a Canadian study aimed at a popular audience, lasted at least until the 1920s (Fleming 2002, p. 181); and its illustrations show that such stores were still important in many small places thirty or more years after that. The challenge for shopkeepers, ever more difficult in the ensuing years, was to offer a diverse stock of goods appropriate to the clientele at acceptable prices, in the face of wider changes in retailing and in the rural economy (for example, farm consolidation and rural depopulation).

To Fernand Braudel, the key commercial trend in the eighteenth century was the emergence of various 'forms of specialized shops'; Abraham Dent's shop (and others like it, which dealt in 'the strangest assortment of goods') were "survivals" (1982, pp. 64, 67). It is true that "lack of specialization" was a defining element of the village shop (Bruegel 2002, p. 164), but Braudel's image makes it difficult to account for the vitality of such shops for another two centuries. What the village shop actually specialised in was a place. As long as such places thrived, shops would too. The shopkeeper's knowledge of, judgements about, and relationships with the people and economy of a particular locality were the fundamentals of success both in shopkeeping and in any of the other local ventures in which rural entrepreneurs like Dent engaged.

Notes

1 For consistency, I generally use "shop" for these enterprises, although in North America it was common to speak of them as country or general "stores." Thus, shopkeeper and storekeeper are also synonyms. Sometimes I speak of these figures as merchants, because that is what they were, albeit not on the scale of large international trading houses.

2 To take a simple example, almost every purchase of a box of "pills" at these stores cost exactly 25¢, an unlikely result if bargaining had been involved (McCalla 2015, p. 83).

3 Even for furs, at the peak of competition in the trade, c.1800, rival posts were often close enough to provide a choice of buyers; before that, sellers could threaten to take their furs to a different post in the following season.

References

Bailey, L.A. (2011), 'Consumption and status: Shopping for clothes in a nineteenth-century Bedfordshire gentry household', *Midland History*, 36 (1), pp. 89–114.

Bailey, L.A. (2015), 'Squire, shopkeeper and staple food: The reciprocal relationship between the country house and the village shop in the late Georgian period', *History of Retailing and Consumption*, 1 (1), pp. 8–27.

Baulant, M. (1987), 'Marchand rural, marchand urban: Le commerce de distribution en Brie aux XVIIe and XVIIIe siècles', in F. Lebrun and N. Séguin (eds.) *Sociétés villageoises et rapports villes-campagnes au Québec et dans la France de l'ouest XVIIe–XXe siècles* (Trois-Rivières: Centre de Recherche en Études Québécoises, Université du Québec à Trois-Rivières) 113–120.

Blondé, B. and Van Damme, I. (2013), 'Early modern Europe: 1500–1800', in P. Clark (ed.) *The Oxford handbook of cities in world history* (Oxford: Oxford University Press) 240–256.

Braudel, F. (1982), *Civilization and capitalism, 15th–18th century, ii, the wheels of commerce* (Siân Reynolds, trans.) (New York: Harper & Row).

Breen, T.H. (2004), *The marketplace of revolution: How consumer politics shaped American independence* (New York: Oxford University Press).

Bruegel, M. (2002), *Farm, shop, landing: The rise of a market society in the Hudson Valley, 1780–1860* (Durham, NC: Duke University Press).

Clemens, P.G.E. and Simler, L. (1988), 'Rural labor and the farm household in Chester county, Pennsylvania, 1750–1820', in S. Innes (ed.) *Work and labor in early America* (Chapel Hill, NC: University of North Carolina Press for the Institute of early American History and Culture) 106–143.

Coquery, N. (2008), 'Les faillites boutiquières sous l'Ancien Régime: Une gestion de l'échec mi-juridique mi-pragmatique (fin XVIIe–fin XVIIIe siècle)', *Revue française de gestion*, 188–189, pp. 341–358.

Cox, N. (2000), *The complete tradesman: A study of retailing, 1550–1820* (Aldershot/Burlington, VT: Ashgate).

Cox, N. (2015), *Retailing and the language of goods, 1550–1820* (Farnham, UK/Burlington, VT: Ashgate).

Cox, N. and Dannehl, K. (2007), *Perceptions of retailing in early modern England* (Aldershot: Ashgate).

Craig, B. (2009), *Backwoods consumers and homespun capitalists: The rise of a market culture in Eastern Canada* (Toronto: University of Toronto Press).

Craig, R. and Schofield, M.M. (1967), 'The trade of Lancaster in William Stout's time', in J.D. Marshall (ed.) *The autobiography of William Stout of Lancaster 1665–1752* (Manchester: Manchester University Press for the Chetham Society) 23–63.

Crerar, A. (ed.) (2007), *Letters of Adam Hope, 1834–1845* (Toronto: The Champlain Society).

Crossick, G. and Haupt, H. (1995), *The petite bourgeoisie in Europe 1780–1914: Enterprise, family and independence* (London/New York: Routledge).

Dépatie, S. (2003), 'Commerce et crédit à l'île Jésus, 1734–1775: Le rôle des marchands ruraux dans l'économie des campagnes montréalaises', *Canadian Historical Review*, 84 (2), pp. 147–176.

de Vries, J. (1984), *European urbanization 1500–1800* (Cambridge, MA: Harvard University Press).

de Vries, J. (2008), *The industrious revolution: Consumer behavior and the household economy, 1650 to the present* (New York: Cambridge University Press).

Drummond, I. (1987), *Progress without planning: The economic history of Ontario from Confederation to the Second World War* (Toronto: University of Toronto Press).

Everitt, A. (1967), 'The marketing of agricultural produce', in J. Thirsk (ed.) *The agrarian history of England and Wales, iv, 1500–1640* (Cambridge: Cambridge University Press) 466–592.

Fleming, R.B. (2002), *General stores of Canada: Merchants and memories* (Toronto: Lynx Images).

Gal, A.M. (2016), 'Grassroots consumption: Ontario farm families' consumption practices, 1900–45', PhD, Wilfrid Laurier University.

Grantham, G. (1989), 'Jean Meuvret and the subsistence problem in early modern France', *Journal of Economic History*, 49 (1), pp. 184–200.

Greer, A. (1985), *Peasant, lord, and merchant: Rural society in three Quebec parishes 1740–1840* (Toronto: University of Toronto Press).

Gulliver, P.H. and Silverman, M. (1995), *Merchants and shopkeepers: A historical anthropology of an Irish market town, 1200–1991* (Toronto: University of Toronto Press).

Gwyn, J. (2015), 'Review of Douglas McCalla: *Consumers in the Bush*'. *Journal of the Royal Nova Scotia Historical Society*, 18, pp. 113–114.

United States Bureau of the Census, *Historical statistics of the United States: Earliest times to the present* (2006). Millennial edition, vol. 1 (Cambridge: Cambridge University Press).

Hoffman, P.T. (1996), *Growth in a traditional society: The French countryside, 1450–1815* (Princeton, NJ: Princeton University Press).

Hofstra, W.R. and Mitchell, R.D. (1993), 'Town and country in backcountry Virginia: Winchester and the Shenandoah Valley, 1730–1800', *Journal of Southern History*, 59 (4), pp. 619–646.

Innes, S. (1988), 'Fulfilling John Smith's vision: Work and labour in Early America', in S. Innes (ed.) *Work and labor in early America* (Chapel Hill, NC: University of North Carolina Press for the Institute of Early American History and Culture) 3–47.

Jenkins, M. (2018), 'The view from the street: The landscape of polite shopping in Georgian York', *Urban History*, 45 (1), pp. 26–48.

Lepetit, B. (1994), *The pre-industrial urban system: France, 1740–1840* (Cambridge: Cambridge University Press and Paris: Editions de la Maison des Sciences de l'Homme).

Main, G.L. (1982), *Tobacco colony: Life in early Maryland, 1650–1720* (Princeton, NJ: Princeton University Press).

Mancke, E. (1995), 'At the counter of the general store: Women and the economy in eighteenth-century Horton, Nova Scotia', in M. Conrad (ed.) *Intimate relations: Family and community in Planter Nova Scotia, 1759–1800* (Fredericton: Acadiensis Press) 167–181.

Martin, A.S. (2008), *Buying into the world of goods: Early consumers in backcountry Virginia* (Baltimore, MD: The Johns Hopkins University Press).

Matson, C. (2006), 'A house of many mansions: Some thoughts on the field of economic history', in C. Matson (ed.) *The economy of early America: Historical perspectives & new directions* (University Park, PA: Pennsylvania State University Press) 1–70.

McCalla, D. (1979), *The Upper Canada trade, 1834–1872: A history of the Buchanans' business* (Toronto: University of Toronto Press).

McCalla, D. (2015), *Consumers in the bush: Shopping in rural Upper Canada* (Montreal/Kingston: McGill-Queen's University Press).

Michel, L. (1979), 'Un marchand rural en Nouvelle-France: François-Augustin Bailly de Messein, 1709–1771', *Revue d'Histoire de l'Amérique française*, 33 (2), pp. 215–262.

Monod, D. (1996), *Store wars: Shopkeepers and the culture of mass marketing, 1880–1939* (Toronto: University of Toronto Press).

Mui, H. and Mui, L.H. (1989), *Shops and shopkeeping in eighteenth-century England* (Kingston/Montreal: McGill-Queen's University Press).

North, S. (2016), '"Galloon, incle and points": Fashionable dress and accessories in Rural England, 1552–1665', in R. Jones and C. Dyer (eds.) *Farmers, consumers, innovators: The world of Joan Thirsk* (Hatfield: University of Hertfordshire Press) 104–123.

Ogilvie, S. (2010), 'Consumption, social capital, and the "industrious revolution" in early modern Germany', *Journal of Economic History*, 70 (2), pp. 287–325.

Postel-Vinay, G. and Robin, J. (1992), 'Eating, working, and saving in an unstable world: Consumers in nineteenth-century France', *Economic History Review*, 45 (3), pp. 494–513.

Pronovost, C. (1998), *La bourgeoisie marchande en milieu rural (1720–1840)* (Sainte-Foy: Les Presses de l'Université Laval).

Ray, A.J. and Freeman, D.B. (1978), *'Give us good measure': An economic analysis of relations between the Indians and the Hudson's Bay Company Before 1763* (Toronto: University of Toronto Press).

Riello, G. (2013), *Cotton: The fabric that made the modern world* (Cambridge: Cambridge University Press).

Santink, J.L. (1990), *Timothy Eaton and the rise of his department store* (Toronto: University of Toronto Press).

Shammas, C. (1982), 'How self-sufficient was early America?', *Journal of Interdisciplinary History*, 13 (2), pp. 247–272.

Shammas, C. (1990), *The pre-industrial consumer in England and America* (Oxford: Clarendon Press).

Smith, T.C. (1973), 'Pre-modern economic growth: Japan and the west', *Past & Present*, 60, pp. 127–160.

Stobart, J. (2010), 'A history of shopping: The missing link between retail and consumer revolutions', *Journal of Historical Research in Marketing*, 2 (3), pp. 342–349.

Stobart, J. (2012), *Sugar and spice: Grocers and groceries in provincial England, 1650–1830* (Oxford: Oxford University Press).

Stobart, J. (2016), 'The village shop, 1660–1760: Innovation and tradition', in R. Jones and C. Dyer (eds.) *Farmers, consumers, innovators: The world of Joan Thirsk* (Hatfield: University of Hertfordshire Press) 89–102.

Stobart, J., Hann, A. and Morgan, V. (2007), *Spaces of consumption: Leisure and shopping in the English town, c. 1680–1830* (London/New York: Routledge).

Stobart, J. and Bailey, L. (2018), "Retail revolution and the village shop, c. 1660–1860', *Economic History Review*, 71 (2), pp. 393–417.

Styles, J. (2007), *The dress of the people: Everyday fashion in eighteenth-century England* (New Haven, CT/London: Yale University Press).

Sweeny, R.C.H., Bradley, D. and Hong, R. (1992), 'Movement, options and costs: Indexes as historical evidence, a Newfoundland example', *Acadiensis*, 22 (1), pp. 111–121.

Vaisey, D. (ed.) (1984), *The diary of Thomas Turner 1754–1765* (Oxford: Oxford University Press).

van den Heuvel, D. and Ogilvie, S. (2013), 'Retail development in the consumer revolution: The Netherlands, c. 1670–c. 1815', *Explorations in Economic History*, 50 (1), pp. 69–87.

Walsh, C. (2008), 'Shopping at first hand? Mistresses, servants and shopping for the household in early-modern England', in D. Hussey and M. Ponsonby (eds.) *Buying for the home: Shopping for the domestic from the seventeenth century to the present* (Aldershot: Ashgate) 13–26.
Walsh, L.S. (1983), 'Urban amenities and rural sufficiency: Living standards and consumer behavior in the colonial Chesapeake, 1643–1777', *Journal of Economic History*, 43 (1), pp. 109–117.
Wermuth, T.S. (2001), *Rip Van Winkle's neighbors: The transformation of rural society in the Hudson River Valley, 1720–1850* (Albany, NY: State University of New York Press).
Willan, T.S. (1970), *An eighteenth-century shopkeeper: Abraham Dent of Kirkby Stephen* (Manchester: Manchester University Press).
Willan, T.S. (1976), *The inland trade: Studies in English internal trade in the sixteenth and seventeenth centuries* (Manchester: Manchester University Press).
Winstanley, M.J. (1983), *The shopkeeper's world, 1830–1914* (Manchester: Manchester University Press).

12
ARCADES, SHOPPING CENTRES AND SHOPPING MALLS

Vicki Howard and Jon Stobart

Introduction

Shopping malls are ubiquitous features of modern life across the globe, but unlike many other retail formats, their origin can be traced to a specific time and place. On 8 October 1956, the first fully enclosed shopping mall with dual department store anchors opened in Edina, just seven miles outside downtown Minneapolis where over the years Minnesotans had to brave snowy winters and steamy summers as they shopped. Designed by architect Victor Gruen, an Austrian expatriate who gained a national reputation in the United States for his visionary shopping centre designs, many of them open-air, Southdale was understood at the time to be an entirely new retail environment. The Southdale Regional Shopping Center made the national news, a *New York Times* article touting 'Shopper's Dream Near Completion'. The article noted its seventy-two stores, two full-size department stores, and generous parking, but what drew most praise was its climate-controlled garden court, three stories high and decorated lavishly with trees, flowers, fountains and sculpture. Planned 'for ease of shopping', according to the national report, Southdale developers rented space to chains like F.W. Woolworth, to supermarkets, and many local merchants. By the mid 1960s, enclosed malls like Southdale were an industry standard in the United States, a planned and centrally managed large-scale commercial development deeply connected to automobile-driven suburbanisation (Spielvogel, 1956, p. 38; Jackson, 1996; Longstreth, 2010, p. 247; Hardwick, 2004, chapter 6).

As this revolutionary retail format spread across the globe both to urban centres and new suburban developments, it adapted and evolved within varying political, social and geographic contexts. With their increased importance in economic and cultural life, shopping centres and malls have drawn the attention of a wide range of scholars from diverse fields, including history, anthropology, sociology and management studies, not to mention architecture and urban planning. Historical and contemporary interpretations of shopping centres, malls and their predecessors, the shopping galleries and arcades of Europe, have varied widely. All agree, however, that market places have always been about more than economic transactions (Hardwick, 2004, p. 1; Stobart, 2008, p. 210; Srivastava, 2015, p. 225). Shopping centres, malls, and by some accounts even earlier organised covered markets, such as galleries and arcades, were key instruments of modern consumer society. Despite national or geographic differences, their shared form and function provide a starting point for discussions about the changing relationship between commercial enterprise and social practice over time.

Shopping galleries and arcades

Internal and regulated shopping galleries were features of commercial and financial exchanges in many cities in early modern Europe. In London, the Royal Exchange, built on Cornhill in the heart of the City in 1566–68, led the way. This was built in the style of the Nieuwe Beurs in Antwerp and was intended to emulate the trading and financial power of that city, but above the arcades that framed the exchange were added galleries containing over 100 small shops, most measuring just 2.3m by 1.5m. Despite some initial reluctance, retailers with shops elsewhere in the city rented stalls in these galleries to take advantage of both the grandeur of the setting and the fact that the exchange quickly became both a centre for business and a social rendezvous (Walsh, 2005). Such was its success that it spawned copies and rivals at Westminster Hall, and the New Exchange (1609), Middle Exchange (1672) and Exeter Exchange (1676), all located on the Strand, some distance to the west of London's traditional retail centre. This proliferation was greeted with alarm by the London Corporation who argued – in terms that are echoed in later concerns about shopping centres – that the New Exchange would 'take all resorts from this place . . . and in tyme will drawe Mercers, Goldsmythes and all other chiefe Traders to settle themselves out the Cittie in those parts . . . to the greate decay of Trade within the Cittie' (quoted in Stone, 1973, p. 87). In reality, the stalls were simply too small to carry a sufficient quantity and range of stock to do serious damage to retailers in the surrounding streets, some of whom took leases on the stalls to benefit from the new types of shopping spawned by the exchange galleries.

Each exchange had its own character, Westminster Hall, for example, appealed to male shoppers on account of its numerous booksellers and stationers, whilst the New Exchange was known as a place where elite women would meet to shop and socialise. Since the galleries' shops were arranged along indoor walkways, shoppers were able to stroll in a leisurely manner, browsing the goods or simply passing time. Indeed, the words used by contemporaries to describe these spaces – walks, galleries and malls – reflects their promenading function. They were about seeing and being seen as well as inspecting and buying goods. The owners of exchanges sought to create a feeling of social exclusivity partly through the grandeur of the architecture and aristocratic associations, and partly by regulating the type of retailer allowed to trade there and the quality of visitor allowed in, with beadles employed to police entry. Despite this, exchanges increasingly gained a less desirable reputation, the preponderance of female shopkeepers being problematic because, as one commentator put it, they sat 'begging of custom with such amorous looks, and after so affable a manner, that I could not fancy they had much mind to dispose of themselves as the commodities they dealt in' (quoted in Adburgham, 1979, p. 15). More succinctly, the Middle Exchange earned the nickname 'Whores' Nest' (Morrison, 2003, p. 34). Perhaps as a result, but more likely because fashionable society and fashionable shopping moved further west, the exchanges gradually withered as a retail format: the Middle Exchange was demolished in 1694 and the New Exchange followed in 1737; the shops in the Royal Exchange were converted to offices.

These same attributes, impacts on behaviour, and contested uses of space have characterised the various forms of internalised retail space that followed the exchanges: arcades, malls and shopping centres. Whether we see these various retail spaces as evolutionary or revolutionary is, in many ways, a matter of perspective, but each offered contemporary shoppers new experiences and opportunities.

Arcades are usually traced back to the Galeries de Bois – part of the retail and public spaces which made up the Palais Royal in Paris. Built in 1786, the Galeries comprised rows of shops separated by covered passageways which were illuminated by skylights. The success of this retail format quickly spawned copies elsewhere in Paris, including the Passage Feydau (1790–91), the Passage du Caire (1799) and the Passage des Panoramas (1800). They also spread rapidly to French provincial towns, including some relatively small centres such as Chambery, Niort and Amiens, all of which had arcades by 1820 (Gillet, 2014). Wherever they were built, the format and the link to theatres and other forms of public entertainment remained strong. England's first arcade, the Royal Opera Arcade (1817) was designed as part of the King's Opera House then being built in the Haymarket in London. It ran between Pall Mall and Charles II Street, parallel to the newly constructed Regent Street, and quickly became a fashionable promenade. As such, it epitomised the function of arcades as a means of facilitating the movement of pedestrians between urban blocks and alleviating traffic on the main thoroughfares. However, its single row of little shops appears to have been insufficient to make it a long-term commercial success (Mayhew, 1865). In contrast, Burlington Arcade, built just one year later in a prime commercial location near to the major shopping nexus of Old Bond Street, was far more successful. It comprised a double row of shops some 178 metres long, the central walkway being illuminated by large skylights and a series of lamps running its entire length. Its main entrance on Piccadilly was marked by a triple-arched classical façade, whilst the shops themselves had large glazed windows some two metres in height. Above each shop was living accommodation for the shopkeeper (Morrison, 2003, p. 99). The arcade was conceived of as 'a Piazza for all Hardware, Wearing Apparel and Articles not offensive in appearance nor smell' (quoted in Adburgham, 1979, p. 101) and its shops were quickly filled with drapers, milliners, haberdashers, booksellers, toy sellers, shoemakers, hosiers, glovers and so on, who sold small luxuries to elite shoppers.

Part of the enduring popularity of Burlington Arcade was undoubtedly down to its careful policing by beadles who enforced a whole series of regulations. Visitors were not allowed to whistle, sing or play musical instruments; they could not carry bulky parcels or open umbrellas, nor could they run or push perambulators. Moreover, the arcade closed at eight o'clock in the evening, discouraging its use as a place of clandestine assignations. In this sense, arcades have much in common with modern shopping malls, both being heavily regulated spaces of consumption, shaped around the architectural and behavioural blue prints of their designers and owners. That said, Burlington Arcade, like the earlier galleries, was not entirely immune to subversive uses. Mayhew wrote in his *Survey of London* that prostitutes haunted the arcade 'ready at a given signal to dart into a nearby shop whose upper floors had rooms furnished to their taste and their purpose' (quoted in MacKeith, 1985, p. 23). These same contradictions fascinated Walter Benjamin; his famous *Arcades Project* focuses (if that is the right word for what is in some ways a scrapbook of observations and anecdotes) on these enclosed semi-public spaces as 'temples of commodity capital', but also as one of the principal habitats of the urban flaneur who wandered the streets, aloof from his surroundings, but observing and judging what he saw (see Savage, 2000). Indeed, it was the combination of consumption and entertainment (both planned and opportunistic) that made the arcades so attractive for such purposes.

Despite the spatial paradox of arcades as spaces that were public and private, designed and subverted, they became a key element of the European retail and urban environment during the second half of the nineteenth century: symbols of modernity and vitality. In metropolitan centres, they were constructed on a monumental scale, most famously in Brussels (Galeries Royales Saint-Hubert, 1847), Milan (Galleria Vittorio Emanuele II, 1867) and Berlin (Kasergalerie, 1873). Further east, another predecessor of the arcade can be found in the *bezistans*, covered retail venues made of stone with vaulted ceilings and domes, which had been built in the market squares of towns in Ottoman controlled areas in southeast Europe since the mid-sixteenth century (see Chapter 23 – Hilton). Similar forms of covered retail passageways were found in Russia by 1785, and arcades proper had spread to north America by the 1820s. America's pioneer was the Westminster Arcade in Providence, Rhode Island (1828) which, unlike its European counterparts, had small shops arranged along two upper story galleries as well as the main walkway at ground level. It opened for only two hours each day so was hardly a major retail venue. More conventional was the Paddock Arcade in Watertown, New York (1850) where only the ground floor was used for shops – the upper floors containing offices. Perhaps most spectacular was the 1890 Cleveland Arcade, a huge development modelled on Milan's Galleria Vittorio Emanuele II, but containing shops on five levels and linked with two large office blocks rather than theatres or other places of entertainment. As in Europe, however, these were places for pedestrians who were brought to these city-centre locations via mass transportation systems, most notably trams and railways.

Arnout (2014) argues that the splendour and scale of these structures formed one of their key attractions for urban authorities in sanctioning their construction – they would be ornaments to the city, augmenting its standing relative to other centres. As such, they were part of the wider process of "civic boosterism" that underscored the construction of magnificent town halls and market halls, as well as leisure and educational facilities. And they were well suited to such purposes; the extensive use of innovative materials and building techniques, most notably the

Figure 12.1 The Arcade, downtown Cleveland, OH

Source: Credit: Photographs in the Carol M. Highsmith Archive, Library of Congress, Prints and Photographs Division.

combination of steel and glass in the construction of their roofs, gave them an air of modernity as well as splendour. Add to this the introduction of gas lighting and the presence of a theatre and several cafes and restaurants, and it is easy to believe the rhetoric of the promoters of the Galeries Royales Saint-Hubert in Brussels, who wrote that 'Paris's most frequented arcades offer no sight livelier than the Galeries St-Hubert; a crowd of strollers and passer-by fills them from morning till night' (quoted in Arnout, 2014, p. 170). Yet they faced the same issues seen in Burlington Arcade; the shopkeepers' desire for regulation and respectability clashing with the status of the arcades as a place of entertainment open to everyone.

There is a further paradox: the grand arcades in Brussels, as well as those in Milan and Berlin, were built at a time when they were already going out of fashion in Paris – replaced by the department store and the broad sweep of open boulevards. This highlights the lack of uniformity of the urban experience across Europe and even within a single country. We thus see the Galeries Royales Saint-Hubert in Brussels prospering into the twentieth century when the Antwerp Cité arcade was struggling. Similarly, there was a burgeoning number of arcades being built in the cities of northern England when the emphasis in London, as in Paris, had moved to department stores. There had been a flurry of building in the 1820s, when arcades were constructed in Hastings, Bristol, Bath, Glasgow and Newcastle (Morrison, 2003, pp. 100–101). In London, various mid-nineteenth-century schemes re-envisaged the arcade on a magnificent scale – part of grandiose schemes to re-imagine the city. That of William Moseley linked an arcade of shops to the construction of an underground railway, whilst Joseph Paxton suggested a 16km glazed arcade that would encircle central London – an idea that re-emerged in Ebenezer Howard's vision of a garden city. However, it was only from the 1870s that arcade building gained real momentum in provincial England and began reshaping the retail and urban landscape, especially in Leeds, Manchester and Birmingham. Again, they served as important pedestrian thoroughfares, almost invariably being built to link streets, whilst offering new commercial space. Many, including the 1873 Barton Arcade in Manchester and the 1898 County Arcade in Leeds, broke with earlier tradition and had two or more stories of shops. Others had upper floors given over to offices or incorporated central rotunda or an enlarged central space providing a spatial and functional focus. The Leyland Arcade in Southport (1896), for instance, originally housed a bandstand as well as palm trees and seating (Morrison, 2003, pp. 102–106).

This kind of provision, plus the inclusion of several stories of shops, blurs the distinction in form between late nineteenth-century arcades and twentieth-century malls – something which seems particularly true of the Cleveland Arcade. However, in providing small premises for independent retailers, arcades formed a complement to high streets (and a contrast to later malls), which were increasingly dominated by large department stores and multiple retailers. That said, by the early twentieth century, when the boom in arcade building had passed – at least in Britain – chain stores like Boots were starting to occupy shops in arcades, rendering them less distinctive as retail spaces.

Shopping centres and malls: American origins

The terms shopping centre and shopping mall are used interchangeably in the United States and, to a lesser extent, in the UK and elsewhere in Europe. Historically, shopping centres referred to planned developments oriented to the automobile that were typically open-air, arranged along a strip or around a courtyard or open area, and situated away from the city centre. The term mall appeared with the rise of the enclosed shopping centre – a format which, as we noted above, might be seen as a development of earlier shopping arcades. In the UK in particular it

Figure 12.2 Barton Arcade, Manchester, UK

Credit: Author's own photograph.

was sometimes associated with regeneration of the city centre, although confusingly, many of these developments were referred to as shopping centres – for example, Birmingham's Bull Ring Shopping Centre (1964). As Longstreth (2010) suggests, any distinction between malls and shopping centres was often semantic and, in any case, was soon lost.

When they first appeared in the United States, shopping centres were a revolutionary way of distributing goods and services. First and foremost, their unique form offered consumers a physical/spatial experience distinct from that of the traditional downtown business district. The central business district or market street, which had long served most shopping needs, was comprised of independently owned and operated businesses housed in architecturally distinct buildings. They were heterogonous, often messy places that evolved over time in an organic fashion to serve the needs of their city and wider trading area. Many downtown department stores, for example, reflected their nineteenth-century origins well into the twentieth and were conglomerations of buildings patched together as the business grew and needed to expand within the confines of the city centre. Within the new commercial complexes, however, all stores were 'designed, built, and operated as a single unit', usually at the same time. Mall owners/managers populated them with tenants who were selected for what they could contribute to the whole (Longstreth, 2010, p. 170). Run together as a business, they promised efficiency and order, in contrast to the chaos of an aging downtown. Centralised administration allowed for standardisation and control of architectural and design features, as well as store placement, so as to shape the consumer experience and maximise profits. As well as being designed and operated as a single unit, they were also promoted as a whole, through the efforts of management and their tenants (Cohen, 1996, p. 1056; Longstreth, 2010, p. 170). This revolutionary form remained consistent over several decades in the shape of three distinct categories of shopping centres in the United States: neighbourhood, community, and regional shopping centres were based on size, make-up and target market (Longstreth, 2010, pp. 173–174). Such clear distinctions are less apparent in Europe, although an informal hierarchy is apparent, notably between older in-town malls and later out-of-town regional shopping centres such as Merry Hill in the West Midlands and Bluewater in Kent.

In the United States, where the shopping mall was born, the industry demonstrated a commitment to automobility. Shopping centres' unique form was in fact a product of the automobile revolution, a response to the challenges of downtown parking and traffic congestion in central business districts as car ownership soared. The first fully planned shopping centre, Kansas City's Country Club Plaza, which opened in the early 1920s, exemplified the emergence of a new automobile orientation in retail construction. A multi-building complex, it was arranged to resemble an idealised village, yet nevertheless was oriented to the motorist, with parking lots and wide streets (Longstreth, 2010, p. 170). Other interwar developments occurred in Los Angeles, with its car culture, spreading housing developments and highways that provided easy access to commercial locations outside the urban core (Hardwick, 2004, p. 95). Before World War II, however, shopping centre development was quite limited. Department stores were expanding outside traditional central business districts, but these early suburban branches were typically stand-alone buildings. Department stores came to play a central role in their development after the war, increasingly establishing suburban branches as anchors first for outdoor shopping centres, then enclosed malls (Longstreth, 2010, p. 163).

Residential decentralisation and suburbanisation, facilitated by private automobile ownership, played a major role in new shopping centre development in the United States. Between 1950 and 1955, the suburban population grew seven times as fast as that of central cities. Decentralised residential patterns were tied to increased automobility as people relied on their personal vehicles to get to work or to travel downtown to shop or do business. Between 1946 and 1955,

Figure 12.3 Country Club Plaza, Kansas City

Credit: Library of Congress, Prints & Photographs Division, photograph by John Margolies, [reproduction number, e.g., LC-MA05-1]

new-car sales in America quadrupled (Tarver, 1957, p. 427; Nicolaide and Weise, 2006, p. 7; Cohen, 2003, p. 123). As postwar automobile-oriented suburbanisation expanded markets, shopping centre numbers skyrocketed, reaching 7,100 by 1963 (Cohen, 1996, p. 1052; Longstreth, 2010, p. 170; Howard, 2015, p. 139). By 1960, government reports described suburban shopping centres as 'the inevitable by-product of the automobile age' (*Impact of Suburban Shopping*, 1960).

Shopping centres' connection to automobility was by no means inevitable, however, as the pervasiveness of central or urban shopping districts in Europe suggests. In part, this was a reflection of better state support for European public transport systems. In addition, it was the product of American regulations that facilitated expansion into the suburbs. Since the Great Depression, the federal government had shaped the geography of American retailing. By pumping money into the suburban housing market through programs that eased home financing, more Americans became homeowners. After World War II, federal policies continued to support the decentralisation of cities, not least through federal and state financed highway building which facilitated the movement out of cities. By 1960, 62% of Americans owned their own homes (Nicolaide and Weise, 2006, p. 4; Hardwick, 2004, pp. 86–87), many of which were in new developments that needed the services that a big shopping complex could provide.

Aided by tax policy, such as the 1954 Internal Revenue Code that favoured new construction, developers responded to this growing demand. The policy allowed investors to depreciate their commercial real estate investments in a manner that encouraged new construction over maintenance or renovation of existing properties. Building a shopping centre required a high level of initial investment with an extended pay-out time. By allowing accelerated depreciation, policymakers gave investors a tax break big enough to overcome these potential barriers. Moreover, the law encouraged turnover, as investors sought repeated deductions with new properties. According to historian Thomas Hanchett, this tax code underwrote shopping mall expansion in the postwar era and was a major contributor to decentralisation, along with suburban home ownership, America's automobile culture and rising racial tension in cities (Jackson, 1996, p. 1115; Hanchett, 1996, p. 1082–1110). American shopping centre developers were also aided by financial institutions, such as insurance companies and pension trusts. Their reliance on these financial institutions influenced their makeup. Developers and department store executives at first preferred that the majority of shopping centre tenants be independents, but demands that merchants have the highest credit rating meant that big chains like J.C. Penney would have an advantage (Howard, 2015, p. 139). The trajectory towards chain organisation within the department store industry influenced the character of malls, which became increasingly standardised after the late 1980s (Howard, 2015).

When they first appeared on the American scene in large numbers in the 1950s, shopping centres seemed to fill pressing needs, both economic and social. Built to serve as both a commercial and a social centre for burgeoning new suburban communities, their function was unique. Architects like Victor Gruen designed them to provide American suburbanites with a new kind of urban experience. At Northland outside of Detroit, for example, Gruen's design evoked a European city, featuring clusters of open spaces that were labelled with names that evoked urban pathways or public space – such as lanes, terraces, courts and malls – all of which were decorated in an idyllic way with colonnades, sculptures and fountains (Hardwick, 2004, pp. 80, 85, 128–130; Cohen, 2003, pp. 262–263). Contemporary shopping centres were built with non-selling spaces, such as community halls that hosted dances, meetings and receptions. Department stores, and in many cases, supermarkets, anchored these developments, meaning they could replace the traditional downtown food market, butcher or corner grocer. In suburban New Jersey, for example, when Bergen Mall and Garden State Plaza opened in 1957 they offered everything that was available downtown. More than just a collection of department stores, specialty shops and restaurants, the New Jersey malls featured every service, from laundry to shoe repair, from banking and stock brokerage to travel and real estate offices. Functioning in many ways as a civic centre for the suburbs, they were home to a Catholic chapel and diverse recreational facilities, such as a movie theatre, ice-skating rink and bowling alley. Children were even made to feel at home with a gymnasium and a playground (Cohen, 1996, p. 1058). Such services and amenities were intended to draw people in and by increasing mall traffic, drive sales volume.

Shopping centres were consciously developed and promoted to function as an alternative to the heterogenous city street and traditional downtown business district. Their American development took place in direct conversation with downtown retail traditions. Typically built on inexpensive land well beyond the central business district, they expanded outward rather than upward, leaving behind the traditional verticality that downtown department stores adopted out of necessity as well as for prestige (Hardwick, 2004, p. 97). Their early architects hoped they would have the appeal of a traditional downtown centre but without the aggravation of limited parking and congested streets. (See illustration in Chapter 5 in this volume: Cross County Shopping Center, Westchester County, New York.) Shopping centres like NorthPark, for example, which opened outside Dallas in 1965, were advertised as 'an attempt to counteract the confusions of the city'. By the mid-1960s, this view of the shopping centre as a solution to 'the plight of cities' and 'unplanned urban sprawl' was widespread (Howard, 2015, p. 142).

In Britain as well, shopping malls were understood to offer an experience in direct contrast with High Street or downtown shopping and its association with urban decay and crime, not to mention inclement weather (Stobart, 2008, p. 206). Some British shopping centre architects, however, turned away from the American-style developed by Victor Gruen. Referencing their parking lots, one of the architects of Britain's visionary 1979 Milton Keynes shopping centre criticised them as 'tarmac machines for spending money, entirely enclosed' (quoted in Gosseye, 2015, p. 213). That said, the shopping centre that was built in Milton Keynes resembled its American counterparts more closely than any other British development (Morrison, 2003, p. 267). 'Pav(ing) paradise to put up a parking lot' was looked down upon by some in the United States when Joni Mitchell sang these words in 1970, but in the emerging neoliberal environment of both nations suburban shopping mall development advanced unabated. There were 22,000 shopping centres in the United States by 1980, and this number had more than doubled by the early twenty-first century (Blaszczyk, 2009, p. 210). Development was slower in Britain. From pioneers in the 1960s, development was steady through the 1970s before accelerating to culminate in the construction of eleven out-of-town regional shopping centres, seven of them built in the 1990s (Pacione, 2005, pp. 255–262). By 2017, there were about 550 shopping centres in the United Kingdom, twenty of them "supermalls" (*The Guardian*, 16 December 2017).

In Britain, most shopping centres appeared as part of programmes of urban development (as at Milton Keynes) or redevelopment (for example, in Bradford and Newcastle in the 1970s or Reading and Kingston-on-Thames in the 1990s). In the United States, though, they were largely suburban enterprises and as such embodied the ills and injustices of American suburban history. Decentralisation took place in a racialised context in the United States. The suburban/urban bifurcation that emerged in contemporary shopping centre discussions reflected the industry's racism, as well as the racially driven demographic shifts taking place in the postwar period. When American department stores considered expanding by opening branches, for example, they generally chased the white, emerging middle-class markets that were racing to the suburbs after World War II (Howard, 2015, pp. 2–3). Unlike downtown emporia, shopping centres and their branch department stores catered specifically to the needs and preferences of this more homogenised group. While marketers were beginning to discover African American consumers through the early postwar period, shopping centres largely ignored them. One exception was the South Center Department Store, which opened in 1928 in Chicago as part of a shopping and entertainment complex. It was white-owned until the late 1960s, when it was bought by an African American developer (Howard, 2015, pp. 54–55).

When African American citizens and retailers came together in the media it was through coverage of civil rights protests, particularly the boycotts of Southern department stores and variety chains like Woolworths where black shoppers faced employment discrimination and segregation in store restaurants and restrooms. Civil rights protests largely bypassed suburban shopping malls during this period. Shopping centre developers single-mindedly sought a middle-class market, which was understood to be white even though the black middle-class was expanding significantly (Howard, 2015, pp. 159–162). To pursue this market, department store branches in these shopping centres did things differently to their downtown parent store, cultivating a controlled, safe atmosphere that was believed to appeal specifically to white, suburban housewives. Suburban branches, as it was understood by the trade press, were 'breaking away from downtown traditions', establishing evening hours, offering novel services, and even competing with the new mass merchandisers like the discount operation. The practice of self-service, led by the grocery trade in the 1930s but also increasingly instituted at downtown department stores, was fully part of this suburban shopping mall experience (Howard, 2015, p. 90). The massive new complexes were meant to appeal to families, not just women, all of whom were encouraged to spend their leisure time wandering between stores, handling the goods if desired, and most important, spending. Indeed, by the early 1960s shopping malls appeared to have had some success in reorienting the experience, as retail and marketing experts noted a change in family buying habits, with the husband becoming a 'more active member of the family purchasing team'. When depicted in advertisements or trade literature, this purchasing team was largely figured as white and middle class (Isenberg, 2004, p. 176; Howard, 2015, "family purchasing team" quote, 143).

Diffusion and diversification of shopping centres: the US and beyond

Shopping malls were an American invention, built on the nation's early and ongoing commitment to private automobile ownership; but, as we have already noted, shopping malls did not stay a uniquely American retailing mode over the second half of the twentieth century. By the 1960s and early 1970s, the father of the American shopping mall form, Victor Gruen, was exporting his ideas back to Europe, his suburban shopping centres appearing outside Vienna, around Paris and the French Riviera, and in Zurich (Hardwick, 2004, p. 221). As many Western and non-Western nations embraced the retail format, they faced different economic, political and social imperatives. In the United States as we have seen, decentralisation was a key force. Department stores and mall developers built "markets in the meadows" in order to follow residential populations shifting from urban cores to the periphery into new housing made possible by mass housing construction methods, affordable automobiles, tax breaks for developers and inexpensive home loans provided through the GI Bill after the war (Hanchett, 1996; May, 1988). Suburbia and mall development emerged in the context of post-World War II prosperity in the United States.

Other nations dealt with differing postwar circumstances. Following World War II in Britain, for example, shopping centre development took place hand-in-hand with larger redevelopment schemes addressing wartime damage and the need to reconstruct town centres and provide housing (Stobart, 2008, pp. 192, 203; Morrison, 2003, pp. 251–273). To a large extent, British department stores, chains, independents and co-operatives maintained a strong presence on the High Street, with shoppers continuing to see downtown as a place to take care of their daily needs (Stobart, 2008, p. 193). Schemes for gathering retailers into specially redeveloped shopping districts or precincts emerged in the 1950s, with the earliest perhaps being the Chrisp Street Shopping Precinct in Poplar, East London in 1951. Many took design clues from the Lijnbaan in Rotterdam, a completely pedestrianised zone rebuilt in 1953 after the city was devastated by wartime bombing. The 1960s saw these shopping precincts emerging in towns that had suffered little damage in the war, but that were committed to modernisation (Morrison, 2003, pp. 251, 258–259; Stobart, 2008, pp. 203–204). This process continued with the development of urban shopping malls from the 1960s into the 2000s. The first of these was the Bull Ring in Birmingham (1964), followed by a succession of others, including the Arndale centres built on a massive scale and in modernist styles in many northern cities. Whilst more sympathetic architecture was adopted from the 1980s, the key role of the shopping mall in reviving the city centre was maintained with schemes such as Touchwood in Solihull (2001) and Liverpool One (2008).

Enclosed, out-of-town shopping malls like Southdale Center in Minnesota were being developed in France by the late 1960s, with early examples being Parly 2 (1969), Velizy 2 (1972) and Rosny 2 (1973), all in the Ile-de-France. Britain was slower to embrace these developments, in part because of much tighter planning regulations, including Green Belt restrictions designed to limit out-of-town developments of any kind. Although out-of-town centres were built near Peterborough (Breton Centre, 1971–72) and Northampton (Weston Favell, 1974) as part of new town expansion schemes, The Brent Cross Shopping Centre, which opened in northwest London in 1976, was the first to really follow the American model in location and scale. It was situated away from established centres of retailing and not part of a larger urban redevelopment plan (Morrison, 2003, pp. 296–297; Miller et al., 1998, p. 2; Gosseye, 2015, p. 212). The mall's design also mirrored the standard US dumb-bell style, with two anchor department stores linked by a two-level mall. It also featured a supermarket, many large chain branches and originally had 3,000 parking spots, all on a 52 acre site. (Miller et al., 1998, pp. 32, 44; Gosseye, 2015, p. 212). By the 1990s, Britain was building very large out-of-town shopping centres, such as Manchester's Trafford Centre (1995–98) and Bluewater in Kent (1999), mirroring earlier American developments with regional malls (Stobart, 2008, pp. 219–222).

While on the surface shopping malls may appear to have the same form and serve the same function across national borders, the context in which they were produced varied widely across space and time. New Town shopping centres, for example like that developed at Milton Keynes in 1979, were intended to serve a civic function and were accordingly built with many non-commercial features and attractive landscaping, as in the United States in the early postwar period (Gosseye, 2015). But unlike purely private commercial developments in the United States, Milton Keynes was the product of a public-private partnership intended to cater to the interests of investors but also to promote particular social and political goals in an era when neoliberalism was beginning to pick apart the welfare state in Britain under Prime Minister Thatcher (Gosseye, 2015). In this, Milton Keynes was perhaps unusual, with most UK shopping malls, especially the larger regional centres, being financed and built by private developers.

Beginning in the 1980s, shopping malls began to face competition from new brick-and-mortar retail formats. In the United States, designer outlet malls like Ontario Mills in California and Sawgrass Mills in Florida were built along highways and attracted bargain hunters willing to drive long distances for fashion labels at a lower price (Farrell, 2003, p. 13). The outlet mall village format spread in the United Kingdom in the following decade, the first being built in 1993 by the shoe manufacturer Clarks on their redundant factory site in Street, Somerset (Morrison, 2003, pp. 293–295). Others quickly followed, many constructed in a quasi-high street format with relatively small stores often built in a vernacular if sometimes anachronistic style. Out-of-town outlet centres came to Japan at the turn of the twenty-first century, with Gotemba Premium Outlets winning an award for its publicity campaign to convince Japanese customers of the benefits of the new retail format (Farrell, 2003, p. 253). More significantly, perhaps, formidable power centres first appeared in the 1970s in the United States (Spector, 2005, p. 111). Comprised of a Walmart or Target, and a row of so-called "category killers", big-box stores that dominated one line of goods, such as toys, hardware or bedding, they marked a turn towards discounts and specialisation (Spector, 2005, p. 110). They were also more firmly embedded in automobile culture. Stores share a parking lot and, unlike a traditional shopping mall with pedestrian passageways between anchors, power centres are 'a cars-only zone' (Spector, 2005, p. 4). While typically associated with American car culture, these commercial developments also prospered in Britain and across Europe, even in countries with a much stronger commitment to public transportation.

Finally, the regional shopping centre, once the largest retail format, faced competition from a new giant, the megamall. The term first appeared in 1979, but only became common in 1986, a year after the first of its kind opened in Alberta, Canada (NYT, "Why Supermall is Superbad", 1979; "A Shoppers Paradise on the Prairie", 1986). Finding its niche in cold climates, where indoor shopping and entertainment complexes provided leisure opportunities in long winters, the 1985 West Edmonton Mall, was followed by the 2.5 million square foot Mall of America outside of Minneapolis, Minnesota in 1992. Anchored by multiple department stores and boasting such things as an ice skating rink, aquarium, water park, rollercoaster rides, movie theatres, hotel and wedding chapel, they serve as tourist attractions, drawing millions of visitors a year. And outdoor "lifestyle centres", distinct from power centres and the traditional postwar mall, grew in popularity during the same time period. Consisting of specialty and big-box retailers, interspersed with fine dining opportunities along a landscaped outdoor walkway, these upscale venues harkened back to the original outdoor shopping centres introduced by architectural visionaries, like Victor Gruen, right after World War II (Sherman, 2008). Not surprisingly, consumer interest in the ordinary indoor shopping malls has been declining since the mid-1990s. In America especially, older enclosed shopping malls have been shut down, converted to alternate uses or demolished by the hundreds since then (Spector, 2005, p. 176).

As the traditional American shopping centre is in decline in the early twenty-first century, a boom in mall construction is underway globally. Russia, India and Latin America have all undergone a retail transformation in their urban centres (Davila, 2012, p. 23; Srivastava, 2015, p. 224; Abaza, 2006, p. 196). In Cairo, Egypt, there were two dozen by 2003 (Abaza, 2006, p. 197) and in Japan several railway companies were instrumental in constructing malls and department stores linked to their city centre terminals (Fujioka, 2014, p. 31). With the rise of major players globally, American influence has lessened. Southeast Asian malls in Kuala Lumpur, Singapore and Jakarta, for example, with their glass elevators and elaborate facades provide a new model for mall development in other countries, like Egypt (Abaza, 2006, pp. 208–209).

In terms of size, the United States is no longer the leader either. In the twenty-first century, megamalls opened in China, a country which now boasts a number of the world's largest malls, reflecting its new consumer economy and expanding middle class. The Golden Resource Mall in Beijing, which opened in 2004, covered six million square feet and became the largest, though other bigger Chinese megamalls arrived quickly on the scene (Campanella, 2008, p. 236). After a shopping mall building boom in China, however, much retail space remains unrented. Overstoring and the astronomical popularity of e-commerce in China will cause many to close by 2020, according to several reports (Minter, 2016; Linder, 2016). Shopping malls in other countries have also suffered from overbuilding, recession and currency devaluation. Vast income

Figure 12.4 Suria KLCC, a shopping centre in Kuala Lumpur, located at the base of the landmark Petronas Towers

Credit: https://pixabay.com-

disparity is to blame in countries like Egypt, where only a minority can afford to shop in the new upscale malls. Like the United States, Egypt has experienced the "dead mall" phenomenon (Abaza, 2006, p. 199, mall quote p. 216). It remains to be seen whether the enclosed shopping mall retail format can withstand all these pressures or whether it will decline as a global trend.

Behaviour, power and space in the shopping mall

As a retail format that has shaped landscapes and transformed economic and social behaviour, it is not surprising that the shopping mall attained a prominent place in American culture, emerging as a positive symbol of postwar suburban consumer abundance. Surrounded by a sea of colourful parked cars, it was a concrete monument to American prosperity. Ubiquity, however, transformed this symbol into a reference point for everything that was wrong in American society. Shopping centres and megamalls have often appeared as the 'apotheosis of American consumerism' (Hardwick, 2004, p. 1). One 1979 observer described them as symbols of 'undisciplined American consumption, showrooms for planned obsolescence' full of 'pumped waterfalls, plastic flowers, filtered air and wired birdsong' that parodied nature (Neill, 1979, p. 20). This type of criticism stems from a critical view of suburban identity. In this view, shopping malls stand for other negative aspects of mass culture, namely the perceived dull homogeneity of suburban living. In part this was a response to their regularised appearance. Unlike the traditional downtown store, which was part of the heterogeneous city, shopping mall formats were quite standardised. This was the result of a number of factors, both practical and strategic. Shopping centre leases during the period sought to control the overall visual effect by requiring tenants to create unified colour schemes and signage. Increasingly they were organised around plain, windowless department stores – boxlike containers with low-key signs and entrances. Centres were regularised into 'a linear sequence of stores facing a front parking lot', laid out in a straight line or bent at one or two points to form a V or divided into two parts into an L shape (Isenberg, 2004, p. 198; Longstreth, 2010, p. 178). The overall effect was a low-slung, windowless shape the monotony of which critics found emblematic of suburban living.

As the shopping mall form made its way into non-Western cultures by the late twentieth century, its meaning continued to evolve and scholarly interpretations continued to diverge. The imposition of standardised Western retail modes, some have argued, have destroyed local cultures and hindered social and family ties (Davila, 2012, p. 23). And yet, while the shopping mall has been seen as an Americanising force – and a negative one at that – it has also found a positive reception. This favourable interpretation has largely hinged on the idea that shopping malls provided privatised public spaces within which there could be a great diversity of experience and potential for social/cultural and political expression. Daniel Miller and others have long argued there are multiple publics even within each mall (Miller et al., 1998, p. 29). Sociologists and others have also emphasised the potential for consumer agency in malls. Looking at non-Western countries, such as Egypt, Turkey and India, scholars have made the point that a wide cross-section of people visit malls, even if they do not shop there (Srivastava, 2015, citing Abaza and Erkip, p. 225).

By focusing on individual consumer practices, it is possible to see malls as a positive source of social interaction and expression of identity (Davila, 2012, p. 23). As did the nineteenth-century urban department store in the United States (Benson, 1988), recent non-Western shopping malls have created newly gendered middle-class spaces for women (Abaza, 2006, pp. 215–216). In India, for example, malls appealed to middle-class women, young and old, providing them with a socially acceptable, safe place for socialising. They also provided a place for courting couples who did not have parental approval. Their appeal was quite wide-ranging in terms of social class as well. The sociologist Sanjay Srivastava has argued that they formed 'meeting points of the promises of urban culture and the aspirations of the hinterlands' and played a role in the lives of the urban poor who, though unable to spend money there, took part in their 'imaginative economies' (Srivastava, 2015, p. 225, 259). In Egypt, young people who live in informal housing or slums find in Cairo's shopping malls a clean space where they can feel they are participating in a better world, imitating through dress and through their presence in the mall a higher social status (Abaza, 2006, p. 216). There are limits, however, dictated by the privatised nature of shopping mall space. As Srivastava (2015, p. 225) suggested, 'there is only so much sociality investment capital can countenance'. Mall owners have had to 'calibrate sociality so that it issues an exchange value', in other words, finding ways to balance the non-commercial activities or actions of mall visitors with spending.

As privatised public spaces, others point out that they reproduce social inequality by policing and excluding people who might not so easily be 'kept at bay in the public street' (Davila, 2012, p. 24). Nevertheless, such scholarship has documented public activities in shopping malls that actively resist their consumerist message and goal. This is the case in Puerto Rico, where the shopping mall industry underwent expansion between 1993 and 2001, and by 2008, was home to 317 malls. This construction boom, as Arlene Davila (2012, pp. 30–31) argues, did not mean that the new retail format was accepted uncritically. This same period not surprisingly saw a steep rise in small retailer bankruptcies, which led to concerns that the island's retail sector was undergoing "Walmartisation". Moreover, the shopping malls were not always used for the purpose for which they were built. Senior citizens used them as meeting places for socialising, with little consumption attached, while unauthorised, outside vendors try to use their open spaces to sell their wares. The major Puerto Rican shopping mall, *Plaza las Americas*, was even the site a major takeover by student strikers who were protesting university tuition fees. Such demonstrations, Davila suggests, are evidence that shopping malls are not necessarily apolitical spaces just for leisure and entertainment. 'These striking performances showcased a key predicament of neoliberalism: that if there are no jobs or accessible public higher education, there cannot be shopping' (Davila, 2012, p. 44).

Envisioning a commercial cultural sphere that is distinct from the political domain, some scholars have argued that the expansion of mass consumer culture has cut into public space. Such encroachment has 'blurred the distinction between arguments made on behalf of political claims and the rationales used for making consumer choices' (de Grazia, 2005, pp. 229–230; Ewen, 1976). Shopping centre development made physical inroads into public space, its paved parking lots and highway access standing in direct contrast with downtown centres that evolved to serve the needs of pedestrians. Unlike the public spaces that served as a community forum for citizens and free speech, shopping malls privileged the rights of private property owners (Cohen, 1996, pp. 1053–1054). Shopping centres were privatised spaces, with entry limited to opening times and behaviour and activities monitored and controlled by security personnel and mall management. In this view, the expansion of this commercial sphere came at the cost of avenues for political expression and action.

Just as scholars have interpreted these commercial spaces differently, seeing them as contested spaces where power relations play out in a variety of ways that change over time, mall management and shoppers themselves have also understood their public function in contrasting ways. A key point of debate in the American context is connected to the issue of free speech and the legal interpretation of shopping malls as public or private space. There is no absolute First Amendment right to free speech in privately owned spaces in the United States. As privatised spaces where the public typically has free entry, shopping malls are potentially the site of leafleting, petitioning, or expressions of a political nature, either through speech or even dress. A key Supreme Court decision (*Pruneyard Shopping Center v Robins*, 1980) argued that state constitutions might protect free speech in such private forums, but that no federal protection was given. As a result of this case, some states amended their constitutions to allow certain kinds of speech in private forums, but others did not. *Pruneyard* meant 'as state law will oblige, shopping centres can be converted into a limited public forum open to political speech of all shades and opinions'. But, in states where no state constitutional protection was offered, malls were able to eject customers or patrons based on their own rules. This was found to be the case in Albany, New York, for example, when a father and son wearing political t-shirts were told to leave the Crossgates shopping mall; the father was arrested when he refused to leave. (Pigeon, 1981; Epstein, 1997, quote p. 35; *New York Times*, 6 March 2003). While the issue seems settled in a legal sense in the United States (state variations/no federal protection), on a daily basis shopping malls continue to be sites of social interaction, stages upon which the power relations to do with race, class and gender are contested and upheld. In a more benign manner, however, malls continue to offer a venue for the sort of activities noted by Davila (2012) in Puerto Rica. While behaviour is regulated by private security guards, malls formed places to meet and socialise for young and old alike, sitting on the benches provided an enjoyable a pleasant and safe environment, free from the normal urban hazards: 'no hassle, no traffic, older kids don't bother you' (Matthews et al., 2000, p. 286).

Conclusion

Malls might be the epitome of late twentieth-century retailing, but their roots lie deep in the shopping galleries and arcades of early modern Europe. While different in their form, scale and location, they share a common thread of planned and regulated space, designed to foster leisurely shopping and with the ability to shape consumer behaviour. In their own times, each has been very successful, shopping malls in particular spreading across the globe very soon after their introduction in postwar US. In this context, they formed a symbol of modernity and of the American dream: a venue in which consumer desires could be formed and satiated in an environment that was safe, enticing and above all convenient. Success can be counted in numbers, but also in the way that malls quickly became central to modern lifestyles and cultural norms. In Europe, and especially in the UK, they took on the additional role of urban renewal, both in a series of New Towns and in the reconstruction and conscious modernisation of city centres. But the mall format was constantly shifting in its location and form, out-of-town and later regional shopping centres have undermined the viability of many downtown malls in the US and a similar problem has emerged in the UK and elsewhere. Just as profound as this devaluation of the mall's economic currency is the tarnishing of its social and cultural credentials, with earlier complaints of uniformity and ennui being overlain with concerns over citizens' rights and the privatisation of urban space. Changing economics have meant that hundreds of malls have closed in the US and shops lie empty in many UK malls, though the problem of vacant premises is less severe than on many high streets. The convenience of the shopping mall, accessed by car, has been replaced by the convenience of online retailers, accessed via the Internet and by vast numbers of delivery vans (see Chapter 5). And yet shopping malls remain places to go for millions of shoppers across the world – places to acquire the trappings of modern consumer society; places to look at both goods and people or simply places to be and be seen.

References

Abaza, M. (2006), 'Egyptianizing the American dream: Nasr City's shopping malls, public order, and the privatized military', in D. Singerman and P. Amar (eds.) *Cairo cosmopolitan: Politics, culture, and urban space in the new globalized middle east* (New York: American University in Cairo Press).

Adburgham, A. (1979), *Shopping in style: London from the restoration to Edwardian elegance* (London: Thames and Hudson Ltd).

Arnout, A. (2014), 'Something old, something borrowed, something new: The Brussels shopping townscape, 1830–1914', in J.-H. Furnee and C. Lesger (eds.) *The landscape of consumption: Shopping streets and cultures in Western Europe, 1600–1900* (Basingstoke: Palgrave Macmillan) 157–183.

Benson, S.P. (1988), *Counter cultures: Saleswomen, managers, and customers in American department stores, 1890–1940* (Urbana/Chicago: University of Illinois Press).

Blaszczyk, R. (2009), *American consumer society, 1865–2005: From hearth to HDTV* (Wheeling, IL: Harlan Davidson).

Campanella, T. (2008), *The concrete dragon: China's urban revolution and what it means for the world* (New York: Princeton Architectural Press).

Cohen, L. (2003), *A consumers' republic: The politics of mass consumption in postwar America* (New York: Knopf Doubleday Publishing).

Cohen, L. (1996), 'From town center to shopping center: The reconfiguration of community marketplaces in postwar America', *American Historical Review*, 101 (4), pp. 1050–1081.

Davila, A. (2012), *Culture works: Space, value and mobility across the neoliberal Americas* (New York: New York University Press).

de Grazia, V. (2005), *Irresistible empire: America's advance through 20th-century Europe* (Cambridge, MA: Harvard University Press).

Epstein, R. (1997), 'Takings, exclusivity and speech: The legacy of *Pruneyard v Robins*', *The University of Chicago Law Review*, 64 (1), pp. 21–56.

Ewen, S. (1976), *Captains of consciousness: Advertising and the social roots of the consumer culture* (New York: Basic Books).

Farrell, J.J. (2003), *One nation under goods: Malls and the seductions of American shopping* (Washington, DC: Smithsonian Books).

Fujioka, R. (2014), 'The development of department stores in Japan: 1900s–1930s', *Japanese Research in Business History*, pp. 11–27.

Gillet, M. (2014), 'Innovation and tradition in the shopping landscape of Parish and a provincial city, 1800–1900', in J.-H. Furnee and C. Lesger (eds.) *The landscape of consumption: Shopping streets and cultures in Western Europe, 1600–1900* (Basingstoke: Palgrave Macmillan) 184–207.

Gosseye, J. (2015), "Milton Keynes' centre: The apotheosis of the British post-war consensus or the apostle of neo-liberalism?', *History of Retailing and Consumption*, 1 (3), pp. 209–229.

Hanchett, T.W. (1996), 'U.S. tax policy and the shopping-center boom of the 1950s and 1960s', *The American Historical Review*, 101, pp. 1082–1110.

Hardwick, M.J. (2004), *Mall maker: Victor Gruen, architect of an American dream* (Philadelphia, PA: University of Pennsylvania Press).

Howard, V. (2015), *From main street to mall: The rise and fall of the American department store* (Philadelphia, PA: University of Pennsylvania Press).

Hu, W. (2003), 'A message of peace on two shirts touches off hostilities at a mall', *New York Times*.

Impact of Suburban Shopping Centers on Independent Retailers, Report of the Select Committee on Small Business United States Senate, 86th Congress 1st Session, Report No. 1016 (United States Government Printing Office, January 5, 1960).

Isenberg, A. (2004), *Downtown America: A history of the place and the people who made it* (Chicago: University of Chicago Press).

Jackson, K.T. (1996), 'All the world's a mall: Reflections on the social and economic consequences of the American shopping center', *American Historical Review*, 101, pp. 1111–1121.

Linder, A. (2016), 'Five years from now, one-third of China's shopping malls will be out of business, report says', *Shanghaiist* (September 8, 2016), Available at: http://shanghaiist.com/2016/09/08/one_third_shopping_malls_gone.php.

Longstreth, R. (2010), *The American department store transformed, 1920–1960* (New Haven, CT: Yale University Press).

MacKeith, M. (1985), *Shopping arcades. A Gazetteer of extant British arcades, 1817–1939* (London: Mansell Publishing).

Matthews, H., Taylor, M., Percy-Smith, B. and Limb, M. (2000), 'The unacceptable flaneur: The shopping mall as a teenage hangout', *Childhood*, 7 (3), pp. 279–294.

Mayhew, H. (ed.) (1865), *The shops and companies of London and the trades and manufactories of great Britain* (London).

Miller, D., Jackson, P., Thrift, N., Holbrook, B. and Rowlands, M. (1998), *Shopping, place and identity* (London: Routledge).

Minter, A. (2016), 'China's empty malls get weirder', *Bloomberg View* (February 17, 2016), Available at: www.bloomberg.com/view/articles/2016-02-17/china-s-empty-malls-get-weirder.

Morrison, K. (2003), *English shops and shopping* (London: Yale University Press).

Neill, P. (1979), 'Why supermall is superbad', *The New York Times* (August 5, 1979).

Nicolaide, B. and Andrew Weise, A. (eds.) (2006), *The suburb reader* (New York: Taylor & Francis).

Pacione, M. (2005), *Urban geography: A global perspective*, 2nd ed., (London: Psychology Press).

Pigeon, S. (1981), 'Freedom of speech: The Florida implications of PruneYard shopping center v. Robins', *University of Miami Law Review*, 35, pp. 559–580.

Savage, M. (2000), 'Walter Benjamin's urban thought', in M. Crang and N. Thrift (eds.) *Thinking space* (London: Routledge) 33–53.

Sherman, L. (2008), 'The world's best shopping malls', *Forbes* (August 1, 2008).

Spector, R. (2005), *Category killers: The retail revolution and its impact on consumer culture* (Boston, MA: Harvard Business School Press).

Spielvogel, C. (1956), 'Shopper's dream near completion', *New York Times* (September 24, 1956), p. 38.

Srivastava, S. (2015), *Entangled urbanism: Slum, gated community, and shopping mall in Delhi and Gurgaon* (Oxford: Oxford University Press).

Stobart, J. (2008), *Spend, spend, spend: A history of shopping* (London: The History Press).

Stone, L. (1973), *Family and fortune: Studies in aristocratic finance in the sixteenth and seventeenth centuries* (Oxford: Oxford University Press).

Tarver, J.D. (1957), 'Suburbanization of retail trade in the standard metropolitan areas of the United States, 1948–54', *American Sociological Review*, 22.

Walsh, C. (2005), 'Social meaning and social space in the shopping gallerie of early-modern London', in J. Benson and L. Ugolini (eds.) *A nation of shopkeepers: Five centuries of British retailing* (London: Tauris) 52–79.

Wood, Z. (2017), 'Global shopping centre giants go on a Christmas buying spree', *The Guardian* (December 16, 2017).

13
BIG-BOX STORES

Stephen Halebsky

Introduction

A twenty-first century urbanite in the developed world can choose from an array of retail formats: slightly faded but still elegant downtown department stores; no-frills dollar stores where everything costs a dollar or less; family-owned and – operated specialty stores that have been in business since the middle of the last century; and discount mass merchandisers operating out of huge single-story rectangular windowless buildings.

Various formats have been associated with different levels of popularity and dominance. Today the big-box store is clearly the dominant retail format in the United States and has made significant inroads into other formats. Among the companies that operate big-box stores there is one that stands apart from the rest. That company, Walmart Stores, Inc., is the nation's biggest retailer (measured by sales, among publicly held companies, *Fortune 500*, 2017), the nation's biggest company (*Fortune 500*, 2017), the world's biggest retailer (*Fortune Global 500*: 2017) and the world's biggest company (*Fortune Global 500*, 2017).

As a result of its economic dominance and the fascination which that has for many people, Walmart has become the subject of a large, multifarious literature, making it difficult to disentangle Walmart and the general phenomenon of big-box stores. The perspective taken here is that Walmart, as the world's biggest company, deserves more attention than other retailers, but in the final analysis Walmart and the other big-box retailers are more alike than different.

I begin with some basic information about Walmart and the other leading big-box retailers. I then provide some historical context, emphasising the period from 1945 to the present and noting the possible effects of neoliberalism, globalisation, technological change, suburbanisation and sprawl. I describe the development of the big-box format, interspersed with the story of Sam Walton, founder of Walmart, and his rise to retail supremacy.

A note on terminology: "Format" is used inconsistently in the literature. Sometimes it is used somewhat narrowly to refer to the material aspects of a store such as its size, shape and placement. Other times it is used more broadly to refer to the entire integrated complex of characteristics – both material and immaterial. I will use it in the latter sense.

What has changed over time? The most salient change, visible to the naked eye, is 'the growth of large national retail chains . . . coupled with a dramatic decrease in the share of retail activity accounted for by small single location or "mom-and-pop" stores' (Jarmin et al., 2005).

Also, stores selling general merchandise (i.e., Walmart, Target, etc.) have gotten larger and the companies that operate these stores are now mostly chains. Industry concentration is now the rule.

Size has brought with it many problems. The actions of Walmart and to a lesser degree other big-box stores have sparked controversy, including local disputes over the siting of superstores, the treatment of the retail workforce and the desirability of Walmart as a contemporary paradigm for the organisation of work and consumption in America.

Retail formats and contexts

Opening his first discount store, Walmart Discount City, in the small town Rogers, Arkansas in 1962, Walton drew on previous innovations. Discounting is a strategy in which 'retail establishment[s] . . . operate on very low margins in order to offer merchandise at prices well below the recognized market level' (Ostrow and Smith 1988). Vance and Scott (1994) suggest that the roots of discounting reach back to the 1930s when supermarkets enthralled customers with their 'inexpensive locations, long hours of operation, and brash advertising' (24). They distinguish three retail formats coming out of the Great Depression: department stores, chain stores and variety stores. Big-box stores like Walmart can be seen as taking elements from each: they are large like department stores; they are standardised chains (or multiples); and they emphasise low prices like variety stores. Managed properly – get the goods cheaply, keep costs down, turnover inventory frequently – discounting could be very profitable. Sam Walton excelled at this strategy and others followed. As of 2018, almost all of the large general merchandise stores operate on the discounting model.

The spread of big-box stores is closely linked to demographic change after World War II. Millions of Americans moved from the central cities to the suburbs where they participated in an auto-centric way of life. This is a high-consumption lifestyle involving shopping centres, malls, and driving. The government's hand was quite visible: suburban home loans guaranteed by the FHA and VA, the financing of shopping centres aided by changes in tax laws (Hanchett 1996) and roadbuilding paid for by the Federal Aid Highway Act of 1956. Big-box stores like Walmart are even more car-centric than the shopping malls of the postwar period. Generally not integrated into a shopping mall, they tend to stand-alone in a type of retail agglomeration known as a power centre, where every customer must drive from store to store.

What makes a store a big-box? From a physical point of view, we have in mind a building that is very large, single-story, windowless, monochromatic, rectangular, with acres of parking – a Walmart. The spread of this format is tied to sprawl – low density development. Local land ordinances often codified these settlement patterns and promoted sprawl. Sprawl consumes huge amounts of land, makes driving virtually mandatory, and is implicated in poor health. By the 1990s, sprawl had become a key issue for national level organisations such as the Sierra Club, the Natural Resources Defense Council, and the National Trust for Historical Preservation (Halebsky 2009). Big-boxes, according to their critics, are the epitome of sprawl because they are rarely sited downtown and consume large tracts of land themselves.

Big-box stores are often part of a global corporation. Currently perched atop the Fortune 500, Walmart has ranked first or second every year since 1999. The company operates 5,443 stores in the US and 6,363 abroad to generate total world sales of $485,873 million, about four times the corresponding amount for Costco, Walmart's closest competitor. Walmart divides its operations into three segments. Walmart US comprises the domestic operations that remain the heart of the Walmart empire and account for 64% of total sales in 2016 (*Walmart Annual Report 2017; Walmart 10K Report 2017*). Walmart has stores in every state. Walmart International operates stores in Africa (326), Argentina (107), Brazil (498), Canada (410), Central America (731), Chile (363), China (439), India (20), Japan (341), Mexico (2411) and the UK (631), which collectively generated 24% of total sales. Sam's Club is the third pillar of the Walmart empire. There are 660 Sam's Clubs, Walmart's version of a warehouse club, which produced 12% of total sales.

Walmart's unheralded emergence as a discounter in 1962 in a small town in the northwestern corner of Arkansas, followed by its rise to the heights of corporate power and influence may appear to be the result of Sam Walton's keen business sense and knack for discount retailing. Walton's success and that of other big-box retailers, however, is best understood when placed in a larger neoliberal context. During the 1970s, a small but determined group of intellectuals, including Milton Friedman and Friedrich von Hayek, began applying neoliberalism to the policy questions of the day. President Reagan and Prime Minister Thatcher were enthusiastic about neoliberalism, which they understood as a necessary reaction against the evils of big government, excessive taxation and unjustified regulations.

The rhetoric of Walmart fits comfortably with the spread of neoliberalism, especially with respect to organised labour. The Walmart culture, as analysed by Copeland and Labuski, is antithetical to unions. Its extreme hostility towards unions continues to be an obstacle to organising retail employees (Lichtenstein 2010; Ortega 2000; Warren, 2011). The proliferation of right-to-work states, whose stronghold is the South where Walmart originated, is evidence of this antagonism. In every state all the workers at a unionised workplace are entitled to the benefits specified in the union contract, regardless of whether they actually join the union or not. In non right-to-work states those who do not join the union must pay an amount equal to union dues. What this means in practice is that unions in right-to-work states are weakened financially, sometimes fatally, because they have a legal obligation to support all employees while receiving dues or an equivalent amount from only from a minority of workers. This sets up a free rider situation in which many workers covered by union contracts opt not to join the union. Thus, unions in right-to-work states are weakened financially. Most of the southern states have become right-to-work states.

Walmart's rise was in part the result of the United States' larger transformation from an industrial to a service economy. When Walton began discount operations in the 1960s, the US still manufactured an enormous amount and variety of goods. As the number of Walmart stores increased the company's purchasing power increased, as evidenced by Walmart's demand that manufacturers sell to Walmart at lower and lower prices. Moreover, as the number of Walmart stores increased the potential advantage of selling to the company increased as well. Realising that it had the upper hand, Walmart pushed its suppliers to cut their prices. Each year Walmart demanded more price cutting, until it became apparent that the only way an American company could meet Walmart's demand was to move its factory to someplace with cheaper labour. This might mean moving to a low-wage right-to-work state. If that was not sufficient the company might have to move its manufacturing to a maquiladora in Mexico. And if that failed the remaining alternative was to move production to China, which had a booming manufacturing sector built on exactly this sort of situation.

Logistics, information technology and Walmart

The rise of the big-box stores coincides with the development of information technology. In some instances, an older invention provided the necessary groundwork for the far-reaching changes that eventually occurred. Self-service, which began in 1916 at a Piggly Wiggly food store in Tennessee, was a prerequisite for discounting. The lowly shopping cart ("trolley") is another example. However, the universal product code (UPC) was a key contemporary technological development which benefited Walmart. Originally developed by (and for) supermarkets, "the bar code" was first used in an actual commercial transaction in 1974. Once it had been established as a viable technology, Walmart and the other large retailers forced it on all their larger suppliers. It sped up checkout and improved inventory management (Leibowitz 1999). The UPC also enabled retailers to collect detailed point-of-sales (POS) information almost instantly, thereby revealing exactly what merchandise was selling – and what was not.

One unanticipated and far-reaching result of these changes was a radical restructuring of the relationship between retailers and manufacturers. As retailers acquired enormous amounts of information about their customers and their shopping habits, they came to realise that now they knew more about their customers than the manufacturers. Retailing had been viewed as a necessary but prosaic intermediary between manufacturers and their customers. It had always been assumed that the manufacturers knew what their customers wanted and what they would pay for it. But when the retailers figured out how to use the data they had collected, they began to call the shots: the outcome was an historic reversal of fortune.

Manufacturers and retailers normally maintained an arms-length relationship based on separate interests and proprietary data. Walton, wanting to increase turnover, proposed to give certain large manufacturers access to some of Walmart's data in exchange for more timely replenishment of merchandise. This was accomplished through EDI (electronic data interchange), a system developed for this purpose. When a store ran out of an item a production order would be initiated automatically, enabling the manufacturer to take the steps necessary to get the product back on the shelf as soon as possible with as little paperwork and as little human intervention as possible. EDI is now used across the industry. It was Walton's genius to see that both manufacturers and retailers could benefit from this arrangement.

Another innovation that increased efficiency is the reconfigured warehouse, known now as a distribution centre. In traditional distribution most new merchandise spent some time warehoused before it reaches its final destination. To have salable goods just sitting in a warehouse, however, is costly for the owner of those goods. A Walmart distribution centre, by contrast, is not intended to be a place where goods are simply warehoused. Rather, it is meant to keep goods moving on their way to the store or stores that will be their final destination. As described by Abernathy *et al.* (1999: 63), a Walmart distribution centre 'consists of bays for inbound and outbound trucks, an automated, fast-moving conveyer network' and a sophisticated information system to control movement from receiving to shipping docks. The purpose of this arrangement, known as cross-docking, is to minimise or eliminate time spent in warehouses.

Containerisation – the practice of using identically shaped, stackable, interchangeable containers to transport merchandise to and from seaports, train depots, and truck terminals – is another advance that aided the big-box stores. The "box" is now the standard method for transporting large amounts of goods throughout the world (Levinson 2016). The increased use of the box has led to the enlargement of the container ships that move the boxes across the waterways of the world (Cudahy 2006).

These advances are associated with store size and company size in various ways, often involving economies of scale and scope. As a general proposition, expensive technology and big-box retailers have a mutually beneficial relationship: big-box retailers are better able to afford sophisticated software and hardware; in turn, this software and hardware allow the big-box companies to order, stock, and keep track of a greater number of SKU (stock-keeping units), which allows big-box stores to appeal to more people. A Walmart supercenter, once established, can sell many different products and services. This is an example of an economy of scope. A large retailer can spread the cost of sophisticated-but-expensive data processing equipment over a large number of transactions at many stores. This is an example of an economy of scale. The most important corollary of increasing size is that large of retailers – those large enough to buy a significant percentage of a supplier's output – can demand to pay for manufactured merchandise at a per unit price below what small retailers pay.

Globalisation of big-box stores

While Walmart may appear to be a singular behemoth, it has counterparts in Europe, notably Carrefour in France and Tesco in the UK. Outside the United States, large boxy stores that sell food and non-food items are known as hypermarkets (this term is used rather loosely). According to the standard account, the first true hypermarket was built in 1963 at Sainte-Genevieve-des-Bois, near Paris, by Marcel Fourneier, Jacques Defforey, and Deni Defforey, who were affiliated with Carrefour. There is evidence, however, that the first European hypermarket was actually built in 1961 in Bruges by the group GB-Inno-BM (see *Brussels Studies*.)

The big-box phenomenon is no longer peculiar to the United States and can be found around the world now. What Walmart and the other boxes – big, medium and small – have in common is a commitment to the rationalisation that stalks the history of retailing. It is evident in the various advances in information technology, in the transformation of distribution from supplier- to retailer-driven, and in the careful attention given to choice of retail formats. The modus operandi associated with big-box stores has become the most common form of contemporary retailing. In spite of the impressive size of stores, the rationalisation of retailing is not complete, and that incompleteness is most easily seen if we take a global view of big-box stores.

Viewed at the global level it is easy to see that whether a store is a big-box store is ultimately secondary to whether it pursues a strategy that is highly rationalised. Being highly rationalised is usually taken to result in a modern way of doing business and a modern way of life. According to the rhetoric, rationalised retailing is modern retailing and is taken to be superior. The traditional is ultimately displaced by the modern.

HP & S argue that the big retailers have become so powerful that they "make the market" for many of the commodities that constitute contemporary society. HP & S don't present a normative argument but simply assume that the highly rationalised big-box format will ultimately dominate all consumer goods markets, and that is for the best in the best of all possible worlds. Put differently, the future will be dominated by "modern consumer markets" (101). A very brief look at a few aspects of globalisation highlights the extent to which rationalisation exerts its force.

There are various reasons for venturing abroad. One reason is the saturation of the home market. This applies especially to Walmart, which has saturated many areas in the South and Midwest. Zook and Graham (2006: 20) report that '96 percent of the US population are within 20 miles' of a Walmart. Another reason is the increased difficulty in obtaining the necessary approvals from planning authorities to build large stores outside of Main Streets and similar local venues.

During the 1960s, the French authorities encouraged suburban living, which included big-box stores. By 1980, there were 541 hypermarts in France. Threatened by this, small shopkeepers and their supporters led three "direct action campaigns" (Cliquet 2000: 186) against the big chains. The number of small independent retailers continued to shrink. Planning restrictions on size and location of retail development are more formidable in Europe than in the US.

To increase sales Walmart must now open stores in cities, in other countries, or both. Walmart has been doing this since 1991 when it began a joint venture with a Mexican company to operate a wholesale club in Mexico City (Walmart 1992). There are differences within Europe. In Germany, for example, there is a culture of searching for the lowest price, while in England convenience and the personal touch of the smaller independent stores are still highly valued. Fernie *et al.* observe that 'Germany has a strong discounter culture, reflected in its large number of hypermarkets and discounters' (Fernie *et al.* 2015: 230–231.)

Walton expanded his empire by carefully building new stores along the front lines of the existing stores, instead of setting up new stores in locations far removed from current operations. He first expanded into areas and markets that were closer geographically and culturally. The big European-based retailers have used this strategy too. Thus, 'the UK favor Ireland. . . ; France target Spain; Germany target Austria; Japan target Hong Kong and Singapore; Australia target New Zealand; and the USA target Canada and Mexico' (Fernie *et al.* 2015: 34). Walmart has pushed thus strategy about as far as it will go, such that the company now has 410 stores in Canada and 2,411 in Mexico (*Walmart 2017 Annual Report*: 63).

This rather conservative strategy is perhaps not surprising given the number of failures (politely called "disinvestment") experienced by the world's leading retailers. Walmart, for example, gave up and pulled out of Germany. It also tried and failed in Argentina, Brazil, Hong Kong, Indonesia and Japan. [Wang (2011)] examines the growth of various retail formats in China over the last twenty years.

Reactions and controversies

Ostensibly nothing more than a place to purchase toothpaste, milk, and other banal commodities, big-box stores have become integral to life in the modern world, while arousing intense debate on a wide range of issues. What is perhaps most striking are the stark differences between the various parties in these debates, many of whom evince little interest in understanding the concerns and arguments of the other side.

Beginning in the 1980s and continuing today, big-box retailers have encountered organised resistance by local citizens to the siting of its stores. Walmart has been the most frequent target of ire, but not the only one. There are many reasons behind these "site fights". One is the simple fact that the big-boxes have gotten bigger, in part because they have added full-sized supermarkets to their full-sized discount merchandise stores. The general trend, with the US in the lead, is for more and more of the landscape to become covered by big-box stores and their even bigger parking lots.

As Sam Walton opened stores farther and farther away from his patch of "Walmart Country" (Moreton 2009: 8) in northwest Arkansas, he encountered local residents who were knowledgeable about Walmart's record in regard to unions and labour, to alleged gender bias, to the problems faced by American manufacturers, to Walmart's effect on downtown and local merchants, and did not want a store in their town or city. Also, as the big-boxes have exhausted small town and suburban locations, they have started to venture into the large cities where they have not received the same welcome as they did in some small towns.

When Sam Walton first encountered resistance he seems not to have taken it too seriously and famously said that

> today we have almost adopted the position that if some community, for whatever reason, doesn't want us in there, we aren't interested in going in and creating a fuss. I encourage us to walk away from this kind of trouble because there are just too many other good towns out there who do want us.
>
> (Walton 1992: 182).

The people of the Ozarks had been active in the anti-chain store movement of the 1920s and early 1930s. Walton, however, was able to neutralise any potential populist threat to his stores by reconfiguring the once-radical culture of the Ozarks into something Moreton (2009) calls "corporate populism" (p. 50).

The announcement that Walmart is planning to come to town often sets off a spirited debate. Walmart and its representatives claim that the new store is desired by the overwhelming majority of local residents who will benefit from low prices, jobs and increased tax revenue. The protestors respond by arguing that two of these three benefits are illusory. Regarding jobs, they argue that the situation is essentially a zero-sum game in which an increase in the number of jobs at a new Walmart will eventually be offset by a loss of jobs elsewhere (i.e., at those stores which will eventually be forced to close). And the same for tax revenue: the increase in income or sales tax from a superstore will be offset by the taxes not paid by other stores, some of whom will eventually go out of business. The protestors also note that the profits generated by the store will be sent back to Bentonville and thus not spent or invested locally. Besides raising doubts about jobs and tax revenue, the opponents often elaborate a series of problems associated with superstore.

A store occupying 180,000 sq. ft. is simply out of scale with everything else in a small town (except other similar stores) (Evans-Cowley 2006). A new Walmart in a typical small town instantly becomes the biggest building in town and is radically incongruent with other local buildings. While huge stores provide retailers with economies of scale, they do not satisfy basic human needs for intimacy and familiarity.

Unless required to meet some specified standard of architectural design, a new superstore will be "architecturally uneventful", in the words of architect John Rohe. Early big-boxes tended to be plain, windowless and monochromatic, with "unimproved" interiors. Recently built stores tend towards a cheap version of postmodernism. Writing in *Harvard Design Magazine*, Dunham-Jones notes that whereas 'downtown department stores were constructed of high quality materials and built to last, Wal-Mart's treatment of its stores and employees as . . . disposable assets . . . exemplifies corporate strategies of flexible accumulation' (Dunham-Jones 1997).

Big-box stores tend to be built in low density zones several miles from downtown ("Main Street" or "High Street"), which means they contribute to the sprawl that has become a nationwide concern. Walmart and the other big-box retailers place their stores where they do because of cost and efficiency: land outside of town is cheaper and single-story buildings can more efficiently accommodate the frequent truck deliveries that are an essential part of the big-box format.

Big-box stores inevitably draw some portion of shoppers away from downtown. This matters because a thriving downtown functions as the civic, social, political and commercial enter of a town. If too many merchants desert downtown, the ramifications can be severe: up to and including the eventual collapse of downtown. One can see evidence of this all over the US.

The local merchants are invested – literally and figuratively – in the local community and have a long-term commitment to it. They tend to be active in their communities to a greater extent than the average resident. A new Supercenter may pose an existential threat to the independent merchants in a small town (Jarmin *et al.* 2005; Peterson and McGee 2000; Stone 1995; Stone *et al.* 2002).

In Europe, by contrast, local planning authorities have been more concerned with the adverse effects of commercial development outside downtown. The shortage of land and its concomitant regulation has been an impetus for large European retailers such as Carrefour to expand outside their national borders.

The local supporters of a proposed new big-box often speak about "modernization". They contrast the small, local independent merchants, who are portrayed as plodding, insular, and old, with the imagined big new store in its big new building. To the big-box supporters the newness and the size are *ipso facto* modern. The meaning of being "modern" is not explained; it is assumed to be superior to whatever is not modern.

Along with the hundreds of siting controversies that have occurred across the country, what has landed big-box stores on the front pages of the nation's news media is their treatment of workers. In Walmart's early days Sam Walton promoted a pseudo-egalitarian approach in which workers were referred to as "associates". As the company grew the personal touch began to disappear and the conflictual nature of employment in the retail industry came to the fore (Adams 2006; Seligman 2006; Lichtenstein 2010; Ortega 2000; Rosen 2006; Bair and Bernstein 2006; Copeland and Labuski (2013). Labour issues at big-box stores – with Walmart as the most visible offender – include employees forced to work off the clock, workers locked in stores during overnight shifts, lack of affordable health insurance and inadequate wages (Copeland and Labuski 2013: 43).

As part of their strategy to minimise costs most of the American big-box stores have taken an extremely hostile stance towards unions. When the butchers at a Walmart in Texas voted to be represented by a union the company quickly discontinued all butchering at all stores. When workers at a Walmart in Canada voted to be represented by a union Walmart promptly closed the entire store. Today there are no unionised retail workers in any Walmart stores in the United States or Canada.

Abstracting from the particularities of each case, what this illustrates, according to labour historian Nelson Lichtenstein, is Walmart's retrograde attitude towards workers. This social policy was put forth in such key pieces of legislation as the National Labor Relations Act of 1935, the Equal Pay Act of 1963 and the Fair Labor Standards Act of 1938, and is ultimately a reflection of the common interests of the American people as expressed through their elected representatives.

What Lichtenstein finds troubling is that Walmart has become

> the template business setting the standards for a new stage in the history of world capitalism. In each epoch a huge, successful, rapidly emulated enterprise embodies a new and innovative set of new and innovative set of technological advances, organisational structures, and social relationships. It becomes the template economic institution of its time.
>
> *(Lichtenstein, 2006: 4)*

US Steel, A&P, General Motors (GM) and IBM were earlier template corporations (p. 5). GM, arguably the most influential company of the twentieth century, differs from Walmart in a fundamental way: GM strove to maintain profitability and provide a rising income for its employees. Walmart, by contrast,

> takes the most potent technological and logistic innovations of the twenty-first century and puts them at the service of an organisation whose competitive success depends upon the destruction of all that remains of New Deal-style social regulation and replaces it . . . with a global system that relentlessly squeezes labor costs.
>
> *(2006, p 4). (See Coclanis [2007] for a pro-labor alternative to Lichtenstein.)*

In 2001, the McKinsey Global Institute, a consulting firm, issued a report about the relationship between low prices, low costs and productivity growth. The report noted the impressive increase in productivity that occurred in the American economy between 1995 and 2000 and found that a substantial portion of this growth occurred in retailing and, furthermore, that 'Wal-Mart's success forced competitors to improve their operations' (p. 2). This report has led to further study of the economic effect of big-box stores.

Another report, released in 2005 by Global Insight, a consulting firm, claimed that Walmart had saved the typical American household $2,329 (or $895 per person) between 1985 and 2004 (Global Insight 2005: 1). Thus, Walmart's ability to squeeze inefficiency out of every part of the supply chain (the "Walmart effect") actually made the country as a whole more efficient. These views are presented very favourably by Vedder and Cox, who see the Walmart phenomenon as essentially another instance of Schumpeter's "creative destruction" which will eventually make everybody better off. From this perspective outsourcing is good for consumers in the developed world because of low prices and good for the developing countries because they can use their relative advantage (low wages) to accumulate capital which can then be employed in capital goods. What Americans may see as severe exploitation of production workers in China is seen by Vedder and Cox as a necessary phase of the economic development of China. More generally low costs, whether through new technology or low wages, translates into higher productivity, which benefits all Americans, even those who dislike Walmart.

If big-box stores put small independent merchants out of business this is taken to reflect either the inevitable replacement of low-productivity firms by high-productivity firms or simply consumer choice, in the sense that if consumers shop at Walmart then, *ipso facto*, a retail sector dominated by Walmart is what they need.

The critics respond by arguing that whilst low prices on consumer items do offset low wages somewhat, they do little to reduce the costs of housing, health care, insurance, education and transportation, which constitute a larger proportion of expenses for most people than do the sundries at Walmart. The earlier studies generally concluded that Walmart and other stores have had an overall negative impact on small towns and on the lives of Walmart employees. A second round of studies has come up with results that are more mixed in regard to the economic impact of superstores. In regard to all matters moral, aesthetic, political and cultural, Vedder and Cox have nothing to say.

Recapitulation

Big-box stores, virtually unknown before the 1960s, have become the leading retail format in the US. Their lineage is uncertain but they appear to have evolved out some combination of chain stores, variety stores and existing supermarkets. While some locate their ancestors in the early supermarkets, others find theirs in the large department stores that remain a fixture of downtown retailing long after their glory days.

The emergence and growth of big-box stores reflect a number of favourable conditions, including a neoliberal political environment in which labour, broadly speaking, is disempowered. New technology, especially in communications, computing and logistics, has enabled large retailers to gain better control of their inventory, containerisation and the mega-ships designed to carry containers, highly automated distribution centres, and logistics in general.

Global big-box stores are prevalent in North America (US, Canada and Mexico), followed by Western Europe and then Eastern Europe, Asia and the developing countries.

Big-box stores pose various threats to the small towns and suburbs where most have been built. In respect of their format, the critics charge them with being ugly, too homogeneous and clashing with local architectural styles. Because they are usually built in or near small towns but not actually downtown they contribute to sprawl, which entails excessive driving, leading to poor health and increased risk of isolation.

After more than twenty years of contention, big-box stores continue to inspire awe and disgust. The former is primarily based on appreciation for the large number of different types of products available and their low prices.

References

Abernathy, F., Dunlop, J., Hammond, J. and Weil, D. (1999), *A stitch in time* (Oxford: Oxford University Press).

Adams, T.J. (2006), 'Making the new shop floor: Wal-Mart, labor control, and the history of the postwar discount retail industry in America'. in *Wal-Mart* and N. Lichstenstein (eds.) *The face of twenty-first century capitalism* (New York: The New Press).

Bair, J. and Bernstein, S. (2006), 'Labor and the Wal-Mart effect'. in S. D. Brunn (ed.) *Wal-Mart World* (New York: Routledge) 99–113.

Cliquet, G. (2000). 'Large format retailers: a French tradition despite reactions', *Journal of Retailing and Consumer Services* 7, pp. 183–195.

Coclanis, P.A. (2007), 'Model change: Wal-Mart, general motors, and the "new world" of retail supremacy', *Labor: Studies in Working-Class History of the Americas*, 4 (1), pp. 49–58.

Copeland, N. and Labuski, C. (2013), *The world of Wal-Mart: Discounting the American dream* (New York: Routledge).

Cudahy, B.J. (2006), *Box boats* (New York: Fordham University Press).

Dunham-Jones, E. (1997), 'Temporary Contracts', *Harvard Design Magazine,* No. 3, np.

'Them Coming and Going,' *Adweek's Marketing Week*, 30 (36), p. 20.

Evans-Cowley, J. (2006), *Meeting the big box challenge: Planning, design, and regulatory strategies* (Chicago, IL: American Planning Association).

Fernie, J., Fernie, S. and Moore, C. (2015), *Principles of retailing*, 2nd ed., (London: Routledge).

Twentieth Century (New York: W. W. Norton) 2015.

Global Insight (2005), 'The economic impact of Wal-Mart', Available at: http://www.ihsglobalinsight.com/publicDownload/genericContent/11-03-05_walmart.pdf

Halebsky, S. (2009), *Small towns and big business: Challenging Wal-Mart superstores* (Lanham, MD: Lexington Books).

Hanchett, T. (1996), 'US tax policy and the shopping-center boom of the 1950s and 1960s,' *American Historical Review*, 101, pp. 1082–1121.

Jarmin, R.S., Klimek, S.D. and Miranda, J. (2005), *The role of retail chains: National, regional, and industry results* (Washington, DC: Center for Economic Studies, Bureau of the Census).

Leibowitz, E. (1999), 'Bar codes: Reading between the lines,' *Smithsonian*, February.

Levinson, M. (2016), *The box* (Princeton, NJ: Princeton University Press).

Lichtenstein, N. (2010), *The retail revolution: How Wal-Mart created a brave new world of business* (New York: Picador).

Lichtenstein, N. (ed.) (2006), *Wal-Mart: The face of twenty-first-century capitalism* (New York: The New Press).

Markusen, A., Hall, P., Campbell, S. and Deitrick, S. (1991), *The rise of the sunbelt: The military remapping of industrial America* (Oxford: Oxford University Press).

McKinsey Global Institute (2001), 'US productivity growth, 1995–2000: Understanding the contribution of information technology relative to other factors,' *McKinsey*, October, Available at: www.mckinsey.com/mgi/productivity/usprod.pdf.

Moreton, B. (2009), *To serve god and Wal-Mart: The making of Christian free enterprise* (Cambridge, MA: Harvard University Press).

Ortega, B. (2000), *In Sam we trust: The untold story of Sam Walton and Wal-Mart, the world's most powerful retailer* (New York: Times Business).

Ostrow, R. and Smith, S. (1988), *The dictionary of marketing*, 2nd ed., (New York: Fairchild Publications).

Peterson, M. and McGee, J. (2000), '"Survivors of W-day"': An assessment of the impact of Wal-Mart's invasion of small town retailing communities.' *International Journal of Retail & Distribution Management* 28, no. 4/5, pp. 170–180.

Rosen, E. (2006), 'Labor and the Wal-Mart effect,' in S. D. Brunn (ed.) *Wal-Mart World* (New York: Routledge) 91–97.

Seligman, B. (2006), 'Patriarchy at the checkout counter: The Dukes v. Wal-Mart Stores, Inc. Class Action suit', in N. Lichtenstein (ed.) *Wal-Mart: The face of twenty-first century capitalism* (New York: The Free Press) 231–242.

Stone, K. (1995), *Competing with the retail giants* (New York: John Wiley).

Stone, K., Artz, G. and Myles, A. (2002), *The economic impact of Wal-Mart supercenters on existing businesses in Mississippi* (Mississippi State Extension Service).

Vance, S. and Scott, R. (1994), *Wal-Mart: A history of Sam Walton's retail phenomenon* (New York: Twayne Publishers).

Walmart Annual Report various years.

Walton, S. (1992), *Sam Walton: Made in America* (New York: Doubleday).

Warren, D. (2011), 'The unsurprising failure of labor law reform and the turn to administrative action,' in T. Skocpol and L. R. Jacobs (eds.) *Reaching for a new deal* (New York: Russell Sage) 191–229.

Zook, M. and Graham, M. (2006), 'Wal-Mart nation: Mapping the reach of a retail colossus,' in S. Brunn (ed.) *Wal-Mart World* (New York: Routledge) 15–25.

PART III

People, processes and practices

14
PENNY RETAILERS AND MERCHANT PRINCES

Susan Spellman

Introduction

When the doors at the corner of Broadway and Chambers Streets opened on 21 September 1846, few in attendance at the much-anticipated event thought themselves at the centre of a retail transformation. Alexander Turney Stewart's "Marble Palace" had drawn shoppers and reporters who for months had speculated about the store's rumoured opulence and grandeur as they watched the austere façade of a four-story structure rise along one of New York City's main thoroughfares. It was the building's location, in fact, that initially caused the biggest stir. 'Well – we are at last actually in the midst of a revolution, and in a short time the East side of Broadway will be as fashionable as the West', one New York journalist surmised ("City Items" 1846). As crowds of women streamed through the front doors they met with 100 uniformed clerks ready to show $1,000 shawls, kid gloves, valuable laces and expensive dresses housed within one of the grandest spaces many had ever shopped. Massive plate glass windows illuminated mahogany counters and maple shelves, while a domed ceiling rose 90 feet above the sales floor supported by Italian marble columns, each topped with a 'cornucopia intertwined with the caduceus of Mercury, the god of commerce' ("Stewart's New Dry Goods Store" 1846). There was no mistaking Stewart's intention with his symbolism. His was a store designed for abundance and profit-making.

Stewart's contemporaries likewise saw benefit in expanding the scope of operations and providing shoppers with plentiful goods and posh spaces. A few doors up on Broadway, James Beck & Company sold an impressive array of expensive embroidery, laces and other stocks estimated to be worth nearly the same $600,000 Stewart claimed ("Fashionable Shopping in New York" 1846). Meanwhile in England, Emerson Muschamp Bainbridge had by 1849 organised his Newcastle-upon-Tyne drapery and dry goods store into twenty-three different departments, and provided a ladies' tea room for female sociability (Mitchell 2014). A few years later in 1852, Parisian entrepreneur Aristide Boucicaut transformed Au Bon Marché from a small notions shop, where he sold laces, ribbons and thread, into a full-scale department store with a wide assortment of merchandise, fixed prices and guaranteed returns (Miller 1981).

By the mid-nineteenth century, the movement towards big retail organisations and mass merchandising was well underway. With its flashy and expansive selling spaces, division into sales departments and one-price system, Stewart's store and methods signalled for some scholars a "retail revolution", a transition from the penny merchants who had directed retail commerce for much of the nation's early history to the merchant princes who would transform shopping from an everyday task to an experience (Leach 1993). While department stores brought about an alteration in the size, scope and methods of some retail operations – particularly in urban locations – many underlying trade principles remained remarkably similar for small and large-scale traders alike. In other words, Stewart and other merchant princes may have built the physical structures that gave rise to mass retailing, but they did so on methodological foundations laid by penny retailers.

Initial forays into retailing history by business and consumption scholars nevertheless led many to the merchant princes. Evaluating department stores and methods, historians focused on identifying signs of "modernity" to help explain the transition to mass retailing during industrialisation in America and Europe (Pasdermadjian 1954; Ferry 1960; Miller 1981; Benson 1986; Leach 1993; Lancaster 1995). Developments such as Stewart's fixed-pricing system, the Bon Marché's guaranteed return policies and the creation of elaborate shopping spaces supposedly demarcated the line between so-called "traditional" penny merchants operating on a small scale and "modern" large-scale retailers. As a result, much of what we understood about retailing in the industrial era centred on Gilded Age, urban department store owners and consumers, despite the overwhelming presence of stores and shoppers who neither operated nor patronised big-city consumption palaces. The emphasis, too, has been on the most successful businessmen and their enterprises. Names like Rowland H. Macy, Marshall Field and H. Gordon Selfridge adorned buildings, wagons and labels for decades, their longevity making them an obvious foundation for tracking long-term trends and innovations. Like most royalty, though, these merchant princes rarely represented the majority of subjects who populated the retail kingdom.

Equating "bigness" with modernity likewise led to characterisations of rural and urban small-scale shops as places where "confusion and disorganization" reigned, making them a seemingly fitting counterpoint for those seeking to explain the rise of the mass market (Tedlow 1990). Yet as more recent scholarship has acknowledged, a remarkable number of small grocers, dry goods dealers, boot and shoe merchants, confectioners, haberdashers and other retailers persisted alongside department and other big stores well into the twentieth century, and in some lines even into the twenty-first century. Were they not just as "modern" as the department store contemporaries? The entrepreneurial men and women (if there were merchant princesses, we have yet to learn their stories) who owned and operated microenterprises tended to operate in the rural and urban niches of the economy. Their persistence has challenged historians in the last twenty years or so to reconceptualise modern business along broader lines that includes not only organisational systems and selling methods, but also technology adoption, merchandising, distribution and contributions to local as well as national economies (Blackford 1991; Wills 2005; Sparks 2006; Gamber 2007; Spellman 2016).

These more recent histories cover both European and US retailing and range in time from the early modern period through the twentieth century. Collectively, they demonstrate that there was no clear break between the so-called "traditional" methods of small retailers and those of their large-scale counterparts. Elements of design and practice such as fancy interiors, alluring displays and show windows, along with cost accounting, departmentalisation and fixed-pricing systems could be found in backwoods shops as readily as urban stores, and often long before department stores made them standard (Walsh 2003, p. 68; Fowler 1998; Spellman 2016). Others have identified elements of "modern" retailing in eighteenth-century England (Mui and Mui 1989; Cox 2000; Stobart, Hann, and Morgan 2007), as well as in the networks and practices of peddlers, open-air markets and fairs of medieval and early modern Europeans (Benson and Ugolini 2003).

Moving away from binary comparisons of "traditional" and "modern", others have begun to consider how small-scale merchants contributed to local, national and global economic, social and cultural systems (Elvins 2004; Wenger 2008; Martin 2008). In so doing, they have illuminated the complicated ways in which retailers became central to the growth and development of communities large and small, and the relationships upon which these economies formed and operated. As a result, our understandings of retail enterprise have expanded beyond store walls to consider the role of commercial exchange within broader and more sophisticated frameworks. While Alexander Stewart's 1846 grand opening may once have marked a transition from old to new, the notion of a nineteenth-century "retailing revolution" in the US and Europe has been complicated by our growing knowledge of the many and varied ways small retailers innovated and implemented many of the methods often associated solely with the era's consumption palaces.

Evaluating the stores, sales methods and distribution strategies of penny retailers and merchant princes reveals as many similarities as differences between the two forms. While there were changes on all three fronts – stores got bigger, sales strategies evolved and distribution systems varied across product lines – there were ties that bound and continue to bind together turn-of-the-twentieth-century entrepreneurs. Indeed, the coexistence of small- and large-scale retailing throughout the period and beyond throws into sharp relief assumptions that industrialisation and its concomitant population, transportation and technology developments elevated consumer demand as prerequisites to the rise of "modern" retail systems. This essay will explore the similarities and differences between penny retailers and merchant princes, their stores, methods and long-term contributions to the development of retailing in the nineteenth and early twentieth centuries. While the focus is primarily on the US and the UK, it will make occasional forays into other markets in an attempt to highlight the multi-faceted nature of retailing in the period.

Penny retailers

Small retail merchants were present in the US from its founding, initially in the form of independent trading posts and later in the shops that emerged in colonial villages and towns. These early outlets furnished shoppers with a wide range of Atlantic World goods, enmeshing both retailers and consumers in a complex international market economy (Martin 2008). In the UK during the eighteenth and early nineteenth centuries, fixed shops catered primarily to wealthy customers, with others relying on public markets to satisfy many of their needs. Specialty craftsmen such as saddlers, cabinet makers, jewellers and clock and watchmakers combined both workshop and retail space as some of the first traders to open storefront locations. Grocers, however, were among the most numerous both in the US and the UK, as the regulated nature of public markets and concerns over sanitation prompted the increased privatisation of food selling (Tangiers 2002; Winstanley 1983; Spellman 2016). Regardless of their specific origins, small merchants dominated retailing in the middle of the nineteenth century and remained so well into the twentieth century. They were key agents in the formation of local, national and international economies. Their stores, sales methods and distribution networks served as templates for commercial exchange and developments that came to characterise the industrial and post-industrial eras.

General stores dominated US retailing in the early nineteenth century. Small and fragmented markets, especially in rural regions, influenced the development of outlets that sold a range of bulk goods from brooms and calicoes to crackers and pickles. Merchants focused on accommodating customers' essential needs, both in cities and in frontier towns. In 1824, New York storekeeper Alexander Walsh, boasted of having a 'large stock of Dry Goods, Hardware, Groceries,

Crockery, Glass, &c &c', in his Lansingburgh shop, and carried 'nearly every article in usual demand, and extending the variety to whatever constitutes the character of a general store' ('Fresh goods' 1824). Rural shops tended to be small free-standing structures approximately 20 by 30 feet, with shelves, hooks and pegs lining the walls. A countertop served as both point of exchange and packaging station in the absence of boxed and canned goods. In urban regions, these same kinds of stores took root in the narrow, but deep street-front buildings that lined board sidewalks. There was little in the way of formal merchandising or display in either country or city shops, but rather a functional arrangement familiar to storekeepers who picked items at the customer's request. Walsh, however, understood his village store in terms that became more common later in the century, announcing the "numerous additions" made to his "*Grocery Department*" ("Stock Renewed" 1825), a nod to Walsh's grasp of organisation.[1] Others like New Orleans dealer William Smith sold items like guava jelly and marmalade in "handsome glass jars", acknowledging the importance of presentation and merchandising in these early days ("Choice Havana Sweetmeats" 1827).

In the US, many of these early proprietors, including Walsh and Smith, conducted both retail and wholesale businesses, buying and selling in large quantities with an eye towards supplying both consumers and other merchants. Wholesaling helped stabilise profits in the wake of unpredictable consumer demands and a reliance on barter to supplement a cash-starved economy. Likewise, few wholesalers in this early period carried the small lots most general storekeepers required. Merchants procured their stock of goods by knitting together nascent distribution networks of commercial intermediaries that required them to travel twice yearly to trade centres in New York, Philadelphia, Boston, Charleston, and other port cities (Spellman 2016). One trip could take up to six weeks of hazardous travel through undeveloped lands by horseback, riverboat, wagon, railroad or an exhausting combination of all (Blackford 1991). Indiana merchant John Brownlee, for example, endured frigid sleigh rides, frozen canals and "very lonely" horseback rides in the 1830s and 1840s as he made his way to commercial centres hundreds of miles away in Pittsburgh and Baltimore.[7] Storekeepers like Brownlee would visit multiple manufacturers, wholesalers, drummers, commission merchants and other retail intermediaries to purchase and arrange shipping for their goods. The commercial networks these entrepreneurial men and women forged supplied the growing nation's interior and established a distribution system utilised for decades to come.

Urban shopkeepers, like those in England, sometimes benefitted from better access to a range of goods. Port cities profited from the regular arrival of both supply ships from abroad and merchants' wagons from the interior, which brought produce and other agricultural products to trade in commercial centres. Liverpool, for example, by the late eighteenth century imported cotton on a large scale in addition to a wide variety of linens and animal skins, lumber, tobacco and wines from around the Atlantic world, and built large warehouses to accommodate this trade. The city opened its ports to a growing number of manufactured and agricultural goods, such as Chinese silks and tea, by the middle of the nineteenth century (Haggerty 2003, p. 108; Milne 2000). The close proximity of urban merchants to these resources reduced travel and transportation costs, potentially increasing profitability. City retailers, however, faced greater competition from a range of large and small merchants who competed for shoppers' attention. Parisian arcades and galleries, along with sizeable drapery shops and English department stores, emerged in the late eighteenth century, giving consumers their first taste of shopping for pleasure as they strolled past window displays (Furnée and Lesger 2014, pp. 11–12). In both the US and England, though, small retail outlets grew significantly over first half of the nineteenth century, expanding rural and urban commerce and opening the door for entrepreneurial men and women who sought to join their ranks.

floors; cigar box lids depicting faraway places topped drugstore counters; and mirrors promoting well-known chocolatiers backed confectioners' shelves. Some shopkeepers drew customers into their stores by creating elaborate window displays that included stuffed and mounted animals, holiday decorations and mounds of shoes, boots, coats and hats. Others, however, went to extra lengths to keep passers-by curious about what delights could be found beyond the glass. Shoppers, for example, delighted in the window display of one Washington, DC druggist who installed a barnyard scene complete with a hen and brood of chicks with dyed feathers, making them appear 'not unlike a lot of animated Easter eggs' ("Easter Window Displays" 1889). While amusements drew attention, during the last quarter of the nineteenth century, abundance became a popular merchandising theme in these rudimentary exhibits. Between 1869 and 1909, the total value of US goods rose from $3.6 billion to over $13 billion, with many viewing the proliferation of consumer goods pouring out of factories as a sign of advancement and material progress (Olegario 2006; Lears 1994). Storekeepers piled high cans, boxes, baskets and bottles in their front windows to tempt customers into their stores, spurring the growth of a consumer market and increasing retailers' bottom lines.

Expansion of the retail market, however, came at a price. Despite advances in manufacturing, advertising and distribution, the risks associated with small-scale enterprise remained, with countless numbers of undercapitalised firms emerging in all lines. This was possible in part because of the structure and function of the retail trade system, which relied heavily on credit. Wholesalers extended generous credit lines to most storekeepers, encouraging them to purchase large stocks for their stores to generate faster turnover rates and greater profits. Retailers likewise took advantage of this system to extend their buying power and financial capacity, with many quickly becoming indebted to several commercial intermediaries, often with disastrous results. Figures from as early as 1858 suggest that in the US, country storekeepers on average owed approximately $14,500 each to wholesalers, a number that sometimes represented four or five times the actual value of a retailer's business capacity (Olegario 2006). Female proprietors were often disadvantaged in this system, as credit reporting firms typically based their assessments on available capital and collective business experience, both of which women in the period generally had limit access (Sparks 2006). Longstanding custom and competitiveness often overruled rationality, however, and wholesalers routinely granted generous credit lines even to those deemed unworthy, thus perpetuating the system.

Retailers in both the US and Britain likewise extended consumer credit as a necessary function of running a small store. Limited availability of hard cash in the US for much of the early and mid-nineteenth century gave rise to systems of barter and credit in small shops. Rural shoppers in both the UK and the US traded produce and livestock for goods and services, additionally maintaining credit lines paid in conjunction with harvest cycles. Wealthy and working-class city shoppers alike regularly held accounts settled on a monthly, quarterly or yearly basis, depending on the proprietor's liberality. In England, co-operative stores adhered to a strict cash-only basis, which sometimes excluded poorer shoppers who relied on credit to make ends meet. While most nineteenth-century merchants understood the advantages of dealing on a cash-only basis, they found it exceedingly difficult to acculturate shoppers to pay before taking their purchases, especially in rural and tightknit towns where such longstanding practices had become an expectation for community members (Spellman 2016).

With retail competition on the rise at the turn of the twentieth century, credit and personal services such as delivery and telephone ordering increasingly became a method small proprietors employed to differentiate themselves in the marketplace. Storekeepers promoted their crediting policies as one of several services that fostered community welfare, while corporate-owned chains were routinely criticised for funnelling their profits to out-of-town management and investors (Spellman 2016). Proprietors selling high-ticket items such as furniture, household goods and jewellery likewise found credit selling one of the only ways to move a profitable quantity of wares in a timely fashion. Clothiers, dry goods dealers and others who marketed essentials routinely found themselves dependent on credit sales to accommodate customers who demanded goods at a quantity and rate that exceeded their budgets. Credit likewise enabled merchants to turn stock faster, an issue particularly acute to those who dealt in perishable goods, and earn customer loyalty. Yet limited capital combined with excessive encumbrances to both creditors and customers often limited the ability of many small merchants to expand their businesses beyond one shop. This became increasingly worrisome as large-scale chain stores and multiples began to emerge in the US and the UK in the early years of the twentieth century, bringing significant changes to retailing.

Looking eastward to Russia, however, the retail landscape had remained remarkably static, with public markets and small shops scattered and large stores rare. While manufacturing firms such as the Singer Company had made inroads by the turn of the twentieth century, establishing upwards of 4,000 outlets across the country, these *magaziny* and other similar outlets catered to a largely metropolitan consumer population. Railroad improvements had made the year-round movement of goods and people faster easier as it had in the West, yet nearly 80% of retail licenses in 1912 were still held by *lavki* – peddlers, street vendors and market stall hawkers – concentrated in major cities (Hessler 2004). These penny merchants faced little competition from the kinds of new retailing forms emerging in the US and Western Europe. Peasants' limited purchasing power combined with a lack of manufacturing and distribution advances stalled commercial development, and was further hampered by the nation's transition to a Communist state. One exception was Moscow's GUM (*Glávnyj Universálnyj Magazín*), the nation's largest retail store. The GUM started in the early nineteenth century as a trading centre filled with small shops housed in one building; by the start of the Russian Revolution in 1917, nearly 1,200 stores occupied the glass-roofed structure. A few years later, the state established the GUM as a model retail store, designed to serve consumers of all classes and advance Bolsheviks' goal of squashing private enterprise. By 1918, Bolshevik leaders had shut down nearly all privately owned stores, concentrating commerce in the hands of the state (Hilton 2011).

While shopkeepers in the newly formed Soviet Union found few commercial paths open, small retailers in the US and Western Europe faced new pressures at the turn of the century from department stores and other challengers. Penny entrepreneurs who once dominated the commercial landscape now saw merchant princes establish themselves as commercial leaders. Men like Stewart, Field, Selfridge and Macy constructed oversized emporiums that drew shoppers with promises of opulent fixtures, abundant goods, courteous salespeople and extensive services. While their buying and selling methods might have appeared fresh to those outside of retailing, many who operated within the commercial space found them to be familiar and tried. It was the scale and scope of these operations that initially distinguished merchant princes from penny retailers. Some, like William Whiteley, a London draper who dared to combine groceries with dry goods under one roof in building the West End's first department store, ran afoul of small dealers for challenging retailing custom (Rappaport 2000). As their imposing structures rose in cities across the US East and Midwest, and in places like London and Paris, millions of urban shoppers lauded their arrival. Countless others, however, continued to patronise the penny merchants who retained the lion's share of the marketplace, particularly in rural and outlying areas. Yet even from afar, most consumers could not help but notice merchant princes' shopping emporiums, as they cast a long shadow over the retail landscape.

Merchant princes

Alexander T. Stewart was no stranger to small-scale entrepreneurship. The Irish-born merchant opened his first dry goods shop in 1823 on Broadway in New York City, not far from City Hall. The space was compact at approximately 12½ feet wide and 30 feet deep, a typical urban street-front store for the period. Like most retail entrepreneurs of his day, Stewart functioned as clerk, bookkeeper and delivery man, taking on every task necessary to carry on trade, with the doors open up to eighteen hours daily. Stewart's willingness to try new methods to attract customers – like other fellow penny merchants – distinguished him from some competitors. In addition to setting fixed prices on his goods, Stewart also instituted liberal return and exchange policies, installed floorwalkers – employees trained to meet customer needs – and applied principles of rapid stock turn and departmental organisation. High stock turn rates soon would become a hallmark of department stores, as merchant princes amassed fortunes on the principles of volume sales and low markups. Unlike many of his smaller contemporaries, Stewart bought from wholesalers on cash terms and frequented "sample lot" auctions, where larger (sometimes damaged) assortments were broken down and sold to the highest cash bidder (Elias 1992). He likewise insisted in receiving cash on delivery from his customers. Upon Stewart's death, the *New York Times* noted that 'buying on credit and selling on credit forced him to the adoption of this rule' after he found himself early on encumbered by creditors. Stewart's cash trading was a luxury he could afford, having inherited a tidy sum of £1,000 in 1823 (approximately £82,000 in 2015) from his Scottish grandfather ("Death of A.T. Stewart" 1876).

Stewart's ample capital and cash policies were some of the many advantages he and other merchant princes exploited to build their retailing empires. First department stores, and later chain stores, represented the expansion and growth of mass production and mass distribution during the last quarter of the nineteenth century. In both the US and the UK, men with big ideas and a keen understanding of retailing methods built grand, multifloored structures designed specifically to move large quantities of goods profitably through calculated organisational and merchandising methods (Howard 2015). While department stores have been credited with pioneering the use of showcases and windows, bargain sales, delivery, parcel wrapping and departmentalised operations, what made them appear fresh and new was the scale and refinement with which they were employed. Merchant princes constructed retailing empires that both presaged and guided the growth and development of consumer culture and society. They did so by creating a new kind of shopping environment focused on female shoppers that encouraged browsing, lingering, and engaging with products, sales staff and other consumers. From dry goods, ready-to-wear, home furnishings and groceries to lunch rooms, phrenology studios and libraries, visitors to these consumption palaces could expect to not only buy what they needed and wanted, but also to be entertained while doing so. While perhaps not revolutionary, department stores and the men who pioneered their development represented a notable departure from established selling norms.

Much like Stewart, many of the era's merchant princes had emerged from the ranks of penny entrepreneurship, with most learning the trade while working as clerks, stock boys and salesmen in various retail establishments before striking out on their own. Marshall Field clerked for a Pittsfield, Massachusetts, dry goods dealer, spending five years sweeping floors, arranging stock and reading *Godey's Lady's Book* and *Hunt's Merchants' Magazine* to learn about women's consumption preferences and general business practices before heading west in 1858 at the age of twenty-one. He furthered his retail education in the frontier town of Chicago with the dry goods firm of Cooley, Wadsworth and Company, eventually becoming a partner and then proprietor of his eponymous store. In 1879, an energetic Harry Gordon Selfridge joined the firm of Marshall Field as a stock boy. The Michigan-born 21-year-old soon after became a wholesale salesmen before being moved to the retail sales floor, where his merchandising ideas earned him a promotion to head of the retail division and later junior partner. Thirty years after joining Marshall Field, Selfridge struck out in 1909 to open his Oxford street emporium in London. Demolishing a host of penny merchants and their shops to clear the city block for his store, Selfridge later noted, 'Bigness alone is nothing, but bigness filled with the activity that does everything continually better means much' (Selfridge 1918). Embarking on a mission to cut costs and vertically integrate, he delegated decision-making to a host of managers who added mills and factories to produce textiles, foodstuffs, glassware and furniture for his enormous store. Selling to London's masses was Selfridge's primary goal, one that he embraced by employing marketing strategies learned during his time with Marshall Field.

Drawing on the bolder, more colourful and assertive style of American advertising, Selfridge conjured up images and copy that cast his store as a theatrical experience, one in which all were welcome to enjoy. Full-page ads extolled the virtues of shopping, encouraging consumers to take in poised mannequins in dramatic window displays and elaborate lighting and grand productions frequently staged in various departments. Selfridge likewise promoted his store to journalists, inviting reporters and editors to indulge in personal tours and private dinners, and cultivated relationships with the press to encourage free advertising in the form of extended editorials in the papers touting his emporium (Rappaport 2000). Not all found the merchant's outspoken and boisterous personality appealing, with some West End competitors deriding Selfridge as "the American hothead" ("Dislike American Hothead" 1912). Addressing critics who speculated that he would never make a go of large-scale American-style retailing England, Selfridge remarked in a 1918 interview about his vigorous advertising campaigns, 'We never could have broken through these traditions. . . . We had to use all we could to break down prejudices. We made people stop, look and listen. Then the store itself did the rest'. Paying upwards of one dollar per copy line, Selfridge credited the power of advertising for making him a merchant prince. 'We are limited only by the limitations of the newspapers', he claimed, 'I will take all [the ad space] they will give' ("Advertising Is Secret" 1918).

Back in the United States, Rowland H. Macy started his first business in 1844, a small Boston thread-and-needle shop that promptly failed. He next embarked on a course of serial entrepreneurship, opening another short-lived Boston shop, a gold-rush trading venture in California and a Haverhill, Massachusetts, dry goods business that also closed. While Field and Selfridge had avoided Macy's trial-and-error method for learning the retail trade by joining established firms, Macy finally cobbled together a winning strategy when he opened his New York City fancy goods shop in 1858. Macy's inclination for diversifying his product lines allowed him to test small quantities of goods before committing to a full-fledged department. He took chances in his first year by adding men's gloves and hosiery and house furnishings to his stocks, later experimenting with imported pocketbooks, picture frames, dolls and jewellery, along with books, garden implements and fancy groceries. More of a seat-of-the-pants buyer than merchandise planner, Macy and his methods were perhaps unorthodox when compared with other department store merchants, but they afforded him flexibility in his offerings and the ability to take advantage of bargain lots. Macy, like many of his contemporaries, travelled regularly overseas in search of fresh stocks and well-priced products to fill his stores. He took chances on velocipedes, potted plants and anything else he thought would sell, enabling him to accommodate a wide range customers' pocketbooks and tastes. Upon his death in 1877, his store conducted over US $1.5 million in annual sales, and featured multiple departments, delivery service and dynamic advertising campaigns that drew customers from across the region. In the following years, several part-owners directed operations before Lazarus Straus and his son Isador Straus took control and grew the company into a nineteenth- and twentieth-century retail giant (Mahoney and Sloane 1966).

Throughout the nineteenth century, retailing ideas and methods flowed like goods across the Atlantic. In addition to department stores, chain stores (or multiples) opened doors for those looking to capture budget shoppers by stocking their stores with large lots of identical products purchased at deep discounts and sold for cheap prices. In the US, George Gilman, founding proprietor of the Great Atlantic and Pacific Tea Company (A&P), has been credited with pioneering the chain grocery model with his 1859 beginnings in New York. By 1878, the firm boasted seventy-eight stores spread throughout the Northeast (Levinson 2011). Gilman's UK counterpart, Scottish-born Thomas Lipton, left his family in 1865 at the age of fifteen bound for the United States. There, Lipton travelled throughout the South labouring first on a Virginia tobacco plantation before finding work as an accountant and bookkeeper on a South Carolina rice plantation, eventually moving north to take a position in a New York grocery store 'run on up to date methods', according to Lipton (Mathias 1967). Upon returning to Glasgow in 1869, Lipton settled into his family's provision shop, applying his newly acquired skills to the trade. When his reticent father hedged at expanding the family firm into a second store, Lipton struck out on his own and opened his first grocery shop in 1872. Inspired by his time in the US, Lipton maintained, 'Every business idea, every successful move I have made has been suggested to me by my observation of American methods' (Matthias 1967, p. 106). This included daring advertising techniques that featured elements such as parading pigs, cheeses and brass bands through public streets to draw attention to store openings, sales and philanthropic efforts.

Much like Selfridge, Lipton's outspoken personality, combined with his flair for self-promotion, aided him in growing his firm at an extraordinary pace. By the end of the century, Lipton boasted over 250 retail outlets across the UK, eventually expanding to thirty-eight countries, including Germany, China, Chile and New Zealand, among others. It was an impressive feat, especially given Lipton's penchant for overseeing every facet of his vast organisational empire. Whereas department store operators like Selfridge employed decentralised management to administer their enormous operations, Lipton preferred to remain the primary decision maker on all matters large and small. This was particularly challenging as Lipton vertically integrated, buying tea plantations in Ceylon, bakeries in the UK, and pork processing facilities in the US. Lipton's insistence on running his business in the style of a sole proprietorship created difficulties for the organisation, with poor business and financial decisions such as ill-advised forays into wines, spirits, and beef extracts, imperilling the firm at the turn of the twentieth century. Ultimately, it was Lipton's expansive tea business, though, that stabilised the firm and garnered the purveyor the recognition he desired. Identifying an untapped market in selling low-priced, high-quality tea to the masses at home and abroad, Lipton established the tea-packing firm of Thomas J. Lipton Company in 1893, and sold his affordable, standardised product in premeasured packets. Lipton was forced out of the company in the 1920s at the age of seventy-six, and his grocery store empire eventually refocused its efforts solely on consumer goods manufacturing, a holdover from Lipton's intense nineteenth-century efforts to vertically integrate and cut production costs (Mathias 1967).

While Lipton was building his grocery empire through bold and brash methods, Earle Perry Charlton was quietly and confidently helping to pioneer the five-and-dime chain movement in the United States. Born in 1863 in Chester, Connecticut, Charlton broke with his family's artisan roots (his father was a blacksmith) and moved to nearby Hartford, Connecticut, to work in a local retail shop. From there he went to Boston, clerking for a penny dealer before taking to the road as a "drummer", or travelling salesman, for Thomas C. Newell, a wholesaler specialising in fancy goods, notions and toys. Eight years after joining Newell's firm, Charlton partnered with Seymour Knox – Frank W. Woolworth's cousin. In 1889, they opened a store in Fall River, Massachusetts, based on the principle of selling a wide variety of merchandise bargain priced at five and ten cents, with nothing over fifteen cents. It was a model Frank Woolworth first introduced in 1879 in Pennsylvania, and one that Charlton would launch into California, the Pacific Northwest and Canada. After splitting with Knox in 1896, Charlton formed E.P. Charlton & Company, and sold nine of his New England stores to Woolworth to capitalise his expansion into Canada. His first store opened in 1900 in Montreal, followed closely with a second and third shop in the same city, along with outlets in Ottawa, St. John, Quebec, Halifax and Amherst, Nova Scotia. By 1910, Charlton boasted thirteen stores throughout Canada and its provinces. Concurrently expanding in the US, Charlton opened his first west coast shop in 1905 in Portland, Oregon, with Los Angeles and San Francisco, California, close behind. Dozens more followed in Washington, Montana, and Utah, with E.P. Charlton & Company operating fifty-three stores in two countries by 1911, yet Charlton continued directing activities from his company's headquarters in Fall River. Nevertheless, the organisation's rapid national and international expansion made it one of the few US retail chain operations in this period conducting business at such vast distances (Charlton and Winius 2001).

Charlton relied on his low-priced merchandise to do much of the selling for him. His bargain prices, Charlton believed, spoke for themselves. Although men like Selfridge and Lipton liked to employ flashy advertising to draw customers, Charlton instead maintained a muted and reserved media presence. Preferring simple copy to announce store openings, he rarely promoted sales or products available in his shops. 'If you have never seen one of these modern, novel, and thoroughly up-to-date "5, 10 and 15¢ stores"', one newspaper post quietly announced, 'it will pleasantly surprise you to see our store and goods' (E.P. Charlton Advertisement 1909). Charlton shunned flashy demonstrations and instead focused on the principles of five-and-dime chain retailing, negotiating deep discounts with manufacturers for large lots of everything from glassware and sheet music to clothes lines and dime banks. He often purchased goods in conjunction with Woolworth and a number of other five-and-dime dealers affiliated with Woolworth, expanding the groups' buying power. While department store merchants like Macy, Field, and Selfridge promoted their emporiums to the middle-class masses, five-and-dime retailers like Charlton pitched their stores and products to the throng of frugal shoppers in search of deals rather than experiences. In a 1929 essay on mass selling, Charlton ascribed the success of five-and-dimes to rapid turnover, allowing companies like his and Woolworth's to profit by making 'the same invested capital work for it eight and one-half times in one year', by turning stock faster than most penny retailers or department stores could muster. It was a risky strategy, Charlton admitted, as 'the moment the public fails to buy fast enough and steadily enough, our whole structure crumbles' (Charlton and Winius 2001).

By 1911, Charlton perhaps thought the gamble too great. When Frank Woolworth proposed a merger with Seymour Knox (who had gone on to open 112 stores on his own), along with his brother Charles Sumner Woolworth, former business partner Fred M. Kirby and William Moore, Charlton agreed, helping to form the conglomerate F.W. Woolworth Company (Pitrone 2003). Charlton retained his original store and Fall River headquarters (which continued to operate under his own name), but chose to retire from the day-to-day ministrations of retailing, and instead served behind the scenes as a vice president of the newly formed corporation. Upon his death in 1930, Charlton had amassed a fortune of over US $30 million, making him one of the era's more notable, if unassuming, merchant princes (Charlton and Winius 2001).

Conclusion

How did some storekeepers grow to become merchant princes while others remained penny retailers? It is impossible to say with any certainty. Several who expanded their retail empires shared entrepreneurial qualities such as a willingness to take risks, a flair for self-promotion, and a pioneering spirit. Yet many small retailers likewise possessed these same characteristics and remained microentrepreneurs. Others might point to the ability of the princes to raise capital, their extraordinary business acumen or their keen understanding of markets and consumers. A quick perusal of any city directory, though, will likely turn up any number of individuals tucked away in small towns who also benefitted from these same insights and abilities, but their names and businesses were familiar only to those locals who patronised the shops. By the same token, there were many who had all the makings and advantages of merchant princes, opened grand stores that catered to shoppers' every whim and failed miserably.

This was the case in 1908 when the D.C. Beggs Company of Columbus, Ohio, failed, making news from Washington, DC, to San Francisco, California. Once touted as "the largest department store in central Ohio", the firm operated by David Carson Beggs boasted fifty departments in an eight-story building some described as "mammoth", and was outfitted with modern conveniences including telephone service ("Independent Telephones Adopted" 1906). Beggs had started in business in the 1870s as a clerk and salesman for local carpet and upholstery dealers. He partnered in the 1890s with another carpet retailer, and together the pair ran a successful trade for several years, with Beggs demonstrating "good business qualities", which included "conscientious work" along with "courteous manners and characteristic energy" ("D.C. Beggs a Successful Carpet Merchant" 1904). Sometime around 1902, Beggs consolidated his operation with another well-known area merchant, bringing together two of the city's largest department stores. Despite his mercantile experience and advantages, however, Beggs's slow customer debt collections, combined with an 'inability to dispose of the huge stock in a short time', forced the company into receivership after only a few years ("Big Department Store Fails" 1908). Just as there was no guarantee of success in the retail trade, there was no secret formula for becoming, or remaining, a merchant prince.

Department store princes and their stores loomed large over the retail landscape by the end of World War I. The overwhelming majority of shoppers, however, never stepped foot inside their lavish interiors or experienced firsthand the plethora of services they offered. Despite their size and scope, the period's department stores, like their smaller counterparts, served largely local markets. Most consumers continued to patronise neighbourhood shops, five-and-dimes, regional outlets and a growing number of chains for most of their needs and wants. Visitors to those stores, knowingly or not, likely experienced department stores' influence on the way products were priced, displayed and arranged. They might also have discerned a difference in the way clerks spoke with them and how their accounts were handled at the sales counter. It is also possible that the floors were a bit cleaner, the walls a slightly more decorated, and the windows filled with attractive arrays of enticing goods. Shoppers may now have strolled from department to department, instead of perusing a single aisle of products. In this way, penny retailers and merchant princes combined to propel retailing in new and significant directions, indelibly altering the commercial landscape at the turn of the twentieth century.

From backwater towns to major metropolises, retailers small and large took note of each other's methods and practices, continuing what worked, modifying what did not and innovating where necessary to increase demand and profitability. Few (if any) penny retailers or merchant princes found themselves driven to modify their methods solely based on either demand or supply, or any other single economic or political development. Rather, their businesses and economic contributions are best understood by acknowledging the opportunities and constraints under which they operated, and the dynamic combination of commercial, social and cultural processes that influenced their choices. While entrepreneurs like Alexander Stewart and other department store moguls often forged their path to prosperity (and failure) through highly capitalised urban enterprises, microentrepreneurs tended to focus on servicing niche economies by providing products and services that catered to local and regional consumers. The complexity of both retail types and the men and women who ran these operations speaks to the need for understanding large- and small-scale commercial development as two sides of the same coin. Both made significant contributions to national and international commerce, with both representing the range of entrepreneurial opportunities open to those willing to take a risk.

Notes

1 Italics in original.
2 John Brownlee to Jane Brownlee, May 13, 1834, folder 2, "Correspondence, 1833–1838," Brownlee Family Papers, 1828–1851, Indiana Historical Society, Indianapolis.

References

Newspaper and journal articles

'Advertising is secret of Selfridge success in London,' 1918, *Gazette-Times* (Heppner, Oregon), 25 July, p. 2.
'Big department store fails,' 1908, *San Francisco Call*, 19 July, p. 21.
'By telegraph,' 1851, *Democratic Banner*, 18 June, p. 3.
'Choice Havana sweetmeats' (advertisement), 1827, *Louisiana Advertiser*, 1 January, p. 4.
'City items,' 1846, *New York Daily Tribune*, 22 September, p. 2.
'D.C. Beggs a successful carpet merchant,' 1904, *Carpet and Upholstery Journal*, 10 October, p. 63.
'Death of A.T. Stewart,' 1876, *New York Times*, 11 April, p. 1.
'Dislike "American hothead,"' 1912, *Evening Star* (Washington, DC), 17 November, p. 10.
'The Dry goods business,' 1857, *Evansville Daily Journal*, 13 August, p. 2.
'Easter window displays,' 1889, *Washington Critic*, 19 April, p. 2.
'E.P. Charlton advertisement,' 1909, *Salt Lake Tribune*, 14 August, p. 11.
'Fashionable shopping in New York,' 1846, *New York Herald*, 26 September, p. 2.
'Fresh goods,' 1824, *Saratoga Sentinel*, 1 September, p. 3.
'Independent telephone service adopted at large department stores at Columbus, Ohio,' 1906, *American Telephone Journal*, 15 December, p. 391.
'News of the week,' 1854, *Spirit of the Times*, 14 November, p. 2.
'Stewart's new dry goods store,' 1846, *New York Herald*, 18 September, p. 2.
'Stock renewed' (advertisement), 1825, *Saratoga Sentinel*, 18 January, p. 4.

Books

Benson, J. and Ugolini, L. (2003), *A nation of shopkeepers: Five centuries of British retailing* (London: I.B. Tauris).
Benson, S.P. (1986), *Counter cultures: Saleswomen, managers, and customers in American department stores, 1890–1940* (Urbana, IL: University of Illinois Press).
Blackford, M.G. (1991), *A history of small business in America* (Chapel Hill, NC: University of North Carolina Press).
Charlton, E.P., III and Winius, G. (2001), *The Charlton story* (New York: Peter Lang).
Cox, N.C. (2000), *The complete tradesman: A study of retailing, 1550–1820* (Burlington, VT: Ashgate).
Elias, S.N. (1992), *Alexander T. Stewart: The forgotten merchant prince* (Westport, CT: Praeger).

Elvins, S. (2004), *Sales and celebrations: Retailing and regional identity in Western New York State, 1920–1940* (Athens, OH: Ohio University Press).

Ferry, J.W. (1960), *A history of the department store* (New York: Palgrave Macmillan).

Fowler, C.L. (1998), *Satisfying popular consumer demand 1775–1815: With specific reference to the dress trades in Hampshire* (Portsmouth: University of Portsmouth).

Furnée, J. and Lesger, C. (2014), *The landscape of consumption: Shopping streets and cultures in western Europe, 1600–1900* (Basingstoke: Palgrave Macmillan).

Gamber, W. (2007), *The boardinghouse in nineteenth-century America* (Baltimore, MD: Johns Hopkins University Press).

Haggerty, S. (2003), 'Women, work, and the consumer revolution: Liverpool in the late eighteenth century', in J. Benson and L. Ugolini (eds.) *A nation of shopkeepers: Five centuries of British retailing* (London: I.B. Tauris) 106–126.

Hessler, J. (2004), *A social history of Soviet trade: Trade policy, retail practices, and consumption, 1917–1953* (Princeton, NJ: Princeton University Press).

Hilton, M.L. (2011), *Selling to the masses: Retailing in Russia, 1880–1930* (Pittsburgh, PA: University of Pittsburgh Press).

Howard, V. (2015), *From main street to mall: The rise and fall of the American department store* (Philadelphia, PA: University of Pennsylvania Press).

Lancaster, W. (1995), *The department store: A social history* (London: Leicester University Press).

Leach, W. (1993), *Land of desire: Merchants power, and the rise of a new American culture* (New York: Vintage).

Lears, T.J. (1994), *Fables of abundance: A cultural history of advertising in America* (New York: Basic Books).

Levinson, M. (2011), *The great A&P and the struggle for small business in America* (New York: Hill & Wang).

Mahoney, T. and Sloane, L. (1966), *The great merchants: America's foremost retail institutions and the people who made them great* (New York: Harper & Row).

Martin, A.S. (2008), *Buying in to the world of goods: Early consumers in backcountry Virginia* (Baltimore, MD: Johns Hopkins University Press).

Mathias, P. (1967), *Retailing revolution: A history of multiple retailing in the food trades based upon the Allied Suppliers group of companies* (London: Longmans).

Miller, M.B. (1981), *The Bon Marché: Bourgeois culture and the department store, 1869–1920* (Princeton, NJ: Princeton University Press).

Milne, G.J. (2000), *Trade and traders in mid-Victorian Liverpool: Mercantile business and the making of a world port* (Liverpool: Liverpool University Press).

Mitchell, S.I. (2014), *Tradition and innovation in English retailing, 1700–1850* (Farnham, Surrey: Ashgate).

Mui, H. and Mui, L. (1989), *Shops and shopkeeping in eighteenth-century England* (London: Routledge).

Olegario, R. (2006), *A culture of credit: Embedding trust and transparency in American business* (Cambridge, MA: Harvard University Press).

Pasdermadjian, H. (1954), *The department store, its origins, evolution and economics* (London: Newman Books).

Pitrone, J.M. (2003), *F.W. Woolworth and the American five and dime: A social history* (New York: McFarland & Company).

Porter, G. and Livesay, H.C. (1971), *Merchants and manufacturers: Studies in the changing structure of nineteenth-century marketing* (Baltimore, MD: Johns Hopkins University Press).

Rappaport, E.D. (2000), *Shopping for pleasure: Women in the making of London's west end* (Princeton, NJ: Princeton University Press).

Selfridge, H.G. (1918), *The romance of commerce* (London: John Lane Company).

Sparks, E. (2006), *Capital intentions: Female proprietors in San Francisco, 1850–1920* (Chapel Hill, NC: University of North Carolina Press).

Spellman, S.V. (2016), *Cornering the market: Independent grocers and innovation in American small business* (New York: Oxford University Press).

Strasser, S. (1989), *Satisfaction guaranteed: The making of the American mass market* (New York: Pantheon Books).

Stobart, J., Hann, A. and Morgan, V. (2007), *Spaces of consumption: Leisure and shopping in the Englishtown, c. 1680–1830* (London: Routledge).

Tangires, H. (2002), *Public markets and civic culture in nineteenth-century America* (Baltimore, MD: Johns Hopkins University Press).

Tedlow, R.S. (1990), *New and improved: The story of mass marketing in America* (New York: Basic Books).

Walsh, C. (2003), 'Social meaning and social space in the shopping galleries of early modern London', in J. Benson and L. Ugolini (eds.) *A nation of shopkeepers: Five centuries of British retailing* (London: I.B. Tauris) 106–126.

Wenger, D.E. (2008), *A country storekeeper in Pennsylvania: Creating economic networks in early America, 1790–1807* (University Park, PA: Pennsylvania State University Press).

Wills, J. (2005), *Boosters, hustlers, and speculators: Entrepreneurial culture and the rise of Minneapolis and St. Paul, 1849–1883* (St. Paul, MN: Minnesota Historical Society Press).

Winstanley, M.J. (1983), *The shopkeeper's world, 1830–1914* (Manchester: Manchester University Press).

15

RETAIL WORKERS AND THEIR UNIONS, 1850–2016

Daniel Opler

In many ways, the history of workers in the American retail industry is very similar to other well-established narratives about American workers. Meagre efforts at unionisation in the nineteenth century led to much more effective strategies and struggles in the 1930s, followed by a serious and rapid decline in workers' power in the later twentieth century. As in other industries, retail workers' control over their jobs and conditions lessened throughout most of the twentieth and early twenty-first centuries. While the story looks slightly different in European countries, there too, one sees the rapid decrease in retail workers' control over their jobs, and the overarching failure of retail workers' unions, although there are a few scattered signs of more powerful retail workers' unions in a few European countries, where unions generally are far more powerful.

If retail workers fit fairly well into these overarching narratives, there are some important aspects of retailing that make the industry unique in labour history. Women workers, for instance, have represented a far higher percentage of workers in the retail industry than in other industries. Also, retail work conditions were often significantly worse than in other industries: retail workers' hours in the nineteenth century were generally significantly longer than in other industries (before a shift to part-time employment reversed this trend, bringing with it a new set of problems), and retail workers' pay was often lower. In addition, the unions in the retail industry, even more so than elsewhere in American labour history, have been noticeably fractured, mired in internal conflict and powerless to effect important changes in workers' lives, even at their height. Finally, the forces that worked to the grave detriment of other workers in the late twentieth century, mechanisation and globalisation, have had far more mixed and complicated effects on retail workers; the challenges workers faced were far more likely to result from suburbanisation, the rise of online retailing and the rise of new retailing strategies such as self-service shopping.

Also unlike many other industries, retail workers are relatively rarely studied. Although there have been a few local studies of retail workers and their unions – especially New York City's left-leaning District 65 and its affiliated locals – and some good studies of retail workers' strikes throughout the country, there has not been a full-length study of retail workers and their unions in almost fifty years. And, while historians' understanding of retail workers continues to grow, it remains largely an incomplete picture, with key developments in retail history largely unexamined.

The AFL era, 1850–1930

Working in nineteenth century retail stores in the United States was, by all accounts, strenuous. Workers in the stores seem to have made even less than workers in factories (Obenauer 1913, 6–7). In addition, store managers were as demanding and patriarchal as any employer of this era. In an 1850 list of instructions issued at one store, the owners warned against smoking and dancing and suggested that 'leisure hours should be spent mostly in reading'. Finally, and most frustratingly for many retail workers, the hours of work were significantly longer than in many factories; a 112-hour work week was the norm for many store workers, in part to make sure that stores remained opened so that other workers who worked long hours would be able to shop after work if they wished (Kirstein 1950, 4–5).

The long workdays meant that some retail workers got involved in labour organisations as early as the 1840s, when New York clerks formed an association specifically targeted at shortening their working hours. The association amassed a great deal of public support, holding mass meetings in Union Square attended by important political figures like Horace Greeley, but did not seem able to shorten working hours. For the next thirty years, clerks at grocery and small dry goods stores throughout the country issued petitions, organised small associations, and wrote letters to newspapers in an effort to convince the public that these long working hours were morally objectionable and should be stopped. Their efforts at getting the public to condemn their long working hours continued throughout the 1870s and 1880s, and spread throughout the country to cities large and small. Despite the decades of effort, however, these public relations campaigns were largely unsuccessful, perhaps because the long working hours of clerks (and the long hours the stores were open) seemed good for the consumers to whom the early closing associations would have had to appeal to have any lasting impact ('Clerks congratulatory meeting' 1863).

The early closing associations were also generally limited to relatively small retail establishments. They did not exist in the great palaces of consumption, the department stores that were an increasingly important part of upscale consumption in America in the late nineteenth century. There were a few reasons for the absence of the early closing associations in the department stores. Certainly gender played a role; the leaders and many of the members of the early closing associations were men, and the women workers of the department stores were somewhat foreign to their organising experience. Equally important was the status of department store workers, who were at least on occasion eligible for promotion to low-level managerial positions, a rarity for any worker in this era, let alone women. But perhaps most important of all, as Susan Porter Benson argued in her landmark study, *Counter Cultures*, workers in the department stores had their own system for challenging employers' power. Women working in these stores, Benson demonstrated, were particularly adept at fashioning a work culture that allowed them all sorts of small perks, defiantly riding the elevators that were reserved for customers, taking full advantage of their charge accounts, and occasionally openly criticising the store to customers if they felt they were ill-treated by store managers. These techniques meant that formal organisations to fight for workers' interests were simply not necessary in the department stores (Benson 1986).

By the end of the 19th century, American department stores had developed into solidly non-union establishments, even as retail workers in other retail establishments, finding their independent early closing associations ineffective, sought permanent unions affiliated with national and international coalitions. As early as 1886, grocery store clerks in New York affiliated their early closing campaigns with the national labour union, Knights of Labor ('Grocery clerks encouraged' 1886). The Knights' collapse later in 1886, in the aftermath of the Chicago Haymarket Bombing and the Red Scare that followed, meant that this affiliation was very short-lived. Beginning in 1890, however, grocery store clerks in the Midwest organised the first permanent retail workers union in the United States, the Retail Clerks International Protection Association (RCIPA), affiliated with the powerful American Federation of Labor (AFL) (Kirstein 1950, 11–13).

In Europe the situation was more complex, and varied widely from country to country. But in Europe as in the United States, the primary concerns seem to have been working conditions and hours rather than wages. In France, the Catholic-inspired Syndicat de Employés du Commerce et de l'Industrie set out to organise workers in the growing department store industry as early as 1887, and won notable successes reasonably quickly. By 1900, French retail workers had forced legislators to pass the seat law, which gave women clerks the right to sit-down when not waiting on customers, and by 1906 they won an even more important legislative victory: the six-day work week for French retail workers. Employers, seeing the writing on the wall, began instituting early closing in France in these years, perhaps forestalling even more legislative action (Miller 2014, 146–147).

Workers in Germany took on similar issues in the late nineteenth century, though with different allies. As early as 1896, women's rights activists spearheaded campaigns for seat laws in Germany, forcing city governments to back down. By 1900, the German Industrial Code was amended to include the requirement that employers had to provide seats for sales clerks, only to run into the problem that most store owners, even if they did follow this code, instituted policies forbidding workers to actually use the seats. At the same time, German retail workers began working on a petition campaign to demand early closing, apparently getting their demands met in at least some cities where they were organised (Adams 1988, 57–59).

In England, employers seemed to have combined the American and French retail practices: workers had extremely long work weeks, ranging from 70 hours a week up to as many as 90 in some suburban stores. There, however, perhaps influenced by the famous upstairs dormitories for workers at the Bon Marché and other French stores, large retailers practiced the living-in method of employment, requiring some 400,000 workers in their stores to live in employer-owned lodgings, often in cramped conditions and in dangerous neighbourhoods. Employers in these circumstances had tremendous power, dismissing workers for such offences as getting married or putting up photographs or other pictures on the walls of the employer-owned housing (Richardson 1979, 5–7). In part in response to this system, in 1891, English retail workers formed the National Union of Shop Assistants, which, a few years later, expanded to the National Amalgamated Union of Shop Assistants, Warehousemen and Clerks.

In both England and the US, the unions set their sights on achieving earlier closing times. In England, the union was part of the formation of the Early Closing Association, which called upon employers to voluntarily establish shorter hours; when this proved ineffective, the union began organising strikes. In the US, by the early 1900s, the RCIPA, drawing on a longer tradition of struggles around the shorter workday, called upon customers to boycott stores that would not grant the 60-hour week. This tactic proved only slightly more effective than any of the other efforts at limiting working hours. They had a few scattered victories in mining towns where they were able to get the support of the comparatively powerful mine workers' unions, but outside of these communities, the union found managers unwilling to limit the number of hours potential customers could shop in their stores (Kirstein 1950, 19).

The early 1900s also saw a short-lived independent union campaign in department stores in the US. Spearheaded by the New York Women's Trade Union League, and bolstered by Progressive reform groups' investigations into the department stores, Macy's workers set up the Retail Clerks Union (RCU), which then attempted to spread to other department stores around New York City. Store managers quickly increased commissions and cracked down on any and all union activity, establishing extensive informant networks, locking store exits near union meetings to physically prevent workers from attending meetings, and firing workers who were involved with the union. The RCU applied for AFL affiliation, but apparently never received it, and all but vanished from the historical record after 1914 (Johnson 2007).

The RCIPA and RCU alike generally avoided calling strikes. The RCU simply did not last long enough to launch any major strikes, and the RCIPA leaders viewed boycotts and public condemnation of recalcitrant managers as far more promising than strikes. Partially this was a sign of the times; strikes were expensive and risky, and many labour leaders were uneasy about their viability as a tactic in labour struggles. But the peculiarities of work in the retail industry might also have played a role; retail establishments, more directly than most other businesses, catered to the public at large and so a boycott could have very immediate, visible and devastating effects, if organised effectively.

Despite the union leaders' disinterest in organising strikes, retail workers did strike on occasion. In Buffalo in 1913, for instance, department store workers went on strike to demand both higher wages and an 8½-hour workday. In that strike, in which the RCIPA was only marginally involved, workers emerged with some important gains; weekly pay was raised to $12 minimum for men and $6 minimum for women, somewhat less than the workers had demanded when they'd begun their strike, though they did not get the hours of work shortened. Other strikes called by the union during the 1910s, most important at stores in Memphis and in St Louis, saw even less success, and by the end of World War I, the union was weaker than ever (Kirstein 1950, 42–49).

In Europe, conditions were more complex. In the United Kingdom, retail workers began striking against the living-in system in the early 1900s. Beginning with the small 1901 strike against William Whiteley's store in London and continuing with strikes throughout the United Kingdom, retail workers began destroying the living-in system. By the beginning of World War I, workers in the UK had largely won the right to choose between room-and-board and wage increases (USDAW 2016). And, following the war, the retail unions in the UK began to expand rapidly, reaching some 86,000 members by 1920, only to collapse again in the postwar economic recession.

In America, while the unions were far weaker than in the UK, workers found that they could have a lot of power without the aid of the union. Especially in the larger department stores, retail managers, in keeping with their patriarchal methods before World War I, created massive "welfare capitalism" programs in the 1920s, offering workers profit-sharing, vacation homes, employer-sponsored pension and health care plans and, quite famously, at Macy's, a free turkey every Thanksgiving. As managers used these tactics to gain greater worker loyalty and discourage turnover, they openly condemned unions as un-American and unwelcome in their stores. The RCIPA, small and not especially powerful, had no effective means to combat these sorts of tactics (Kirstein 1950, 48).

It is also worth noting that American retail jobs were strictly segregated throughout the late nineteenth early twentieth centuries. While African American and other non-white workers often had jobs in the stores, especially in larger department stores, these jobs fell into two categories: either behind the scenes or in servile positions, as washroom attendants, cleaning staff and elevator operators. African American workers were not employed in sales generally, except in the few African American owned stores in segregated neighbourhoods. (Even these stores were sometimes the sites of racial violence. A famous lynching took place in Memphis, Tennessee in 1892, when three African American men opened a grocery store that might take customers away from a nearby white-owned store; it was this case that first drew the attention of journalist

Ida B. Wells to lynching, and launched her career as an anti-lynching activist.) By and large, the unions did nothing to challenge this situation.

The Great Depression and World War II would dramatically change the situation of retail workers in America and beyond. These decades would mark the end of retail unions in Axis-controlled countries, and a new respect for their tremendous service in the UK during the war. At the same time, in the US, these years would bear witness to the rise in the power of unions within the retail industry, introduce different retail strategies with profound effects on workers' situation, see the first major challenges to segregated hiring practices and would forever transform the conditions of retail workers.

Unions ascendant, 1930–1950

The Great Depression saw a tremendous increase in strikes against retail stores. With national support for workers and unions growing rapidly in the early Great Depression, workers were more willing to go on strike than ever before. The largest strike of the early Depression years took place in Milwaukee, a centre of radical labour activism. In September 1934, Milwaukee retail workers at several different stores applied for RCIPA membership, and in November of that year they demanded a union contract at the large Boston Store. When management refused, workers went on strike, hitting the store at the beginning of the Christmas shopping season. Store managers applied for and received an anti-picketing injunction, and the strike became a war of attrition, with store managers taking out advertisements in the city's papers condemning the union, and with workers resorting to breaking windows and throwing stink bombs into the store to drive away customers. By January 1935, the strike was over, with workers receiving merit-based raises and with most workers receiving their jobs back. Workers received neither the level of raises nor the union representation they had demanded (White 2016).

More important, though equally unsuccessful in most regards, were a series of small strikes in New York City that would lead to the creation of a more radical retail workers' union, the retail branch of the Office Workers' Union. Affiliated with the Communist-led Trade Union Unity League, the Office Workers' Union defied all the accepted wisdom of retail organising, setting its sights on the upscale department stores as well as the lower-priced stores where the RCIPA had previously been successful. When managers at the S. Klein's store, a cut-rate department store on Union Square, fired a number of workers for union organising, workers at Klein's went on strike; within a few days, workers at the competing Ohrbach's store went on strike as well (Opler 2002).

The strikes were dramatic ones. The strikers took advantage of Communist-affiliated allies to transform the stores and Square alike into a battleground, decorating statues with picket signs, etching strike slogans into the store windows, handing balloons with strike slogans on them to the children of customers, recruiting writers and actors to join their picket lines on special strike "theme days", introducing white mice into the stores to frighten customers, and interrupting charity banquets at which the store owners spoke. Again and again, the strikers found ways to capture the public imagination, enough so that by 1935 there was a play based on the strikes, *The Klein-Ohrbach Strike*, produced by the important Workers Laboratory Theatre, and by 1936, there was a novel based on the strikes, Leane Zugsmith's *A Time To Remember*. Despite the attention they received, the strikes were not successful. At both stores, workers got reinstatement, and at Ohrbach's workers got a verbal promise of reduced hours. At both stores, however, managers laid off workers in the weeks and months after the strikes had taken place, marking a serious defeat for the radicals. After these and other similarly devastating losses, the Office Workers' Union merged with an RCIPA local to create the important Local 1250, which would become a major force in organising department store workers in New York City into unions (Opler 2002).

If the dramatic strikes of the early Depression years were largely unsuccessful, that would change in the late 1930s, when organising and striking resulted in permanent and powerful unions. The key moment in retail unions' history occurred in early 1937, when, in the aftermath of sit-down strikes at auto and rubber plants, workers at five-and-dime stores went on a sit-down strike in Detroit, Michigan. Locking themselves inside Woolworth stores, and singling out Woolworth heiress Barbara Hutton as a target for their ire, the Detroit Woolworth workers quickly made headlines throughout the country. This tactic played nicely into the radical worldview of the 1930s, which often singled out wealthy women as particularly greedy, wasteful and deserving of contempt, and throughout the Woolworth strikes, workers played up the contrast between the hardworking female Woolworth clerks and the wealthy, lazy, spoiled Barbara Hutton, both with songs invoking Hutton's name and with what became their favourite chant in some of the stores on strike, 'Barbara Hutton, she gets mutton! Woolworth workers, they get nothin'!' (Frank 2012; Opler 2007).

The strikes spread. In New York City, former OWU organisers started to pay more attention to workers at five-and-dime stores, and in March 1937 they wound up leading massive sit-down strikes in a number of New York five-and-dime stores, capturing the front pages of newspapers and attracting tremendous attention (and eventually pressuring New York City Mayor Fiorello LaGuardia and others to intervene on behalf of the workers). Unlike in the earlier strikes, the Woolworth strikes ended with contracts, raises, and improvement in working hours. After years of defeats and compromises, unions had finally won a clear-cut victory in the retail industry. Influenced by these victories, a group of more politically moderate RCIPA insurgents in New York City abandoned the AFL, joining with the former OWU leaders in forming a union that would eventually become the CIO's retail union, the Retail, Wholesale, and Department Store Union (RWDSU) (Opler 2007).

These same years also marked the beginnings of effective labour organising in San Francisco's retail industry. As early as 1936, organisers for the powerful west coast branch of the International Longshoreman's Association had led small strikes of warehouse workers in five-and-dime stores, and in 1937 these strikes spread to the sales workers. That year, as workers did in five-and-dime stores throughout the rest of the country, workers launched a massive strike against Woolworth stores in San Francisco that won workers better conditions, better hours, and union recognition. In 1938 this campaign culminated in a still larger strike against twenty-seven of the largest department stores in San Francisco in an effort to win all retail workers in the city shorter work weeks, store-wide seniority policies and union contracts (Reagan 2016).

The 1938 San Francisco strike was an important if not entirely victorious one. The strikers resorted to tactics similar to those used in earlier New York City strikes, making them as dramatic as possible. Female picketers wore their best dresses to the picket lines, and the *New York Times* suggested that, at least on the first day, the picket lines looked more like "fashion shows" than anything else, with the strikers engaging in dance steps, chatting with passers-by and keeping the mood as light as possible. This light mood did not last long; the strike became a violent one within days, with workers and police (and sometimes workers and store managers as well) fighting on the streets outside of the stores. For two months, workers kept the stores shut down, until they reached a somewhat weak compromise, accepting a seniority clause but giving up on the shorter workday and union shop clauses. Despite this weak compromise, the strike meant that the Department Store Employees Union (DSEU) was in San Francisco to stay, and the city's retail trade would remain unionised for years to come (Reagan 2016; Kirstein 1950).

Following the massive retail workers' uprisings of 1937 and 1938, the retail workers unions saw gains across the country. In Denver, Newark, Philadelphia, Pittsburgh, Boston, and Providence, retail workers voted to unionise. But the bulk of the retail unions' strength was always in San Francisco and New York City. In these cities, most of the major stores were unionised – in New York, managers at Macy's, Gimbels, Hearns, Bloomingdale's and Sterns all signed contracts with the CIO, perhaps in hopes of avoiding the unpleasant strikes that had shaken so many other stores in these years. In San Francisco the Emporium, Hale Brothers and J.C. Penney stores (among many others) all signed contracts with the AFL's RCIPA. The unions' accomplishments were important ones – some of the largest stores in the country's largest cities were now union stores, and they would remain so for many years to come. At the same time, it's important to note the limits of this organising drive; retail workers' unions never achieved anything close to the size or power of the unions in the auto or steel industry, and there were a number of stores – especially more downscale stores and grocery stores – that remained largely untouched by unionisation drives even in this era (Kirstein 1950).

Retail employers also faced a challenge to their segregated hiring practices in the 1930s. While at the largest New York City stores, down on 34th Street, racial segregation remained virtually unchallenged (despite the radical politics of many of the leaders, the retail workers unions did almost nothing on this issue, preferring to focus on more standard labour issues like wages and hours), during the Great Depression African Americans did begin organising to push retailers to offer more jobs to African American workers in the famous "Don't Buy Where You Can't Work" Campaigns. Beginning with struggles against Chicago Woolworth stores in the late 1920s and expanding into New York City in the 1930s, this campaign pitted African American consumers against retailers who owned stores in their neighbourhoods. With the support of important activists like Adam Clayton Powell, Jr., the campaign was eventually successful enough that every major store in Harlem employed at least one African American worker by the end of the 1930s (Greenberg 1997).

As with other workers, then, the Depression era marked some important gains for retail workers. However, retail workers still faced some important obstacles, especially with regard to the major labour legislation of the 1930s. Until 1941, courts were reluctant to apply the Wagner Act, which protected workers' right to choose their own unions, to retailing. Even more important, the Fair Labor Standards Act of 1938, which established the 40-hour week, the minimum wage, an end to child labour, and other important reforms, explicitly exempted retail workers, so long as their work was primarily related to intrastate commerce (*New York Times* 1938, 1, 1941, 28).

As a result, most retail workers lacked the eight-hour day, and the length of the workday, a concern throughout their history, continued to be a sticking point. This issue of the length of the workday became a key issue for an unexpected 1941 strike against New York's Gimbels store, led by the radicals who had left the Office Workers Union and now joined with the CIO. Gimbels, like Macy's and other upscale department stores, catered to a largely upper-class and wealthy clientele.

That did not stop the workers, however, from engaging in some fairly militant tactics in the strike, releasing pigeons into the store and taking their picket lines right into the store in order to cause disruption and force customers out. These sorts of tactics proved effective, and the workers won the eight-hour day, but also earned the local union the tremendous ire of store managers. Gimbels' managers, who had signed a union contract precisely because they hoped the more moderate national CIO leaders could help them avoid this sort of disruption, were furious, and happily testified in state hearings later that year against the radicals leading their local unions.

Figure 15.1 Sales clerk and customer examining a dress at Saks Fifth Avenue store following a fashion show presented by the Chrysler Girls' Club of the Chrysler Corporation in 1942.

Source: Siegel, A. S., photographer. (1942) Detroit, Michigan. Girl and sales lady examining a dress at Saks Fifth Avenue store following a fashion show presented by the Chrysler Girls' Club of the Chrysler Corporation. Detroit Michigan United States Wayne County, 1942.

Source: Spring. [Photograph] Library of Congress

In Europe, as always, things were different, depending especially on what country one was in. In countries occupied by the Axis powers, unions were made illegal and driven out of existence in the 1930s and early 1940s. In the United Kingdom, however, retail unions, now under the umbrella of the National Union of Distributive and Allied Workers (NUDAW), had grown quite large, with around 200,000 members, and increasingly powerful. Their role as non-essential workers during the war would mean that they were frequently drafted, and some estimates suggest that as many as 100,000 of these members served in the armed forces during the war (Richardson 1979, 144–145).

In the US, World War II and the early Cold War years severely weakened unionisation in the retail industry. Many of the most militant organisers left the stores; men left for the front or sometimes for other war industry jobs, and women, who before the war had no more promising job opportunities, now found work in war production plants a lucrative alternative to the stores. At the same time, the political divisions between moderate Democrats, who ran the national RWDSU, and the more radical voices who were often in charge of the more successful locals, especially in New York, began to surface more clearly in the war and postwar years.

The earliest signs of major internal conflict within the RWDSU took place amidst a major labour conflict, at the Montgomery Ward store in Chicago. Montgomery Ward chairman Sewell Avery, a fierce opponent of the New Deal and especially of the government's involvement in his business, rejected the federal government's insistence that he allow workers at Montgomery Ward stores in Chicago to unionise peacefully during the war. After some unproductive efforts at negotiation with Avery, the federal government took over Montgomery Ward stores and allowed workers to form unions, only ceasing their involvement in the store management after the war was over. The strike sharply divided the union. Local leaders who were affiliated with the Communist Party condemned the strike, committed as they were to defeating Hitler at all costs, while national leaders who were moderate Democrats tended to celebrate their victory against the store managers (Phillips 2013, 84–87).

The divisions got significantly worse after the war. At first, there were serious efforts by the radical and local leaders to collaborate, but with the passage of the 1947 Taft-Hartley Act that required non-Communist union leaders to sign affidavits stating explicitly their lack of membership in the Communist Party, the divisions greatly worsened. In 1948, as early Cold War paranoia took hold of the country, national CIO leaders vocally condemned Communist influences in the New York local unions and participated, although reluctantly, in a House Un-American Activities Committee investigation into the role of Communists in the retail and wholesale trade in New York City.

Adding to the CIO's political troubles were two major structural changes in the American retail industry. During the war, due to labour shortages, retail managers increasingly experimented with self-service retailing, which allowed customers direct access to merchandise and eliminated the need for some salespeople, in some cases allowing stores to run with half the salespeople as the full-service stores (Ziskind 2003, 58). This would expand in the postwar years, spreading to Europe as well by the late 1950s (USDAW 2016). In addition, as suburbanisation became more and more prominent in the United States in the late 1940s and early 1950s, store managers increasingly focused on the suburban market, opening up new branch stores that were separate from the cities that had so often been the union's strength.

In New York, the centre of the RWDSU's strength but also the centre of the union's political struggles, the combination of political disarray and the transformation of the retail industry was disastrous. Retail union organisers attempted again and again to organise in the suburban branch stores, but these efforts were problematic. For one thing, the stores were often located in malls rather than on public streets, which made picketing more difficult. For another, there were fewer workers available to picket. In the city, as historian Minna Ziskind has demonstrated, workers could picket neighbouring stores during their lunch breaks; they could not do so in the suburbs, where the unions lacked support. They set up a few picket lines here and there where store managers proved fiercely intractable, but these picket lines were poorly staffed and had no real effect on the stores' function. By the late 1950s, Ziskind writes, 'admissions of responsibility [for the union's failures in the suburbs] were almost routine parts of meetings'. The union's presence in the suburban branch stores would always be limited, and one of their major bases of strength – the big department stores – was rapidly fading in importance, as the stores became increasingly reliant upon the branch stores for sales and profits (Ziskind 2003, 65).

However, despite these important setbacks, there were clear signs of progress, especially for the RCIPA in this era. In 1944, a new leader, James Suffridge, took over the RCIPA, and became an important force in the industry. Suffridge, a veteran of struggles in the Oakland grocery workers' unions, quickly worked to centralise power in the union, and modernise operations.

Politically moderate (he was a registered Republican, but routinely supported Democratic candidates for office), Suffridge had some important qualities that his predecessors in the RCIPA had lacked. He was a fierce proponent of integration, and had long since refused to allow segregated locals in the union, and insisted upon organising white and non-white workers alike into the union. He was also extremely savvy about the importance of chain stores to the retail industry, and by the late 1940s he set about hiring large numbers of organisers to work directly for his international union, circumventing the locals in an effort to organise the national chain stores that were increasingly dominating the retail industry. Finally, Suffridge was, by all accounts, a militant leader, more than willing to have workers go on strike if it meant a chance for a better contract. (Harrington 1962, 13–42; Zielinski 2001).

Suffridge's rise coincided with other events that demonstrated that the AFL would leave the war in a more militant fashion. In Oakland, California, workers at the Kahn's and Hasting's stores struck under RCIPA leadership in 1946, part of a massive postwar strike wave. Truck drivers from the AFL's Teamsters refused to cross the picket line to deliver goods to the store, but store managers employed non-union trucking companies to try to break the strike. It was a serious error: some 100,000 workers in Oakland declared themselves on strike, closing all stores except for pharmacies and grocery stores, taking over traffic, banning all non-union members from downtown Oakland, and carefully monitoring those stores that remained open for any signs of price gouging (Kirstein 1950; Lipsitz 1994, 148–152).

The unions also attempted to expand internationally, especially in Canada. Beginning in 1948, the RWDSU participated in a major drive to organise at Eaton's in Toronto, the largest department store in Canada (and Canada's third largest employer). The campaign was problematic from the get-go; the RWDSU was still reeling from the struggle over communism in the US, and the Canadian store managers used that to their great advantage to paint the union as a whole as a Communist-inspired movement. To make matters worse, as Donica Belisle has demonstrated, the union's emphasis on masculine rhetoric and male figures did not match the largely female workforce at Eaton's. The result was that the campaign at Eaton's, the largest union drive in Canadian history, was a dismal failure (Belisle 2005).

More importantly, though by far the least studied aspect of retail workers' history, the RCIPA and RWDSU both found some important successes in the grocery industry in this era. In the early 1940s, the RCIPA extended into grocery stores throughout the Philadelphia area, including victories against such chains as A&P and Food Fair, and in other scattered cities throughout the country. By the early 1950s, grocery stores in most major cities – Los Angeles, Chicago, Cleveland, Detroit and St Louis, were largely unionised (*New York Times* 1940, 26; Zundel 1954, 306).

This did not mean that retail workers were getting significantly higher wages or that their conditions were improving dramatically. If anything, the 1950s and 1960s saw retail workers' wages stagnating, with workers making an average of $1.68 an hour in the early 1960s, well below the $2.25 in manufacturing and other trades (Schaffer 1963). Additionally, a sizable minority – around 1/3 – of retail workers continued to work more than 44 hours a week. While a far cry from the 112-hour work week workers had faced in the nineteenth century, the long workdays that had been the impetus for unionisation in the nineteenth century had continued well beyond the rise of unions in retailing. These long work hours came at least sometimes with unions' support; in union stores, workers received additional bonuses for working longer hours, and got time-and-a-half for working on Sundays. In addition, some union organisers took the view that by allowing retail chain stores to stay open later (especially with the increased wages), they would undercut smaller non-chain stores that were generally non-union, thus allowing union membership numbers to grow (Walsh 1993, 50). And, whether they opposed these conditions or not, developments of the late twentieth century would mean that retail workers' unions were facing a long and steady decline in the coming years.

Towards the twenty-first century: Walmart and globalisation

The late twentieth and early twenty-first century have not been promising for retail workers. Working hours, wages and discrimination continue to be key parts of working in the retail industry, while unions have faded in importance, leaving workers with limited ability to change their working conditions.

By far the most important development in retailing in the late twentieth century was the rise of Walmart and other big-box stores. Corporations like Target and Walmart expanded rapidly in the 1980s and 1990s to become the most important players in the retail industry. Their model of the big-box store – low prices, low overhead and low wages combined with a very high sales volume – became the new hallmark of the retail industry, which had massive implications for retail workers.

Store managers at these big-box stores have taken tremendous measures to prevent workers from organising unions in their stores. In the late 1970s and 1980s, for instance, when the Teamsters made tremendous strides in a unionisation campaign among Walmart distribution centres, company managers threatened to close the warehouses if the workers voted to support the union in a National Labor Relations Board election. In 2000, when meat cutters at Walmart stores began organising under the auspices of the United Food and Commercial Workers, Walmart announced that they would no longer employ meat cutters at all in their stores, requiring customers instead to buy pre-cut meat (Lichtenstein 2009, 128, 137).

If Walmart is most notorious for its anti-union practices, it is by no means alone. Target stores made a small splash in 2014 when their anti-union video, "Think Hard: Protect Your Signature" was leaked to the public. The video warned employees that if unions came in they would destroy Target's "fast, fun and friendly culture". More seriously, when workers at Target stores did organise, as did workers at a store in Valley Stream, New York, Target management crusaded relentlessly against the union, warning that the store might well close if it was unionised; then, after the workers voted against unionisation, and the National Labor Relations Board ordered a second election, store managers actually did close the store for six months, leading up to a massive defeat for the union in the election that followed (Becker 2014).

These anti-union practices have forced union organisers to turn to other techniques to fight on behalf of workers. Most important here are the recent campaigns for the $15 minimum wage, the Fight for Fifteen movement. With support from the Service Employees International Union (SEIU), the Fight for Fifteen movement has successfully skirted the challenges of gaining union recognition in extremely difficult conditions by working on behalf of workers who are, by and large, not unionised. By focusing on the minimum wage, the SEIU's movement has become remarkably successful, especially among fast food workers, but also increasingly among convenience store workers (DePillis 2016).

Workers also continue to struggle around the length of the workday. Nelson Lichtenstein reports that Walmart managers routinely require workers to put in more than 40 hours a week, and to alter workers' time cards so that no over time needed to be paid. Workers respond to this old problem with time-honored solution: looking for new jobs and stealing from the stores whenever possible. Here, too, in recent years, workers have turned to more formal methods of protest. Especially important here are the strikes and protests around stores that remain open on Thanksgiving weekends. Beginning in 2011, the union-sponsored campaign, OUR Walmart, organised Black Friday strikes on the very busy shopping day directly after Thanksgiving. As

Jess Guh pointed out in *Counterpunch*, this was a new strategy for the labour movement. The strikes did not include enough workers to slowdown or even greatly complicate store operations; they also had no appreciable effect on customers' desire to shop on Black Friday. What they did instead was raise public awareness of Walmart's labour issues. Accompanying stories on store-sponsored food drives for Walmart employees drove home the point that the unions were trying to make, that Walmart's labour policies were simply unacceptable (Guh 2014).

Big-box stores' presence has also meant that other retail establishments have changed their employment practices. In 2003, supermarket managers at three different chains in southern California announced they were cutting wages and benefits in order to compete more effectively with Walmart. Workers, longstanding members of the UFCW, declared a strike against the stores in response, significantly slowing down business at 900 stores in the state. From October 2003–February 2004, the stores and unions fought bitterly, only to negotiate their way to a compromise that meant a two-tiered hiring system.

Dire as the situation looks for retail workers, the two most serious challenges facing workers in other industries, globalisation and mechanisation, have had far more complicated effects on American retail workers. In the retail industry, globalisation has taken two primary forms. First, large retail businesses based in the US and Europe have systematically displaced smaller firms in the rest of the world. While globalisation began in Europe, American firms began the process in earnest in the 1990s, and quickly became important players. Walmart, for instance, has opened stores (sometimes under different names) in dozens of countries, including Argentina, Brazil, China, India, Japan, Mexico and South Africa. But unlike in other industries, because of the very nature of retailing, globalisation does not mean that the US stores are likely to close as a result of the now-global reach of the store managers. The second aspect of globalisation in retailing is the import of products made all over the world. Again, while this has dramatic and serious effects on American manufacturing industry, its effect on retail workers is negligible.

For all its importance, then, globalisation has simply not been a major factor in the working lives of American retail workers. It has obviously impacted workers in other countries, though the effects have been extremely complex. In a 2006 study on retailing in Mexico, for instance, Charles Tilly and José Luis Álvarez Galván found that the retail sector as a whole in Mexico was not a promising one for workers, with low pay and company unions that are so powerless that at several stores, workers were uncertain if they were even in a union. However, they also found that Walmart's role in Mexico is not, as it has been in the United States, as a leader in the fight to keep unions out of retailing and drive down wages, but rather as a participant in a much more common, mainstream business practice of company unionism and low wages (Tilly and Galván 2006).

Things are even more complex when one gets beyond Mexico. In a more global study of Walmart's employment practices, Tilly found that in most of the world, Walmart's wages are at or near (and in several cases, even above) industry standards (Tilly 2007). A 2006 study by Yuko Aoyama and Guido Schwarz suggests that part of this is because retailing doesn't work like other industries – so much of it is controlled by customer expectations that foreign-owned retailers have to act, to some extent, like local retailers (Aoyama and Schwarz 2006, 290–291), making globalisation in retailing a more complicated phenomenon than in manufacturing.

Like globalisation, mechanisation has had mixed effects on retailing. There have been efforts at using mechanisation to reduce labour costs, to be sure. When computerised price tags and Universal Product Codes (UPC's) were introduced in the 1970s and 1980s, many feared it would mean a severe reduction in the number of workers employed in retail stores, a change that never took place. Similarly, in the late 1990s and especially early 2000s, many major stores introduced self-checkout options for consumers. However, the machines were so unreliable and unwieldy that by the early 2010s, several store chains, most notably the Albertsons grocery stores, gave up on the machines altogether. Self-checkout remains key to Walmart and other cut-rate stores, but many retailers' focus on customer service means self-checkout is incompatible with their business model.

Other forms of mechanisation, though still in their infancy, are likely to have more serious effects on retail workers. The rise of Internet sales, for instance, has meant major store closings, with major retailers from Office Depot and Sports Authority to Macy's either closing down stores, cutting back on over time or going out of business entirely (Close 2016).

While the rise of Walmart and the Internet of course represent new factors in the lives of retail workers, most of the struggles that American retail workers face are issues they have faced since the nineteenth century. Wages, for instance, continue to be a major problem for retail workers. According to the Bureau of Labor Statistics, retail workers made an average of $17.87/hour in September 2016, significantly below the $25.79 that was the national average. The $17.87/hour makes retail workers the lowest paid workers in any employment sector except for leisure and hospitality, which included fast food and restaurant workers (Bureau of Labor Statistics 2016).

Like low pay, issues of racial inequality also continue to plague the industry. According to a 2015 study conducted by Demos and the NAACP, African American and Latino retail workers were disproportionately underrepresented in management positions, and overrepresented in the lowest-paying retail jobs, such as cashier positions. In addition, according to the same study, African American and Latino employees made between 75–90% of what white employees made in corresponding positions (Ruetschlin and Asante-Muhammad 2015).

Gender inequality likewise continues to play an important role in the retail industry. This was especially central in the famous *Sears* case, where the Equal Employment Opportunity Commission (EEOC) argued that statistically, women were severely underrepresented in the relatively lucrative commission sales jobs. After years of hearings (the charges were first filed in 1973, but the case was not heard by the court until 1984, and the decision not issued until 1986), the Court found that the EEOC's statistical analysis did not, in itself, prove discrimination. Whether or not Sears discriminated against women in these jobs, however, the statistics did demonstrate conclusively that women in retailing did face severe inequality. This has not changed in the intervening decades; a 2015 study by the Institute for Women's Policy Research found that retail saleswomen made 71.2% as much as their male colleagues, as opposed to the 81.1% of their colleagues' salaries made by women in other fields (Institute for Women's Policy Research 2016).

Retail workers also face new problems, most important among them the rise of part-time employment. A 2013 study cosponsored by the Retail Action Project and the Murphy Center for Labor Studies found that between 2003 and 2013, the number of involuntary part-time workers (part-time retail workers looking for full-time work) had more than tripled in number; by March 2014, 7.4 million American workers were involuntary part-time workers, many of them in the retail industry. To make matters worse, managers in many stores have introduced just-in-time scheduling, which requires workers to be available for work on less than 24 hours' notice and often gives workers very little notice about whether they will have any work at all the next day, making scheduling anything outside of work tremendously difficult (Luce, Hammad, and Sipe 2016).

Retail work has, unquestionably, changed over the century and a half during which workers have attempted to organise to make their lives better. The rise and fall of unions, however, seems to have not been the driving factor in these changes. Economic and population shifts, changing marketing strategies and a changing business environment have all played a role in making the situation of retail workers today markedly different than that of the nineteenth century clerks who began organising. Unfortunately, those changes have not, on the whole, substantially improved retail workers' always difficult circumstances.

References

Adams, C. (1988), *Women clerks in Wilhelmine Germany* (Cambridge, UK: Cambridge University Press).

Aoyama, Y. and Schwarz, G. (2006), 'The myth of wal-martization: Retail globalization and local competition in Japan and Germany', in S. Brunn (ed.) *Wal-Mart world: The world's biggest corporation in the global economy*, 1st ed., (New York: Routledge) 275–292.

Becker, B. (2014), 'Taking aim at target: West Indian immigrant workers confront the difficulties of big-box organizing', in R. Milkman (ed.) *New labor in New York: Precarious worker organizing and the labor movement*, 1st ed., (Ithaca, NY: Cornell University Press) 25–48.

Belisle, D. (2005), 'Exploring postwar consumption: The campaign to unionize Eaton's in Toronto, 1948–1952', *The Canadian Historical Review*, 86 (4), pp. 641–672.

Benson, S. (1986), *Counter cultures: Saleswomen, managers, and customers in American department stores, 1890–1940* (Urbana, IL: University of Illinois Press).

Bureau of Labor Statistics, US Department of Labor (2016), *Average hourly and weekly earnings of all employees on private nonfarm payrolls by industry sector, seasonally adjusted.* [online] Available at: www.bls.gov/news.release/empsit.t19.htm (Accessed 9 October 2016).

Close, K. (2016), '12 major retailers closing stores like crazy', [online] *money.com*. Available at: http://time.com/money/4386499/retail-stores-closing-locations/ (Accessed 24 September 2016).

DePillis, L. (2016), 'It's not just fast food: The fight for $15 is for everyone now,' [online] *Washington Post.* Available at: www.washingtonpost.com/news/storyline/wp/2014/12/04/its-not-just-fast-food-the-fight-for-15-is-for-everyone-now/ (Accessed 4 October 2016).

Frank, D. (2012), *Women strikers occupy chain store, win big* (Chicago: Haymarket Books).

Greenberg, C. L. (1997), *Or does it explode?* (New York: Oxford University Press).

Guh, J. (2014), *Walmart Black Friday strikes.* [online] *CounterPunch.* Available at: www.counterpunch.org/2014/12/01/walmart-black-friday-strikes/ (Accessed 23 September 2016).

Institute for Women's Policy Research (2016), *Fact sheet: The gender wage gap by occupation 2015 and by race and ethnicity.* [online] Available at: www.iwpr.org/publications/pubs/the-gender-wage-gap-by-occupation-2015-and-by-race-and-ethnicity/at_download/file (Accessed 24 September 2016).

Johnson, V.M. (2007), '"The rest can go to the devil": Macy's workers negotiate gender, sex, and class in the progressive era', *Journal of Women's History* 19 (1), pp. 32–57.

Kirstein, G. (1950), *Stores and unions: A study of the growth of unionism in dry goods and department stores* (New York: Fairchild Publications).

Lipsitz, G. (1994), *Rainbow at midnight* (Urbana, IL: University of Illinois Press).

Luce, S., Hammad, S. and Sipe, D. (2016), *Short shifted.* [online] Available at: http://retailactionproject.org/wp-content/uploads/2014/09/ShortShifted_report_FINAL.pdf (Accessed 24 September 2016).

Miller, M. (2014), *The Bon Marché: Bourgeois culture and the department store, 1869–1920*, 1st ed., (Princeton, NJ: Princeton University Press) 146–147.

New York Times (1863), 'Clerks' congratulatory meeting', 14 March, p. 9.

New York Times (1886), 'Grocery clerks encouraged', 8 March, p. 8.

New York Times (1938), 'Andrews defines exempt employees', 20 October, p. 1.

New York Times (1940), 'Clerks end strike at 1500 groceries', 13 November, p. 26.

New York Times (1941), 'Stores now held in labor act scope', 14 January, p. 28.

Obenauer, M. (1913), *Hours, earnings, and duration of employment of wage-earning women in selected industries in the District of Columbia* (Washington, DC: G.P.O).

Opler, D.J. (2002), 'Monkey business in union square: A cultural analysis of the Klein's-Ohrbach's strikes of 1934–5', *Journal of Social History*, 36 (1), pp. 149–164.

Opler, D.J. (2007), *For all white-collar workers: The possibilities of radicalism in New York City's department store unions, 1934–1953* (Columbus, OH: Ohio State University Press).

Phillips, L.A.W. (2013), *A renegade union* (Urbana, IL: University of Illinois Press).

Reagan, M. (2016), 'The 1937 and 1938 San Francisco retail strikes', *Libcom.org*. Web. 22 Aug. 2016.

Richardson, W. (1979), *A union of many trades*, 1st ed., (Manchester: Union of Shop, Distributive, and Allied Workers).

Ruetschlin, C. and Asante-Muhammad, D. (2015), 'The retail race divide: How the retail industry is perpetuating racial inequality in the early 21st century', [online] *Demos and NAACP*. Available at: www.demos.org/sites/default/files/publications/The%20Retail%20Race%20Divide%20Report.pdf (Accessed 9 October 2016).

Schaffer, H. (1963), 'Changes in employee earnings in retail trade, June 1961–June 1962', *Monthly Labor Review*, 86 (7), pp. 802–807.

Tilly, C. (2007), 'Wal-Mart and its workers: *NOT* the same all over the world', *Connecticut Law Review*, 39 (4), pp. 1–19.

Tilly, C. and Galván, J.L.Á. (2006), 'Lousy jobs, invisible unions: The Mexican retail sector in the age of globalization', *International Labor and Working-Class History*, 70 (1), pp. 61–85.

USDAW (2016), *USDAW 125th Anniversary booklet*. [online] Available at: http://dtp.usdaw.co.uk/Usdaw-125th-Anniversary-Booklet/ (Accessed 17 January 2017).

Walsh, J. (1993), *Supermarkets transformed* (New Brunswick, NJ: Rutgers University Press).

White, J. (2016), 'Milwaukee sales clerks strike for wage increases, 1934 | Global nonviolent action database', *Nvdatabase.swarthmore.edu*. Web. 15 Aug. 2016.

Zielinski, G. (2001), 'Union leader James Suffridge dies', *Washington Post*. Web. 22 Aug. 2016.

Ziskind, M. (2003), 'Labor conflict in the suburbs: Organizing retail in metropolitan New York, 1954–1958', *International Journal of Labor and Working-Class History*, (64), pp. 55–73.

Zundel, R. (1954), 'Conflict and co-operation among retail unions', *The Journal of Business*, 27 (4), pp. 301–311.

16
RETAIL MANAGEMENT

Martin Purvis

Introduction

All retailers, no matter where and when they traded, and on whatever basis and scale, will have had managerial decisions to make; about the location of their business, how best to obtain and manage stock, what to sell and at what price, what forms of payment to accept, how to keep costs in check and how to record receipts and expenses. Nor were such decisions simply a function of routine trading. Many retailers would have reflected more strategically on whether and how to expand their business; by selling new lines, by greater promotional activity, by employing more staff, and by investing capital in larger or additional premises. Only latterly, and chiefly in bigger businesses, have such decisions become the preserve of senior staff specifically identified as managers, working within an organisational structure which distanced them from the shop floor. At other times, as remains true for many small retailers today, the full range of managerial responsibilities has been assumed by a single proprietor, or by an owning family, still closely involved in everyday trading.

Yet, for all its importance in ensuring that goods flow efficiently from producers to consumers, retail management has rarely been subjected to sustained historical investigation. Despite Chandler's (1977, 1990) example, retailing receives short shrift in most mainstream business and management histories. Nor have calls for closer connections between studies of past and present been widely answered by researchers interested in contemporary retail management (Alexander 2016; Savitt 1989). Retail historians, meanwhile, have frequently focused on the outcomes of managers' decisions – evident in the development of new forms and formats, and the rise and fall of specific businesses – rather than exploring managerial structures and decision-making processes. Only gradually has such work begun to engage with wider arguments about the implications of management for organisational performance (Alexander 2015). Retail history is, moreover, partial in its coverage; paying disproportionate attention to individual larger businesses. Company histories and biographies of leading retailers are also inconsistent in quality. Some are rich in empirical detail; but too many are uncritical and formulaic, offering few managerial insights. Given the limited documentation of past practice, especially for smaller family-owned businesses, redressing the balance is not easy.

Yet not all is gloom. We can draw on a rich literature which, whilst often chiefly concerned with other matters, illuminates aspects of managerial practice and the evolution of management structures in retailing. As noted this literature reveals most about the workings of the large-scale retail businesses of the modern era, which frequently grew beyond the managerial capabilities of any single individual. It is thus amongst department stores and multiple retailers that we often find the clearest evidence of managerial innovation, of the complexity of change as an experimental and contested process, and of the impact of management decision-making on business performance. Much of the following discussion focuses, therefore, on retailers' responses to the challenges of managing at scale, and of co-ordinating increasingly large and spatially dispersed branch networks, during the century between 1850 and 1950.

We cannot, however, assume that major stores have always maintained the highest managerial standards, or that effective retail management has ever been confined to such operations. The demise of familiar brands since the financial crash of 2008 confirms that even substantial retailers can be undermined by inadequate, inflexible or complacent management. Equally important is that we recognise the part played in modern retailing by a multitude of smaller shopkeepers. Although often dismissed as laggards, independent retailers sometimes displayed managerial skills that rivalled their larger counterparts. Indeed, their ideas and methods arguably exerted a greater influence than is generally acknowledged upon the "revolutionary" forms of large-scale retailing that developed from the nineteenth century onwards. This chapter thus attends initially to retail management amongst independent businesses, before turning to department and chain store development. In so doing it considers not only the ways in which key aspects of retail management evolved between the eighteenth and the mid-twentieth centuries, but also why such change appeared necessary and how it was enacted. Geographically, greatest attention is paid to Western Europe and North America, but discussion of the transmission of ideas between particular national contexts will take us further afield.

Managing on a small scale – independent retailers

Small-scale retailing has generally been characterised by organisational simplicity, with managerial functions being discharged by a single owner, or owning family. Indeed, small business structures often echoed those of the family; with proprietors exercising "parental" supervision over the work of relatives, and of apprentices and other paid employees, who sometimes formed part of the retailer's household. In other respects, however, the differing levels of competence exhibited by individual shopkeepers, the variety of circumstances in which they operated and the wide range of trades involved, make it difficult to discern common managerial characteristics. Before the advent of industrialised mass production, retailers were often judged as much for their knowledge of the products which they sold, and for their skills in producing and processing their own merchandise, as they were for more abstract understanding of business organisation. Perhaps partly as a result, efforts to characterise independent retailers often imply only a limited interest in the finer points of retail management, or in the pursuit of managerial innovation.

At times and places when independent shopkeepers have been most numerous – particularly in the expanding urban settlements of nineteenth- and twentieth-century Europe and North America – only a minority made more than a marginal living. Retailing presented few entry barriers, so that small ventures were frequently started by individuals with little or no capital, education or commercial experience. Success was represented by the establishment of an enduring business, even if this entailed long working hours and the exploitation of family labour. But reports from Britain, Germany and the United States indicate that thousands of shopkeepers failed every year; defeated not just by growing competition, but also by their own flawed understanding of purchasing, stock control, account keeping and credit management (Douglas 1935; Strasser 1989). Such naivety was rarer amongst more substantial independent retailers. But the competent management of routine business which apparently characterised this latter group has often been taken as confirmation of the innate conservatism of established family firms. The proprietors of such businesses – including the Banbury shopkeepers studied by Stacey (1960) – are portrayed as risk averse, disdainful of modern business methods, unwilling to countenance expansion that would erode their personal proprietorial control and ultimately more concerned with preserving their social status than with maximising profits.

Whilst claims about the limitations of shopkeepers' managerial and entrepreneurial abilities are often justified, they cannot be taken as a judgement upon all independent retailers (Phillips and Alexander 2005; Spellman 2016). A minority of individuals – blessed with greater ability, ambition and good fortune than their neighbours – created substantial businesses. Indeed, the origins of many department and chain stores can be traced to a single modest shop. Nor was independent retailers' ability to confound predictions of their demise entirely a product of inertia, or of the legal protection afforded by some governments. Successful shopkeepers may have exhibited little formal understanding of managerial principles, but experience and knowledge of the community which they served provided invaluable insights into which items their customers would demand most frequently, the prices they could afford to pay, how best to present goods and the creditworthiness of potential purchasers (de Grazia 2005; Spiekermann 2006). Such knowledge, moreover, was applied not just to maintaining a store's existing business, but also to developing new lines and services, even if only on a modest scale. These are aspects of retailing about which we know frustratingly little, largely because of the lack of documentary evidence. Recent research has, however, drawn on sources including diaries, account books, advertising and trade publications to reveal something of shopkeepers' practices in specific contexts. As the following sections discuss, such work confirms the managerial sophistication of some independent retailers; both in pioneering ways of working that were subsequently more fully developed by others, and in adapting the methods of larger businesses for their own purposes.

Foreshadowing retail revolution

Our knowledge of retailers' methods in eighteenth- and early nineteenth-century England chiefly reflects the practices of relatively prosperous traders selling higher-order goods in major urban centres. These individuals doubtless exhibited a degree of managerial ability and a capacity for innovation that were rare amongst contemporaries. But some practices first identified amongst metropolitan traders have also been detected in humbler provincial contexts (Stobart and Hann 2004; Walsh 1995). Even if they were atypical these progressive retailers provide valuable evidence of the emergence of recognisably modern commercial practice (Walsh 1999). Taking advantage of the decay of legal and customary constraints upon retailing, and spurred on by an associated increase in competition, many displayed 'enterprise and adaptability' both in day-to-day business and in expanding their trading activities (Cox 2000, p. 227).

Such enterprise is evident in the unusually full surviving records of provincial shopkeepers William Stout of Lancaster and Abraham Dent of Kirkby Stephen in Westmorland; both of whom developed complex and geographically extensive networks of suppliers so as to secure a wide range of goods at advantageous prices (Stobart 2012). Contacts were also cultivated as sources of intelligence about changing fashions, new goods and the wider state of trade. Progressive retailers, particularly in trades such as drapery and footwear, were equally active in marketing their wares to potential purchasers; investing in shop fittings and lighting, and developing window displays (Riello 2006; Walsh 1995). Shopkeepers also attended to the internal organisation of their stores; as a direct contribution to increased operational efficiency and as a means of conveying their managerial skills to customers. The creation of structured systems for the storage and display of goods allowed retailers to demonstrate the range of their stock, minimise losses caused by damage or contamination, and improve customer service by ensuring that items could be readily located. Indeed, some larger eighteenth-century businesses found it advantageous to organise their premises as a series of separate areas dealing with particular categories of goods, each with their own specialist staff. Such traders foreshadowed the organisational practices of later department stores in other ways. Fixed prices and cash-only sales speeded up transactions and reduced the need for close proprietorial supervision. It thus became easier to delegate routine transactions to employees and apprentices, whether within a single store, or – as was true of emergent footwear chains trading in Regency London and provincial centres including Brighton, Bath, Norwich and Liverpool – in branch outlets (Riello 2006).

Little of this would have been possible without careful bookkeeping and attention to financial management; whether in respect of supplier payments, customer credit or receipts for goods sold. Standards in such matters must have varied enormously. But mathematics and basic accountancy formed part of the education received by more substantial English tradesmen from at least the sixteenth century onwards. Indeed, it was in this field that some of the earliest commercial textbooks were produced to disseminate good practice, including double-entry bookkeeping. Business success was thus, in part, a product of what later centuries would formalise as management training, communicated between the generations in trading families, between masters and apprentices, but also through instruction manuals. The most famous of these books, Daniel Defoe's *The Complete English Tradesman*, with its comments on shop location and design, the importance of civility to customers, managing credit and bookkeeping, was thus a prototype for many retail management textbooks (Cox 2000; Stobart 2012).

Rising to the competitive challenge

If eighteenth-century shopkeepers pioneered modern retail methods, a focus on the later nineteenth and early twentieth centuries reveals independent retailers' ability to respond positively to challenging circumstances. Efforts to ensure their own survival in competitive markets led shopkeepers to explore ways to increase operational efficiency, boost sales and reduce costs. In some contexts, moreover, shopkeepers abandoned their traditional individualism to cooperate with other retailers – locally and nationally – and with manufacturers and suppliers. Independent retailers were potentially enthusiastic adopters of new technologies, provided that they appeared relevant and affordable. Automatic cash registers, produced in the United States from the 1880s onwards, were one such technology, promising an immediate check on the competence and honesty of sales staff, and greater ease and accuracy in account keeping. Indeed, it was independent shopkeepers, rather than large-scale retailers, who made greatest initial use of cash registers and whose experience contributed to the technology's refinement (Spellman 2016). At the same time, in both Europe and the United States, the trade press and technical manuals offered shopkeepers practical advice about other ways to boost their business, including innovations in advertising and display, modernisation of their premises and reorganisation of store layouts (Alexander et al. 1999; Cochoy 2010).

Independent traders were thus exposed to arguments for a rational approach to retailing which paralleled developments, explored below, in department and chain store management. But documentary limitations frustrate efforts to gauge the extent to which shopkeepers' outlook and methods changed in practice. Particular proposals – including self-service, which increasingly featured in advice to American grocers during the mid-twentieth century (Cochoy 2016; Deutsch 2010) – represented too decisive a break with tradition for some retailers to countenance. Nor did those who saw the commercial logic of new methods always possess the financial and organisational means to implement them. Even relatively modest changes probably spread slowly and selectively, at least initially. Work on the take-up of cash registers, using manufacturers' sales records, confirms that early adopters were a tiny minority of all shopkeepers in the United States (Spellman 2016). Aggressive marketing, especially by the National Cash Register Company, extended demand to Western Europe, Latin America, Australia, New Zealand, South Africa and Japan by the 1900s. But annual sales in specific national contexts rarely numbered more than a few hundred (Haberstroh 2013). Germany proved a receptive market; but even here barely half of all retail establishment had a cash register by the 1920s. Indeed, only a quarter of German retailers reportedly kept regular accounts; a situation mirrored in Britain and the United States (de Grazia 2005; Douglas 1935; Tedlow 1990).

Technical and managerial innovation by individual shopkeepers was, however, reinforced by strategic alliances with other retailers, wholesalers and manufacturers. Initially such operations were often defensive, aiming to kerb competition and price cutting. But joint initiatives developed in ways that contributed positively to retail modernisation. In interwar Britain some local trade associations collaborated with Art Schools and Technical Colleges to provide instruction in window dressing and display; others coordinated joint advertising and promotional initiatives. The latter included shopping festivals, intended not just as a stimulus to trade, but also as an encouragement to shopkeepers to raise service standards and to invest in modernising their premises. Efforts to replicate the vertical integration and scale economies achieved by larger retailers, through joint purchasing of stock and requisites such as wrapping paper did not, however, flourish in Britain. By contrast Germany, with its traditional regard for the *Mittelstand*, proved fertile territory for co-operative purchasing amongst independent retailers. Local ventures established during the late nineteenth century subsequently combined to create national associations. Two of the largest such co-operatives, Edeka (founded in 1907) and Rewe (established in 1926) were still substantial forces in German grocery retailing when converted into corporate entities in the 1980s (Wortmann 2004). Retailer purchasing co-operatives also took root in the United States from the 1880s onwards, particularly in the drug and grocery trades.

Alternative joint-buying initiatives were promoted by wholesalers keen to protect their own sales. In their most developed form these operations created voluntary symbol groups which involved independent shopkeepers in identifying with a common brand. The implications of membership for retail management extended beyond the central contractual relationship between retailer and supplier. Shopkeepers surrendered some of their independence as they were expected not only to make a minimum weekly stock purchase, but also to uphold common service standards and to display group signage. In some instances members were required to purchase equipment supplied by the group, or to submit trading figures in a prescribed fashion. In return, however, they gained access to centrally provided services, including advertising and publicity material, insurance, managerial training and advice about business modernisation. The influence of voluntary symbol groups was greatest in the United States, where operations such as Royal Blue Stores and the Independent Grocers Alliance emerged in the 1920s; and in parts of continental Europe, particularly the Netherlands, where groups including SPAR expanded rapidly from the 1930s (Deutsch 2010; Jefferys and Knee 1962). By contrast, such organisations did not take off in Britain until the 1950s. They were eclipsed little more than a decade later by the rise of the supermarket, and the spread of cash and carry wholesaling as a more flexible means of reducing independent retailers' costs (Fulop 1962). However, some of the functions which voluntary groups provided elsewhere, in particular the modernisation of publicity and display, and a willingness to supply small retailers at competitive prices, were partially fulfilled by major manufacturers.

Managing on a large scale – department stores

If growing competition created managerial challenges for independent shopkeepers, the development of large-scale retailing produced its own distinctive difficulties. The department stores which emerged in nineteenth-century Europe and North America, and subsequently spread elsewhere, were retail businesses on a scale that had few precedents. Their appeal reflected, in large part, the diversity of goods sold at affordable prices. Commercial success therefore required contacts with multiple suppliers; the search for volume at competitive prices often leading to direct dealing with producers. The department store's business model also demanded fast stock turnover. Operational systems had thus to be capable of handling a large volume of business; and of working effectively at speed when dealing with the transfer of physical goods, and associated flows of orders, invoices and payments. Store premises, too, were substantial; encompassing not only spaces for selling, but also for the production, inspection, pricing and storage of goods, for mail-order trading, for financial and administrative functions and for staff facilities, sometimes including residential accommodation (Iarocci 2014; Whitaker 2011). Such businesses became major employers. By the early 1920s, Macy's of New York had 12,000 permanent employees, whilst Bresee's, a small-town store in upstate New York, had nearly 200 on its payroll (Graham 2000; Howard 2008). This increasing scale and complexity of operations prompted managerial innovation.

In practice the growth of individual businesses was often incremental. Many major stores had modest origins; as wholesale dealers which started selling on a retail basis, or as drapers which added lines in jewellery, fancy goods and furniture. Expansion, moreover, often reflected an opportunistic search for new business, rather than pursuit of a grand strategy (Miller 1981). Managerial developments tended to have a similarly experimental and evolutionary character. At times stores drew inspiration from other large organisations, including railways and the military. But there were also important continuities with the managerial ethos of the family firm, not least in the importance of store founders and their heirs as the public face of the business – projecting an image variously as commercial visionary, showman and paternalist – and as the ultimate, even dictatorial, authority sanctioning all key decisions (Belisle 2011; Miller 1981). In some smaller department stores, such as Bresee's in upstate New York and Power's of Montana, individual proprietors retained direct control over routine operations, as well as strategic decision-making (Klassen 1992; Howard 2008). But expansion usually required the recruitment of additional managerial expertise, at senior levels and throughout the store. Responsibilities within this hierarchy were defined by the individual's place in an increasingly formal division of stores into sub-units or departments, each with their own management team.

The origins of the departmental model are unclear and, as previously noted, probably predate the department store per se. The model was, however, applied at least as early as the 1840s by growing stores such as A.T. Stewart of New York, creating an organisational structure that arguably would 'have looked efficient even by modern standards' (Resseguie 1965, p. 314). Some departments dealt with functions, including financial record-keeping and store maintenance, which served the business as a whole. But at Stewarts, as elsewhere, the operation's core was constituted by a series of merchandising departments specialising in particular lines of goods. Each was headed by a buyer, responsible not only for sourcing goods from suppliers, but also for setting retail prices and all aspects of selling. Buyers' powers did not usually extend to staff recruitment, which was handled centrally by the store superintendent; but they were frequently influential in determining the staffing levels and personnel of their own departments (Benson 1986). Considerable authority was thus conferred on buyers; reflecting a belief that business success was dependent on skilled buying of fashionable and keenly priced goods by individuals with specialist knowledge of their own particular lines of trade. Selling, by comparison, was regarded as a secondary function.

The managerial model which came to be associated with the late-nineteenth-century department store was something of a hybrid in terms of the relationships which it fostered. As stores expanded they became bureaucratic and impersonal workplaces. Operational efficiency was seen to require a clear, if increasingly complex, division of labour. Alongside sales staff, stores employed a growing body of other workers, including window dressers, stock controllers, cashiers, bookkeepers, seamstresses, packers, cleaners, maintenance engineers and delivery drivers. Effort was invested in standardising and documenting the tasks that each would perform. Indeed, workers were increasingly judged on the basis of their conformity with these norms, which often extended to matters of personal appearance and morality. Application and efficiency, especially amongst sales staff, were encouraged by linking reward to performance. Commission on sales was a necessary supplement to low basic pay, and longer-term loyalty was fostered by systems of internal promotion to supervisory and managerial positions. By contrast, even trivial misdemeanours – including, at Macy's of New York, unauthorised sitting and talking – could prompt instant dismissal. This emphasis on discipline and conformity was, however, tempered by efforts to refashion the personal bonds between employer and employee which characterised smaller family firms. Institutionalised paternalism – evident in subsidised meals, health, educational and leisure programmes, staff benevolent funds and celebratory social events – encouraged staff to identify themselves as part of an extended family constituted by the store and its owners (Benson 1986; Miller 1981).

Stores were also structural hybrids, combining centralised direction of functions including personnel management and financial accounting with significant autonomy for individual merchandising departments. It was a model which initially secured success, but which contained the seeds of later tensions. The identification of buyers as temperamental and authoritarian figures is a recurring theme in writings about department stores. Inter-departmental relations, moreover, were often unhealthily competitive, with buyers prioritising the interests of their own fiefdom over those of the wider store (Benson 1986). The operation of stores as a fractious collection of quasi-autonomous units was widely tolerated on both sides of the Atlantic – including Macy's of New York and Bon Marché of Paris – whilst sales and profits continued to grow. Some stores, indeed, leased out particular departments to other specialist retailers (Perkins and Freedman 1999). It was thus understood that units with store-wide functions were intended chiefly to relieve buyers of burdensome distractions, rather than to constrain their activities. Even financial accounting had a relatively lowly status in most nineteenth-century department stores as an exercise in routine record keeping.

Proprietors and senior managers, keen to ensure that popular merchandise was always available, but without accumulating costly stock surpluses, attempted some control over buyers. This usually entailed setting limits to individual buyer's spending or, in the case of John Wanamaker of Philadelphia, restricting external advertising to goods deemed worthy of carrying the store's name (Perkins and Freedman 1999). Despite internal opposition, the distance between some American stores and metropolitan suppliers also encouraged them to depute buying duties to resident agents in New York and Chicago. But proprietors generally lacked both the means and inclination to subject buyers' performance to closer scrutiny. Store-wide costs were frequently allocated to merchandise departments in proportion to their sales, without regard to their specific origins. Stock-taking, meanwhile, was a laborious and infrequent process which did little to inform future planning, or to highlight poor purchasing by buyers (Walsh and Jeacle 2003). This managerial ethos changed only slowly even in stores which, like Bon Marché of Paris, were by the 1880s compiling statistics for sales and other indicators of departmental performance (Miller

1981). Senior figures perhaps understood the potential managerial value of such information, but few felt the need for greater intervention.

Experiments in "scientific" management

Attitudes would, however, change later in the nineteenth century as major stores struggled to sustain their growth. Initially this encouraged greater attention to selling; prompting innovation such as the bargain basement, popularised by Filene's of Boston, and a modest redistribution of authority from departmental buyers to the store superintendent responsible for staffing. Often the superintendent acquired an enhanced status as the head of a newly constituted team of floorwalkers who supervised the daily work of departmental sales staff. Intended to reinforce customer service standards, such developments risked creating organisational confusion. Lines of authority were blurred as sales staff appeared answerable to two superiors, often falling foul of antagonism between buyers and floorwalkers. More substantial reforms were thus required to enable department stores to respond to increased retail competition, the effects of suburbanisation and transport improvements and wider economic volatility.

As governments and manufacturing industry were drawn to the writings of Frederick W. Taylor and other advocates of workplace planning and rationalisation, so leading retailers also came to see a solution to their own difficulties in "scientific" management (Jacobs 2007). Such thinking was not entirely new; department stores were early adopters of technological innovations – including telephones, escalators and pneumatic cash transfer systems – which promised to increase the speed and efficiency of particular tasks. Moreover, some individual businesses had previously used sales and stock holding records to inform purchasing decisions. Marshall Field's wholesaling division in Chicago began working in this way in the 1870s, and its methods perhaps spread to its customer stores in smaller American cities (Twyman 1954). Former Marshall Field employee Gordon Selfridge implemented a similar system when establishing his own London store in 1909, in turn influencing Harrods and other British retailers (Scott and Walker 2012). In Germany, meanwhile, Salman Schocken of Kaufhaus Schocken independently devised an organisational structure which employed a central statistical office to monitor income and expenditure, and to support managerial decision-making (Lerner 2015). Only gradually, however, did such experiments come to be accepted as normal working practice. Research into the rationalisation of retail management was published at least as early as the 1900s. But even in the United States, where such thinking originated, change in retail practice became widespread only during the interwar years (Walsh and Jeacle 2003). Thus, Graham (2000, p. 285) identifies Lillian Gilbreth's work with Macy's between 1925 and 1928 as the first close collaboration between a store and a 'bona fide scientific management consultant'. Such initiatives were encouraged by the depression of the early 1920s; declining retail profits being widely, if often unfairly, attributed to poor purchasing by departmental buyers. Efforts to eliminate waste and promote efficiency thus assumed an increasing importance.

Much of Gilbreth's work with Macy's focused on efforts to increase the economy with which individual workers executed routine tasks. Macy's own staff subsequently applied similar principles to store planning; recording, for example, customer movement patterns to identify optimum locations for particular sales departments, lifts and elevators. In Paris, meanwhile, Galeries Lafayette first engaged with scientific management in an effort to rationalise the operations of an associated clothing plant (Champsaur and Cailluet 2010). The wider application of "science" to retailing, however, had particular implications for the role and status of departmental buyers. Reliance on their individual judgement about stock gave way to a conviction that purchasing must be informed by systematic analyses of past sales and research into consumers' tastes and preferences. Only in this way, advocates of scientific management claimed, could retailers ensure that their stores would always be full of the goods which their customers wanted to buy, in exactly the right mixture of styles, sizes and colours. Informed purchasing and developments such as the model stock plan – promoted by Boston store proprietor Edward Filene as a means to streamline stocks by focusing on the fastest selling and most profitable items – promised not only to maximise sales, but also to reduce costs by making it easier to order goods in bulk, minimising the capital locked up in accumulated stock, and reducing the need to discount slow-selling merchandise (Savitt 1999).

Crucially, this new perspective identified the store as a whole as the primary operational unit. Evolving ideas about managerial structures were captured in a series of interwar publications. In particular, the ideas of Paul Mazur (1927) – an American retailer turned banker and consultant – became a model for department store organisation. Although stores still appeared to their customers as a series of product-based departments, Mazur outlined a managerial structure which grouped activity across the entire operation into four functional divisions: merchandising (buying and selling goods); communications (advertising, display, promotional activities); store management (personnel, stock storage and inventory control, customer deliveries, maintenance); and a controlling division responsible for financial accounting (see Figure 16.1). The size and importance of their workforce subsequently led many stores to identify personnel management as a separate division. But this refinement does not alter the main implication of Mazur's work; authority would henceforth be wielded by those individuals who headed the major store-wide divisions.

Mazur's model promised greater rationality in internal organisation, reducing costs, eliminating duplication, and placing key functions under the supervision of senior specialists. In practice it did not always enable stores fully to achieve these goals; tensions often remained between buying and selling staff within newly established merchandising departments (Wood 2011). But the reformed structure addressed the primary concerns of proprietors and senior managers. Buyers with product expertise and supplier contacts remained important figures, but increasingly they worked to execute store-wide purchasing strategies defined by merchandise managers. Central control of staff recruitment, training and retention was also confirmed. Equally significant was the emphasis placed on the collection and analysis of financial information about all aspects of store operations; as a means of reviewing current performance and to inform future planning. Employees were increasingly judged on the extent of their contribution to growing store revenues, or reducing operational costs. Regular sales and profits reviews also became a vital means of maintaining the discipline which stores sought to impose on buyers. New accounting techniques were thus important managerial tools. In particular, the retail price method of inventory control allowed a constant check to be kept on stock levels, and the ready identification of losses due to theft or the discounting of surplus stock (Savitt 1999; Walsh and Jeacle 2003). The interwar years thus saw the elevation of the financial controller, or company accountant, to a prominent role in store management.

Scientific management did not claim to increase sales and profits only by enabling stores to make informed stocking decisions. A similar logic was applied to the allocation of store staff and floor space, aiming to focus resources on the fastest selling and most profitable merchandise. In parallel, the emergent science of psychology promised greater understanding of what motivated customers to buy and how sales staff could encourage purchasing (Chessel 1999). Salesmanship training therefore sought not only to improve product knowledge and service standards, but also to teach staff to recognise supposed customer types, each of which required handling in particular ways to maximise sales. Engagement with psychology extended to staff recruitment with the aim of identifying individuals with the greatest aptitude for particular tasks. This was often allied to wider efforts to promote a more positive labour regime, emphasising staff retention and

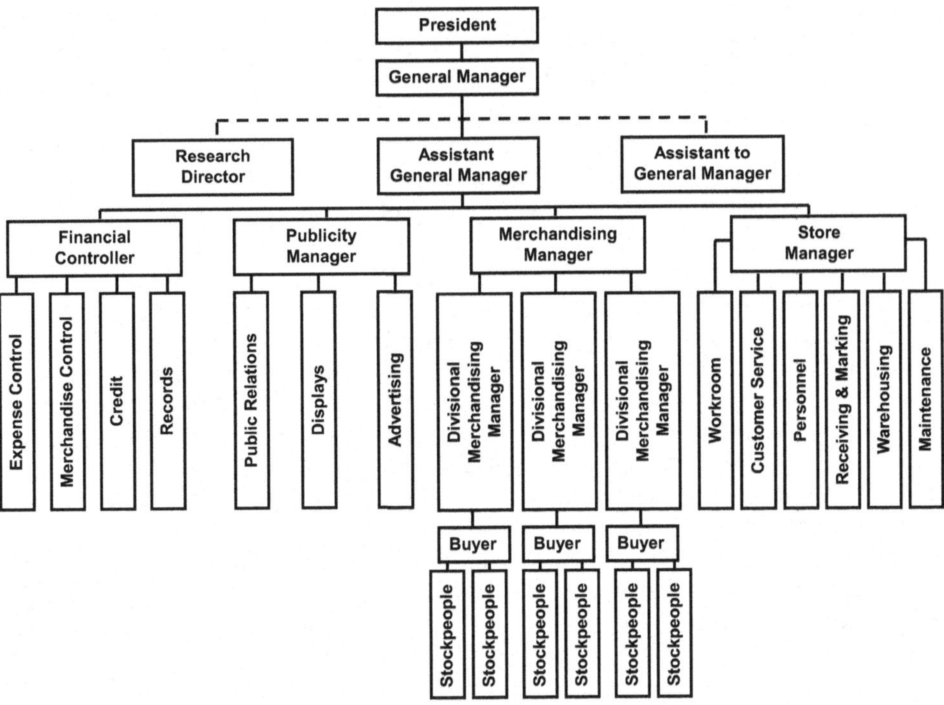

Figure 16.1 Mazur's Organisational Plan for Department Store Management

Source: Adapted from P. Mazur, *Principles of Organisation Applied to Modern Retailing*. New York NY: Harper, 1927.

welfare. Analyses of work routines thus promised not just efficiency, but also an improved working environment, greater job satisfaction and reduced staff fatigue (Graham 2000). In parallel, training and internal communications grew in importance as a means of encouraging identification with the business. Stores established staff magazine; including Filene's of Boston (*The Echo*), individual branches of the Hudson's Bay Company (*The Bay Builder, The Bayonet and The Beaver*) and Brown, Muff of Bradford (*The Beam*) (Miller 2006). Scientific management thus reinforced the logic of established forms of institutionalised paternalism, whilst rendering them more systematic (Miller 1981). Additional resources were invested in health care, pensions, sick pay, sports and social facilities and paid holidays; whilst in the 1900s Shepard's of Providence and Filene's of Boston were amongst the earliest stores to appoint managerial staff with specific welfare responsibilities. A minority of businesses, including John Lewis of London, went further by instituting employee profit-sharing (Cox 2010). But pay scales generally became more regular, promotion processes more transparent and discipline less arbitrary (Belisle 2007; Benson 1986).

From America to the world

Retailing's embrace of scientific management was initially an American phenomenon, pioneered by stores including Macy's of New York and Filene's of Boston. Senior business figures not only refined their own operations, but also encouraged efforts to identify and disseminate managerial best practice. Major stores sponsored the creation of departments of commerce and business as centres for research and teaching at American universities, including Harvard and

New York (Leach 1993). Edward Filene also helped to create groupings amongst stores themselves, including the National Retail Dry Goods Association (founded in 1911) and the Retail Research Association (dating from 1917), aiming to foster interest in scientific management and to collect data to inform continuing investigation.

Recent research has helped to trace the spread of efforts to promote scientific management from North America to Europe, Japan, Australia and New Zealand (de Grazia 2005; Roberts 2003). Although little was published elsewhere during the interwar decades, American writings on "scientific" retailing were read increasingly widely. A German translation of Mazur's work on store management was, for example, published in 1928. Training manuals and other documents created by stores themselves also circulated internationally; the collection amassed by the personnel manager of the David Jones store of Sydney, Australia included material from the United States, Canada and Britain (Miller 2006). At the same time leading department stores in other national contexts began to strengthen their own institutional links. British stores, for example, established the Retail Distributors Association in 1920. By the early 1930s the Association was co-operating with the London School of Economics to produce an annual survey of store operating costs similar to the pioneering analysis undertaken by the Harvard Bureau of Business Research (Scott and Walker 2012).

Evidently, too, the interwar years saw a growth in direct international exchanges between leading industry figures. Store owners and senior managers from Europe, Japan, Australia, New Zealand and elsewhere visited the United States to study developments firsthand (Champsaur and Cailluet 2010; Maeda 1998; Roberts 2003). Trans-Atlantic links, along with British and Swedish influences, were also important in the development of France's first retail training school, under the aegis of the Paris Chamber of Commerce (Chessel 1999). Edward Filene, meanwhile, was an ardent internationalist; in politics as well as commerce. He visited Europe frequently, developing extensive personal and professional links with department store owners; and championing institutions such as the International Chamber of Commerce. In the late 1920s, Filene's own philanthropic foundation supported Emile Bernheim, of *L'Innovation* department store in Brussels, in his efforts to establish what would become the International Association of Department Stores (IADS). Unlike many international projects the IADS was not wrecked by the deteriorating economic and political climate. Meetings and exchanges of statistical information were supplemented by a system of critical store visits which aimed to provide member firms with comprehensive advice about potential operational improvements (Pasdermadjian 1950).

Yet whilst the general pattern of contacts is relatively well-known, understanding of the spread of particular ideas and innovations remains partial. Few of the individuals or organisations involved in early efforts to render retail management scientific have been the focus of sustained or recent research. Pasdermadijan's (1950) history of the IADS is dated and reveals more about the principles of scientific management than it does about the Association's impact on store management. In Britain work using data collected by the Retail Distributors Association has shed new light on the economics of department store trading, challenging claims that stores failed to match the efficiency gains made elsewhere (Scott and Walker 2012). But in most cases we still know little about how such gains were achieved, the specific influences which inspired them, or the degree to which it was necessary to adapt internationally circulating ideas to reflect specific local circumstances.

There are, however, good reasons to think that change during the interwar years was neither swift nor universal. Whilst IADS membership was multinational – including representatives from France, Belgium, the Netherlands, Britain, Sweden, Denmark, Germany, Italy and Spain – it never exceeded ten stores. The Association's impact was, therefore, limited beyond a self-selecting retail elite (Champsaur and Cailluet 2010; de Grazia 2005). Stores, moreover, were not equally willing to share commercially sensitive information through such organisations. Communication constraints may thus partly explain why techniques such as the retail price method of inventory control were not always implemented effectively when first introduced into new national contexts (Jeacle and Walsh 2008). Even in the United States, smaller stores such as Bresee's in New York State changed their managerial structures and practices only slowly; not necessarily because senior staff were unaware of new thinking, but because they questioned its relevance for their own business (Howard 2008). Indeed, such a stance was arguably logical, given evidence of the problems created for the Hudson's Bay Company in Canada when scientific management principles were applied without regard for local market conditions (Monod 1986). Restructuring of the managerial hierarchy was also a source of tensions within retail businesses. Store controllers' assertion of their new authority was sometimes accompanied by attacks on the competence and honesty of departmental buyers. Buyers, in turn, resented their subordination, so that companies' efforts to implement new accounting and stock control systems could turn into long-running battles (Benson 1986; Jeacle and Walsh 2008).

Labour and gender historians also offer an important critical appraisal of the motivations for, and impacts of, new approaches to personnel management. Such work challenges accounts of welfarism as evidence of employer benevolence that appear in company histories. Instead a picture emerges which emphasises managerial self-interest; the desire to create a more docile and efficient workforce, to deflect external criticism of previous labour practices and the associated threat of state regulation, and to obstruct the spread of trade unionism. Welfare policies may also have exacerbated gender inequalities. This was not just because a predominantly male management became a paternalistic provider of benefits to a dependent and increasingly female workforce. Male and female employees were often treated differently, with women being exposed to a welfare regime which was arguably infantilising in stressing their need for protection (Belisle 2007). Whilst recreation and training for men focused on career development, provision for women placed greater emphasis on promoting middle-class notions of social respectability and their future roles as wives and mothers. This is not, however, to imply uncritical acceptance of these values by employees, despite their enthusiasm for the associated benefits. Sometimes, as was true of Australian stores studied by Reekie (1987), workers asserted their own control over provision such as convalescent funds. More generally, staff magazines were used to express employees' frustration about the regulation of their working lives. Workers also challenged managerial expectations about conduct by establishing their own collective standards. Although individual studies disagree about the extent of such behaviour, practices such as deliberate inattention to customers and theft of goods from the store sometimes assumed significance as forms of resistance to managerial control (Belisle 2007; Benson 1986).

Managing at a distance – multiple retailing

Early twentieth-century interest in the application of "science" to retail management was not confined to department stores. Leading multiple retailers were equally enthusiastic advocates of intelligent purchasing, rigorous stock control, planned allocation of store space and staff, cost monitoring, and innovations in personnel management (Purvis 2015). Again, ideas pioneered in the United States found their way to Europe and elsewhere. In part this reflected the overseas expansion of American retail capital; Woolworth's, for example, exported its five-and-dime store model to Britain (from 1909) and Germany (from 1927) (Godley 2003). A decade under American ownership also prompted improvements in stock control and the supervision of local store managers at Boots, Britain's largest retail chemist (Chapman 1974). But European retailers were increasingly active in emulating the formats and managerial methods of popular American stores. This was evident in the interwar transformation of Marks and Spencer from an ailing former penny bazaar into a successful variety store chain. But the fixed-price format was also taken up more widely across Europe, not least by existing department stores in Germany, France, Belgium and Italy, concerned that they would otherwise be excluded from emerging mass markets (Furlough 1993). A similar story can be told about the later trans-Atlantic journey of self-service retailing in the grocery trade, and its managerial implications both at company level and in the individual store (Schröter 2008; Shaw et al. 2004).

Growth and the logic of centralisation

All manifestations of multiple retailing, however, posed distinctive managerial challenges as businesses considered how best to coordinate the operation of growing, and increasingly geographically dispersed, branch networks. The individual department stores already discussed were, of course, sometimes part of retail chains, created by mergers or the expansion of city-centre stores into secondary shopping districts. But these were often loose alliances, each outlet retaining its own independence. Multiple retailing, by contrast, usually involves significant managerial centralisation; with decisions about the location, funding and design of stores, operating practices, retail pricing, advertising and promotion, financial accounting and, especially, stock acquisition, being taken at the company's headquarters (Alexander 1997; Tedlow 1990). Indeed, centralisation is frequently seen as vital to multiple retailing's success, given its role in creating a coherent operation with a strong brand identity; in fostering relative organisational simplicity based on procedures common to all stores; and in securing economies of scale and scope, not just in sourcing stock, but also in business administration and store construction (Perkins and Freedman 1999).

In practice, however, the logic of centralisation was tempered by other considerations. Too great a degree of uniformity risked demoralising staff and alienating customers by creating stores which appeared impersonal, and insensitive to consumers' varying tastes and financial means. Growth might, moreover, create a business so large and complex that it could not be directed effectively by a single owner, or central management team. In the early 1900s, Jesse Boot could still claim personal knowledge of branches throughout his 300-strong chain of chemist's shops, located in some 150 English towns. But administrative lapses increased over the following decade as Boot aged, whilst store numbers increased by 50% (Chapman 1974). The managerial challenge presented by multiple retailing varied with the commercial and geographical scale of specific businesses. Multiples operating on a local or regional basis, and selling a limited range of basic goods, might be dealing with an essentially homogeneous market that could be served by centrally controlled clone stores. The same was less likely to be true of businesses selling individually more expensive items or fashion goods, and of retailers who aspired to trade nationally or internationally. But, large or small, most multiples faced questions about the distribution of decision-making power between company headquarters, individual branches and any intermediate layers of management. The difficulty which companies experienced in determining the most appropriate managerial balance between these various levels is an important theme in Chandler's (1977, 1990) work on corporate structures. Subsequent research, although uneven in its coverage, has explored the ways in which businesses addressed these issues, and the impact of particular geographical contexts, market conditions, company histories and individual personalities on their decision-making.

The multiple retailers which emerged in Western Europe and North America in the late nineteenth century varied in their origins. Some, some including the British footwear chain

Stead and Simpson, were established by consumer goods producers as outlets for their products, and were thus initially managed as divisions of what were essentially manufacturing companies. Others grew out of earlier franchising systems, as producers, including the Singer Sewing Machine Company, sought greater control over retail sales. Many consumer co-operatives also represented a form of multiple retailing, distinctive both in the collective ownership of the business by its customers and the consequent potential for conflict over a society's direction between paid managers and elected representatives of the consumer members (Wilson et al. 2013). Most multiple retailers, however, traced their origins back to a single store owned by the company's founding family.

Initial branch development was often limited, sporadic and localised. Family members and trusted assistants were installed as managers of the new stores, working under close proprietorial supervision (Raucher 1991). The American retailer J.C. Penney was distinctive in adopting a model of co-ownership in which new store managers became partners in the business, helping to fund expansion in return for a share of the profits. But here, too, new men were accepted only at the personal discretion of Penney and his lieutenant E.C. Sams (Curry 1993). Success, however, encouraged Penney's to attempt large-scale expansion. Such growth required outside investment, whilst also making it difficult for any individual to maintain direct control over the entire branch network. It was at this point, therefore, that many family businesses were formally incorporated. For Penney's, which made the move in 1913, this entailed the reconstitution of a loosely articulated series of overlapping partnerships into a single corporation. At the same time proprietors drew on the experience of family members and other allies to develop a more substantial and organised company head office (Kruger 2012; Bookbinder 1993 explores a similar phase in Marks and Spencer's development). Such offices would become populated by specialist staff with expertise in areas including buying, product development and testing, transport and logistics, advertising and display, property acquisition and finance. With store-level management no longer in the hands of the proprietor's close confidents, multiple retailers also invested effort in standardising branch operations. Store managers and their staff were thus expected to abide by systems of rules and regulations akin to those which governed department store operations (Raucher 1991).

The task of ensuring that individual branches maintained expected service and performance standards was frequently devolved to a new group of experienced staff who functioned as intermediaries between company headquarters and local stores. These inspectors or superintendents usually oversaw territorially defined districts, paying regular visits to the stores under their supervision. As well as monitoring the conduct of routine business and advising managers about store improvements, inspectors also communicated orders and information from head office throughout the branch network, and ensured the return flow of trading reports. At best this was a recipe for decisive, if somewhat dictatorial, management, fostering consistent standards and driving continued expansion. But, as the following section details, companies suffered as their commercial development exposed the limitations of established operating practices and managerial structures.

Searching for new structures

By the interwar years some multiple chains, particularly in the United States, had become too large and geographically dispersed to be managed effectively from a single head office. Rather than countenance unauthorised operational variations by individual store managers, companies opted for planned decentralisation. The Great Atlantic and Pacific Tea Company (A&P), which by the mid-1920s operated over 14,000 grocery stores across the United States, was amongst the first to review its structure. From 1925, greater managerial responsibility was devolved to six operating divisions, each accountable for around 2,500 stores, and charged with ensuring that day-to-day trading was tailored to local market conditions. Yet the internal distribution of power remained strongly in favour of a head office dominated by A&P's owners, the Hartford brothers. Divisional managers were expected to uphold company policy on stocking, pricing and advertising, and to defer to head office in matters including the establishment or improvement of stores. The consequent mismatch between the distribution of responsibility and power would become a focus of discontent within the company (Walsh 1986).

Sears Roebuck, too, experienced protracted managerial uncertainty during the interwar years (Chandler 1990). The company's concentration of buying and all other major management functions in Chicago – reflecting its origins as a mail-order retailer – proved increasingly problematic during the later 1920s as Sears reacted to competition by establishing a national chain of over 300 stores selling furniture, electrical appliances and other consumer durables. This development strained the capacity of the company's existing systems. But it also raised questions which the central management team was ill-equipped to answer; about branch location, manager recruitment and the selection of goods to reflect local demand. Efforts to resolve these difficulties led to extended experimentation with alternative management structures. Decentralisation during the early 1930s proved abortive as ambiguity regarding the respective powers of the company's financial, merchandise and operational managers in Chicago and new tiers of regional management responsible for the branch network created conflict and duplication of effort. A brief return to centralisation was followed by an attempt to devolve much greater responsibility to individual store managers. It was not, therefore, until the 1940s that Sears implemented an enduring solution which saw full multi-functional authority transferred to five new territorial divisions. Under this devolved model the centre played a largely advisory and strategic role; decisions about store development and operation, including inventory, sales promotion, financial management, personnel, and maintenance were taken at territorial level. The structure preserved the ultimate logic of multiple retailing as all stock was still ordered through the merchandise department in Chicago. However, territorial and store managers gained the freedom to devise stocking plans and pricing strategies that were appropriate for their particular markets.

The example of Sears Roebuck reveals the difficulties which businesses faced in responding to managerial challenges unmatched in the previous experience of most retail executives. Indeed, Chandler (1990) advances the wider claim that companies tend to make significant changes in managerial structures only when forced to do so by serious threats to their development strategy. Chandler's study also highlights the role of specific individuals in promoting, or obstructing, change. In particular, he identifies the importance of Sears' long-serving President, Robert E. Wood, as the originator of the new retail strategy, but also as someone whose tendency to value the personal abilities of individual managers over the development of systematic management structures complicated the company's search for a solution to its problems. The greater degree of centralisation maintained throughout this period by Sears's leading competitor, Montgomery Ward, can similarly be linked to the autocratic tendencies of its CEO, Sewall Avery.

Other examples confirm that there was no singular solution to the challenge of managing at a distance. As Woolworth's developed its British operations from 1909 onwards it retained the divisional structure which characterised its American parent, with district offices in Liverpool, Birmingham and London (Seaton 2009). The same model was not, however, adopted by their British rival Marks and Spencer which, although it employed district store inspectors, continued to stress direct contact between head office and branch managers. But Marks and Spencer's evolution from penny bazaar to variety retailer saw increasing emphasis placed on the experience of store managers, who were charged with ensuring that their own outlet carried stock which reflected the specifics of local demand, and with supplying sales intelligence to inform purchasing by the company's central buyers. Managers who failed to show the expected judgement and application were just as likely to be reprimanded by head office as those who appeared too independent (Purvis 2015).

Such diversity survived into the postwar era. As Alexander's (2015) study of British grocery chains Tesco and Sainsbury confirms, the histories and circumstances of particular companies, and the personalities and prejudices of their individual leaders continued to shape management structures. Only with the development from the 1980s onwards of computerised systems that allow real-time monitoring of sales and automatically generate stock replenishment instructions has there been a general shift towards close centralised control over the operations of individual stores. Yet studies of today's supermarket chains suggest that store managers value the limited freedoms which they retain in matters of stocking and product promotion (Fuller et al. 2009). Some, indeed, seem to seek ways to subvert, at least symbolically, centralised corporate control. Experimentation and contestation have not entirely receded into managerial history.

Conclusion

Across retailing as a whole there has always been greater variety in managerial systems and competencies – from the ordered to the chaotic; the collaborative to the dictatorial; the simple to the complex – than any brief survey can convey. The functioning of particular businesses, both large and small, has often reflected the personalities of individual owners and managers. Retail development from the eighteenth century onwards has, however, posed a series of common managerial challenges. For the independent retailer such challenges were largely a reflection of growing competition, which hastened the end of some businesses, whilst encouraging others to emulate the efficiencies and scale economies that underpinned the success of department and chain stores. But the growing scale of retail operations created its own difficulties, which often saw direct proprietorial control give way to an increasingly complicated managerial hierarchy, populated by individuals responsible for particular functions within a large store, or for the performance of specific stores within an extensive network. The division of major businesses into components that could be comprehended by individual managers solved one set of problems, but often created others; not least regarding communications, and the balance to be struck between the centralisation and devolution of decision-making power. Attempts to promote organisational efficiency and coherence led many large retailers to place faith in performance data, and associated technologies for its acquisition and analysis. Most also sought to redefine relationships between managers and shop floor staff, through the formal codification of working practices and the creation of systems of pay and rewards intended to foster company loyalty. Such managerial changes were, however, often adopted in a piecemeal fashion. The application of "science" to retail management was, initially at least, a rather hesitant process, sometimes resisted by vested interests.

So much is clear from the growing body of research on retail history. But, as noted at the outset, much of this work is the product of a primary concern with the evolution of retail systems and the history of particular businesses. More systematic study is therefore required of the managerial systems which underpinned the development of modern retailing; perhaps particularly to illuminate the part played by the multitude of currently anonymous managers in the establishment of retail chains and department stores.

References

Alexander, A. (1997), 'Strategy and strategists: Evidence from an early retail revolution in Britain', *International Review of Retail, Distribution and Consumer Research*, 7 (1), pp. 61–78.

Alexander, A. (2015), 'Decision-making authority in British supermarket chains', *Business History*, 57 (4), pp. 614–637.

Alexander, A. (2016), 'The study of British retail history: Progress and agenda', in D.G.B. Jones and M. Tadajewski (eds.) *The Routledge companion to marketing history* (Abingdon: Routledge) 155–172.

Alexander, A., Benson, J. and Shaw, G. (1999), 'Action and reaction: Competition and the multiple retailer in 1930s Britain', *International Review of Retail, Distribution and Consumer Research*, 9 (3), pp. 245–259.

Belisle, D. (2007), 'Negotiating paternalism: Women and Canada's largest department stores, 1890–1960', *Journal of Women's History*, 19 (1), pp. 58–81.

Belisle, D. (2011), *Retail nation: Department stores and the making of modern Canada* (Vancouver: University of British Columbia Press).

Benson, S.P. (1986), *Counter cultures: Saleswomen, managers and customers in American department stores 1890–1940* (Champaign, IL: University of Illinois Press).

Bookbinder, P. (1993), *Simon Marks: Retail revolutionary* (London: Weidenfeld and Nicholson).

Champsaur, F.B. and Cailluet, L. (2010), 'The great depression? Challenging the periodization of French business history in the interwar period', *Business and Economic History On-Line*, 8, pp. 1–21.

Chandler, A.D. (1977), *The visible hand: The managerial revolution in American business* (Cambridge, MA: Belknap Press of Harvard University Press).

Chandler, A.D. (1990), *Strategy and structure: Chapters in the history of American industrial enterprise* (Cambridge, MA: MIT Press).

Chapman, S. (1974), *Jesse Boot of Boots the Chemists: A study in business history* (London: Hodder & Stoughton).

Chessell, M.-E. (1999), 'Training sales personnel in France between the wars', in G. Crossick and S. Jaumain (eds.) *Cathedrals of consumption: The European department store 1850–1939* (Aldershot: Ashgate) 279–298.

Cochoy, F. (2010), 'How to build displays that sell', *Journal of Cultural Economy*, 3 (2), pp. 299–315.

Cochoy, F. (2016), *On the origins of self-service* (Abingdon: Routledge).

Cox, N. (2000), *The complete tradesman: A study of retailing, 1550–1820* (Aldershot: Ashgate).

Cox, P. (2010), *Spedan's partnership: The story of John Lewis and Waitrose* (London: Labatie).

Curry, M.E. (1993), *Creating an American institution: The merchandising genius of J.C. Penney* (New York: Garland).

de Grazia, V. (2005), *Irresistible empire: America's advance through twentieth-century Europe* (Cambridge, MA: Harvard University Press).

Deutsch, T. (2010), *Building a housewife's paradise: Gender, politics, and American grocery stores in the twentieth century* (Chapel Hill, NC: University of North Carolina Press).

Douglas, I. (1935), 'Retail trade statistics in different countries', *Journal of the Royal Statistical Society*, 98 (3), pp. 455–496.

Fuller, A., Kakavelikas, K., Felstead, A., Jewson, N. and Unwin, L. (2009), 'Learning, knowing and controlling the stock: The nature of employee discretion in a supermarket chain', *Journal of Education and Work*, 22 (2), pp. 105–120.

Fulop, C. (1962), *Buying by voluntary chains and other associations of retailers and wholesalers* (London: Allen & Unwin).

Furlough, E. (1993), 'Selling the American way in interwar France: "Prix uniques" and the salons des arts menagers', *Journal of Social History*, 26 (3), pp. 491–519.

Godley, A. (2003), 'Foreign multinationals and innovation in British retailing, 1850–1962', *Business History*, 45 (1), pp. 80–100.

Graham, L. (2000), 'Lillian Gilbreth and the metal revolution at Macy's, 1925–1928', *Journal of Management History*, 6 (7), pp. 285–305.

Haberstroh, S. (2013), "The sun never sets on national cash registers': The international operations of the National Cash Register Company, 1885–1922', unpublished MA thesis, Miami University.

Howard, V. (2008), '"The biggest small-town store in America": Independent retailers and the rise of consumer culture', *Enterprise and Society*, 9 (3), pp. 457–486.

Iarocci, L. (2014), *The urban department store in America 1850–1930* (Farnham: Ashgate).

Jacobs, M. (2007), *Pocketbook politics: Economic citizenship in twentieth-century America* (Princeton, NJ: Princeton University Press).

Jeacle, I. and Walsh, E. (2008), 'A tale of tar and feathering: The retail price inventory method and the Englishman', *Accounting, Business and Financial History*, 18 (2), pp. 121–140.
Jefferys, J.B. and Knee, D. (1962), *Retailing in Europe: Present structure and future trends* (London: Macmillan).
Klassen, H.C. (1992), 'T.C. Power & Brothers: The rise of a small western department store 1870–1902', *Business History Review*, 66, pp. 671–722.
Kruger, D.D. (2012), 'Earl Corder Sams and the rise of J.C. Penney', *Kansas History*, 35, pp. 164–185.
Leach, W. (1993), *Land of desire: Merchants, power and the rise of a new American culture* (New York: Vintage).
Lerner, P. (2015), *The consuming temple: Jews, department stores and the consumer revolution in Germany 1880–1940* (Ithaca, NY: Cornell University Press).
Maeda, K. (1998), 'The innovativeness and adaptability of department stores in Japan: Birth, growth, maturity and crisis', *Japanese Yearbook on Business History*, 15, pp. 45–73.
Mazur, P. (1927), *Principles of organization applied to modern retailing* (New York: Harper & Row).
Miller, D. (2006), 'Strategic human resource management in department stores: An historical perspective', *Journal of Retailing and Consumer Studies*, 13, pp. 99–109.
Miller, M.B. (1981), *The Bon Marché: Bourgeois culture and the department store, 1869–1920* (Princeton, NJ: Princeton University Press).
Monod, D. (1986), 'Bay days: The managerial revolution and the Hudson's Bay Company department stores 1912–1939', *Canadian Historical Papers*, 21 (1), pp. 173–196.
Pasdermadjian, H. (1950), *Management research in retailing: The International Association of Department Stores* (London: Newman Books).
Perkins, J. and Freedman, C. (1999), 'Organisational form and retailing development: The department and the chain store, 1860–1940', *Service Industries Journal*, 19 (4), pp. 123–146.
Phillips, S. and Alexander, A. (2005), '"An efficient pursuit": Small-scale shopkeeping in 1930s Britain', *Enterprise and Society*, 6, pp. 278–304.
Purvis, M. (2015), 'Direction and discretion: The roles of centre and branch in the interwar management of Marks and Spencer', *History of Retailing and Consumption*, 1 (1), pp. 63–81.
Raucher, A. (1991), 'Dime store chains: The making of organization men, 1880–1940', *Business History Review*, 65 (1), pp. 130–163.
Reekie, G. (1987), '"Humanising industry": Paternalism, welfarism and labour control in Sydney's big stores 1890–1930', *Labour History*, 53, pp. 1–19.
Resseguie, H.E. (1965), 'Alexander Turney Stewart and the development of the department store, 1823–1876', *Business History Review*, 39 (3), pp. 301–322.
Riello, G. (2006), *A foot in the past: Consumers, producers and footwear in the long eighteenth century* (Oxford: Oxford University Press).
Roberts, E. (2003), '"Don't sell things, sell effects": Overseas influences on New Zealand department stores, 1909–1956', *Business History Review*, 77 (2), pp. 265–289.
Savitt, R. (1989), 'Looking back to see ahead: Writing the history of American retailing', *Journal of Retailing*, 65 (3), pp. 326–355.
Savitt, R. (1999), 'Innovation in American retailing, 1919–39: Improving inventory management', *International Review of Retail, Distribution and Consumer Research*, 9 (3), pp. 307–320.
Schröter, H.G. (2008), 'The Americanisation of distribution and its limits: The case of the German retail system, 1950–1975', *European Review of History*, 15 (4), pp. 445–458.
Scott, P. and Walker, J. (2012), 'The British "failure" that never was? The Anglo-American "productivity gap" in large-scale interwar retailing: Evidence from the department store sector', *Economic History Review*, 65 (1), pp. 277–303.
Seaton, P. (2009), *A sixpenny romance: Celebrating a century of value at Woolworths* (London: 3d and 6d Pictures).
Shaw, G., Curth, L. and Alexander, A. (2004), 'Selling self-service and the supermarket: The Americanisation of food retailing in Britain, 1945–60', *Business History*, 46 (4), pp. 568–582.
Spellman, S.V. (2016), *Cornering the market: Independent grocers and innovation in American small business* (New York: Oxford University Press).
Spiekermann, U. (2006), 'From neighbour to consumer: The transformation of retailer-consumer relationships in twentieth-century Germany', in F. Trentmann (ed.) *The making of the consumer. Knowledge, power and identity in the modern world* (Oxford: Berg) 147–174.
Stacey, M. (1960), *Tradition and change: A study of Banbury* (Oxford: Oxford University Press).

Stobart, J. (2012), *Sugar and spice: Grocers and groceries in provincial England, 1650–1830* (Oxford: Oxford University Press).

Stobart, J. and Hann, A. (2004), 'Retailing revolution in the eighteenth century? Evidence from north-west England', *Business History*, 46 (2), pp. 171–194.

Strasser, S. (1989), *Satisfaction guaranteed: The making of the American mass market* (Washington, DC: Smithsonian Institute).

Tedlow, R.S. (1990), *New and improved: The story of mass marketing in America* (Oxford: Heinemann).

Twyman, R.W. (1954), *History of Marshall Field & co. 1852–1906* (Philadelphia, PA: University of Pennsylvania Press).

Walsh, C. (1995), 'Shop design and the display of goods in eighteenth-century London', *Journal of Design History*, 8 (3), pp. 157–176.

Walsh, C. (1999), 'The newness of the department store: A view from the eighteenth century', in G. Crossick and S. Jaumain (eds.) *Cathedrals of consumption: The European department store, 1850–1939* (Aldershot: Ashgate) 46–71.

Walsh, E.J. and Jeacle, I. (2003), 'The taming of the buyer: The retail inventory method and the early twentieth century department store', *Accounting, Organizations and Society*, 28, pp. 773–791.

Walsh, W.I. (1986), *The rise and decline of the Great Atlantic and Pacific Tea Company* (Secaucus, NJ: Lyle Stuart).

Whitaker, J. (2011), *The department store. History – design – display* (London: Thames and Hudson).

Wilson, J.F., Webster, A. and Vorberg-Rugh, R. (2013), *Building co-operation: A business history of the Co-operative Group, 1863–2013* (Oxford: Oxford University Press).

Wood, S. (2011), 'Organisational rigidities and marketing theory: Examining the US department store c.1910–1965', *Service Industries Journal*, 31 (5), pp. 747–770.

Wortmann, M. (2004), 'Aldi and the German model: Structural change in German grocery retailing and the success of grocery discounters', *Competition and Change*, 8 (4), pp. 425–441.

17
MULTIPLE RETAILERS

David Delbert Kruger

On the rural high plains of Wyoming in 1902, 7,000 feet above sea level and thousands of miles from the urban centres of London and New York City, a 26-year-old sales clerk named James Cash Penney unveiled his first department store. The wooden location had no utilities and was merely 25 x 45 feet in size, the modest fruition of a frugal partnership between Penney and two older mentors who had trained him for the venture. However, after grossing nearly $29,000 his first year, the young clerk acquired a stake in a second Wyoming store 90 miles away, subsequently using profits from both stores to open a third store in Wyoming by 1904. At the time, the largest city in which Penney operated had just 4,000 residents; the other two locations had fewer than a thousand. Even so, Penney's fledgling retail chain was poised to rapidly expand across the United States over the next three decades. By 1914, the *New York Times* had taken notice of his then-fifty store chain, tracking Penney down for a personal interview on one of his buying trips to the city (Kruger, 2017, pp. 11–29, 83). Seven years later, Penney's network of 312 small-town J.C. Penney stores were collectively outselling what was then the largest single store in the world, Macy's behemoth flagship in New York City. The difference, of course, was that it had taken Penney and his small-town stores only nineteen years to reach that mark. By 1929, James Cash Penney had successfully created North America's first transcontinental department store chain, replicating 1400 of his stores across every state, in cities as large as Chicago and agricultural towns as small as Shamrock, Texas, with total sales of nearly $210 million (Lebhar, 1963, pp. 12–14; J. C. Penney, 1985).

When it comes to examining department stores in the twenty-first century, multiple operations have clearly become the rule as opposed to the exception. Since the 1980s, they have accounted for nearly all of department store sales in the United States, as opposed to just 17% in 1929 (Howard, 2015, p. 193). Around the world, mass retailers such as Walmart and Carrefour, each begun as a single store in the early 1960s, have replicated their retail stores on a global level, with Walmart operating 11,500 supercenters and discount stores across twenty-eight countries worldwide, and Carrefour adding the same quantity of its own hypermarkets across thirty countries (Walmart, 2017; Carrefour Group, 2017). Walmart has clearly become the world's largest retailer in volume and revenue, generating $482 billion in sales, nearly $366 billion more than its next closest global competitor, Costco. Despite its rural Arkansas origins, almost 26% of Walmart's revenue now comes from outside the United States (National Retail Federation, 2017). Traditional department stores of the nineteenth century have also evolved, for better or for worse, from autonomous monolithic flagships into formidable multi-unit chains today. J.C. Penney has since retreated from its apogee of more than 2000 locations in the 1970s while it and upscale competitor Macy's still operate roughly 800 stores apiece, while younger competitor Kohl's operates nearly 1,200 and upscale discounter Target nearly 1,800 (Macy's, 2017). Within the United Kingdom, Britain's House of Fraser operates in a similar fashion to Macy's, though on a comparably smaller scale, with sixty locations throughout the United Kingdom and Abu Dhabi, while Canada's Hudson's Bay company envelops 460 stores on both sides of the Atlantic (House of Fraser, 2017; Hudson's Bay Company, 2017). Even British grocer Tesco has evolved into the realm of a chain department store, with nearly 500 Tesco Extra hypermarkets concurrently functioning as some of the largest physical stores in England, complementing Tesco's more than 6,000 other units across eleven countries (Clark and Chan, 2014). German grocer Lidl likewise operates 10,000 units across twenty-seven countries, with aggressive plans to enter the United States no later than 2018 (Wilson, 2017).

While single-unit retailers have existed since the beginning of commerce, they have become an almost microscopic entity in this chain store dominated world of the twenty-first century. Nevertheless, the genesis of multi-unit retailers is anything but a recent phenomenon, preceding the current retail scene by anywhere from 400 to 2,200 years. Retail historian John P. Nichols noted in his early history of chain stores that the multi-unit concept was actually utilised by Chinese merchant On Lo Kass as early as 200 B.C., as well as through the early efforts of the Mitsui group of Japan and later the wealthy Fugger family of Germany. Even current department store chain Hudson's Bay Company began its operation as a multi-unit retailer from its 1670 inception, originally as a network of fur trading outposts around North America (Nichols, 1940, p. 13). In many ways, Hudson's Bay Company can be seen as one of the first global retail chains as well, authorised by a British charter under King Charles II encompassing present-day Canada as well as the Pacific Northwest of the United States. These early retail units of Hudson's Bay Company were certainly not chic department stores, but they did provide basic retail services and merchandise for both early European immigrants as well as indigenous people of the First Nations (Newman, 1989).

By the nineteenth century, however, a different type of customer began to emerge on both sides of the Atlantic, far more affluent with a propensity to pay with currency over pelts or goods in trade. In response to the decline of its fur trading operations, Hudson's Bay Company gradually began to evolve into the conventional department store chain for which it is known today. Similarly, the seeds for many of today's successful department store chains were likewise sown throughout the nineteenth century. Dickins & Jones, an upscale British store most recently subsumed by House of Fraser, can trace its origins as far back as 1790 while House of Fraser's Jolly's department store dates to 1830 (Clark, 2013). Lord & Taylor, now operated as a subsidiary of Hudson's Bay, has its roots in New York City in 1826. Harrods of London and Holt-Renfrew of Canada can both trace their origins to the 1830s, while a number of American department store operations currently enveloped under the ubiquitous Macy's nameplate long predate the 1858 founding of R.H. Macy's initial store in New York City, much less Macy's Herald Square flagship of 1902. One of Macy's more recent acquisitions, the F.R. Lazarus chain, had its multi-unit roots in a singular Ohio department store originating as early as 1832, while another, Thalheimer's, dated back to a Virginia department store established in 1842. Across the Atlantic, Arnott's, a department store nameplate now under Selfridge's, likewise began as a single Irish operation as early as 1843, while British department store Lewis's of Liverpool came into being thirteen years later. Contemporary American chains like Belk and J.C. Penney can likewise be traced back to a single department store in the nineteenth century as well, with William Henry Belk's first location originating in 1888 and Penney's chain indirectly emerging from his mentor Thomas

Callahan's first Golden Rule location in 1889 (Covington, 1988; Penney, 1931, pp. 20–25; Curry, 1993, pp. 65–79, 98–100; Kruger, 2017, pp. 18–22).

Despite the large number of modern department stores with origins in the early 1800s, chain store historian Godfrey M. Lebhar delineates the first significant era of multiple retailers as a historical period of 1859–1900, when retail pioneers of multi-unit operations truly got their start as single-unit proprietors. 'The history of the chains', wrote Lebhar optimistically in 1962, 'is replete with instances of merchants who, once they realised the limitations of single-store operation, found that the road to unlimited volume presented practically no obstacles' (p. 14). The beginning of this first era certainly coincided with the disruptive innovation of one particular American merchant, George F. Gillman, and his partner, George Huntington Hartford. Gillman was never in the department store business, but the expansion of his retail operations from one single location into the formidable Great Atlantic & Pacific Tea Company is what set his retail efforts apart from any predecessor, and largely served as an example for multiple retailers that followed his lead. By 1865, just six years after Gilman had opened his first store, he had successfully expanded its retail operations across twenty-five separate locations. By 1880, his Great Atlantic & Pacific Tea Company, or "A&P" as its stores were commonly known, had topped 100 locations, and by 1900 had reached 200. Yet Gillman and Hartford were far from finished with this multi-unit strategy for A&P. Over the first three decades of the twentieth century, the A&P chain would go on to reach unprecedented heights beyond such modern titans as Carrefour and Walmart, with more than 10,000 locations by 1924, and more than 15,000 by 1927. By 1929, the A&P chain had topped $1 billion in annual sales. The sheer scope and success of the Great Atlantic & Pacific Tea Company is impressive even by today's standards, and it certainly shattered the limitations for what retail operations could ultimately become (Lebhar, 1963, pp. 33–36; Walsh, 1986; Levinson, 2011).

Early American discount stores and their respective chains were typically not considered or classified as department stores until the late twentieth century. However, like the multiple retail outlets of the Great Atlantic & Pacific Tea Company, they provided a multi-unit blueprint for department stores to eventually follow. One of the most notable, Woolworth's, began as a single "five-and-dime" store in 1878, first failing in New York before successfully retrenching in Pennsylvania the following year. Unlike its retail counterparts, Woolworth's stores offered a less upscale yet vastly broader selection of merchandise for a clientele largely comprised of factory workers, farmers and immigrants – its chief appeal being wider varieties and lower prices. Large selections of tinware, notions, novelties, and candy were grouped in each store according to fixed prices of either five cents or ten cents. Woolworth's best-selling items included pots, pans, toys, wash tubs, towels, handkerchiefs, and ladies hair ribbons and accessories. Mass production innovations in manufacturing continued to drive down the cost of potential merchandise, and Woolworth's was subsequently able to incorporate additional five and ten cent product lines into its already vast store inventories (Winkler, 1940, pp. 15–16, 53). As the number of Woolworth stores exponentially grew, brothers Frank and Charles Woolworth soon realised they could each efficiently operate their own Woolworth chains, as friendly competitors sharing resources and taking advantage of merchandise discounts through volume purchasing. Rather than each brother expanding entirely on his own, however, Charles Woolworth teamed up with friend Fred Kirby to branch into the nearby city of Wilkes Barre, while Frank Woolworth partnered with their cousin Seymour Knox to branch into nearby Reading. Around the same time, in 1882, competitor John McCrorey founded his first discount store in Scottsdale, Pennsylvania, re-spelling it as "McCrory's" and rapidly expanding to five Pennsylvania locations by 1885. Across the Atlantic in 1884, Michael Marks likewise opened the first of his retail establishments under the name "Penny Bazaar", teaming up with cashier Thomas Spencer to launch their Marks and Spencer chain of stores in 1894 (Tse, 1985, pp. 13–25). By 1912, the Woolworth brothers had created an organisation of nearly 600 separate locations in the United States, consolidating them under the "F.W. Woolworth" name, while McCrory's operated ninety-three.

More importantly, however, both Woolworth's and McCrory's inspired other entrepreneurs to follow their leads, with competitor Samuel H. Kress beginning his S.H. Kress stores in 1896, also in Pennsylvania, while former McCrory partner and Kmart founder Sebastian Kresge began his S.S. Kresge chain the following year in Michigan and Tennessee. Despite the later starts of Kress and Kresge, their chains had each expanded to more than eighty stores by 1912, with Kress exceeding McCrory's by the end of that year. Like Woolworth's and McCrory's, these chain stores of Kress and Kresge also catered to a price-conscious customer base, with wide varieties of merchandise priced no higher than 10 cents, including pots, pans, home furnishings, fashions, novelties and candy (Kresge, 1979, pp. 7, 31). The successes of these four discount chains spawned similar additional chains. In 1906, former McCrory clerk George Murphy had already unveiled his first G. C. Murphy store in Pennsylvania while Pennsylvania native William T. Grant unveiled the first of his W.T. Grant stores in Massachusetts. By 1912, Murphy and Grant had expanded their chains to eighteen and twelve locations, respectively, with many more to follow in the years ahead. Former S.H. Kress clerk John Josiah Newberry likewise branched out on his own in 1911 with his Pennsylvania-based J.J. Newberry chain. All of these early discount chains would eventually have a formidable presence across the United States. Frank Woolworth had even taken his chain to the United Kingdom in 1909, successfully expanding from one location in Liverpool to six locations in England by the end of the year, with more than twenty-eight Woolworth's locations operating across the Kingdom in just three years. Woolworth even referred to his first global locations as "3 pence and 6 pence" shops to translate the value of the American "five-and-dime" concept to British consumers (Lebhar, 1963, pp. 36–43).

Multi-unit organisation came earlier to the department store field outside of the United States. David Lewis of Great Britain, not to be confused with the John Lewis department store chain today, was in many ways ahead of his contemporaries in the United Kingdom as well as his American counterparts. After creating his Lewis's of Liverpool department store in 1856, Lewis eventually augmented his longstanding flagship with another location in Manchester in 1877, followed by additional locations in Sheffield and Birmingham the following decade. Even after the death of Lewis in 1885, his department store chain would likewise remain ahead of its American counterparts in the early twentieth century, expanding to additional stores in Glasgow, Leeds, Leicester and Hanley in Stoke-On-Trent, a full fifteen years before the chain acquired Selfridge's in 1951 (Patterson, Hodgson, and Shi, 2008, pp. 29–45).

While John Wannamaker of Philadelphia and the Hecht brothers of Baltimore had each opened additional department stores outside of their flagships during the nineteenth century, with respective locations in New York City and Washington, DC, these moves were largely aberrations within the United States. Likewise, Colorado-based May Company's 1899 acquisition of E.R. Hull & Dutton of Cleveland, Ohio, which it later re-branded under the May name, was equally unusual for its time. Prior to the twentieth century, most of the family-run department stores in the United States, along with Harrods and even House of Fraser in the United Kingdom, remained autonomous retail institutions, with operations primarily centred on a single flagship department store within its respective city. Typically, the flagship location existed within the same city where the department store founder had humbly begun, though these majestic singular stores grew increasingly larger and more opulent as the nineteenth century progressed. Although some – like Wannamaker's and its Philadelphia competitor Strawbridge & Clothier, Virginia's Thalheimer's, Liverpool's Owen Owen and Northern Ireland's Austin's of Derry – remained autonomous family operations for well over 100 years, an overwhelming majority inevitably joined or were absorbed by department store conglomerates in the twentieth century, retail consolidations that would eventually lead to the "Macyfication" of hundreds of American department stores in the twenty-first century (McDonald, 2016).

Multi-unit retailing took shape differently across rural and urban regions over the nineteenth century. In urban America, the modern department store was certainly well in place by 1890, with palaces of consumption such as Macy's, Marshall Field's and Wannamaker's evolving far beyond utilitarian outlets that simply sold necessities to their customers (Howard, 2008, p. 459). By contrast, emerging agrarian towns in the Midwest and West were largely served by autonomous country or general stores, with limited selection and inventories typically provided through merchandise jobbers, "middlemen" that brokered merchandise to these outlets at a typically higher cost (Kline, 2000). Mining companies in boomtowns throughout the American West likewise tended to control the entire retail scene for any community adjacent to and dependent upon their industrial operations. Credit was freely available in these existing rural stores, a perk over Thomas Callahan's cash and carry philosophy in his Golden Rule syndicate, though it certainly came at a price for rural customers, who were often subjected to higher costs, limited selection, and perpetual debt, all for lack of a better shopping alternative (Setzer, 1985). If rural shoppers wanted variety, service and value beyond what their local retail establishments were offering, they were typically forced to utilise mail order catalogue warehouses such as Sears Roebuck or Montgomery Ward to span the retail gaps of their bucolic communities. Ironically, Sears Roebuck and Montgomery Ward had absolutely no interest in operating physical department stores as a result of their extensive mail-order business in rural America, functioning essentially as the late nineteenth- and early twentieth-century equivalents of Amazon.com until the mid-1920s (Lichtenstein, 2009, pp. 16–17; Moreton, 2009, p. 17). Yet, as historian Nelson Lichtenstein points out, 'farmers and small-town folk always preferred to fondle, squeeze, and handle the products they bought, rather than just imagine how they would feel' (p. 17).

Multi-unit organisation provided particular advantages for rural retailers in the United States. As a sales clerk in the rural Golden Rule stores of Thomas Callahan, James Cash Penney realised that such limiting retail conditions in smaller cities and towns provided an amazing opportunity for multiple locations across those communities. From 1897–1900, Callahan had provided both mentorship and inspiration to the younger Penney through his own fledgling Golden Rule chain and the roughly six stores he was operating, particularly selecting and selling quality merchandise at the then lower markup rate of 20%, while maximising the number of times his small stores could turnover their inventories each year. Although he was not in the five-and-dime business, Callahan's focus on sales volume and inventory turnover was in many ways a precursor to modern discount merchants who likewise embraced high volume on low profit margins for their multi-unit chains (Kruger, 2017, p. 20). By 1901, Callahan and his partner William "Guy" Johnson, a former sales clerk Callahan had mentored in Colorado, were collectively grooming Penney to open his first department store in rural Wyoming, a location which came to fruition in the town of Kemmerer the following year. Ultimately, the two partners put up 2/3 of the initial investment, with Penney providing the remaining third out of personal savings and loans. Penney would then run his Golden Rule store as part of their chain, entirely on a cash and carry basis, with profits divided among the three owning partners and future expansion coming through the reinvestment of store profits. By 1904, at the age of twenty-eight, Penney was operating two additional Wyoming locations for Callahan and Johnson, and by 1907, he had completely bought out their interests in the three stores, preparing to expand his own chain in the years that followed. 'Three stores were much more responsibility than I had imagined shouldering at that stage of my experience as a merchant', Penney (1950) later reflected. 'Along with managing, I had to select and train men, and more, and more, men' (p. 58).

Figure 17.1 J.C. Penney Store #3 (Cumberland, WY).

Source: J.C. Penney Company Records, DeGolyer Library, Southern Methodist University, Dallas Texas

In the United States, rural markets and small-town entrepreneurs were central to the rise of the multi-unit retail format. Several merchants associated with the early development of J.C. Penney played a significant role in chain store development. One in particular, a Kansas farmboy named Earl Corder Sams, had been fascinated by retailing since early childhood and, at the age of seventeen, even convinced his father and two local businessmen to finance a local department store under his management. After successfully managing the single-unit store for a few years, however, Sams became discouraged with the limited opportunities for personal or professional growth. 'In looking around for a much bigger opportunity', Sams (Seventy-Sixth United States Congress, 1940, p. 559) later reflected, 'an employment agency told me about a man named J.C. Penney who had a store in the little coal camp of Kemmerer, Wyo., and who had a vision of something beyond a single small store' (p. 559).

Out of curiosity, Sams began corresponding with Penney, eventually securing an interview in Wyoming. Although Penney had scaled his retail operation back to just two locations in 1907, Sams was intrigued by Penney's ambitious vision for its future, particularly the idea of his store clerks not only becoming managers for additional store openings, but partnering with Penney in sharing store profits and training additional employees, whom Penney explicitly called "associates", for the same opportunities. By 1909, Earl Corder Sams had opened a new Golden Rule store for Penney in Eureka, Utah, the fifth location in Penney's retail chain. By the end of that year, Sams was able to reinvest his profits from their Eureka store in additional locations Penney planned to open, typically through partnerships between Penney, Sams, and the young

Figure 17.2 J.C. Penney Store #300. J.C. Penney exiting antique car at new (re)location. (Kansas City, KS).

Source: J.C. Penney Company Records, DeGolyer Library, Southern Methodist University, Dallas Texas

sales clerk they had trained to manage the new location. By 1910, the two men had doubled the size of Penney's chain to fourteen locations. By 1912, they had added twenty more, generating $2.1 million in annual sales across the chain. Five years later, Penney's company was operating out of a New York City headquarters with 177 locations generating $14.9 million in sales, with some of these stores established more than 3000 miles away from Penney's office (Kruger, 2012, pp. 164–185).

From 1917, the year Penney recommended Earl Corder Sams as company president, until Sams's death in 1950, he quietly led the J.C. Penney Company behind the enigma of the company founder, a period in which Sams concurrently mentored a young J.W. Marriott, Sr. into the global entrepreneur Marriott would ultimately become. Yet the impact of Earl Corder Sams on J.C. Penney stores and chain stores in general was undeniable. Over the course of his thirty-three years as president and chairman of the board at J.C. Penney, he took Penney's company from 177 department stores to more than 1,600, increasing company sales from $8.4 million to nearly $1 billion, a growth rate of more than 10,000% (J. C. Penney, 1985; Lebhar, 1963, p. 17). Even the company founder himself was quick to give credit to his younger partner in making his enterprise the nationwide chain it ultimately became. 'If I had insisted on keeping personal control of the Penney Company', Penney would later write in his 1950 autobiography, 'we would still be merely a small chain of stores scattered through the Middle West' (p. 95). Sams had long developed a reputation as a skilled merchandiser, selecting not only attractive inventories

Figure 17.3 E. C. Sams and J. C. Penney

Source: J.C. Penney Company Records, DeGolyer Library, Southern Methodist University, Dallas Texas

but making the stores themselves a pleasant shopping environment. He held enough credibility and clout to criticise Penney's earliest stores as "junky" and lacking uniformity, upgrading and standardising such elements as merchandise buying and management training as well as store layouts and appearances. His 1917 creation of a company magazine, the *Dynamo*, promoted a corporate culture and shared outstanding management and merchandise presentation ideas among stores and associates across the expansive chain; British variety chain Marks and Spencer would take a similar approach in 1927, beginning their *Management Bulletins* and later *Sparks* magazine to be distributed to their numerous employees across their many stores (Purvis, 2015, pp. 63–81). In a pre-digital world, such forms of communication were essential to standardising and co-ordinating best practices from the home office across multiple units, and in many cases eliciting feedback from disparate store employees in response to the content of the publications. In the case of J.C. Penney, it was quite common for Sams and even Penney himself to personally follow up with individual store managers during their period of rapid expansion, even as their department store chain approached more than a thousand locations.

Aside from establishing a corporate real estate department, one of Earl Sam's particular innovations during the 1920s was the creation and replication of a store prototype known as the "Cortland", a J.C. Penney store with departments easily identifiable from the front entrance, under a high-ceiling sales floor augmented by an additional merchandise balcony elevated above the back of the store.

J.C. Penney stores utilising the Cortland layout could be adjusted to fit new or existing buildings in the disparate main streets of their respective communities, serving cities of more than 50,000 residents or farm towns with populations barely above 1,000 (J. C. Penney, 2001). By 1929, a year in which he planned to open 500 additional J.C. Penney stores, Sams was quick to emphasise the company's multi-unit identity as well as the localised service and selection from each store manager in press releases and advertisements. Throughout the interwar period, Penney and Sams continued to work in tandem on developing company policy while empowering each local store manager within their growing chain (Kruger, 2012, pp. 175–182).

In many ways, the management approach and leadership arrangement of Penney and Sams was strikingly similar to that of Britons Simon Marks and Israel Sieff, particularly as the latter duo transformed Marks and Spencer from the Penny Bazaars of Simon's father into a chain of respectable variety stores poised to dominate the retail landscape of Great Britain (Tse, 13–26; and Purvis, 67, 74–75). Even with the economic setbacks of the Great Depression across the United States, Earl Sams continued positioning J.C. Penney department stores for additional locations and markets throughout the 1930s, notably large metropolitan cities the company had traditionally avoided. By the end of the Great Depression, Sams was bringing J.C. Penney stores to customers in farm towns of hundreds and urban cities of millions, giving the company more department store locations than any retail chain in the world (Kruger, 2012). Likewise, Simon Marks and Israel Sieff had moved Marks and Spencer stores into considerably larger facilities, even referring to them as "superstores" long before the term became commonplace among later retail chains (Tse, 1985, pp. 24–25; Purvis, 2015, pp. 67–68).

Figure 17.4 J.C. Penney Store #113. Cortland prototype layout. (Williston, ND, 1941).

Source: J.C. Penney Company Records, DeGolyer Library, Southern Methodist University, Dallas Texas

"From Ocean to Ocean"

1400 Department Stores

Where Economy of Distribution and Large Group Buying Make Possible Important Savings to Millions of Families

WHEN our New Store throws open its doors, it will present an entirely new idea in Distribution Service.

First of all, it will be a Local Service Institution, attuned to local needs, in harmony with local projects, manned by local people.

It will be a better local store because of its National Resources, making possible Economy in Buying and Operating.

Most important of all, this Store will have an individually selected stock of goods—not standardized—not just like that of any other J. C. Penney Company Store—but bought by our Manager for this Store and for this Community.

The folks who buy at this New Store will buy here—not because it is part of a National Organization, not because we have other Stores extending "from Ocean to Ocean"—but because of WHAT THIS STORE CAN DO FOR THEM! And that is as it should be. We expect to build this business strictly on the merits of THIS STORE and its Service to you.

But because of our National Relation to the World's Markets, and because of our ability to effect very large savings in everything we buy—because of these things—we expect to make our Local Store Service more convincingly apparent than would otherwise be possible.

J. C. PENNEY COMPANY, Inc.

KENYON, MINNESOTA

Figure 17.5 J.C. Penney Newspaper Ad, 1929

Source: J.C. Penney Company Records, DeGolyer Library, Southern Methodist University, Dallas Texas

Within the United States, the J.C. Penney chain had already been in operation before large conglomerates of multiple flagship department stores began to surface in the early twentieth century. Of course, each of the flagship department stores within these conglomerates had previously functioned as single-unit retail enterprises, nearly all of them autonomously originating in the nineteenth century. However, the success of a national department store chain like J.C. Penney illuminated the operational efficiencies and growth that could certainly come from a multi-unit operation. Not only could management, merchandising, training, customer service and store design be standardised and streamlined, but economies of scale could likewise be achieved through the increased buying power of multiple stores (Kruger, 2017, pp. 18–26, 83).

The visible success of J.C. Penney's department store chain across rural America had also forced the mail order giants of Sears Roebuck and Montgomery Ward to transition into department store chains as well, rather than continuing solely as catalogue warehouses. Sears would finally unveil its first retail store in 1925, twenty-three years after Penney had opened his first store in Wyoming. Montgomery Ward would follow the next year (Lebhar, 1963, pp. 16–17; Emmet and Jeuck, 1950, pp. 338–357; Weil, 1977, pp. 993–994; Latham, 1972, pp. 70–73). Neither company, however, had any interest in remaining single-unit operations. From 1925 to 1930, Sears had expanded from just eight department stores to 351. Over that same period, Montgomery Ward had gone from ten to 554. Nevertheless, even these impressive numbers were greatly eclipsed by J.C. Penney, which was operating nearly 1,400 stores at the time. Despite the fact that J.C. Penney had no catalogue operations until 1964, the collective buying power of its small-town department stores allowed it to competitively match that of Sears and Wards, who were still trying to perfect their physical retail locations. In early 1929, Montgomery Ward and Sears Roebuck both proposed merging with J.C. Penney to capitalise on their respective strengths (Emmet and Jeuck, 1950, pp. 652–653; Beasley, 1948, pp. 126–137). Although Earl Sams declined merging J.C. Penney with either company, he continued to advocate on behalf of the entire chain store industry, even in congressional testimony, arguing that chain stores were an inevitable component of American progress, the commercial agents for perpetually improving the quality of American life (Sams, 1929, pp. 17–18).

Despite the immense growth of department store chains like Sears, Montgomery Ward and J.C. Penney during the early twentieth century, chain stores were far from being universally popular across every public sector, particularly during the 1920s and especially during the 1930s. As early as 1920, American author Sinclair Lewis (1920) had already articulated his own disdain for their presence in his satirical novel *Main Street*. By 1923, growing widespread opposition to their pervasive expansion organised into what later became known as the anti-chain store movement. Independent merchants were largely behind the anti-chain store movement, seeing the growth of chain stores not just as a threat to their own economic viability, but a replicated, homogenous blight against the unique commercial environments within their local communities. By 1927, the anti-chain store movement had gained enough popular and political traction that four states successfully passed anti-chain store laws, essentially in the form of additional taxes levied against these multi-unit operations. To a lesser extent, labour unions also lent their support to the movement primarily to improve wages and the standard of living on behalf of unionised retail workers themselves. By the 1930s, negative reactions against this "chain store menace" had garnered significant media attention and publicity, and more than twenty additional states, along with a number of local municipalities, began passing their own anti-chain store laws as well. Texas Congressman Wright Patman was perhaps the most prominent anti-chain store crusader on a national level; after successfully advocating federal anti-chain legislation on behalf of smaller, independent retailers, Patman ambitiously proposed a nationwide chain store tax in 1938, which failed to pass Congress but nonetheless caught the attention of chain store supporters and opponents alike (Scroop, 2008, pp. 925–949).

Historian Daniel Scroop would later describe the anti-chain store movement as a "species of populist anti-monopolism", a grassroots political effort against the large-scale tendencies that were increasingly concentrating economic and political power in empires of production as well as consumption (pp. 925–938). While the anti-chain store movement did notch a number of successes during its apogee in the early 1930s, notably behind the support of Wright Patman as well as Supreme Court Justice Louis D. Brandeis, it was ultimately unable to counter the growing power of organisations such as the American Retail Federation, which aggressively lobbied for influence on behalf of the increasingly powerful chains of stores (Scroop, 2008, pp. 932–938). Chain store advocates like Earl Corder Sams had also helped turned the tide of popular support for chains, advocating low prices for consumers, better opportunities for employees, improved distribution for producers, and enhanced economic development for communities in which chain stores could freely operate (Kruger, 2012, pp. 178–181).

Although chain stores accounted for only 17% of the nation's trade in 1929, more than half of all department stores in the United States had become multi-unit operations by 1948, with Montgomery Ward operating 621 of its own locations, Sears Roebuck operating 623, and J.C. Penney overseeing a whopping 1,600 (Lebhar, 1963, pp. 409–410, 415). A similar rise of multi-unit operations was likewise taking place within the United Kingdom during that same interwar period, with the percentage of chain store sales doubling in the nineteen years leading up to 1939 (Jefferys, 1954; Purvis, 2015, p. 64). Over the next three decades, the conquest of the independent department store in the United States would become a *fait accompli*, with nearly 100% of department stores being chain stores in nature by the 1980s (Howard, 2015, p. 193).

With the anti-chain store movement all but neutralised by 1940, the multi-unit retail format was readily poised to become a central player in postwar suburban development. Prior to World War II, retail activity across the United States had been anchored primarily to the central business districts of cities and towns. The prominence of these "downtown" centralised retail districts, in many cases the only shopping districts these cities had ever known, was a continued validation for independent flagship department stores that essentially anchored them. Yet the concept of suburban branch department stores augmenting downtown flagships had already begun to emerge among a few department store firms. In 1941, twelve of fourteen department store executives believed that developing branch suburban stores would become a major trend in American retail. Lord & Taylor had already unveiled one of the first suburban branch department stores that year, more than 20 miles east of New York City in the Long Island suburb of Manhasset. Dorothy Shaver, a female Lord & Taylor executive, had been instrumental in establishing this branch store, significantly larger than any of its predecessors. Once Shaver assumed leadership of Lord & Taylor in 1945, she not only became one of the first women to ever lead such a firm, but continued the process of successfully opening similarly large branch stores (Oakes, 1957; Smithsonian, 2012). By 1948, Earl Corder Sams had likewise begun preparing J.C. Penney for suburbia with his first J.C. Penney store prototype outside of a central business district, in a shopping centre along the outskirts of St Louis, Missouri (Kruger, 2017, p. 264).

Multi-unit retailers significantly contributed to the growth of the postwar suburban shopping centre. In 1950, for example, retail conglomerate Allied Stores made the unusual move of hiring prominent Seattle, Washington, architect John Graham, Jr. to design a shopping centre around one of their proposed Bon Marché branch department stores, creating what became the first suburban shopping centre in the Pacific Northwest. Four years later, Austrian-born architect Victor Gruen began designing massive shopping malls to accommodate booming suburban populations and particularly, the automobiles and freeways that took them to and from their suburban homes. Large department stores such as J.L. Hudson in downtown Detroit capitalised on Gruen's ideas by financing and anchoring one of his first centres twelve miles north of its flagship store, a retail development called "Northland Center" that showcased a massive four-level, 470,000 square foot Hudson's branch department store as its centrepiece. In 1956, Minnesota-based Dayton's department stores enlisted Gruen to create what is arguably regarded as America's first indoor shopping mall in the Minneapolis suburb of Edina, anchored by a 238,000 square foot branch department store nine miles southwest of Dayton's flagship store. Given the immediate success of these large suburban locations, Hudson's and Dayton's were naturally eager to open additional stores in similar suburban centres. By the end of the 1960s, Hudson's would operate twenty-one stores in Michigan alone. Other flagship department stores previously confined to city centres likewise began financing the development of suburban shopping centres throughout the United States, opening prominent branch stores to augment their downtown locations (Hardwick, 2008). By 1959, Sears Roebuck created its own subsidiary, Homart, chiefly to carry out many of the ideas Victor Gruen had pioneered. Homart then began planning and developing regional shopping malls throughout the United States, creating gigantic new spaces not only for its suburban Sears stores, but competing department store chains as well, while other suburban shopping mall developers such as A. Alfred Taubman, Ernest Hahn and Edward DeBartolo, Sr. continued to woo additional department store branches and chains into their proposed centres (Howard, 2015; Longstreth, 2010).

Even as branch locations outside of the local flagship became *en vogue* for larger cities and their burgeoning suburbs, department store firms themselves were not entirely at the vanguard of suburban shopping. In many ways, such innovations were largely led by discount stores in the 1950s, pioneering the massive suburban operations that have become so commonplace in twenty-first century retail. One of the first of these discount chains had the unwieldy name of "Two Guys from Harrison", a sprawling superstore started by the Hubschman brothers in Harrison, New Jersey, which offered full lines of appliances and later hardlines, softlines and grocery items at discount prices. By 1948, 27-year-old entrepreneur Eugene Ferkauf unveiled E. J. Korvette, his first attempt at creating a suburban discount store. Six years later, Ferkauf unveiled an unusual 90,000 square foot store on what had previously been a potato field in Long Island, New York, and the success of that store led to four additional Korvette's locations by 1956, which Ferkauf multiplied to twelve by 1958. Ferkauf referred to E.J. Korvette as a Discount Department Store, but in contrast to its traditional predecessors, his locations took the then-unusual approach of sprawling spartan sales floors, virtually no personalised customer service, and an expansive free parking lot to keep cars and customers coming and inventories turning (Barmash, 1981). 'If [Ferkauf] could make a one-dollar profit selling a refrigerator', explained historian David Halberstam, 'he could make a million-dollar profit selling a million of them' (Martin, 2012). Ferkauf's highly unusual and successful stores quickly inspired fellow entrepreneur Carl Bennett to create his own Caldor discount chain in suburban New York. Ferkauf would likewise become a significant influence for Sam Walton in rural Arkansas during the following decade (Lichtenstein, 2009, pp. 26–29).

Throughout the latter half of the 1950s, an American discount retailing period that predated Walmart, Kmart and Target, a number of formidable discount chains began to emerge nationwide, eager to replicate the success of early chains like E.J. Korvette, Two Guys and Caldor. Within the Northeast, chains such as Zayre, Topps, Twin Fair, Ames, Mammoth Mart, Bradlees and Turn Style all began to roll out their large suburban prototypes. Gibson's Discount Center, a Texas-based chain, likewise established itself with locations across the Midwest and South, while California-based chains White Front and GEMCO emerged along the Pacific coast. Although each of these firms were clearly chains of suburban discount stores, some, such as Ann & Hope of Rhode Island, King's of Massachusetts and Hills of Ohio, explicitly referred to themselves as department stores. By 1962, discount chains like Korvette's and its many competitors had gained so much credibility in American retail that *Time Magazine* put Eugene Ferkauf on one of its covers, along with the headline "Consumer Spending: Discounting Gets Respectable" (Time, 1962).

By the 1960s, traditional department stores were not only opening branch locations in suburban malls, but creating their own multi-unit subsidiaries that could compete with the growing numbers of suburban discount stores. Indianapolis-based L.S. Ayres was one of the first American department stores to develop its own discount chain; the 1961 opening of their first Ayr-Way store was significant in that it predated Sam Walton's first Walmart location by nine months. Minnesota-based department store Dayton's likewise developed Target as their "upscale discount chain" the following year, virtually the same time as traditional discounters S.S. Kresge and F.W. Woolworth unveiled their respective Kmart and Woolco suburban discount stores. Even J.C. Penney got into the discount store business with its Treasury and Treasure Island outlets. Of all the significant American discount chains that opened their doors in the 1960s, Arkansas-based Walmart and Wisconsin-based Shopco (now Shopko) were among the few spearheaded by single entrepreneurs. Most of the others had grown out of existing retail chains dating back to the nineteenth century.

The openings of shopping malls and discount stores in burgeoning American suburbs certainly provided additional multi-unit possibilities for single-unit retailers, especially department stores that had previously been confined to one flagship location. However, such suburban proliferation had also come at the expense of the urban retail core where most department stores had begun and thrived. Without the capital to expand, the ongoing vulnerability of many local department stores led to their increasing absorption by prominent retailing syndicates such as Allied Stores, Associated Dry Goods, Federated and Mercantile, as well as Macy's and May Company. Even non-retail companies such as British American Tobacco, through its Batus subsidiary, were positioning themselves to become major department store syndicates by the 1970s, eventually acquiring such formidable chains as Gimbell's, Saks Fifth Avenue and Marshall Fields. Shopping mall developer A. Alfred Taubman also began acquiring entire department stores such as Wannamaker's and Woodward and Lathrop in order to vertically integrate them into his own ongoing real estate activities. Upstart merchant William T. Dillard likewise began expanding his fledgling retail chain by acquiring Arkansas competitors Gus Blass, Pfeiffer's and Oklahoma department store Brown-Duncan (Rosenberg, 1988, pp. 46, 61–62).

Within the United States, rising newer department store chains such as Wisconsin-based Kohl's and California-based Mervyn's became nimble multi-unit operations with a clear preference for suburban locales and growth. Even Arkansas-based Dillard's, while buying up flagship and branch stores across the Midwest and South, increasingly worked with Homart and other shopping mall developers after 1964 to ensure their new stores were well-positioned in suburban centres as well (Rosenberg and Rao, 1989, pp. 230–236). Montgomery Ward, which had conservatively opened almost no new stores since the early 1940s, likewise renewed their expansion in the 1960s with an emphasis on becoming a shopping mall anchor. And under the leadership of CEO William "Mil" Batten, J.C. Penney aggressively began developing massive store prototypes specifically to anchor suburban shopping malls, selling full offerings of hardlines merchandise as well as softlines, and providing multiple services from beauty salons to automotive service centres. With sales floors exceeding 200,000 square feet, some of these J.C. Penney stores were more than 200 times the size of the first one James Cash Penney had opened in 1902 (Kruger, 2017, pp. 251, 264–265).

Within Ireland, businessman Arthur St. John Ryan concurrently began his own "Penney's" department store chain in 1969, initially in Dublin before rapidly opening additional locations throughout the country. However, Ryan's successful department store chain was a completely separate entity from that of the eponymous American merchant, who happened to still be alive and active in his company at 94 years of age. As Ryan began eying expansion into the United Kingdom and beyond, he was soon forced to open his non-Irish locations under the new name of Primark; J.C. Penney had apparently registered the "Penney's" name across other European countries in the event of his own worldwide expansion (Finn, 2015). Ironically, J.C. Penney would never open a store in the United Kingdom, but Primark would eventually cross the Atlantic into North America, taking over the former Filene's flagship location in Boston as its American flagship location in 2015, and even anchoring a shopping mall opposite the very first of James Cash Penney's own full-line stores in a shopping mall outside Philadelphia (Di Stefano, 2015).

Suburban discount store chains had already surpassed conventional department stores in sales volume since 1965 and continued to leave department stores behind throughout the 1970s (Howard, 2015, p. 171). Within the United States, S.S. Kresge's Kmart stores had quickly emerged at the head of this dynamic group, largely through the innovation and direction of Kresge executive Harry S. Cunningham. Cunningham not only created the Kmart store prototype in 1962, but successfully replicated its low-margin, high volume, and self-service locations across eighteen additional states and Canada by 1963, with 338 Kmart locations across the United States, Canada, Puerto Rico and Australia by 1969. By the time Cunningham retired from S.S. Kresge in 1972, he had increased company sales from $450 million to more than $3.8 billion, a financial windfall that facilitated the company's move to a new headquarters complex in suburban Detroit (Kresge, pp. 248–49). Cunningham's successor, Robert E. Dewar, would continue Cunningham's momentum by aggressively opening a thousand more Kmart locations across the United States and abroad from 1972–1979 (Eichenwald, 2000). By contrast, Sam Walton kept Walmart a largely regional discount chain over that same period, slowly expanding from eighteen stores in Arkansas, Oklahoma and Texas to nearly 300 by the end of the 1970s (Schuster, 1981). Target, the discount arm of Dayton-Hudson department stores, had likewise expanded to roughly 100 stores over the same decade, though its atmosphere as an upscale discounter allowed it to anchor regional shopping malls that might have otherwise snubbed a discount store in their centre. By 1975, Target stores were generating more revenue than Dayton's and Hudson's department stores combined, and by 1977, Kmart stores were accounting for 95% of S.S. Kresge's sales, prompting the eponymous company to change its name to Kmart Corporation, a prelude to a similar name change Target would eventually bring to the Dayton-Hudson Corporation at the close of the twentieth century (Kresge, 1979, p. 372; Dow Jones Newswire, 2000).

Throughout the 1970s, the rise of multi-unit suburban discount chains continued to eat away at the remaining market share of traditional department stores. By the 1980s, a stagnant American economy further weakened many department store chains, making longstanding operations and even entire department store conglomerates extremely vulnerable to takeover or permanent closure. The "Macyfication" of American department stores in the twenty-first century, where the homogenised Macy's nameplate, merchandise, management, culture and shopping atmosphere subsumed previously autonomous department stores from Abraham & Straus to ZCMI, was merely the fruition of seismic retail consolidations that began occurring in the 1980s. Throughout that particular decade, conditions in American banking, commerce and government had largely been shaped by a spirit of neoliberalism that enabled such drastic and ultimately destructive "mega-mergers" of entire retail conglomerates to finally occur (Howard, 2015, pp. 203–218). By 2006, the aftershock from this neoliberalism on the American department store landscape was visibly evident, as once-independent retail institutions had not only been acquired by Macy's, but completely re-branded under the Macy's nameplate and its iconic red star. From 2006–2017, Macy's additionally began shutting down nine of the historic flagship locations it had recently acquired, many of them department store locations more than 150 years old. Unfortunately for Macy's and the many stores it absorbed, declining sales and profits in recent years now threaten to make the entire chain a victim of its own appetite for conquest and expansion. In February 2017, Hudson's Bay Company, the global department store conglomerate that predated the existence of Macy's by nearly 200 years, announced plans to aggressively takeover the longstanding American retailer (Kestenbaum, 2017). Macy's capitulation to Hudson's Bay Company is not yet a certainty, but if it does come to fruition it will finally give Hudson's Bay Company the title of world's largest department store chain – in addition to their historic mantle of being the world's oldest.

Gigantic hypermarket stores have likewise come to dominate the twenty-first century landscape of multi-unit stores, competing with department stores, discount stores, grocery stores, and even entire shopping centres as one-stop shopping destinations. While the concept of merging grocery, hardlines and softlines under one roof was already evident as early as the 1940s, when the Two Guys from Harrison chain incorporated such disparate merchandise into their massive New Jersey locations, such comprehensive merchandising has now become the primary thrust of global retailers like Carrefour and Walmart. Within the United Kingdom, traditional grocers such as Tesco have expanded their hypermarket prototypes as well, with Tesco Extra locations rivalling the size and scope of Carrefour's Hypermarkets and Walmart's Supercenters (AEW Architects, 2012). Even Groupe Casino, a French firm dating back to a nineteenth century grocer, has likewise morphed into a formidable hypermarket competitor, with nearly 130 of its own Hyper Géant Casino locations to complement its network of 12,000 other stores across Europe and South America (2017). Michigan grocer Meijer has likewise become a competitor for Walmart Supercenters and Super Targets among six Midwestern states, with 231 Meijer superstores now in operation (2017).

In conjunction with hypermarkets, the prominence of large membership warehouses in multi-unit retailing is also a relatively recent phenomenon, with Costco becoming not only the leader of that store category within the United States, but the second largest retailer in sales across the entire world. Costco itself was not created until 1983, but the roots of the membership warehouse industry, and really Costco itself, technically date back to 1954, when entrepreneur Sol Price created Fedmart, a membership-only retail store operating out of a former warehouse in San Diego, California. Price, an attorney by trade, had inherited the warehouse and developed Fedmart after being impressed by an unusual competitor, Fedco, then a single non-profit membership store that had opened in 1948. Sol Price's first Fedmart store was so successful that he opened a second location in Arizona the following year, followed by a third in Texas the year after. Under Price's leadership, Fedmart continued its multi-unit expansion into seventy stores over the next two decades, while pioneering his innovative ideas such as in-store pharmacies and optical centres, as well as selling gas to its member-customers at wholesale prices. When Sol Price was forced out of Fedmart in 1976, he responded by creating Price Club, a new chain of membership stores that fully embraced his concept of warehouse retailing, with merchandise sold in bulk quantities inside a utilitarian warehouse atmosphere. By 1982, Fedmart had gone out of business, while Price Club had nearly doubled its earnings every year, spawning ambitious competitors imitating Sol Price's membership warehouse model.

In 1983, James D. Sinegal, one of Price's former employees at Fedmart, created Costco while Walmart founder Sam Walton unveiled Sam's Club, each of them multi-unit membership warehouse chains explicitly inspired by Sol Price's ideas and concepts. When a journalist asked Sol

Price how it felt to be considered "the father" of so many retailing innovations for his own emerging competitors, he humorously replied, 'I really wish I had worn a condom' (Stone, 2013). By 1984, Massachusetts-based BJ's Wholesale additionally began similar warehouse club operations as a successful subsidiary of Zayre discount stores. Sam's Club had already acquired a number of regional membership warehouses as well, and keen competition among other competitors led to the merger of Sol Price's and James Sinegal's respective chains in 1993, ultimately combining them under the Costco name in 1997. By the year 2000, Costco and Sam's Club

Figure 17.6 Jim Sinegal and Sol Price

Source: Photo courtesy of ©Michael Christmas Photography.

had established their membership warehouses throughout the United States, while regional competitor BJ's Wholesale operated primarily along the Atlantic region, outperforming and outliving its parent company Zayre.

Today, Costco clearly dominates the membership warehouse industry within North America, with more than 600 locations across the United States, Canada and Mexico. In addition, Costco's retail empire has likewise transcended the Atlantic and the Pacific, with nearly thirty stores in the United Kingdom, as well as multiple locations across Spain, Japan, South Korea, Taiwan and Australia. With nearly $120 billion in annual sales along with a reputation for treating its employees with dignity and respect, Costco has become the second largest retailer in the world, ahead of fellow global competitors Carrefour, Schwartz and Tesco (National Retail Federation, 2017). While Walmart remains significantly ahead of Costco in number of stores and total sales worldwide, its Sam's Club warehouses have continued to lose ground to Costco and to a lesser extent, regional competitor BJ's Wholesale. Despite Sam's Club operating more than 600 locations across the United States, nearly half of the total number of membership warehouses nationwide, Sam's Club accounts for just 37% of the total sales within that category. Even with 200 locations across Mexico, Brazil and China, slumping sales have forced Walmart to withdraw Sam's Club operations from both Canada and the state of Rhode Island, and increasingly shut down additional locations across the United States since 2010 (Ritter, 2010; Campbell, 2016; Wahba, 2016).

In the twenty-first century, when postmodern retail institutions like Amazon.com have clearly ascended as merchandising dynasties, the multi-unit demise of prominent "bricks and mortar" predecessors is glaringly self-evident. Long gone from the scene are such household names as Montgomery Ward in the United States, Eaton's in Canada and Lewis's of Liverpool. Likewise absent are the pioneering multi-unit discount chains of F.W. Woolworth and innovative discounters such as E.J. Korvette. The Great Atlantic & Pacific Tea Company, in many ways the model for the modern, multi-unit chain, itself fell into bankruptcy and ultimately went from a high of 15,737 "A&P" locations in 1930 to a grand total of zero by 2016 (Lebhar, 1963, p. 365, Barron, 2015). Other once-dominant industry titans such as Sears Roebuck and Kmart, the top two retail chains in the United States until Walmart overtook them in 1990, have not only been forced to merge with each other as Sears Holdings Corporation, but desperately hold on for their very survival as their sheer numbers of stores, sales and market share continue to erode. In 2013, J.C. Penney nearly fell into bankruptcy as a result of its own $4 billion loss in sales and $1 billion net loss on the year due to poor company leadership, forcing the company to shutter nearly eighty department stores from 2014–2016, with plans to close at least 130 more by the end of 2017 (Kruger, 2017, pp. 280–281; Loeb, 2017). In late 2016, Macy's likewise announced plans to close roughly 100 of its nearly 800 remaining locations by the end of 2017. Even retail juggernaut Walmart is not impervious to change and occasional failures across its own multi-unit empire, with failed global ventures into Germany, India, Russia and South Korea (Berfield, 2013). In 2016, Walmart was forced to close about 1% of its global store fleet, and shut down 152 stores of various formats within the United States as disparate competitors continue to provide time-saving shopping alternatives to visiting Walmart's massive Supercenters (Wahba). Dollar General, despite its modest Tennessee roots and exponentially smaller stores, already has 13,000 locations in the United States alone, outnumbering both Walmart or Carrefour worldwide; its $22 billion in revenues also place the tiny discounter ahead of department store chains such as Kohl's, J.C. Penney and Dillard's, and nearly on par with Macy's (Mergent Online, 2017).

The poet T.S. Eliot, a cosmopolitan resident of both the United Kingdom and the United States, once penned the line that 'Time present and time past are both perhaps present in time future, and time future contained in time past' (1943). Through the retail lens of the twenty-first century, Eliot's twentieth-century statement certainly appears to be apropos for multiple retailers on both sides of the Atlantic. Most notably, the Hudson's Bay Company, brought to life by the efforts of Prince Rupert and the 1670 signature of King Charles II, today oversees 461 department store locations across North America as well as Europe, including Germany's Galeria Kaufhof chain and such American institutions as Saks Fifth Avenue and Lord & Taylor, with a takeover bid of the Macy's empire still in play at the time of this writing (Kestenbaum, 2017). Walmart, the world's number one retailer with 11,500 locations and more than $482 billion in annual sales, likewise has its own historical roots in James Cash Penney's rural Wyoming enterprise, a 114-year-old department store chain that first employed and inspired Sam Walton and his younger brother Bud in the early 1940s (Kruger, 2017, pp. 9–10, 285). Ironically, of the thousands of department stores Penney would ultimately open, his first one within the remote Wyoming community of Kemmerer still remains in operation at the time of this writing, competing against the likes of both regional Walmart Supercenters and global online retailers such as Amazon.com (Kruger, 2017, p. 296).

In hindsight, the history of multiple retailers can really be seen as a succession of innovative merchants perpetually responding to the needs of ever-changing customers, adapting and borrowing new ideas from each other in the process, and creating and replicating new types of stores to better meet those needs. As chain store innovator Earl Corder Sams remarked in 1929, 'We could not bring all of our customers to one store so we have taken the store to the customers' (Kruger, 2014, p. 331). Nearly eighty years later, global retail visionaries like Jeff Bezos are additionally proving that a retail firm with virtually no physical stores can generate more than $100 billion in annual sales worldwide. Amazon.com is but one example of the postmodern convergence of technology and multi-unit retailing, where anyone anywhere can be a customer, and any screen in front of that customer can be a number of stores. Such infinite possibilities in multi-unit retailing were well beyond even the wildest dreams of earlier masterminds such as James Cash Penney, David Lewis, George Gilman, Frank Woolworth, Simon Marks and Dorothy Shaver – and yet, for better or worse, the present and the future of multiple retailers is merely the continuance of retailing ideas and methods they each set in motion.

References

AEW Architects (2012), *Tesco Walkden, Phase I.* [online] Available at: www.aewarchitects.com/tesco-walkden/TESCO Walkden (Accessed 10 March 2017).

Barmash, I. (1981), *More than they bargained for: The rise and fall of Korvettes* (New York: Chain Store Publishing).

Barron, J. (2015), 'A.& P. Bankruptcy means New York, Chain's Birthplace, will lose last store', *New York Times.* [online] Available at: www.nytimes.com/2015/08/02/nyregion/a-p-bankruptcy-means-new-york-chains-birthplace-will-lose-last-store.html?_r=0 (Accessed 10 March 2017).

Beasley, N. (1948), *Main street merchant: The story of the J. C. Penney company* (New York: McGraw-Hill).

Berfield, S. (2013), 'Where Wal-Mart isn't: Four countries the retailer can't conquer', *Bloomberg.* [online] Available at: www.bloomberg.com/news/articles/2013-10-10/where-wal-mart-isnt-four-countries-the-retailer-cant-conquer (Accessed 10 March 2017).

Campbell, T. (2016), 'What 4 closed Sams cubs tell us', *Kantar Retail.* [online] Available at: http://us.kantar.com/business/retail/2016/what-sams-club-closures-tell-us/ (Accessed 10 March 2017).

Carrefour Group (2017), *Carrefour official website.* [online] Available at: www.carrefour.com/content/carrefour-stores-worldwide (Accessed 10 March 2017).

Clark, N. (2013), 'The decline of the British department store', *BBC.* [online]. Available at: www.express.co.uk/news/uk/445772/The-decline-of-the-British-department-store (Accessed 10 March 2017).

Clark, T. and Chan, S.P. (2014), 'A history of Tesco: The rise of Britain's biggest supermarket', *London Telegraph.* [online] Available at: www.telegraph.co.uk/finance/markets/2788089/A-history-of-Tesco-The-rise-of-Britains-biggest-supermarket.html (Accessed 10 March 2017).

Covington, H.E. (1988), *Belk: A century of retail leadership* (Chapel Hill, NC: University of North Carolina Press).

Curry, M.E. (1993), *Creating an American institution: The merchandising genius of J.C. Penney* (New York: Garland).

Di Stefano, J. (2015), 'Primark replaces Sears in King of Prussia', *Philadelphia Inquirer.* [online] Available at: www.philly.com/philly/blogs/inq-phillydeals/Primark-.html (Accessed 15 October 2016).

Dow Jones Newswires (2000), 'Dayton Hudson plans to change name to target, reflecting chain's success', *Wall Street Journal.* [online] Available at: www.wsj.com/articles/SB947776079405742850 (Accessed 10 March 2017).

Eichenwald, K. (2000), 'Robert E. Dewar, 77, who led Kmart in 70's expansion, dies', *New York Times.* [online] Available at: www.nytimes.com/2000/09/11/business/robert-e-dewar-77-who-led-kmart-in-70-s-expansion-dies.html (Accessed 10 March 2017).

Eliot, T.S. (1943), *Burnt Norton. Four quartets* (New York: Harvest Books/Harcourt Brace).

Emmet, B. and Jeuck, J.E. (1950), *Catalogues and counters: A history of Sears, Roebuck and company* (Chicago, IL: University of Chicago).

Finn, C. (2015), 'A household Irish name built from Humble Beginnings: The Penneys story', *TheJournal.ie.* [online] Available at: www.thejournal.ie/penneys-business-1957209-Mar2015/ (Accessed 10 March 2017).

Groupe Casino (2017), *Groupe Casino's official website.* [online] Available at: www.groupe-casino.fr/en/activities/geant-casino-hypermarkets/ (Accessed 10 March 2017).

Hardwick, M.J. (2008), *Mall maker: Victor Gruen, architect of an American Dream* (Philadelphia, PA: University of Pennsylvania Press).

HBC.com (2017), *Hudson's Bay company official website.* [online] Available at: http://www3.hbc.com/hbc/about-us/ (Accessed 10 March 2017).

HouseofFraser.co.uk (2017), *House of Fraser official website.* [online] Available at: www.houseoffraser.co.uk/store+locations/M098_STORE_LOCATIONS,default,pg.html (Accessed 10 May 2017).

Howard, V. (2008), '"The biggest small-town store in America": Independent retailers and the rise of consumer culture', *Enterprise & Society*, 9 (3), pp. 457–486.

Howard, V. (2015), *From Main Street to mall: The rise and fall of the American department store* (Philadelphia, PA: University of Pennsylvania Press).

Hudson's Bay Company (2015), 'Writing our own story: A company of adventurers', Annual Report of the Hudson's Bay Company, Hudson's Bay Company, Toronto, ON, Canada.

J. C. Penney Company (1985), *Store opening/closing date lists.* [list] Southern Methodist University, DeGolyer Library, J. C. Penney Company Archival Records Collection, Dallas, TX.

J. C. Penney Company (2001), *Store history for J. C. Penney Store #476 – Downtown Cortland, New York.* [computer file] Southern Methodist University, DeGolyer Library, J. C. Penney Company Archival Records Collection, Dallas, TX.

Jefferys, J.B. (1954), *Retail trading in Britain 1850–1950* (Cambridge, UK: Cambridge University Press).

Kestenbaum, R. (2017), 'How to understand Macy's possible acquisition by Hudson's Bay', *Forbes.* [online] Available at: www.forbes.com/sites/richardkestenbaum/2017/02/03/how-to-understand-macys-possible-acquisition-by-hudsons-bay/#3df85eb66340 (Accessed 10 March 2017).

Kline, R. (2000), *Consumers in the country: Technology and social change in rural America* (Baltimore, MD: Johns Hopkins University Press).

Kresge, S.S. (1979), *The S. S. Kresge story* (Racine, WI: Western Press).

Kruger, D.D. (2012), 'Earl Corder Sams and the rise of J. C. Penney', *Kansas History*, 35 (3), pp. 164–185.

Kruger, D.D. (2014), 'J. C. Penney in the land of enchantment: The evolution of a national department store in twentieth-century New Mexico', *New Mexico Historical Review*, 89 (3), pp. 321–358.

Kruger, D.D. (2017), *J. C. Penney: The man, the store, and American agriculture* (Norman, OK: University of Oklahoma).

Latham, F.B. (1972), *1872–1972 a century of serving customers; The story of Montgomery Ward* (Chicago, IL: Montgomery Ward).

Lebhar, G. (1963), *Chain stores in America, 1859–1962* (New York: Chain Store Publishing).

Levinson, M. (2011), *The great A&P and the struggle for small business in America* (New York: Hill & Wang).

Lewis, S. (1920), *Main Street: The story of Carol Kennicott* (New York: Harcourt Brace).

Lichtenstein, N. (2009), *The retail revolution: How Wal-Mart created a brave new world of business* (New York: Henry Holt).

Loeb, W. (2017), 'J. C. Penney faces reality: The future of retailing is uncertain', *Forbes*. [online] Available at: www.forbes.com/sites/walterloeb/2017/02/27/j-c-penney-faces-reality-the-future-of-retailing-is-uncertain/#669a376322c5 (Accessed 10 March 2017).

Longstreth, R. (2010), *The American department store transformed, 1920–1960* (New Haven, CT: Yale University Press).

Macys.com (2017), *Macy's incorporated official website*. [online] Available at: www.macysinc.com/for-investors/store-information/store-count/2016/default.aspx (Accessed 10 May 2017).

Martin, D. (2012), 'Eugene Ferkauf, 91, dies; Restyled retail', *New York Times*. [online] Available at: www.nytimes.com/2012/06/07/business/eugene-ferkauf-founder-of-e-j-korvette-chain-dies-at-91.html (Accessed 10 March 2017).

McDonald, H. (2016), 'Austins of Derry closes doors after 186 years' trading', *Guardian*. [online] Available at: www.theguardian.com/uk-news/2016/mar/08/austins-of-derry-closes-doors-after-186-years-trading (Accessed 10 March 2017).

Meijer.com (2017), *Meijer incorporated official website*. [online] Available at: www.meijer.com/custserv/store_locator.jsp (Accessed 10 May 2017).

Mergent Online (2017), *Retail – General merchandise/department stores competitor report* [data set] (Fort Mill, SC: Mergent) Online. (Accessed 10 March 2017).

Moreton, B. (2009), *To serve God and Wal-Mart: The making of Christian free enterprise* (Cambridge, MA: Harvard University Press).

National Retail Federation (2017), *2017 top 250 powers of global retailing*. [online] Available at: https://nrf.com/news/2017-top-250-global-powers-of-retailing (Accessed 10 March 2017).

Nichols, J.P. (1940), *The chain store tells its story* (New York: Institute of Distribution).

Newman, P.C. (1989), *Empire of the Bay: An illustrated history of the Hudson's Bay company* (New York: Viking).

Oakes, C.L. (1957), *Managing suburban branches of department stores* (Palo Alto, CA: Stanford School of Business).

Patterson, A., Hodgson, J. and Shi, J. (2008), 'Chronicles of "customer experience": The downfall of Lewis's Foretold', *Journal of Marketing Management*, 24 (1–2), pp. 29–45.

Penney, J.C. (1931), *J.C. Penney: The man with a thousand partners* (New York: Harper & Row).

Penney, J.C. (1950), *Fifty years with the golden rule* (New York: Harper & Row).

Purvis, M. (2015), 'Direction and discretion: The roles of centre and brank in the interwar management of marks and spencer', *History of Retailing and Consumption*, 1 (1), pp. 63–81.

Ritter, I. (2010), 'Sam's Club closings shows it lags behind Costco, BJs', *CBS Moneywatch*. [online] Available at: www.cbsnews.com/news/sams-club-closings-shows-its-lag-behind-costco-bjs/ (Accessed 10 March 2017).

Rosenberg, L.J. (1988), *Dillard's: The first fifty years* (Fayetteville, AR: University of Arkansas Press).

Rosenberg, L.J. and Rao, C.P. (1989), 'William T. Dillard: A pioneer merchant in suburban shopping centers', *Essays in Economic and Business History*, 7, pp. 230–236.

Sams, E.C. (1929), *Yesterday, to-day, and to-morrow* (address delivered at the Dallas and Tulsa Sessions of the J. C. Penney Company Spring Convention). [pamphlet] Southern Methodist University, DeGolyer Library, J. C. Penney Company Archival Records Collection, Dallas, TX.

Schuster, L. (1981), 'Wal-Mart chief's enthusiastic approach infects employees, keeps retailer growing', *Wall Street Journal*.

Scroop, D. (2008), 'The anti-chain store movement and the politics of consumption', *American Quarterly*, 60 (4), pp. 925–949.

Setzer, C. (1985), *Fire in the hole: Miners and managers in the American coal industry* (Lexington, KY: University of Kentucky Press).

Seventy-Sixth United States Congress (1940), *Excise tax on retail stores* (Washington, DC) p. 559.

Smithsonian Institute (2012), *Dorothy Shaver (1893–1959): The first lady of retailing*. [pdf] (Washington, DC: Smithsonian Institution). Available at: http://amhistory.si.edu/archives/WIB-tour/dorothy_shaver.pdf (Accessed 10 May 2016).

Stone, B. (2013), 'Costco CEO Craig Jelinek leads the cheapest, happiest company in the world', *Bloomberg*. [online]. Available at: www.bloomberg.com/news/articles/2013-06-06/costco-ceo-craig-jelinek-leads-the-cheapest-happiest-company-in-the-world (Accessed 10 May 2017).

Time (1962), 'Discounting gets respectable', *Time Magazine* (53), cover.

Tse, K.K. (1985), *Marks and Spencer: Anatomy of Britain's most efficiently managed company* (New York: Pergamon Press).

Wahba, P. (2016), 'Walmart to close 152 U.S. stores, affecting 10,000 jobs', *Fortune*, p. 1. [online]. Available at: http://fortune.com/2016/01/15/walmart-stores-closings/ (Accessed 10 March 2017).
Walmart.com (2017), *Walmart stores incorporated official website*. [online] Available at: http://corporate.walmart.com/our-story/our-locations (Accessed 10 March 2017).
Walsh, W.I. (1986), *The rise and decline of the great Atlantic & Pacific Tea company* (Secaucus, NJ: Lyle Stuart).
Weil, G.L. (1977), *Sears, Roebuck, U.S.A.: The great American catalog store and how it grew* (New York: Stein and Day).
Wilson, M. (2017), 'German Grocery giant to make a big U.S. debut ahead of schedule', *Chain Store Age*. [online] Available at: www.chainstoreage.com/article/german-grocery-giant-make-big-us-debut-ahead-schedule (Accessed 10 March 2017).
Winkler, J.K. (1940), *Five and ten: The fabulous life of F. W. Woolworth* (New York: Robert M. McBride).

18
CO-OPERATIVE RETAILING

Mary Hilson, Silke Neunsinger and Greg Patmore

Introduction

In its most basic form, consumer co-operation is a form of resource pooling. Individuals – often though not exclusively those of limited means – contribute to a common fund, which can then be used to purchase goods in bulk and thus at a discount, for redistribution between the members (van der Linden 2008: 133). As such, consumer co-operatives may be small-scale and informal, for example when members of a shared student household pool their resources to buy a 20kg sack of rice in preference to each individual buying their own 500g bag. But consumer co-operatives may also become very large organisations manufacturing, distributing and retailing goods to millions of members and handling annual volumes of trade turnover that easily rival that of any other retailing business.

Most of the consumer co-operative societies discussed here began as small community initiatives but later grew into regional or national federations. Often referred to by popular names – such as the "Co-op" or "Brugsen" to give the English and Danish examples – it is these established co-operatives that are the main focus of this chapter. The chapter draws on our knowledge of consumer co-operatives in different national contexts, but above all on the examples presented in our volume *A Global History of Consumer Co-operation since 1850: Movements and Businesses* (Hilson, Neunsinger and Patmore 2017). While as far as possible we try to consider co-operative retailing in a global perspective, a Eurocentric bias has to some extent been unavoidable, reflecting the much better developed historiography on European consumer co-operation (in languages that we can read).

As Marcel van der Linden has noted, the pooling of resources in a co-operative is one strategy available to consumers of limited means to resist market failures in a capitalist system and secure supplies of scarce essential goods (van der Linden 1994).[1] For this reason, consumer co-operatives have often been conceived as alternatives to capitalist systems for the distribution and supply of goods. Moreover, consumer co-operatives are also often characterised by the idea of members' democratic influence and a bottom up approach. There are also examples of consumer co-operatives started and operated by the state, such as those in the USSR and the socialist states of Eastern Europe, but consideration of these is beyond the scope of this chapter. Consumer co-operatives were sometimes associated with liberal self-help strategies in the second half of the nineteenth century, but around the turn of the twentieth century they became aligned with working-class socialist movements in many countries. In 1910, the Second International formally recognised co-operatives as a means in the class struggle, though the question of political affiliation has remained deeply controversial for many co-operatives. Co-operatives have generally needed to operate within the market economy and to compete with other retailers, even if their leaders were often ambivalent about the strategies which this implied.

This ambivalence forms a central theme for our chapter. We consider co-operatives as organisations that combine the features of businesses and social movements, with varying degrees of balance between the two (Jensen 2016). To what extent are consumer co-operatives part of the capitalist retailing sector and to what extent have they tried to provide an alternative to it? How have they sought to reconcile their functions as businesses operating in a competitive retailing market with their aspirations to challenge capitalist retailing, distribution and consumption? How have they adapted to changes in the sector and how successful has this been?

The growth of co-operative retailing c.1860–1914

The story of the Equitable Rochdale Pioneers Society founded in December 1844 is well-established in the mythology of the international co-operative movement. The consumer co-operative movement in nineteenth-century Europe was however a multi-centred phenomenon which emerged more or less simultaneously in a range of different contexts. Examples of co-operative stores could be found in France, Switzerland and Britain during the 1830s and Italy from the 1850s. Often these were relatively short-lived experiments, formed in response to temporary periods of high prices or food shortages, but they were also linked to the radical political movements of the 1830s and 1840s (Battilani 2017; Degen 2017; Hilson 2017a; Lambersens et al. 2017). Similar initiatives also appeared outside Europe, for example in Canada (MacPherson 2017).

The main period of growth for consumer co-operatives in Europe started in the 1860s, as a result of several factors. First, it was stimulated by the transnational circulation of ideas and innovations in response to economic and social change. Often these exchanges were mediated through personal contacts and many of the national histories of co-operation reserve a special place for the individual pioneer who 'discovered' co-operation abroad and transplanted the idea to his [sic!] national context. Knowledge of co-operative ideas also moved across borders with migrants. Examples include Belgium, where co-operatives were established by labour migrants and political refugees from northern France during the 1850s (van Goethem 2017) but above all in the Americas and Australia, where consumer co-operatives were the result of "white" trans-Atlantic migration and part of the resources used by immigrants to help them establish new lives (Balnave and Patmore 2017; MacPherson 2017; Patmore 2017; Vuotto et al. 2017).

Secondly, and often triggered by these transnational exchanges, the establishment of a suitable legislative framework for co-operatives was an important stimulant to co-operative organisation. Early nineteenth-century co-operative societies tended to be formed as associations or mutual (friendly) societies, or as joint-stock companies. Legal arrangements varied considerably in how co-operatives were defined and the extent to which the legislation defined co-operative principles. For example, the flexibility of Belgium's 1873 law did little to shield co-operative societies from the effects of bad management, while Germany's co-operative law in 1889 improved the statutory arrangements for auditing co-operative businesses but at the same time banned them from trading with non-members (van Goethem 2017; Prinz 2017). In some cases co-operatives developed in the absence of legal recognition of their businesses as co-operatives, for example in Italy where such legislation was not introduced until 1911 (Battilani 2017).

What then was a consumer co-operative according to the various legal codes? Finding a definitive statement of co-operative principles before the International Co-operative Alliance (ICA) established one in 1937 is difficult, but most co-operatives shared several distinctive features. First, co-operatives were a form of business partnership, but in contrast to the other nineteenth-century innovation, the joint stock company, they generally placed limits on the individual ownership of share capital. Second, most co-operatives contained within their rules some provision for democratic control, usually expressed in the principle of "one member one vote". Third, even before the Rochdale Pioneers consumer co-operatives had begun to adopt the practice of distributing the trading surplus to members in proportion to patronage. The advantage of this approach, as Michael Prinz has noted, was that 'it was set against the logic of spontaneous co-operation' (Prinz 2003: 19); in other words it contained a built-in incentive for members to patronise the co-operative stores. It was also favoured by social reformers for helping to encourage thrift and in some parts of Europe, such as Britain, the quarterly dividend or "divi" became an extremely important part of working-class household economies from the second half of the nineteenth century (Gurney 1996). The dividend was sometimes a source of friction between co-operative societies and their opponents: co-operators argued the surplus generated through mutual trading was not technically profit and thus should not be taxed but during the interwar period many governments, under pressure from the lobbies of private traders, insisted that this was not the case (e.g. Gurney 2015).

From the 1860s therefore co-operative stores became part of the retailing landscape in many European towns and cities. In most cases they started very modestly as small and simple stores, sometimes located in temporary premises and trading for limited hours only. Their stock consisted above all of essential foodstuffs and many co-operative societies, such as the famous Vooruit society in Ghent and Solidar in Malmö, began trading as co-operative bakeries (van Goethem 2017; Friberg 2005). With bread as with other goods, co-operatives were partly a response to concerns about the quality and safety of food in industrial cities and co-operative societies made much of their ambition to supply pure, unadulterated food at fair weights and measures.

Consumer co-operation was by no means exclusively an urban phenomenon, however. In Scandinavia co-operative development was stimulated by new legislation in the 1860s and 1870s which ended the monopoly of the towns on retail trade. By the early twentieth century the co-operative store was as much a feature of the villages of rural Denmark and Finland as it was of the working-class neighbourhoods of cities like Hamburg, Manchester or Turin (Hilson 2017b). This meant that the line between agricultural and consumer co-operatives was often blurred, as for example where co-operative societies supplying agricultural equipment also offered groceries to their farmer members. Elsewhere, however, consumer co-operatives faced apathy or even hostility in the countryside, for example in Ireland or the Scottish Highlands (King and Kennedy 1994; Watts 2017). Meanwhile, especially in settler societies such as Canada and Australia, co-operative stores often emerged to serve the needs of particular occupational communities, such as those associated with mining areas or railway junctions (Balnave and Patmore 2017; MacPherson 2017).

It is difficult therefore to generalise about patterns of co-operative success and failure in the nineteenth century. Consumer co-operation flourished in Ghent, where the Vooruit society had developed an extensive network of stores and other activities, but as Geert van Goethem has shown attempts to transplant this system to the other Flemish cities of Antwerp and Zele ended in failure (van Goethem 2017). Co-operatives could be strengthened through their connection to already established working-class "networks of solidarity" as was the case in Portugal (Freire and Pereira 2017), but attempts to link them more closely to the labour movement were a source of controversy and division in many parts of Europe. There are also examples of consumer

Figure 18.1 Bakers Lennart Lindmark and Åke Granström with the 'Derby' baking machine. Co-operative bakery, 17 July 1946. Many consumer co-operatives began trading as bakeries and prided themselves on their use of the most modern, hygienic and efficient equipment.

(Courtesy of the Swedish Labour Movement Archives and Library)

co-operatives that reflected ethnic or linguistic solidarities, for example in North America where they were associated with Finnish settler communities or in Bohemia where there were separate German and Czech-speaking co-operative federations (Patmore 2017; Reich 2006).

By the turn of the twentieth century consumer co-operatives were expanding rapidly, not only in the size of their membership and trade, but also in the nature and ambition of their businesses. The largest urban co-operative societies served tens of thousands of members. Their share of retail trade in any particular locality is difficult to measure accurately, but one estimate suggests that the British consumer co-operatives accounted for between 7 and 9% of national retail trade, rising to about 17% of the grocery sector (Wilson, Webster and

Vorberg-Rugh 2013: 99). The co-operative proportion of trade was probably significantly higher in particular localities.

Co-operative expansion was facilitated by three innovations. First, with some exceptions where legislation prevented co-operative societies opening more than one store, co-operatives pursued horizontal integration, so that many larger cities had multiple branches of stores run by a single co-operative society. Second, co-operative societies expanded their trade beyond the initial focus on basic foodstuffs: they had specialist departments for butchery, dairy produce and groceries; they also sold non-food goods such as clothes and larger items such as furniture and bicycles. Many offered a range of other services to their members, including insurance, banking and savings, pharmacies, funerals, recreational activities, education and even holidays. Third, co-operative societies were pioneers of vertical integration, establishing central organisations for the wholesale purchase of goods and also for their manufacture. Spearheading these developments was the English Co-operative Wholesale Society (CWS), founded in 1863. The CWS' foundation was possible only after a legislative amendment allowed co-operatives to form federal structures, but thereafter it grew rapidly from its beginnings in the north of England. By the turn of the century it had developed an extensive network of depots and warehouses not only across England and Wales (there was a separate wholesale society for Scotland) but also internationally, including bases in Denmark, France, Ireland, Australia and New Zealand (Webster, Wilson and Vorberg-Rugh 2017). It also manufactured branded goods at its own factories, including biscuits, sweets, boots and shoes, soap and tea, to name just a few (Wilson, Webster and Vorberg-Rugh 2013: 80–81). Its impressive headquarters in Manchester became a destination for co-operative visits from abroad, so much so that its influence deserves to be considered as important as that of Rochdale.

Co-operative retailing in the interwar period

World War I was a turning point for consumer co-operatives in many parts of Europe. Even in non-belligerent countries the food shortages and consumer price rises caused by the war necessitated government intervention in the regulation and distribution of the food supply. Co-operatives were incorporated into these efforts, in recognition of the fact that they had an infrastructure for food distribution that private retailers lacked. This also meant that their membership and volume of trade rose substantially. But the situation also sharpened conflicts over the production and distribution of food and many European countries saw a mobilisation of consumers – especially working-class women – protesting against what they saw as profiteering by the producers and distributors of food (Davis 1996; Hunt 2010). Some consumer co-operatives found themselves on the frontline of these conflicts. In Finland for example the unity of a co-operative movement containing both producers' and consumers' co-operatives could no longer be sustained, and the movement split in 1916 with the formation of a new co-operative union for the working-class consumer societies (Hilson 2017b). In Britain, co-operators' dissatisfaction with the government's treatment of their movement led to a decision to engage directly in political action and the formation of the Co-operative Party in 1918 (Adams 1987).

Leaving these political difficulties aside, from the end of the war co-operatives faced new challenges. First, the disruption to international trade threatened the international supply chains on which co-operatives relied to secure many of their goods. Many co-operators accepted free trade as an article of faith, which they hoped would be restored as quickly as possible as normal activities resumed after the war. For this purpose, efforts were made within the ICA to found an International Co-operative Wholesale Society (ICWS) to promote trade between co-operative societies in different countries, but this proved difficult and despite various initiatives the

ICWS did little more than undertake some limited bilateral activities during the interwar period (Friberg 2017). But there was one notable example of success in international co-operative trading, namely the Scandinavian Co-operative Wholesale Society (Nordisk Andelsforbund, NAF) established by representatives of the three Scandinavian co-operative wholesale societies in 1918 with the aim of creating a stronger position for the Scandinavian co-operative wholesales in international markets.[2] NAF established a trading office in London in 1921, and during the interwar period it was to become a significant importer of goods such as coffee and dried fruit to the Nordic region (Hummelin 1998).

Second, although the acute trade disruptions immediately following the war subsided, co-operators were widely aware that they were also facing new challenges resulting from longer-term changes in the capitalist economy. In terms of co-operative retailing these can be summed up in terms of three related developments: concentration and the rise of trusts and monopolies; increased horizontal integration with the rise of large retailers and chain stores; increased vertical integration which in turn implied the rise of marketing, branding and advertising. All of these changes had been evident before the war of course and at times they had brought the co-operative movement into conflict with its capitalist rivals. An example is the Swedish margarine manufacturers' attempted boycott of Kooperativa Förbundet (KF) in 1909–10, which led KF to establish its own production of margarine, while the English CWS fought a similar battle with Lever Brothers in 1910–11 (Kylebäck 1974; Wilson, Webster and Vorberg-Rugh 2013: 115–120).

Historians of the co-operative movement have been divided in their assessments of how successfully co-operative retailers responded to these challenges. Pessimists have highlighted the difficulties co-operatives faced in maintaining their market shares without losing their distinctiveness as co-operative businesses. Thus, Furlough (1991) describes how the French co-operative movement gained in membership and volume of trade following the war, but its concessions to 'waltzing with the capitalists', as she put it, amounted to a defeat of the co-operative aspirations to establish an alternative culture of consumption that had flourished before the war. Similarly in Britain, although the interwar period marked in many ways the high point of the movement in terms of its membership and influence it was already showing some signs of the problems that were to beset it after World War II: fragmentation and local rivalries between societies; difficulties in adapting its products to the demands of mass consumerism. While co-operation was able to make some advances in the south, including London, there were also ominous signs of falling sales in its traditional strongholds in the north of England (Purvis 1999, 2009). The decision to embrace political activism was seen by some as a defeat for the movement and a sign of its loss of confidence in the power of voluntarism to effect social and economic change (Youngjohns 1954; cited in Carbery 1969).

As this suggests, while co-operation was forced to respond to changes in commercial retailing, it also faced political challenges. Firstly, the growth of state welfare benefits such as pensions and accident insurance removed what was in some cases an important incentive to join the local co-operative society (van Goethem 2017). Secondly, especially in the wake of the Great Depression, co-operatives were threatened by the political mobilisation of their commercial opponents. In some parts of Europe this took the relatively mild form of legislation that was hostile to co-operative trading, for example making co-operative trading surpluses liable to taxation (Gurney 2015). But elsewhere these challenges were far more serious, where attacks on co-operatives formed part of the wider challenges to democracy and the eventual fall of democratic regimes. In Austria, Germany and Italy for example there were examples of vandalism and attacks on co-operative stores, with the co-operatives eventually incorporated directly into the authoritarian regimes with a consequent loss of autonomy (Battilani 2017; Brazda et al.

2017; Prinz 2017). Likewise, consumer co-operatives were also incorporated into the distribution structures of new authoritarian regimes in Spain and Portugal (Freire and Pereira 2017; Medina-Albaladejo 2017).

Against this rather gloomy picture there are also grounds for a much more optimistic interpretation of co-operative history in interwar Europe. First, there is evidence to suggest that co-operative retailers were able to respond to the challenges and to maintain both the strength of their businesses and their significance and influence as social movements. As Robertson (2010) has shown, during the interwar period consumer co-operative societies flourished as a ubiquitous part of everyday life in Britain, not only through their network of stores, but also through the broad range of social, recreational and education activities that they provided. Robertson also finds evidence that the co-operative aspiration to offer an alternative to capitalist trading persisted. These included for example the movement's ambitions to operate as a model employer, or its continued emphasis on the quality and trustworthiness of its goods (Robertson 2010).

Second, there are also examples of how co-operative businesses were able to respond with some success to the new business challenges in the retail sector, including vertical and horizontal integration and the branding and advertising of co-operative goods. Even before World War I, some of the larger urban co-operative societies such as Vooruit constructed lavish central stores to rival the capitalist department stores (Scholliers 1999; see also Morrison 2003: 153–155). Co-operative thinkers were initially hostile to advertising, which they regarded as symptomatic of capitalism's tendency to mislead consumers and create false desires. But they could not afford to ignore it. Jonsson (2017) shows how from the early twentieth century Swedish KF began to take seriously the need not only for advertising but also related questions, including the packaging and branding of its goods and the design and layout of its stores. Unlike the efforts of its capitalist rivals, co-operative advertising was conceived not as manipulative or misleading but as part of strategies to educate its member-customers in rational consumption (Jonsson 2017; Aléx 1994). Co-operative advertising campaigns were thus designed to draw attention to the quality, purity and trustworthiness of co-operative goods, in other words to give consumers *information* about the goods that they bought.

KF can be considered a leader not only in this field but more generally as an example of a highly successful co-operative retail business during the interwar period. For Brazda and Schediwy (2011a), comparing the business successes and failures of co-operatives across Europe, KF epitomised the switch towards the professionalisation of management in the co-operative movement after 1918, which in turn emphasised the need for business efficiency and rationality alongside the more traditional co-operative values of solidarity and community. In the case of KF this can be seen in its efforts to centralise the movement and co-ordinate its development, for example through promoting the mergers of local co-operative societies; its investments in advertising, stock display, staff training and shop design; its strategies for co-ordinating its purchases internationally through NAF and above all the extension of its own manufacturing undertakings as part of a conscious and highly publicised strategy to tackle the problem of monopoly. Beginning with its successful defeat of the margarine boycott in 1909–10, and continuing after the war with the establishment of its own manufacturing plants for flour, sugar refining, matches, galoshes, linoleum and lightbulbs, KF was able to resist successfully the attempts of international cartels to monopolise the market and in doing so to force consumer prices for these commodities down. Its success in doing so was used by its leaders as an argument for how co-operation contributed to maintaining competition and thus business efficiency in free markets that were increasingly threatened by monopolies (Hilson 2018).

Third, the 1930s also saw a resurgence of interest in consumer co-operation outside Europe, including Canada, which Ian MacPherson (2017) has described as a golden age of Canadian co-operatives, and the US (MacPherson 2017; Patmore 2017). The Great Depression generally encouraged criticism of the prevailing business system and the search for alternatives based on service rather than profit. The Co-operative League of the USA (CLUSA) estimated that the membership of US consumer co-operatives grew 40% from 1929 to 1934. Central associations of local co-operatives and regional federations were formed to undertake joint purchase and to market bulk items such as petrol, while youth leagues and women's guilds were founded to encourage young people and women to join the movement. African Americans formed co-operatives in locations such as Chicago and Harlem, which was also the headquarters for Young Negroes' Co-operative Leagues (Gordon Nembhard 2017). Examples of external influences on these developments include a visit to the US by the Japanese Christian co-operator Toyohiko Kagawa, which attracted considerable interest, and publicity surrounding the co-operative educational work of the Reverend Dr Moses Coady at Antigonish in Nova Scotia (Fitzpatrick-Behrens and LeGrand 2017; MacPherson 2017; Patmore 2017).

The US co-operative movement also faced a favourable political situation, with support from President Roosevelt and renewed interest from the labour movement. In 1933, Roosevelt issued an Executive Order exempting all 'bona fide and legitimate cooperative organization' from the prohibitions of rebates and discounts under the National Industrial Recovery Act (NIRA) (Patmore 2017). The President sent a mission to Europe in July 1936 to report on co-operative developments in Europe, especially in Sweden where they were regarded as a "middle way" (Knapp 1973: 391). The US co-operative movement also found a renewed level of support from the trade unions. The American Federation of Labor (AFL) welcomed the resurgence of the consumer co-operative movement, noting the benefits of co-operatives for workers in cutting out the middle-man and ensuring the quality of goods and reducing prices by minimising waste. Meanwhile, business groups such as the Chamber of Commerce of the United States watched the growth of consumer co-operatives with concern, noting that it was 'improper for government agencies to extend preferential treatment' to them, as they were 'but another form of competitive force' seeking to win the patronage of consumers (Patmore 2017).

Co-operative retailing since 1945

Espen Ekberg has noted that in the postwar years some consumer co-operative movements were able to survive or strengthen their market share while others went into decline. The survival of consumer co-operatives is linked to their ability to confront three major transformations or revolutions in the food retail market. Ekberg focuses on the German, British and Nordic experiences to illustrate his argument, with the German experience being one of failed adaptation, the British case being one of delayed adaptation and the Nordic cases being ones of partially successful adaptation, albeit in different ways (Ekberg 2012a, 2017; Balnave and Patmore 2015: 1134–1138).

Firstly, co-operatives have had to adapt their store formats to meet the "supermarket revolution" with the growth of self-serviced supermarket and hypermarket retailing. Before these changes co-operative stores were small and specialised, located close to the consumer and relying upon personal counter service. Now food is largely sold on a self-service basis and the average size of stores has increased, while the overall number of stores has fallen. Meeting this challenge successfully requires sufficient capital formation to purchase the land required to build supermarkets and hypermarkets, with sufficient space for car parking. While the German co-operative movement was quick to launch self-service stores, they failed to consolidate these gains and transfer trade to larger supermarkets and chains (see also Prinz 2017). There was also declining shareholder capital and an increased reliance on borrowed capital. The British co-operatives, despite having also had an initial lead, lost their initiative. There were also problems with raising capital for extension and in both the British and German co-operatives there was some hostility to the supermarket format. The Norwegians by contrast were able to retain their initial lead in self-service and raise sufficient capital for extension through a co-operative savings programme launched in 1954. Unlike Germany and the UK, the competition from conventional retailers was less fierce in Norway (Ekberg 2012a: 1006, 1009–1015).

While Ekberg does recognise the importance of shareholder capital, Menzani and Zamagni (2010) have suggested that improved capitalisation has been an important factor allowing Italian co-operatives to flourish since the 1970s. A favourable legal environment has assisted this, for example with laws that exempt undistributed profits set aside in indivisible reserves, which are the assets owned by the co-operative that can never be divided among members, from corporate taxes. This allowed co-operatives to fund further expansion from self-financing (Menzani and Zamagni 2010: 105–106).

The second important challenge according to Ekberg was the 'chain store revolution', which related to the growth of large standardised, integrated and centralised retail chains. In the 1950s West European independent retailers would own one or more stores and operate them on a non-standardised and autonomous basis, receiving supplies from a variety of stores. This organisation had fundamentally changed by the end of the century with retail chains having several hundred branches marketed under the same brand. Inflationary pressures in the 1970s increased the costs of holding stocks on the premises and improvements in delivery techniques reduced the need for on-site warehousing. Large supermarket chains in the US and UK developed Regional Distribution Centres or centralised depots. Technological developments at the cash register, such as price scanning, allowed better supply forecasting and an emphasis on "demand pull" rather than supply push. The headquarters of the chain store supermarkets became responsible for buying and negotiated on behalf of all stores in the chain. These developments paved the way for large cost savings, the increased efficiency and productivity of operations and cheaper prices (Ekberg 2012a: 1006; Hallsworth and Bell 2003).

According to Ekberg, the German co-operative movement's two national associations, its wholesale and union, failed to co-ordinate their activities and had very different attitudes to key issues such as logistics and amalgamation. There was also a breakdown in the relationship between the wholesale society, GEG (Grosseinkaufs-Gesellschaft Deutscher Consumvereine) and the retail societies, with the latter developing their own warehousing and buying procedures. The British co-operative movement also remained highly fragmented until 1993 when the CWS with three other societies formed the Co-operative Retailing Group to buy supplies for the member organisations (see also Secchi 2017). However the regional societies soon formed a separate buying group, the Consortium of Independent Co-operatives, a development which highlighted continuing tensions within the movement. By contrast the Norwegian co-operative movement did not face the impact of the chain store revolution before the 1980s, but these changes were already underway in the Norwegian co-operative movement, which launched Norway's first fully integrated retail/wholesale chain in 1990 (Ekberg 2012a: 1009–1015).

Ekberg has also developed three organisational models to explain the success or failure of co-operative movements since World War II in the face of competition from large, centralised conventional retail chains. These are the federal, hybrid and non-federal models. The non-federal model involves merging all independent consumer co-operatives into one organisational unit. Examples of this included Konsum Austria and Co-op AG in Germany, which were formed to avoid financial difficulties. The hybrid model involved the amalgamation of societies into

Figure 18.2 New co-operative convenience store in Årsta, 1948. In many parts of Europe co-operatives were the pioneers of retailing innovations such as the introduction of self-service during the 1940s, but later lost out to their capitalist rivals.

(Courtesy of the Swedish Labour Movement Archives and Library)

larger units with a national wholesaler having centralised control over commercial operations. This type of model was a transitional model for the UK, which since 2000 has moved towards a fully centralised non-federal model. The federal model emphasises merging small local co-operatives into larger regional units, with the national federations focusing on wholesaling and manufacturing and ensuring the integration and standardising of operations through contractual arrangements. An example of this can be seen with the NKL in Norway. This approach reinforces a traditional federal model that has served the consumer co-operatives since the nineteenth century (Ekberg 2012b).

The successful Italian experience reinforces Ekberg's recognition that the organisational structure of co-operatives can be important for the survival against competition from conventional large retail chains. In Italy the smaller co-operatives merged into larger co-operatives in order to have sufficient capital to manage the modern supermarkets and hypermarkets. Battilani (2017) argues that this process transformed the Italian consumer co-operatives during the 1950s and 1960s and made the second half of the twentieth century the golden age of the Italian consumer co-operative movement. Menzani and Zamagni (2010) view co-operative networking as another strategic factor that allowed the Italian movement to flourish. The networking between co-operatives has allowed them, for example, to achieve a critical mass in the market.

Outside Europe there were some examples of decline and major collapses of significant co-operatives, in countries such as Australia, New Zealand and the US (Balnave and Patmore 2008: 103–104; Cooper and Mohn 1992). One particularly notable example of collapse was the Berkeley Consumer Co-operative, which was the largest consumer co-operative in the US, formed in 1937. Following rapid expansion during the 1950s and 1960s, during which it also became a centre for consumer activism and education, the co-operative's finances deteriorated during the 1980s and in 1988 it had to file for bankruptcy (Patmore 2017). The reasons for its decline and collapse are indicative of the problems faced by many consumer co-operatives in the postwar period. They include: problems resulting from its expansion policy and attempts to incorporate non-co-operative businesses after 1962; bitter political divisions within the co-operative; the turnover of co-operative management; difficulties in relationships with wholesalers and problems with the quality of produce; the competitiveness of the retail sector and the loss of member support (Patmore 2017).

Survival and revival

While there has been an emphasis of the significance of networking among co-operatives, some co-operatives have survived where co-operative movements and networks have collapsed. One factor that Ekberg does not highlight is the links between co-operative societies and their local communities. Several scholars have recently attributed the continued appeal of surviving consumer co-operatives to their link to the community, particularly in rural areas (Balnave and Patmore 2015: 1138). As Nicole Robertson has noted 'for some of its members, the role of a co-operative society within a community extended beyond the realms of grocery shopping' (Robertson 2010: 213). The survival of what Balnave and Patmore describe as 'outsider co-ops, which are not linked to any co-operative retailing networks' can be seen for example in Germany, where the co-operative eG operates more than 200 supermarkets in five states, and the Community Co-operative Store (Nuriootpa) in the Barossa Valley of South Australia (Balnave and Patmore 2015: 1133).

The Nuriootpa co-operative was able to survive the "supermarket challenge" and highlights the need to focus on capitalisation as an important explanation for the survival of retail co-operatives. The Co-op successfully retained sufficient capital to expand and update its facilities

Figure 18.3 An example of recent success: the Barossa Co-operative Mall in South Australia, 2009. (Courtesy of Richard O'Leary).

to build modern supermarkets and provide a range of services. Its funds also gave it sufficient capital to purchase suitable property for both the required supermarket floor space and appropriate car parking facilities. This also allowed it to buy-out land that could provide potential floor space for competitors. It successfully tightened up the provision of credit facilities so that this did not become a major liability for the Co-op. Second, the Co-op was able to survive the 'chain store revolution'. Like other surviving Australian consumer co-operatives, as an outsider co-operative the Nuriootpa Co-op does not fit the organisational models developed by Ekberg. The Nuriootpa Co-op represents a fourth model of co-operative organisation built around non-co-operative business brand franchising. The Co-op became a franchisee for the Foodland and later IGA (Independent Grocers of Australia) supermarket chains to ensure access to supply chains and broader marketing campaigns. It became a franchisee for a range of products including hardware and carpets and franchising also became a mechanism for blocking other potential franchises setting themselves up in the Barossa Valley. The Co-op also rapidly adopted innovations such as computerised price scanning to ensure minimal inventories and respond to consumer demand. Third, the Nuriootpa Co-op survived the "consumer revolution". The appeals of co-operative ideology and dividend payments became less important in attracting and retaining members. The Co-op found it necessary to rely on sales and promotions to maintain custom and compete with other retailers. While there was a declining level of participation in the Co-op through AGMs for instance, Co-op members would take advantage of the democratic governance of the Co-op if there were major issues of concern. The Co-op's survival was also linked to its close association with the local community. The Co-op's origins lay in a community movement formed in Nuriootpa in 1936 to develop local facilities such as parks and swimming pools. While there was a major early disagreement within the Co-op as to how much of the Co-op's surplus should be diverted into community projects, the Co-op Committee of Management provided funding for a range of activities, including sporting associations and youth services. They also promoted the retail profile of the Barossa Valley by forming alliances with other retailers. The Co-op through its advertising broadened its appeal by highlighting the importance of members shopping locally for the economic survival of Nuriootpa and the Barossa Valley (Balnave and Patmore 2015: 1150).

While the established consumer co-operatives collapsed in a number of countries following World War II, there have also arisen smaller community-based co-operatives. These focus on organic, natural and local foods, rekindling the nineteenth-century co-operative concerns with the provision of quality and safe food. Disillusion with capitalism during the late 1960s and 1970s led to the formation of new consumer co-operatives in Australia and the United States. Protestors against the Vietnam War, environmentalists, community control advocates and civil rights activists saw co-operatives as a symbol of the counterculture. Some of these co-operatives have been able to prosper by specifically focusing on organic foods and locally produced goods. In the United States current examples include the GreenStar Co-operative Market at Ithaca, which was founded in 1971 and had 8,000 members in 2011, and the New Pioneer Food Co-op in Iowa City, which was also founded in 1971 and has more than 11,000 members. The growth of these consumer co-operatives followed the earlier pattern of establishing regional associations and then forming the National Co-operative Grocers' Association (NCGA) in 1999. By 2012 there were 121 food co-operatives, which operate 160 stores in thirty-four states and have combined annual sales of approximately over $1.4 billion. The states that have largest numbers of these co-operative stores in 2011 were Minnesota (nineteen), Washington (seventeen) and California (eleven) (Patmore 2017). By contrast, against a background where two leading conventional retail supermarket chains control 80% of the Australian grocery market share, there are only a small number of these food co-operatives in Australia and there has been no attempt to form an organisation on the scale of the NCGA. A notable example in Australia is Alfalfa House in Sydney, which is a member-based co-operative with a one-off joining fee. The co-operative provides discounts for members who volunteer their labour in the store (Balnave and Patmore 2015: 1139; Battilani, Balnave and Patmore 2015: 65).

Outside of Europe and Western countries, there has been a continuing interest in consumer co-operatives in developing and less industrialised countries. In Argentina the Sociedad Cooperativa Obrera Limitada (CO) began a regional expansion in 2006 that was still continuing in 2016. Against the background of extreme state neoliberal reforms and consequent rising unemployment in Argentina during the 1990s and 2000s, a movement of worker-owned factories commenced in 1998 when 190 workers occupied Metallurgical and Plastic Industries of Argentina, a medium sized factory, to stop its closure and turned it into a workers' co-operative. This movement grew rapidly and by 2010 there were approximately 205 occupied factories, which were mainly small to medium sized companies, in industries ranging from chocolate manufacturing to metallurgic products. The worker co-operatives have linked up with consumer co-operatives in 2016 to construct an online purchasing platform that will allow the two co-operative sectors to interact and trade with one another. In South Korea, political democratisation in 1987 and economic growth provided a favourable climate for the growth of consumer co-operatives. The total number of co-operative members increased from 70,000 in 1999, when the consumer co-operation law was enacted to 630,000 by late 2010. They have played an important role in promoting ethical consumerism, support for domestic wheat production, fair trade and trade with other co-operatives (Kim 2017; Rossi 2015; Voinea 2016; Vuotto, Verbeke and Caruana 2017).

An important event that raised the profile of the co-operative movement generally was the declaration of 2012 by the United Nations as the International Year of Co-operatives. One country where the Year had an impact was Australia, where national co-operative organisation was weak and co-operatives had a low political profile. In July 2013, a new organisation called Business Council of Co-operatives and Mutuals (BCCM) was launched to represent the whole sector, including consumer co-operatives. The BCCM successfully lobbied the Australian Senate for the first major federal inquiry into Australian co-operatives and mutuals, with a favourable report delivered in March outlining seventeen recommendations including the need for national statistics and the better representation of the sector in government policy discussions. All major Australian political parties, with the exception of the Liberal Party, adopted the recommendations without qualification as part of their policies for 2016 federal elections (Balnave and Patmore 2017: 466; Commonwealth of Australia Senate 2016).

Co-operative retailing: between movements and businesses

Co-operative movements started to become a global phenomenon in retailing during the second half of the nineteenth century, during a period of European expansion that implied the adaptation of local models of co-operation to European models. Ideas of co-operation were circulated through different media: international organisations, political and social movements, migration and trade. The co-operative movement's democratic ideal of shared responsibilities and rights with a set of relatively simple rules meant that it was easy to adapt to places of white settlement. Co-operative retailing was also seen as an important strategy for self-help, especially during periods of scarcity.

Although there are many similarities between consumer co-operatives worldwide we need to analyse their development in relation to specific historical contexts in order to understand the diversity of forms that they take. Consumer co-operatives have been started not only as grassroots initiatives, but also with the support of the state or other institutions. State intervention could mean support for the movement, such as in those cases where laws facilitated new initiatives, but also demanded formalised auditing of co-operative businesses. State intervention could also mean oppression of the democratic elements of the movement, or even in some cases that consumer co-operatives became illegal or were forced to abandon co-operative principles.

Much of the historiography has been rather pessimistic about the long-term possibilities for consumer co-operatives to present a lasting and viable alternative to capitalist retailing. Writing in the 1990s, Ellen Furlough and Carl Strikwerda acknowledged the importance of co-operation as an historic alternative to capitalist retailing, but argued that the significance of this alternative had declined in the late twentieth century, due to the inability of co-operatives to respond to 'the powerful commercial and cultural challenges of capitalist consumer culture' (Furlough and Strikwerda 1999: 5–6). This thesis of decline seemed to be borne out by the high-profile and sometimes terminal difficulties of once-powerful consumer co-operative businesses in for example Germany, Austria, France and Britain during the 1980s (Brazda and Schediwy 2011b [1989]). Our comparative study suggests a more diverse picture. First, co-operative businesses – just like any form of business – are never static but constantly evolving and adopting new forms. In many communities in Europe and North America in the early twenty-first century there were examples of new types of consumer co-operatives, often local, small-scale and formed in response to new consumer preferences for goods and especially food that was locally, ecologically or otherwise ethically produced. Second, the picture of drastic decline in consumer co-operatives after 1945 is profoundly Eurocentric. We still lack research about the history of consumer co-operatives in many parts of the world, but there is plenty of scattered evidence to suggest that they continue to play a role, especially in helping consumers of limited means secure scarce goods in the market (Birchall 1997; Shaw 2014).

Notes

1 Other strategies include boycotts and unilateral (often illegal) actions to adjust the price or quantity of goods, for example through looting or appropriation.

2 The two Finnish wholesales joined in 1928; the Icelandic wholesale in 1949.

References

Adams, T. (1987), 'The formation of the co-operative party reconsidered', *International Review of Social History*, 32 (1), pp. 48–68.

Aléx, P. (1994), *Den rationella konsumenten: KF som folkuppfostrare 1899–1939* (Stockholm/Stehag: Brutus Östlings Bokförlag Symposion).

Balnave, N. and Patmore, G. (2008), '"Practical utopians": Rochdale consumer co-ops in Australia and New Zealand', *Labour History*, 95, pp. 97–110.

Balnave, N. and Patmore, G. (2015), 'The outsider consumer co-operative: Lessons from the community co-operative store (Nuriootpa), 1944–2010', *Business History*, 57 (8), pp. 1134–1154.

Balnave, N. and Patmore, G. (2017), 'Rochdale consumer co-operatives in Australia and New Zealand', in M. Hilson, S. Neunsinger and G. Patmore (eds.) *A global history of consumer co-operation since 1850: Movements and businesses* (Leiden: Brill), 456–480.

Battilani, P. (2017), 'Consumer co-operation in Italy: A network of co-operatives with a multi-class constituency', in M. Hilson, S. Neunsinger and G. Patmore (eds.) *A global history of consumer co-operation since 1850: Movements and businesses* (Leiden: Brill), 584–613.

Battilani, P., Balnave, N. and Patmore, G. (2015), 'Consumer co-operatives in Australia and Italy', in A. Jensen, G. Patmore and E. Tortia (eds.) *Cooperative enterprises in Australia and Italy: Comparative analysis and theoretical insights* (Florence: Firenze University Press).

Birchall, J. (1997), *The international co-operative movement* (Manchester: Manchester University Press).

Brazda, J., Jagschitz, F., Rom, S. and Schediwy, R. (2017), 'The rise and fall of Austria's consumer co-operatives', in M. Hilson, S. Neunsinger and G. Patmore (eds.) *A global history of consumer co-operation since 1850: Movements and businesses* (Leiden: Brill), 267–295.

Brazda, J. and Schediwy, R. (2011a), 'Consumer co-operatives on the defensive: A short overview', in J. Brazda and R. Schediwy (eds.) *A time of crises: Consumer co-operatives and their problems around 1990* (Wien: Fachbereich für Genossenschaft, Universität Wien) 13–42. Available at: https://genos.univie.ac.at/fileadmin/user_upload/genossenschaftswesen/Genos/consum.pdf (Accessed 29 August 2016). First published 1989.

Brazda, J. and Schediwy, R. (eds.) (2011b), *A time of crises: Consumer co-operatives and their problems around 1990* (Vienna: Fachbereich für Genossenschaftswesen. Wien: Fachbereich für Genossenschaft, Universität Wien) Available at: https://genos.univie.ac.at/fileadmin/user_upload/genossenschaftswesen/Genos/consum.pdf (Accessed 29 August 2016). First published 1989.

Carbery, T.F. (1969), *Consumers in politics: A history and general review of the co-operative party* (Manchester: Manchester University Press).

Commonwealth of Australia Senate, Economics References Committee (2016), *Co-operative, mutual and member owned firms* (Canberra: Commonwealth of Australia).

Cooper, D. and Mohn, P. (1992), *The greenbelt co-operative: Success and decline* (Davis, CA: Centre for Co-operatives, University of California).

Davis, B. (1996), 'Food scarcity and the empowerment of the female consumer in world war I Berlin', in V. de Grazia and E. Furlough (eds.) *The sex of things: Gender and consumption in historical perspective* (Berkeley, CA: University of California Press) 287–310.

Degen, B. (2017), 'Consumer societies in Switzerland: From local self-help organizations to a single national co-operative', in M. Hilson, S. Neunsinger and G. Patmore (eds.) *A global history of consumer co-operation since 1850: Movements and businesses* (Leiden: Brill), 614–641.

Ekberg, E. (2012a), 'Confronting three revolutions: Western European consumer co-operatives and their divergent development', *Business History*, 54 (6), pp. 1005–1015.

Ekberg, E. (2012b), 'Organization. Top down or bottom up? The organisational development of consumer co-operatives, 1950–2000', in P. Battalani and H.G. Schröter (eds.) *The co-operative business movement, 1950 to the present* (Cambridge: Cambridge University Press) 222–242.

Ekberg, E. (2017), 'Against the tide: Understanding the commercial success of Nordic consumer co-operatives, 1950–2000', in M. Hilson, S. Neunsinger and G. Patmore (eds.) *A global history of consumer co-operation since 1850: Movements and businesses* (Leiden: Brill), 698–726.

Fitzpatrick-Behrens, S. and LeGrand, C. (2017), 'Canadian and US catholic promotion of co-operatives in central America and the Caribbean and their implications', in M. Hilson, S. Neunsinger and G. Patmore (eds.) *A global history of consumer co-operation since 1850: Movements and businesses* (Leiden: Brill), 145–175.

Freire, D. and Pereira, J.D. (2017), 'Consumer co-operatives in Portugal: Debates and experiences from the nineteenth to the twentieth century', in M. Hilson, S. Neunsinger and G. Patmore (eds.) *A global history of consumer co-operation since 1850: Movements and businesses* (Leiden: Brill), 296–325.

Friberg, K. (2005), *The workings of co-operation: A comparative study of consumer co-operative organization in Britain and Sweden 1860 to 1970* (Växjö: Växjö University Press).

Friberg, K. (2017), 'A co-operative take on free trade: International ambitions and regional initiatives in international co-operative trade', in M. Hilson, S. Neunsinger and G. Patmore (eds.) *A global history of consumer co-operation since 1850: Movements and businesses* (Leiden: Brill), 201–225.

Furlough, E. (1991), *Consumer cooperation in France: The politics of consumption 1834–1930* (Ithaca, NY: Cornell University Press).

Furlough, E. and Strikwerda, C. (1999), 'Economics, consumer culture and gender: An introduction to the politics of consumer co-operation', in E. Furlough and C. Strikwerda (eds.) *Consumers against capitalism? Consumer cooperation in Europe, North America, and Japan, 1840–1990* (Lanham, MD: Rowman & Littlefield Publishers) 1–65.

Gordon Nembhard, J. (2017), 'African American consumer co-operation: History and global connections', in M. Hilson, S. Neunsinger and G. Patmore (eds.) *A global history of consumer co-operation since 1850: Movements and businesses* (Leiden: Brill), 176–200.

Gurney, P. (1996), *Co-operative culture and the politics of consumption in England, 1870–1930* (Manchester: Manchester University Press).

Gurney, P. (2015), "The curse of the co-ops': Co-operation, the mass press and the market in interwar Britain', *English Historical Review*, 130 (547), pp. 1479–1512.

Hallsworth, A. and Bell, J. (2003), 'Retail change and the United Kingdom co-operative movement – new opportunity beckoning?', *The International Review of Retail, Distribution and Consumer Research*, 13 (3), pp. 306–311.

Hilson, M. (2017a), 'Rochdale and beyond: Consumer co-operation in Britain before 1940', in M. Hilson, S. Neunsinger and G. Patmore (eds.) *A global history of consumer co-operation since 1850: Movements and businesses* (Leiden: Brill), 59–77.

Hilson, M. (2017b), 'Consumer co-operation in the Nordic Countries, c.1860–1939', in M. Hilson, S. Neunsinger and G. Patmore (eds.) *A global history of consumer co-operation since 1850: Movements and businesses* (Leiden: Brill), 121–144.

Hilson, M. (2018), *The international co-operative alliance and the consumer co-operative movement in Northern Europe, c. 1860–1939* (Manchester: Manchester University Press).

Hilson, M., Neunsinger, S. and Patmore, G. (eds.) (2017), *A global history of consumer co-operation since 1850: Movements and businesses* (Leiden: Brill).

Hummelin, K. (1998), *Nordisk andelsförbund NAF 1918–1993* (Köpenhamn: Nordisk Andelsforbund).

Hunt, K. (2010), 'The politics of food and women's neighbourhood activism in first world war Britain', *International Labor and Working-Class History*, 77 (1), pp. 8–26.

Jensen, K. (ed.) (2016). *Brugsen – en anderledes forretning?* (Albertslund: Samvirke).

Jonsson, P. (2017), 'From commercial trickery to social responsibility: Marketing in the Swedish co-operative movement in the early twentieth century', in M. Hilson, S. Neunsinger and G. Patmore (eds.) *A global history of consumer co-operation since 1850: Movements and businesses* (Leiden: Brill), 642–667.

Kim, H. (2017), 'The break off and rebirth of the consumer co-operative movement in Korea', in M. Hilson, S. Neunsinger and G. Patmore (eds.) *A global history of consumer co-operation since 1850: Movements and businesses* (Leiden: Brill), 353–378.

King, C. and Kennedy, L. (1994), 'Irish co-operatives: From creameries at the crossroads to multinationals', *History Ireland*, 2 (4), pp. 36–41.

Knapp, J. (1973), *The advance of American co-operative enterprise: 1920–1945* (Danville, IL: The Interstate).

Kylebäck, H. (1974), *Konsumentkooperation och industrikarteller* (Stockholm: Rabén & Sjögren).

Lambersens, S., Artis, A., Demoustier, D. and Mélo, A. (2017), 'History of consumer co-operatives in France: From the conquest of consumption by the masses to the challenge of mass consumption', in M. Hilson, S. Neunsinger and G. Patmore (eds.) *A global history of consumer co-operation since 1850: Movements and businesses* (Leiden: Brill), 99–120.

MacPherson, I. (2017), 'Patterns, limitations and associations: The consumer co-operative movement in Canada, 1828 to the present', in M. Hilson, S. Neunsinger and G. Patmore (eds.) *A global history of consumer co-operation since 1850: Movements and businesses* (Leiden: Brill), 431–455.

Medina-Albaladejo, F.J. (2017), 'Consumer co-operatives in Spain (1860–2010): An overview', in M. Hilson, S. Neunsinger and G. Patmore (eds.) *A global history of consumer co-operation since 1850: Movements and businesses* (Leiden: Brill), 326–352.

Menzani, T. and Zamagni, V. (2010), 'Co-operative networks in the Italian economy', *Enterprise & Society*, 11 (1), pp. 98–127.

Morrison, K.A. (2003), *English shops and shopping: An architectural history* (New Haven, CT: Yale University Press).

Patmore, G. (2017), 'Fighting monopoly and enhancing democracy: A historical overview of US consumer co-operatives', in M. Hilson, S. Neunsinger and G. Patmore (eds.) *A global history of consumer co-operation since 1850: Movements and businesses* (Leiden: Brill), 507–526.

Prinz, M. (2003), 'Structure and scope of consumer co-operation in the 20th century: Germany in the English mirror', in P. Verbruggen and L. Soubry (eds.) *Consumerism versus capitalism? Co-operatives seen from an international comparative perspective* (Ghent: Amsab-ISG) 15–50.

Prinz, M. (2017), 'German co-operatives: Rise and fall 1850–1970', in M. Hilson, S. Neunsinger and G. Patmore (eds.) *A global history of consumer co-operation since 1850: Movements and businesses* (Leiden: Brill), 243–266.

Purvis, M. (1999), 'Crossing urban deserts: Consumers, competitors and the protracted birth of metropolitan co-operative retailing', *The International Review of Retail, Distribution and Consumer Research*, 9 (3), pp. 225–243.

Purvis, M. (2009), 'Retailing and economic uncertainty in interwar Britain: Co-operative (mis)fortunes in North-West England', in E. Baigent and R.J. Mayhew (eds.) *English geographies 1600–1950: Historical essays on English customs, cultures and communities in honour of Jack Langton* (Oxford: St John's College Research Centre) 127–143.

Reich, A. (2006), 'Economic interests and national conflict: The relationship between Czech and German consumer cooperatives in Czechoslovakia between 1918 and 1939', in T. Lorenz (ed.) *Cooperatives in ethnic conflicts: Eastern Europe in the 19th and early 20th century* (Berlin: Berlin Wissenschafts-Verlag), pp. 263–282.

Robertson, N. (2010), *The co-operative movement and communities in Britain, 1914–1960* (Farnham: Ashgate).

Rossi, F. (2015), 'Building factories without bosses: The movement of worker-managed factories in Argentina', *Social Movement Studies*, 14 (1), pp. 98–107.

Scholliers, P. (1999), 'The social-democratic world of consumption: The path-breaking case of the Ghent cooperative vooruit prior to 1914', *International Labor and Working-Class History*, 55, pp. 71–91.

Secchi, C. (2017), 'Affluence and decline: Consumer co-operatives in Post-War Britain', in M. Hilson, S. Neunsinger and G. Patmore (eds.) *A global history of consumer co-operation since 1850: Movements and businesses* (Leiden: Brill), 527–547.

Shaw, L. (2014), "Casualties inevitable': Consumer co-operation in British Africa." ARAB Working Paper 6, Stockholm: Arbetarrörelsens arkiv och bibliotek. Available at: http://www.arbark.se/wp-content/dokument/2014/12/shaw-casualties-inevitable.pdf, (Accessed 31 July 2018).

Van der Linden, M. (1994), 'Working-class consumer power', *International Labor and Working-Class History*, 46, pp. 109–121.

Van der Linden, M. (2008), *Workers of the world: Essays towards a global history* (Leiden: Brill).

Van Goethem, G. (2017), 'The Belgian co-operative model: Elements of success and failure', in M. Hilson, S. Neunsinger and G. Patmore (eds.) *A global history of consumer co-operation Since 1850: Movements and businesses* (Leiden: Brill), 78–98.

Voinea, A. (2016), 'Argentinian co-ops collaborate to launch central purchasing platform', *Co-operative News*, 20 April. Available at: www.thenews.coop/103974/news/co-operatives/argentinian-co-op-collaborate-to-launch-a-web-based-central-purchasing-platform/, (Accessed 10 August 2016).

Vuotto, M., Verbeke, G. and Caruana, M.E.C. (2017), 'Consumer co-operatives in a changing economy: The argentine case', in M. Hilson, S. Neunsinger and G. Patmore (eds.) *A global history of consumer co-operation since 1850: Movements and businesses* (Leiden: Brill), 481–506.

Watts, D.C.H. (2017), 'Building an alternative economic network? Consumer cooperation in Scotland from the 1870s to the 1960s', *Economic History Review*, 70 (1), pp. 143–170.

Webster, A., Wilson, J.F. and Vorberg-Rugh, R. (2017), 'Going global: The rise of the CWS as an international commercial and political actor, 1863–1950: Scoping an agenda for further research', in M. Hilson, S. Neunsinger and G. Patmore (eds.) *A global history of consumer co-operation since 1850: Movements and businesses* (Leiden: Brill), 559–583.

Wilson, J.F., Webster, A. and Vorberg-Rugh, R. (2013), *Building co-operation: A business history of the co-operative group 1863–2013* (Oxford: Oxford University Press).

19

BY MAIL AND RAIL

A history of mail order commerce

Howard R. Stanger

Mail-order houses revolutionised distribution in the decades after the Civil War and contributed to the rise of consumer society in the United States (Chandler, 1977; Strasser, 1989; Barron, 1997; Ayers, 1992). Mail-order catalogues (often called "Farmer's Bibles"), along with country stores and county fairs served as important modernising "agents of change" in rural buying and selling in the late nineteenth and early twentieth centuries. By using the expanding railroad and telegraph networks, the steamship, and improved postal services, they extended their reach nationally to sell manufactured consumer goods to a growing population with rising incomes. By 1910, roughly 10 million Americans annually shopped by mail (Schlereth, 1989, 1992). While mail order businesses emerged in other western nations, it developed first and most extensively in the United States (Nystrom, 1919, p. 292; Nystrom, 1930).

The origins of mail order

Mail order became big business very quickly after the Civil War, with two names dominating the field: Aaron Montgomery Ward and Richard Sears. Ward started with the prosperous dry goods firm of Field, Palmer & Leiter, out of which grew the famous Chicago department store Marshall Field's. After clerking there, he worked as a travelling salesman for a St Louis dry goods wholesaler, which gave him the opportunity to hear farmers' dissatisfaction with limited selections and prices high. He also saw how the use of middlemen added to the final cost of goods sold. Ward returned to Chicago with the idea of selling goods a different way – through a mail-order general store (Latham, 1972, *1872–1972: A Century of Serving Consumers*; Boorstin, 1973a). Along with his partner and brother-in-law George R. Thorne, Ward established the first general mail order company – Montgomery Ward & Company (Montgomery Ward or Ward), in 1872.

Mail order firms relied upon their catalogues to do the selling. Montgomery Ward's single-page price list contained 163 items shipped "subject to examination". Dissatisfied customers could return items free of charge – "Satisfaction or your money back!" The company also gained the trust of distant consumers by offering testimonials from representatives of farmer organisations like the Grange and other satisfied customers, and with personally signed correspondence. Early customers were concentrated in the Midwest. When settlers pushed west in search of cheaper land, the catalogue followed them. Over the years, the "Big Book" grew in size, such that by the end of the 1880s Ward offered over 24,000 items in a fat 540-page catalogue. A workforce of over 300 clerks handled 750,000 letters and transactions worth over $1 million in Ward's seven-story "bee hive" on Michigan Avenue. By the turn of the century, the catalogue grew to 1,200 pages with 17,000 illustrations that required 2,000 clerks to handle two million customers (Thorne, 1920; Boorstin, 1973a, 1973b, p. 123; Cronon, 1991, pp. 335–336; Tedlow, 1990, p. 285; Miller, 1996, pp. 246–247).

Montgomery Ward's rapid success outraged merchants and wholesalers who doubted the firm's legitimacy. On November 8, 1873 the *Chicago Tribune* published an article titled, 'Grangers beware. Don't Patronize Montgomery Ward & Co. – They are Dead-Beats'. But under threat of lawsuit and its own investigation, the newspaper issued a retraction writing that its attack was "grossly unjust" and that the company 'is a bona fide firm, composed of respectable persons, and doing a perfectly legitimate business in a perfectly legitimate manner' (quoted in Cronon, 1991, p. 335). Ward's low prices came from the high volume of goods purchased at a discount, the absence of a retail store and a salesforce. Its money-back guarantee made buying through the impersonal mail and personal correspondence earned consumers' trust. At maturity, mail-order houses and chain stores were also able to lower their selling prices with centralising buying and management, turning over inventory rapidly and employing modern accounting systems (Cronon, 1991; Koehn, 2001, pp. 99–100).

For almost two decades Montgomery Ward stood alone as the nation's mail-order general store until Sears, Roebuck & Company (Sears Roebuck, or Sears) overtook it early in the twentieth century. (Emmet and Jeuck, 1950; Tedlow, 1990). Founded by Richard Warren Sears, as a mail order firm selling watches, it quickly expanded. In 1887, Sears hired Alvah C. Roebuck, a skilled watchmaker from Indiana, expanded his product line of jewellery and started advertising in magazines and newspapers. (Boorstin, 1973a; Strasser, 1989; Tedlow, 1990; Miller, 1996). After a few years in and out of business, Sears reconnected with Roebuck to start a new firm, Sears, Roebuck & Company, in 1893. (Two years later, complaining of stress and illness, Roebuck sold his share to Sears for $25,000.) In addition to watches and jewellery, they sold silverware, firearms, sewing machines, clothing and other merchandise from a 196-page "wish book" that advertised the company as the "Cheapest Supply House on Earth". A year later, when the firm moved back into a five-story building in Chicago, its catalogue expanded to over 500 pages and to almost 800 pages in 1897. In 1895, the year that saw Roebuck's departure, the company sold $750,000 worth of goods. By 1900, Sears passed Ward to become the largest mail-order house in the world (Emmet and Jeuck, 1950, p. 39; Strasser, 1989: Miller, 1996, p. 249).

The Sears catalogue is an iconic part of American culture now, but it changed over time, reflecting the increasing corporatisation of business. From 1887 to 1895, both the company and the catalogue reflected Sears's personality, 'with all his flamboyance, his almost intuitive feeling for the farmer's idiom, his knowledge of what items would sell and what would not'. From 1895 until 1908, according to the firm's historians, the catalogue reflected the

> new-found corporate stature of the company and its steadily expanding size, the trend towards "truth in advertising" with somewhat more accurate and more detailed descriptions of the merchandise, and the great systemization of the entire business of producing the book.
>
> *(Emmet and Jeuck, 1950, p. 85)*

By 1900, Sears was the largest advertiser in the world via its catalogue, with related expenditures rising from $400,000 in 1898 to $3.5 million in 1908. The catalogue was the main mode of advertising, but there were others like circulars and probably newspapers. Advertising contributed to the company's financial success. In 1891, the first year of available data, sales were almost $138,000 with profits slightly over $30,000. At the end of June 1908, a depression year, sales jumped to almost $41 million and profits to over $2 million. In 1908, the year that Richard Sears sold his share of the company for $10 million (he died six years later at age 50 with an estate valued at $17.5 million or $436 million in 2016 dollars), Sears Roebuck employed 8,500 employees and had close to five million customers. Sales passed $100 million in 1915 and profits crested in 1919 at $18.9 million. By 1920, at mail order's peak, sales topped $245 million, slightly more than double Montgomery Ward's. Staffing levels more than doubled between 1908 to 1920 to 21,652 (Casson, 1908, p. 514; Emmet and Jeuck, 1950, pp. 290, 295; Tedlow, 1990, pp. 264, 273, 280).

Organisational and operational changes also contributed to Sears's early success. One immediate problem executives had to solve was how to handle the sheer volume of orders that arrived daily. The high volume overwhelmed the firm's capacity to handle them and led to delayed shipments, errors and excessive product returns, high employee turnover, and inter-departmental coordination problems. The solution came in the form of a "scheduling system", the brainchild of plant superintendent and later vice president Otto C. Doering, who benefited from the opening of a much larger and more modern mail-order plant on Chicago's West Side, in 1906. Using principles of scientific management, special-purpose machinery, assembly lines, a network of train tracks, gravity chutes, conveyors and other devices, and a new methods department that continually refined the system, Doering pulled off and engineering triumph that enabled employees, in twenty-seven discrete steps, to ship orders within 48 hours. The sophistication and efficiency of the scheduling system attracted Henry Ford's attention, who visited the plant to personally inspect Doering's methods (Emmet and Jeuck, 1950, pp. 131–136; Mahoney and Sloane, 1966, p. 230).

Sears Roebuck also made a number of organisational changes beginning in the first decade of the twentieth century. It launched a buying office in New York City (1902) and its first branch plant (1906) in Dallas, which published its own catalogue. Two others followed before 1921 – Seattle (1910) and Philadelphia (1920). It also began selling through an agent in Mexico City in 1908. By 1899, the company sold an increasing array of goods from twenty-four different departments and four divisions – wearing apparel, domestics, hardlines and miscellaneous (Emmet and Jeuck, 1950).

As the largest marketer in the world, Sears Roebuck took the risk out of manufacturing for its suppliers by guaranteeing steady demand, allowing manufacturers to increase plant capacity, lower unit costs, and limit marketing expenses. Sears also assumed financial interests in at least nine factories by 1906 and thirty-one by the end of World War I. It integrated backward only out of necessity (Emmet and Jeuck, 1950; Tedlow, 1990).

In addition to operating efficiencies, Sears also was able to lower selling prices by an average of 22% by removing middlemen from the distribution process. It also continued to experiment with selling techniques. In 1905, it shipped two dozen catalogues to customers in good standing in Iowa who agreed to distribute them to twenty-four neighbours and supply their names to the company. In return, they received premium gifts. Personalised selling work well enough that Sears chose to "Iowize" the nation. Circulation of the catalogue – along with its heft – grew from about 1.6 million in 1902 to 3.8 million in 1905 and to almost 6.6 million in 1908 (Tedlow, 1990, pp. 269, 273–274). Beginning in 1910, Sears began offering instalment buying on some of its hardlines like pianos, cream separators, gas engines, and farm implements. The period between 1917 and 1921 was known as the "No Money Down" era at Sears. Over the next decade, additional items were added to the list of items eligible for instalment purchases. New to Sears, instalment buying was becoming increasingly popular during this time. For example, 'Montgomery Ward sold on instalment (sic) terms, and another Chicago mail-order concern – Spiegel's – specialised entirely in instalment selling by mail. Many department stores, however, and so-called "quality" retailers held back on instalment selling until the 1930's', when Philadelphia department store Wanamaker's initiated a revolving credit plan that became the standard department store credit plans (Emmet and Jeuck, 1950, p. 274).

Montgomery Ward also thrived from its founding into the twentieth century and settled in as the second largest mail-order house in the nation. Ward tallied $8 million in sales in 1900, the year that Sears surpassed it. One year earlier, Ward completed a new office building on Michigan Avenue. The Ward Tower, at twenty-five stories, was taller than any building west of Philadelphia. The company also built a massive mail-order plant along the Chicago River, which, at the time, was the largest commercial building in the world. Ward continued to do well through the 1910s, when sales reached $62 million. They exceeded $100 million in 1920 (Latham, 1972, pp. 44–47, 62–64).

Overall, the American mail-order industry did very well in the years before 1921. Total sales rose from $31 million in 1899 to $165 million in 1909 and further to $543 million in 1919. The two general merchandisers were in a class by themselves. For example, Sears (43%) and Ward (18%) combined for over 60% of national mail-order volume in 1919. The next largest firm, The National Cloak & Suit Company, also of Chicago, was a distant third (7.3%). Other prominent mail-order houses included Chicago-based Spiegel, and the Buffalo's Larkin Company, whose administration building was designed by Frank Lloyd Wright, his first commercial commission. In addition, there were about 1,200 mail-order concerns operating in the country in 1900 and 2,500 in 1919, including many specialty firms and large urban department stores that had mail order units. Yet even with 10 million mail-order customers, mail-order sales registered only about 4% of total retail sales at their apex (Nystrom, 1919, pp. 290–291; Chamber of Commerce of the United States, 1931, pp. 28–33; McNair, 1931, p. 31; Smalley, 1961, pp. 384–385; Leach, 1993, p. 45; Stanger, 2000).

Montgomery Ward and Sears Roebuck were the leaders in general merchandise mail order, but there were other important companies that made significant contributions to the development of mail order. One of them was the Larkin Company (Larkin) of Buffalo, New York. Established by John D. Larkin in 1875 to manufacture soaps, the company initially sold its goods through the normal channels of middlemen. In 1885, it retired all its salespeople and began selling via the mail in support of its new "factory-to-family" strategy whose motto, "The Larkin Idea: save all cost that adds no value", was widely advertised through multiple channels.

Because it was a hybrid manufacturer-mail-order house, contemporary retail scholar Paul Nystrom referred to Larkin as a firm of "unique character".

Around 1890, the company created the Clubs of Ten, a selling plan run by "Larkin Secretaries" – mostly married women who used their social networks – family, friends, neighbours – to solicit bulk orders in return for valuable premiums for club members, including additional ones for club organisers. The premiums were more valuable to members than the soaps and household products that Larkin sold for cash. (Nystrom, 1919, p. 185; Stanger, 2000, 2008). The success of Larkin Clubs is revealed in the growth of sales, from about $220,000 in 1892 to $15.3 million in 1906. In addition to innovative selling techniques, the company's success can also be attributable to its progressive employee relations and the creation of a strong corporate culture of "Larkinites" – employees, managers and executives *and* customers. Larkin executive Darwin Martin, head of mail-order operations, hired Frank Lloyd Wright to design a modern office building for the company that opened in 1906. It was Wright's first commercial commission.

Similar to the mail-order giants, Larkin Company's sales grew steadily during the first two decades of the twentieth century and peaked at $28.6 million in 1920. Despite adding a chain of

Figure 19.1 Larkin Company Catalog, 1917. Whereas most of the large mail-order houses were headquartered in Chicago because of its extensive railroad network and access to its rural consumer base the Larkin Company was headquartered in Buffalo, N.Y., also a significant railroad town. Larkin's "Factory-to-Family" business model relied on an extensive network of unpaid "Secretaries" who organised buying clubs through which they took bulk orders in exchange for premiums to stock a middle-class family.

Source: Author's Collection.

food stores, department stores, and other retailing ventures beginning in 1918, sales and profits continues to trend downward during the 1920s and 1930s (Stanger, 2000, 2008, 2010).

Another innovative mail-order firm that opened for business in Chicago, in 1882, as a retailer of furniture and household furnishings was Spiegel, May, Stern Co., originally known as Spiegel House Furnishings. Spiegel combined aggressive selling and instalment buying mainly for its mostly foreign-born lower-middle and working-class customers who lived in industrial south-side districts, where it operated two branch stores, populated by mostly foreign-born residents. It expanded its geographic reach over time and employed the motto "We Trust the People – Everywhere" to reflect its ambitions. While national mail-order sales declined by $89 million between 1919 and 1929, Spiegel's rose 204 per cent even though it faced direct competition from Sears and Ward, which also adopted instalment credit plans (Smalley, 1961, p. 401; Smalley and Sturdivant, 1973, pp. 123, 129–130, 149). According to company historian Orange Smalley,

> The role played by Spiegel, May, Stern . . . in providing the preliminary education in modern installment credit, making it easy to obtain and relatively painless to use, and in helping to overcome the ethical and moral barriers to the use of credit for improving living standards must be regarded as being fundamentally important,

and was largely responsible for the company's success heading into the challenging years of the 1920s and 1930s (1961, p. 401; Smalley and Sturdivant, 1973). Spiegel moved in and out of retailing a few times during the twentieth century and emerged primarily as a successful mail-order firm by the mid-twentieth century.

In addition to Sears, Ward, Larkin and Spiegel, there were many smaller ones scattered around the country that specialised in areas such as household goods, plows, auto supplies, jewellery, sporting goods, and more. Department stores and wholesalers also operated mail-order units. Montgomery Ward's Robert E. Wood surveyed his firm's competitors in 1920. Among the department stores he identified included Altmans, Gimbels and Wanamakers in the East, and the Boston Store of Chicago. Other prominent department stores that operated mail order included Wanamaker's Philadelphia Strawbridge & Clothier, Chicago's Marshall Field's and New York's Macy's. More worrisome to Wood were the growing chain stores, particularly J.C. Penney, whose stores were concentrated in small Western towns. Writing about department stores' early mail-order business, a contemporary department store-executive noted,

> The mail-order trade as associated with Department Stores began in a very small way; it began with a few requests from customers out of town asking for samples and prices of certain goods, a few letters of enquiry regarding one thing and another.

While there is evidence that department stores scaled back mail-order operations in the 1910s, department store historian Vicki Howard points out that large urban department stores added mail-order divisions during the 1920s (Phillips, 1901, p. 62; Wood, 1920, "Past, Present and Future of the Mail Order Business", Robert E. Wood Papers, Montgomery Ward and Company, 1919–1923, Herbert Hoover Presidential Library, West Branch, IA; Worthy, 1986).

One former mail-order executive noted in 1928,

> When you stop to think about it, there is hardly a class of merchandise that is not being sold through the mails, the chief reason is that this method is proving most economical for the distribution of merchandise to the ultimate consumer.

Among the most common goods were books and magazine subscriptions, jewellery, seeds and garden products, medical preparations, cosmetics, clothing and accessories, tools, novelties, foods and musical instruments (Wadsworth, 1928, p. 28; Nystrom, 1930; Cherry, 2008, *Catalog: The Illustrated History of Mail-Order Shopping*). One of the most expensive and unique items sold through the mail was homes.

Houses were an important marker of middle-class status. By removing middlemen, mail-order firms were able to lower the price of a home permitting more families to purchase them (Moskowitz, *Standard of Living*, 2004, p. 5). Houses that arrived by train were marketed on a large scale through catalogues between the years 1906 and 1983, although their origins can be traced to architectural plans books that were sold by mail after the Civil War. New York City-based architects Palliser and Palliser, which published its first book in 1876, were the industry's pioneers, but Robert Shoppell of New York City perfected the Pallisers' techniques and established mail-order house plans as a major business. Plans books permitted homeowners to acquire the benefits of trained architects without paying their fees. The industry matured during the 1890s and helped to create America's suburbs. As significant,

> The mail-order plan brought high standards of design and the latest architectural trends to countless middle-class homeowners and builders. Houses built from such plans reflect not only the aesthetics of their era but also the new technologies that placed in the hands of the middle class those amenities formerly reserved for the wealthy.
> *(Garvin, 1981, p. 334; Schweitzer and Davis, 1990; Culbertson, 1992)*

The first large mail-order company to sell pre-cut homes was the North American Construction Company, founded by brothers William and Otto Sovereign, of Bay City, Michigan, in 1906. In 1913, after ownership changes, the company changed its name to Alladin, after the mythical genie who built a castle overnight for his master. Equating the family unit to a small business, Alladin advertised its homes as good investments. Its cash-only policy kept prices low, but Alladin also offered financing options. Former Larkin Company advertising innovator Elbert Hubbard wrote promotional materials for the company: 'Here is an absolute safe deal for the financier. A good workingman should own his own home. By doing so, he becomes a better citizen and a better workman' (Moskowitz, 2004, pp. 137–138; Hunter, 2012).

Alladin was also able to keep home prices affordable through scientific management and thriftiness. Its 1915 catalogue declared: 'What Henry Ford has done for the motorist, ALLADIN has done for the home builder'. Standardisation did not prevent Alladin from offering homebuyers sixty possible design options. Similar to Sears, Ward, Larkin and others, Alladin promoted the absence of middlemen – "Manufacturers Create Value – Middlemen Add Cost" – in its appeal to its rural customers. As well, Alladin shared with other prominent mail-order houses its desire to make the company part of its customers' extended family. In the 1910s, Alladin requested of its homebuyers to provide the names of potential customers who might join the Alladin "family" in exchange for cash and other rewards. These methods proved successful for Alladin, which remained in business until 1983 (Moskowitz, 2004, pp. 143, 156, 169, 173; Hunter, 2012).

Sears Roebuck was the largest mail-order home seller during its time in that segment between the years 1908 and 1940. It claimed to have sold 30,000 houses by 1925 and nearly 50,000 in 1930. Its 1939 catalogue bragged that, 'over one hundred thousand families, or approximately half a million people, are living in Honor Bilt Modern Homes today' (quoted in Stevenson and Jandl, 1986, p. 19). By comparison, Alladin sold a little more than 50,000 units in its 75-year history. Until 1928, it sold three-fourths as many homes as Sears (Schweitzer and Davis, 1990, p. 14).

Sears began selling building materials by mail in 1895 and, around 1900, created the Modern Homes Department. It issued its first mail-order home catalogue, called *Book of Modern Homes and Building Plans*, in 1908. The 1915 edition offered 109 plans, with five of them pre-cut kits. By 1917, most of Sears' plans were for pre-cut kit houses. As its business expanded, Sears purchased lumber and millwork facilities. Its Philadelphia branch provided an eastern base for the Modern Homes operations. Beginning in the 1910s, it offered financing terms for its homes – typically five years at 6% interest. Sears and others also sold homes to corporations and organisations. To provide more personal service to buyers, it opened ten sales offices between 1919 and 1925. Sears capitalised on the national urban housing boom during the 1920s, and by 1930 it employed 350 salespeople in forty-eight sales offices, all east of the Mississippi River and north of the Mason-Dixon Line. The Depression hurt Sears when many of its financed homes went into foreclosure. Sears ceased financing homes in 1935, but it never fully recovered and ended its mail-order homes business in 1940 (Emmet and Jeuck, 1950; Schwartz, 1985; Stevenson and Jandl, 1986, pp. 20–23; Hunter, 2012, p. 24).

Not to be outdone by its larger rival, Montgomery Ward began offering home building plans in a catalogue in 1909 or 1910. Ward's 80-page 1912 catalogue showed sixty-six home designs. It adopted the *Wardway Homes* name in 1918. Unlike Sears, Ward did not own or operate housing production facilities, but subcontracted for them. Ward's early homes were manufactured in Bay City, Michigan. Beginning in 1917, the well-known mail-order homes company, Gordon-Van Time, produced Ward's homes. The last known reference to Ward's home catalogue appeared in 1931 when, like Sears, unpaid mortgages brought down the Wardway Homes division (Schweitzer and Davis, 1990; Hunter, 2012).

The Great Depression spelled the end of mail-order home sales for Sears and Ward. Additional factors contributed to the demise of other companies in subsequent decades.

> With a declining market due to demands for on-site delivery, the development of tract housing, and the growing popularity of prefabricated and mobile housing, the pre-cut (mail-order) home gradually faded away.... Alladin, the pioneers of the mass-marketed kit home, hung on until 1983: the first company in business also had the distinction of being the last.
>
> *(Hunter, 2012, p. 59)*

Accounting for the rise and success of mail-order commerce

The rise and success of mail order between the years between 1870 and 1920 can be attributed to a constellation of factors, both external and internal to these firms. Beginning in the last quarter of the nineteenth, new technologies and production methods enabled factories to turn out a high volume of standardised goods at increasingly lower costs. Total private production rose a phenomenal 318% between 1900 and 1920, with almost two-thirds of the gain occurring between 1915 and 1920. Demographics also proved to be significant. Population growth – natural and immigration – and lower household size created demand for factory-made products. Many of these people were concentrating into cities. The US population rose from 31.5 million in 1860 to 92.4 million in 1910, with the overwhelming majority living on farms. The rural population continued to grow in absolute numbers until 1920, although as a percentage of the total population it fell from 71.8% in 1880 to 48.8 in 1920, the first year the percentage of Americans living in urban areas exceeded those living in rural areas. Rural consumers were mail order's main customers. Moreover, a high degree of literacy and new printing technologies facilitated the high circulation of printed matter, including catalogues, newspapers and magazines, all of which carried lots of advertisements for consumer goods (Emmet and Jeuck, 1950, pp. 12, 194; Smalley, 1961, pp. 378–379; Tedlow, 1990; Strasser, 2006). According to business historian Susan Strasser,

> The economic effects of these demographic changes were compounded with a general rise in disposable income, with the rising expectations and standards of living promoted by the new products and by the developing advertising industry, and with the triumph of a culture of mass consumption. Increasingly, Americans satisfied their needs entirely through the market.
>
> *(2006, p. 33)*

As with other mass retailers – the department store and later the chain store – mail order also benefited from mid-nineteenth century developments in transportation and communication, especially the expansion of railroad and telegraph networks. Extensive rail networks made the Windy City the mail-order capital of the nation after 1870. By the end of the nineteenth century, there were almost 200,000 miles of track in the United States. A decade later trackage increased by another 25%. Unlike department and chain store customers who arrived on foot or a variety of wheeled conveyances, mail-order customers lived in distant rural areas and could only be reached by mail and rail (Emmet and Jeuck, 1950, p. 11; Chandler, 1977; Cronon, 1991).

Railroad development speeded up and made mail delivery more reliable, which led to sharp reductions in postal rates and increased mail usage for business correspondence, catalogues and packages. The one-cent postal card was established in 1873, while the two-cent rate on first-class letters began in 1883. Both aided mail-order companies, as did the federal government's permission to allow them to send their catalogues and other advertising materials at very low second-class mail rates (Nystrom, 1930; Chandler, 1977, pp. 195–196). Still, as late as 1890, fewer than 20 million of the 75 million people who lived in the United States had mail delivered free to their doors. The rest had to visit their local post office to pick up their mail. After free delivery was tried in cities, in the 1860s, farmers began agitating for the same service (Fuller, 1964; Boorstin, 1973b; Gallagher, 2016).

It was not until the Philadelphia department store merchant John Wanamaker became Postmaster General in 1889 that the movement for free rural delivery mail service accelerated. Wanamaker believed that connecting the rural population with modern society was important. He argued that, by allowing farmers to work their farms instead of taking long breaks to pick up their mail at the nearest post office was crucial to their economic viability. As a businessman who traded by mail, he also saw the possibility of economic stimulus by drawing more potential customers into a national marketplace through newspapers, magazines and catalogues. At the same time, the government could close thousands of small, unprofitable post offices. The Grange and newspaper publishers also supported free delivery, while country merchants, small-town newspaper editors, mail-carrier contractors and postmasters in small offices, and the express companies and their congressional allies opposed it (Boorstin, 1973b; Gallagher, 2016; Leonard, 2016).

Wanamaker left office in 1893, but the momentum he helped to create led Congress to authorise funds in 1896 for the creation of a few experimental rural free delivery (RFD) routes. Within a year there were forty-four routes operating in twenty-nine states. In 1902, President Theodore Roosevelt made RFD a permanent postal service. Initially costly to operate, RFD became a highly successful addition to the postal system. Historian Daniel Boorstin contends that it was 'one of the greatest administrative achievements of the later nineteenth century' (1973b, p. 132; Gallagher, 2016, p. 131; Leonard, 2016).

The success of RFD concerned its opponents, primarily the private express companies – which feared that once rural Americans had free home letter delivery, they would agitate for home parcel delivery. The express firms – Wells Fargo, American Express, United Express Company and Adams Express – were only permitted to drop off packages at the nearest freight train station, which might be miles away from one's home. In addition, the maximum weight for an individual parcel permitted to be sent through the US Mail was four pounds. The express companies handled heavier packages. Wanamaker lobbied for a government parcel post but he was unsuccessful in the face of stiff resistance from the express companies, rural merchants, Parcel Post League, and the Chicago-based organisation American League of Associations (ALA), which had Marshall Field's as a member. The ALA represented mercantile interests who feared their businesses would suffer in the face of expanded mail-order markets. Presidents Roosevelt and William Howard Taft, rural congressmen, and Western and Midwestern farmers endorsed parcel post legislation to benefit farm families. The mail-order giants remained silent during the five years of debates (Emmet and Jeuck, 1950; Fuller, 1964; Boorstin, 1973b; Simon, 1974). In general, the conflict over parcel post – and mail order in general – that peaked between 1910 and 1912 'provoked one of the most vigorous policy debates of the early twentieth century' (Kielbowicz, 1994, p. 81).

After intense congressional debates, the farmers' lobby prevailed when President Taft signed the Parcel Post Act in August 1912 that enabled packages weighing up to eleven pounds be sent via US Mail. The Act went into effect on 1 January 1913. John Wanamaker sent the first package from the Pennsylvania Railroad's West Philadelphia Station to Taft in the White House. Within the first year, 300 million packages were shipped. Parcel post legislation spelled the doom of the rural merchant and was a boon to mail-order houses, which saw their profits climb from $40 million in 1908 to $250 million in 1920. The Post Office Department reported in 1938 that Parcel Post rose to second place in postal revenues and was 'the greatest extension of Postal facilities in world Postal history' (quoted in Emmet and Jeuck, 1950, p. 189; Boorstin, 1973b, p. 134; Simon, 1974; Gallagher, 2016; Leonard, 2016, p. 85).

Parcel Post, more than RFD, became one of the two key ingredients to mail-order's strong market during its "golden age" between 1908 and 1925. The other was the strength of the farm sector, which was stimulated mainly by industrialisation and urbanisation in both the United States and Europe. Its golden age, between 1900 and 1920, overlapped and reinforced with mail order's. According to rural historian David Danbom,

> The years between 1870 and 1900 were a time of dramatic expansion for American agriculture. By virtually every measure, agriculture doubled in size during that remarkable period. The number of farms increased from 2.66 million to 5.74 million. Acres of land in farms jumped from 407,735 million to 841,202 million. And the total value of farm property rose from $9.4 billion to 20.4 billion.
>
> *(1995, p. 132)*

In addition, between 1900 and 1910 the prices of agricultural products increased by nearly half. World War I further raised farmers' material wealth. The index of wholesale farm prices more than doubled between 1915 and 1920. Combined with good harvests, farmers' cash receipts rose from $5.7 billion in 1910 to a peak of $14.6 billion in 1919. Farmers spent their new-found wealth improving their farms, making their homes more livable, updating community infrastructure and purchasing new consumer goods from mail-order catalogues and elsewhere (Emmet and Jeuck, 1950, pp. 191–192; Danbom, 1995, Kline 2000).

In addition to the economic benefits that mail order millions of customers – lower prices, a money-back guarantee, a wide assortment of useful and stylish goods, speedy delivery, browsing and shopping convenience – there were also social and cultural ones. In the late nineteenth, early twentieth centuries when Montgomery Ward's and Sears Roebuck's catalogues made their way into rural southern homes via RFD and Parcel Post, they not only increased purchasing options for both whites and blacks, but they also 'placed the consuming practice of blacks beyond local white knowledge and control' and gave them cover to make private purchases free of discrimination in stores. Upset that blacks might patronise mail-order houses instead of local, white-owned shopkeepers spread rumours that Ward's and Sears were black-owned and sold by mail to avoid being seen by the public (Rips, 1938; Hale, 1998, p. 179).

Catalogues also touched other aspects of daily life on farms and in small towns by reducing they and their families' isolation: 'To many farmers and their families the catalogue was magazine, newspapers, radio, movie – all rolled into one – providing entertainment, education, and excitement' (Rips, 1938, pp. 57–58). The "Farmer's Bible" also acted as general store and an encyclopedia in many rural schoolhouses. Children learned math by calculating orders, geography from postal zone maps, and drawing by tracing the products and models. The "Big Books" also as served as home almanacs because they often contained inspirational stories, poetry, short stories, poetry, and household and farming tips. In 1946, the Grolier Society, the prestigious book and graphic arts club, selected the mail-order catalogue as one of the 100 outstanding American books of all time. Catalogues also has been the subject of novels, songs and parodies (Schlereth, 1989, 1992).

Small retailers rise up: opposition to mail-order

The success of Montgomery Ward and Sears Roebuck, and other mail-order firms inspired protests and general opposition that peaked during the debates over parcel post legislation between 1910 and 1912. Opposition to mass retailing was nothing new. During the 1880s and 1890s, urban shopkeepers protested department stores, calling for special taxes and laws that would restrict the number of lines of merchandise department stores could carry. The phenomenal growth of chain stores during the 1920s and 1930s also stimulated fierce opposition from shopkeepers and their allies to stop the "chain store menace". These attempts to tax, regulate, and legislate these larger and more efficient businesses out of existence generally failed, as did those directed at mail-order houses (Strasser, 1989; Bean, 1996, p. 26).

Around 1900, small-town merchants went on the offensive against the mail-order giants. Refusing to call Montgomery Ward and Sears Roebuck by name, they instead referred to them as "Monkey Ward" and "Shears and Rawbuck". They claimed they sold shoddy merchandise and employed slave labour. Southern merchants also spread rumours that Ward's and Sears were black-owned. Other mail-order houses also met various forms of resistance. Local newspaper editors railed against them for "making commercial graveyards of once prosperous towns", while local "trade at home" campaigns encouraged residents to patronise local businesses. Midwestern commercial associations banded together in the Home Trade League of America, while local newspaper editors railed against these "foreign" firms. Relying less on political action, the merchants and their allies used moral suasion and public demonstrations, such as catalogue burnings (Rips, 1938; Emmet and Jeuck, 1950; Strasser, 1989; Bean, 1996, pp. 23–24; Barron, 1997).

In general, these campaigns achieved very little. Farmers were not natural allies of the country merchant, whose prices were high and selection low. Farmers lobbied for parcel post, while

Figure 19.2 "You Stay Away from Here", 1914. Small retailers and their allies organised and railed against the market power and size of the large mail-order houses, ultimately with little success owing to the benefits consumers derived from them.

Source: Library of Congress, mph.3b 43886, ca. 1914, Lot 7690.

merchants opposed it. Mail-order firms protected customers and suppliers by shipping goods in plain brown paper wrapping and refusing to print their suppliers' names in their catalogues. They also effectively employed public relations against false claims, invited the public to inspect their operations, and sold the virtues of their business methods to an accepting public. In general, as business historian Jonathan Bean observes, the

> verbal heat generated by the controversy over department stores and mail-order catalogues was out of all proportion to the amount of market share that small retailers lost to these mass-marketers. As late as 1920, (they) accounted for less than 10 percent of total retail sales.
>
> *(Rips, 1938; Emmet and Jeuck, 1950; Strasser 1989; Bean, 1996, p. 25; Barron, 1997)*

Trouble on the farm: the declining fortunes of mail order after 1920

Mail order declined after 1920 for a number of reasons. Changing demographics cut into mail order's traditional rural markets. Farmers' economic troubles combined with the attractiveness of cities during the 1920s to quicken the pace of rural-to-urban migration (Emmet & Jeuck, 1950; Danbom, 1995; Neth, 1995; Kline, 2000; Abbott, 2007). The growth of suburbs also hurt mail order firms. The suburban population rose from 9.1 to 15.2% of total population. Both urban and suburban residents had increasing access to department, chain and specialty stores. These stores attracted consumers with print and radio advertisements, dazzling store and window displays, updated styles, branded products, low prices and frequent sales events. Between 1919 and 1929, chain stores increased their market share from 4% to 20% of total retail sales. By 1935, they received 23% of all retail sales (Emmet and Jeuck, 1950; Bean, 1996, p. 26; Spellman, 2016, pp. 151–52). And of course, the automobile increased shopping options, expanded the trading zones and brought mail-order businesses into direct competition with other types of retailers (Emmet and Jeuck, 1950, p. 317; Abbott, 2007).

In addition to more intense retail competition, mail-order firms were beset by a number of problems, such as the high cost of catalogue production and distribution, the most profitable use of catalogue space, increasing sales per catalogue, addressing customer complaints, processing returns, and reducing the time period between when a customer first views the catalogue to the actual purchase of items because the typical life of a catalogue was only six months. The latter issue made it hard to carry extensive lines of fashion items that changed rapidly. In addition, in a period of falling prices, fixed catalogue prices were injurious to the bottom line. Store-based retailers were better suited to capitalise of the latest fashions and could attract potential customers with show window displays and discounted merchandise (Nystrom, 1930; Tedlow, 1990).

By the first half of the 1920s, the major mail-order houses had responded to their declining competitiveness by opening retail stores and making changes to their mail-order operations. Yet even with these adjustments and with store sales included, mail-order, in 1928, comprised only 3 to 5% of total retail sales, with Sears and Ward's accounting for 40% of that total (Nystrom, 1919, p. 291; Chamber of Commerce of the United States, 1931, pp. 28–33). By 1939, Montgomery Ward's retail and catalogue sales were strong, although it took the latter ten years to pass their 1926 peak. At the outbreak of World War II, Ward operated 650 retail stores, nine catalogue houses and 183 catalogue stores (Latham, 1972).

Postwar mail-order in the United States

On the eve of World War II, there were 434 firms classified as "mail order", which comprised only 1% of total retail sales. Sears Roebuck and Montgomery Ward accounted for the majority of mail-order sales, with the next two largest firms – Spiegel and Chicago-based Aldens – taking a significant share of the rest. The other 430 concerns were mainly small, specialty houses, that combined for a small percentage of total sales but would grow in the decades after World War II (Emmet and Jeuck, 1950, pp. 2–3; McNair and May, 1976, pp. 36–37).

By the latter part of the 1970s, catalogue sales comprised only a tiny part of Sears's total sales, even though it distributed 315 million catalogues annually (Worthy, 1986; McNair and May, 1976; Weil, 1977, pp. 252–255). During this period, Sears's historic competitor, Montgomery Ward, saw its relative standing decline. In 1945, Ward held 41.7% share of the mail-order market, while Sears captured 50.7%. By 1951, Sears increased its share to 66.1%, while Ward's declined to 28%. Overall, Sears's sales volume was two-and-a-half times that of Ward's and had almost twice the net profits. By the mid-1950s, according to historian Richard Tedlow, 'Ward was only a shadow of its former self. It would never rise again' (Tedlow, 1990, pp. 332–336; Michman and Greco, 1995, pp. 27–28). In 1985, the company closed its 113-year-old catalogue business (Montgomery Ward, 1972; Michman and Greco, 1995).

While traditional retailers were affected by new forms of retail and the rise of suburbs and regional shopping centres, mail-order firms experienced a comeback as a growing number of urban consumers had greater access to catalogue desks and phone service available in urban and suburban retail stores. Overall, catalogue sales rose from $608 million to $1.2 billion between 1944 and 1954. This growth exceeded that of general merchandise sales. The large catalogue houses – Sears, Ward and Spiegel – accounted for the major share of aggregate sales, but specialty mail-order firms who sold books, records, and novelties expanded their share of the market after 1945 (Smalley and Sturdivant, 1973, p. 272).

The experiences of Sears, Montgomery Ward and Spiegel since the late 1960s, however, reflected the rapidly changing retail environment brought about by the entrance of large discount retailers, the blurring of retail segments, the expansion of specialty catalogues, a slowdown in the macro-economy, technological changes in operations and distribution and business trends such as conglomeration and financialisation. While Montgomery Ward has vanished from the scene and Sears limps along as a struggling company- and Internet-based retailer, Spiegel, after 150 years, is now a female-owned company that operates catalogues and online businesses under the Spiegel, Newport News and FX brand names.

Mail order outside the United States

Mail-order commerce has existed in a more limited form in other Western nations since the nineteenth century. Experiences have been determined in part by land mass size and demographics, as well as infrastructural developments, literacy and consumer demand. Mail order in France, Germany and England shared some similarities to the American and former British colony model in terms of infrastructure, consumer culture and roots in department store-based retailing, but there also were differences.

Canada's experience with mail order paralleled the United States to some degree. Canada was the home of two major mail-order houses – Eaton's and Simpson's – whose origins were in small-shop and department store retailing. Founded by Timothy Eaton and Robert L. Simpson, respectively, these businesses benefited from the constellation of factors noted above (Glazebrook et al., 1969; Benson 1992a, b; Belisle, 2011). According to historian John Benson, '(d)epartment store entrepreneurs (played) a leading role in the development of late nineteenth- and early twentieth-century retailing. But they did so less by their opening of city-centre shops, than by their establishment of nationwide systems of mail-order selling' (1992b, p. 193). As in the United States, Canadian mail-order retailers encountered serious competitive threats and declining sales in the 1920s and 1930s owing to economic depressions, the rise of chain and other types of retail stores and wider automobile ownership (Monod, 1996, pp. 211–214, 342; Kopytek, 2014, pp. 112–114).

Canada's postwar growth in population and the economy fueled Eaton's general expansion into Canada's major cities, and in the suburbs and smaller towns, but retailers faced a changing business environment. Department stores pushed into the suburbs beginning in the 1950s. In response, Eaton's opened catalogue desks and stores like Sears and Ward. But by the 1970s, Eaton's catalogue business was unprofitable and in trouble. By January 1976, after merger talks with J.C. Penney collapsed, Eaton's shuttered its mail-order business, including 400 catalogue sales offices (Kopytek, 2014).

The history of mail order in Australia is similar to Canada's. Both nations were former British colonies, which retained cultural and commercial connections to England. Both were geographically large countries with mainly rural and farm populations who were mail-order's target customers. The largest mail-order businesses had origins as city-based retail shops that grew into large department stores that established separate mail-order businesses. In addition, the success of mail order was enabled by similar infrastructural developments in transportation, postal services, communication and rising literacy and incomes (Kingston, 1994; Webber and Hoskins, 2003; McArthur, 2005). Australia's main mail-order houses were units of Sydney's largest department stores, such as Anthony Hordern, which, like most large department stores, had their roots as draperies and ironmongeries. According to historian Howard Wolfers, 'Horderns' large red catalogue was probably the best known of the catalogues. It is said that some country people viewed it as a shopping "Bible"' (1980, p. 25). Other prominent Sydney-based department stores with significant mail-order units included David Jones, McDowell's, Walton's, Farmer's and Clark's. Around 1900, these stores were expanding to become "universal providers" or "emporia". Collectively, these family-owned stores were referred to as the "kings of Fortune" (Pollon, 1989; McArthur, 2005).

While mail-order commerce reached their zenith around 1920 in the United States in Canada, mail order in Australia was more resilient through two World Wars and the Great Depression. This was partly attributed to the country's scattered population, relative social isolation, and limited access to goods. It was only after World War II when takeovers obliterated Sydney's family-run big stores that the catalogue trade weakened. During that period, the influx of variety stores and shopping centres into country town also adversely impacted the trade of the country stores, which responded by updating and modernising their businesses. Their department store analogues faced growing competition during the second half of the twentieth century from chain stores and other retailing formats (Pollon, 1989; Webber and Hoskins, 2003; McArthur, 2005).

Mail-order commerce in continental Europe developed in similar fashion to the countries once part of the British Dominion, especially in France and Germany where it was derivative of department stores. The 1844 Petit Saint-Thomas catalogue might be one of the first in France, but it was Paris's Bon Marché, the largest department store in France, where mail order was most developed. Aristede Boucicaut, a former employee at Petit Saint-Thomas, joined with Paul Videau as co-proprietors of the Bon Marché in 1852. Backed by a financier, Boucicaut bought out Videau's share in 1863 and transformed Bon Marché into one the world's first department stores in 1869 (Miller, 1981). The Bon Marché developed an extensive mail-order business beginning around 1871. For the 1894 winter season, the store mailed 1.5 million catalogues, with 700,000 targeting potential provincial customers, and 260,000 sent abroad. For a white sale only, Bon Marché distributed almost one million catalogues in 1910. The store had customers in four continents (Miller, 1981, pp. 61–63).

Alfred Chandler (1990) noted that while modern transportation and communications networks precipitated a revolution first in distribution and then in production in both the United States and Britain, in Germany it was the other way around – infrastructural developments spurred innovation in production, while changes in distribution were more derivative than innovative. He also suggested that there were more mail-order firms in Germany than in Britain but they were smaller in size. The same was true for German mass retailing in general compared with the United States and Britain.

Germany's retail market was transformed rapidly during the period between 1871 and 1914, a period of similar transformation in other major western nations. Industrialisation, urbanisation, population growth, rising literacy, an improving standard of living and transportation and communication developments enabled the growth of large-scale retailing. As occurred in other countries, the rise of large retailers sparked intense opposition from small retailers and their allies (Gellately, 1974; Shaw, 1992).

German mail order was rooted in department stores and emerged in the second half of the nineteenth century. In some cases, it accounted for close to one-third of a store's total sales. In the interwar years, the specialty mail-order house arose in Germany and in other parts of Europe, although some existed prior to 1914. By the late 1920s, specialty mail-order firms were active in Germany as well as in Sweden, Switzerland and Britain. In Germany, and to some extent throughout Europe (with the exception of Britain and Sweden), mail-order houses tended to be small and confined to a narrow group of merchandise, such as textiles and cigars. Still, they relied on economies of scale, small price markups and fast stock turn to offer lower prices and a greater variety of goods than traditional retailers (Jefferys and Knee, 1962, pp. 62–63; Gellately, 1974).

Mail order in Germany achieved the biggest growth in sales and share of the retail trade after World War II, rising to 4% of total retail sales (versus 1% in the typical European nation). The large general mail-order house was largely responsible for this growth. Typically employing roughly 3,000, it used the catalogue and a system of agents who called on potential customers, who were increasingly urban residents, a noticeable shift from its historic rural base. By the early 1960s, new developments in mail order occurred, including a move by some food voluntary chains and buying groups into catalogue and order desk sales (Jefferys and Knee, 1962).

By contrast, British mail order showed the greatest deviation from other countries because of its urban, working-class customer base that relied on instalment payments to make purchases through part-time selling agents bound to customers through different types of social networks. It also is the only country for which there has been a comprehensive study of the history of mail order (see Coopey et al., 2005). The relatively large general mail-order firms that developed in Britain began selling a narrow set of goods, typically watches, clocks and jewellery in the 1880s. A few had origins as department stores. The pioneers were Fattorini and Sons in Bradford which, as early as the 1850s, encouraged relatively affluent working men to establish "watch clubs" where each member was required to make a weekly payment, and Kays of Worcester. William Kilbourne Kay, Kay's founder, took control of an established firm of jewellers and watchmakers in the early 1880s and began to sell watches to railroad workers. The club system eventually transitioned into general mail order selling. (This also occurred at Fattorinis beginning around 1890.) By 1907, Kay's success led it to create a separate business and warehouse to support mail order. Club organisers gradually became travelling agents who recruited part-time, commission-based agents. Kay's established an agency department in 1886. By 1908, Kay's had about 500,000 customers (Coopey et al., 1999, p. 263).

Fattorinis and Kays soon met competitive challenges from Freemans – established in 1906 – John Myers and John Enrico Fattorini, who left his family's company to create Grattan Warehouses in 1912. By this time Fattorinis had changed its name to Empire Stores. The interwar years witnessed additional growth in British mail order, which, like in other Western nations, also began to be challenged by chain stores. Two important new mail-order entrants during these years included Great Universal Stores (GUS), which had its origins in Manchester in 1900 and established a mail order business in 1920. Under the leadership of Isaac Wolfson, GUS grew significantly. The second important firm was Littlewoods Mail Order Stores, founded by John Mores in 1932. Littlewoods began selling by mail in 1937. Despite the growth of mail order into the 1930s, total mail order sales in Britain were estimated to be only about 1% by the decade's end. However, the "Big Five" "universal providers" – Empire, Freemans, Grattans, GUS – which purchased Kay's in 1937 – and Littlewoods – accounted for over 80% of mail-order sales by the early 1960s, during mail order's heyday between the 1950s and 1960s (Coopey et al., 1999, pp. 262–263; Coopey et al., 2005, p. 37).

As in other countries, infrastructural and economic developments facilitated the growth of British mail order. Changes in postal services were critical. First, in 1881, the creation of postal orders provided people without access to a chequebook a secure way of paying for goods by mail. By the end of the century over 80 million postal orders were being issued annually. Second, the Post Office (Parcels) Act of 1882 offered reliable, low-cost parcel delivery service to home-based consumers. In its first year, the Post Office transported 20.6 million parcels; by the early 1890s, the number almost doubled. In addition, economic conditions benefitted mail-order firms. Real wages for workers rose and food prices stabilised, enabling working families to devote more disposable income to consumer goods (Coopey et al., 2005, pp. 15–17).

By the early 1900s, British mail order's distinctive features were clear. Watch clubs grew to become universal providers. Club organisers became part-time sales agents who earned commissions – roughly 10% of sales. Travellers canvassed working-class neighbourhoods to recruit local agents, and urban working-class customers purchased a wide variety of goods on instalment plans. Mail-order houses exploited social networks between agents and customers to limit bad debts. The agency system suited British conditions where firms were selling to consumers who already had easy access to small retail shops and larger co-operative stores (Coopey et al., 1999; Coopey and Porter, 2001; Coopey et al., 2005).

British mail order firms developed largely independent of American influence because the large American mail-order houses operated under conditions quite different from their British counterparts. None was of comparable size to the American giants. In 1919, for example, Britain's largest mail-order firm, Kay's, handled 1,200 parcels a day, or about 1% of Sears's daily volume. Differences in customers – rural in the United States and urban in Britain – distance from customers and the scale of operations (both greater in the United States) led British mail-order companies to borrow from the Americans only on a piecemeal basis, mainly in the areas of systematising and rationalising business operations and labour management via scientific management and the Bedaux incentive pay system (Coopey and Porter, 2001).

British mail order also deviated from the American experience in that it reached its zenith in the decades following World War II, not around 1920 as in the United States. World War II caused hardships in Britain and limited consumer spending on non-essential items. It was not until the early 1950s that normalcy returned and workers' newfound affluence led them to spend more on a growing bounty of consumer goods. In the late 1950s, conservative British Prime Minister Harold Macmillan (1957–1963) declared that British workers 'had never had it so good' (Coopey, 2012, p. 117).

British mail-order houses successfully accommodated this wave of consumer demand and experienced a "golden age for catalogue" between 1950 and 1980. Two significant trends enabled mail order to thrive during this time. The first was a shift from male to female catalogue selling agents. By 1967, there were an estimated 2.5 million active part-time agents. Related, social changes at home gave women more power over the purse. The second was the establishment of new, often modernist-inspired, housing complexes. According to Coopey,

> (i)n these new environments, new groups of women reassembled and formed new friendships, new social groups. In this burgeoning world which was to see the development of new configurations of social interactivity amongst couples and families, the

catalogue took its place alongside the Tupperware party as an opportunity to shop, but also an opportunity to be sociable.

(Coopey et al., 2005, p. 56; Coopey, 2012, pp. 117–118)

Conclusion

In the 1990s, mail order was significantly restructured with the arrival of the home computer – the PC – and the Internet. Old-line mail-order houses, however, failed to initially capitalise on these technologies. They did eventually adjust to the world of Internet commerce, though the field is currently in flux and the future remains unknown (Coopey et al. 2005; Coopey, 2012, pp. 125–126).

The emergence and flowering of mail order in the last few decades of the nineteenth century was dependent upon a number of economic, demographic, cultural and political factors. Among the most significant ones that were common to a number of Western nations included improvements in transportation and communications, new and expanded postal services, population growth, rising literacy and disposable income and mass production. The role of entrepreneurs who imagined and created mail-order businesses must not be underestimated.

The success of mail order provoked opposition from small retailers and their allies. Despite their efforts, consumers preferred the cornucopia of lower-priced goods available to them in large catalogue books. Initially, buying goods sight unseen from a distant mail-order house raised suspicions, but entrepreneurs gained consumers' trust with folksy messages and money-back guarantees.

Compared with those in other western industrialised nations, the American mail-order houses – Sears Roebuck, Montgomery Ward, Spiegel and Larkin, in particular – were significantly larger and often served as inspiration or as models to mail-order entrepreneurs in other countries. Mail order reached its zenith around 1920 in the United States, Canada and New Zealand, while German and British mail order peaked after World War II. Old and especially new forms of retail forced mail-order firms to respond by moving into store retailing, modernising their mail order operations and making other strategic and tactical decisions. They generally adapted to their competitive environments, but their "pure" mail-order operations declined relative to other marketing channels.

The experiences across nations reveal that mail-order sales comprised only anywhere between 1 and 5% of total retail sales. Yet mail order's impact was far greater in helping to spread a culture of consumption, make available many new kinds of products, improve retail management across multiple sectors and to reduce the urban-rural divide countries with large land mass and scattered populations.

While the traditional form of mail order has long ceased to exist, mail order continues to live on through the billions of catalogues that find their way into people's mailboxes, and especially through Internet commerce. Instead of writing and mailing a hand-written order form to a mail-order house, consumers now order goods by a click of a computer mouse or a tap on the screen to place their orders. Those orders can now be processed almost immediately and, in some cases, delivered the next day. While mail order is dead, the catalogue lives on.

References

Abbott, C. (2007), *Urban America in the modern age: 1920 to the present* (Hoboken, NJ: Wiley-Blackwell).

Ayers, E.L. (1992), *The promise of the New South: Life after reconstruction* (New York: Oxford University Press).

Barron, H.S. (1997), *Mixed harvest: The second great transformation in the Rural North, 1870–1930* (Chapel Hill, NC: University of North Carolina Press).

Bean, J.J. (1996), *Beyond the broker state: Federal policy toward small business, 1936–1961* (Chapel Hill, NC: University of North Carolina Press).

Belisle, D. (2011), *Retail nation: Department stores and the making of modern Canada* (Vancouver: University of British Columbia Press).

Benson, J. (1992a), 'The North-American scene: Canada', in J. Benson and G. Shaw (eds.) *The evolution of retail systems, c. 1800–1914* (Leicester: Leicester University Press) 35–48.

Benson, J. (1992b), 'Large-scale retailing in Canada', in J. Benson and G. Shaw (eds.) *The evolution of retail systems, c. 1800–1914* (Leicester: Leicester University Press) 186–198.

Boorstin, D.J. (1973a), *The Americans: The democratic experience* (New York: Random House).

Boorstin, D.J. (1973b), 'A. Montgomery Ward's mail-order business', *Chicago History,* 2 (3), pp. 142–152.

Casson, H.N. (1908), 'The marvelous development of the mail-order business', *Munsey's Magazine,* 38 (4), pp. 513–515.

Chamber of Commerce of the United States (1931), *Distribution in the United States: Trends in its organization and methods.* Washington, DC.

Chandler, A. (1977), *The visible hand: The managerial revolution in American business* (Cambridge, MA: Belknap Press of Harvard University Press).

Chandler, A. (1990), *Scale and scope: The dynamics of industrial capitalism* (Cambridge, MA: Belknap Press of Harvard University Press).

Cherry, R. (2008), *Catalog: The illustrated history of mail-order shopping* (New York: Princeton Architectural Press).

Coopey, R. (2012), 'Credit, community and technology', in R. Jessen and L. Langer (eds.) *Transformations of retailing in Europe after 1945* (Aldershot, UK: Ashgate) 115–126.

Coopey, R., O'Connell, S. and Porter, D. (1999), 'Mail order in the United Kingdom c. 1880–1960: How mail order competed with other forms of retailing', *The International Review of Retail, Distribution and Consumer Research,* 9 (3), pp. 261–723.

Coopey, R., O'Connell, S. and Porter, D. (2005), *Mail order retailing in Britain: A business and social history* (Oxford: Oxford University Press).

Coopey, R. and Porter, D. (2001), 'Did Bradford have anything to learn from Chicago? American influences on mail order retailing in Britain', in M. Kipping and N. Tiratsoo (eds.) *Americanisation in 20th century Europe: Business, culture, politics,* Vol. 2. (Lille, France: Université Charles de Gaulle) 277–279.

Cronon, W. (1991), *Nature's metropolis: Chicago and the great west* (New York: W.W. Norton).

Culbertson, M. (1992), 'Mail-order house and plan catalogues in the United States, 1876–1930', *Art Documentation: Journal of the Art Libraries Society of North America,* 11 (1), pp. 17–20.

Danbom, D.B. (1995), *Born in the country: A history of rural America* (Baltimore, MD: Johns Hopkins University Press).

Emmet, B. and Jeuck, J.E. (1950), *Catalogues and counters: A history of Sears, Roebuck and company* (Chicago: University of Chicago Press).

Fuller, W.E. (1964), *RFD: The changing face of rural America* (Bloomington, IN: Indiana University Press).

Gallagher, W. (2016), *How the post office created America* (New York: Penguin).

Garvin, J.L. (1981), 'Mail-order house plans and American Victorian architecture', *Winterthur Portfolio: A Journal of American Material Culture,* 16 (4), pp. 309–334.

Gellately, R. (1974), *The politics of economic despair: Shopkeepers and German politics, 1890–1914* (London: Sage).

Glazebrook, G.P. de T., Brett, K. and McErvel, J. (1969), *A shopper's view of Canada's past: Pages from Eaton's catalogues, 1886–1930* (Toronto: University of Toronto Press).

Hale, G.E. (1998), *Making whiteness: The culture of segregation in the South, 1890–1990* (New York: Pantheon Books).

Hunter, R.L. (2012), *Mail-order homes: Sears homes and other kit houses* (London: Shire Publications).

Jefferys, J.B. and Knee, D. (1962), *Retailing in Europe: Present structure and future trends* (London: Palgrave Macmillan).

Kielbowicz, R.B. (1994), 'Rural ambivalence toward mass society: Evidence from the U.S. parcel post debates, 1900–1913,' *Rural History,* 5 (1), pp. 81–102.

Kingston, B. (1994), *Basket, bag and trolley: A history of shopping in Australia* (Melbourne: Oxford University Press).

Kline, R.R. (2000), *Consumers in the country: Technology and social change in rural America* (Baltimore, MD: Johns Hopkins University Press).

Koehn, N.F. (2001), *Brand new: How entrepreneurs earned consumers' trust from*

Wedgwood to Dell (Boston, MA: Harvard Business School Press).

Kopytek, B.A. (2014), *Eaton's: The trans-Canada store* (Charleston: The History Press).

Latham, F.B. (1972), *1872–1972: A century of serving consumers: The story of Montgomery Ward* (Chicago: Montgomery Ward).

Leach, W.R. (1993), *Land of desire: Merchants, power, and the rise of a new American culture* (New York: Pantheon Books).

Leonard, D. (2016), *Neither snow nor rain: A history of the United States postal service* (New York: Grove Press).

Mahoney, T. and Sloane, L. (1966), *The great merchants: America's foremost retail institutions and the people who made them great* (New York: Harper & Row).

McArthur, E. (2005), *Towards a theory of retail evolution: An Australian history of retailing in the early twentieth century* (Sydney: University of Technology Sydney).

McNair, M.P. (1931), 'Trends in large-scale retailing', *Harvard Business Review*, 10 (1), pp. 30–39.

McNair, M.P. and May, E.G. (1976), *The evolution of retail institutions in the United States* (Cambridge, MA: Marketing Science Institute).

Michman, R.D. and Greco, A.J. (1995), *Retailing triumphs and blunders: Victims of competition in the new age of marketing management* (Westport, CT: Quorum Books).

Miller, D.L. (1996), *City of the century: The epic of Chicago and the making of America* (New York: Simon & Schuster).

Miller, M. (1981), *The Bon Marché: Bourgeois culture and the department store, 1869–1920* (Princeton, NJ: Princeton University Press).

Monod, D. (1996), *Store wars: Shopkeepers and the culture of mass marketing, 1890–1939* (Toronto: University of Toronto Press).

Moskowitz, M. (2004), *Standard of living: The measure of the middle class in Modern America* (Baltimore, MD: Johns Hopkins University Press).

Nystrom, P.H. (1919), *Retailing selling and store management* (New York: D. Appleton and Company).

Nystrom, P.H. (1919 & 1930), *Economics of retailing: Institutions and trends* (New York: The Ronald Press).

Neth, M. (1995), *Preserving the family farm: Women, community, and the foundations of agribusiness in the Midwest, 1900–1940* (Baltimore, MD: Johns Hopkins University Press).

Phillips, W.B. (1901), *How department stores are carried on* (New York: Dodd, Mead & Company).

Pollon, F. (1989), *Shopkeepers and shoppers: A social history of retailing in New South Wales from 1788* (Sydney: Retail Traders' Association of New South Wales).

Rips, R.E. (1938), *An introductory study of the role of the mail order business in American history, 1872–1914* (Chicago: University of Chicago).

Schlereth, T.J. (1989), 'Country stores, county fairs, and mail-order colleagues: Consumption in rural America', in S.J. Bronner (ed.) *Consuming visions: Accumulation and display of goods in America 1880–1920* (New York: W.W. Norton) 339–377.

Schlereth, T.J. (1992), *Victorian America: Transformations in everyday life, 1876–1915* (New York: Harper Perennial).

Schwartz, D.M. (1985), 'When home sweet home was just a mailbox away', *Smithsonian*, 16 (November), pp. 90–101.

Schweitzer, R.A. and Davis, M.W.R. (1990), *America's favorite homes: Mail-order catalogues as a guide to popular early 20th-century houses* (Detroit: Wayne State University Press).

Shaw, G. (1992), 'The European scene: Britain and Germany', in J. Benson and G. Shaw (eds.) *The evolution of retail systems, c. 1800–1914* (Leicester: Leicester University Press) 17–34.

Simon, A.H. (1974), 'The battle for parcel post: The western farmer vs. the eastern mercantile interests', *Journal of the West*, 13 (4), pp. 79–89.

Smalley, O.A. (1961), 'Market entry and economic adaptation: Spiegel's first decade in mail order', *The Business History Review*, 35 (3), pp. 372–401. Available at: jstor.org/stable/3111476 (Accessed 12 April 2016)

Smalley, O.A. and Sturdivant, F.D. (1973), *The credit merchants: A history of Spiegel, inc* (Carbondale, IL: Southern Illinois University Press).

Spellman, S.V. (2016), *Cornering the market* (New York: Oxford University Press).

Stanger, H. (2000), 'From factory to family: The creation of a corporate culture in the Larkin company of Buffalo, New York', *Business History Review,* 74 (3), pp. 407–433. Available at: www.jstor.org/stable/3116433 (Accessed 22 November 2016)

Stanger, H. (2008), 'The Larkin Clubs of Ten: Consumer buying clubs and mail-order commerce, 1890–1940', *Enterprise & Society*, 9 (1), pp. 125–164.

Stanger, H. (2010), 'Failing at retailing: The decline of the Larkin company, 1918–1942', *Journal of Historical Research in Marketing*, 2 (1), pp. 9–40. Available at: www.emeraldinsight.com/1755-750X.htm.

Strasser, S. (1989), *Satisfaction guaranteed: The making of the American mass market* (New York: Pantheon Books).

Strasser, S. (2006), 'Woolworth to Wal-Mart: Mass merchandising and the changing culture of consumption', in N. Lichtenstein (ed.) *Wal-Mart: The face of twenty-first-century capitalism* (New York: The New Press) 31–56.

Stevenson, K.C. and Jandl, H.W. (1986), *Houses by mail: A guide to houses from Sears, Roebuck, and company* (New York: Wiley-Blackwell).

Tedlow, R.S. (1990), *New and improved: The story of mass marketing in America* (New York: Basic Books).

Thorne, R.J. (1920), 'The mail-order business', in S. Crowther (ed.) *The book of business* (New York: P.F. Collier & Son Company) 22–35.

Wadsworth, R.K. (1928), *Handbook on mail order: Selling and merchandising* (Chicago: The Dartnell Corporation).

Webber, K. and Hoskins, I. (2003), *What's in store? A history of retailing in Australia* (Sydney: Powerhouse Publishing).

Weil, G.L. (1977), *Sears, Roebuck, U.S.A.: The great American catalog store and how it grew* (New York: Stein and Day).

Wolfers, H. (1980), 'The big stores between the wars', in J. Roe (ed.) *Twentieth century Sydney: Studies in urban and social history* (Sydney: Hale & Iremonger) 18–33.

Wood, R.E. (1920), 'Past, present and future of the mail order business', Robert E. Wood Papers: Montgomery Ward and Company, 1919–1923, Herbert Hoover Presidential Library, West Branch, IA.

Worthy, J.C. (1986), *Shaping an American institution: Robert E. Wood and Sears, Roebuck* (Urbana, IL: University of Illinois Press).

20

AT THE MARGINS? ITINERANTS AND PEDLARS

Laurence Fontaine

Introduction

In dictionaries as well as in literature, the pedlar is an ambiguous figure, hard to fit into straightforward categories. In France, the word was first used to mean one who traversed the town selling pictures and loose printed sheets. Second, it was applied to the itinerant rural tradesman who had been known up until then as a *petit mercier, porte-balle, marcelot* or *mercelot*. The first meaning refers to a recognised trade – albeit an unimportant one – whereas the second is nothing more than another way of saying "tramp" or "trickster" (Furetière, 1690). It was only from the second half of the eighteenth century that rural peddling acquired the status of a trade; in the 1762 *Dictionnaire de l'Académie* it appeared as *mercier* rather than just *petit mercier*. Nonetheless, the pedlar remained a disturbing figure who was on the fringes of society and someone to be guarded against.

In England, the word developed in the opposite direction. Chapman was originally a generic term for anyone who bought and sold merchandise. Often the word was modified by the addition of the adjective "petty" which denoted the beginnings of a hierarchy between the well-off merchants of Manchester and Yorkshire, who rode all over the country to deliver their wares to shopkeepers, and the lowliest pedlars who, pack on back, travelled cross-country to far-flung villages. In the seventeenth century and the first half of the eighteenth century, petty chapmen were described as those who 'buy up commodities of those that sell by wholesale and sell them off dearer by retail, and parcel them out'. This term had an equally pejorative connotation: 'Hawking . . . has its derivation from the spying, thievish habits of the bird and man. They also acquired a reputation for ruffianism and brigandage' (Westerfield, 1915, pp. 314–315).

In Spain the pedlar was known as *gabacho*, the coarse man from the mountain of the North; in Italy he was the *merciajuolo* or *merciajo*; and in the Ticino region he is variously recorded in legal records as *mercante, girovagho, trafficante, pertegante* or *cromero* (Corominas, 1954; Pecori, 1980, Fietta, 1985). In Germany each town had its own name for him; as well as the more general term of *Hausierer*, he was also known by the fashion in which he plied his trade – hence, *Gänger*, he who walks; *Ausrufer*, he who shouts in the street; and *Hockerer*, he who squats down. Some pedlars were associated with small luxuries, and were thus called *Tündler*, or they were known quite simply as *Gaukler* or charlatans (Augel, 1971).

Echoing these definitions, right up to the end of the nineteenth century, the pedlar was depicted in literature as a rogue or trickster, half merchant and half thief. He was someone who belonged to another world, who sold both the stuff of everyday life and the stuff of dreams. He came from far away and possessed secret knowledge; his misdeeds were compensated by his clever trickery. If names and images reflect the diversity of their figures they can however be regrouped in two different categories: one is embedded in a larger network of people from the same origin; the other encompasses poor local men and women of the places, who, for lack of work, survived through reselling all kind of food and clothes.

Pedlars and networks of migrants

From the time it first appeared right through to the mid-nineteenth century, peddling was primarily dominated by the mountain dwellers. Indeed, for Western Europe, a map showing the origins of the first migrant merchants reveals three main places: the Alpine curve, the Pyrenees and Scotland. Since the Middle Ages, pedlars from the high Alpine valleys had established a presence on the trade routes. Savoyards from the North and men from the Valle d'Aosta moved to the centres of commerce on the Swiss plateau and the mid-Rhine region (Martin, 1942; Gothein, 1892). The east-west trade movements, between Italy and Spain, had swept the Southern Alp valleys (Fontaine, 1996). In the sixteenth century, the migrant merchants from the great Italian lakes moved on – some towards the North and others towards Southern Italy and Sicily (Merzario, 1984). Finally, from the seventeenth century onwards, the migrants from the South – the "welches" – met up with an influx of northern European merchants from Brabant in Holland (Hemmert, 1979). Scotland scattered her merchants, pedlars, leather craftsmen and weavers across all of northern Europe to Poland, Denmark, Sweden and Norway. The first settlements date back to the second half of the fifteenth century when Scots were to be found on both sides of the Channel, in western France, Norway and the Baltic (Riis, 1988; Grosjean and Murdoch, 2005). Quantifying these pedlars is an impossible task given the inexact and debatable nature of the statistical evidence. However, the fact that the confusion between geographical origins and professional activity ran so deep that a German merchant would find himself called *der Deutscher Italiener* and that in Denmark the word *scot* meant a pedlar provides us with another means of measurement.

These commercial organisations operated on two levels. The first was made up of familial relatives, supported a family banking system and, through opening warehouses and shops in the city, created a vast geographical web. The second level was a distribution network linked to migratory movements. It had a rigid hierarchical structure and was based upon temporary migration and the labour of men from the home village. At the first level, the Giraud family, originally from La Grave in Oisans in the Dauphine, were part of a Protestant merchant network which can be partially reconstructed from Jean Giraud's record book, kept at the end of the seventeenth century. It extended over Switzerland, northern Italy, southern France and Spain: between Lyon, Geneva, Mantua, Perpignan and Cadix. The Brentano family originally came from the valleys surrounding Lake Como and relied on four family branches: the Brentano-Gnosso, the Brentano-Toccia, the Brentano-Cimaroli and the Brentano-Tremezzo. In the Tremezzo branch of the family, the first Brentano to come to Frankfurt was Martino. In 1662, he obtained permission to sell his citrus fruits from a table, as a *Hockerer*, sharing this privilege with the old and infirm. His son Domenico, born in 1651 in Tremezzo, developed the business in partnership with his brothers-in-law and in 1698 opened a shop in Frankfurt. At the beginning of the eighteenth century, members of the Brentano family established themselves in Amsterdam, Bingen, Brussels, Koblenz, Cologne, Constance, Cracow, Diez, Frankfurt, Fribourg,

Heidelberg, Mannheim, Mainz, Nuremberg, Rothenburg, Rotterdam and Vienna. If we also add to the above the towns where their relatives had opened shops, then their establishments covered all of northern Europe (Augel, 1971). Scottish merchant migration proceeded along similar lines (Spufford, 1984). Mathew Cuming, for example, travelled in England between 1683 and 1686. Profiting both from his income and from the credit to which he then had access, Cuming loaded up his ass with bundles of material, which he then took to London to sell in order to finance the importation of dyes from Holland, and to get a share in a boat bringing sugar and tobacco from Virginia. He thus broke into the world of "big business" and prepared to venture onto the Continent.

At the core of many networks at this upper level of activity was a family banking system, which bound the network together and enabled it to maximise resources, since each member invested the best part of the family fortune into the firm. Commercial inter-marriage was therefore one of the cogs in a mechanism which aimed to protect the banking system and the loyalty that each member felt towards the merchant network. Exceptions to this rule were the result of compromises that the migrants had to make in order to gain access to markets in the countries where they settled. These family networks organised themselves into very flexible firms, which could be set up and disbanded in response to commercial necessity, death and the relative wealth or poverty of its members. Therefore, despite settlement in the towns, it was still a question of temporary migration: progressing imperceptibly from one activity to another more important and remunerative one, the length of absence being in proportion to these variables.

In order to develop their businesses, these merchants relied on village migration. At the top of the hierarchical structure were generally relatives of members of the organisation who, having completed their apprenticeship, remained in the service of the business until they had the capital necessary to set up their own business or take a share in the company employing them. Alongside the relatives, the merchants had numerous apprentices. These young men, sons of members of the organisation or of their relatives, came to undertake their apprenticeship as packmen. There were sometimes a fair number of them in the host town, generating complaints from native merchants, who complained that all these young men not only were not registered with the town authorities but also peddled their wares with impunity.

On the lower level of commercial organisation were a great many pedlars. A hierarchy also became apparent within this group. At the top were travelling merchants who did not have shops, but who were always referred to as "merchants" and numbered amongst the richest inhabitants of their home villages. From the end of the seventeenth century, notaries' deeds concerning travelling merchants demonstrate the essential role of these men as a pivot between the two halves of the organisation. In the lowlands they were part of the network developed by shop-owning merchants from whom they got their supplies. One only needs to examine the stocks held by the merchant shopkeepers, and all is revealed. In the two shops and the stockroom he had opened in Lyon, Jacques Berard had 195 pairs of stockings, twenty dozen bonnets, 360 woollen bootlaces, lots of braid, ribbons, laces of all possible colours and fabrics: cordillat, cadiz, serge, drugget, calico, canvas, ratine, muslin, wool, woollen cloth and homespun. Documents confirm the pedlars as clients since most of Berard's debtors were the same rich pedlars from the Alpine valleys himself came from.

In the mountain villages, the wealthy travelling merchants acted as intermediaries through whom one could trade in winter. Pierre Gourand, from Clavans in the Dauphine, owed more than three hundred *livres* to Jean and Daniel Horard, merchants of Mizoen in the form of four obligations dating from 1665, 1668, 1670 and 1672. The Horard family, linked by marriage to the Berards and other trading families, were responsible for the Burgundy link in the network of upper Dauphine merchants. In his turn, Gourand acted as a link between the families in the village and the merchant network of which he himself was part. He did so by finding work for other migrants, providing them with merchandise and acting as banker and intermediary between them and more important merchants with whom, as with the Horard brothers, he enjoyed a special relationship. These pedlars, who were very much a part of the economic life of the village, were the pivots of the village migratory system.

In their turn, the packmen, who stocked up from the factories and warehouses established in the town by their compatriots, employed servants and apprentices. However, unlike other members of the company, the pedlar's employees were not allowed any opportunity to line their own pockets: they were forbidden to act as wholesalers or retailers on their own behalf or to lend money (the other method of building up one's own business); moreover, any social activities likely to divert them from their work – such as dancing, playing billiards or going to the theatre – were forbidden. The Perroman company from Savoy made use of this structure from the end of the fourteenth century to distribute textiles, scythes, metals, saffron and saltpetre, which they imported in bulk; the packmen collected fresh supplies from a storehouse set up by their employer in the shop or hostel of a compatriot (Guichonnet, 1948).

Even allowing for exaggeration, the complaints that the German towns and guilds made regularly to the Diets indicate how far the peddling hierarchies had extended. At the Diet of Zurich in 1516, Schwyz, from German Switzerland, denounced

> those persons who travel around the region, hawking their cheap goods, from village to village, from farm to farm and from house to house, up hill and down dale. So much so that no home is safe: they worm their way in with their servants and children – even the lowliest of them has three or four. They also beg and live off the backs of the poor, without paying a pfennig to a single innkeeper.
>
> *(quoted in Augel, 1971, pp. 193–194)*

In the seventeenth century, the local spice merchants took every opportunity of denouncing Italian and Jewish organisations that used five or six boys to distribute their products, on public holidays as well as working days. The boys stopped off in inns, wriggled their way into the houses of the middle classes on wedding days and knocked on every door. Danish rulings in the fifteenth and sixteenth centuries forbidding Scottish merchants to send their apprentices and servants to hawk their wares in the surrounding countryside also bear witness to the existence of links between the now sedentary business community and the trade done by itinerant pedlars who originated from the same village. From North to South, the existence of peddling reveals the extent of recruitment which bound the migrant community together and included even its poorest members.

These small business networks had a certain number of common characteristics. They relied on commercial diversity: merchants and pedlars traded in all types of merchandise, depending on demand and commercial opportunities, although most families had a specialty which often had its roots in the produce of their home region – the southern Tyrol for carpets, Lake Como for citrus fruits or the Upper Dauphine for gloves. Three factors forced them to offer a wider selection of goods: the desire to reach a larger clientele by offering the widest possible range of products; methods of payment in which exchange and barter played a large part; and the search for new or forbidden goods, which would mean larger profits. Thus, in 1692, the stock list for Antonio Brentano's shop in Nuremberg revealed that he had on sale salted herrings, salmon, beef, cheese, tobacco and prunes. At his death eleven years later this also included 1537 pounds of coffee, 67 pounds of tea, 65 pounds of truffles, potatoes, oil, candy sugar, cotton, paper, Spanish and Rhenish wine, and Dutch and Spanish tobacco. During the same period, Carl Brentano's shop contained casks of capers, figs, salted lemons, Parmesan, bay leaves, rice, nuts, almonds, olives, oil, lemonade, 180 pounds of chocolate, a cask of dried truffles, four barrels of truffles in oil, Spanish wine, Brazilian tobacco, 34 pounds of Spanish snuff, two boxes of rubber, a barrel of indigo, a small cask of cochineal, 140 caskets of blue and pink wood, three bales of cotton and sixteen bales of silk. Moreover, the peddling organisations turned trade circuits to their advantage. Pedlars sold their goods on credit, demanding repayment in the form of buying or renting fields or as a share of the harvests which they stored there in the village in rented cellars and barns. In this way they multiplied their access to other markets and short-circuited a certain amount of trade between town and countryside.

One final aspect of these merchant organisations is that both men and merchandise circulated and worked on the fringes of the law. This constant is, of course, the most difficult to establish, even if one can hazard a guess at the profits gained from the skill with which these men manipulated the rules. Goods were transported along routes where it was possible to avoid customs and tolls, especially when some of the goods were of smuggled origin, as was the case with raw wool and, in particular, tobacco which was grown on a large scale (despite the ban on this) in the Alpine valleys of Lombardy and processed in the towns of the Rhine where the laws were more flexible (Caizza, 1965). As soon as a new market opened up or circumstances allowed (in particular during times of war), smuggling and illicit warehouses multiplied. The wealthiest pedlars tried as hard as possible to avoid paying costly registration fees in cities, thus confusing both urban and peddling hierarchies. A society based on order and status here came up against the organisational logic of the peddling network; thus, as soon as one or two members of the family firm were legally established in the city, the others saw no advantage in paying duties and taxes which they would have to add to the sale price of their goods. It was also a sign that they did not yet share urban values. These same merchants were careful not to register with the local administration the vast number of young men who came to work for them several months of the year, nor to purchase status for them. A substantial amount of the profits no doubt came from the accumulation of all such fraudulent practices and irregularities.

The eighteenth century: a return to the regional areas

The balance between locations was the basis of the migratory structure, at the centre of which were several powerful families from the home villages. Because of this structure, despite the constant friction with the sedentary merchants and in defiance of the political moves to contain them and change their trading practices, the links established at the end of the Middle Ages between town wholesalers and itinerant pedlars from the same region lingered until the end of the eighteenth century. Long before this, however, the vast peddling networks had become fragmented and withdrew to regional areas. The chronology of this withdrawal, a result of the encounter between internal changes in the adopted country and those in the home villages, had its own logic and periods of inertia: the break-up was sometimes abrupt and sometimes the result of a gradual change, depending on the region. But by the end of the eighteenth century, this transformation had been accomplished everywhere.

In the French and Savoyard Alps, the first crack in the migratory system was a political one. In France the affirmation of royal sovereignty, centred on religious unity and the war, upset the balance of the mountain economy between 1685 and 1715. The decision to go into exile taken by the majority of the peddling elite and a significant proportion of the Protestant population of the villages threw the networks into disarray. The war brought its own difficulties and the Treaty of Utrecht established for the first time a border between the two sides of the mountains. In Savoy, the conflict between the Sardinian states and the French monarchy forced the merchants to choose sides. The French Revolution and the Napoleonic Wars completed the process of fragmentation, but the flow was already greatly reduced through the combined effects of national politics, municipal obstacles and the merchants' growing lack of interest in the highlands. The networks which had been built up between Scotland and the Baltic States suffered the same fate, despite renewed activity during the Jacobite uprisings of 1715–1745. The dominant position occupied by the Dutch in Baltic commerce for over a century and the opening up of the English market following the Act of Union with Scotland had already signalled the decline of Scottish merchant and pedlar migration: since emigration was no longer as widespread, men gradually integrated into new communities and, towards the end of the eighteenth century, the transformation was accomplished in Poland and Denmark. The renewed activities of the sea adventurers can be traced in the customs records, where names changed after a number of decades (Smout, 1968). The same phenomenon had occurred a century earlier in Sweden where political expediency had led to gradual integration into native families via settlement and marriage.

Conversely, those peddling networks that were organised around the east-west commercial axis and that looked towards Mediterranean Europe, benefited from the shift of the main trade movements towards the Atlantic coast and continued to profit from commercial structures which remained weak in the Iberian peninsula. Families from Briançonnais and Queyras, for instance, forced to abandon the Italian market in the eighteenth century, now directed their attention in the opposite direction, towards Spain, Portugal and their American colonies. Other migratory movements took advantage of the change of direction in the peddling networks to set up their own commercial organisations, as did men from the Auvergne and the Bas Limousin in Spain (Poitrineau, 1985). Similarly, ethnic minorities – particularly Jews – took a further step towards integration by moving into the place left vacant by the Italians and Savoyards and by extending their activities towards Western Europe.

The break-up of many large networks brought about change within the profession of travelling merchant. Although the timing varied from country to country – starting from the early seventeenth century in England and in the eighteenth century in France and in the Rhine regions – the geography was always the same, with border mountain regions or outlying areas providing most pedlars. In France, pedlars came from the Alps, the Pyrenees and the Massif Central area as well as from the Jura mountains and from Brittany. In Britain, although migration was less dominated by the highlands because of the existence of a peddling structure organised around the industrial zones, nonetheless Scotland still accounted for the largest number of pedlars, In Belgium it was the Hainaut region which upheld the old tradition, and in Italy, pedlars always came from the Alps or the central region of the Apennine mountains. Whilst the origin of pedlars had changed little, however, the new structure very different. It was distinguished by an increase in the number of pedlars; by the use made of pedlars by all urban commerce and no longer just by the village elite who had settled in the towns; by the wider range of goods offered by the pedlars; and by the disappearance of the multiple transactions involving the pedlar (in which payments in foodstuffs and goods bypassed other markets) in favour of credit alone.

The increase in the number of pedlars was evident everywhere, although it is impossible to determine precise numbers. That England had an early start is obvious, as much from the upsurge in numbers as by the subsequent decline, which had begun even before peddling in France really took off. England thus had a century's head start over the Continent: from the end of the seventeenth century the distribution network covered by the travelling merchants had reached the furthest corners of the land, whilst on the Continent the rural areas had only been partially conquered. In France, the growth in numbers was significant from the 1760s onwards: whilst notaries' records had referred only to 'merchants' in the seventeenth century; from the eighteenth, 'pedlars' appeared in droves. There was a commensurate hardening of definitions, merchants being distinguished from merchant-pedlars and from pedlars (Fontaine, 1991, pp. 43–46). This upsurge was the consequence of the general development of urban business; pedlars no longer worked solely for merchants who came from the same valleys as themselves but also bought their stock from other city merchants who used pedlars to further their own business concerns. This new development brought with it other changes: the better-off pedlars neglected the products of family industry to devote themselves solely to the resale of goods; the less well-off, who were selling their craftsman's knowledge, gradually abandoned this in favour of city goods. Thus the knife-grinders and scissor-sharpeners tended to give up these humbler professions and concentrate solely on trading.

Eventually large quantities of a new product – printed material – became part of the pedlar's range of wares. Initially this was distributed from centres of production in eastern France and the German regions of the Rhine, from Paris and Lyon; by the mid-eighteenth century it had reached most rural areas. Before specific peddling networks were built up around it, printed matter was an extra commodity much valued by pedlars of haberdashery. Trading in prohibited books became a very attractive business for the pedlars since there were large profits to be had. Paul Malherbe, a Norman pedlar linked to the *Société Typographique de Neuchatel*, ordered books from Neuchatel, stored them in a secret warehouse and resold them to pedlars because they were

> the goods with the biggest turnover at the moment . . . the pedlars are extremely eager for this type of book; they earn far more than on other works, because the price is perfect, a snip given the demand for the book.
>
> *(Darnton, 1987, p. 130)*

The same appetite for prints can be traced for England (Spufford, 1981, pp. 111–128).

In the mid-eighteenth century, most large towns in northern and central France boasted a bookseller-cum-printer who catered for pedlars. At the same time as printed material was finding its way into the haberdasher's backpack, certain regions were beginning to specialise in this type of peddling: Cotentin and Briançonnais in France and the Ticino valley in Italy. Indeed, in the eighteenth century, peddling on a large scale – where the entire population of the home village benefited from the network of shops established by the wealthiest families – was only made possible by the market for printed material. This durability is explained by the choice of product: printed material was a new commodity, very much sought-after, likely to bring in substantial profits and one where there was a market for both legal and smuggled goods. In 1754, François Grasset, formerly chief clerk with the Cramer booksellers in Geneva, wrote in a letter to the director of the French library that:

> The bookselling trade in Spain and Portugal, as well as that of many Italian towns, is totally controlled by the French; all of them from a village in a Briançonnais valley in the Dauphiné. Active, hard-working and moderate, they make successive trips to Spain and almost always marry amongst themselves . . . not only is the bookselling trade in their hands, but also the market for geographical maps, prints, clock-making, cloth, printed calico, stockings, hats and so forth.[1]

And Grasset was right: they dominated the market for print material in Portugal and Spain and hold a good share of it in Italy (Fontaine, 1996, pp. 50–72). However, if the network emanating from the Briançonnais appears to be the most important, it was not by any means the only one. The Remondini publishers ofVenice, originally from Bassano, made their mark in the second half of the eighteenth century by means of a similar network. De Lalande, in his book *Le Voyage en Italie*, points to the printing operation run by the Remondini family as the largest establishment of its kind in Europe and the only one to have a completely integrated production process, from the paper manufacture to the sales network (Lefrançois de Lalande, 1769). The firm employed a thousand workers, 1,500 business correspondents in Italy and a further fifty in Europe and more than 2,000 travelling salesmen, all originally from the Ticino valley. Similarly, a peddling network for books and other printed material developed in northern France around Cotentin. It also had an international dimension especially strong in northern Europe (Casselle, 1978, pp. 84–85; Sauvy, 1967).

A flexible typology

The best criterion for distinguishing between types of travelling merchant during this period concerns the way in which the trip was financed. This allows us to identify three groups of pedlars in terms of the security they could offer to the city merchants in return for the goods supplied. The importance of the amount of credit allowed thus serves to distinguish the half-starved pedlars with nothing to offer from the regular pedlars who had enough property to guarantee their loans and the merchant-pedlars who, with a solid financial base, could travel by cart and open shops. A typology such as this has two distinguishing features. On the one hand it is flexible: the pedlar who carried a pack could hope to attain the higher ranks of the profession; for many, it was seen as a career with scope for progression, even as far as opening a shop in the city. On the other hand, these different types of pedlar were bound together as much by family ties as by the business links that existed within the profession. Alongside these three a new model emerged in England: the "Manchester Man", who heralded a radical innovation in that his ties with his home community were relaxed in favour of the firm for which he worked on a virtually exclusive basis. Four groups then, each with their own methods of selling, obtaining their supplies and attracting customers.

The sociological diversity was greatest amongst the destitute pedlars, since they had nothing to offer as security against goods and credit. Their trade thus slipped easily through the net of interdependency and restraints which bound other pedlars together. Three sub-groups can be identified: those who, in villages where there were craftsmen and pedlars, had been expelled from credit circles; those who came from villages which specialised in the sale of devotional images, where the profession came within the framework of family interdependency, like the *santari* from Campli in Italy or the *chamagnons* from the Jura; and finally, the blind, who in Spain succeeded in obtaining a virtual monopoly for themselves in the sale of printed sheets (Trifoni, 1989, pp. 113–120; Darmon, 1972; Botrel, 1973, 1974). The first group took any work which came along, and in between jobs went hawking their wares and begging. Their ties with the home village had not been broken and their temporary itinerancy was primarily an economy of absence – a saving of the bread that they would not be there to eat in the village in winter. For these pedlars, who were half-beggar, half-tramp, more important than the goods was the act of selling itself. They put on a show and sold entertainment and dreams. They were not seeking one-to-one contacts with purchasers nor the intimacy of the home, but public square and fairs – places where people passed through, times of festivity when a crowd might form around them. The *cantastores*, the charlatans, teeth-pullers, hernia-shrinkers and Bergamasque maskers spread prophecies as they travelled from one town square to another in Italy. Those from the Ticino region who sold pictures and small booklets threaded them onto a piece of string and told their story using a hazelnut twig to illustrate the tale. In Germany such pedlars resorted to large illustrated boards (*Bild*) the tale of which he told as he sold his booklets; as did his French counterpart (Niccoli, 1987; Passamani and Manfredi, 1972; Duval, 1991). On these fringes of entertainment were to be found the destitute vagrants who exhibited curiosities, such as the marmot which accompanied the mountain dwellers of the Savoy region; the bear which certain dwellers of the Pyrenees brought with them; or the Mohawk Indian put on display by a Jewish pedlar from England in 1765. Acrobats, organ grinders and bear-tamers from the mountain villages of Tuscany all became familiar figures in the city (Endelman, 1981, pp. 113–126; Sarti, 1985).

The regular pedlar, who had established suppliers, faithful customers and enough of an inheritance to guarantee his credit, was the pedlar *par excellence*. Generally speaking, he set out between the end of August and the end of November, depending on the demands of farm labour, the dates of the livestock markets and the number of people in the household. These pedlars stocked up primarily at the shops opened by émigrés, then made up the rest of their stock from other merchants. They made the bulk of their purchases from the former and borrowed from them much of the money they would need for their campaign, forging strong relationships that were often built up over successive generations (Fontaine, 1996). In contrast to the scattered nature of suppliers of goods in France, London was the place where many minor English merchants filled their packs. At the end of the seventeenth century, over three-quarters of the supplies of fabrics were still bought there. The city was also the major centre for the redistribution of porcelain imported from China (Weatherill, 1986, pp. 51–76). To the supplies purchased in London were added more specialised products from the provinces. At his death, Thomas Teisdale of Lincoln owed £192 to five London merchants; he made up the rest of his stock in Glasgow (for Scottish cloth), Manchester (for needles and small articles of ironmongery) and Newport (for braid). Long-standing personal relationships developed between pedlars and London suppliers to the point where certain among the latter remembered their "faithful" pedlars when they died and left them some money so that they might buy a mourning ring in memory of them (Spufford, 1984, pp. 79–80). These packmen generally undertook one or two small-scale predetermined trips. They kept account books. Knowledge of the places and the people went hand in hand with another relationship, one as much economic as cultural – that of credit. This was the basis of the relationship between the pedlar and the villagers: they paid him back over the year, in dribs and drabs, payment being made when the pedlar turned up again, and always coupled with a further purchase and thus further credit.

The merchant-pedlar who rented a shop seldom withdrew from the migrant network or abandoned his former practices; on the contrary, he was prepared to go back on the road if business went badly. However, to consolidate his success, he employed the newest sales technique, using for instance the press as an advertising medium and if he was a bookseller he would have catalogues printed (Da Gama Caeiro, 1980; Fontaine, 1996, pp. 140–163).

The new figure to emerge in seventeenth-century England was the Manchester Man. He could be distinguished from the traditional pedlar by the way in which he obtained his supplies, through his customers and sales techniques. The Manchester Man was a pedlar working for a factory, who did not travel from door to door but from shop to shop, He remained an itinerant merchant, but the vital difference was that he operated as a middleman between manufacturers in the north of England and retailers, shopkeepers and pedlars across the country. As early as 1685, the existence of the Manchester Men was well-established. They criss-crossed England with their mules or horses loaded with cheap fabrics and clothes, ironmongery and cutlery, to which assortment they also added watches and almanacs. A bell worn by the lead horse signalled the arrival of the convoy. As an intermediate stage in the distribution network, they sold in bulk to shopkeepers and to pedlars who they met when visiting fairs, thus competing with London merchants for the custom of itinerant merchants. They all attended the fairs, which became places where deals were struck between, on the one hand, the London merchants or their agents and the Manchester Men and, on the other, the pedlars, who took this opportunity to settle their previous debts and to obtain the necessary goods for their next campaign. The London merchants, like the Manchester Men, offered extensive credit to the packmen. In addition, the Manchester Man, who in the eighteenth century was one of the preferred agents of the manufacturers as they set out to create a mass market, played on his respectability, creating the illusion that he had the same social status as an established merchant. To lend substance to this impression, he had ostentatious decorated visiting cards and headed notepaper printed, which he left with businesses to indicate that he had called, or published in the local newspapers to advertise his imminent arrival (McKendrick, Brewer and Plumb, 1982, pp. 77–89; Westerfield, 1915, pp. 313–314).

The demise of the profession

Marginalised in the business world and discredited in the home villages, peddling began to decline as early as the eighteenth century in England and from the middle of the nineteenth in France. Following the rejection of organisations based on extended family groups and the withdrawal into a narrower family structure, the end of the profession was marked by a double breakdown which put an end to all future development: both family tradition and credit structures were demolished. This final stage reveals that, behind the continued use of the term pedlar, there lay a radically different way of thinking and of operating as a migrant merchant.

During the twenty years that followed the great agricultural crises seen in mid-nineteenth century France, definitive emigration supplanted seasonal emigration and the basis of peddling fundamentally shifted. An analysis of the censuses of 1896 and 1901 for the peddling villages in the valleys of the Oisans reveals that the profession, which up until then had been passed down from father to son, now only survived on the margins of families. Only single men who belonged to atypical families still practiced the profession: brothers living together or men who were the only wage-earners in the family. Moreover, an analysis of the records for military conscription for this same group of villages highlights another aspect of this marginalisation: one-third of the conscripts who had been pedlars had engaged in the trade only occasionally and the majority only peddled for a year or two before or after military service, or returned home and became packmen after having failed in other careers (Fontaine, 1991, pp. 43–68).

Certain traditional pedlars, however, managed to continue in their profession for a few decades longer. In each peddling region there were a few families who turned their attention to a new specialisation or by selling new or luxury goods. In the Dauphine, haberdashers became opticians, seed merchants or florists; in the Pyrenees they became booksellers; in the Auvergne, wine merchants; in the southern parts of the Black Forest they peddled glass jewellery; on the other side of the Rhine it was pictures. In the Apennine valleys of Lucques, pedlars became known as *figurinai* because they sold plaster figures. There was a wide range of specialities and the organisation of itinerant trade was not confined to one single model since, depending on the markets canvassed, the goods offered and the village traditions, either the old way of doing things was resurrected, or original ways of selling were invented to fit in with the new economic constraints of the end of the nineteenth century.

The most profitable forms of specialisation combined luxury goods with the conquest of new markets. The florist-pedlars from the Oisans in upper Dauphine offer an excellent example. Originally from traditional families of cloth merchants and haberdashers, they gradually discovered new markets, new customers, and new ways of selling and financing their expeditions. The florists sold all sorts of fruit and ornamental trees, decorative plants, rosebushes and various sorts of bulbs and seeds. They packed them in sturdy wooden boxes, added a few baskets, and picked a destination, depending upon the time of year when they were setting out. Those who set out in autumn headed for Latin America, the Mediterranean basin or the Middle East; those who could only leave at the beginning of winter went to countries where spring came later: the Northern States and Russia. Jean-Pierre Magne, one of the first great florists, born in 1806 in Mont-de-Lans in the Dauphine, travelled all over Europe from Ireland to the Baleares, North Africa, Egypt, Russia and Brazil; he also took over seven trips to the eastern part of the United States, from the Great Lakes to New Orleans. Claude Chouvin, born in 1853 in the neighbouring village of La Garde, travelled to Mexico, North America and Canada and then specialised in trading with Latin America. Others went as far as the borders of Russia and of Iran. Their target customers were dignitaries and the rich middle classes: their sales pitch combined evocations of luxury and the exotic. Once they had reached their chosen destination, they set out to look for a shop to rent in a busy shopping street and went about advertising their presence. In Latin America, where the rich middle class was relatively large, they placed advertisements in the newspapers; in Russia and Egypt, where those in power constituted a limited elite, before putting their wares on display they first presented them to the local dignitary in the hope that by gaining favour with the prince they would attract the small number of people of standing into their shop. Whatever the circumstances, they had to make a sale quickly: customers were few and the plants either withered or demanded too much attention. They hoped to sell most of their stock within a month at most, off-loading the remaining plants at one or two smaller towns on the way back.

As well as the plants, they offered dreams to the bourgeoisie. Their sales pitch primarily targeted the imagination: they had calling cards and invoice slips printed which created the impression that their shop was a branch of a large business which counted amongst its customers the most important people in France; they hung pictures of flowers in their shops, generally painted with stencils, reproducing the descriptions in the advance catalogues they published. The flowers, seeds, bulbs and the bare trees advertised as being on sale took on surprising and unexpected shapes and colours in their promotional material: green and blue roses in the shape of a turban, up to 14 centimetres wide, three-coloured hyacinths, gentians with thousands of red flowers, strange orchids, flowering ferns and so on.

The financial structure of their business was similar to that of other pedlars, in that they approached the important people in the valleys for backing. However, there three were important differences. First, their suppliers were outside of this circuit, the merchant-pedlars borrowed money, but never merchandise. Second, because the initial capital outlay was large and involved cash payments for stock, business associations involved more people than for other types of peddling: the florists set out in groups of three or four, and sometimes more; their partnership was usually agreed verbally and lasted for the duration of the journey; two months after the merchants returned home they settled their accounts and dissolved the partnership. Third, this type of business made use of nascent banking services, whether for insuring their goods or transferring money. More than any other type of peddling, the flower trade was an extremely risky business with uncertain profits. The merchant could lose his merchandise at any point in his campaign; but profits were in proportion to the risks taken and sometimes enormous. These pedlars thus managed to get round the major problems which beset pedlars who travelled in France: by choosing countries with loose business networks and a rich clientele who were able to pay cash, they were able to continue practicing the profession profitably without being constrained by the traditional shackles of debt. However, the economic slump that hit South

America at the end of the nineteenth century was the final factor in dissuading florists from a profession which had been depreciated despite the potential earnings: families wanted no more itinerancy but saw success in terms of a settled life and a fixed income, even if it was a small one (Fontaine, 1996, pp. 152–156).

The death of peddling in Europe, marked by the great variety of pedlars, can be seen as symbolic of the migrant merchants' final attempts to adapt to the explosion of new sales methods, which were forcing them to the fringes of the market. The increasing number of sales outlets, new distribution networks, the opening up of the rural areas and, of course, the rapid development of mail order all made them redundant as intermediaries.

Peddling as a resource for the poorest everywhere in early modern Europe

The migrant pedlars have never been the only ones to sell in the streets since reselling small goods was the first survival strategy for the unemployed and for people who were rejected from trade organisations. Moreover, many shopkeepers sent their wives and servants to peddle their merchandises illegally in other districts of the city or at its outskirt (Montenach, 2013; Van den Heuvel, 2007). Street vendors were part of two important markets: food and second-hand objects. Indeed, next to the official food markets, myriads of hawkers criss-crossed streets and markets, went up and down staircases and entered inns. The housing conditions of most people were such that they had no place for storage or even for cooking and all kinds of small traders sold meat directly from slaughterhouses outside the capital, as well as cheese, milk, fruit and vegetables (Reynald, 2002). Some stood behind a table, others moved with a basket or tray, and still others sold from a cart. Furthermore, cities developed a vast chain of sellers and resellers, both men and women, who recycled leftovers from well-to-do houses. Water carriers and drink vendors completed the picture (Fontaine, 2014).

The peddling of foodstuffs was largely handled by women. In Nuremberg in the sixteenth century, the market was full of women selling food, candles, even books and pictures. Their small-scale retail operations included the distribution of household production, but they also sold exotic items of long-distance trade such as citrus fruits, dyestuffs and spices. They shared this market with the networks of Italian peddlers and, like in Paris, they were active in the urban peddling of books, engravings and news (Merry Wiesner, 1981, pp. 3–13; Beauvalet-Boutouyrie, 2001, p. 282). Permitting these small traders to exist was a political strategy employed by the city to give them the means to support themselves and thus avoid falling back on charitable institutions. This strategy of reserving to the poor segments of small retail was very common in European cities, but they were generally allowed to sell only one kind of merchandise – the distribution of official news being the most common.

To access the needed capital to buy their merchandise, most of them had to borrow from usurers on a day to day basis. Louis-Sébastien Mercier, an acute observer of the small Parisian economy, recounted that the latter set up their agencies around markets and that the women merchants were to accept collective liability:

> He [the usurer] then goes to an out-of the-way house, to a room where there is only one bad carpet, a pallet, three chairs and a crucifix. There he grants an audience to sixty women, – vulgar food sellers, street hawkers and fruit sellers. Then he speaks to them in a stiff voice: "My friends, as you can see, I am not better off than you; here is my furniture, here is the bed I lie on when I come to Paris; I give you my money and rely on your conscience and religion; as from you I have no signature, you know, I can

> ask nothing of the law. I am useful for your trade; and when I lavish my trust, I must have my surety. So be all of you jointly liable, and swear in front of this crucifix, the image of our divine Saviour, that you shall do me no wrong, and that you shall faithfully return to me that what I shall entrust to you". All the vulgar food sellers and fruit sellers raise their hands, and swear to strangle the one who would not be faithful in payment: dreadful oaths are taken and long signs of the cross made.
>
> *(Mercier, 1994b, pp. 548–551)*

Caught between the will to let the poor earn a living and the desire to keep prices low for the working-class population, urban authorities have tried to regulate the activity of numerous resellers and fought against the immediate resale of goods. In France, the hours during which resellers could operate in the market were regulated to give people the time to buy, carry and sell their small produce (Petrowiste, 2004, pp. 316–320; Duval, 2001, p. 327). In Spain, small resellers and regraters (regatones) were either not permitted to sell in the market or strict restrictions were placed on them to avoid the very widespread practice of purchase and immediate resale. In London and urban Holland restrictions were also taken against food hawkers (Blasquez, 1996, p. 118; Van den Heuvel, 2016, pp. 94–95).

As consumer credit was formally forbidden in many parts of Europe, pawn broking was the major tool to access it, creating a micro-economy in which clothing circulated as a form of currency, and was rented out and pawned according to need. Women were at the heart of these markets: their social roles, in an incompletely monetarised economy and in a legal environment which marginalised them, explain why they were active, along with recognised guilds and migrant networks in the sale and resale of used clothes. In Paris, for instance, in 1725 the female second-hand dealers were between 6000 and 7000 (Fontaine, 2008, pp. 104–111; Roche, 1989, pp. 328–344).

From the eighteenth century, in these societies where the poor hardly counted, new values marginalised them even further. Health and safety requirements were imposed, requiring more capital investment to adhere to the new standards. As and when they were imposed, women would, for lack of rights and capital, be replaced increasingly by men and by sedentary merchants. On the other hand, city dwellers pushed municipal authorities to domesticate the street and the market by facilitating the movement of people so that the air and the water could be cleansed of unpleasant smells and noxious air, and the street and pavements cleared of cumbersome street vendors. Louis Sébastien Mercier echoed these new values in his description of the markets of Paris in 1799. Not a single one found favour in his eyes: on top of their 'hideous and repulsive appearance', he lamented that to access the merchandise, 'you have to lay yourself open to the sharp tongue of sellers, resellers and sub sellers'. He then denounced the links between the official merchants and the vendors from the countryside which spoiled the only pleasant market of Paris: 'Why does the quadrangular Marché des Innocents, so vast and so airy, with easy exits, only present to the people a forbidding row of umbrellas that eager farmers rent at a hundred louis per year from wretched rag dealers?' (Mercier, 1994a, pp. 1296–1299).

Finally, the establishment of a patent law in France obliged all sellers and resallers to pay a tax which the poorest could not afford. One of two women accused of selling clothes without a patent at a fair in 1796, invoked the paltriness of her business: 'of such little value that she had not been liable for a patent'. The counsel for the two women stated that they had no other choice to survive because

> the woman Moreau, a housewife and mother, who owned nothing and who only put on sale her own meagre belongings as well as those of her husband and goods

entrusted to her by a female patented trader . . . that she is obliged to sell to feed her family.

As for her sister, the counsel explained,

indigent and crippled, she is not in a position to earn her living in any other way but by making rags for children out of old clothes . . . that she is in the habit of going to the markets of Paris and the areas nearby and that she was never asked whether she had a patent.

In his conclusion, he emphasised the extent to which such practices were common for

the Moreau women and the girl Toutain are like many other citizens from all the communes of the Republic who like them made children's rags with the old clothes they get as they are in no position to pay for the least patent, most of their businesses not even being equivalent to the price of the smallest patent.[2]

These women and all the petty street vendors were also victims of the official merchants' determination to keep their monopoly on trade (Fontaine, 1991, pp. 85–95; Van den Heuvel, 2015). Mercier castigated the confiscation of goods of men and women trying to benefit from the market to earn their livelihood:

There is nothing more common and nothing which dishonours our legislation more. One often sees a commissioner with bailiffs running after a rag seller or a small ironmonger carrying a portable shop. A woman is publicly stripped of the forty odd pairs of breeches she is carrying on her back and her head. Her old clothes are confiscated in the name of the majestic community of secondhand clothes dealers . . . a man in a jacket carrying something wrapped in his coat is arrested. What do they confiscate? New shoes that the poor man had hidden in a teatowel. The shoes were taken away by order, this sale becoming prejudicial to Parisian cobbling.

(Mercier, 1994b, pp. 143–144)

This tells us clearly that the survival of men and women living hand to mouth depended on the market and trade, for at the time everyone was more or less a trader. But this access to the market was one thing the big players always wanted to keep for themselves. From the Middle Ages, they obtained regulations directed at excluding migrants, women and all those looking to derive from selling a small additional income or simply the means to survive. At the end of the *Anciene Regime* and in the nineteenth century, the new standards of hygiene requiring greater capital reinforced the dominance of the sedentary traders, for the poor, who lived on small transactions and small productions, could not conform to them. The fact that market activity was the livelihood of the poorest mattered little at that time and the State compounded matters further by taxing them to meet its monetary needs and to control the itinerant sellers and their ware.

Notes

1 Bibliothèque Nationale, Ms. Fr. 22130, fo. 37, November 1754.
2 Archives Nationales, BB 18822 Justice Seine et Marne, quoted by Cobb, R. (1985). *La Mort est dans Paris*, Paris: Chemin Vert, pp. 170–171.

References

Archives Départementales de Isère, 1J 1102, *Livre de raizon apartenant à Moy Jean Giraud de Lagrave où est contenu mais affaires emparticulier. Comancé le 17 janvier 1670 à Lion.*

Archives Nationales, BB 18822 Justice Seine et Marne, quoted by Cobb, R. (1985). *La Mort est dans Paris* (Paris: Chemin Vert) 170–171.

Augel, J. (1971), *Italienische Einwanderung und Wirtschaftstätigkeit in rheinischen Städten des 17. und 18. Jahrhunderts* (Bonn: Röhrscheid).

Beauvalet-Boutouyrie, S. (2001), *Etre veuve sous l'Ancien Régime* (Paris: Belin), p. 282.

Blasquez, A. (1996), 'Foires et marchés ruraux en Castille à l'époque moderne', in C. Desplat (ed.) *Foires et marchés dans l'Europe médiévale et moderne* (Toulouse: Presses universitaires du Mirail) 105–127.

Botrel, J.-F. (1973, 1974), 'Les aveugles colporteurs d'imprimés en Espagne', *Mélanges de la casa de Vélasquez*, 9, pp. 417–482 and 10, pp. 233–271.

Caizza, B. (1965), *Industria e commercio della republica veneta nel XVIII secolo* (Milan: Banca Commerciale Italiana).

Casselle, P. (1978), 'Recherche sur les marchands d'estampes parisiens d'origine cotentinoise à la fin de l'Ancien Régime, Comité des travaux historiques et scientifiques', *Bulletin d'histoire moderne et contemporaine*, 11, pp. 74–93.

Corominas, J. (1954), *Diccionario Crítico Etimológico de la Lengua Castellana* (Bern: Francke).

Da Gama Caeiro (1980), 'Livros e livreios franceses em Lisboa nos fins de setecentos e no primeiro quartel do seculo XIX', *Anais da Academia Portuguesa da História*, Lisbon, IIa serie, II (26), pp. 301–327.

Darmon, J.-J. (1972), *Le colportage de librairie en France sous le Second Empire* (Paris: Plon).

Darnton, R. (1987), 'Un colporteur sous l'Ancien Régime', in *Censures, de la Bible aux larmes d'Eros* (Paris: Centre Georges Pompidou).

Duval, G. (1991), *Littérature de colportage et imaginaire collectif en Angleterre à l'époque des Dicey (1720–v1800)* (Bordeaux: Presses Universitaires de Bordeaux).

Duval, M. (2001), *Foires et marchés en Bretagne de l'Antiquité à la fin de l'Ancien Régime* (Paris: Royer éditions).

Endelman, T. (1981), "L'activité économique des juifs anglais', *Dix-huitième siècle*, 13, pp. 113–126.

Fietta, I.E. (1985), 'Con la casetta in spalla: gli ambulanti di Tessino', *Quaderni di cultura alpina*, (23), pp. 4–111.

Fontaine, L. (1991), 'Family cycles, peddling and society in upper alpine valleys in the eighteenth century', in S. Woolf (ed.) *Domestic stategies: Work and family in France and Italy 17–18th century* (Cambridge: Cambridge University Press).

Fontaine, L. (1996), *History of pedlars in Europe*, translated by Vicki Whittaker (Cambridge: Polity Press).

Fontaine, L. (2008), *The moral economy. Poverty, credit and trust in early modern Europe*, translated by Punam Puri (New York: Cambridge University Press).

Fontaine, L. (2014), *Le marché: Histoire et usage d'une conquête sociale* (Paris: Gallimard), pp. 70–101.

Furetière, A. (1690), *Dictionnaire universel* (The Hague, The Netherlands).

Gothein, E. (1892), *Wirtschaftsgeschichte des Schwarzwaldes und der angrenzenden Landschaften* (Strasbourg: J. K. Trübner).

Grosjean, A. and Murdoch, S. (2005), *Scottish communities abroad in early modern Europe* (Leiden/Boston, MA: Brill).

Guichonnet, P. (1948), "L'émigration alpine vers les pays de langue allemande', *Revue de Géographie alpine*, pp. 553–576.

Hemmert, D. (1979), 'Quelques aspects de l'immigration dans le comté de Bitche, fin du XVIIe siècle, début XVIIIe', in *Actes du 103e Congrès national des Sociétés Savantes, Nancy-Metz, 1978, Histoire moderne et contemporaine* (Paris: Imprimerie Nationale) 41–56.

Laterza, P.B. and Manfredi, R. (eds.) (1972). *Stampe per via. L'incisione dei secoli XVII–XIX nel commercio ambulante dei tesini* (Calliano: Arti grafiche).

Lefrançois de Lalande, J.J. (1769), *Voyage d'un François en Italie dans les années 1765 et 1766* (Paris: A Venise (et se trouve à Paris) chez Desaint, libraire, rue du foin, MDCCLXIX).

Martin, K. (1942), 'Die Savoyische Einwanderung in das alemannische Süddeutschland', *Deutsches Archiv für Landes und Volksforschung*, VI (4), pp. 647–658.

McKendrick, N., Brewer, J. and Plumb, J.H. (1982), *The birth of consumer society: The commercialization of eighteenth century England* (Bloomington, IN: Indiana University Press).

Mercier, L.S. (1994a), *Le Nouveau Paris* (Paris: Mercure de France), original edition from 1798.

Mercier, L.S. (1994b), *Tableau de Paris*, edited by J.-C. Bonnet, 2 volumes (Paris: Mercure de France), first edition published between 1781 and 1789.

Merry Wiesner, W. (1981), 'Paltry peddlers or essential merchants? Women in the distributive trades in early modern Nuremberg', *The Sixteenth Century Journal*, XII (2), pp. 3–13.

Merzario, R. (1984), 'Una fabbrica di uomini: L'emigrazione dalla montagna comasca (1650–1750)', *Mélanges de l'École française de Rome*, 96 (1), pp. 153–175.

Montenach, A. (2013), 'Legal trade and black markets: Food trades in lyon in the late seventeenth and early eighteenth centuries', in D. Simonton and A. Montenach (eds.) *Female agency in the urban economy: Gender in European towns, 1640–1830* (New York/London: Routledge) 17–34.

Niccoli, O. (1987), *Profeti e popolo nell'Italia del Renascimento* (Rome-Bari: Laterza).

Pecori, G. (ed.) (1980). *Gridi nelle strade fiorentine* (Florence: Liberia Editrice).

Petrowiste, J. (2004), *À la foire d'empoigne: Foires et marchés en Aunis et Saintonge au Moyen Âge (vers 1000–vers 1550)* (Québec/Toulouse: Université francophone d'été Saintonge/CNRS-Méridiennes).

Poitrineau, A. (1985), *Les "Espagnols" de l'Auvergne et du Limousin du XVIIe au XIXe siècle* (Aurillac: Mazel-Malroux).

Reynald, A. (2002), *Le grand marché: L'approvisionnement alimentaire de Paris sous l'Ancien Régime* (Paris: Fayard).

Riis, T. (1988), *Should Auld Acquaintance Be Forgot . . . Scottish-Danish Relations. c. 1450–1707*, 2 Vol. (Odense: Odense University Press).

Roche, D. (1989), *La culture des apparences: Une histoire du vêtement XVIe–XVIIIe siècles* (Paris: Fayard).

Sarti, R. (1985), *Long live the strong. A history of rural society in the Apennine mountains* (Amherst, MA: University of Massachusetts Press).

Sauvy, A. (1967), 'Noël Gille dit La Pistole, marchand forain libraire roulant par la France', *Bulletin des bibliothèques de France*, mai, pp. 177–190.

Smout, T.C. (1968), 'The Glasgow merchant community in the seventeenth century', *Scottish Historical Review*, 47, pp. 53–71.

Spufford, M. (1981), *Small books and pleasant histories: Popular fiction and its readership in seventeenth-century England* (London: Methuen).

Spufford, M. (1984), *The great reclothing of rural England, Petty chapmen and their wares in the seventeenth century* (London: Hambledon Press).

Trifoni, M. (1989), 'I "santari": Venditori itineranti di immagini devozionali a Campli e nel teramano', *La Ricerca Folklorica*, 19, pp. 113–120.

Van den Heuvel, D. (2007), *Women & entrepreneurship. Female traders in the Northern Netherlands, c. 1580–1815* (Amsterdam: Aksant Academic Publishers).

Van den Heuvel, D. (2015), 'Policing peddlers: The prosecution of illegal street trade in eighteenth-century dutch towns', *The Historical Journal*, 58 (2), pp. 367–392.

Van den Heuvel, D. (2016), 'Food, markets and people: Selling perishables in urban markets in pre-industrial Holland and England', in M. Calaresu and D. van den Heuvel (eds.) *Food Hawkers: Selling in the streets from antiquity to the present* (Oxon: Routledge) 84–106.

Weatherill, L. (1986), 'The business of middleman in the English pottery trade before 1780', *Business History*, 28, pp. 51–76.

Westerfield, R.B. (1915), *Middlemen in English business, particularly between 1660 and 1760 reprint* (New York: David & Charles).

PART IV

Geographical variations

21
RETAIL HISTORY
United States and Canada

Bettina Liverant

Today it is the ability to sell things and not the ability to make them that drives consumer goods manufacturing and propels the economy forward. In both the United States and in Canada, the barriers of time and space that used to constrain selling and buying have disappeared. Driven by the search for profit, entrepreneurs evolve their business practices and competitive strategies. New retail formats emerge and older ones adapt. Before the 1860s, most retailers served local and regional markets. Selection was limited, transportation expensive, and the availability of goods determined in large part by the dealings of a wholesalers and middlemen. Now we occupy "landscapes of consumption" that provide for and encourage spending. Having internalised our role as consumers, we are comfortable spending our leisure time in shopping environments even when we are not shopping (Ritzer, 2010). Airport terminals have been reconfigured as shopping centres; the store is a critical component of many museum operations; fitness clubs sell "wellness" including classes, equipment and clothing. Non-store retailing has expanded dramatically, changing *what* as well as *how* we buy.

The processes of making, distributing and selling have been systematised and standardised. The American discount model has driven down wages and levels of service as well as prices and profit margins. Competition for consumer dollars has also generated counter movements to rationalisation in the form of "enchanted" settings, including stores with elaborate themes, personalised shopping experiences, and warehouses piled to the ceilings with goods, a fantasy of abundance presented as great bargains (Ritzer, 2010). The largest chains account for the most sales by retail dollar but small store formats have proven highly resilient and account for more transactions. Approximately 95% of American retail businesses employ fewer than fifty people and operate only a single location (National Retail Federation, 2017). Even as large-format retailers restructure and close, small store ownership, whether as an independent owner or as a franchisee, remains a dream for many, driven by the desire for independence as well as income.

For all its success, retail is experiencing a "malaise". Although the retail sector is one of the largest private employers in both countries, labour productivity lags behind other sectors. Median real hourly wages of retail workers have declined since 2007. Retailers require fewer workers even as more things are being sold: indeed the gap between retail sales and retail jobs is growing. There is an over abundance of physical stores, a problem exacerbated by the rapid growth of e-commerce. Canada is a smaller, less wealthy market that generally lags behind developments in American retailing by a decade or more. Disparities in the penetration of innovations and consumer preferences between two countries seen as substantially the same highlight the importance of demographics, location, government policy, culture and even weather in shaping the particulars of retail at any time. All this is to say that retailing as it has developed in the United States and Canada is complex, heterogeneous and now ever present.

Colonial narratives

In recent decades, widely held images of self-sufficient pre-industrial households living in relative isolation have been contradicted by new evidence found in store account books, tax rolls, court cases, probate inventories and diaries. Colonial consumers and early retailers lived on the margins of Atlantic capitalism but they participated in extended, often global, networks of exchange. Indeed rural retailers are increasingly being cast as 'economic and cultural innovators, the central agents of social transformation in their communities' (Nobles, 1990, p. 113; Perkins, 1991; Bushman, 1994; McCalla, 2015).

There was broad similarity in retailing across British North America and the American colonies before urbanisation and industrialisation. Retailing in the pre-industrial period did not follow the European model. There was no transfer of medieval markets, market squares, or craft guilds from the Old World to the New. The term "store" as a place of commerce where supplies and goods were kept and sold was unfamiliar to the British, who used the term "shop" as the place where goods were made and displayed for sale. The difference in terminology is significant: most storekeepers were involved in both retailing and collecting goods for export. Dual purpose stores appeared where the staple trade was strongest: collecting cotton in the tidewater south, furs in the north, and wheat in the middle colonies in the early decades of the eighteenth century. In more settled regions, or where the staple trade was less important, back country general stores collected surplus agricultural produce and home production, sometimes for the personal use of the shopkeeper, but often to be resold locally or exported beyond the community, placing shopkeepers in the role of marketing agents. Purpose-built retail stores appeared in the more settled regions of New England as early as 1750, but in less developed or back country regions it was common for stores to be owned and operated by the "great man" or "principal man" in the community alongside other commercial enterprises. Running a general store adjacent to, for example, a mill or forge, on a plantation (in the southern colonies), or alongside a woollen mill (in Upper Canada), attracted customers and generated income and employment for the community. The chain store format was also present in the colonial period. Some chains were family based, but some partnerships were much larger, including those opened by Scottish and English merchants in Virginia and Maryland and fur trading posts-cum-general-stores operated by the Hudson's Bay Company. By the late eighteenth century, then, retailing already involved salaried employees and managers keeping accounts for distant head offices (Shammas, 1990; Perkins, 1991; Benson and Shaw, 1992; Carlos and Lewis, 2002; O'Leary et al., 2002; McCalla, 2015).

Careful studies of day books kept by early country stores challenge assumptions about book credit, payment in kind and pricing. Once seen as evidence of underdevelopment, book credit is now regarded as evidence of economic diversification, allowing for complex transactions when currency and banks were in short supply. Credit was extended to individuals and also to commercial operators and innkeepers. Credit might be repaid in cash or by a wide range of goods in kind, including labour, wood and home production undertaken specifically for commercial exchange. Book credits facilitated exchanges between third parties, as when person A owed a debt to person B, but instead paid the storekeeper who recorded a credit for B. Credit was especially important in Canada, where winter slowdowns routinely meant that 10 to 20% of the workforce was unemployed for six months at a time, complicated even more by fluctuations in the resource-based economy (Mancke, 1995; McCalla, 2015).

Although the volume of business during the settlement period certainly fluctuated, the emphasis on producing goods for export and the relatively high ratio of men to women inhibited household self-sufficiency. As a result, regardless of class or location, early North Americans were shoppers. Geographic concentration varied considerably: a large country store in the mid nineteenth century might see 200 or 300 people a year, while a small store might have a customer base of fifty. With a limited customer base and slow stock turn, there was little incentive to innovate bookkeeping methods. Account books recorded "who owed how much to whom" but were not used to calculate profit or loss (Craig, 2009, p. 125). Debts could be carried for years with little payment. Although prices were not marked, recent studies of account books show that prices for regularly purchased basic commodities such as sugar, tea, coffee, salt, flour and after mid-century a growing number of brand name goods, were consistent from customer to customer well before the era of the mass merchandizer: as early as the 1830s in at least some country stores in the American Midwest and rural Upper Canada. Bargaining was common for goods such as imported cloth, dishes and hardware where variations in quality allowed for negotiation, but contrary to long held assumptions, not all prices were determined by haggling (Norris, 1962; Shammas, 1990; Deutsch, 2010; McCalla, 1997, 2015a, 2015b).

Colonial consumers, including First Nations consumers, were discerning and selective, with choices in what to buy and where to buy it. Most storekeepers faced competition, whether from nearby stores, peddlers or retailers in larger towns where farmers took produce to market. Carole Shammas calculates that although most stores were very small, there were more retail outlets per capita in mid-eighteenth century New England than existed in the United States in 1929, in 1967 or in 1985 (Shammas, 1990, pp. 275–276). Even in the north, Hudson's Bay Company managers complained of competition, particularly from independent merchants who left the Company to set up their own stores. The competitive advantage of one store over another lay in the willingness to extend credit, the acceptance of goods in lieu of cash, and in the selection of goods for sale, but not generally in price (Shammas, 1990; Martin, 2000; O'Leary et al., 2002; McCalla, 2015a). Stores served a broad range of customers. Women are present in account ledgers, charging goods as wives and daughters to the accounts of husbands and fathers, and also as economically independent widows and single women. In the American South and Midwest, African American slaves purchased goods on book credit in back country stores. First Nations consumers were listed by name in the ledgers of the Hudson's Bay Company. This is not to overstate equalising nature of shopping. Country stores were primarily places of male sociability; and, as historian Ann Smart Martin observes, participation in retail commerce did not change status in other arenas of life. However, commercial transactions bound people together. When goods were behind the counter and a high percentage of sales depended on credit, each purchase represented a personal exchange between storekeeper and customer (Perkins, 1991; Monod, 1996; Martin, 2000, 2008; Carlos and Lewis, 2001, 2002; McCalla, 2015a).

In hundreds of villages and small towns and in sparsely populated regions on the frontiers of settlement, itinerant peddlers supplemented the country general store. Historians have crafted different, although certainly complimentary, narratives of peddling north and south of the border. Surveying the Canadian scene, John Benson stresses the importance of peddling (and also of small shops) as a way of life as well as a source of goods. Street-selling persisted, even in the face of legal restrictions, well into the twentieth century in urban Canada, filling gaps in the retail system and in the job market, providing income to those on the margins of society. Most often, Benson asserts, the 'decision to sell was born of poverty and misfortune . . . [peddling] was the last resort of the unskilled, the unemployed, the very young, and the very old, the sick, the injured and the victimized' (Benson, 1985, p. 80). It was also often the first resort of European and Asian immigrants with few alternatives. Peddling required little start up capital and held significant competitive advantages: selling at the door, charging low prices (often for lower quality goods), dealing in small volumes (desirable in cities where cash and ice box space were often limited) and operating when stores were absent or closed.

American historians have been more interested in peddlers as agents of commercial development and social change. David Jaffe and Jackson Lears discuss peddlers as the advance guard of consumer society, pointing to thousands of young men peddling clocks and tinware across the United States in the decades following the War of 1812. By mid-century, many peddlers were travelling regular circuits as salaried employees and commissioned agents, selling for wholesalers and manufacturers, bringing news, new kinds of goods and cosmopolitan market culture to rural homesteads, building up demand where none existed, and promoting the message of social transformation through bought goods. A successful wagon peddler might begin the autumn season with goods worth $300 to $2,000 (about the same value of inventory as a small country store) and turn a 100% gross profit over two or three months before returning home to settle debts and arrange for new supplies. As population densities rose and rural transportation networks improved, peddling developed into a primarily urban occupation, involving pushcarts and semi-permanent stalls rather than packs and wagons.

Tensions between fixed stores and peddlers were endemic. Storekeepers regularly demanded the imposition of regulations and licensing fees, objecting that peddlers, who did not have to pay taxes or store upkeep, were unfair competitors. High fees simply encouraged evasion. Peddling, unlike waged labour, promised adventure, opportunity and the possibility of social mobility. Many peddlers did achieve modest economic success. A few rose to open department stores or scrapyards; a very few became retail manufacturers or financiers (Jaffee, 1991; Lears, 1994; Blackford, 2003; Howard, 2008; Diner, 2015).

Pre-industrial urban

Greater population densities allowed for specialisation but store formats prior to the 1830s were much the same in town and countryside, shaped by similar needs to store, protect and display inventory, to serve customers, and keep records. In towns with populations of 1,000 or more, small specialty shops clustered along Main Street. Prices were not posted; however, notices in colonial newspapers might list prices when announcing the arrival of new shipments. Although small urban retailers were less likely to take goods as payment in kind, they still made anywhere from one-half to two-thirds of their sales on credit and continued to grant credit long after chain stores had stopped doing so. Goods that did not sell became dated and dusty. Clearance sales were not unheard of but were not common. Much like peddling, storekeeping was an occupation with relatively low barriers to entry. Inventory holding costs could be significant but storekeepers could live where they worked, operating from an open window or a front parlour. Women were active in colonial retailing. Indeed small business historian Mancel Blackford proposes that gender imbalances during the settlement period created opportunities for women. Blackford estimates that perhaps half of all American retailers in this early period were female, although restrictions on property ownership often meant they operated shops as partners of husbands or as widows. Steady economic expansion after 1830 widened possibilities for women as independent storekeepers but by the late nineteenth century changing social expectations, lack of capital and the burden of low credit ratings began to constrain opportunities in both American and in Canada. Growth in female entrepreneurship was increasingly limited to small shops, often in sectors like dressmaking, stationary, millinery and fancy goods already under threat

Figure 21.1 Peddler E.H. Farrell with his cart. Inscribed on back: "This Load, when ready for Fall Business, weighs about 6000 pounds/Makes four trips a year./I have driven this for 20 years/over same ground, striking 15 villages./E. H. Farrell". c.1910.

Source: The Connecticut Historical Society, 2000.198.34.

from mass merchandisers. As the size of business enterprises continued to grow, businesswomen were often shouldered aside by better financed and better connected male entrepreneurs. By the later decades of the 19th century, women entering the retail labour force found jobs as salesgirls and department supervisors, but seldom in the ranks of management or owners (Monod, 1996; Blackford, 2003; Baskerville, 2008; Deutsch, 2010; Hodge, 2014).

Mass retailing: more customers, more goods

Retailing changed dramatically between 1860 and 1920 as new formats emerged in response to changes in production, distribution and demand. Industrialisation in manufacturing and food processing increased the amount of product to be sold and made new kinds of goods available in new ways. Immigration accelerated in both America and Canada. In the United States, only fourteen cities had more than 100,000 residents in 1860; by 1920 the number had risen to sixty-eight. Prior to 1871, Montreal was the only Canadian city with a population greater than 100,000 and 84% of the population lived in rural areas. By 1921 the population was evenly divided between urban and rural dwellers, six cities now had populations in excess of 100,000. Although purchasing power in both countries was concentrated in rapidly growing urban centres, rural dwellers, no less than urban dwellers, were interested in new consumption opportunities. Business historian Alfred Chandler emphasises a third factor: modernisation of transportation and communication systems made it possible to co-ordinate flows of materials and goods at speeds and volumes required to achieve economies of scale (Chandler, 1984).

As productivity rose, manufacturers confronted the prospect of over-production. Companies such as Procter & Gamble, Libbey Foods, General Mills, Johnson & Johnson, Singer Sewing Machines and Coca-Cola devised mass market strategies to sell higher volumes at lower markups by hiring travelling salesmen, publishing catalogues, and developing new styles of packaging and recognisably modern advertising campaigns. The mechanics of bottling, canning, packaging and labelling improved and became less costly. Literacy rates rose. Legislation passed in 1905 protected trademarks, making them a clearer indication of quality. The transition to prepackaged branded products was critical in "unleashing retailing's potential", to use business historian Barry Boothman's phrase, lowering costs in transportation, storage, labour and display, and opening the way to self-service (Strasser, 1989; Livingston, 1994; Carden, 2013; Isenstadt, 2014; Boothman, 2016, p. 135).

Some new products replaced goods that had been locally produced or homemade; others were technologically complex and required explanation. The Singer Sewing Machine Company, for example, pioneered the franchised selling agency and the consumer instalment plan to finance sales of its new sewing machines, and devised new types of accounting and statistical controls to maximise the benefits of vertical integration. By 1905, Singer employed twice as many workers in the marketing of its machines as it did producing them (Chandler, 1962; Bucheli et al., 2010).

Individual merchants also recognised that the economics of retailing were changing. There were more goods to sell and more customers to buy them. In the 1860s and 1870s, dry goods and general store merchants in the largest cities began adding new departments, services, and flare to the selling process. In the 1870s and 1880s, other entrepreneurs recognised that improvements in railroads made it possible to reach out to customers in farms and small towns through catalogue sales. Closer to the turn of the century, other visionary businessmen recognised the advantages that could be gained by aggregating the operations of many small stores and began to aggressively add new units in locations with high foot traffic. These new formats emerged separately and exploited the opportunities of growing markets differently, but their innovators all understood that turnover and cash flow rather than high profit margins were the key success. Each time a good was sold, the capital invested was freed up and could be reused to buy more goods, which could in turn be sold and replaced (Strasser, 1989; Jacobs, 2005).

Often dubbed "machines for selling", department stores, chain stores and mail order houses transformed the economic exchanges that lay at the heart of retailing. With large staffs, growing inventories and more customers, transactions were necessarily depersonalised. Customers could of course enter country general stores and urban specialty stores freely, but there was an implied obligation to buy. Exchanges in mass retailing were more anonymous, changing the selling process. Set, marked prices simplified transactions and lowered costs. Staff was specialised and professionalised if needed, but generally low-waged and unskilled. The discretion to extend credit to unfamiliar customers shifted to new credit departments or was stopped altogether in favour of cash-only sales. Liberal exchange policies helped build consumer confidence in unknown and, in the case of mail order, unseen sellers.

All mass merchandisers adopted some form of departmentalised organisation. With better organisation and fixed prices, retailers had a better sense of which goods generated the highest profits. Management of labour, inventory and operations were centralised and became more sophisticated. Efficiency became the watchword of business enterprise. Advances in transportation and communication improved the flow of goods, reducing delivery times and shipping costs. The ability to buy goods from manufacturers and wholesalers in large quantities enabled retailers to negotiate better prices and sell branded goods more cheaply. Mass manufacturers such as Singer integrated forwards, becoming involved in marketing to increase the volume and predictability of sales. Mass merchandisers integrated selectively backwards into manufacturing, creating private-label brands to insure supply and control the costs of key products. By 1906, Sears owned wholly or in part sixteen manufacturing plants (Chandler, 1962). Modernised accounting systems tightened control over costs.

Price consciousness was built into mass merchandising (Jacobs, 2005). Whether displayed on store tags or listed in catalogues, all goods had clearly marked prices. Although department stores positioned themselves as upscale environments, they aggressively advertised loss leaders, clearance sales and promotions. Macy's was famous for its price wars. Filene's was known for its bargain basement. The Montgomery Ward mail order company maintained that its low prices were possible because the company paid no rent, employed no "high-priced salesmen", sold nothing on time and eschewed all fakery in favour of simple business efficiency (Blanke, 2000, p. 195). Chains promised and delivered no frills shopping and lower prices. Mass retailers educated consumers about economies of scale. Department store founder Edward Filene explained that he could offer fur coats at low prices 'Because we are unusually large dealers . . . we sell on the basis of a small profit on a large volume – rather than a large profit on a small volume' (Jacobs, 2005, p. 22). The Maze, a San Francisco department store, put it even more directly in a 1891 advertisement,

> We are with the people first, last and all the time . . . the more we can sell the larger we can buy, and the larger we can buy the cheaper we can sell, and the cheaper we can sell the more you can save.
>
> *(Whitaker, 2015)*

The additional characteristic that mass merchandisers shared was physical size. In 1902, Marshall Field's (Chicago) and Macy's (New York) opened new flagship stores, each with over one million square feet of floor space (more than five times the size of a 2016 Walmart Supercenter). In 1904, Marshall Field's had a workforce of between 8,000 and 10,000 employees, and served 250,000 customers in a day. Filene's new 1912 store, designed by a reknown architect, featured thirteen elevators carrying an average of 10,000 shoppers from floor to floor every hour. America's largest mail order companies operated vast plants in the middle of the continent. Sears Roebuck's new 1906 plant – the largest business building in America at the time – used assembly line methods to process 100,000 orders each day – more than an early American merchant would have filled in a lifetime. By the 1920s, A&P, the largest of the grocery chains, had almost sixteen thousand stores reaching from coast to coast. Operating organisations of great size and complexity, mass merchandisers mobilised capital at a scale not previously associated with retailing. Over time, as they organised the distribution and sale of mass production to consumers, retailers integrated rural and urban consumers into a vast and largely homogeneous market, differentiated more by the purchase of good/better/best than by differences of kind (Boorstin, 1973; Chandler, 1984; Strasser, 1989, 2014; Tedlow, 1990; Koehn, 2001, Boothman, 2016).

Mass retailing also changed the culture of shopping. Emphasising the shopping experience, department stores strengthened the association between shopping and leisure. Customer service was handled strategically, with amenities added to give more reasons to visit, linger and socialise. Department stores promoted themselves, and rapidly gained acceptance, as a new kind of community institution with social and cultural significance beyond mere commerce. Their restaurants became meeting places; their exhibition spaces held educational events. Purchasing modern clothing in a department store was a rite of citizenship for many immigrants (Leach, 1993).

Ordering goods by mail from limited range catalogues circulated by specialty stores dated back to colonial times; but in the 1860s, Aaron Montgomery Ward began to aggressively promote the general merchandise catalogue as a saver of time and money to rural and small town "consumers in waiting". Like department stores, mail order companies grew by adding new lines of goods. By 1904 Montgomery Ward was distributing three million catalogues, over 1,000 pages nationwide, each weighing 4 pounds (1.8 kg), selling everything that could be packaged and delivered. The arrival of the latest catalogue, soon nicknamed the "the wish book", became a highlight of rural life.

The third "machine for selling" was the chain store. Renting small spaces in high-traffic locations, chain stores focused on a limited range of fast-selling goods, undercutting their competition on price and convenience. In the chain store business, price policies and merchandise policies were one and the same. Chains did not stock much in the way of apparel; instead they sold small necessities like canned foods, boxed cereals, cigarettes, gum, toothpaste, pots and pans, and other household goods with brand name labels that urban customers valued. The key to low prices was standardisation: in goods, advertising, store layout and work routines. These in turn opened the way to the most significant innovation of the chain store format: self-service. The greatest benefits of the self-service format turned out to be cultural: given freedom to browse without pressure to buy or wait for service, shoppers bought more. Moreover, customer satisfaction increased: no one felt that some customers received better service than others; and the tensions associated with personal scrutiny, class, race and ethnicity between storekeepers and customers were reduced (Chandler, 1977; Deutsch, 2010; Hamilton et al., 2011; Levinson, 2011; Carden, 2013; Hamilton and Phillips, 2014).

Despite early similarities, Canada industrialised later than the United States; markets remained smaller and more dispersed. Smaller retail formats had longer staying power. Department stores diversified earlier, reaching out to working-class as well as middle-class customers, circulating catalogues to urban as well as rural households, and opening branch stores decades before most of their American counterparts. Eaton's opened its first branch in 1905. By 1930, it was operating a network of forty-seven retail stores and a nationwide catalogue sales system with over 100 order offices. Eaton's was Canada's third largest employer and one of the largest retailers in world (measured by revenues). Marshall Field's did not open its first branch store until 1928; Wanamaker's and Bloomingdale's did not open branches until the late 1940s (Wright, 1992; Monod, 1996; Belisle, 2011; Boothman, 2016).

Consolidation, new prototypes and resistance

As the rate of conventional growth slowed in the 1920s and 1930s, retailers responded in a number of ways. The drive to increase efficiencies of scale fuelled a wave of mergers and acquisitions financed by the selling of common shares. Large grocery chains began consolidating stores, combining five or six small stores to create a single, more sophisticated supermarket. As store counts shrank, sales figures actually rose. Recognising the growing impact of urbanisation and automobile ownership, Sears Roebuck and Montgomery Ward opened their first fixed stores in the mid-twenties, following their customers to new suburban locations with low land costs, to become the first nation-wide department store chains in America (Chandler, 1962, pp. 233–234).

New pro-types appeared, laying the groundwork for postwar innovations. In California, filling stations added grocery sales to create super service stations. In the American Midwest, a few property developers began building small "community" shopping centres adjacent to upscale residential developments, with storefronts set back from the street to allow for automobile parking. On both coasts (and about a decade later in Canada), independent local retailers began opening large stores outside of the central business district, adapting self-service "no-frills" shopping to non-fashion staples and household goods. Unencumbered by management systems and willing to ignore government regulations and middle – class shopping conventions, discount warehouses extended opening hours and attracted customers with ample free parking, fanfare and festivities, selling brand merchandise below the accepted retail price. When investment rose again after World War II, chains of grocers and real estate developers would seize on these different precedents (Longstreth, 1997).

The rise of mass retailing generated strong opposition from independent merchants who began forming associations in the 1880s, calling for limits on store hours and fair trade acts to prevent large retailers from using advantages of size to sell goods at reduced prices. Loss leaders, for example, were condemned as morally objectionable. Independent retailers did, on an individual basis, go bankrupt; however, there was no transition from small to large formats. In the face of competition from mass retailers, independents adapted, often borrowing techniques developed by mass merchandisers to better organise, display and manage their businesses. Some independents formed voluntary chains, buying collectively and operating under common policies and brand names. Neighbourhood grocery-cum general stores also flourished, opening in

Figure 21.2 Interior view of Jenkins' Groceteria, Calgary, Canada, c.1918. Henry Jenkins brought self-service to Canada, in part as a solution to labour shortages created by World War I. By 1929, Jenkins Groceteria Ltd was a vertically integrated corporation operating a chain of thirty stores across southern Alberta known for self-service and low prices.

Source: Glenbow Archives, NA 4501-4.

working class and ethnic communities well into the interwar years in America and even later in Canada, where patterns of distinct ethnic neighbourhoods continued longer.

During the depression, some shoppers shifted to less expensive goods, buying in small lots, and on credit – practices that helped sustain neighbourhood retailers through difficult times. Others, dependent upon relief vouchers, favoured the anonymity of chain stores. The growing burden of government regulation during depression and wartime also favoured larger retailers. This was particularly the case in America, where retailers faced new demands for record keeping, collecting sales taxes, and compliance with pricing codes mandated by New Deal legislation. Larger stores and chains were also better able to manage wartime labour shortages. The difference between small stores and large stores, many historians have argued, was not adherence to tradition but access to capital. Ultimately chains had more staying power, greater managerial expertise and the funds to implement innovations on an ongoing basis (Walden, 1989; Cohen, 1990; Benson and Shaw, 1992; Monod, 1996; Haupt, 2012; Deutsch, 2010; Krulikowski, 2014; Scott and Walker, 2011, 2014; Boothman, 2016).

After the war, conversion back to a peacetime economy occurred very rapidly in the United States, with the government supporting mass consumption through a broad range of policy initiatives, including G.I. benefits, mortgage insurance and highway construction. The Canadian government implemented similar policies but at reduced levels, instead prioritising growth through exports and capital investment. Both countries experienced postwar prosperity but American growth was more rapid and widespread, boosted by increases in the supply of goods as well as rising incomes. New household formation and postwar expectations, fuelled by television, generated widespread demand for consumer goods in both countries. Car ownership exploded: by 1960, 79.5% of American and 66% of Canadian households owned at least one motor vehicle, 20% of American and 10% of Canadian households had two or more (Owram, 1996, p. 70; Oak Ridge National Laboratory, 2016, Table 8.5).

As late as 1950, most shopping precincts were still pedestrian oriented, with parking separated from the store. Within twenty-five years, the way most Americans and Canadians shopped was largely transformed. Retailing decentralised as investment flowed towards supermarket grocery stores, shopping centres, "big-box" or warehouse styled stores and small franchises – all part of the distinctive new geography of postwar suburbia (Jackson, 1996; Longstreth, 1999).

Chain and independent grocery stores rapidly converged on a common "supermarket" format, growing in size to accommodate a full range of packaged products (including dry goods, meat, fish, and greengroceries traditionally sold in bulk in different stores), brightly lit, with automatic doors and wider aisles to accommodate shopping carts, rows of open shelving to display packaged, prepared and canned goods, and new cases for refrigerated and frozen foods. A successful supermarket, historian Sandy Isenstadt observes, was the outcome of "packaging, pricing, and parking" (Isenstadt, 2014, p. 25). The pursuit of low overhead and high volume sales drew retailers to suburban locations where land costs were lower and ample parking ensured a large customer base. Food was produced, packaged and marketed to be sold in supermarket settings, transforming what people ate as well as how they shopped. New stores opened with tremendous fanfare. The 1952 opening of a Dominion Store in a mid-sized Canadian city featured a string quartet, guests arriving by limousine and an orchid for each female customer. Between 1948 and 1958, the number of American supermarkets doubled; overall grocery store sales rose more rapidly than either population growth or per capita income (Hamilton and Phillips, 2014). Growth was more moderate in Canada, where the level of expenditure rose in tandem with gains in personal income (Boothman, 2011, p. 12; Marling, 1994; Shapiro, 2005; Deutsch, 2010).

In the late 1950s, Cold War rhetoric positioned the grocery supermarket as symbolic of the American way of life and the superiority of American capitalism. The 'freedom to touch, see, smell and feel merchandise' was celebrated as 'a form of economic democracy' that would increase sales and in turn reduce costs and prices, expanding markets, creating jobs and improving nutrition (Hamilton 2014). Cold war rhetoric was less pronounced in Canada, but newspapers and magazines similarly celebrated modern abundance and conveniences.

The rise of the American shopping centre as a new retail format depended upon the needs of suburban households, widespread automobile ownership and the decisions of property developers willing to make large investments with extended payback periods. The non-selling spaces were attractively designed to entice shoppers. Developers preferred to fill the retail spaces with well-known specialty chains rather than local independents, reasoning that chains provided greater financial stability, attracted tenants for multiple locations and helped draw customers.

Canada has had a somewhat different shopping centre experience. With stronger downtowns, less freeway development, less racial tension, somewhat better public transit and more restrictive land use policies, a greater proportion of shopping centres were built in the city core (10% in Canada versus 1% in the United States). Canadian developers also benefited from differences in land use regulations and business practices that limited direct competition and overbuilding. Because less than a dozen development corporations control the majority of Canada's regional malls, centres are carefully spaced in relation to one another in a pattern of "mutual avoidance". Moreover, when compared with the United States, Canada has 25 to 35% fewer malls, generating significantly higher sales per square foot of mall space (Simmons, 1991).

In terms of mall design, Canada was a leader in the development of urban indoor shopping networks that connect retail centres, office towers, apartment buildings, hotels and entertainment venues. These networks grew incrementally: underground in Montreal (beginning in 1962) and above ground in Calgary (with construction beginning in the 1970s). The world's first freestanding megamall, West Edmonton Mall (WEM), was also Canadian. Built in stages beginning in 1985, WEM was designed with a then unique combination of large-scale recreation, shopping, hotel and convention facilities, including indoor amusement and water parks, an NHL-size ice skating rink, a small lake with mini-submarine rides, a scale replica of Columbus's Santa Maria and a marine show with dolphins and sea-lions. WEM was developed for consumer tourism as well as to compete in the local retail market. All three retail formats emerged as different responses to the challenges of a northern climate.

Traditional shopping malls faced increased competition beginning in the 1970s from a popular new retail format: the big-box store. The formula was straightforward: a large, freestanding single-story building surrounded by ample parking, selling a wide range of product loosely arranged in departments. Customers enter stores that are little more than "big-boxes", collected goods in shopping carts with minimal assistance, and took them to a single point of sale. Specialised "big-box" chains soon followed: Toys 'R' Us, Home Depot, Chapters, Circuit City and others. Although not every big-box retailer positioned itself as a discounter, selling a broad range of goods in a focused category in a warehouse-like setting created efficiencies of scale and lower prices that turned them into "category killers" in the 1980s and 1990s, eliminating most of their traditional small store competitors. The big-box shopping experience was and remains largely private, focused on the "anonymous experience of commodity acquisition" based primarily on price. The pursuit of low prices eroded the long-term relationships that once characterised retail exchanges, replaced by minimum-wage "greeters" and extended warranties (also a retail profit centre), commodifying the bonds of trust that once linked customer and storekeeper (Isenstadt, 2014, pp. 26–27).

The discount chain Walmart became the sector leader though its relentless commitment to a regime of everyday low prices (EDLP) rather than sale prices, achieved by eliminating, reducing and re-organising every stage of the retail process. Since the opening of its first store, Walmart

Figure 21.3 West Edmonton Mall. The world's first freestanding megamall, combining large-scale recreation, shopping, hotel and convention facilities, opened in Edmonton, Canada in 1985. It is still North America's largest shopping mall.

Source: Daniel Case, GNU.

has made low prices the centre of its brand identity, aggressively cutting budgets for interior decor, shelving, store exteriors, parking lots, advertising, maintenance and above all payroll. As these stringencies were combined with innovations in logistics, Walmart gained substantial price advantages over its competitors. Streamlining the checkout process with scanners and bar code technology made it possible to operate much larger stores; more importantly, the point-of-sale data was used to analyse purchasing patterns and refine product ordering. By the 1980s, sophisticated computer networks, a private communications satellite and the world's largest retail data warehouse connected all operating units and suppliers directly to Walmart's corporate headquarters. Warehouses were replaced by distribution centres and innovations in cross-docking, reducing the time goods spent on the road. In the late 1980s, Walmart began to side-step traditional wholesalers, building direct relationships with vendors and sourcing goods wherever cheap labour and lax government regulation lowered costs, most notably China. Walmart benefitted from and accelerated the shift to container shipping, disempowering long-shore unions by moving goods directly through to its distribution centres. Walmart became America's largest retailer in 1990. By 2002, Walmart was America's largest corporation by sales revenue and America's largest private sector employer, an indication of changes in the composition of the American economy as well as the company's strategic prowess. Global chains like Walmart no longer "push" what manufacturers make but determine what they make. Jay Fitzsimons, Walmart senior vice president and treasurer, explained, "The misconception is that we are in the retail business, but in reality we are in the distribution business" (Khade and Lovass, 2009, p. 1; Bonacich, 2006; Lichtenstein, 2006, Hamilton et al., 2011; Carden, 2013).

Walmart and similar big-box chains were at the forefront changes in quantity, pricing and speed, but they were not alone. In the 1970s, retail warehouse clubs appeared, selling a limited array of products at highly discounted prices in wholesale quantities to customers willing to pay an annual fee to simply walk through the door. Costco, now the dominant warehouse club, never advertises, seldom carries multiple brands of the same product and offers little or no customer service. Off-price retailers like T.J. Maxx (in America), Winners (in Canada) and department store discount branches like Nordstrom Rack rapidly gained market share after the 1980s recession. By obtaining product from cancelled orders, overruns, retailer returns, end-of-season closeouts and their own private labels, off-price retailers move a high volume of inventory quickly in bargain basement settings, cultivating a treasure hunt experience by offering a changing assortment of recognised brand name, fashion-oriented apparel and household goods at below regular store prices. The success of these formats, now seen by many as convenient alternatives to traditional department stores, suggests the normalisation of discounting – and the commitment to branded goods – by consumers struggling to meet expectations with stagnant wages through periodic recessions (Kaikati, 1985).

Big-box and warehouse club stores began as stand alones but much of their growth since 2000 has been in vast "power centers" located adjacent to major highway interchanges on the urban peripheries of large cities. This is a new retail format, accessed almost entirely by private transportation, that groups together half a dozen or more freestanding super-sized boxes with a sprinkling of small boxes and small strip plazas housing smaller retailers, fast food chains, banks and professional offices. Collectively, stores gain visibility and improved regional access, but each remains its own destination, reached directly from a common expanse of parking. Power centres typically draw on a 100 km radius, attracting business away from older malls, big-box stores, and downtowns (Hernandez and Simmons, 2006).

For decades, competition on the basis of price led to bigger stores and increased concentration of ownership. In the 1990s, over expansion, changing shopping patterns, excess debt taken on to finance expansion, and periodic recessions forced many of the original big-box chains into bankruptcy (Lal and Alverez, 2011; Boothman, 2016). As store sizes grew and competition intensified, many of the largest retailers responded by becoming less specialised: grocery giants like Loblaw's Superstore introduced general merchandise; discount stores like Walmart and Target moved into food sales; drugstores added cosmetics, electronics, consumer goods and convenience foods in attempt to grab a larger share of consumer spending. The use of private-label store brands increased, promising consumers equal quality at lower prices by reducing marketing costs. With little room to cut further, some discounters took the opposite approach: upscaling to present better quality goods in more compelling ways.

Meanwhile non-store shopping was on the rise, including a resurgence in catalogue shopping in the 1970s and 1980s among specialty retailers (e.g. Land's End, L.L. Bean, Restoration Hardware), the expansion of television shopping (including infomercials and dedicated home shopping channels), more vending machines and by the 1990s, multiple forms of e-commerce. The rapid growth of non-store formats was made possible by a succession of digital innovations that reduced costs and increased transaction speeds and consumer capabilities, beginning with bank-issued credit cards (1950s), 1–800 numbers (1960s), delivery times shortened by UPS and Fed-EX (1970), the Internet (1980s), personal computers (1980s), graphic web browsers and smart phones (1990s).

E-commerce grew dramatically after 1990. Entrepreneurs devised new ways to sell traditional products (including both department store-style sites like Amazon.com and specialised niche retailers); new ways to sell entirely new products that displaced traditional products (e.g. Netflix, ITunes); new market-making sites that allowed anyone to become a seller as well as a buyer of goods (e.g. eBay and Craig's List); and online sites operating as extensions of physical stores. Freed from physical stores, consumers access goods without regard to store hours or geography and in quasi-anonymity. Online shopping also provided new capabilities in research, including price matches and access to detailed product information, such as videos and product reviews. From the perspective of the retailer, pure online selling reduces fixed overhead costs and broadens the market. E-commerce especially lowered barriers for small players, enabling them to reach out globally. However, as many established retailers discovered, e-commerce also has drawbacks, reducing opportunities for impulse buying, upselling and bundling sales that traditionally increased profits per visit.

Canadian consumers embraced the Internet but lagged in their acceptance of online shopping, preferring to use the web for research and buy in-store. Several explanations have been suggested: American consumers perceive they can buy anything online, in part due to the presence of thousands of small online retailers. Canadian retailers have been slower to establish an online presence, likely due to smaller markets and higher shipping costs. Meanwhile, Canadian consumers ordering goods from outside the country face additional import taxes and fees.

Small format retailing did not disappear in the postwar period; there was, however, a shift from independent ownership to franchising. Franchising offers many of the advantages of the chain store format, including brand recognition for an increasingly mobile population, bulk buying and support in developing a clearly defined business, albeit one with high start up costs. Franchises multiplied rapidly after the war, driven in part by veterans using their separation pay to open small businesses. Fast food chains, convenience stores, pet supplies, photo shops, hardware stores and many others sprang up along major roads, in strip plazas and later in power centres. By 2010, one in twelve businesses and nearly half of all retail sales (broadly defined) in the United States occurred in a franchise.

Market saturation and emerging technologies

Decades of expansion, slow economic growth, changing demographics and transformative digital technologies raise questions about retail saturation. Mall visits are declining at a stunning rate: from 35 million in 2010 to 17 million in 2013, according to the real estate research firm Cushman and Wakefield. By 2012, nearly 35% of empty retail space in America was in the big-box format. Growth in store size seems to have peaked, with customers resisting the inconvenience and overall unpleasantness of the experience. How much square feet is enough? In 1999, America averaged 18.45 square feet of retail space per person. By 2017, America had approximately 24 square feet of retail real estate per person, while Canada has only 16 square feet per person (Lal and Alvarez, 2011; Hernandez and Lau, 2014; Rupp and Smith, 2017). Retailers are shifting from mass to targeted marketing, selling identities and experiences rather than simply cheap goods. Engagement is seen as the key to making sales and building customer loyalty. Retailing is becoming omnichannel: physical stores and websites offer different but complimentary shopping experiences with opportunities for customisation. As retailers become brand managers, the physical store becomes only one part of the brand experience, designed to create memorable customer experiences. Some companies that began as online only retailers are opening brick and mortar showrooms, where consumers can "try before they buy".

For decades American retailers focused on productivity at the "back end", using information technology to improve the logistics of inventory management, supply, distribution and staffing.

Reducing costs and adding square footage were fundamental to high volume, low-margin strategies. Many of the productivity gains associated with digital technologies are in the customer-facing "front end" of retail: websites, social media, click and collect, the use of mobile phones to research merchandise, compare prices and pay without waiting in line (Hortacsu and Syverson, 2015).

There are also new kinds of brand-oriented retailers. In the 1980s, American manufacturers began to close their factories, outsource their manufacturing, and concentrate on design and merchandising. Companies such as Nike and Stuart Weizmann used to actually make shoes; computer companies like Apple used to make computers. As the profit margins in manufacturing shrank and became increasingly dependent upon labour costs and working conditions problematic from a customer relations' point of view, manufacturers began to open retail stores and sell product through their own online platforms as well as through other retailers. The largest profits in many consumer goods are to be had in retailing rather than in manufacturing (Klein, 2009; Hamilton, 2014). With domestic markets approaching saturation, retailers have internationalised, looking to carry their competitive advantage to new markets and achieve economies of distribution on a global scale. Competition for mall space is driving rents upwards. Following the passage of the US-Canada Free Trade Agreement (NAFTA) in 1994, huge American companies competing on the basis of price and marketing savvy overwhelmed Canadian retailers, many still operating as small family-run firms. American retailers now dominate significant segments of the Canadian market, including the general merchandise (e.g. Walmart and Costco), electronics (e.g. Best Buy), and home improvement (e.g. Home Depot and Lowes). Canadian-based retailers continue to dominate the pharmaceutical and grocery sectors. In the early 1990s, foreign controlled firms represented less than 3% of Canadian retail sales; by 2011, 53% or sixty-six of the top 124 retailers in Canada were foreign owned, the majority American based. Of the retail chains that closed in Canada between 2008 and 2014, 77% were Canadian owned, while 62% of stores that opened in that time were American. Internationalisation has also seen large European and Asian retailers (including H&M, Zara, Ikea and Uniqlo) enter American and Canadian markets, selling on-trend goods at affordable prices. Adopting the just-in time lean inventory model pioneered by American retailers these companies developed a new category of "fast fashion" (Burns and Rayman, 1995; Industry Canada, 2013; Freeman, 2014; Boothman, 2016).

The value proposition for consumers is changing. Shoppers are making decisions on price and quality in multiple formats: buying some goods online, with or without visiting a physical store, patronising discounters for some goods and luxury retailers and local small shops for others. The increasing diversity of retail formats has been a consistent theme. Meanwhile, the share of total consumer expenditures spent on material goods has declined while that spent on leisure time, entertainment, travel and self-enhancement has increased dramatically. As a sector, retail has traditionally been one of low labour productivity and low wages. Most gains come through the entry of new, more efficient firms and the exiting of less-efficient firms, and successful firms adding new stores. Once established, retailers, for the most part, have been slow to recognise changing circumstances. More than 75% of the top fifty retailers in Canada and the United States during 1980 were no longer in the group, or no longer existed three decades later (Boothman, 2016, p. 146). For 150 years, larger floor areas (in single stores and in growing chains) were associated with more customer trips and increased sales. Transformations in supply chain management, the rise of e-commerce and changes in consumer preferences and shopping patterns are challenging long held models, demanding new strategies and forcing change (Stephens, 2013, Lutz, 2016).

References

Baskerville, P. (2008), *A silent revolution? Gender and wealth in English Canada 1860–1930* (Montreal: McGill-Queen's University Press).

Belisle, D. (2011), *Retail nation* (Vancouver: University of British Columbia Press).

Benson, J. (1985), 'Hawking and peddling in Canada, 1867–1914', *Histoire sociale- Social History*, 18 (35), pp. 75–83.

Benson, J. and Shaw, G. (1992), *The evolution of retail systems, 1800–1914* (Leicester: Leicester University Press).

Blackford, M.G. (2003), *A history of small business in America* (Chapel Hill: University of North Carolina Press).

Blanke, D. (2000), *Sowing the American dream* (Athens, OH: Ohio University Press).

Bonacich, E. (2006), 'Wal-Mart and logistics revolution', in N. Lichtenstein (ed.) *Wal-Mart: The face of twenty-first century capitalism* (New York: The New Press).

Boorstin, D. (1973), *The Americans: The democratic experience* (New York: Random House).

Boothman, B.E.C. (2011), 'Mammoth market: The transformation of food retailing in Canada, 1946–1965', *Journal of Historical Research in Marketing*, 3 (3), pp. 279–301.

Boothman, B.E.C. (2016), 'Distributive orders: The evolution of North American retailing', in D. Jones and M. Tadajewski (eds.) *The Routledge companion to marketing history* (New York: Routledge) 131–150.

Bucheli, M., Mahoney, J. and Vaaler, P. (2010), 'Chandler's living history: The visible hand of vertical integration in nineteenth century America viewed under a twenty-first century transaction costs economics lens', *Journal of Management Studies*, 47 (5), pp. 859–883.

Burns, D.J. and Rayman, D.M. (1995), 'Retailing in Canada and the United States: Historical comparisons', *The Service Industries Journal*, 15 (4), pp. 164–176.

Bushman, R. (1994), 'Shopping and advertising in Colonial America', in C. Carson, R. Hoffman, and P. Albert (eds.) *Of consumimg interests: The style of life in the eighteenth century* (Charlottesville: University Press of Virginia) 233–251.

Carden, A. (2013), 'Retail innovations in American economic history: The rise of the mass-market merchandisers', in R. Parker and R. Whaples (eds.) *Routledge handbook of major events in economic history* (New York: Routledge) 402–414.

Carlos, A.M. and Lewis, F.D. (2001), 'Trade, consumption, and the native economy: Lessons from york factory, Hudson Bay', *The Journal of Economic History*, 61 (4), pp. 1037–1064.

Carlos, A.M. and Lewis, F.D. (2002), 'Marketing in the land of Hudson Bay: Indian consumers and the Hudson Bay company, 1670–1770', *Enterprise & Society*, 3 (2), pp. 285–317.

Chandler, A.D. (1962), *Strategy and structure* (Cambridge, MA: MIT Press).

Chandler, A.D. (1977), *The visible hand: The managerial revolution in American business* (Cambridge, MA: Harvard University Press).

Chandler, A.D. (1984), 'The emergence of managerial capitalism', *Business History Review*, 58, pp. 473–503.

Cohen, L. (1990), *Making a new deal: Industrial workers in Chicago, 1919–1939* (New York: Cambridge University Press).

Craig, B. (2009), *Backwoods consumers and homespun capitalists* (Toronto: University of Toronto Press).

Deutsch, T. (2010), *Building a housewife's paradise: Gender, politics, and American grocery stores in the twentieth century* (Chapel Hill, NC: University of North Carolina Press).

Diner, H. (2015), *Roads taken: The great Jewish migrations to the new world and the peddlers who forged the way* (New Haven, CT: Yale University Press).

Freeman, S. (2014), 'The Canadian shopping mall: Neither Canadian nor a mall, anymore', *The Huffington Post*. Available at: www. huffingtonpost.ca/2014/06/27/canadian-shopping-mall-retail-brands-dying_n_5534651.html.

Hamilton, G., Senauer, B. and Petrovic, M. (eds.) (2011), *The market makers: How retailers are reshaping the global economy* (Oxford: Oxford University Press).

Hamilton, S. and Phillips, S. (2014), *The kitchen debate and cold war consumer politics* (Boston, MA: Bedford/St. Martin's Press).

Haupt, H.G. (2012), 'Small shops and department stores', in F. Trentmann (ed.) *The Oxford handbook of the history of consumption* (Oxford: Oxford University Press).

Hernandez, T. and Lau, S. (2014), *The evolution of major shopping centres in Canada: 1996–2013* (Toronto: Centre for the Study of Commercial Activity).

Hernandez, T. and Simmons, J. (2006), 'Evolving retail landscapes: Power retail in Canada', *The Canadian Geographer*, 50 (4), pp. 465–486.

Hodge, C. (2014), *Consumerism and the emergence of the middle class in Colonial America* (New York: Cambridge University Press).
Hortaçsu, A. and Syverson, C. (2015), 'The ongoing evolution of US retail: A format tug-of-war', *The Journal of Economic Perspectives*, 29 (4), pp. 89–111.
Howard, V. (2008), 'The biggest small-town store in America: Independent retailers and the rise of consumer culture', *Enterprise & Society*, 9 (3), pp. 4457–4486.
Industry Canada (2013), *Consumer trends update: Canada's changing retail market* (Ottawa: Industry Canada).
Isenstadt, S. (2014), 'The spaces of shopping: A historical overview', in D. Andrews (ed.) *Shopping: Material culture perspectives* (Newark, NJ: University of Delaware Press) 1–32.
Jackson, K.T. (1996), 'All the world's a mall: Reflections on the social and economic consequences of the American shopping center', *The American Historical Review*, 101 (4), pp. 1111–1121.
Jacobs, M. (2005), *Pocketbook politics: Economic citizenship in twentieth-century America* (Princeton, NJ: Princeton University Press).
Jaffee, D. (1991), 'Peddlers of progress and the transformation of the Rural North, 1760–1860', *The Journal of American History*, 78 (2), pp. 511–535.
Kaikati, J. (May 1985), 'Don't discount off-price retailers', *Harvard Business Review*, 63 (3), pp. 85–92.
Khade, A. and Lovass, N. (2009), 'Supply chain performance: A case of WalMart's logistics', *International Journal of Business Strategy*, 9 (1).
Koehn, N. (2001, revised 2002), 'Marshall Field and the rise of the department store', Harvard Business School Case 801–349.
Klein, N. (2009), *No Logo* (Toronto: Vintage).
Krulikowski, A. (2014), 'The shop around the corner: Change, continuity, and the corner grocery store', in D. Andrews (ed.) *Shopping: Material culture perspectives* (Newark, NJ: University of Delaware Press) 89–109.
Lal, R. and Alvarez, R. (December 19, 2011), 'Death knell for the category killers?', *Harvard Business Review*.
Leach, W.R. (1993), *Land of desire: Merchants, power, and the rise of a new American culture* (New York: Pantheon Books).
Lears, T. (1994), *Fables of abundance* (New York: Basic Books).
Levinson, M. (2011), *The great A&P and the struggle for small business in America* (New York: Hill & Wang).
Lichtenstein, N. (ed.) (2006), *Wal-Mart: The face of twenty-first-century capitalism* (New York: The New Press).
Livingston, J. (1994), *Pragmatism and the political economy of cultural revolution, 1850–1940* (Chapel Hill, NC: University of North Carolina Press).
Longstreth, R. (1999), *The drive-in, the supermarket, and the transformation of commercial space in Los Angeles, 1914–1941* (Cambridge, MA: MIT Press).
Longstreth, R. (1997), 'The diffusion of the community shopping center concept during the interwar decades', *Journal of the Society of Architectural Historians*, 56 (3), pp. 268–293.
Lutz, A. (August 31, 2016), 'American malls are dying faster than you think – and it's about to get even worse', *Business Insider*.
Mancke, E. (1995), 'At the counter of the general store: Women and the economy in 18th-century horton, Nova Scotia', in M. Conrad (ed.) *Intimate relations: Family and community in planter Nova Scotia* (Fredericton: Acadiensis Press) 167–181.
Marling, K. (1994), *As seen on TV: The visual culture of every day life in the 1950s* (Cambridge, MA: Harvard University Press).
Martin, A.S. (2000), 'Commercial space as consumption arena: Retail stores in early Virginia', in S. McMurry and A. Adams (eds.) *People, power, places: Perspectives in vernacular architecture* VIII (Knoxville: University of Tennessee Press) 201–218.
Martin, A.S. (2008), *Buying into the world of goods: Early consumers in backcountry Virginia* (Baltimore, MD: Johns Hopkins University Press).
McCalla, D. (1997), 'Retailing in the countryside: Upper Canadian general stores in the mid-nineteenth century', *Business and Economic History*, 26 (2), pp. 393–403.
McCalla, D. (2015a), 'We aint "gentlemen" merchants: The country retailer in Upper Canada', *History of Retailing and Consumption*, 1 (2), pp. 140–148.
McCalla, D. (2015b), *Consumers in the bush: Shopping in rural upper Canada* (Montreal & Kingston: McGill-Queen's University Press).
Monod, D. (1996), *Store wars: Shopkeepers and the culture of mass marketing, 1890–1939* (Toronto: University of Toronto Press).
National Retail Federation (2017), *Retail's impact*. Available at: https://nrf.com/advocacy/retails-impact.

National Transportation Research Center (2016), *Transportation energy data book* (Knoxville, NY: Oak Ridge National Laboratory) Available at: cta.ornl.gov/data.

Nobles, G. (1990), 'The rise of merchants in rural market towns: A case study of eighteenth-century Northampton, Massachusetts', *Journal of Social History*, 24 (1), pp. 5–23.

Norris, J.D. (1962), 'One-price policy among antebellum country stores', *The Business History Review*, 36 (4), pp. 455–458.

O'Leary, M., Orlikowski, W. and Yates, J. (2002), 'Distributed work over the centuries: Trust and control in the Hudson's Bay company, 1670–1826', in S. Kiesler and P. Hinds (eds.) *Distributed work* (Cambridge, MA: MIT Press) 27–54.

Owram, D. (1996), *Born at the right time: A history of the baby boom generation* (Toronto: University of Toronto Press).

Perkins, E. (1991), 'The consumer frontier: Household consumption in early Kentucky', *The Journal of American History*, 78 (2), pp. 486–510.

Ritzer, G. (2010), *Enchanting a disenchanted world*, 3rd ed. (Thousand Oaks, CA: Pine Forge).

Rupp, L. and Smith, M. (January 24, 2017), 'Retail malaise puts pressure on U.S. chains to shutter stores', *Globe and Mail*, Tuesday, p. B8.

Scott, P. and Walker, J. (2011), 'Sales and advertising expenditure for interwar American department stores', *Journal of Economic History*, 71 (1), pp. 40–69.

Scott, P. and Walker, J. (2014), 'The service cost – Unit value retail continuum and the demise of the American 'five and dime' variety store, 1914–1941', Henley Discussion Paper Series. Available at: www.henley.ac.uk/research/research-centres/the-centre-for-international-business-history.

Shammas, C. (1990), *The pre-industrial consumer in England and America* (Oxford: Clarendon Press).

Shapiro, L. (2005), *Something from the oven: Reinventing dinner in 1950s America* (New York: Penguin).

Simmons, J. (1991), 'The regional mall in Canada', *Canadian Geographer/Le Geographe canadien*, 35 (3), pp. 232–240.

Strasser, S. (1989), *Satisfaction guaranteed: The making of the American mass market* (New York: Pantheon Books).

Strasser, S. (2014), 'Woolworth to Wal-Mart: Mass merchandising and the changing culture of consumption', in D. Andrews (ed.) *The material culture of shopping* (Newark, NY: University of Delaware Press) 1–32.

Stephens, D. (2013), *The retail revival: Reimagining business for the new age of consumerism* (Mississauga: Wiley).

Tedlow, R.S. (1990), *New and improved: The story of mass marketing in America* (New York: Basic Books).

Walden, K. (1989), 'Speaking modern: Language, culture, and hegemony in grocery window displays, 1887–1920', *The Canadian Historical Review*, 70 (3), pp. 285–310.

Whitaker, J. (2015), *Reviews in history, review of Vicki Howard, from main street to mall: The rise and fall of the American department store*. Available at: www.history.ac.uk/reviews/review/178.

Wright, C. (1992), "Feminine trifles of vast importance': Writing gender into the history of consumption', in F. Iacovetta and M. Valverde (eds.) *Gender conflicts: New essays in women's history* (Toronto: University of Toronto Press) 229–260.

22
WESTERN EUROPE (INCLUDING SCANDINAVIA)

Ilja Van Damme

Introduction

For anyone browsing through forecasts on shopping trends and consumer behaviour, the future of the European retail sector looks gloomy. Predictions of the effects of an online retail boom and simultaneous decline of high streets and town centres, loom large in both specialised reports and general news coverage. Future shopping is believed to become weightless, effortless, timeless and placeless. In the meantime, our individual consumer preferences will be ever more effectively tracked, analysed and catered for in a brave new world of big data management and social media advertising. It is curious how, in predicting the next-step in retailing, the past is often evoked as ultimate proof and justification. After all, does not history tells us how, every fifty years or so, retailing undergoes a significant disruption and change: a "retail revolution" of some sorts? Well, not necessarily: the history of retailing also tells quite another story. Although talk of revolutions certainly abounds in historical retail narratives, such interpretations are not necessarily insightful in comprehending the future of retailing, let alone its past. In fact, it can be seriously questioned whether dividing retail history into something before and after will move any understanding of retail change fundamentally forward. It blots out strong continuities, complexities and contradicting variations in time and place. Moreover, by casting retail history in a traditional–modern dichotomy, historians fail to study and appreciate the act of shopping in its long-term and changing social and cultural contexts.

The last twenty years, however, have seen a liberating revision in approaches. Long-term, comparative knowledge regarding Western European retail diversity has matured enormously in empirical breadth and conceptual precision (for instance: Blondé et al., 2006; Furnée and Lesger, 2014). We now understand better how retailing fitted into medieval and early modern societies, and how shopping in the past differed from today. Important to such reinterpretations has been an acknowledgement of the centrality of the urban framework as both backdrop of retail development and agent of urban lifestyles centred around market-oriented exchange and consumption (Stobart, 2008; Blondé and Van Damme, 2013: 251–253). With estimated mean urbanisation percentages of more than 75%, contemporary Western Europe is believed to be one of the most densely urbanised regions in the world (Clark, 2013: 16). The long-running importance of cities and towns, indeed, has been a mainstay in Western European history; and starting in the Middle Ages, but gaining in significance from the renaissance-period onwards, the retail sector is believed to have been crucial for the continuous social and economic livability of European cities. Part of this dynamism, it will be argued in this chapter, was precisely related to the emergence of shopping as distinct lifestyle or habitus of the social and cultural milieu that is the Western European city. The fact that these strong and long-running ties between urban lifestyles and market-oriented exchange and consumption continue to dominate and structure modern life until today, at least partly explains why inner-city, recreational shopping still thrives in Western Europe. It has continued to do so, despite the actual and predicted revolutionary disruptions caused by large-scale, "out-of-town" retail sprawl and the arrival of the Internet age (Weltevreden et al., 2005: 824–841).

This chapter provides a broad chronological overview to explain how shopping unfolded and developed against an emerging urban Europe between roughly 1000 A.D. and today. Its geographical focus will be on Western Europe as a whole, trying to flesh out generic evolutions and trends. In doing so, however, certain strongly urbanised regions – England, France, Italy, the Low Countries – will pop up more frequently as others, which is due to their historic importance in retail developments and our more advanced knowledge of these places in general. The European countryside remains under-theorised and under-researched within retail history; but it was also later and less commercialised than European cities and towns. What follows, then, is a straightforward chronological account of the European entanglement between shopping and urbanism. It begins by questioning why certain European regions and places had more elaborate and multidimensional retail landscapes than others, and how consumption and shopping needs to be interpreted in the medieval period. It then looks at the centrality of shopping for emerging urban lifestyles from the renaissance period and onwards into the nineteenth century. In a third and last section, it questions the extent to which shopping practices altered during the nineteenth and twentieth centuries, what was driving such changes and how these evolutions will affect our retail futures. The chapter does not go so far as claiming that the level of urbanisation and spread of urban consumer cultures is the only or even the most important causal variable in engendering retail change in Western Europe. In the following, we also touch on other generic variables like political interference, institutional and economic embedding, cultural change and rising standards of living, among others. However, focusing on the history of shopping as being essentially part of an emerging urban lifestyle, does have the advantage of simultaneously describing change and assigning meaning to more than 1,000 years of retail development.

Shopping and the rise of cities

Three persistent myths still haunt commonsensical interpretations of retailing in the past. The first of these starts from the assumption that living standards before 1800 were basically stuck at a persistent low level, making the material conditions for all but a wealthy few 'no higher than for our ancestors of the African savannah' (Clark, 2007: 38). Following up, a second claim states how pre-industrial consumers nurtured only basic subsistence needs and desires. Notwithstanding evidence of markets, shops and commercial buildings in Ancient and Classical sites, the basic mode of living of our rural predecessors in Western Europe is believed to have been one of poverty, self-sufficiency and making do. Hence, and finally, retailing – if existent at all – was thought to be traditional, meaning ill-developed, small and aimed at distributing necessities (Jeffreys, 1954: 1, 5–6). In short, the reasoning goes that before the nineteenth century, people simply provisioned themselves and bought goods in a "natural" manner, that is straight from producers. Only modernity and its ensuing "retail revolutions" nurtured shoppers: hedonistic pleasure seekers with the means and mentality to consume an ever-growing material plenty provided by an ever more extended sales machinery (Campbell, 1987: 77–96).

The word "shopping" in this modern sense – with its social and cultural overtones of leisurely browsing, publicly and spatially interacting with people and seeing and being seen by an urban crowd – only starts appearing in European dictionaries and lexicons from the middle of the eighteenth century onwards (Cox and Dannehl, 2007: 145–147). Yet, the phenomenon to which one commonly refers with the term was obviously of a much older date than is sometimes assumed. For Western Europe, shopping, and all its associated social and cultural meanings, had come of age in the centuries following 1000 A.D. This happened first in northern and central Italy and somewhat later in the cities and towns situated around important waterways like the Themes, Loire, Seine, Scheldt, Meuse and Rheine in North-West Europe. These fertile and well-connected lands were becoming, from an early date, the commercial and urbanised heartland of Europe, clearly evolving differently from the more rugged and isolated terrains in the north (parts of Scotland and most of Scandinavia) and the south of Europe (Spain and Portugal). The eleventh-fourteenth centuries were crucial for the European "blue banana" (the early urbanised regions stretching from Italy over the Alps towards the Rhineland, the Low Counties and the south of England), since it saw the rise of a dynamic, hierarchical network of central places: a system of small towns and rapidly expanding urban centres where markets, shops and shopping became truly quintessential "hallmarks of urban life" (Carlin, 2007: 491).

The old-idea that the manorial system of early medieval Europe lacked any commercial embedding and was essentially autarkic in nature, has long been abandoned. The sporadic mention of local artisans – smiths, potters, thatchers – leads us to the conclusion that fewer households and agrarian settlements were as self-sufficient and subsistence-oriented as once thought (Devroey et al., 2013: 49). Yet it was mostly from the eleventh century onwards that European settlements (as in England or the Low Countries) received market and fair rights, commodity staples and commercial legislation, sometimes also city rights. This strengthened government control and taxation of existing trades and, even more importantly, stimulated the European market-oriented economy more generally (Britnell, 2009). In the bigger European centres – scattered between the Loire and the Rhine, and in northern and central Italy – retailing extended both in time and space, markets being organised at least twice a week in different places in town and arranged by specialisation (fish, grain, vegetables, dairy products, meat, etc.) (Stabel, 2001: 797–817). Evolutions like these were not only a reflection of population size, which was always lower in the more remote and rural regions of Europe like Scandinavia or inland France and Spain. They also attested to regional wealth accumulation in the wake of the expanding European textile trades, growing and diversifying household demands for marketed goods, and intense and longer trade connections that brought in luxuries from further away. The largest cities, such as Paris, London, Ghent or Venice, distributed valuable and fashionable comparison goods for which customers were willing to cross larger distances and for which retailers needed a minimal high demand to supply them. An English Latin teacher, John of Garland, walking along the streets, quays and bridges of early thirteenth-century Paris, for instance, noticed shoe sellers, girdlers, saddlers, shield makers, buckle makers, soap sellers, knife peddlers, hatters, glovers and all sorts of specialised food sellers; his list of professions goes on page after page, listing in total over sixty different trades and multitudes of small-sale activities (Carlin, 2007: 509–517).

It would be wrong, however, to equate the nature and character of medieval consumption and shopping with present-day practices and sensibilities. Most buying and selling still took place outside, in broad daylight; and this was no different in the urbanised and more rural and isolated pockets of Europe. Retailing in European medieval towns and cities was not only concentrated around specialised open-air market squares (see the chapter of Guardia et al. in this volume), but widespread along residential streets, at bridges or in any other highly frequented urban corridor between the centre and the gates that opened up to the food-producing countryside. At mid thirteenth-century Winchester, in southeast England, retailers could use the entire network of streets within the walls, including the cemetery of its cathedral during the markets and fairs (Keene, 1985: 579–580). Sellers set up stock at fixed locations during market-days, often just in front of people's houses, and sale-places were organised around different food categories and artisanal specialisations. Similar developments in other cities and towns indicate that provisional market stalls on the street began to take on a semi-permanent character and sometimes had moved inside. A city like thirteenth-century Antwerp in the Low Countries – at the time a middle-sized town of around 10,000 inhabitants – had solid market facilities in civic buildings for almost every important sale-category: bread, meat, butter and cloth (Van Damme and Van Aert, 2014). Food houses or halls – and the Paris example is probably the most famous one – offered retailers opportunities to stock up, customers shelter for bad-weather and protected the wares from the sun and rain. Other functions could also be combined: in the rooms above the *Broodhuyse* (Breadhouse), the Antwerp urban government took up its first permanent residence, symbolically presiding over trade in the most important food category of the medieval menu.

In the meantime, shops also started to materialise in the best trade-connected European cities and towns, often for specific, imported product categories that were not sold on the market (fine cloth and fashion accessories, groceries, wine) or linked to the workshops of jewellers, silversmiths, tailors and the like, catering for wealthy urban classes. Most durable and valuable goods, including the widespread resale of used, second-hand belongings – an important way for stocking-up households – were distributed out of shops. By the thirteenth century, even the smallest European towns were dotted with shops of retailers and craftsmen selling on a year-round basis, although it would again be wrong to compare these spaces with their modern counterparts (Keene, 2006: 131). Shops were tiny and resembled in many ways the fixed booths on market places or market halls, and customers were not supposed to enter, the shop often being too cramped and stuffed with merchandise anyway. Sale transactions normally took place through an open window facing the street, with external shutters, that could be closed and locked up at night, functioning both as stall board for displaying wares and as canopy above.

Differences with present-day shopping, however, reach deeper than architectural and spatial aspects. Everyday buying and selling in medieval towns and cities in Western Europe took place

Figure 22.1 Market scene with sale of fowl, taking place on the Meir of sixteenth-century Antwerp, Belgium.

(Courtesy of Museum Plantin-Moretus | Prentenkabinet, Antwerpen)

along the lines of a flexible and adaptive set of rules, regulations and morals that owed much to the European-wide spread of Christian beliefs and ideals. In larger towns and cities, rules and regulations reflected, firstly, the emerging guild ordering of production, trade and commodity-sales during the fourteenth and fifteenth centuries, especially in countries like Italy, France, Germany and the Low Countries. It fragmented the retail landscape in a multidimensional structure of trades and professions of a formally recognised or informal kind, each with their own specialisations and privileged access to and control of the market (or precisely a lack of it). However, many of these guild codes also pointed towards deeper and much older conventions and ethics: norms, ideologies and agreements about the nature and character of market exchange and consumption. The moral order of the European medieval market economy – enshrined in canonical and statutory laws – was replete with Christian dogma and beliefs about fairness, justness, honesty and trust. Within this shopping ontology, commerce and consumption had to be reconciled with a moral mode of virtuous behaviour that, in principle at least, steered the individual actions of both buyers and sellers (Stabel, 2007: 53–69; and the chapter by Dyer this volume).

For good moral conduct, open-air market trading was taken as the quintessential ideal of honesty and transparency, both in town and country. In his *Livre des métiers* from around 1270, the Paris official Etienne Boileau described how goods that were sold on the market could be compared, inspected and weighed against each other, thus leading to a 'fair and just price for both the rich and the poor' (cited in Braudel, 1979: 15). Moreover, urban markets were always closely controlled by urban officials and guildsmen supervising the use of weights, measures and money being used during the exchange. Tellingly, the openness of dealings also extended to the customer, who could be publicly sanctioned as well if his shopping behaviour flaunted social norms and codes. It is no coincidence that central market places were also used for public trials and punishments throughout Western Europe by both the Church and secular authorities. The kind of semi-public shops that were common in medieval towns also stood open to inspection by guildsmen and customers; not to be trusted – although frequently part of commercial dealings – were inns, taverns and other more private, domestic spaces. Trade here was often associated with forestalling, artificial price arrangements, hoarding and shady affairs – accusations which extended well into the early modern period.

Despite its strikingly different social and cultural embedding compared with today, shopping and consumption had become firmly part of the urbanised landscape of Western Europe by about 1350, especially in the regions from central Italy to the Midlands of England. Both profit-seeking conduct of retailers and individualised material desires centred around an expanding world of goods, and were mediated and discussed in the growing urban centres. All of this took place amidst a world that remained predominantly characterised by its Christian beliefs and noble ranks and by a fragile but all-important and dominant agrarian economy. Nowhere better could such curious concord be observed than at fairs. As a "high mass" of commerce, entertainment and material plenty, these events often coincided with religious festivities (like Ascension Day or Pentecost) and usually followed the rhythms of the dominant agrarian cycles – at the end of the summer, after harvesting and at the end of spring, when the wool of sheep was brought to town. During fair times peddlers and international traders flocked to town and brought in small luxuries and exotic goods not readily available for the rest of the year. Moments like these also attracted noblemen and their extended court retinues. Rather than having their servants do the day-to-day shopping, the elites went to see the available goods in person as part of an enjoyable stroll through town, and they did so in groups: to see and to be seen (Keene, 2006: 138–142). Most famous are the many descriptions of *La Sensa*, the fair associated with the feast day of the Ascension in Venice. In 1493, Beatrice d'Este, Duchess of Bari and married to the important Sforza family of Milan, reported in a letter home how she had enjoyed the dazzling sights of plenty:

> shops of spices and silks and other merchandise, all in good order and in great quality and quantity of the most diverse goods . . . we saw everything piece by piece, which was a great pleasure, for there was an infinite quantity of most beautiful jewels . . . and found such a magnificent show of beautiful glass, that we were fairly bewildered and were obliged to remain for a long time.
>
> *(Welch, 2006: 47)*

Significantly, while the duchess looked, touched and sighed over the exquisite merchandise, she did not buy or bargain: she was there performing a social ritual of viewing and being viewed by urban Venetian society. Goods could always be paid for and delivered later at her palace.

When compared to the rest of Europe – even the more urbanised and economically well-developed places – Venice played in a league of its own in the fifteenth century. However, the behaviour of Beatrice does have broader significance since it points to important social and cultural changes that had begun influencing the conduct of Italian and other Western-European urban elites from the end of the Middle Ages. As will become clear in what follows, shopping and market-oriented consumption became increasingly linked to the social and cultural habitus of emerging renaissance cities and early modern towns.

The pleasures of shopping

The late Middle Ages were not only a time of warfare, hunger and pestilence on the European Continent; in many ways, it was also a gilded age of wealth concentration, blossoming arts and luxury industries, and one of changing mores and morales around shopping and consumption (Blondé and Ryckbosch, 2015: 105–124). Described as the first age of fashion, this period saw a growing concern about increasing materialistic lifestyles in European cities (Welch, 2005). Signifying these paradoxes and tensions, countries like Italy, France, England and Germany issued sumptuary laws – as early as 1157 in the case of Genoa. These grew in frequency throughout the fourteenth and fifteenth centuries, but gradually petered out afterwards. Such a legislative offensive indicated rising urban wealth and a willingness of more citizens to spend their money on conspicuous expensive and eye-catching goods and designs – the traditional symbolic domain of the feudal elites (Howell, 2010: 208–260). However, if the Church and the State were alarmed by the flagrant flaunting of material identifiers of social standing, their justifications for doing so were simultaneously eroded and out-of-date. The moral dogmas and ideologies of the medieval Church were now re-interpreted and complemented – if not challenged – by competing humanistic discourses on the proper handling of luxury goods and worldly desires. In the opinion of the Venetian renaissance writer Giovanni Fabrini, writing in 1547, avarice was condemnable, but so was prodigality, the 'excessive spending, without order, without method, without measure' (cited in Guerzoni, 1999: 336). Consumption, comparison shopping and worldly display had to become a pleasurable and aesthetic pursuit, a cosmopolitan and elitist, civilised pastime which demanded both restraint and indulgence, study and refinement and above all taste. Being recognised as *a la mode* – something which was done in the open and judged by a knowing and inquisitive urban crowd – became *de rigeur* in renaissance and early modern cities and towns. These evolutions lifted the important advisory function of retailers and commercial middlemen in finding the right piece of attire or fashionable set of furnishings.

Retailing and commerce in general was rescued from its *odium* that had inspired age-old negative perceptions about profit-making and the widespread use of credit, practices that took centre stage in everyday contacts between buyers and sellers (Howell, 2010: 261–297). City governments of fifteenth-century Bruges, sixteenth-century Antwerp and seventeenth-century Amsterdam simply linked their urban policies and futures to the interests of the merchant community at large. In astrological prognostications circulating in sixteenth-century Antwerp, for instance, it was clearly stated how peaceful and good trading concurred with heavenly alignments that promised social peace and prosperity. Such an outspoken ideology of commerce (Kint, 2000: 213–222) eventually gave way to a proper elevation of the commercial classes into ruling urban bodies, a practice which was also widespread along the coasts of North-Western Europe and the Baltic area, with the rise of the Hanseatic League, uniting cities like Lübeck, Hamburg, Bergen, London, etc. It was in places like these that commerce and lifestyles built around consumption and shopping were forcefully engraved in the material, institutional and socio-cultural fabric of cities.

The net effect of all this was a booming retail sector which, in the wake of an expanding and globalising international trade in the sixteenth century, grew and diversified as never before. Newly market squares, impressive market halls and purpose-built commercial buildings – exchanges with ground and upper floors fitted for shopping premises and specialised arcaded salerooms or courtyards for luxury trades – appeared in growing Renaissance cities from Seville to Augsburg and from Copenhagen to Florence. Although figures are difficult to come by, fragmentary evidence for this period indicates how the total number and relative importance of shopkeepers in urban societies was also on the rise, and this for both expanding and declining economies in Western Europe (Blondé and Van Damme, 2010, 2015). Overall, however, the physical environment and shopping experiences found in cities began to diverge. At the top of the shopping hierarchy sat the important European court and capital cities and the international and financial trading hubs. The much humbler provincial towns and rural market centres in the north of England, parts of France, Germany and for most of the Iberian and Scandinavian peninsula, only started to cast off their medieval veil from the middle of the eighteenth century onwards or even later. In the meantime, London had evolved into a shopping world of its own, while Paris took over from smaller fashion producers in Italy and the Low Countries from the late seventeenth century onwards as Europeans' ultimate fashion and luxury house.

An intensification of both retailing and shopping in the renaissance and early modern times, grew from the basic infrastructure and institutions that had already taken shape in the centuries before. Markets that were once situated at the outskirts of the medieval town had now taken on a central position and fixed location within an expanding urban area. The busy retail activity taking place in the centrally located main streets – with peddlers also circulating through market areas and adjacent streets – remained the rapidly pumping heart of cities and towns until well into the nineteenth-century (see Mitchell's chapter in this volume). When population growth continued, new market squares became integral to renaissance and baroque plans of urban extension and Italian inspired *renevatio* and improvement (Calabi, 2004: 40–91). These new markets functioned mainly as central provisioning places for foodstuffs on a neighbourhood level; other types of commercial exchange and shopping had moved indoors in shops, halls, shopping galleries and arcaded salerooms. Shops and market-trade did not grow at the detriment of each other in the early modern period, but fulfilled complementary functions and catered for additional needs and desires. Previously, certain regulations in Italy and the Low Countries had existed about shops being ordered to close their doors during market-days and fairs, but such prescriptions were less common and adhered to as early modern era progressed.

Close connections between markets and shops could be observed in early modern retail geographies, with the busy market centre being perceived as a prime location for shopkeepers to intercept potential customers. As Jacques Savary (1675, vl.1: 247–248) indicated in his widely read treatise on *Le Parfait Négociant*, a good location was crucial for a retailer to prosper. He cleverly observed for seventeenth-century Paris how the growth of cities created recognisable locational patterns and spatial clusters following retail specialisations. This meant that modern notions of the general accessibility of the city centre were already understood and recognised by early modern retailers of durable, upmarket products and luxury goods. Similarly, seventeenth-century retailers also acknowledged the special accessibility of, for instance, crossroads, bridges and prestige buildings, and the arterial accessibility of major thoroughfares and access routes leading to and from the centre (Lesger, 2011). Meanwhile, retailers of daily necessities like bread and groceries had dispersed evenly over town, catering regularly from corner shops to the adjacent streets and neighbourhoods. Workshops and ateliers of producing guildsmen, for which contacts with passers-by were less essential, had moved to cheaper and less visible side- and back-streets. Socially differentiated zones and main shopping streets had also taken shape in and around the medieval centre of Paris, with the opulence and splendour of the Rue Saint Honoré in the wealthy northwest contrasting starkly with shops in the less affluent south-eastern quarters of the city (Coquery, 2014).

Variety in shopping locations also corresponded with differences in the outlook, form and interiors of early modern shops which had much in common with their medieval predecessors: in Seville, as in other towns in Europe, they were narrow and with low ceilings, but sometimes had a mezzanine or second room above (Calabi, 2004: 104). However, as early modern times progressed, shops became recognisable sites of display, seduction and exchange, especially again in the more populated, wealthier and noble court-connected cities and capitals of Europe (Stobart et al., 2007; Walsh, 2014). Shops signs signalled their presence to passers-by, the shop normally being on the ground floor facing the street, with the retailer often living above and behind their commercial premise. These types of fixed shop differed in design and display of goods, which normally corresponded to conventions in the various branches of the retail industry, and to social pressures to keep up appearances with the broader area. Thus, a grocer's shop was different from a *magazin à la mode*, while a baker in a wealthy neighbourhood had to conform to other norms and rules to one in a poorer street. In general, shops had grown bigger, with a growing tendency to service clients within the shop rather than through the window. Window display, decorations and fashioning of the interior space were the subject of growing attention. Particularly in bigger cities like Paris and London, early eighteenth-century commentators like Daniel Defoe and Louis-Sébastian Mercier ridiculed the wasteful frivolousness of shopkeepers who invested in glazed windows, opulent furniture, gilded cornices, mirrors, chandeliers and glass-fronted cases simply to make 'a show to invite customers' (cited in Blondé and Van Damme, 2007: 336). In smaller provincial towns and in the countryside, shops had a more functional outlook with a counter dominating its interior and various cupboards, containers and shelves displaying the merchandise.

For a modern onlooker, most early modern shops probably looked spartan, dull and unattractive, but such interpretation misses the social and cultural context of what shopping was all about in this period. Whether taking place at a market, in a hall, on the street or in a shop, an extended and vivid intercourse between buyer and seller always took centre stage and was mainly aimed at negotiating such abstract notions as trust, probity, order and reputation (Van Damme, 2015). Goods had to be unwrapped or unpacked; explanations given about their provenance, quality and quantity; prices had to be negotiated, and in many cases credit arrangements agreed. For overcoming crucial information asymmetries relating to both creditworthiness and a heterogeneous and opaque product market, building up at least some personal bonds between buyer and seller was of key importance. Such social ties – which at least had the potential of being vested on mutual, long-term beneficial grounds – helped to mediate consumer complaints in the case of fraud, product defects or complaints, and assured the retailer that outstanding bills would be periodically paid. It can even be argued that direct contacts between consumers and their trustworthy providers became more important as material choice widened via a proliferation of fashions and new goods during the seventeenth and eighteenth centuries. Within a socially intricate and increasingly fashionable Western European urban context, the retailer could become the much-needed guide, steering the customer away from the perils of bad taste and social failure.

As the eighteenth century drew to its close, shopping had become a publicly accepted and celebrated leisure pursuit of a polite and worldly elite living within an urban framework (Berry, 2002; Stobart, 2008: 92–96). Undoubtedly, well-to-do households still employed servants to do their daily provisioning and called upon trustworthy craftsmen, tailors and upholsterers to refashion their eighteenth-century bodies and abodes at home. Advice literature of the time, however, also makes clear that performing out-of-doors shopping was increasingly considered an acquired skill of good household management (Walsh, 2008). In travel guides as well, upper tier readers were invited to delight in pleasurable window shopping and polite browsing. In a time when Enlightenment authors like Mandeville were declaring private vices to have public benefits, growing numbers of European citizens – both man and women – threw off any remaining religious and moral fetters for an unapologetically materialistic pursuit of happiness through shopping and leisure in the urban public space.

Urban governments all over Europe responded to these widening sensibilities by stimulating urban renewal and redesign for leisure consumption: new pavements, street lighting, cleaner streets, and sports facilities, promenades, operas, theatres, coffeehouses and adjacent shopping streets were laid out in towns across Europe, from Bath in England to Naples in Italy to Norrköping in Sweden (Borsay and Furnée, 2016). Thus, eighteenth-century urban lifestyles centred around consumption and shopping not only altered urban space in Western Europe and more rural Scandinavia, but also changed the very notion of time as well: leisure and non-working hours were "consumed" by strolling in shopping streets and visiting recreational places for theatre, music, reading, drinking, walking and sports. The urban *flaneur* needed only to speed up his pace to become that much talked about *persona* of the nineteenth-century city (Blondé and Van Damme, 2013: 253).

Not everywhere in Europe were these changes as visible and as pronounced. Norwich in England or Besançon in France had not changed much during the eighteenth-century, and both looked around 1800 very much like the centuries before (Furnée and Lesger, 2014: 5). But overall, small cities everywhere boosted a greater number and variety of shops with a wider range of goods on offer. A growing segment of the eighteenth- and early nineteenth-century population in Leuven, a small university town in what soon would become Belgium, engaged in shopkeeping. Tellingly, this growth included craftsmen who had switched from manufacturing to resale and food sellers (such as butchers) who had abandoned collective forms of sale via markets and halls for retailing through individual shopping premises (De Wilde, 2015: 105). In the countryside as well, village shops started popping up more frequently (Van den Heuvel and Ogilvie, 2013). Annual fairs had lost much of their commercial appeal for both rural and urban dwellers or had transformed into more entertaining affairs aimed at showing and selling livestock or drinking and eating local staples. But the demographic boom in the European countryside after c.1750 triggered urban shopkeepers to extend their business of selling coffee, tea and other imported small luxuries to their rural surroundings on a quasi-permanent basis. Whereas before, many urban based hawkers and petty chapmen had supplied rural consumer needs and desires, fixed village shops – nothing new in themselves – started multiplying in number and enlarging their stock at the same time as agricultural enclosures, rural modernisation and proto-industrial activities were transforming the European countryside. The material wants and desires of rural households thus became part of a widening and in origin urban consumer culture and "habitus" (De Vries, 2008). With commercialisation spreading everywhere and a countryside prepped to become an appendage to a once restricted and urban consumerism, a new age of mass provisioning and recreational shopping was duly in the making.

Shopping for the masses

As cities spilled over in the countryside due to industrialisation and suburbanisation, and modern transport and communication networks drew rural and urban worlds together, age-old retail provisioning systems had to respond to growing product supply and consumer demand (Benson and Shaw, 1992; Alexander and Akehurst, 1998). This urge to innovate and change business practices and retail management in the nineteenth-century was felt most acutely in the European food trades. Initially, with food being essential to the growing labouring poor and aspiring middle classes, boomtowns and expanding cities reacted similarly to previous rounds of European population pressure in the past. New (covered) markets and impressive glass-and-steel market halls were erected from Barcelona in the south of Europe to Odense in the north as a clear expression of civic pride and changing shopping sensibilities (Mitchell, 2014: 153–170; Fava et al., 2016; Toftgaard, 2016, and the chapter by Guardia et al. in this volume). Although, in the vision of nineteenth-century urban reforms, public markets needed to comply to new rules regarding sanitation and social order, their continuous functioning and even proliferation at the neighbourhood level attested to their success and efficiency in selling fresh foods to the urban masses.

Soon, however, the organised and regulated tradition of open-air and covered market trading had to be supplemented more intensely by decentralised and more "liberal" ways of selling food. "Old-school" urban peddlers, streets-sellers and other peripatetic retailers – the much maligned "pushcart evil" – were only part of the solution, and not a very respectable one at that. Somehow, peddlers never succeed in fencing off their medieval *odium* of being untrustworthy and a nuisance. With growing nationalist anxieties about vagabondage and migration in the nineteenth century, their continuous existence in the modernising Western European consumption landscape was eventually doomed. Instead, with the abolishment of guilds and their restrictions at the end of the eighteenth-century, food selling could be taken up more freely through individual and fixed butcher's shops, bakeries, grocers, fish-shops and so on. Food shops – and shops in general – multiplied, diversified and dispersed throughout growing nineteenth-century cities and suburbs. In Antwerp in 1838, for instance, there were fewer bakeries active than around 1567, at the height of the city's expansion in the early modern period. However, when population started rising again in the second half of the nineteenth-century in the wake of resurgent port activity and incipient industrialisation, the number of bakeries tripled in less than twenty years.

More fundamentally, food shops and grocers could become organised under the umbrella of retail chains and co-operatives from c.1870s onwards. These were new forms of retail organisation and management that tried to offer a large-scale solution to a large-scale problem, namely catering standardised and sometimes branded foodstuffs and groceries (including newly "industrialised" wares, like meat extracts, margarine, conserves and canned food) in a recognisable and trustworthy shopping environment. In Belgium, for instance, a family of local grocers became one of the pioneers of the European multiple food retailing by founding Delhaize Frères & Cie 'Le Lion' (Van den Eeckhout and Scholliers, 2011). Their principle was simple: multiplying their grocery stores in each city and town by using recognisable architecture, well-trained staff and an easy to spot logo of a lion. Local branches were supplied by the new steam boats and trains from a central depot, which allowed for economies of scale, and eventually cheaper prices for customers. In other countries as well, the combination of aggressively advertising quality at lower prices proved successful for many a long-lived retail chain like Sainsbury's, Maypole Dairies and Lipton's.

As with retail chains, co-operatives bought in large quantities or started to produce their own food themselves (like bread) to secure, first and foremost, standardisation, trustworthiness and quality at a time of rapidly changing and industrialising product markets (see the chapter of Hilson et al, this volume). As one of the first co-operative societies in England, the Rochdale Society of Equitable Pioneers, put it: they existed 'to secure un-adulterated food, goods of pure quality and guaranteed weight, at the regular trade prices' (cited in Stobart, 2008: 134). The secondary objective of co-operatives – and in this they clearly differed from the more commercially-oriented retail chains – was to improve the material conditions of the struggling working classes. Customers had to become members of the co-operative and any commercial profits were directed to programmes of social and moral improvement. Co-operatives thus became entangled in social politics and were powerful instruments in the hands of late nineteenth-century dominant political ideologies (Chatriot et al., 2004).

Increasing mass standardisation, advertising and branding of commodities, controlling the quality and prices of goods: all had a huge impact on the role of small shopkeepers. Whereas the eighteenth century had seen the rise to pre-eminence of shops in almost all branches of the retail industry, this shopping growth had taken place with only modest productivity gains (De Vries, 2008: 170). Households in the city and in the countryside made use of shops not because they reduced transaction costs – buying at shops was normally more expensive than goods offered at markets, at household auctions or from peddlers – but because they provided essential information and assistance to consumers adrift amidst a rapidly globalising and changing world of goods. In the nineteenth century, however, the crucial and long-running advisory function of small shopkeepers started to change, as did their social position and standing. The training,

Figure 22.2 Exterior of the multiple retailer Le Lion Delhaize Frères & Cie, Huidevettersstraat 49 Antwerp, Belgium, c.1905

(Courtesy of the Archives Delhaize Group, Brussels)

Figure 22.3 Interior of Le Lion Delhaize Frères & Cie, Huidevettersstraat 49 Antwerp, Belgium, c.1905 (Courtesy of the Archives Delhaize Group, Brussels)

knowledge and skills of keeping shop declined, since standardised, homogenised and institutionally protected and guaranteed product brands began to carry goods into the minds and homes of the customer, especially from the last quarter of the nineteenth century onwards (Van Damme, 2015: 100). If they wanted to survive in this competitive, post-guild-organised, nineteenth-century retail business, individual shopkeepers needed to attract attention and become much more efficient in doing business.

The result of these evolutions was most clearly noticeable in the rise of bigger shops that attached growing attention to style and service. Bigger glazed windows – a technique that became more manageable and affordable after 1840 – opulent interiors and well-behaved, well-dressed and well-spoken shop assistants made a great show to attract wealthy customers. In such premises, prices could be fixed, ticketed and advertised because customers were expected to pay upfront in cash. Although these practices were not unfamiliar in the eighteenth century, shop-keeping in the nineteenth century increasingly relied on cash sales to reduce prices and rapidly turnover stock; because the risk of outstanding credit debts was reduced, the shopkeeper aimed for smaller percentage returns, but higher turnover. Shipping in new goods, trends and fashions each year – and in bigger cities like London and Paris even each season – became the norm. Shopkeepers also began to use the newspaper advertisements more regularly and persuasively than before, calling attention to their address and existence and the alluring, new and wide variety of stock they had for sale (Stobart et al., 2007: 171–188; Lyna and Van Damme, 2009).

Enterprising and ambitious shopkeepers sought out new, fashionable locations of urban improvement, such as around the new market halls or within the new covered arcades and galleries that first appeared in capital cities like Paris and London at the end of the eighteenth century, and became the rage from Prague to Berlin and from The Hague to Madrid in the last quarter of the nineteenth century. Along the main street or newly built boulevards and shopping streets of Brussels and Berlin, nineteenth-century shops jockeyed for more space and for the most lavish and eye-catching *étalages* (Spiekermann, 2000).

Around these improved shopping streets one could find the first department stores in the last quarter of the nineteenth century, including Au Bon Marché, La Samaritaine, Harrods, Swan and Edgar (see Elvins's chapter in this volume). Far from being revolutionary, department stores grew organically out of fashionable and large textile shops or bazaars, although they changed the game completely by being bigger, more lavishly decorated and architecturally astonishing and innovating, introducing, for instance, escalators and elevators at the turn of the century (Crossick and Jaumain, 1999: 1–45). The world of the department store was aimed at bringing in many branches of business within huge and impressive premises. Its intention was to impress its mainly middle and upper-class visitors with a dazzling "dream world" of goods and fashions: a high-charged commercial, yet luxurious atmosphere that was heavily commented upon for inciting frenzy and fatigues with the feeble-hearted, usually stereotyped as women. In reality, the "shopping machines" as described by Emile Zola, H.G. Wells and other Victorian commentators, were top-heavy, costly and not infrequently suffered from bankruptcies. The most successful and long-lived of their kind soon realised that cutting costs and aiming at a less wealthy clientele was the way forward. Especially from the beginning of the twentieth century, department stores started offering goods in more diverse price ranges to attract mass audiences, a trend which continued and crystallised further in the economically precarious Interbellum with the rise of discount retail chains, penny bazaars and dime stores.

The most significant change, however, had again taken place in the minds and behaviour of the shoppers themselves. With gradually improving living standards and rising wages from c.1870 onwards – the precise date varying from country to country – the old, elitist leisure pursuit of shopping was transformed into an altogether more democratic, recreational pastime for the masses. The character and meaning of shopping as urban habitus was once more transformed in the course of the nineteenth century, with its dated stress on respectability and politeness giving away to an altogether more brash commercialism and unapologetically materialism. This was the world that Karl Marx famously despised in *Das Kapital* for being obsessed with "commodity fetishism": a society fixated with the aesthetic and pleasurable characteristics of goods and alienated from moral and socio-ecological considerations like labour-relations, ecological costs, etc. In the rising Fordist mode of production at the start of the twentieth century, spending wages on a rapidly expanding material output became in a sense more ethical as saving for hard times. Deficit spending, institutionalised in society by the growing popularity of instalment credit and in the Interbellum by Keynesian welfare policies, became the new dogma of Western societies.

In retrospect, much of the late nineteenth century and Interbellum attitude to the pleasures of spending and shopping was crucial in transforming the European retail landscape into one of quintessentially mass consumption. The Cold War climate after WWII was not likely to alter such materialistic mentality (Jessen and Langer, 2012; Trentmann, 2016: 272–354). In a propagandistic display of capitalistic superiority, money needed to roll when people were going out and rising incomes needed to be spend on an ever-expanding consumer output. During the economic growth spurt of the 1950s and 1960s, this newly acquired affluence in Western European countries was not to be questioned; rather, it should be wholeheartedly endorsed and promoted by the nascent welfare states. The coming of this age of mass consumerism was symbolised on the retail scene by the arrival of American-style big-box supermarkets (Lescent-Giles, 2005: 188–211). These were architecturally uninspiring buildings, both outside and inside; their real miracle was the way in which they stocked, apparently effortlessly, an ever-growing plethora of products in a maze-like ordering of abundance. Within supermarkets customers learned not to ask questions and not to be served, but to embrace the freedom of self-choosing, self-assessing and self-servicing their preferred product brands in individualised shopping trollies. The age-old contact with the retailer was normally only to be reserved for cashing-out, but even that moment of interaction began to be replaced from the 1970s onwards by systems of electronic, and eventually computerised checking-out and self-payment. By pioneering automation and information technologies, successfully managing increasingly global and complex logistic-chains, and collecting a mass of data on consumer behaviour, supermarkets could stock their shelves in spectacularly cost-efficient ways that initiated further price declines. As a result, powerful retail consortia and supermarket chains like Tesco in the UK, Carrefour in France and Ahold in the Netherlands started dominating the overall distribution system, squeezing out or absorbing smaller retailers and neighbourhood grocers in cities and suburbs alike. In 2000, for instance, more than 70% of all food sales in Germany, Austria and Belgium were handled by up to five big supermarket companies (Lescent-Giles, 2005: 207).

Supermarkets, in combination with an increased personal mobility born of growing car ownership, changed post-WWII shopping in other ways. Physically and geographically speaking, supermarkets created a world in which shopping and dwelling became separated from each other, with supermarkets – and later the even bigger hypermarkets and shopping centres and shopping villages – increasingly being erected in no-man's-land at the outskirts or even outside cities and towns; only reachable by motorised transport. Retail sprawl was accelerated in the 1960s and 1970s by suburban consumer demand, concomitant growth ambitions of investors to build bigger and bigger retail spaces, and local politicians wanting to boost employment in their municipalities. The arrival of all sorts of retail parks, constructed alongside high-tech hubs of production, and conveniently situated near highway and motor exists, provided late twentieth-century buyers with an unrivalled abundance of car park space and opportunities for single-purpose shopping trips. Whereas before, provisioning had been part of an almost daily work-schedule, families now economised on shopping trips by overloading their cars and newly arrived household fridges and freezers with all that supermarkets could offer. Thus, retail decentralisation in Western Europe pushed consumers in ever larger herds to peripheral, off-centre located mega-stores, which also started selling furniture, electronics, hardware and so on.

The effects of these centripetal evolutions on the old inner-city cores of Western Europe were varied and depended largely on the preventive actions taken by national governments (Davies, 1995; Guy, 1998: 953–979). In Belgium and France, for instance, socio-economic restrictions to protect urban and suburban small-scale retailing proved eventually ineffective against retail sprawl. Germany, the Netherlands and to a lesser extent the UK adopted stricter urban planning policies to uphold much more successfully the historically grown shopping centrality of European cities and towns and the protection of open green spaces. In general, shopping in European cities and towns has suffered from retail decentralisation in the last fifty years, but not to such an extent that the historically grown liveability of cities and towns was as seriously threatened or hollowed-out as in the United States.

Within cities and towns, things were also changing. Large-scale destruction in WWII – as in Rotterdam or Dresden – gave modernist planners and retail developers ample scope for rebuilding the city centre in accordance with their aesthetics, ideals and principles. Even without wartime damage, retail modernisation and modern urban rebuilding became a rallying call in the 1950s and 1960s, from Sweden to England to Switzerland. Uniform and often all too clinical inner-city shopping malls and high streets were the result of this. In form and function this postwar rebuilding, ironically enough, transposed off-centre retail formats to the centre, but without the car convenience and ample retail space that an out-of-town location could provide. From the 1980s and 1990s onwards the deteriorating, but always picturesque historic core itself

Figure 22.4 Front cover of the Grand Bazar supermarket annual report 1957–1958, Antwerp, 1958. The skyscraper and car complement post-WWII shopping.

(Courtesy of Erfgoedbibliotheek Hendrik Conscience, Antwerpen)

was increasingly thought to have tourist value for visitors and shoppers. With urban heritage and rejuvenation becoming linked to economic policies attracting fresh investments and tourists and gentrified newcomers, luxurious and pedestrian friendly shopping precincts, leisure and cultural quarters were created. These consisted typically of a variety of shops, restaurants and cafés, with a mix of cultural and recreational amenities brought in. Shopping in the centre of Amsterdam, Barcelona or Milan had to equal a sort of recreational and experience-rich environment that no dull retail park or out-of-town shopping centre could hope to imitate. However, upscaling of historical city centres also had its downsides: with real estate prices skyrocketing all over Europe, small corner shops and residential functions gradually disappeared from the historic core altogether, which now increasingly concentrated the same exclusive and fashionable food and shopping outlets of the same big, international branches and retail conglomerates (from Apple to Zara). These evolutions again created a situation where shopping became detached from dwelling, with the city centre transforming into one giant, clean and video surveillanced consumer theme-park (Miles, 2010: 142–163).

Due to this growing spatial polarisation of the European retail landscape between a shopping centre and shopping periphery, all the residential neighbourhoods in between – and even smaller towns and villages – saw a decline in even the most basic retail functions. In certain less wealthy urban districts, empty shop-space was taken over by a very active, but also quite specific form of ethnic and migrant entrepreneurship (for example halal butchers, Turkish bakeries, Polish delis, oriental furniture stores) who equally began to claim their right to the European cities and towns from the 1970s onwards. But aging, middle-class consumers saw their habitual tobacconist, butcher or greengrocer succumb to the combined pressures of centralisation and peripheralisation of shopping.

For these older people – living in villages, small towns or retail-depleted urban neighbourhoods – it is still unclear if the new computer and Internet-driven modes of shopping will improve their personal access to goods. Internet shopping can in a sense be seen as a warped offspring of mail-order shopping that has been institutionalised in Europe since at least the end of the nineteenth-century. However, post or mail-order shopping never enjoyed the same sort of popularity that buying through the Internet now enjoys, especially with younger generations of European. Internet sales on websites like Amazon or eBay are growing at such a pace that the very existence of the physical act of going shopping is now openly being questioned. Research, however, indicates that the use of the Internet is often complementary and additional to the actual performance of going to shops and streets, markets and malls (Stobart, 2008: 232–235). In hindsight of more as 1,000 years of entanglement between places and shopping, such conclusion probably comes as no big surprise.

Conclusion

This chapter has argued how shopping, understood as meaningful public and spatial activity, flowered in medieval times as a direct result of fervent urbanisation and rapid economic development in the so-called "blue banana" of Europe. In Italy, France, the Low Countries and England, new market and shopping space was created to provision a growing, dense and socially diverse urban population. More fundamentally, shopping connected daily and weekly routines of commercial exchange and consumption to the social and cultural life of cities. Shopping, so to speak, became part and parcel of an urban habitus: a market-oriented lifestyle which became common and was increasingly also tolerated and refined within an urban milieu. Whereas the classic feudal forces of church and nobility were initially hesitant to embrace, such evolutions in what was still very much an agrarian world – and even tried to stop the tide by way of moral creed and sumptuary legislation – the new urban elites eventually appropriated and justified shopping as a civilised, renaissance pastime.

Within an expanding and globalising commercial economy, retail, shopping and consumption formed the structural backbone of many European towns and cities in the early modern period.

This was most evident in the court and capital cities which formed part of the much older, densely urbanised and economically areas of Europe. Thus, a clear urban hierarchy became recognisable with Atlantic ports and European court and capital cities having the most extended and multidimensional shopping infrastructure and consumption-based economy in the sixteenth and seventeenth centuries. From the eighteenth century onwards, increasing commercialisation of leisure time and leisure space, and growing and diversifying consumer demand in general, also changed smaller towns and even rural settlements. Village shops popped up everywhere and urban fashions became something to be acquainted with, whether living in a capital city or in the provinces.

Modern times again brought significant changes in the sense that shopping was transformed into an altogether more democratic and mass-oriented pursuit. The basic retail infrastructure showed strong continuities with the early modern period in both location and practices, but became increasingly geared towards cost- and time-efficiency. Economies of scale became important to respond to growing, standardised supply and increasing consumer demand. The social and cultural paradoxes that have arisen after WWII are related to the fact that, within the mass affluence of societies today, more people in Europe can consume more goods than ever before with increasing ease and convenience. Never before, however, has the alienation from the wider social and ecological consequences of shopping and market-oriented consumption been so great. Whereas throughout history, direct, physical contacts between buyers and sellers dominated shopping practices, the role of the retailer has gradually diminished and is now on the verge of entirely vanishing behind the pixels of an anonymous computer screen. Shopping has also become largely spatially divorced from dwelling, with cities and regions being divided in strict commercial and residential zones. Of course, many overlapping worlds continue to exist, testified, for instance, by the periodic popularity of neighbourhood and farmers' markets, and the rise of a multitude of ethnic shops in increasingly diversified Western European neighbourhoods and suburbs. Often, however, such local markets and shops are provisioned by the same dominant global commodity streams and powerful retail concerns that have a suffocating grip on distribution. The current global distribution system has become enormously cheap, efficient and convenient, but only the future can tell if what be seen as alienating retail and spatial organisation will be tenable in a time of worldwide urban change and reordering.

References

Alexander, N. and Akehurst, G. (1998), 'Introduction: The emergence of modern retailing, 1750–1950', *Business History*, 40, pp. 1–15.

Benson, J. and Shaw, G. (eds.) (1992), *The evolution of retail systems* (Leicester: Leicester University Press).

Berry, H. (2002), 'Polite consumption: Shopping in eighteenth-century England', *Transactions of the Royal Historical Society*, 12, pp. 375–395.

Blondé, B. and Ryckbosch, W. (2015), 'In splendid isolation: A comparative perspective on the historiographies of the material renaissance and the consumer revolution', *History of Retailing and Consumption*, 1 (2), pp. 105–124.

Blondé, B., Stabel, P., Stobart, J. and Van Damme, I. (eds.) (2006), *Buyers and sellers: Retail circuits and practices in medieval and early modern Europe* (Turnhout: Brepols).

Blondé, B. and Van Damme, I. (2007), 'The shop, the home, and the retail revolution. Antwerp, seventeenth-eighteenth centuries', *Citta e Storia*, 2 (2), pp. 335–350.

Blondé, B. and Van Damme I. (2010), 'Retail growth and consumer changes in a declining urban economy: Antwerp (1650–1750)', *Economic History Review*, 63 (3), pp. 638–663.

Blondé, B. and Van Damme, I. (2013), 'Early modern Europe: 1500–1800', in P. Clark (ed.), *The Oxford handbook of cities in world history* (Oxford: Oxford University Press) 240–257.

Blondé, B. and Van Damme, I. (2015), 'Beyond the retail revolution: Trends and patterns in 17th- and 18th-century antwerp retailing', in M. Belfanti (ed.) *Retail trade: Supply and demand in the formal and informal economy from the 13th to the 18th century* (Firenze: Firenze University Press) 219–239.

Borsay, P. and Furnée, J.H. (eds.) (2016), *Leisure cultures in urban Europe, c. 1700–1870: A transnational perspective* (Manchester: Manchester University Press).
Braudel, F. (1979), *Civilisation Matérielle, Economie et Capitalisme XVe–XVIIIe siècle*, 2: Les Jeux de l'Echange (Paris: Colin).
Britnell, R. (2009), *Markets, trade and economic development in England and Europe, 1050–1550* (London: Routledge).
Calabi, D. (2004), *The market and the city: Square, street and architecture in early modern Europe* (Aldershot: Ashgate).
Campbell, C. (1987), *The romantic ethic and the spirit of modern consumerism* (London: Wiley-Blackwell).
Carlin, M. (2007), 'Shops and shopping in the thirteenth century: Three texts', in L.D. Armstrong, I. Elbl and M.M. Elbl (eds.) *Money, markets and trade in late medieval Europe: Essays in honour of John H.A. Munro* (Leiden/Boston, MA: Brill), pp. 491–537.
Chatriot, A., Chessel, M.-E. and Hilton, M. (eds.) (2004), *Au nom du consommateur: Consommation et politique en Europe et aux Etats-Unis au XXé siècle* (Paris: Editions La Découverte).
Clark, G. (2007), *A farewell to alms: A brief economic history of the world* (Princeton, NJ: Princeton University Press).
Clark, P. (2013), 'Introduction', in P. Clark (ed.) *The Oxford handbook of cities in world history* (Oxford: Oxford University Press) 1–24.
Coquery, N. (2014), 'Shopping streets in eighteenth-century Paris: A landscape shaped by historical, economic and social forces', in J.H. Furnée and Clé Lesger (eds.) *The landscape of consumption: Shopping streets and cultures in Western Europe, 1600–1900* (Basingstoke: Palgrave Macmillan) 57–77.
Cox, N. and Dannehl, K. (2007), *Perceptions of retailing in early-modern England* (Aldershot: Ashgate).
Crossick, G. and Jaumain, S. (1999), 'The world of the department store: Distribution, culture and social change', in G. Crossick and S. Jaumain (eds.) *Cathedrals of consumption: The European department store, 1850–1939* (Aldershot: Ashgate) 1–45.
Davies, R.L. (ed.) (1995), *Retail planning policies in Western Europe* (London: Routledge).
De Vries, J. (2008), *The industrious revolution: Consumer behaviour and the household economy, 1650 to the present* (Cambridge: Cambridge University Press).
Devroey, J.-P., Wilkin, A. and Gautier, A. (2013), 'Agricultural production, distribution and consumption around the Noth Sea, 500–1000', in L. Van Molle and Y. Segers (eds.) *The agro-food market: Production, distribution and consumption* (Turnhout: Brepols) 13–65.
De Wilde, B. (2015), 'Expanding the retail revolution: Multiple guild membership in the southern low countries, 1600–1800', in M. Belfanti (ed.) *Retail trade: Supply and demand in the formal and informal economy from the 13th to the 18th century* (Firenze: Firenze University Press) 91–112.
Fava, A., Guardia, M. and Oyon, J.L. (2016), 'Barcelona food retailing and public markets, 1876–1936', *Urban History*, 43 (3), pp. 454–475.
Furnée, J.H. and Lesger, C. (2014), 'Shopping streets and cultures from a long-term and transnational perspective', in J.H. Furnée and C. Lesger (eds.) *The landscape of consumption: Shopping streets and cultures in Western Europe, 1600–1900* (Basingstoke: Palgrave Macmillan), 1–15.
Guerzoni, G. (1999), 'Liberalitas, magnificentia, splendor: The classic origins of Italian renaissance lifestyles', in N. De Marchi and C.D.W. Goodwin (eds.) *Economic engagements with art* (Durham, NC/London: Duke University Press) 332–378.
Guy, C.M. (1998), 'Controlling new retail spaces: The impress of planning policies in Western Europe', *Urban Studies*, 35, pp. 953–979.
Howell, M.C. (2010), *Commerce before capitalism in Europe, 1300–1600* (Cambridge: Cambridge University Press).
Jeffreys, J. (1954), *Retail trading in Britain, 1850–1950: A study of retailing with special reference to the development of co-operative, multiple shop and department store methods of trading* (Cambridge: Cambridge University Press).
Jessen, R. and Langer, L. (2012), 'Introduction: Transformations of retailing in Europe after 1945', in R. Jessen and L. Langer (eds.) *Transformations of retailing in Europe after 1945* (Farnham: Ashgate) 1–18.
Keene, D. (1985), *Survey of medieval Winchester* (Oxford: Clarendon Press).
Keene, D. (2006), 'Sites of desire: Shops, selds and wardrobes in London and other English cities, 1100–1550', in B. Blondé, P. Stabel, J. Stobart and I. Van Damme (eds.) *Buyers and sellers: Retail circuits and practices in medieval and early modern Europe* (Turnhout: Brepols) 125–153.
Kint, A. (2000), 'The ideology of commerce: Antwerp in the sixteenth century', in P. Stabel, B. Blondé and A. Greve (eds.) *International trade in the low countries (14th–16th Centuries): Merchants, organisation, infrastructure* (Leuven: Leuven University Press) 213–222.

Lescent-Giles, I. (2005), 'The rise of supermarkets in twentieth-century Britain and France', in C. Sarasua, P. Scholliers and L. Van Molle (eds.) *Land, shops and kitchens: Technology and the food chain in twentieth-century Europe* (Turnhout: Brepols) 188–211.

Lesger, C. (2011), 'Patterns of retail location and urban form in Amsterdam in the mid-eighteenth century', *Urban History*, 38 (1), pp. 24–47.

Lyna, D. and Van Damme, I. (2009), 'A strategy of seduction? The role of commercial advertisements in the eighteenth-century retailing business of antwerp', *Business History*, 51 (1), pp. 100–121.

Miles, S. (2010), *Spaces for consumption* (London: Sage).

Mitchell, I. (2014), *Tradition and innovation in English retailing, 1700–1850: Narratives of consumption* (Farnham: Ashgate).

Savary, J. (1675), *Le Parfait Négociant, ou Instruction Générale pour ce qui regarde le Commerce*, 2 Vol (Paris: Louis Billaine).

Spiekermann, U. (2000), 'Display windows and window display in German cities of the nineteenth century: Towards the history of a commercial breakthrough', in C. Wischermann and E. Shore (eds.) *Advertising and the European city: Historical perspectives* (Aldershot: Ashgate) 139–171.

Stabel, P. (2001), 'Markets in the cities of the late medieval low countries: Retail, commercial exchange and socio-cultural display', in S. Cavaciocchi (ed.) *Fiere e mercati nella integrazione delle economie europee, secc. XIII–XVIII* (Florence: Le Monnier) 797–817.

Stabel, P. (2007), 'Negotiating value: The ethics of market behaviour and price formation in the late medieval low countries', in M. Boone and M. Howell (eds.) *In but not of the market: Movable goods in the late medieval and early modern economy* (Brussels: Paleis der Academiën) 53–69.

Stobart, J. (2008), *Spend, spend, spend: A history of shopping* (Stroud: Tempus).

Stobart, J., Hann, A. and Morgan, V. (2007), *Spaces of consumption: Leisure and shopping in the English town, c. 1680–1830* (London: Routledge).

Toftgaard, J. (2016), 'Marketplaces and central spaces: Markets and the rise of competing spatial ideals in Danish city centres, c. 1850–1900', *Urban History*, 43 (3), pp. 372–390.

Trentmann, F. (2016), *Empire of things: How we became a world of consumers, from the fifteenth century to the twenty-first* (London: Allen Lane).

Van Damme, I. (2015), 'From a "knowledgeable" salesman towards a "recognizable" product? Questioning branding strategies before industrialization (Antwerp, Seventeenth to Nineteenth Centuries)', in B. De Munck and D. Lyna (eds.) *Concepts of value in European material culture, 1500–1900* (Aldershot: Ashgate) 75–102.

Van Damme, I. and Van Aert, L. (2014), 'Antwerp goes shopping! Continuity and change in retail space and shopping interactions from the sixteenth to the nineteenth century', in J.H. Furnée and Clé Lesger (eds.) *The landscape of consumption: Shopping streets and cultures in Western Europe, 1600–1900* (Basingstoke: Palgrave Macmillan) 78–103.

Van den Eeckhout, P. and Scholliers, P. (2011), 'The Belgian multiple grocer: Delhaize le Lion and its clientele, 1867–1914', *Essays in Economic and Business History*, 29, pp. 87–100.

Van den Heuvel, D. and Ogilvie, S. (2013), 'Retail development in the consumer revolution: The Netherlands, c. 1670–c. 1815', *Explorations in Economic History*, 50 (1), pp. 69–87.

Walsh, C. (2008), 'Shopping at first hand? Mistresses, servants and shopping for the household in early-modern England', in D. Hussey and M. Ponsonby (eds.) *Buying for the home: Shopping for the domestic from the seventeenth century to the present* (Aldershot: Ashgate) 13–26.

Walsh, C. (2014), 'Stalls, bulks, shops and long-term change in seventeenth- and eighteenth-century England', in J.J.H. Furnée and Clé Lesger (eds.) *The landscape of consumption: Shopping streets and cultures in Western Europe, 1600–1900* (Basingstoke: Palgrave Macmillan) 37–56.

Welch, E. (2005), *Shopping in the renaissance: Consumer cultures in Italy 1400–1600* (New Haven, CT/ London: Yale University Press).

Welch, C. (2006), 'The fairs of early modern Italy', in B. Blondé, P. Stabel, J. Stobart and I. Van Damme (eds.) *Buyers and sellers: Retail circuits and practices in medieval and early modern Europe* (Turnhout: Brepols) 31–50.

Weltevreden, J., Atzema, O. and Frenken, K. (2005), 'Evolution in city centre retailing: The case of Utrecht (1974–2003)', *International Journal of Retail & Distribution Management*, 33, pp. 824–841.

23

RETAILING IN RUSSIA AND EASTERN EUROPE

Marjorie L. Hilton

Scholars of retailing and consumerism in non-Western countries likely have encountered the skeptical question, "Did a consumer culture even *exist* there?" After all, the traditional narrative of the emergence of a retail industry and culture that privileges the consumer supposes a necessary historical link between capitalism and mass consumption, and presents the department store as the foundation. This conventional view holds that any proto-, quasi- or non-capitalist society cannot possibly qualify as a consumer society. Within this school of thought, the idea of socialist consumerism is especially absurd, because citizens of the formerly communist Eastern Europe are assumed to have consumed little indeed, besides the spectre of empty store shelves and long queues for shoddy, unfashionable goods. But this narrow definition excludes the rich history of buying, selling and consuming in socialist countries, and more recently historians of the region have complicated our understanding of how societies of all kinds are shaped by these seemingly prosaic activities. Every society engages in trade and all individuals consume and, as they do, political structures and social relationships are established, norms and values constructed, and group and individual identities formed. If we think of the retail sector as a cultural system, not merely governed by ideology or economic laws, with the power to act as both agent and medium of social organisation and cultural training, the study of retailing and shopping can reveal the patterns of people's everyday lives and the societies in which they lived, regardless of ideological bent.

As more scholars have explored the history of retailing and consumption in Eastern Europe, they have also challenged the dominant view of life in communist societies. For decades, research was influenced by the totalitarian model, a top-down approach developed during the early Cold War, which assumed that political rhetoric and state policies primarily defined socialism in practice. Reliance on the totalitarian model contributed to a perception of citizens as subjected to the singular will of the communist party-state, unable to resist leaders' determination to control their every move and thought. More current research has shown that, although the communist state's one-party system, censorship, and planned economy certainly imposed constraints and hardships on citizens, the centralised management of retailing and consumption was as significant to the survival of communism in Eastern Europe, as to its collapse (Reid, 2002; Crowley and Reid, 2010; Stitziel, 2008). It has become clear that as citizen-consumers struggled to cope with the material realities of daily life, they re-interpreted, appropriated or rejected the state's ideological claims and frequently circumvented laws or forced state officials to make concessions. Thus, state and society shaped each other. On one hand, the reinvention of the retail economy provided communist officials a means of "selling socialism" to the masses, with the goal of material progress, and fostering unity, especially in multi-ethnic countries (Hilton, 2012, p. 10; Patterson, 2011, p. xvii). On the other hand, promises of a higher standard of living raised and later frustrated consumers' expectations when the policies officials pursued failed to deliver the goods (Chernyshova, 2013, pp. 202–203; Patterson, 2011, p. 17). Given these stakes, any attempt to understand Eastern European communism would be incomplete without a consideration of the social, political and cultural roles played by retailers and consumers.

Origins of the retail industry, 1750–1914

The development of the retail industry in Russia and Eastern Europe largely mirrored trends that unfolded in Western Europe and North America, at least prior to World War I. Permanent retail shops date to at least medieval times. For example, in cities and towns of the Russian Empire, small open-ended shops called *lavkas* carried a limited inventory of similar kinds of goods. Affluent urban residents could also order custom-made clothing, shoes, boots and hats from artisans' workshops. Outside of cities and towns, rural dwellers produced most of the things they consumed, only travelling to markets for things they could not make or occasionally purchasing novelty goods or small luxuries from travelling peddlers. In such rural settings, a *lavka* operated like a general store, stocking a wide assortment of goods. Whether urban or rural, shopkeepers usually displayed merchandise haphazardly, seldom devising elaborate displays or advertising in newspapers. Instead they "called" to passers-by, pressing them to enter their shops, and haggled with them over prices (Hilton, 2012, pp. 14–30; Ruane, 2009, pp. 115–138; Patterson, 2011, pp. 49–51).

By the late eighteenth century, larger, well-appointed stores with more formal operating procedures opened to sell stylish clothing, furs, toiletries, crystal, jewellery and specialty items to the emerging prosperous classes. These Eastern European variants of the *magasin* appeared first in Russia in the fashionable quarters of Moscow and St Petersburg, and initially were operated by German, French and Jewish merchants. Later, leading Russian companies, including Perlov tea merchants, Sorokoumovskii furriers and Abrikosov confectioners opened *magasins* alongside their non-Russian colleagues. To be sure, Eastern Europe had fewer *magasins* than Western Europe, due to the smaller number of urban residents and relatively smaller amount of business investment; however, over time dozens of stylish boutiques and haberdashers lined the central streets of Warsaw, Kiev, Odessa and other major cities (Ruane, 2009, p. 119; Hilton, 2012, p. 20).

As shopping districts emerged, some *magasin* owners clustered their stores under one roof, forming arcades. The idea to house several shops within one structure was not an entirely novel concept, though. In Ottoman South-Eastern Europe, *bezistans*, covered retail venues made of stone with vaulted ceilings and domes, had been built in market squares since the mid-sixteenth century (Sarajevo Museum, 2016). Russia's "rows" existed centuries before the advent of the arcade. St Petersburg's *Gostinyi dvor* dated to 1785 and Moscow's Upper Trading Rows on Red Square had served as the city's major commercial site since the reign of Ivan the Terrible (Bogdanov, 1988; Hilton, 2012, p. 34; Razmadze, 1893). Over time, these forerunners of the arcade transformed into the reinforced steel and glass structures admired throughout Europe in the mid- to late nineteenth century. By the late nineteenth century, department stores arrived in Eastern Europe's major cities. Moscow's Muir & Mirrielees began as a haberdashery and grew into a department store by 1885 (Pitcher, 1994). In Germany, the Jewish Wertheim family opened a haberdashery in 1875, later expanding the sales floor to make room for elaborate merchandise displays and adopting policies of cash payment, fixed prices and exchange and return privileges. Several others, including Karstadt and *Kaufhaus des Westens* opened later and did a thriving business (Ladwig-Winters, 2000, pp. 1–2). In 1894, two Czech businessmen opened Kastner & Öhler, the first department store in the Austro-Hungarian Empire (Kastner & Öhler, 2016). Jabłkowski Brothers operated Poland's largest department store in Warsaw and later opened one in Vilno (Dom Towarawy Bracia Jabłkowscy, 2015). Many department stores caused a sensation when they opened and some became urban landmarks, as famous for their architecture and attractions as merchandise. Budapest's Paris, for example, featured a rooftop café, which was converted into a skating rink in the winter (Hungarian Architecture, 2016). The rebuilding of Muir & Mirrielees in 1908, following a fire, as an elaborate three-story edifice on Theatre Square reflected its pretension as the "The Leading Department Store in Russia" (Hilton, 2012, p. 86).

As conspicuous symbols of a nascent urban mass culture that promoted leisure, materialism, individuality and social mobility, department stores provoked debate. Middle-class liberal thinkers tended to extol the department store as a rational, efficient business model and argued that department stores could educate customers in good taste, thereby elevating the population's aesthetic sensibilities and minimising the potential for poor purchasing decisions. Some, including Paul Wöhre, author of a book on Wertheim, applauded the mixing of social classes on sales floors, where "all were equal before the cash register" (Breckman, 1991, p. 490). Mikhail Sobolev, a Russian political economist, made similar arguments (Sobolev, 1900). Conservative social commentators, who viewed the department store as a foreign import and a threat to tradition, a stable social order and national identity, however, argued that department stores drove small shopkeepers out of business and warned that the desire to emulate the lifestyle of wealthy elites would financially and morally ruin the working class. In fact, despite the size and high-profile of department stores, small retailers and specialty shops continued to account for more than 80% of total retail sales well into the twentieth century (Ladwig-Winters, 2000, p. 6). Social critics also worried about the department store's effect on women, whom they deemed most vulnerable to its perils and temptations (Breckman, 1991, pp. 495–496, Hilton, 2012, pp. 124–131; Felski, 1995). Anti-Semitism also manifested itself in these debates. Christian German merchants perceived in the department store an instrument of Jewish domination, and they defamed Wertheim and others as "bazaars" and hazardous workplaces. The persistence of such criticism eventually prompted Prussia and other German states in 1900 to impose a tax on department stores whose annual sales exceeded 400,000 marks. *Kaufhaeusers*, whose owners were mostly non-Jewish, were exempted, even though some had an even higher sales volume (Ladwig-Winters, 2000, p. 3) In the Russian Empire, the charter of the Upper Rows Trading Company forbade Jews to purchase shares in the company (Hilton, 2012, p. 55).

Despite concerns, Eastern Europe's retail sectors developed customs, idioms and rituals that gave rise to a distinctive culture of exchange. One of the most striking elements of Russia's retail culture was the blending of commerce, Orthodoxy and tsarism. Icons hung inside stores and on the front of market stalls and booths. Orthodox merchants set their businesses by the Church calendar, traditionally ending the retail year during Easter week and undertaking new business ventures on auspicious religious dates. Even after the Upper Rows reopened and traditional ways of buying and selling were disallowed, religion remained ensconced, in the form of four large icons embedded over the arcade's main entrances. Any milestone that a firm reached – the beginning of construction of a new building or an anniversary – was celebrated with a formal ceremonial blessing. Even non-Orthodox Christian merchants, for example, the French Catholic owners of A. Ralle & Company and Protestant heirs of Muir & Mirrielees, staged ceremonial blessings. Moreover, as time went on, the ritual became more elaborate and publicised in newspapers, thus making the connection more visible. In addition, the retail trade was also deeply intertwined with the Russian state, and the public display of the affiliation was common. Some merchants, including Smirnov & Sons, eagerly sought and won the title "Purveyor to the Court of His Imperial Majesty", an honor that essentially served as a royal endorsement and entitled a firm to display the Romanov seal on storefronts and product packages and in ads. Rather than subjugating national identity through Westernisation and secularisation, Russia's leading retail merchants immersed their firms in religion and politics, creating a uniquely Russian entity (Hilton, 2012, pp. 87–91; West, 2011, pp. 63–71).

War, revolution, and the invention of socialist retailing, 1914–21

With the start of World War I in 1914, trade relationships and commercial networks were disrupted. Russia's "continuum of crisis" (Holquist, 2002, pp. 2–3), which began with the outbreak of war, followed by two revolutions in 1917 and a civil war lasting until 1921, which wrecked the economy and drastically altered retailing and patterns of consumption. As supplying and equipping the army took priority in Russia, consumer goods of all kinds disappeared from stores and, as war wore on, many retail businesses closed. Consumers adapted through panic buying, speculation, queueing and the formation of co-operatives. When rumours of profiteering circulated and inflation spiralled, stores sometimes became sites of conflict, rioting and looting (Alpern Engel, 1997). The tsarist state also engaged in extraordinary measures during the war, confiscating and nationalising businesses owned by German and Austrian nationals, deemed "enemy subjects", and searching and closing stores owned by other foreigners such as the American company Singer. Some expropriations were carried out with the help of crowds, and sometimes they attacked stores with foreign-sounding names, including Kunst & Al'bers, owned by two German-Russian subjects (Lohr, 2003, pp. 77–81). The state also targeted Jewish-owned businesses, including an Odessa firm categorised as a "foreign Jewish firm" (Hilton, 2012, p. 178). In all, more than 1,000 businesses, mostly small- and medium-sized commercial firms, voluntarily closed, changed ownership or were forcibly liquidated (Lohr, 2003, p. 67).

Marxists had based the idea of a centralised, planned economy on an industrial base, giving scant attention to retail distribution or consumption. Yet, since communism's ultimate goal was the redistribution of wealth and resources, the retailing of consumer goods could not remain in private hands. The new communist government, which took power in October 1917, began with the seizure of the buildings, merchandise and equipment of the largest private firms, including retailers like Muir & Mirrielees. In November 1918, private trade was abolished and shortly thereafter the Upper Trading Rows were closed. The takeover of prominent, successful retail premises aimed to destroy the old power structure, and writers for the state newspaper depicted these acts as the joyful overthrow of a bourgeois, feminine realm and installation of a collective enterprise where working-class men engaged in the task of rebuilding the economy on behalf of the previously disenfranchised (Hilton, 2012, pp. 84–85).

Civil war broke out in 1918, bringing more store closings and expropriations, as well as famine, extreme shortages, class-based rationing and widespread deprivation. The population also declined, due to the emigration of many wealthy merchants and millions of deaths from war and famine, and urban dwellers fled to the countryside. As a result, most retail businesses ceased to exist, and norms of buying and selling were rendered obsolete. Consumers learned to obtain scarce goods through unconventional or illegal means and to navigate or circumvent new, state-imposed commercial regulations and protocols. Buying on the black market or from "bagmen", men or women who went to the countryside to procure goods and returned to the city to sell them, became most people's primary source for bread, food and manufactured goods, many stolen from state inventories. Despite frequent raids and arrests, black-market trade persisted throughout the civil war. Citizens also relied on acquaintances with connections, sold their own personal items, and queued in front of stores hours before they opened. Over time, these new tactics became normalised and integral parts of a Soviet citizen's daily life (Ball, 1987, pp. 33–34, 110–118; Hessler, 2004, pp. 49–50).

As the civil war wound down in early 1921, V.I. Lenin announced the Party's New Economic Policy (NEP), which sought to restore the economy by allowing limited private manufacturing and retailing, alongside state-owned businesses, and permitting peasants to sell surplus produce at markets. Later that year, state and municipal authorities organised state-run manufacturing and retailing enterprises. Mossel'prom sold foodstuffs via an extensive and diverse network of outlets, including stores, kiosks and mail-order, as well as through vending machines and street vendors. At the same time, the state resumed its nationalisation campaign and began to reorganise, rename, and operate the largest, most successful pre-revolutionary firms. And in December 1921, the Council of People's Commissars established the State Department Store (GUM) and located it in the arcade of the Upper Trading Rows. Mostorg, under local party authority, opened a department store in the Muir & Mirrielees store. Similar processes were underway in Ukraine, where the state-owned firm Larek opened shops in Kiev, Odessa and other cities. Private individuals were initially reluctant to start businesses, but after further restrictions were lifted in 1922, more private stores and restaurants opened, many run by former merchants or shop assistants (Ball, 1987, pp. 20–24, 90–91; Hilton, 2012, pp. 198–199).

GUM, founded as a model retail enterprise, became the centrepiece of the communist state's plan to create a socialist retail economy and working-class culture of consumption. Presenting itself as a universal provider with "Everything for Everybody", GUM operated dozens of stores of varying sizes, most located in cities, including Moscow and St. Petersburg and their suburbs, Saratov, and Ekaterinburg. Some stores opened in the provinces, though most were small and poorly stocked. The flagship store on Red Square led the campaign to "retail the revolution", in other words, to carry out economic struggle against private enterprise, democratise consumption and promote values, norms and behaviours compatible with a modern socialist society. In essence, GUM was intended to achieve nothing less than economic, social and cultural transformation (Hilton, 2012, pp. 195–198, 209–211).

The concept of socialist retailing was fraught with ideological and practical complexities, however. The communist goal of wealth redistribution implied bringing the comforts and delights of the modern world to those previously denied them. Moreover, mass consumption was increasingly viewed as an index of economic and socio-cultural progress. Because communism positioned itself as an alternative to capitalism, fulfilling consumers' needs and wants was essential, even though encouraging the accumulation of material possessions posed a threat to the ultimate goal of equality. This tension between material progress and the ideal of social egalitarianism divided communists, and meant that policies towards retailing and consumption were ambiguous and vacillated. Debates ensued over rational norms of consumption: what exactly did humans need, and how should they consume in order to create an appropriately socialist life? State commercial officials also considered how goods should be bought and sold (Hilton, 2012; Merkel, 2008; Merkel, 2010; Bren and Neuburger, 2012; Crowley and Reid, 2010). Far from merely imitating capitalist institutions or simply adding socialist slogans to a capitalist mix, they reinvented retailing, developing new operating principles and procedures that operated according to their own logic. New terms signified the changed conditions. "Workers of the counter" no longer romanced "shoppers" with affable chitchat or drew them into haggling matches. Fixed prices became the law, and workers "issued" goods to "consumers" or "satisfied" their requests. A retail transaction was to be a professional, straightforward exchange, without any pretense of

Figure 23.1 GUM department store in Russia. Citation. Recent photo of the former Upper Trading Rows, Moscow. The arcade, initially built in the 1880s–90s, was nationalised after the 1917 revolution and renamed GUM (The State Department Store). It is no longer a state-run enterprise and is now called The Main Department Store.

Source: www.pexels.com

superiority or grovelling. The three-queue system, which required customers to wait in three separate lines in order to make a purchase, became standard protocol. Finally, the ceremonial blessing and other religious observances, which had pervaded the pre-1917 retail sphere, disappeared from public life. The establishment of Lenin corners inside state stores may have taken their place, though they do not seem to have been widely publicised. Together, changes in sales terminology, procedure and devotional rituals highlighted the shift from a retail culture reliant on personality, persuasion and private profit to one based on collective rights, codified procedures intended to ensure equal treatment, and a mediating state (Hilton, 2012, pp. 228–240).

State retailing was not an easy sell, however. Although the state succeeded in reducing the private sector's share of total retail sales from 78% in 1922–23, to 42% in 1924–25, to 37% in 1926–27, the gain was achieved largely through coercive measures and discriminatory tax policies rather than the merits of its network of stores (Nove, 1992, p. 99; Ball, 1987, pp. 68–82). State retailers often found themselves outmanoeuvred by more savvy, resourceful private traders or their bottom lines undermined by inexperienced or corrupt officials and employees. Despite images of GUM as a first-rate retailer with an extensive reach, retailing remained largely in the hands of street venders and individuals who sold things from stalls, kiosks or tables (Ball, 1987, pp. 109–121; Hessler, 2004, p. 105). GUM and other state enterprises also suffered from chronic underfunding, a situation that led to descriptions of many of its stores as dirty, "depressing", understocked and lacking the most popular goods, and its sales workers as inept, rude and dishonest. Not surprisingly then, even those customers served by GUM accused the firm of failing to deliver on its promises. Complaints of rudeness, pricing irregularities, favouritism and arbitrary, inefficient and bureaucratic procedures, as well as shortages, poor selection and shoddy merchandise, were common (Hilton, 2012, p. 251, 260).

After Josef Stalin consolidated power in the late 1920s, a tax on "superprofits" drove most remaining private companies out of business and GUM was closed (Ball, 1987, pp. 72–79; Hessler, 2004, pp. 145–147). All private trade was not prohibited, however. The brutal collectivisation drive and strict grain requisitions led to the breakdown of agriculture and famine. To manage this crisis, the state imposed in 1931 a discriminatory system of rationing, which assigned larger rations to educated specialists, state and party officials and workers in vital industries and denied ration cards to peasant producers, who made up 80% of the population. A two-tiered distribution network further entrenched hierarchy and privilege. "Open" shops sold basic goods to anyone with the currency to buy them, while "closed" stores and cafeterias served individuals entitled to scarce and luxury goods. As a concession, in 1932, the state legalised outdoor markets, renaming them "collective-farm markets" for the sale of peasant produce and artisanal goods. These markets essentially replaced small private retail stores and shops and they thrived in the following decades, as consumers spent from one-third to one-half of their earnings there (Hessler, 2004, pp. 185–193; Hessler, 1998, pp. 521–522). Thus, despite the ideological contradictions markets presented to the goal of a centralised, state-run, industrialised economy, the production and retailing of agricultural and other consumer goods remained primarily in the hands of small-scale operators. Likewise, unequal access remained a feature of the retail economy, even though it undermined the ideal of equality and produced resentment.

At the same time, the state launched another campaign to establish "cultured trade". Torgsin stores, originally founded in the late 1920s to serve foreigners, opened showcase stores in Moscow and Leningrad that stocked the best Soviet-made products and imports. Soon, Torgsin expanded to 1,500 locations across the USSR and began to sell ordinary foodstuffs like bread to anyone with foreign currency, gold, diamonds, antiques or another valuable exchange medium. Stores outside of the capitals were small, dirty and lacking any exemplary qualities, and devised to drain citizens of personal assets, which the state needed to buy industrial equipment (Osokina, 1999; Hessler, 2004, pp. 200–201). New model department stores also appeared. Leningrad's Dom Kooperatsii and Moscow's Central Department Store (TsUM), opened in 1933 in the best pre-1917 buildings, the latter in the refurbished former Muir & Mirrielees. Later, smaller, less-well stocked TsUM outlets opened in other cities, and plans were drawn up to open branches in the non-Russian republics (Hessler, 2004, p. 202). Stores designated as flagships operated according to a special set of rules. Instead of receiving all of its merchandise from central distribution, Moscow's TsUM, for example, had its own children's clothing factory and fashion atelier, which created custom-made dresses, tailored suits, hats, shoes and accessories in small quantities. Most large department stores in cities, as well as factories and trusts, also operated in-house fashion workshops and clothing factories (Gronow, 2003, pp. 87–97, 101–103). TsUM strived to offer its clientele a cultured shopping experience. Sales employees were instructed to address shoppers in courteous tones and to assist them with product information and fashion advice. Incentives were awarded to employees who achieved heroic levels of sales, delivered high-quality customer service or created innovative merchandise displays. Commercial officials also sought to upgrade model stores and stay current with contemporary trends. In the 1930s, delegations travelled to London and Berlin and to Macy's in New York to observe store layout, merchandise displays and customer service. Upon their return, TsUM official introduced home delivery and other new customer services (Hessler, 2004, pp. 205–207). Gender played a role in this campaign for cultured trade. Women comprised more than half of sales workers in urban areas by 1939 because officials assumed they inherently possessed domestic skills and traits like kindness and consideration that would advance cultured selling (Randall, 2008, pp. 74–81, 91–97).

These premier retailers conveyed the message that Soviet citizens could enjoy "common luxuries", though this exclusive world of goods was enabled by gross inequality, exploitation and violence. The state privileged a new urban elite, showering them with higher salaries, extra rations, furnished apartments, vacations at health spas, dachas and other material rewards, while denying access and even food to the majority of the population. While TsUM's atelier provided elite urban customers with the latest fashions adapted from French and British magazines and Gastronom and Bakaleia sold them champagne, chocolate truffles and ice cream, most Soviet citizens shopped in small, poorly equipped stores that offered little selection and few services. Things were worse in the countryside, where co-ops selling staple goods and tools were often the only retail outlets. Peasants had to travel to towns and cities to buy other things. In the worst years of the famine, when millions died of starvation and disease, many stores lacked bread, potatoes and vodka, though efforts to mass-produce cheap luxury goods proceeded apace. Even in better years, workers spent most of their earnings on necessities, not items for leisure or pleasure, except perhaps an occasional box of candies. For many peasants, even simple luxuries remained out of reach (Gronow, 2003, pp. 25, 33, 100–103; Hessler, 2004, p. 209). Markets developed spontaneously to meet the majority of the population's needs. Some, such as collective-farm markets, had been sanctioned by the state. Others, like the black market, were not. Non-sanctioned outlets rectified some of the flaws of the centralised economy by supplying most consumers with goods and, thus, were grudgingly tolerated by authorities, but they deprived the state of revenues and resources (Hessler, 1998, pp. 521–522).

Elsewhere in Eastern Europe in the 1920s and '30s, conservatives and nationalists were also remaking the retail economy based on rhetoric and policies that advantaged some citizens, at the expense of others. After the National Socialists came to power in Germany in 1933, Jewish-owned department stores were subjected to policies of Germanisation, which meant non-Jewish ownership, non-Jewish employees and a Germanised name. The Party assigned Nazi representatives to each department store to ensure that no Jews were employed and launched a boycott campaign against department stores. The Ministry of Finance issued marriage loans, in the form of purchase coupons, to German couples, stipulating that they could not be used at Jewish-owned businesses or at any *warenhaeuser*, regardless of owner. Despite these measures, except for the year 1933, Wertheim maintained its sales volume. In Berlin, sales even rose. The transfer of Jewish-owned department stores to German hands began in 1934, when Georg and Martin Tietz were forced to resign and sell their shares in Hermann Tietz Company, which was renamed Hertie. Jewish shareholders were eventually forced to sell their shares at below-market value, Jewish managers and employees dismissed, and party members took over management of the firm. Wertheim and Karstadt, Germany's largest retailer, underwent the same process (Ladwig-Winters, 2000). After Austria's annexation in 1938, the owners of Kastner & Öhler were similarly dispossessed, and their firm renamed Alpenlandkaufhaus (Kastner and Öhler, 2016).

In some other countries, the retail sector continued to expand and even thrive. In March 1939, even as Germans began to occupy Czechoslovakia, White Swan, Prague's only full-assortment department store, opened. At the time, it was the largest glass-covered space in central Europe and the only building in Prague with an interior escalator. The store offered many customer amenities, including a public terrace and child care, as well as a terrace where employees could spend their lunch break (Bílá labuť). Soon, this vitality would be interrupted, and the entire region would undergo drastic and devastating change.

War and postwar reconstruction, 1945–53

The German invasion and occupation wrought unprecedented and widespread devastation throughout Eastern Europe. Trade relationships were disrupted and transportation and commercial networks destroyed, ushering in extreme shortages and rationing. In Soviet territory, especially Belarus, Ukraine, Russia and the Baltics, a "freewheeling" expansion of private trade occurred. Throngs of private individuals sold goods obtained through various, often illegal means, at markets and even inside state stores such as TsUM, where they competed with sales workers for customers. In many places, citizens resorted to bartering or sold whatever they could to purchase basic goods like milk. Most also engaged in "survivalist violations of the law", stealing petty amounts from the workplace or travelling to the countryside to buy food to resell (Judt, 2005, pp. 15–17; Hessler, 1998, pp. 522–525; Hessler, 2004, pp. 280–286). By war's end in 1945, the production of consumer goods in the USSR had shrunk to 59% of the prewar level and 85% of retail stores in the occupied territories had been destroyed (Hessler, 1998, p. 527, 522). Many stores outside of the USSR had also been destroyed, including Berlin's former Wertheim and Hermann Tietz and Warsaw's Jabłkowski Brothers. People throughout Eastern Europe faced hunger, homelessness and a lack of heating, fuel and other basic necessities. As inflation skyrocketed, many currencies had collapsed. Occupying regimes, seeking to avoid the postwar deprivation and desperation that had led millions throughout the region to support extremist politics in the 1930s, tried, above all, to control prices (Landsman, 2005, p. 16; Pence, 2008, p. 289).

When communist states were being established throughout the region in the late 1940s, their new leaders understood that to win widespread support, they would have to end privation and reconstruct societies. As the Stalinist model of economic transformation was either imposed or adopted, communist leaders established central economic organs to carry out rapid industrialisation and convert privately owned businesses, farms, and resources into state-owned property. Levels of development varied throughout the region, but, generally speaking, the impact was dramatic. In Poland, for example, the number of private retailers fell from 131,218 in 1947 to 7,567 in 1955 (Crowley, 2000, p. 32). To adequately provision the population, in 1947, the Soviet Military Administration in Germany's Soviet zone introduced Soviet-style "closed distribution", which allowed workers in important industries and offices to buy rationed foods and other consumer goods in company stores and cafeterias. The following June, officials in the German western zones enacted currency reform and, seemingly overnight, all kinds of food products and consumer goods appeared in previously empty shop windows. Even though wage freezes and the reduction of people's savings, due to currency reform, prevented most from buying much, the image of prosperity and abundance set an upbeat tone. (Landsman, 2005, pp. 32, 38–39) To counter the West's currency reform and provide a more effective means of distribution, in October 1948, the German Economic Commission in East Germany formed *Handelsorganisation* (HO), a state-run commercial enterprise modelled on the USSR's model ventures and devised to help establish socialism. HO stores initially sold non-rationed goods like coffee, tea, chocolate, liqueurs, lingerie, cameras and radios. Rationed goods, for example, meat, eggs, butter, milk and cheese, continued to be sold at private stores and co-ops. Prices on HO merchandise were set just below black market prices to discourage consumers from buying goods through unofficial channels and to prevent privateers from buying and reselling HO merchandise. According to this strategy, private retailing would eventually be eliminated and centralised state retailing would triumph (Pence, 1999, pp. 498, 501; Landsman, 2005, pp. 57–58).

Publicised images of "socialist consumption", intended to signal the move from austerity, accompanied the opening of the first HO in East Berlin in 1948. According to a newspaper report, police were called to control the crowd of thousands impatiently waiting for the doors to open, and once inside shoppers, grateful for the state's protection from black marketeers, snapped up shoes, sweaters, stockings, socks and other goods, despite high prices (Pence, 1999, pp. 497–500). This idealised story, which neglected to mention the store's disorganisation and lack of bright lighting, suggests that officials were aware of the West's "shop-window politics" and eager to make a good impression. In reality, most workers could not afford to buy many things, though some expressed support for HO's campaign against the black market and confidence that profits would fund reconstruction and life would gradually improve. Others complained that prices were too high, while some doubted that HO would be able to combat the black market (Pence, 1999, pp. 499–500). By the end of its first year, HO seemed poised to deliver on its promises. The chain had overfulfilled its sales plan and increased the number of its retail stores, restaurants, cafes and hotels to 343. By March 1951, that number grew to 2,294 (Landsman, 2005, p. 69). However, HO did not receive the level of funding needed to satisfy consumer demands and turn stores into showcases of consumption. When Soviet Deputy Premier Anastas Mikoyan visited the flagship HO in the early 1950s, he praised the selection of fine watches, typewriters, and stockings, but observed that the store, with its small, dark sales floors and unfriendly atmosphere, lacked a world-class character (Landsman, 2005, pp. 123–124).

Reconstruction and economic restructuring were also underway in Poland, where, in 1949, urban planners unveiled a plan to rebuild downtown Warsaw. Architects had designed a multipurpose complex of apartment buildings, offices and retail stores to signal the arrival of a modern collective lifestyle. Stores and shops, to be located on the ground floors of the new buildings, featured marble and other costly materials, comfortable furniture where customers could relax while workers attended to them and candelabra in the jewellery shops. By the time the complex was partially completed in 1952, other state-run stores were opening, including Pedet (short for Universal Department Store) and Delikatesy, which sold imported coffee, sweets, Soviet champagne and other delicacies. Jabłkowski Brothers, refurbished and reopened as a state store in 1951, sold children's clothing and toys (Crowley, 2000, pp. 34–37; Dom Towarawy Bracia Jabłkowscy, 2015).

Eastern Europe's central planned economies managed reconstruction and large-scale economic development fairly well in this period, although coercion and force were used to expropriate property. Yugoslavia, which by 1948 was communist, but not part of the Soviet Bloc, as well as Bulgaria and Romania, experienced among the highest rates of growth in the region. Poland and Hungary rapidly expanded their industrial sectors, while in Czechoslovakia the pre-existing industrial economy developed further, urbanisation increased, and an educated middle class emerged. Party leaders in the Soviet Union sought to normalise the economy and daily life by eliminating the rationing system, increasing production of consumer goods, and reducing workplace distribution points by building more state stores. As these efforts to create centralised state-owned retail sectors proceeded throughout the region, many consumers continued to buy staple foods and other essential goods from market venders and individuals operating illegally (Judt, 2005, p. 170; Hessler, 2004, p. 304; Hessler, 1998, p. 533).

Building a modern socialist consumer society, 1953–1979

After a series of crises in the early 1950s, several communist states began to seriously address consumer issues. In East Germany (German Democratic Republic or GDR), anger over long lines and criticisms of the government's prioritisation of industrial production precipitated a barrage of complaints and even a few acts of violence against salespeople (Landsman, 2005, p. 105). In early 1953, the Council of Ministers formed the State Commission for Trade and Supply to hear from average shoppers about their concerns and represent their needs to economic officials. At the same time, the state established the right of consumers to present their complaints to officials and to receive a response. Over the ensuing years, women, aware of the gap between the state's claim of female emancipation and the daily realities of wage discrimination and shopping, wrote the majority of complaint letters. Expressing frustration over high prices and the lack of good quality, fashionable clothing in a range of popular sizes, they demanded respect for the rights of consumers. Rural women voiced other complaints, among them the lack of stores in the countryside and the privileged access of industrial workers (Pence, 2008, pp. 296–297; Stitziel, 2008, pp. 265–271). Despite these efforts, demonstrations erupted in June, when 300,000 citizens, angry about shortages and HO's high prices demanded the dissolution of the GDR. Suppressed by Soviet forces, the protests nonetheless made clear that consumer issues could not be neglected. That fall, chastened policymakers introduced the New Course, which reduced prices on thousands of items, meat and milk, as well as clothing and bicycles; however, when consumption of butter, sugar and other basic goods rebounded a few years later, they shifted resources back to heavy industry (Pence, 2008, pp. 306–307).

Delivering a higher standard of living became even more important to the legitimacy of communist governments after a wave of revolts broke out following Joseph Stalin's death in March 1953, and again after Nikita Khrushchev's 1956 "secret speech" denouncing Stalin's crimes. After the rebellions were suppressed, Party leaders once again tried to stabilise their governments with consumer-friendly policies, and they relaxed travel restrictions that promoted cultural exchange between Eastern Europe and the West. The Soviet government signalled the start of a new era with the renovation and re-opening of Moscow's GUM on December 24, 1953. GUM was less a department store and more a collection of shops and counters selling everything from men's and women's clothing, accessories, fabrics, cosmetics and jewellery to carpets, bicycles, stationery and school supplies. Still, the retailer became the USSR's premier retailer, as evidenced by its Section 100, a clothing store housed on the top floor that was only open to the party elite (GUM). In Hungary, where a major revolt erupted in 1956, Party leader János Kádár launched reforms, popularly known as "goulash communism", devised to "buy back" the support, or at least compliance, of the population through, among other things, a promise to deliver the latest appliances and electronics – vacuum cleaners, refrigerators, washing machines and televisions. Moreover, Hungary's commercial officials encouraged manufacturers to respond to consumers' wants and needs, rather than simply fulfilling the state's centralised plan, and to market their brands in order to spur competition and win customers' loyalty (Dombos and Pellandini-Simanyi, 2012, pp. 325–326; Greene, 2014, pp. 113–114, 119–120; Patterson, 2012, pp. 122–123). Yugoslavia, arguably, created the most affluent, consumer-oriented society in Eastern Europe. Tito, Yugoslavia's leader, had broken with Stalin as early as 1948 and thereafter opened the country to the West, even as private stores were nationalised and the Communist Party retained a monopoly on politics. In the 1950s, central economic planning was limited to the establishment of long-term goals and some market mechanisms were introduced (Patterson, 2011, pp. 3–4, 123; Luthar, 2006, p. 235).

Improving the quality of life was also key to Khrushchev's avowed intention to fight the Cold War on a new cultural front. Khrushchev and other leaders had, in fact, begun to make good on this promise. Millions of prefabricated apartment buildings were built, providing tens of millions of families their own private dwellings and generating demand for home furnishings and appliances. Moscow's GUM opened a fashion atelier that turned out tens of thousands of custom-made items a year, as well as in-store fashion salons that offered personal assistance to shoppers and shops that specialised in silk, women's hats, fur coats and perfumes. Fashion ateliers also opened in major cities of the Soviet republics, numbering almost twenty by the late

1960s. Despite their prodigious output, however, ateliers and workshops did not produce nearly enough items to meet consumers' growing demand (Bartlett, 2010, p. 139; Gronow and Zhuravlev, 2010, pp. 127–129). The construction of high-end stores that represented socialist progress and a contemporary, prosperous lifestyle were particularly important in the GDR, Hungary and Czechoslovakia, where downtown commercial districts had previously thrived and suppressed rebellions left citizens angry and resentful. They were critical in Berlin, where proximity to the West forced East German officials to try to match the consumerist policies of West Germany. After West Berlin's Kurfürstendam shopping avenue dubbed itself the "shop window of the West", Khrushchev pledged to make East Germany a "showcase" of socialist splendour (Landsman, 2005, p. 12; Patterson, 2012, p. 120). Prague's House of Fashion opened in 1956 to retail small collections of high-fashion clothing, imported from abroad or produced by special workshops, in a modernist setting of glass walls, Sputnik-style chandeliers and minimalist furniture, and in 1959, Sibylle – Berlin's first boutique – was hailed as a "ladies' paradise". (Bartlett, 2010, p. 145, 147, photo, p. 148). These gestures were not enough to stop the tens of thousands of East Germans who were fleeing to the West each year, or reduce cravings for Western food, clothing and music on sale in West Berlin, however. In response, in August 1961, communist leaders closed the border between East and West Berlin.

In the mid-1960s, increased imports and new economic theories stressing profit as an indicator of socialist efficiency renewed an emphasis on consumption (Salmon, 2006, p. 191). In this atmosphere, the number of department stores and luxury retailers grew rapidly. The HO was reinvented as two new chains of luxury stores. Exquisit sold high-fashion clothing made exclusively for the chain from imported fabrics and retailed them via hundreds of boutiques named Yvonne, Jeannette, Chic or Madeleine to invoke Parisian chic. Delikat retailed fine foods at high prices. These stores' elegant interiors, discreet window displays, and attentive sales personnel provided exclusive shopping experiences for elites whose motivation and loyalty the government prized. Over the years "Ex" and "Posh Nosh", as they were known became popular among average workers, who ventured there to buy something special on occasion (Landsman, 2005, p. 213; Merkel, 2010, pp. 64–65, 67; Bartlett, 2010, p. 147, 150).

Some countries expanded and diversified their retail economies more fully than others, and certain cities such as Budapest, with its many boutiques, shops and department stores, earned a reputation as a shopper's paradise (Patterson, 2012, p. 123). Budapest's Skála attracted more than 50,000 customers a day, on average, in its first days. The chain, which operated more than sixty stores across the country and became a favourite of consumers looking for trendy apparel, styled itself "One step ahead of fashion – in Skála" (Patterson, 2012, pp. 127–128). The Luxus department store, opened in 1963 in Budapest's prestigious Vörösmarty, specialised in high-priced, elegant clothing, including fur coats (Dombos and Pellandini-Simanyi, 2012, p. 325; Bartlett, 2010, p. 147). Fehérvár Department Store presented shopping as an exciting venture, with the claim that "Something is always happening in the Fehérvár Department Store!" (Patterson, 2012, p. 128). Állami Áruház, Corvin, and Rainbow guaranteed convenience, with the promise that consumers would find the largest selection and could buy everything in one place (Patterson, 2012, pp. 123, 129). Hungary's retailers, like those elsewhere, trained sales workers to be courteous and attentive, but they were also encouraged to compete with other stores, even those within the same chain. As the head of the Domestic Trade Ministry advised, 'A resourceful, enterprising seller takes every opportunity to make the buyer or perspective buyer feel that *this* store is different than the others, that buying in *this* store is somehow more favorable' (Greene, 2014, p. 120). Czechoslovakia, Yugoslavia and even Poland also established relatively upscale or diversified retail sectors and attracted shopping tourism (Kotva, 2016; Bartlett, 2010, p. 185; Patterson, 2012, pp. 125, 131; Crowley, 2000, pp. 41–42; Gorsuch, 2006, p. 218). As retail merchants in the

West, created new kinds of retail venues, Eastern European retailers sent delegations abroad to investigate and often adopted them too. Warsaw's Supersam, a self-service supermarket opened in 1959, featured a stylish curved canopy over the entrance and illuminated sales floor (Crowley, 2000, p. 42). The expansion of self-service retailing in the GDR was slow at first, but by late 1961, there were nearly 13,000 such stores (Landsman, 2005, p. 188). When more citizens began to own cars, the NAMA chain opened an 8,700 square foot store in Zagreb's suburbs with parking lots, and expanded to sixteen locations, including smaller cities (Patterson, 2012, p. 125). More consumer services also became available. In the USSR, Houses of Everyday Living offered hairdressing and other salon services, as well as a laundry service and custom-clothing atelier (Gronow and Zhuravlev, 2010, p. 130; Chernyshova, 2013, p. 38). Study groups were also sent to the West to observe consumer service providers. One East German group travelled to Sweden to investigate dry cleaners, shoe repair shops and other services (Landsman, 2005, p. 196).

Budding consumerism concerned some within the socialist elite, whose lifestyle debates questioned whether fulfilling individualist consumer desires was, after all, one of socialism's goals. (Dombos and Pellandini-Simanyi, 329–35). Nevertheless, attempts to satisfy ever-changing consumer demands continued in the late-1960s to mid-1970s, when the Communist Party's rhetoric about improving living standards turned into a "consumer boom", that brought an unprecedented standard of living to several Eastern European countries (Chernyshova, 2013, p. 3). New home construction expanded, while rising wages and artificially low prices allowed most consumers to furnish their new dwellings and equip them with televisions and appliances (Chernyshova, 2013, p. 176). More people could also afford to buy some fashionable clothing and enjoy champagne on special occasions, while those with "pull" could acquire televisions, cars and refrigerators. Indeed, many urban dwellers began to regard the achievement of a better lifestyle a "right", and they expected the state to keep prices on basic goods low so that they could afford to buy "common" luxuries. Leaders, who had learned that shortages and even small price increases could provoke demonstrations and riots, enacted policies that enabled consumers to fulfil more of their desires. In the GDR, the Soviet Union, Poland and elsewhere, leaders increased imports, price subsidies, wage increases and spending on social services, financing it all primarily through Western creditors (Landsman, 2005, pp. 214–216; Chernyshova, 2013, pp. 2–3, 32; Mazurek, 2012, p. 299). At the same time, these policies raised expectations and made social status and hierarchies even more visible and more clearly defined by access to and ownership of status goods. Fur coats and hats, for example, were on prominent display at GUM and TsUM and became common items of desire among Soviet consumers, with different kinds of furs a marker of status (Tikhomirova, 2010, pp. 295–297; Chernyshova, 2013, pp. 104–105). More exclusive specialty shops and boutiques also appeared and sold mini-skirts, paisley fabrics, platform shoes and jeans to young consumers (Chernyshova, 2013, pp. 154–155). As a result of these developments, many consumers became more discriminating and more often refused to buy furniture, clothing and electronics that did not suit their tastes. This tendency was encouraged by the black market, which expanded and began to deal mostly in high-quality foreign goods. More members of the urban middle classes were also permitted to travel abroad, often for business, and many returned home to sell items they had bought abroad. Over time, as the number of individuals involved in unofficial sales increased, the state suffered enormous financial losses (Bartlett, 2010, p. 239; Chernyshova, 2013, pp. 30, 101, 192).

Despite the steady, incremental progress made in raising the standard of living, chronic shortages continued, largely because manufacturers had little incentive to produce the "little things" of daily life or to prioritise consumer goods. The clothing sold in elite shops and boutiques rarely were mass produced because factory directors preferred to meet their production quotas by producing standardised goods, instead of upgrading equipment to produce clothing and other items that changed according to fashion trends (Chernyshova, 2013, pp. 147–152; Landsman, 2005, p. 195). Even model retailers like GUM and CENTRUM repeatedly reported shortages of all kinds of desirable goods and, although the 400 Exquisit shops that had opened in the GDR by the 1980s netted a significant income for the state, they never satisfied demand (Bartlett, 2010, p. 239; Patterson, 2012, p. 126). To obtain the clothing they wanted, many consumers hired dressmakers and tailors to make clothing shown in magazines, or sewed for themselves at home (Stitziel, 2008, pp. 256–265). Those living outside of cities travelled to urban or regional centres to shop, and more people throughout the region flocked to Hungary, Yugoslavia, Poland and the GDR, as well as the West. Yugoslavs, who had the right to travel abroad freely, made monthly or seasonal shopping tours to Italy, Austria and Greece (Luthar, 2006, p. 230). Residents of less prosperous countries engaged in other kinds of cross-border trade. Women in Romanian villages went to Hungary to sell things, either stolen from the state or bought through connections, at prices lower than average in Hungary, and to buy coffee and other products that, by the late 1970s, had vanished from Romania's stores (Chelcea, 2002, p. 23). As the number of people making such trips grew, so did the number of people who became aware of the West's higher standard of living.

Changes in the global economy created even greater problems. When global recession hit, Western creditors cut off credit to Eastern European states. To make up the deficit, communist states began to export more goods, resulting in mass shortages. By the late 1970s and 1980s, consumers, who had become accustomed to expect access to an ever-greater variety of shopping experiences and goods, increasingly encountered empty store shelves. They managed as before, by impulse and panic buying, hoarding, carrying around an *avoska* ("just in case" bag), gaining access to hard-to-get items via connections or relatives living abroad and selling things to and buying from friends and colleagues (Crowley and Reid, 2010, p. 10).

The 1980s: consumerism and the collapse of communism in Eastern Europe

Decades of promises of material abundance had raised and then frustrated consumers' expectations, and by the early 1980s, disillusionment and dissatisfaction set in, undermining collective values and the legitimacy of communist governments. The life experiences and conservatism of most top communist officials played a significant role. Wedded to Marxism, they prioritised the needs of the working class, even as they strove to satisfy middle-class material desires, and failed to introduce fundamental economic reforms or invest in new industries, as was occurring in the West. Each country faced a different set of obstacles and challenges. Mikhail Gorbachev's ascension to power in the USSR in 1985 and his introduction of *perestroika* may seem a necessary corrective, but economic reforms undermined the "social contract" that had been premised on the state's promise to provide, without offering a new one (Cook, 1992; Bren and Neuburger, 2012, pp. 12–13). In the GDR, shortages reappeared at roughly the same time as travel restrictions were eased and West Germany opened its Intershops to East Germans, who once again faced the disparity in retail offerings and living standards (Landsman, 2005, pp. 216–218). The Polish state's rationing of meat, shoes and cigarettes contributed to the frustrations that inspired the formation in 1980 of Solidarity, a Polish trade union independent of the state and eventual mass political opposition movement (Mazurek, 2012, p. 299). Even Yugoslavia's relatively prosperous, consumerist lifestyle began to unravel after Tito's death in 1980 (Patterson, 2011, pp. 20, 42–43). Citizens throughout the region coped by joining any queue, with the intent to buy whatever was for sale and trade it for something else. In many places, people took a second job or second shift to cope with inflated prices (Bren and Neuburger, 2012, p. 13; Crowley and

Reid, 2010, p. 16; Mazurek, 2012, p. 299). The situation became most dire in Romania. Nicolae Ceauşescu's nationalist rhetoric and austerity measures, including his policy of paying off foreign loans through increased exports, led to strict rationing of meat, sugar, cheese and milk, as well as electricity and gasoline, and the disappearance of the trappings of a modern society, for example, refrigerators, vacuum cleaners and operational elevators. In this desperate situation, Romanians became even more dependent on personal connections and the black market, where American whiskey, jeans and cigarettes served as currency (Massino, 2012, p. 228; Chelcea, 2002, p. 22). 1989 brought the collapse of communism and end of the experiment in socialist modernity.

Retailing did not play a direct role in these monumental events, but retailers played no small part in exposing the gap between the promise of a modern socialist society and the inequities and material realities of the majority of people's lives. Founded to symbolise socialist modernity, model stores like HO and GUM turned out to be mere facades for the state's reinstitution of inequality and hierarchy (Hilton, 2012, p. 284; Pence, 1999, p. 514). Thus, it can be argued that communist regimes failed to 'provide a politically stable solution to the problem of consumer desire' (Zatlin, 1997, p. 380).

Conclusion

Over the previous centuries, the retail trade played a significant role in shaping Eastern European politics, society and culture. Despite ideological shifts, ways of buying, selling and consuming were used to establish power structures and enact socio-economic transformation, and they were understood to signify social and gender norms, cultural practices, and the meaning of "modern". In the years since 1989, the retail industry has helped to define the post-communist era. The former flagship GUM, now a private enterprise that retains the acronym, but calls itself The Main Department Store, has become a high-fashion shopping mall, populated by luxury brands such as Hermés, Louis Vuitton, Manolo Blahnik and Tiffany & Co. The firm's website vaunts its heritage and, in recounting the arcade's nearly 125-year history, refers to this "monument of architecture" as an "integral part of Russia's history" and "symbol of Moscow" (GUM, 2016). TsUM has also restyled itself as an upscale retailer of brands such as Dolce & Gabbana, Jimmy Choo and Valentino (TsUM). Around Moscow, the Ritz-Carlton sits on the former site of the state-run Intourist Hotel. Jaguar dealerships, Prada boutiques and other luxury retailers line the main boulevards. Yet, the material world of communism has not been forgotten. Nostalgia for and curiosity about a bygone era and way of life have even proved saleable. GUM shoppers can take a break at a Soviet-style café or cafeteria, while tourists in Krakow can sample Polish snacks, beer and vodka in a communist-era restaurant, tour the city in a vintage Trabant and visit an apartment preserved from the 1970s (Crazy Guides, 2017). Every city seemingly has dozens of stores selling communist-themed souvenirs and T-shirts. Yugo-Nostalgia celebrates Iskra electronics and appliances, Ledo and Pekabela ice cream treats, Hambi fast-food restaurants and Konzum/Unikonzum, Zagreb's first self-service grocery stores (Patterson, 2011, pp. 323, 326). Clearly, the retail industry expresses more about a society than its current ideological or political system.

Acknowledgements: My thanks to the editors and to Kala Dunn and Christine Varga-Harris for their suggestions.

References

Alpern Engel, B. (1997), 'Not by bread alone: Subsistence riots in Russia during world war one', *Journal of Modern History*, 69 (December), pp. 696–721.

Ball, A. (1987), *Russia's last capitalists: The NEPmen, 1928–1929* (Berkeley, CA: University of California Press).

Bartlett, D. (2010), *Fashion east: The spectre that haunted socialism* (Cambridge, MA: MIT Press).

Bílá Labuť, Available at: www.bilalabut.cz/page/about-us/, October 26, 2016.

Bogdanov, I.A. (1988), *Gostinyi dvor*, Leningrad.

Breckman, W.G. (1991), 'Disciplining consumption: The debate about luxury in Wilhelmine Germany, 1890–1914', *Journal of Social History*, 24 (3), pp. 485–505.

Bren, P. and Neuburger, M. (eds.) (2012), *Communism unwrapped: Consumption in cold war Eastern Europe* (New York: Oxford University Press) 3–19.

Chelcea, L. (2002), 'The culture of shortage during state socialism: Consumption practices in a romanian village in the 1980s', *Cultural Studies*, 16 (1), pp. 16–43.

Chernyshova, N. (2013), *Soviet consumer culture in the Brezhnev Era* (London: Routledge).

Cook, L.J. (1992), 'Brezhnev's "social contract" and Gorbachev's reforms', *Soviet Studies*, 44 (1), pp. 37–56.

Crazy Guides Communism Tours (2012), Available at: www.crazyguides.com/, May 31, 2017.

Crowley, D. (2000), 'Warsaw's shops, stalinism, and the thaw', in S.E. Reid and D. Crowley (eds.) *Style and socialism: Modernity and material culture in post-war Eastern Europe* (New York: Berg).

Crowley, D. and Reid, S.E. (2010), 'Introduction', in D. Crowley and S.E. Reid (eds.) *Pleasures in socialism: Leisure and luxury in the Eastern Bloc* (Evanston, IL: Northwestern University Press) 3–52.

Dom Towarawy Bracia Jabłkowscy (2015), Available at: www.dtbj.pl/, October 28, 2016.

Dombos, T. and Pellandini-Simanyi, L. (2012), 'Kids, cars, or cashews? Debating and remembering consumption in socialist hungary', in P. Bren and M. Neuburger (eds.) *Communism Unwrapped* (New York: Oxford University Press) 325–350.

Felski, R. (1995), *The gender of modernity* (Cambridge, MA: Harvard University Press).

Gorsuch, A.E. (2006), 'Time travelers: Soviet tourists to Eastern Europe', in A.E. Gorsuch and D.P. Koenker (eds.) *Turizm: The Russian and East European tourist under capitalism and socialism* (Cornell: Cornell University Press) 205–226.

Greene, B. (2014), 'Selling market socialism: Hungary in the 1960s', *Slavic Review*, 73 (1), pp. 108–132.

Gronow, J. (2003), *Caviar with champagne: Common luxury and the ideals of the good life in Stalin's Russia* (New York: Berg).

Gronow, J. and Zhuravlev, S. (2010), 'Soviet luxuries from champagne to private cars', in D. Crowley and S.E. Reid (eds.) *Pleasures in Socialism* (Evanston, IL: Northwestern University Press) 121–146.

GUM. Available at: https://gum.ru/history/, October 28, 2016.

Hessler, J. (1998), 'A postwar perestroika? Toward a history of private enterprise in the USSR', *Slavic Review*, 57 (3), pp. 516–542.

Hessler, J. (2004), *A social history of Soviet Trade* (Princeton, NJ: Princeton University Press).

Hilton, M.L. (2012), *Selling to the masses: Retailing in Russia, 1880–1930* (Pittsburgh, PA: University of Pittsburgh Press).

Holquist, P. (2002), *Making war, forging revolution: Russia's continuum of crisis, 1914–1921* (New York: Cambridge University Press).

Hungarian Architecture, Department of Public Building Design at the Technical University of Budapest (2016), Available at: http://hazai.kozep.bme.hu/en/parizsi-nagy-aruhaz-budapest/, October 28, 2016.

Judt, T. (2005), *Postwar: A history of Europe since 1945* (New York: Penguin).

Kastner & Öhler. (2016), Available at: www.kastner-oehler.at/ueber-uns/geschichte/, October 28, 2016.

Kotva. (2016), Available at: www.od-kotva.cz/en/anniversary, October 23, 2016.

Ladwig-Winters, S. (2000), 'The attack on Berlin department stores *Warenhaeuser* after 1933', in D. Bankier (ed.) *Probing the depths of German antisemitism: German society and the persecution of the jews, 1933–1941* (New York: Berghahn Books) 1–21.

Landsman, M. (2005), *Dictatorship and demand: The politics of consumerism in East Germany* (Cambridge, MA: Harvard University Press).

Lohr, E. (2003), *Nationalizing the Russian empire: The campaign against enemy aliens during world war I* (Cambridge, MA: Harvard University Press).

Luthar, B. (2006), 'Remembering socialism: On desire, consumption and surveillance', *Journal of Consumer Culture*, 6 (2), pp. 229–259.

Massino, J. (2012), 'From black caviar to blackouts: Gender, consumption, and lifestyle in Ceauşescu's Romania', in P. Bren and M. Neuburger (eds.) *Communism Unwrapped* (New York: Oxford University Press) 226–249.

Mazurek, M. (2012), 'Keeping it close to home: Resourcefulness and scarcity in late socialist and postsocialist Poland', in P. Bren and M. Neuburger (eds.) *Communism Unwrapped* (New York: Oxford University Press) 298–320.

Merkel, I. (2008), 'Alternative rationalities, strange dreams, absurd utopias: On socialist advertising and market research', in K. Pence and P. Betts (eds.) *Socialist modern: East German everyday culture and politics* (Ann Arbor, MI: University of Michigan Press) 323–344.

Merkel, I. (2010), 'Luxury in socialism: An absurd proposition?' in D. Crowley and S.E. Reid (eds.) *Pleasures in Socialism* (Evanston, IL: Northwestern University Press) 53–70.

Muzei Sarajeva, Available at: http://muzejsarajeva.ba/en/, October 23, 2016.

Nove, A. (1992), *An economic history of the USSR, 1917–1991* (New York: Penguin).

Osokina, E. (1999), *Za fasadom Stalinskogo izobiliia: raspredelenie i rynok v snabzhenii naseleniia v gody industrializatsii, 1927–1941* (Moscow: Rosspen).

Patterson, P.H. (2011), *Bought & sold: Living and losing the good life in socialist Yugoslavia* (Ithaca, NY: Cornell University Press).

Patterson, P.H. (2012), 'Risky business: What was really being sold in the department stores of socialist eastern Europe?', in P. Bren and M. Neuburger (eds.) "handels-" *Communism Unwrapped* (New York: Oxford University Press) 116–139.

Pence, K. (1999), 'Building socialist worker-consumers: The paradoxical construction of the handels-organisation – HO, 1948', in P. Hübner and K. Tenfelde (eds.) *Arbeiter in der SBZ – DDR* (Essen: Klartext Verlag) 497–526.

Pence, K. (2008), 'Women on the verge: Consumers between private desires and public crisis', in K. Pence and P. Betts (eds.) *Socialist Modern* (Ann Arbor, MI: University of Michigan Press) 287–322.

Pitcher, H. (1994), *Muir & mirrielees: The Scottish partnership that became a household name in Russia* (Cromer, UK: Swallow House Books).

Randall, A. (2008), *The Soviet dream world of trade and consumption in the 1930s* (New York: Palgrave Macmillan).

Razmadze, A.S. (1893), *Torgovye riady na Krasnoi ploshchadi v Moskve*, Kiev.

Reid, S.E. (2002), 'Cold war in the kitchen: Gender and the de-stalinization of consumer taste in the soviet union under Khrushchev', *Slavic Review*, 61 (2), pp. 211–252.

Ruane, C. (2009), *The empire's new clothes: A history of the Russian fashion industry, 1700–1917* (New Haven, CT: Yale University Press).

Salmon, S. (2006), 'Marketing socialism: Inturist in the late 1950s and early 1960s', *Turizm*.

Sarajevo Museum, Sarajevo Canton, Federation of Bosnia and Herzegovina, Available at: http://muzejsarajeva.ba/en/, October 28, 2016.

Sobolev, M. (1900), 'Universal'nye magaziny i bazary, kak iavlenie noveishago torgovago oborota', *Mir Bozhii*, 4, pp. 114–130.

Stitziel, J. (2008), 'Shopping, sewing, networking, complaining: Consumer practices and the relationship between state and society in the GDR', in K. Pence and P. Betts (eds.) *Socialist Modern* (Ann Arbor, MI: University of Michigan Press) 253–286.

Tikhomirova, A. (2010), 'Soviet women and fur consumption in the Brezhnev Era', in D. Crowley and S.E. Reid (eds.) *Pleasures in Socialism* (Evanston, IL: Northwestern University Press) 283–308.

TsUM. Available at: www.tsum.ru/, May 17, 2017.

West, S. (2011), *'I shop in moscow': Advertising and the creation of consumer culture in late Tsarist Russia* (DeKalb, IL: Northern Illinois University Press).

Zatlin, J.R. (1997), 'The vehicle of desire: The trabant, the wartburg, and the end of the GDR', *German History*, 15 (3), pp. 358–380.

24

RETAILING IN AUSTRALIA AND NEW ZEALAND

Historical perspectives through the distinctive lens of innovation

Dale Miller

Introduction

At its heart, retailing is about exchange. However, the contexts and consequences of exchange vary from country to country, region to region and era to era. This chapter explores some unique aspects of Australian and New Zealand retailing during the nineteenth and twentieth centuries with a particular focus on changes over time. Consistent with Hollander et al. (2005), rather than a timeline of significant events, the chapter proceeds by discussing innovations and distinctive forms, particularly department stores, and the shift from the corner store to supermarkets and superstores. Retailing in Australia and New Zealand has been remarkable for changes over time, responding to global trends and local needs and introducing innovations large and small, which are sometimes idiosyncratic responses to the specific retailing context in the region.

The 1800s saw the emergence of retailing in the nascent settlement including in Sydney (e.g. Pollon, 1989). The scope of this chapter is confined to retailing per se, with less attention to the broader distribution channel which covers wholesalers, suppliers and shopping centres, where for example, Westfield, which originated in Australia, is a major global player in the shopping centre/mall domain (Westfield, c. 2000). Moreover, retailing developed in Australia both in parallel with, and in contrast to, developments in other countries (compare with, for example: Hower, 1943; Kimbrough, 1952; Miller, 1981; Nasmith, 1923; Nesbitt, 1993; Nystrom, 1915; Pound, 1960; Resseguie, 1962, 1965; Rees, 1969; Santink, 1990; Siry, 1988).

By drawing on multiple sources, the distinctive features of retailing in Australia and New Zealand can be explored. It is noteworthy at the outset, that although relatively geographically and culturally close, the two countries also display some particular differences. The sources include a range of academic works, archival materials, celebratory tomes and newspaper accounts and advertising. There are also oral histories made with retail employees, interviews with retailers and family memories to add depth to the more formal works. One concern for researchers is the difficulty in accessing archival materials (Miller, 2006b). The nature of business with intergenerational management of private companies, mergers, acquisitions and bankruptcies for example, means that with a few notable exceptions, accessible systematic archival collections are rare in the Australian and New Zealand context.

Did retailing in Australia and New Zealand develop differently or similarly to the development in other countries such as England, Scotland, Canada and the US? The brief answer is yes to both parts of the questions. There were many similarities and some distinctive differences. Does this question matter? The answer here too is yes. Why? Various researchers continue to call for further studies in retailing history (e.g. Alexander, A., 2010; Alexander, N., 1997; Hollander, 1986). As well, studies are emerging for example such as Alexander's work on British retailing (Alexander, 2011; Godley & Hang, 2012), and the examination of European department store retailing (Crossick & Jaumain, 1999; Miller, 1981). However such studies do not stretch to include Australia or New Zealand. Notwithstanding, some researchers are examining various aspects of retailing and marketing in Australia (e.g. Bailey, 2015; Miller, 2005; Miller & Merrilees, 2001, 2002, 2004, 2016). However, the dearth of business history and economic history study options reduces the scope for advanced research, (see Friedman & Jones, 2012 for example, who identify only two courses which include Australian business history).

The history of retailing or related aspects such as mass marketing, and the evolution of fashion, featured in various works that emerged particularly in the 1980s and 1990s (e.g. Kingston, 1994; Lancaster, 1995; Macpherson, 1963; Maynard, 1994; Perkins & Freedman, 1999; Perkins & Meredith, 1996; Pitcher, 1994; Santink, 1990; Strasser, 1989; Wendt & Kogan, 1952). Many works about retailing in Australia and New Zealand are more like company biographies or panegyrics. They are often celebratory in nature and linked to milestones or anniversaries. Examples include a focus on major retailers like Anthony Hordern and Sons (Hordern, 1985; Redmond, 1938), Foy & Gibson (Davies, c. 1946), Mark Foy's Ltd (Mark Foy's, 1935), David Jones (Bartlett, 1946; Cullen, 2013; Jones, 1956; O'Neill, 2013) and Georges (Cooper, A., 2014). Various exhibitions have been curated about shopping heritage (McCann, 2002; Webber et al., 2003).

Many contemporary retailers echo these acknowledgements of the past on their websites, as a means of building reassurance for their customers and other stakeholders such as suppliers, and as part of developing their corporate brand (Cooper et al., 2015; Miller, 2011, 2014). The focus has often been the department store format. Even so, works on specific department stores and retailers are relatively rare in Australia and New Zealand, although those available offer insights to the dynamic nature of retailing (for example, Barber, 2005; Brash et al., 1985; Dunstan, 1979; Hordern, 1985; Marshall, 1961; Millen, 2000; Warrender, 1972).

In the 1990s, several authors noted that only a modest volume of academic research supported the few Australian celebratory published works on specific department stores and their owners (Merrilees & Miller, 1996; Perkins & Freedman, 1999; Perkins & Meredith, 1996). However, related research is emerging, for example about the development of shopping malls in Australia (Bailey, 2015; Merrilees et al., 2016: 264–266). While outside the scope of this work, they provide insight into early innovations in this format, such as their inclusion of supermarkets, a marked contrast to planned shopping malls in other countries like Canada, where supermarkets tend to stand alone. While lagging behind developments in the United States by about a decade, the first planned shopping centres opened with department stores and supermarkets as anchor tenants, the first Australian mall being Chermside (Queensland) in 1957 and the first New Zealand mall being Lynnmall in West Auckland. This new format included novel services such as 'drive in parking' (Merrilees et al., 2016). Bailey (2015: 368) notes that while shopping malls inhabit a significant space in urban and regional landscapes, and they 'are deeply embedded in the social and cultural life of communities', they have not capitalised on their brand heritage as part of their marketing.

Australian economic historians have tended to focus on commodities produced through primary industries or related services such as stock and station agencies, and on manufacturing generally or in specific industries like steel (Ville & Merrett 2000). Kingston (1994) gives an Australian perspective on the history of shopping overall. She highlights the dramatic changes that occurred in the twentieth century for the consumer, the most obvious being the escalation of mass merchandising.

This study is grounded in the emergence of modern retailing, which is well-documented (e.g. Alexander & Akehurst, 1999). From the 1850s, or even earlier, the routes to modern retailing were emerging. In some ways, the developments in Australia and New Zealand paralleled changes in European and North American retailing. However, the relative remoteness of both countries predicated unique responses including how they offered credit, managed long supply chains and refined labour practices in an increasingly formal regulatory environment.

Growth of the department store

Historically, the department store was a very successful and innovative form of retailing. Several authors note that only a modest volume of academic research supports the few Australian self-congratulatory published works on specific department stores and their owners (Clarke & Rimmer, 1997; Merrilees & Miller, 1996; Perkins & Freedman, 1999; Perkins & Meredith, 1996). In the Australian and New Zealand contexts, the early department store retailers had emigrated predominantly from England, Scotland and Wales to set up new businesses. They maintained links with "home" and thus were able to use those relationships to help with sourcing and with trends. Sometimes, they were able to make visits back to "the old country", noting in diaries all the changes and advances that they observed.

In a descriptive work, Ferry (1960) drew on his extensive retailing career as a template for his department store mini-cases studies focused on department stores in the US, Britain and parts of the British Empire (Canada, Australia, New Zealand and South Africa). He provided evocative snapshots of the histories and features of many department stores, suggesting a familiarity developed through his business networks, personal connections, and acute observations. In Australia, two major waves occurred. The early drapers and milliners from the 1820s to 1840s, including Farmer & Co., Anthony Hordern & Sons, and David Jones, had developed into department stores by the early 1880s. *David Jones* began as a Sydney drapery store in 1838, and grew in physical store size, scope of merchandise and services, and small-scale manufacturing (custom tailoring and millinery for example) during the next five decades (Horton, n.d). The transition from drapery to department store was gradual but inexorable, with the expansion of selling, storage and manufacturing spaces through acquiring leases or freehold of adjacent buildings. In 1887, the opening of a large new store on an expanded original location marked its ascendency to department store status in terms of size, scope and organisation. Anthony Hordern & Sons had its roots in Ann Hordern's millinery shop, and flourished to become the largest physical store in the country (Barnard, 2015); like its major contemporaries it was an early adopter of new technologies such as the pneumatic tube for moving cash, change, accounts and orders round the store.

The second wave comprised new Sydney entrants such as Grace Bros and J. Marcus Clarke from the mid-1880s to the early 1900s, and included Myer in Melbourne in the period from 1910 to 1920. The opening of suburban and rural draperies, some of which developed into independent department stores or small chains supplemented these principal waves. Larger department store chains later acquired many of the independent department stores, while others failed, with changing social and economic conditions especially in rural areas. Of the many department stores that existed as strong and vibrant firms up to the 1960s, only two names remain, David Jones (forty-three stores) and Myer (sixty-seven stores).

In the early 19th century, David Jones introduced European merchandising methods to urban markets when he opened the David Jones firm's first Sydney outlet in 1838, operating it

Figure 24.1 Interior of Finney Isles store, Brisbane, 1910

Citation: John Oxley Library, State Library of Queensland Neg: 110549.

as a retail and wholesale drapery. As the business expanded, building renovations and extensions were frequent. By the mid-1870s, Edward Lloyd Jones I (one of David Jones' sons) was instituting changes that were appearing in dry goods stores and emerging department stores. His trips abroad especially to England often stimulated changes. Family members and members of the former partnership dominated the first Board of Directors on incorporation in 1906 (Horton, n.d.).

By the late nineteenth century, department store retailing in Sydney increasingly mirrored Europe and the United States with respect to the architectural and technological advances during this period. The store was partly fashioned on British lines, inspired by Whiteley's and others and also American stores including Macy's. In 1887, an opulent new full-scale department store replaced its 'higgledy piggledy' predecessor (Miller & Merrilees, 2016). There were many innovative features of the new store, including greater size, more floors (including a third floor devoted to workrooms) more departments, a modern passenger lift, a semiautomatic version of the not yet invented pneumatic tubes for moving cash around the store (amusingly, customers' dogs would chase the wooden balls as the latter tore along the metal tracks) and more innovative merchandising practices (Miller & Merrilees, 2016). The last included showrooms using new lighting; showcases with more open displays of merchandise; some areas of "tout ensemble" display. All of these represented a more customer convenient method of presenting and displaying merchandise and an enhanced buying experience for the customer (Miller & Merrilees, 2016). Greater size enabled a greater variety of choice, as a type of one-stop shopping, enabling, in the words of 1887 advertising, buyers 'to see in a few moments a larger range of designs than heretofore' (Miller & Merrilees, 2016).

Figure 24.2 Electric trams, George Street, David Jones corner

Citation: Tyrrell Collection, Museum of Applied Arts and Sciences.

Expansion continued under the direction of the next generation of family ownership in the early twentieth century, and drew in part on British and American influences. Edward Lloyd Jones II and his brother Eric entered the firm on the death of their father, Edward (1844–1894). They were relatively junior in age and experience and they depended in part on the other partners who pursued a *status quo* approach, continuing rather than changing business practices, until incorporation in 1906 when E.L. Jones II became Chairman of the Board. The firm moved into the mail order business, building additional floors at the store and consolidating what had been dispersed workrooms in a large new factory in 1914 in an inner Sydney suburb (Surry Hills). World War I and the early 1920s economic recession hindered plans for a new flagship store. Finally, the dramatic state-of-the-art store opened in 1927, in Elizabeth Street, Sydney, a few blocks away from the 1887 store, which continued to trade. Saks Fifth Avenue, New York and Selfridges' 1909 London store influenced the design of this store significantly (DJA: Horton, 2000; O'Neill, 2013). Percy Best from Selfridges paid a visit to the firm, sharing his expertise and commenting favourably on some aspects of the operations (DJA; Miller, 2006a: 247). The new store became the flagship store because of its size, architecture, modernity and the scope of merchandise, and remains the flagship store in 2018. The George Street store built in 1887 was extended in 1906 and renovated extensively in 1935. In 1938, the firm built a further store diagonally opposite the flagship Elizabeth Street store, giving it three stores within the city.

As the firm expanded, the management culture changed, bringing contemporary European methods of merchandise assortment and merchandise acquisition into the firm. In terms of

Figure 24.3 Anthony Hordern & Sons Palace Emporium, Brickfield Hill, Sydney, 1935

Citation: Mitchell Library, State Library of New South Wales.

leadership, Charles Lloyd Jones was a complex and charismatic person according to some contemporary accounts (DJA Newspaper Clippings) and was widely travelled, with a strong interest in retail developments worldwide. Clarence Edwards joined the firm in 1901, from Swan and Edgar, and with experience in the Manchester department of Woollands (Knightsbridge). His role was General Manager, and Charles Lloyd Jones claimed that Edwards acted as a necessary brake on some of Charles' creative ideas. His key contribution to the firm was his understanding of the nature of the business, particularly merchandise assortment and procurement, and he was therefore very involved with the firm's buyers.

The David Jones case indicates American and European influence in terms of architectural and technological changes between the late nineteenth and early twentieth century. Its labour practices, however, took place in a different historical context, yet nevertheless some similarities can be seen. In the Australian context, the notionally egalitarian society with its convict roots and its anti-servitude creed still exhibited elements of a unique paternalistic management as discussed by various authors (including Kingston 1994; MacCulloch, 1980; Pragnell, 2001; Reekie 1987, 1993). Charles Lloyd Jones, head of David Jones, described this relationship between owner and staff in positive terms:

> Frankly I believe in the kind of relations between employer and employee which, for want of a better word, is called "paternalism", although I know this is anathema to some people . . . in any case nothing would deter us from treating our employees as members of a vast 'family'. There should be more between employer and employee than the payment of good wages for good work.
>
> *Charles Lloyd Jones (DJA)*

In other ways, however, Australian retailers followed a larger industry trend towards professionalisation and scientific management seen in American department stores by World War I. In the context of their times, the motivations and practices at David Jones were innovative and progressive (Miller, 2006a).

At David Jones, the growth of business gave impetus to acquiring expertise to develop and implement the Board's visions. Various means were used to obtain this crucial organisational capability. By the 1920s and 1930s, emerging literatures on popular management and retailing were extensive. They were augmented by seminal academic works such as Nystrom's work (1915) on the economics of retailing and his book on retailing operations. The Alexander Hamilton Institute prepared handbooks and courses, and their Modern Business Series contained twenty-four volumes, including topics on organisation and control and Marketing and Merchandising (McNeill Collection: The Editors & In Collaboration with Butler and Swinney, 1918). The books were designed to be used 'as part of the modern business course and service of the Alexander Hamilton Institute' (McNeill Collection, The Editors et al., 1918). Some of their publications remain in the McNeill Collection, a collection within the Archive of the books held by David McNeill the Staff Manager for more than fifty years. Their presence together with Rydges journals, books on character analysis using phrenology and many other related books suggests an interest by senior management in, if not a theoretical framework for, a structured approach to business and staff management.

Other ways in which the firm accumulated corporate expertise included their own benchmarking activities and general lectures by prominent academics such as Professor G. Elton Mayo on work stress in 1921 and benchmarking visits to overseas' retailers. Percy Best from Selfridges spent some time with David Jones, sharing his expertise and commenting favourably on some aspects of the operations. In New Zealand, in salesforce training staff were encouraged to focus not so much on the products for sale but the effects for the customer such as in the case of shoes, selling comfort and the benefits of walking (Roberts, 2003).

Parallel to the 19th century development of the department store was another major mass retailer: mail order. The mail order catalogue was a significant innovation, as it met the needs of the remote rural customers in developing countries such as the US (Emmet & Jeuck, 1950) and Canada in the late 1880s. With the exception of Waller (1992), little Australian or New Zealand research has appeared despite the immense importance of this shopping channel to many customers, and indeed to the retailers' business growth and success. The introduction of the catalogue meant that the retailers were operating in multiple channels and the department stores, or Universal Providers as they were termed, tended to publish their catalogues annually or six monthly, and to distribute them widely. They also sought to reassure customers with extensive information about policies, returns, warranties, delivery and sizing, and in later years, even samples of fabrics. The Anthony Horderns catalogue was legendary, being the size of about two house bricks, containing everything the consumer of the day could want or desire.

The David Jones Mail Order catalogue was the one company publication that bridged the late 1800s and the twentieth century. It was internal to the firm in terms of its preparation and the consequences for staff when customers responded to it, but it was targeted at customers, especially those who could not visit the store frequently. The catalogue became a significant integrating communication mechanism, linking the Board, the staff and the customers. The catalogues communicated the essence of the firm to the staff. Various staff were involved in merchandise selection, the catalogue preparation and the filling of orders. Thus, the catalogue embodied for staff the firm's strategies and conveyed concepts of service and fashion, and basic practices such as how the customers should order goods and what the delivery terms and arrangements were.

Mail order was one form of advertising David Jones utilised; Ladies periodicals were another. Department stores had long been dependent on advertising in other nations and the Australian industry was no different. In the early twentieth century, Australia saw a shift towards more graphic and extensive modern advertising. Charles Lloyd Jones had taken over responsibility for advertising in 1905. Over several years, he drew on his knowledge gathered overseas, his artistic ability, his growing understanding of the firm and his senior position, to escalate the advertising effort and budget. David Jones placed advertisements in ladies magazines, selected journals and newspapers on a regular basis. The very choice of magazines sent a message to the staff. The firm shunned tawdry or tasteless press, preferring respectable daily newspapers and genteel magazines, whose perceived readers were consistent with the image the Executive had of the store's preferred customers. The messages in the advertisements were about fashion, merchandise variety, value, quality and service, invoking the store's longevity and reputation as symbols of trustworthiness and social standing. Many activities had to support the advertisements, including previous merchandise selection and acquisition, store displays, selling staff knowledge and policies about returns, delivery and credit.

The rise of supermarkets as a retailing powerhouse

Supermarkets are the second of the mega trends in Australian retailing history. As of 2017–2018, supermarkets are a major economic powerhouse, not just in retailing but across sectors. Indeed, the contemporary retailing landscape is dominated by the two components of supermarkets and superstore specialist stores. Supermarkets may seem a humble and ordinary part of the shopping landscape and few people might imagine that they are such a powerful force. However, the timid image of supermarkets has changed much in recent years with all sorts of community issues being raised against the large supermarket corporate giants in Australia. In particular, small communities (like Maleny in Queensland) often protest the arrival of large, chain supermarkets that threaten the peaceful lifestyles of residents, and the viability of small retailers like butchers and greengrocers. Equally, there is much social unrest when supermarkets squeeze small suppliers, on the prices paid to dairy and egg farmers.

The modern supermarket emerged in the US in the 1930s, however in Australia it was a post-World War II development, as the major cities expanded with many new suburbs catering to the rise in families and the baby boom, in the late 1950s and early 1960s. Primarily emerging from the grocery category, the supermarket introduced modernity and excitement to what was a small, traditional, personal service format. New technology in the form of modern layout and refrigeration represented a major innovation effort at the time (Humphrey, 1998). It is hard to imagine now that more than sixty years earlier, the first supermarkets created excitement and a party-atmosphere, with large crowds queuing to get in and see for themselves firsthand what a modern supermarket looked like.

Although most supermarkets emerged from a traditional grocery origin, in Australia the current two dominant supermarkets had their roots forty to fifty years earlier in the variety store format [Coles in 1914 (Sydenham, 1993), and Woolworths in 1924 (Murray, c. 1999)]. By the late 1950s, variety stores essentially split into supermarkets and discount department stores, at first within the one store location and then shifting into stand-alone locations for each. Other predecessors including the corner store and the self-service grocer, a development which derived from the full-service grocer prevalent up to the 1930s. More recently, supermarkets have expanded their product range to include more dry goods and homewares, reminiscent of the variety store.

As Humphrey (1998) shows, the emergence of the supermarket was a major format and technological innovation, a disruptive change. Thus, innovation is critical in explaining the explosive rise from the staid grocery trade category. Innovation has continued to characterise the supermarket industry. This fact may seem surprising to many as supermarkets per se seem the antithesis of entrepreneurship and dynamism. On the contrary, unexpectedly it is one of the fastest growing retail categories over the past thirty years, despite the limited budget allocation to food.

A major innovation in the supermarket industry occurred from the mid-1980s. From that point, mega-size supermarkets were introduced, akin to the superstores in specialist stores. The average size of Australian supermarkets grew from 800 square metres in 1985 to 4000 square metres in 1995 (Merrilees & Miller, 1997). The innovation was not merely the greater size, but also the inclusion of larger fresh food sections and also generally more modern displays and appearances (Merrilees & Miller, 1997).

The changes through innovations in the supermarket category continue. The two leading supermarket corporations, Woolworths and Coles, have been particularly innovative. Merrilees and Miller (2001a) demonstrate their high level of innovation, including a major role in ushering in the fresh food revolution to the supermarket category; ever-more creative visual presentations; online stores (in 1996–97), financial services and insurance services. In contrast in the Australian context, attempts to introduce European-style hypermarkets have not succeeded, although warehouse retailers including Costco are finding a niche in urban areas.

A corollary of the rise in supermarkets has been the demise of the traditional grocer. In 1961–62, there were only 200 supermarkets in Australia compared to 33, 000 small grocery retailers Merrilees and Miller (1996). By 1968–69, there were 650 supermarkets, accounting for a third of grocery sales. By the mid-1970s the number of supermarkets had grown to 1000. Further, by the mid-1990s the share of supermarkets exceeded 95% of the grocery sales, reaching 99% by 2000. There are very few small grocers left out of the original 33,000 in the early 1960s. Some small grocery firms operate as part of a broader (more independent) supermarket chain. However, the traditional grocery trade operator has all but vanished. Occasionally, a couple of traders open up a new innovative mode of grocery store such as a focus on gourmet food, but these stores are rare and generally not sustained over time. The period saw the rise of the convenience store such as 7-Eleven in urban areas, and especially in city centres, and the 2001 arrival of the smaller yet powerful players such as Aldi, which is now in the top three Australian supermarket retailers, and has over 470 stores (Aldi, 2017; Roy Morgan, 2017).

Superstores

Superstores or category killers in specialised retail categories are the third of our mega trends in Australian retailing history. Today, as of 2018–2019, superstores are a major economic powerhouse, not just in retailing but across sectors. Indeed, the contemporary retailing landscape is dominated by the two components of supermarkets and superstore specialist stores.

In the 1990s, the economic recession in Australia influenced consumers to explore a greater variety of retailers in their quest for value for money. As well, they became more amenable to destination shopping where they were willing to travel further to gain better prices and greater ranges of merchandise (Jarratt, 1998; Polonsky & Jarratt, 1992). This predisposition created a receptivity to the introduction of superstores in Australia.

In tracing the history of the emergence of superstores, the first major Australian article on superstores identified 1993 as a watershed in superstore activity (Merrilees & Miller, 1997).

Prior to 1993 there were just a few superstore categories, including hardware (e.g. BBC Hardwarehouse), furniture (e.g. IKEA) and sporting goods (e.g. Rebel Sports). The entry to Australia of Toys 'R' Us from the USA ushered in a wave of other categories. Consequently by the mid-1990s there were ten retail categories where superstore format had twenty or more outlets: toys, sporting goods, hardware, furniture, cinema, car washes, clothing, stationery, videos and pharmacies (Merrilees & Miller, 1997).

The key benefits of superstores include a wider range of goods and lower prices and often a more interesting design of store that allows more movement and freedom by the consumer. As such, the superstore is a major, disruptive innovation in the specialty retailing categories. Compared to traditional stores, the superstore is often between five and ten times bigger. So potentially each time a superstore is built, it supplants say ten small traditional stores. The economic advantage of the superstore is impressive, which explains the rapid development in Australia from the mid-1990s in so many retail categories. Innovation triggered economic success for the retailers and acceptance by consumers.

The competitive power of the superstore format is demonstrated in a study where consumer perceptions were contrasted across superstores and traditional stores in two categories (toys and hardware) (Merrilees & Miller, 2001c). The superiority of the superstore was evident from the consumer perceptions. The superior format design was a critical factor. The superstores had more powerful and interesting visual displays, more use of colour and lighting, more use of merchandise packaging as part of the displays, more use of in-store price scanners and promotions and so on. The entire character of the shopping experience had changed.

The past twenty-five years have seen the continued advance of the superstore format, not just in the ten initial categories but across virtually every other specialist category, including pets, books and baby goods.

Other retail categories

The story so far told in this chapter of Australian retailing history is that of three giants in retailing: department stores, supermarkets and superstores in specialist categories (see Brash et al., 1985; Miller, 2005; 2006a; Miller & Merrilees, 2002, 2004, 2013, 2016).

A corollary of the emergence of retailer giants in these three dominant areas is the demise of many small retailers. Specialty retailers have a long history in Australia. In the early stage of colonisation, retailing was very small scale and fragmented, and included small drapery and grocery stores. Hundreds of small drapers were eliminated in the nineteenth century; over 30,000 small grocery trade businesses were unable to compete against the modern supermarkets; and tens of thousands of small specialty retailers have been unable to compete against the mega-size superstores. Very few of these stories have been documented. We know little about how some may have simply accepted their lot while others may have resisted and perhaps introduced changes and innovations in their own way.

Although there are relatively few academic studies about individual retailers, Australian menswear retailer, *Gowings*, is an exception. For example, Miller and Merrilees (2001) tell the story of the iconic Sydney menswear store Gowings. The research complemented a celebratory history of the firm (Gowing, 1993). Research on the retail strategy that Gowings used from the firm's inception in the 1860s until the late 1990s, shows the range of innovations deployed mainly in Sydney's Central Business District (CBD) location over four generations (Miller & Merrilees, 2001).

Gowings was founded in 1868 and quickly gained a reputation as a relevant, somewhat quirky and down to earth retailer. Innovation was a major part of their evolution and a major factor in their longevity. The role of marketing and organisational capabilities including innovation were sufficient in the Gowings story for Miller and Merrilees (2001) to develop a model of retail longevity from the case material evidence (including advertising archives). Another article (Crittenden & Wilson, 2002) has since replicated the Miller and Merrilees (2001) Great Merchant Model of Retail Longevity.

The structure of retailing has changed dramatically. Traditional specialist stores remain, providing they are not too close to an existing superstore. Location convenience and personal service remain as possible advantages. However, an ominous sign for the remaining traditional stores is the leading superstores exhausting prime sites, and so considering an ever-wider territory for expansion. This strategy can be viable because of extensive car ownership and a willingness to travel for destination shopping in Australia. Additionally, some superstores are adding a smaller, junior version of the format which again increases the chances of encroaching into places where the traditional stores have retreated to. Michael Hill, the New Zealand jewellery chain, has made a significant impact in the Australian market and is a strong example of a small-outlet size specialty retailer being modern and innovative.

The main real counters that traditional stores have to the superstore threat is for them to be innovative and to offer more personalised customer serviced. Traditional stores in key cutting and jewellery have responded by joining branded chains and modernising where possible. Innovation is both a threat (from the superstores) and a counter-attack (when the traditional stores innovate). Innovation has a role to play in most retail categories.

Australia and New Zealand have participated in retail trends globally, influenced by other national models but also shaping others as well. The unique challenge to far-flung retailers in the nineteenth and twentieth century was to manage the paradox between being somehow up to date with trends, products and services in the major capitals such as London, Paris and New York, and yet somehow respond to local needs, local opportunities and local constraints (Miller, 2005). The transference of fashion especially couture was often mediated by the department stores, such as in the example of department stores in Toronto, where some Parisian fashion could be ordered (Palmer, 2001). Several authors explore the impact of transnational influences on the development of Australian and New Zealand department stores (Miller, 2005; Miller & Merrilees, 2016) and find that while there were significant and identifiable global influences, there were equally very recognisable local innovative responses, and thus glocalisation might best describe developments (see also, Svennson, 2001). Retailing in Australia and New Zealand has also made an impact globally. Scholars like Wellington Chan (1996) have demonstrated the transference of knowledge from Sydney to Asia, for example, via the development of the Sincere and Wing On department stores in Hong Kong, Canton and Shanghai. Chinese Australian merchants wanted to take modern business methods to China and were even inspired by architecture of David Jones and Anthony Horderns (Chan, 1996; Godley & Hang, 2016; Miller, 2005). As an aside, some of those department store buildings from the first half of the twentieth century can still be found on Nanying Road in Shanghai.

The impacts: an historical perspective

Disruptive innovation in marketing channels is best seen from a longitudinal view and historical analysis is an ideal way of doing this. One rationale for the current chapter is to highlight the role of innovation in retailing, that is, the marketing channel. All the innovations discussed in our historical journey are tantamount to disruptive innovations. The department store was much larger than its predecessor drapery stores. Not only was the size of the store and the product range greater, the price was somewhat lower initially, and the scope of customer services was expanded including the provision of credit, delivery and lay-by (lay-away). Thus, department stores were a disruptive change to the prevailing drapery businesses. Similarly, supermarkets were disruptive to the grocery trade stores, and they effectively eliminated them from business within a few decades. Superstores were disruptive to the small traditional specialist stores, rendering many of them uncompetitive. In short, an historical longitudinal discourse provides a powerful lens into a very modern phenomenon: disruptive innovation.

Conclusion

The chapter is structured to focus on what the author identifies as the three giant retail categories that have dominated the past 200 years of Australian retailing. Department stores, supermarkets and superstores are the three retail categories representing the dominant format for two key eras: first, the century-plus up to 1950 (dominated by department stores), and second, the subsequent seven decades to the present (dominated by supermarkets and superstores). Taken at face value, department stores and supermarkets seem unlikely candidates for superstar status. The current somewhat negative perception of department stores (even whether they can survive) should not distort their previous stellar status. Similarly, supermarkets might be dismissed by many shoppers as boring and basic, but they remain a dominant economic force in Australian and New Zealand retailing.

The capability of these three categories to achieve superior status is closely linked to their innovation ability and to change over time. Innovation has been a theme linking the parts of this chapter. All three retail categories have achieved high status because of superior innovation. That is a salient lesson for contemporary retailers and other businesses. Moreover, they achieved acceptance of their innovations by adopting glocalisation, proactively responding to global trends and local needs.

References

Aldi (2017), 'Who we are', Available at: https://corporate.aldi.com.au/en/about-aldi/. (Accessed 21 November 2017).

Alexander, A. (2010), 'Past, present and future directions in the study of the history of retailing', *Journal of Historical Research in Marketing*, 2 (3), pp. 356–362.

Alexander, N. (1997), 'Objects in the rearview mirror may appear closer than they are', *The International Review of Retail, Distribution and Consumer Research*, 7 (4), pp. 383–403.

Alexander, N. (2011), 'British overseas retailing, 1900–60: International firm characteristics, market selections and entry modes', *Business History*, 53 (4), pp. 530–556.

Alexander, N. and Akehurst, G. (eds.) (1999), *The emergence of modern retailing 1750–1950* (London: Frank Cass).

Bailey, M. (2015), 'Written testimony, oral history and retail environments: Australian shopping centers in the 1960s', *Journal of Historical Research in Marketing*, 7 (3), pp. 356–372.

Barber, S. (2005), *Sidney myer, a life, a legacy* (Melbourne: Myer Family Investments).

Bartlett, N. (1946), 'Charles Lloyd Jones: The art of the honest draper', *Daily Telegraph* (25 May), pp. 16–17.

Barnard, E. (2015), *Emporium: Selling the dream in Colonial Australia* (Canberra: NLA Publishing).

Brash, N., Burke, A. and Hoeben, C. (1985), *The model store 1885–1985, Grace Bros: 100 years serving Sydney* (McMahons Point, NSW: Kevin Weldon & Associates).

Chan, W.K.K. (1996), 'Personal styles, cultural values and management: The sincere and wing on companies in Shanghai and Hong Kong, 1900–1941', *Business History Review*, 70 (2), pp. 141–166.

Clarke, I.C. and Rimmer, P. (1997), 'The anatomy of retail internationalisation: Daimaru's decision to invest in Melbourne, Australia', *The Service Industries Journal*, 17 (3), pp. 361–382.

Cooper, A. (2014), *Remembering Georges: Stories from Melbourne's most elegant store* (Melbourne: Melbourne Books).

Cooper, H., Merrilees, B. and Miller, D. (2015), 'Corporate heritage brand management: Corporate heritage brands versus contemporary corporate brands', *Journal of Brand Management*, 22 (5), pp. 412–430.
Crittenden, V. and Wilson, E. (2002), 'Success factors in non-store retailing: Exploring the great merchants framework', *Journal of Strategic Marketing*, 10 (4), pp. 255–272.
Crossick, G. and Jaumain, S. (1999), *Cathedrals of consumption: The European department store 1850–1939* (Aldershot: Ashgate).
Cullen, J. (2013), *The extraordinary life of Charles Lloyd Jones: Painter, Patron and Patriot 1878–1958* (Melbourne: Palgrave Macmillan).
Davies, S.C. (1946), *Foy's Saga: An account of the genesis and progress of the house of Foy & Gibson (W.A.) Limited . . . in Commemoration of Their Jubilee October 1895 to October 1945* (Perth, WA: Sands & McDougall).
Dunstan, K. (1979), *The store on the hill* (Melbourne: Palgrave Macmillan).
Emmet, B. and Jeuck, J.E. (1950), *Catalogues and counters: A history of Sears, roebuck and company* (Chicago: University of Chicago Press).
Ferry, J.W. (1960), *A history of the department store* (New York: Palgrave Macmillan).
Friedman, W. and Jones, G. (eds.) (2012). *Guide to business history course worldwide* (Cambrige, MA: Harvard Business School, Business History Initiative).
Godley, A. and Hang, H. (2012), 'Globalisation and the evolution of international retailing: A comment on Alexander's 'British overseas retailing, 1900–1960'', *Business History*, 54 (4), pp. 529–541.
Godley, A. and Hang, H. (2016), 'Collective financing among Chinese entrepreneurs and department store retailing in China', *Business History*, 58 (3), pp. 364–377.
Gowing, S. (1993), *Gone to gowings* (Sydney: State Library of New South Wales Press).
Hollander, S. (1986), 'A rearview mirror might help us drive forward – a call for more historical studies in retailing: Guest editorial', *Journal of Retailing*, 62 (1), pp. 7–10.
Hollander, S., Rassuli, K.M., Jones, D.G.B. and Dix, L.F. (2005), 'Periodization in marketing history', *Journal of Macromarketing*, 25 (1), pp. 32–41.
Hordern, L. (1985), *Children of one family: The story of Anthony and Ann Hordern and their descendants in Australia, 1825–1925* (Sydney: Retford Press).
Hower, R.M. (1943), *History of Macy's of New York, 1858–1919: Chapters in the evolution of the department store* (Cambridge, MA: Harvard University Press).
Humphrey, K. (1998), *Shelf life: Supermarkets and the changing cultures of consumption* (Cambridge: Cambridge University Press).
Jarratt, D. (1998), 'Modelling outshopping behaviour: A non-metropolitan perspective', *The International Review of Retail, Distribution and Consumer Research*, 8 (3), pp. 319–350.
Jones, C.L. (1956), 'The history of David Jones limited', *Bulletin of the Business Archives Council of Australia*, 1 (1), pp. 1–10.
Kimbrough, E. (1952), *Through Charley's door* (New York: Harper).
Kingston, B. (1994), *Basket, bag and trolley: A history of shopping in Australia* (Melbourne: Oxford University Press).
Lancaster, B. (1995), *The department store: A social history* (London: Leicester University Press).
MacCulloch, J. (1980), ''This store is our world': Female shop assistants in Sydney to 1930', in J. Roe (ed.) *Twentieth century Sydney: Studies in urban and social history* (Sydney: Hale & Iremonger) 166–178.
Macpherson, M.E. (1963), *Shopkeepers to a nation: The Eatons* (Toronto: McClelland and Stewart).
Mark Foy's Ltd (1935), *The romance of the house of Foy: Golden Jubilee of Mark Foy's Ltd Sydney 1885–1935* (Sydney: Mark Foy's Ltd).
Marshall, A. (1961), *The gay provider: The Myer story* (Melbourne: F.W. Cheshire).
Maynard, M. (1994), *Fashioned from penury: Dress as cultural practice in Colonial Australia* (Cambridge: Cambridge University Press).
McCann, J. (2002), *A lot in store: Celebrating our shopping heritage* (Sydney: NSW Heritage Office and NSW Ministry for the Arts Moveable Heritage Project).
Merrilees, B. and Miller, D. (1996), *Retailing management: A best practice approach* (Melbourne: RMIT Press).
Merrilees, B. and Miller, D. (1997), 'The superstore format in Australia: Opportunities and limitations', *Long Range Planning*, 30 (6), pp. 899–905.
Merrilees, B. and Miller, D. (2001a), 'Innovation and strategy in the Australian supermarket industry', *Journal of Food Products Marketing*, 7 (4), pp. 3–18.
Merrilees, B. and Miller, D. (2001b), 'Radical service innovations: Success factors in retail pharmacies', *International Journal of New Product Development & Innovation Management*, 3 (1), pp. 79–91.
Merrilees, B. and Miller, D. (2001c), 'Superstore interactivity: A new self-service paradigm of retail service?' *International Journal of Retail & Distribution Management*, 29 (6), pp. 379–389.

Merrilees, B., Miller, D. and Shao, W. (2016), 'Mall brand meaning: An experiential branding perspective', *Journal of Product and Brand Management*, 25 (3), pp. 262–273.

Millen, J. (2000), *Kirkcaldie & stains: A Wellington story* (Wellington: Bridget Williams Books).

Miller, D. (2005), 'Diverse transnational influences and department stores: Australian evidence from the 1870s – 1950s', in A. Sedlmaier (ed.) *Jahrbuch Fur Wirtschaftsgeschichte: From department store to shopping mall: Transnational history / Vom Warenhaus zur Shopping Mall: Einzelhandel Transnational [Economic History Yearbook]* (Berlin: Akademie Verlag) 17–40.

Miller, D. (2006a), 'Strategic human resource management in department stores: An historical perspective', *Journal of Retailing and Consumer Services*, 13 (2), pp. 99–109.

Miller, D. (2006b), 'Marketing perspectives on the value and conduct of archival research', *Canadian Journal of Marketing Research*, 23 (1), pp. 47–55.

Miller, D. (2011), 'Building customer confidence in the automobile age: Canadian Tire 1928–1939', *Journal of Historical Research in Marketing*, 3 (3), pp. 302–328.

Miller, D. (2014), 'Brand-building and the elements of success: Discoveries using historical analyses', *Qualitative Market Research: An International Journal*, 17 (2), pp. 92–111.

Miller, D. and Merrilees, B. (2001), '"Gone to Gowings" – an analysis of success factors in retail longevity: *Gowings* of Sydney', *Service Industries Journal*, 20 (1), pp. 61–85.

Miller, D. and Merrilees, B. (2002), 'Innovation processes in an early entrepreneurial department store: *David Jones* 1906–1927', in *Research at the marketing/entrepreneurship interface* (Chicago: Institute for Entrepreneurial Studies University of Illinois at Chicago) 374–392.

Miller, D. and Merrilees, B. (2004), 'Fashion and commerce: A historical perspective on Australian fashion', *International Journal of Retail & Distribution Management*, 32 (8), pp. 394–402.

Miller, D. and Merrilees, B. (2013), 'Historical ambidextrous marketing: Antipodean perspectives', Paper presented at CHARM 2013, Copenhagen. It was awarded the *Stanley C. Hollander Best Paper Award.*

Miller, D. and Merrilees, B. (2016), 'Department store innovation: David Jones Ltd., Australia, 1876–1915', *Journal of Historical Research in Marketing*, 8 (3), pp. 396–415.

Miller, M.B. (1981), *The Bon Marché: Bourgeois Culture and the Department Store 1869–1920* (London: Allen & Unwin).

Murray, J.C. (1999), *The woolworths way: A great Australian success story 1924–1999* (Edgecliff, NSW: Woolworths).

Nasmith, G. (1923), *Timothy Eaton* (Toronto: McClelland & Stewart).

Nesbitt, R. (1993), *At Arnotts of Dublin, 1843–1993* (Dublin: A. & A. Farmar)

Nystrom, P. (1915), *The economics of retailing*, 1919 ed. (New York: The Ronald Press).

O'Neill, H. (2013), *David Jones 175 Years* (Sydney: NewSouth University of New South Wales Press).

Palmer, A. (2001), *Couture & commerce: The transatlantic fashion trade in the 1950s* (Vancouver: UBC Press in Association with the Royal Ontario Museum).

Perkins, J. and Freedman, C. (1999), 'Organisational form and retailing development: The department and the chain store 1860–1940', *Service Industries Journal*, 19 (4), pp. 123–146.

Perkins, J. and Meredith, D. (1996), *Managerial development in retailing: The department and the chain store, 1860–1940* (Sydney: University of New South Wales School of Economics).

Pitcher, H. (1994), *Muir & Mirrielees: The Scottish partnership that became a household name in Russia* (Cromer, UK: Swallow House Books).

Pollon, F. (1989), *Shopkeepers and shoppers: A social history of retailing in New South Wales from 1788* (Sydney: Retail Traders' Association of New South Wales).

Polonsky, M. and Jarratt, D. (1992), 'Rural outshopping in Australia: The Bathurst-Orange region', *European Journal of Marketing*, 26 (10), pp. 5–16.

Pound, R. (1960), *Selfridge: A biography* (London: Heinemann).

Pragnell, B.J. (2001), '"Selling consent": From authoritarianism to Welfarism at David Jones, 1838–1958', PhD thesis. University of New South Wales, Sydney.

Redmond, T. (1938), *The history of Anthony Hordern and sons limited* (Sydney: Anthony Horderns' Print).

Reekie, G. (1987), 'Humanising industry: Paternalism, welfarism and labour control in Sydney's big stores 1890–1930', *Labour History*, 53, pp. 1–19.

Reekie, G. (1993), *Temptations: Sex, selling, and the department store* (St. Leonards, NSW: Allen & Unwin).

Rees, G. (1969), *St Michael: A history of marks and spencer*, 1973 Revised ed. (London: Pan Books).

Resseguie, H.E. (1962), 'The decline and fall of the commercial empire of A. T. Stewart', *Business History Review*, 36 (Autumn), pp. 255–286.

Resseguie, H.E. (1965), 'Alexander Turney Stewart and the development of the department store, 1823–1876', *Business History Review*, 39 (Autumn), pp. 301–322.

Roberts, E. (2003), 'Don't sell things, sell effects: Overseas influences in New Zealand department stores, 1909–1956', *Business History Review*, 77 (2), pp. 265–289.
Roy Morgan (2017), 'Aldi hits new high in supermarket wars', *Press release*, 17 May. Finding no. 7234. Available at: www.roymorgan.com/findings/7234-woolworths-coles-aldi-iga-supermarket-market-shares-australia-march-2017-201705171406. (Accessed 21 November 2017).
Santink, J.L. (1990), *Timothy Eaton and the rise of his department store* (Toronto: University of Toronto Press).
Siry, J. (1988), *Carson Pirie Scott: Louis sullivan and the Chicago department store* (Chicago: University of Chicago Press).
Strasser, S. (1989), *Satisfaction guaranteed: The making of the American mass market* (Washington, DC: Smithsonian Institution Press).
Svennson, G. (2001), 'Glocalization of business activities: A "glocal" strategy', *Management Decision*, 39 (1), pp. 6–18.
Sydenham, D. (1993), 'Coles, Sir George James (1885–1977)', in *Australian dictionary of biography*, National Centre of Biography, Australian National University, published first in hardcopy 1993, Available at: http://adb.anu.edu.au/biography/coles-sir-george-james-9788/text17299. (Accessed 19 October 2017).
Ville, S. and Merrett, D. (2000), 'The development of large scale enterprise in Australia, 1910–64', *Business History*, 42 (3), pp. 13–43.
Waller, D. (1992), 'Shopping by post: The early development of mail order in Australia', *Journal of Direct Marketing Association*, 8 (1), pp. 24–28.
Warrender, P. (1972), *Prince of merchants: The story of sir Norman Myer* (Melbourne: Gold Star Publications).
Webber, K., Hoskins, I. and McCann, J. (2003), *What's in store? A history of retailing in Australia* (Sydney: Powerhouse Publishing in Association with the New South Wales Heritage Office).
Wendt, L. and Kogan, H. (1952), *Give the lady what she wants! The story of marshall field & company* (South Bend, IN: And Books).
Westfield, C. (2000), *The westfield story: The first 40 years* (Sydney: Westfield Holdings).

Sources

From the David Jones archive

Used with permission of David Jones Ltd and in consultation with the Archivist, Barbara Horton.

BRG 1/32/1–6: *Board Minutes.*
BRG 1/69 *50th Anniversary.*
BRG 1/577 Historical Notes on David Jones & Co. and David Jones Ltd.
BRG Annual Reports and Chairman's Addresses.
BRG R1/31/0–6 Rough Minutes of Board Meetings.
PRG 1/7a, 1862 *Journal* of Edward Lloyd Jones: Notes made in London, Scotland, Ireland and Paris April/August (Transcription); PRG 1/7: Original of PRG 1/7a.
PRG 1/8c.1874 Edward Lloyd Jones: Notes in *Diary.*
PRG 1/9a 1876 E. L. Jones Journal on the occasion of his visit to America and London 7th April to 16th September 1876 (Transcription); PRG 1/9 Original of PRG 1/9a.
PRG 2/80
PRG 2/80 (25a) 1958. *Customers Are Human*, by Charles Lloyd Jones in Collaboration with Desmond Robinson (unpublished).

Reports

Harwood, A. 1913 Commissioned Report.
Harwood, A. 1913 Commissioned Report – Responses to the Board.

Historical notes and articles

Horton, B. (c. 2000) Personal communications with C. B. L. Jones re influence of Saks 5th Avenue on development of 1927 store design.
Horton, B. (n.d.) The Management of David Jones Co 1838–1906.

Jones, C.L. (1948), *David Jones idea of doing business: As outlined by "C. L."*; Reprint of Talk given in 1946.
Jones, C.L. (1956), 'The history of David Jones Limited', *Bulletin of the Business Archives Council of Australia*, 1 (1 May), pp. 1–10.

The catalogue collection

Most catalogues from their inception in 1899 are available. They emphasise both products and services.

The McNeill collection

The McNeill Collection (McNC): the materials include published reference works (books, journals), McNeill's original speeches and lectures prepared for training programme, photographs and extensive materials from other department stores especially from outside Australia.

McNeill Collection: The Editors & In Collaboration with Ralph Starr Butler and John B. Swinney, 1918. Marketing and Merchandising. *Modern Business Series*. New York: The Alexander Hamilton Institute. Accessed in the David Jones Archive, 2006.

Newspaper clippings collection

Newspaper clippings have been collected over an extensive period. They include advertisements by *David Jones* and press reports; Bartlett N. 1946. Charles Lloyd Jones: The Art of the Honest Draper. *Daily Telegraph* (25 May): 16–17.

Oral history collection

Oral History Collection (OHC). This collection was generally developed by the Archivist with former members of staff

Staff newspaper collection

Covers all the variously named internal staff newspapers including:

Between Ourselves 1916, Issues 1 and 2.
Between Ourselves from 1919, numbering starts at Volume 1, Issue 1.
The Dajonian Monthly
David Jones Store News

25

HISTORY OF RETAILING IN LATIN AMERICA

From the corner store to the supermarket

Martín Monsalve Zanatti

The big department stores of the nineteenth century transformed the urban structure, culture of consumption and ways of doing business in the major Latin American capitals. Nowadays, shopping malls have left the middle- and upper-class neighbourhoods to reach a larger mass of consumers, and for the first time supermarkets enjoy a high level of participation in the region's food distribution channels. In this chapter we will give a brief overview of the history of retailing in Latin America, describing the transition from monumental city-center department stores to the expansion of supermarkets throughout the urban space. We draw on national cases for the analysis of each stage in this history, as they provide a broader explanation of the period. Likewise, given the specificities of the subject, we place emphasis on a cultural approach, as well as one involving commercial strategies.

The development of modern retailing is a phenomenon that emerged in Latin America during the late nineteenth century as part of the first globalisation, but the system was not consolidated until the middle of the last century. Moreover, it was not until the second half of the 1990s that the sector underwent explosive growth. Two of the issues that we stress in this overview are how the sector's commercial strategies are configured based on tensions between the global and the local, and how these strategies seek to address specific problems such as market size, or competition with multinational companies using local resources.

We start by presenting a review of the literature on the culture of consumption in Latin America, which will serve as an introduction to our overview of retail history. Then, we provide a general outline of the periodisation of retail in the region, before drawing on secondary sources to sketch out the main characteristics of each of the stages in question.

Background: a review of the history of consumption in Latin America

Historical studies on consumption in Latin America are still in their early stage and have been heavily influenced by economic, anthropological and, in recent times, cultural studies. According to Trentmann & Otero-Cleves, this is because studies on consumption in the region have centred on three factors. The first is the prevalence of the study of export economies within economic and social history approaches, which saw more importance being given to production than to consumption. The second is based on the assumption that Latin America is an economically backward region, and thus that it is lacking in consumers. Finally, the preconception that the Latin American population tends to imitate foreign patterns of behaviour (tastes) (Trentmann & Otero-Cleves, 2017: 20).

Despite these preconceptions, in recent years an interesting historiography has grown up around consumption in Latin America, which can be grouped into three broad categories, or stages. The first, formative category continues to work from the conceptual framework of Latin America as an exporter of raw materials and an importer of manufactured products; the second is based on national case studies and seeks to elaborate upon the path opened up by its predecessors; and the third locates its analyses of consumption in gender debates, identity politics and conceptions of social dignity. That said, a historiographical agenda for the history of consumption has still to be established.

As proposed explicitly by Trentmann and Otero-Cleves (2017), initial studies on consumption in Latin America were heavily influenced by the notion of the so-called Latin American "exporter model". Thus, analyses were preoccupied with the production of raw materials and their impact on consumers in the European or North American markets. However vast its contributions may have been, the pioneering study by Sidney Mintz, *Sweetness and Power* (1985), works from this standpoint, as do the more recent studies on raw materials or global commodities, as well as the excellent research on supply chains presented by Steven Topik, Carlos Marichal & Zephyr L. Frank, in *From Silver to Cocaine: Latin American Commodity Chains and the Building of the World Economy, 1500–2000* (2006). Paul Gootenberg's *Andean Cocaine: The Making of a Global Drug* (2008) provides another example.

The analyses that truly open up the study of consumption in the region are those of Arnold Bauer & Benjamin Orlove, *The Allure of the Foreign: Giving Importance to Imports* (1997), and A. Bauer, *Goods, Power and History: Latin American's Material Culture* (2001). Bauer charts a history of consumption from the era of conquest through to the end of the twentith century. His study provides an analysis of consumption and its techniques, as well as its relations with culture and the impact of imported goods in different contexts (Morales, 2005: 178). That is, Bauer shifts the focus away the exporter model to enquire into the impact that goods produced in Europe and the United States have had on Latin American societies. Taking their lead from Bauer, the most recent studies on national cases such as Manuel Llorca (2014) and Ana María Otero (2017) have shown that Latin Americans are not passive consumers of foreign goods, and so European traders should adapt to local needs and tastes (Trentmann & Otero-Cleves, 2017: 21–22).

In keeping with this pattern of national histories but from a perspective more closely linked to economic history, several studies have analysed the formation of a society of local consumption and its influence on industrialisation during the first globalisation (Rocchi, 1998). Such works complement the analyses of interaction between final consumers and commercial intermediaries in the creation of local and international markets (Lluch, 2015).

A third historiographical strand has focused on the development of a culture of consumption and new consumers. A good example of this approach is Steven Bunker's *Creating Mexican Consumer Culture in the Age of Porfirio Díaz* (2014), in which the author analyses big stores and the publicity associated with consumption during the *Porfiriato*. Bunker studies the emergence of a society of consumption as part of the construction of the idea of modernity in Mexico. The most important contribution of this strand, however, lies not in its analyses of the ideas of modernity, but, as proposed by (Pérez, 2017; Trentmann & Otero-Cleves, 2017), in the study of consumption as one of the mechanisms of gender and/or class identity, how consumption contributes to the formation of a civic culture and political participation, and how it is linked to notions of social dignity (Elena, 2011, Milanesio, 2013). Another example is the initial study of the relationship between middle-class identity and consumption in Maureen O'Dougherty's *Consumption Intensified: The Politics of Middle-Class Daily Life in Brazil* (2002).

The book by Natalia Milanesio, *Workers Go Shopping in Argentina: The Rise of Popular Consumer Culture* (2013) is perhaps that which best exemplifies the aforementioned iterations, because, on the one hand, it develops the idea of how the emergence of workers as new consumers in Argentine society was fundamental to the legitimisation of President Juan Domingo Perón's regime. And on the other, the irruption of workers as new consumers forced publicists to change their techniques and create a new culture of consumption. Moreover, Milanesio points out that the importance of the domestic space in Peronist politics gave housewives from working-class families a leading role (Pérez, 2017: 33).

This review of the literature on consumption sets the scene for our history of retail in the region. However, if the historical analysis of Latin American consumption in general still lacks a concrete agenda, the study of the history of retail in particular remains in its beginnings (Bunker, 2010). As such, in this chapter we present a general review of the history of retail in the region, based on the existing literature for the cases of Chile, Colombia, Mexico and Peru. We approach the histories of these national cases for each of the periods in the development of retail in Latin America, from the end of the 1900s through to the first decade of the twenty-first century.

Periodisation of the history of retail in Latin America

Modern retail took root in Latin America in the late nineteenth century, in the period known as the first globalisation. During this formative stage, the main actors were generally immigrants from Europe who turned their old stores into supermarkets and/or department stores. This phenomenon first occurred in the region's most populous urban centres, such as Mexico City and Buenos Aires, but quickly spread to other major Latin American cities (Reardon & Berdegué, 2002: 93).

The 1950s marked the start of the consolidation of supermarkets and department stores, while the first shopping malls opened their doors in the 1960s. This was a period that coincided with urban growth and industrialisation in the region, which saw workers become the "new consumers" (Milanesio, 2013). This obligated the supermarkets to leave the city centres and penetrate not only middle- and upper-class districts, but also working-class neighbourhoods. However, this process did not occur at the same time in each of the countries in the region. The period ended with the external debt crisis and the inflationary processes that hit the Latin American economies in the 1980s.

The sector experienced significant growth following the liberalisation of the Latin American economies in the 1990s, which involved both a process of regional internationalisation and the arrival of large international chains to countries in the region. During this period, first supermarkets and then shopping malls expanded into neighbourhoods in the urban peripheries inhabited by the lower-middle and working classes. Finally, it is important to note the growth of self-service or convenience stores during the 2000s, including the likes of OXXO in Mexico, Tambo in Peru and Big John and Ok Market in Chile.

It should be noted that marketing channels known generically as "traditional" or "informal" have existed across all of these periods, and until very recently dominated the commercialisation of goods. These include *bodegas*, traditional stores engaged in the sale of miscellaneous retail products; markets, places where retail and wholesale traders operate, are grouped into unions or associations, and to a certain extent conserve the "traditional" channels of exchange of goods; and street hawking.

Figure 25.1 Supermercado, Chile

Source: Código: MC0069705/BN 1074891, Autor: Cardoso, Armindo, Titulo: Supermercado Almac, Año: 1973, URL: http:www.memoriachilena.cl/602/w3-article-128267.html

Figure 25.2 Bodega E. Wong

Source: Photo courtesy of Eric Wong

The first department stores and supermarkets, 1890–1950

There is a long tradition of exchange and commerce in Latin America, which in one way or another has influenced the development of retailing in the region (Bunker, 2010). Mexico and Peru, historical centres of indigenous civilisation in the region, had different traditions of exchange that predated the invasion of the Spanish conquistadors. Markets or *tanguis* were spaces of commercial transactions in Mesoamerica, while forms of exchange or bartering measured in the provision of work predominated in the Andes. Following the establishment of the dominion of the Spanish Crown, trade expanded throughout the region.

In the colonial cities, commerce took place through street hawking, markets, *pulperías* and *cajones*. The *pulperías* were stores usually located on street corners where a wide variety of products were sold. These are the forebears of what came to be known in the twentieth century as bodegas. In the post-independence era through to the mid-twentieth century, these establishments were often run by European or Asian immigrants: in the Peruvian case, the Italians and Chinese.

Meanwhile, the *cajones* were stores based on the ground floor of buildings, generally found in the major plazas of the cities. They sold threads, buttons, padlocks, footwear, textiles and so on. In the years immediately following the independence of the Latin American countries, *cajones*

Figure 25.3 Augusto Fernando Oechle.

Source: Peruvian National Library

tended to specialise in the sale of a single product, or goods that were in some way related. In the case of the rural sector, these stores acted as trading houses that supplied capital goods to farmers and ranchers, connecting them to the international market (Fernández & Lluch, n.d.). For various reasons, among them the scarcity of low-denomination currency, most sales during the colonial and post-independence periods in the region were by credit; as Bunker notes for the Mexican case, this practice would prove to be highly influential on modern retailing in the region (2014).

In the early decades of the nineteenth century, a new wave of European immigration reached Latin America. Many of these immigrants acquired *cajones* in the centres of major cities, in some cases specialising in the sale of certain products, such as clothing. Little by little the *cajones* evolved into stores that displayed their products in glass cabinets or behind the counter. This made the merchandise more visible, but it meant that consumers did not have direct access to it. Prices were not fixed and so were subject to constant haggling (Bunker, 2010: 43). These stores were to play a fundamental role in the development of retailing in Latin America during the first globalisation.

In the case of Mexico, it was the stores run by a group of immigrants from the commune of Barcelonnette in France that were instrumental to the creation of department stores in the country. The Barcelonnette entrepreneurs diversified their investments across the fields

Figure 25.4 Almacenes, Peru.
Source: Peruvian National Library

of clothes manufacturing, banking, and beer, cigarette and paper production in several Mexican cities. But their most significant investments for the history of retailing lay in converting the old colonial *cajones* into retailers resembling the Parisian fashion stores, which later became the first department stores in Latin America (Bunker, 2010, 2014; Galindo, 2013; Valerio, 2016).

One such store was "Fábrica de Francia", opened in the 1860s by Alexander Raynaud and V. Gassier from Barcelonnette. Years later, the two partners sold the store to the Parisians Joseph Tron and Joseph Leautaud, who in 1891 turned it into "El Palacio de Hierro": Mexico's first department store. Notably, they soon faced competition from similar businesses such as "El Puerto de Veracruz" (opened in 1897) and "El Puerto de Liverpool" (1898), followed by several others (Bunker, 2014).

In the case of Argentina, the experience was similar to Mexico's. Thus, for example, in 1883, Lorenzo Chaves from Chile and the Englishman Alfredo Gath founded a store selling menswear made from English fabrics. They branched into women's clothing soon after, turning "Gath y Chaves" into a department store in 1901. In the Peruvian case, the main player was a German immigrant, Augusto Fernando Oechle, who in the late 1900s opened a store selling threads, lace, and buttons imported from Europe, to which he later added textiles, perfumes, decorative items and toys. The growth of his business prompted Oechle to open Peru's first department store in 1917.

All of these businesses, with the exception of Oechle, expanded considerably, spawned branches and competed with similar stores. Yet these companies could not rely solely on the sale of European imports to the upper classes from those countries as a means of expanding and competing. They needed a strategy to reach a broader mass of consumers and be able to sell at scale.

One pattern that many of the Mexican and Argentine department stores followed was to initiate a process of backward vertical integration and invest in clothes production for sale in their stores. Consumption of clothes had increased markedly in both countries at the start of the 1900s, sparking the development of a garment industry (Rocchi, 1998: 540). In the case of Mexico, department stores such as El Palacio de Hierro also benefited from low labour costs in the manufacturing sector. The stores based much of their clothes-making strategy on producing copies of French and other European products (Bunker, 2010: 47).

Department stores in Mexico, and in Latin America in general, changed the consumption experience of an entire sector of society. Indeed, not only were store buildings enormous, but they were also spaces in which consumers could enjoy the innovations of modernity, such as electrical lighting, elevators, etc., free of charge. They were also able to view products in glass display cases or behind the counter under no obligation to buy. Unlike their counterparts in Europe and the United States, consumers in Latin America had no direct contact with the products on sale (Bunker, 2010: 51–53).

Bunker (2010, 2014) notes that the transition to fixed prices denoted by labels was one of the hardest changes for Mexican consumers, more accustomed to haggling, to accept. However, embracing and promoting the sale of credit, as well as integrating into the country's religious and political calendar, were two characteristics that set Mexican department stores apart from the French models on which they were based. The publicity strategies the stores designed were aimed at reinforcing the idea of a negotiated modernity, whereby they sold a modern lifestyle adapted to the particularities of the cultural world of contemporary urban consumers.

Just like the department stores, supermarkets in Latin America can also trace their roots to the old colonial *cajones* converted into stores during the nineteenth century. Likewise, European immigrants played an important role (Moreno, 2012). The best analysis of the rise of supermarkets so far available is that by D. Aristizábal García (2017), on the Colombian case. Of the European traders who came to Colombia in the early 1900s, the Catalan José Carulla stands out. To begin with, the bulk of Carulla's business activities were centred on exporting coffee, rubber and tobacco to Europe, and the sale of imported products to the Bogotá elite. As the years went by, the latter field came to dominate through his store, "Carulla y Compañía". Between 1930 and 1940, Carulla established a chain of stores known as "Escudo Catalán", which followed the pattern of the region's early stores in that they were places of encounter and conversation for consumers as much as buying and selling. For Carulla, gaining customer loyalty owed more to the warmth of the service than it did to price levels (Aristizábal García, 2017: 144). World War II changed the outlook for the Carulla family's businesses by making it impossible to import European products, while new commercial techniques were introduced to the city of Bogotá. At the start of the 1940s, the Steurs, a family of Czech origins who had fled the war in Europe, opened a store in Bogotá called "Tienda Internacional Americana" in which they applied all of the advances they had learned from American retailers – such as shelving, showcases and counters. Thus, Carulla decided around the same time to adopt the new ways of promoting merchandise, and changed his business focus to supplying Bogotá's internal market with Colombian products. In the early 1950s, his son, José Carulla Soler, went on a trip to the United States and Mexico to learn about supermarkets and the self-service system. Years later, Carulla Soler would open the family group's first supermarket in the city of Bogotá. The strategy was accompanied by a series of measures to "educate consumers" in the use of the new service. Leaflets were produced with instructions on how to make the best use of shopping carts, for example. The Carullas transformed their business in short order, establishing other supermarkets in Colombia and abroad within the decade. In addition, Colombia attracted US department stores such as Sears Roebuck, completely changing the consumption habits of the Andean country's upper and middle classes (Aristizábal García, 2017: 147–148).

In sum, the European immigrants who arrived in Latin America from the late 1900s to the early 2000s were fundamental to the formative stage of retailing in the region, because they acted as intermediaries between the new cultures of consumption in Europe and the United States, and the commercial traditions of the Latin American countries. Both department stores and supermarkets adapted to a situation in which they had to compete with traditional marketing channels such as bodegas and markets, where price negotiation was central. Department stores, for their part, embarked upon backward vertical integration processes to lower costs and enable competitive pricing. However, at a time of globalisation, department stores and supermarkets became a meeting point in which global notions of modernity interacted with local traditions, as proposed by Bunker (2014) and Aristizábal García (2017).

The consolidation of retailing in Latin America, 1950–1990

The postwar years in Latin America marked a period of state-led economic development upon which industrialisation processes were founded; the urban population had outgrown the rural by the end of the period, the middle classes consolidated themselves in countries such as Argentina, Chile, Mexico and Brazil, women acquired more economic independence and political rights, and workers became the great new sector of consumption following their incorporation into the region's formal economy (Bulmer Thomas, 1994; Elena, 2011; Milanesio, 2013). In this context, marketing channels based on department stores and supermarkets took root, and a new actor emerged in the form of the shopping mall. However, traditional channels such as bodegas, markets, and street hawking remained the primary mechanisms through which most of the population obtained their consumer goods.

In this section we will continue with the case of Colombian supermarkets before moving on to the particular experience of Peru. The aim of selecting these cases is to analyse the learning experiences and the dissemination of knowledge around the retail business, and how even during this period of consolidation the negotiation between traditional and modern styles endured.

As we saw in the previous section, the 1950s marked the definitive entry of supermarkets into Colombian retailing. However, this process of consolidation involved a steep learning curve for both the owners of the establishments and the consumers. One of the main problems was that many potential customers, despite the printed material and the educational notices, preferred to stick with the traditional markets and bodegas. The Carulla-run supermarkets had difficulties in securing customer loyalty, but they were not alone. Sears had to close their Medellín branch because once the novelty of experiencing "modernity" had passed, locals opted to return to their direct and personal dealings with the traditional stores. The firm's branches were bought by the Toro family, owners of what went on to become the Éxito supermarkets (Aristizábal García, 2017: 149).

The supermarket system was consolidated in Colombia during the 1960s and 1970s and several new local chains emerged, leading to fierce competition. According to Aristizábal García (2017: 150–151) this compelled owners to constantly improve their knowledge through trips abroad and participation in talks, such as those given by Bernardo of the National Cash Register company in the United States. Thereafter, the owners shared what they had learned with their employees. The Carullas were among those who embraced the new learning mechanisms, establishing more formal links with the National Supermarket Association in the United States. This gave them an advantage over their competitors in terms of acquiring knowledge and marketing.

Towards the end of the 1970s, the supermarket owners looked for ways of making the shopping experience more pleasant for consumers with a view to boosting their sales. Thus, they experimented with combining the practices of the old stores with those of the US supermarkets. The Éxito supermarket owned by the Toro family began to combine the sale of food staples with garments and household appliances. In the 1980s, the Colombian supermarket sector concerned itself primarily with expanding into working-class areas by promising access to modernity at affordable prices. Finally, it is important to note the interest in adapting supermarket architecture to local culture (Aristizábal García, 2017: 152–154).

We have followed the proposal of Colombian historian Aristizábal García closely because her analysis demonstrates how the evolution of the self-service model was a product of the experiences of owners, who acted as bridges between the North American culture of consumption and the desires and aspirations of their customers. Just as Bunker argues for the case of Mexican department stores, Colombian supermarkets were symbols of modernity that negotiated with local consumers to achieve acceptance by the population and thus assure profitability.

Returning to Oechle and the Peruvian case, at the start of the twentieth century the department store continued its expansion among the upper and upper-middle classes in the city of Lima. Unlike his Mexican counterparts, Oechle had no interest in incorporating the working classes into the "world of the modern consumer". The economic growth undergone by the county between 1950 and 1963 (Sheahan, 2001: 29), and the consequent consolidation of a professional middle class in Lima, seemed to prove him right. Perhaps with this pattern in mind, in 1953 the brothers Aldo and Orlando Olcese opened Peru's first supermarket, itself called "Súper Market", in Miraflores – a district where the upper and middle classes converged. Aldo Olcese had studies Business Administration at Texas University in the United States, where he "conceived of the idea . . . based on the North American models" (Sheahan, 2001: 34). The company sustained a solid rate of growth in the subsequent decades, with ten branches in Lima by the time it was expropriated by the dictatorship of General Juan Velasco in 1972. In parallel, other supermarket chains were established, such as Monterrey (1952) and Scala (1958). Probably attracted by the growth of retailing in Peru, Sears, Roebuck opened its first Lima store in 1955. Later, the supermarkets Gálax, Todos and Tía followed, always located in middle- or upper-class districts of the city of Lima (Suarez, 2011: 156). These companies led the market until their absorption by Grupo Wong in 1994.

The history of the E. Wong supermarket in Peru, founded on the notion of combining the self-service model with the traditions of the neighbourhood bodega, helps to deepen the study of how the culture of retailing was gradually introduced in Latin American countries and developed into the boom of the 1990s. However, the case is atypical of the Peruvian and Latin American experience insofar as the E. Wong group – which went on to lead the retail sector in Peru until its sale in 2007 to the Chilean transnational Cencosud – was founded by Chinese immigrants.

The first generation of the family, headed by the founder Erasmo Wong, opened a bodega in Avenida Dos de Mayo in the district of San Isidro in 1942, under the name of Wong. Located as he was in an upper-class district and in a business in which prices did not vary significantly, Erasmo Wong reasoned that his advantage over the competitors should lie in the warmth of the service he provided to his customers. This idea governed the approach of the second generation when they opted to convert the old bodega into a supermarket, which was followed by a second branch in the district of Miraflores in 1983, at a time when inflation and the economic crisis were starting to hit established competitors (Uber Grosse, 2006).

The second generation rapidly understood that, given the economic environment, they would not be able to compete on prices with the established supermarkets. Therefore, they opted to compete on the level of product quality and personalised attention. To achieve both objectives, they sought to lend their supermarkets the feel of an upmarket bodega. Thus, for example, they designed their supermarkets without the generic rectangular aisles, and included special compartments for liquor and delicacies. Moreover, despite the self-service model, supermarket staff were urged to offer customers special attention. This compelled the company to provide its employees with ongoing training, which set it apart from the competitors. To an even greater extent than in the Mexican and Colombian cases, from the mid- to late-twentieth century, tradition and modernity came together to create a consumer experience that distinguished Wong from its competitors, who were more preoccupied with emulating "the American way of life".

In 1994, E. Wong acquired the Gálax and Todos stores, displacing them from the market. This gave the company an enormous advantage over the rest of the field. But to safeguard the company's identity, it needed to assure the same quality of service in a greater number of stores, and to this end it set up the Training Center for E. Wong Workers in 1996 (Calado, Castro, & Lossio, 2004).

Wong's biggest challenge in the 1990s lay in expanding the supermarket model to the peripheries of Lima, which were still largely supplied through traditional channels. To do so, it needed to lower prices, even if this meant a deterioration in service quality. To this end the company created the Hipermercados Metro brand as a platform for selling staples at wholesale prices, opening the first Metro supermarket in the working-class district of Chorrillos in 1992. Later, more Metro supermarkets followed in working-class downtown neighbourhoods. But the biggest milestone was the entry of Hipermercados Metro into the district of Independencia in the north of Lima, as this marked the first time that a very low-income population – but whose numbers equated to high aggregate demand – was included in the supermarket circuit. The business was a success, and the supermarket contributed to the north of Lima's ongoing commercial development (Calado, Castro, & Lossio, 2004: 164). Moreover, the Wong group was responsible for the expansion of supermarkets to all social sectors of the Peruvian population, and not just in the city of Lima. This paved the way for the expansion of other Latin American supermarket chains into Peru, which, somewhat ironically, ended up pushing the Wong Group out of the supermarket business in 2007 – although the Wong and Metro brands were retained by their new owners, Cencosud.

The expansion of supermarkets in Latin America, 1990–2000

This stage in the history of retailing is characterised by the departure of supermarkets, convenience stores, department stores, shopping malls, pharmacies and home improvement stores from the middle- and upper-class neighbourhoods of Latin American cities. Shopping malls, for example, have become one of the major urban landmarks, and a space of interaction for city populations (Sassano, 2015).

Particularly striking is the progress made by supermarkets and convenience stores in seizing large market shares from more traditional distribution channels such as market and bodegas. This process can be explained by a combination of changes that took place in Latin American societies between 1980 and 2000. Of particular note was the rise in the urban population, the increasing entry of women to the workforce, the liberalisation of the food supply starting from the 1990s and the growth of average per capita income at the beginning of the twenty-first century (Reardon & Berdegué, 2002: 95).

The expansion of the sector has been accompanied by intense competition between domestic companies, leading to a series of mergers and acquisitions. Moreover, the growth in the Latin

American economy attracted foreign direct investment to the retail sector, especially in the case of the largest economies in the region. Thus, major international chains such as Walmart, Carrefour and Royal Ahold took advantage of the market concentration process initiated by local chains, and ended up controlling the sector in Argentina, Brazil and Mexico (Reardon & Berdegué, 2002: 98).

Chilean retail companies are the exception to this process in that they managed not only to compete successfully with the big transnational chains, but embarked upon their own regional internationalisation process, establishing operations in the likes of Argentina and Peru. In this section we focus on the Chilean case to understand how local companies responded to the challenge posed by a new process of globalisation.

The development of the retail sector in Chile was one of the most extensive in the region, despite the comparatively small size of the market. This involved the emergence of a large number of companies that had to compete fiercely with one another and develop competitive advantages to stay afloat in the domestic market. Chilean retail companies then leveraged these capacities to expand into other regional markets.

Chile was one of the first countries in Latin America to implement market reforms that included openness to international markets, state deregulation, and privatisations. As a result, Chilean companies underwent a restructuring process almost 20 years before their regional counterparts. Thus, at a time when most Latin American companies were still adapting to the liberal reforms of the 1990s, Chilean firms were already internationalising by expanding into neighbouring countries, especially Argentina and Peru. These first attempts were not all that successful, and in some cases the companies in question were forced to sell their investments to US or European competitors.

As we have noted, the competition from foreign retail firms was very strong. Walmart entered the Mexican market in 1991 and 4 years later expanded into Argentina and Brazil. Carrefour also consolidated its market position in these two countries. Royal Ahold, for its part, partnered with Grupo Velox of Argentina, which gave it directorial control of the Disco and Santa Isabel supermarkets, allowing it to access the markets of Argentina, Chile, Paraguay and Peru (Calderón Hoffmann, 2006: 158).

But the Chilean retailers successfully saw off the challenge posed by the expansion of these international operators. In 1999, for example, the US company J.C. Penney sold its assets in Chile to Almacenes París; while in 2001 Home Depot sold its operations in the country to local rival Falabella; and in 2003 Carrefour offloaded its branches to D&S and Royal Ahold transferred its operations to Cencosud. For Calderón Hoffman, there are two main reasons for the success of Chilean retail companies in this period. The first is the financial business lines of these firms, and the second is the adoption of an integrated retail model (Calderón Hoffmann, 2006).

The development of financial retail by issuing credit cards to customers was one of the main innovations of the Chilean retailers, serving as a means of financing their operations and gaining customer loyalty. The success of these activities spurred companies to open their own financial institutions, such as Banco Falabella (1998), Banco Ripley (2003) and Banco Paris (2004), which allowed them to expand their business further. In turn, the construction of an integrated retail mechanism was not as direct as the first process identified by Hoffman and was very closely linked to the firms' experiences of internationalisation.

Cencosud's internationalisation process began in the 1980s when it started operations in Argentina, leading to the creation in that country of the Jumbo chain of hypermarkets. But more important was its construction of the Unicenter shopping mall in the 1990s. In 1993, Cencosud introduced its line of home improvement stores, Easy, in Argentina and Chile simultaneously. For the rest of the decade, Cencosud concentrated its growth on the real estate sector in Argentina, which would later allow the company to build and run the biggest shopping malls in that country. Moreover, in 2002 Cencosud took over Home Depot's four Argentine branches, and the firm took leadership of the country's home improvement sector as a result. Meanwhile, Falabella expanded more cautiously into the Argentine market by establishing branches of its department stores in Mendoza, San Juan and Córdova. Its arrival in Buenos Aires came with the opening of a branch in Unicenter. But Falabella's most successful internationalisation experience was its incursion into the Peruvian market in 1995, the outcome of which prompted its domestic rival, Ripley, to open stores in Peru 2 years later (Calderón Hoffmann, 2006: 161–162).

The development of the Chilean retailers was stalled by the difficulties experienced by the Argentine and Peruvian economies around 2000. According to Calderón Hoffman, this forced the Chilean retail companies to diversify – as opposed to specialising – into various sectors, which allowed them to develop synergies to strengthen their businesses and reinvest abroad once the situation improved. Thus, they gradually developed a retail circuit around six fundamental lines of business: department stores, supermarkets, home improvement stores, banking, credit card administration and real estate operations, generally manifested in the construction of shopping malls (2006: 169).

As we have seen, each of the stages in the history of retailing in Latin America were characterised by episodes in which companies or consumers reacted to cultural and economic stimuli from outside the region. In this section, unlike in the others, the emphasis has not been on the negotiation of ideas of modernity as a starting point, but on how Latin American companies developed successful strategies to compete internationally.

Conclusion

Throughout this brief history of retail in Latin America, we have seen how department stores, supermarkets and shopping malls became spaces in which ideas of modernity were negotiated with local traditions in a globalised world. The European immigrants who gave rise to modern retailing in Latin America, or the descendants of Chinese immigrants who revolutionised Peru's supermarkets, acted as intermediaries between these tensions.

During the stages of emergence and consolidation of retailing in Latin America, the process of acquiring techniques and devising commercial strategies owed much to the intuition of the business owners and managers. Using family contacts or friendships abroad, attending conferences, going on field trips, joining international associations: trial and error were the most common methods of learning about the business. Moreover, one of the main challenges, above all during the early decades, lay in getting customers used to the self-service system.

Finding mechanisms to expand the reach of "modern" retailing among the population constitutes a constant tension. Vertical integration at the start of the last century was one of the mechanisms used to lower the cost of products, and in the first years of this century, store credit cards have been a common method employed. But it was the population and economic changes in Latin American countries that enabled the expansion of supermarkets and department stores into the working-class sectors towards the end of the 1990s.

Finally, a recent phenomenon is the concentration of the retail sector and the preponderance of transnational operators in the region, the counterpoint of which has been the regional expansion of Chilean retailers through the integration of different branches of the business.

References

Ablin, A. (2012), 'El supermercadismo argentino', *Alimentos Argentinos-Min*, 2.

Aristizábal García, D.M. (2017), '"Supermercados made in". Conexiones, consumo y apropiaciones. Estados Unidos y Colombia (siglo XX)', *Historia Crítica*, 65, pp. 139–159, doi:dx.doi.org/10.7440/histcrit65.2017.07.

Ayerdis, M. (2004), 'Consumo, poder e identidad a finales del siglo XIX e inicios del XX en Nicaragua (una aproximación)', *ihnca.*

Bauer, A.J. (2001), *Goods, power and history: Latin America's material culture* (Cambridge: Cambridge University Press).

Bauer, A.J. (2002), *Somos lo que compramos: historia de la cultura material en América Latina* (Mexico: Taurus).

Bauer, A.J. and Orlove, B. (eds.) (1997). *The allure of the Foreign: Imported goods in postcolonial Latin America* (Ann Arbor, MI: University of Michigan Press).

Bulmer Thomas, V. (1994), *Economic history of Latin America since independence* (Cambridge: Cambridge University Press).

Bunker, S.B. (2010), 'Transatlantic retailing the Franco-Mexican business model of fin-de-siecle department stores in Mexico City', *Journal of Historical Research in Marketing*, 2 (1), pp. 41–60.

Bunker, S.B. (2014), *Creating Mexican consumer culture in the age of Porfirio Díaz* (Albuquerque: University of New Mexico Press).

Calado, A., Castro, M., Lossio, F., et al. (2004), 'Las tiendas E. Wong: Un análisis organizacional', *Debates en Sociología*, 29, pp. 160–186.

Calderón Hoffmann, A. (2006), 'El modelo de expansión de las grandes cadenas minoristas chilenas', *Revista de la CEPAL*, 90, pp. 151–170.

CEPAL. (2005), *América Latina: Urbanización y Evolución de la Población Urbana, 1950–2000* (Santiago de Chile: ONU).

Cerdà Troncoso, J.F. (2011), *Análisis de correspondencia entre los patrones de localizacion y comportamiento del mercado en la industria supermercadista: Santiago de Chile 1958–2000.* Universidad Politécnica de Cataluña

Ciccolella, P. (2000), 'Distribución global y territorio. Modernización y concentración comercial en Argentina en los años noventa', *Economía, Sociedad y Territorio*, 2 (7).

Di Nucci, J. and Lan, D. (2008), 'Globalización y modernización del comercio minorista argentino en la década de los noventa', *Huellas*, 12.

Elena, E. (2011), *Dignifying Argentina: Peronism, citizenship, and mass consumption* (Pittsburgh, PA: University of Pittsburgh Press).

Fernández, A. and Lluch, A. (n.d.), 'Comercio y redes de comercialización mayoristas y minoristas en la Argentina de comienzos del siglo XX', *Fuentes*, 1885 (25), p. 8.

Galindo, J. (2013), 'The economic expansion of an elite business family of french origin in Central Mexico in the first half of the Twentieth Century', *Enterprise & Society*, 14 (4), pp. 794–828, doi:10.1093/es/kht039.

Gootenberg, P. (2008), *Andean Cocaine: The making of a global drug* (Chapel Hill, NC: University of North Carolina Press).

Gore, E. (2009), *Conocimiento Colectivo: La formación en el trabajo y la generación de capacidades colectivas* (Ediciones Granica). Available at: https://books.google.com.pe/books?id=oAU5DAAAQBAJ.

León, O. (2007), 'Las tiendas de autoservicio y la pugna por el mercado', *Comercio Exterior*, 57 (12), pp. 46–57.

Llorca-Jaña, M. (2014), *The British textile trade in South America in the Nineteenth Century* (Cambridge: Cambridge University Press).

Lluch, A. (2015), *Las manos visibles del mercado: intermediarios y consumidores en la Argentina (siglos XIX y XX)* (Rosario: Prohistoria).

Milanesio, N. (2013), *Workers go shopping in Argentina: The rise of popular consumer culture* (Alburquerque: University of New Mexico Press).

Mintz, S.W. (1985), *Sweetness and power: The place of sugar in modern history* (New York: Penguin).

Morales, E.P. (2005), 'Arnold J. Bauer, Somos lo que compramos: Historia de la cultura material en América Latina, México', *Historia y Sociedad*, (11), pp. 177–181.

Moreno, J. (2003), *Yankee don't go home! Mexican Nationalism, American business culture, and the shaping of modern Mexico, 1920–1950* (Chapel Hill, NC: University of North California Press Books).

Moreno, J. (2012), 'Los españoles y la revolución comercial mexicana: las cadenas de supermercados, 1921–2011', *Investigaciones de Historia Económica*, 8 (2), pp. 69–82.

O'Dougherty, M. (2002), *Consumption intensified: e politics of middle-class daily life in Brazil* (Durham, NC: Duke University Press).

Otero-Cleves, A.M. (2017), 'Foreign machetes and cheap cotton cloth: Popular consumers and imported commodities in nineteenth-century Colombia', *Hispanic American Historical Review*, 97 (3), pp. 423–456.

Pérez, I. (2017), 'Consumo y género: una revisión de la producción historiográfica reciente sobre América Latina en el siglo XX', *Historia Crítica*, 65, pp. 29–48, doi:dx.doi.org/10.7440/histcrit65.2017.02.

Reardon, T. and Berdegué, J.A. (2002), 'La rápida expansión de los supermercados en América Latina: desafíos y oportunidades para el desarrollo', *Revista Economía*, (49), pp. 85–120.

Reyna, M.L. (2006), 'De la tiendita al supermercado: los comerciantes chinos en América Latina y el Caribe', *Nueva Sociedad*, 203, pp. 128–137.

Rocchi, F. (1998), 'Consumir es un placer: La industria y la expansion de la demanda en Buenos Aires a la vuelta del siglo pasado', *Desarrollo Económico*, 37 (148), pp. 533–558.

S/A La evolución del retail desde el principio de los tiempos. (n.d.). Available at: www.peru-retail.com/especial/la-evolucion-del-retail-desde-el-principio-de-los-tiempos (Accessed 14 August 2017).

S/A La historia del Retail en Chile. (n.d.). Available at: www.eclass.cl/articulo/45296/la-historia-del-retail-en-chile (Accessed 14 August 2017).

Sassano, S. (2015), 'Imagen, localización y evolución de los centros comerciales en Argentina: un estudio de caso', *Documents d'Anàlisi Geogràfica*, 61, pp. 409–432.

Semana Económica. (n.d.), *El nuevo orden del retail*. Available at: http://semanaeconomica.com/article/sectores-y-empresas/comercio/250367-el-nuevo-orden-del-retail/ (Accessed 14 September 2017).

Sheahan, J. (2001), *La economía peruana desde 1950: buscando una sociedad mejor*, 19 Vol (Lima: Instituto de Estudios peruanos).

Suárez Rojas, L.A. (2011), *Mercados y mercaderes: hacia una antropología de las prácticas económicas* (Lima: Tesis de licenciatura en la Universidad Mayor de San Marcos).

Topik, S., Marichal, C. and Frank, Z.L. (2006), *From silver to cocaine: Latin American commodity chains and the building of the world economy, 1500–2000* (Durham, NC: Duke University Press).

Trentmann, F. and Otero-Cleves, A.M. (2017), 'Presentation. Paths, detours, and connections: Consumption and its contribution to Latin American history', *Historia Crítica*, 65, pp. 13–28, doi:dx.doi.org/10.7440/histcrit65.2017.01.

Uber Grosse, C. (2006), 'Innovación al servicio al cliente en el Grupo de Supermercados Wong: Una historia de éxito peruano', *The Journal of Language for International Business*, 17 (2), pp. 105–123.

Valerio Ulloa, S.M. (2016), 'Almacenes comerciales franceses en Guadalajara, México (1850–1930)', *América Latina en la Historia Económica*, [S.l.], 23 (1), pp. 68–89, ene. 2016. doi:http://dx.doi.org/10.18232/alhe.v23i1.64.

Vergara, R. (2012), *Caso: Supermercados en Chile* (Valparaiso: Universidad Catolica de Valparaiso).

26

CARAVANSERAI TO CARREFOUR

The retail history of the Middle East, 600–present

Omar Foda

The burning of the Arcadia Mall and the looting of Carrefour in Cairo sit as peripheral events in the January 2011 movement in Egypt (Amar 2011; Press 2011; Chmaytelli 2015). The movement is remembered for the mass mobilisation of Egyptians in the country's squares, the iconic chants and signs and the steadfastness of the people in the face of tanks and tear gas. If any fire is associated with the movement it is the burning of the Napoleonic Institut d'Egypte (Press 2011). Nevertheless, the burning and looting of these venues in 2011 evokes the last time Cairo burned in 1952. In that year, as Nancy Reynolds details in *A City Consumed: Urban Commerce, the Cairo Fire, and the Politics of Decolonization in Egypt*, the fire-starters and looters targeted many European-style department stores and retail venues. The targeting was symbolic of the greater politicisation of retail during the decolonisation of Egypt. One could make the same proclamation about the targeting of Arcadia Mall and Carrefour. It signalled that retail and its venues were not collateral damage to the political happenings in Egypt, but were politicised as much as the squares, mosques and government buildings.

The politicisation of the retail sector in the Middle East, however, has not been limited to Egypt or the colonial/post-colonial period. From the very foundations of Islam until the present day, buying and selling, and the venues where these transactions took place, have been inseparable from the politics that surrounded them. This connection manifested itself in government regulation of retail spaces, countrywide boycott of products and active scenes of violence in retail venues. As I argue, there was never a time where retail was not a concern of those ruling and those hoping to rule. This connection was only amplified by the fact that mass consumption, and its attendant ideologies, erupted in a colonial context in the Middle East (Cohen 2004).

This political reality means that by analysing the typology of retail markets in the Middle East, we not only see who was selling what, and to whom, but grasp the historical interaction of state and society. Since retail markets generally abide by the rule of "sell what people want to buy", they offer a more honest look at the reality on the ground in the Middle East during the pre-modern, early modern, colonial and post-colonial eras.

Nevertheless, there are a few caveats with this study, which through a four-part analysis aims to map retail markets in the Middle East from 600 to the present. First, when I refer to the Middle East, I am referring to the area south of the Danube and north of Aden and between the Atlantic Ocean and the Indus river. Second, the topic of coverage is so large that

I can only discuss general trends and concepts. It goes without saying that exceptions exist for most everything discussed here. Third, the sources for this history are still being discovered. Much remains obscure, and perhaps will be forever so. This is especially the case with rural retailers, whose markets have generally remained outside the purview of study. Finally, the definition of retail I use is broad and applies to any venue that traded or sold goods to individual consumers.

Retail in the Islamic World, 600–1750

For the uninitiated, it may come as a surprise that the *Quran*, the foundational Islamic text, deals with such a mundane matter as trade, but this was standard practice for a religion that aimed to guide its followers in both worship and day-to-day activities. The *Quran* engages with the concept of trade on two levels. First, it frequently employs the vocabulary of the market in its teachings (O'Meara n.d.). For example, 'We shall set up scales of justice for the day of judgement' (Q 21:47) (O'Meara n.d.). Second, it lays out some of the basics of a religiously valid transaction.

The outlines of sale laid out in the *Quran* were supplemented by the *hadith*, the collection of sayings and actions of the Prophet Muhammad and his companions. The *hadith* contains pertinent sayings on all variety of business-related matters, including: sales and trade; hiring; transference of a debt; business by proxy; loans; freezing of property; bankruptcy; and mortgaging (Bukhārī 1987).

From these two bases, an entire ruling structure emerged that blurred religious and secular authority, as did the legal system, Islamic Law (*shari'a*), that supported it (Constable 1994, p. 113). As a result, Muslim rulers from the seventh to the eighteenth centuries, in one way or other, were charged with the maintenance and protection of the *suq* (market, bazaar). The nature of their intervention could take varied forms. Leaders could step in to protect local food supplies, keep an eye on foreigners, prevent the export of certain goods or just to raise revenue (Constable 1994, p. 112). The involvement of the government in the market was best embodied in the position of the *muhtasib*, the market inspector, who was to make the relationship between retailer and buyer a fair and honest one.

The position of *muhtasib* was a feature of all Muslim empires from the eighth until the nineteenth century. Somewhere between a judge and chief of police, he would monitor prices and reprimand those who overcharged the rate set by the market. His methods of enforcement entailed beatings, parading offenders through the streets, confiscating faulty goods and even banishing repeat offenders from the markets. He was a government official, chosen for his outstanding moral probity and knowledge of Islamic jurisprudence (*fiqh*), although, unlike a *qadi* (judge), mastery was not required. He worked with the judges and police and would often have deputies to cover markets that were too large for one individual. However, his jurisdiction and interests were limited to the urban markets and even there, he did not have the power to determine prices. (Cahen *et al.* n.d.).

Under the Ottomans and the Persians, he took on additional functions like the enforcement of fixed prices (Turk. *narh*, Per. *tas'ir ajnas* list of fixed prices), which came either from a direct government order or through agreement with artisans (Floor 1987). While the *muhtasib* and the *narh* regulated prices, it was the institution of the guild that was the strongest regulator of artisans and retailers in the period from 1500 to 1750 (Faroqhi 2009, p. 31). Guilds appeared sometime during the fourteenth century in Persia and in the late fifteenth or sixteenth century in the Ottoman Empire and were involved in the production, marketing and taxing of crafts in urban areas (Rafeq 2008, p. 109). Guilds were generally organised hierarchically, with the headman (Tr. *kethüda/kahya*, Ar. sheikh, Per. *kadkoda*) at the top. Below the headman was the master (*al-ustadh* in Persian, shortened into *usta*, or *al-mu'allim* in Arabic), the journeyman (*al-sani'*) and the apprentice (*al-ajir* or *al-mubtadi'*) (Rafeq 2008, p. 108).

In Ottoman domains in the seventeenth and eighteenth centuries, guilds, in response to the greater cost of opening shops and less demand for their products, tried to limit the number of shops opened through the *gedik* system. A *gedik*, which meant "gap" or "slot", was a heritable 'workshop along with its contents, such as tools, instruments, raw materials and perhaps finished goods and the right to do business in this shop' (Faroqhi 2009, p. 119). It typically passed from father to son, or the top journeyman if the master craftsman had no son. It was a court-granted right and could not be bought or sold (Faroqhi 2009, p. 119). A similar institution appeared, called the *haqq-e bonica,* in Persia in the Qajar period for similar reasons, but was not as widespread as the *gedik* (Floor 1987).

Types of spaces

The *muhtasib*, the guilds, and the *gedik* were primarily urban institutions, but retail markets in the period from 600 to 1750 in the Islamic world went beyond the cities. Retail markets were generally organised in a solar central-place system (Clancy-Smith, 1994, p. 28; Barbara K. Larson 1985, p. 498). To understand what that means in the Middle Eastern context, it useful to map a typology from the rural exterior to the urban centre.

The terms *suq*, *çarşı* and bazaar roughly correspond to the English word "market". They, like the English term, could cover a vast array of places where commercial business happened, and, in some instances, even covered a single shop. Although there was a significant amount of overlap, the terms corresponded to the ruling language. Thus in Arabic speaking domains, *suq* predominated, in Ottoman domains, *çarşı*, and in Persianate domains, bazaar.

The simplest type of market, and the one located in the smallest rural population centres was the periodic market. Staged on private property, in exchange for a fee, it would meet on a designated day of the week and would be organised by product. Friday markets staged near the village mosque were quite popular because of their ability to draw people together, but these types of markets were not exclusive to that day nor to that locale. In fact, nearby markets would often co-ordinate their schedules so that a particular area could have a market every day of the week (Mohieddin 1998, pp. 302–303). They mainly provided the rural peasantry an opportunity to exchange locally produced agricultural products and household essentials (Larson 1985, p. 501). Besides peasants selling to other peasants, there were also probably Bedouins, professional village traders and local merchants.

As we move to a more densely populated area like a village or a town, the market maintained similar features (periodic, on private property, organised by product and dominated by the peasant), but everything was on a larger scale. In addition, the market featured products produced by local artisans (and guilds, after they appeared) and imported goods. These markets were also where agricultural goods would start moving up the chain towards urban centres. Merchants would move goods from these markets towards the provincial town, which sat at the centre of these small markets in a solar pattern (Larson 1985, p. 501).

As we move from the town, but before we reach the city, it was the *khan* that dominated. This was a one to two-story enclosed structure with fixed walls, a monumental gate, and an open courtyard with a water source. It was variably called a *khan, funduq, samsara, wakala, hawsh* and the most familiar caravanserai, and was an essential feature of commerce in the Islamic world between 600 and 1750 (Bianquis *et al.* n.d.). The *khans* dotted the trade routes of the Islamic world in the intermediary spaces between centres of populations. They served as the junction point between rural and foreign production and urban consumption (Elisséeff n.d.). In this capacity, their most critical role was as a safe haven and way station for caravans and other overland traders. Their solid walls, limited entrances, and access to water meant that they could be closed off from the surrounding world, keeping the goods, horses and merchants safe in isolated areas.

Although they were vital to the flow of goods through the paths of trade in the Islamic world, *khans* were also a feature of its urban spaces. In the city, the *khan* was, as opposed to a way point, the endpoint or a depot (Elisséeff n.d.). There, a large amount of merchandise could be sold either semi-wholesale or retail and distributed to the markets throughout the city. Depending on the city, it could be situated at the gates or inside of them, but there was always a connection to the world outside. The features that made it an ideal safe haven on trade routes made it an excellent segregation point for the rulers of the city. They were a place where rulers could tax or tariff goods, isolate undesirables or house foreign merchants and their goods (Elisséeff n.d.). They were also a place where *muhtasib* could verify the quality of the goods to be sold. The use of the market as an administrative site in the city paralleled the rural markets, which were also places to collect taxes and perform other administrative duties (Mohieddin 1998, p. 308). Beyond the *khan*, the urban retail scene in the Islamic world from 600 to 1750 was characterised by two common institutions: permanent booths and covered markets.

These urban markets, would be under the watch of the *muhtasib* and had their own guilds. However, this would change as the Ottoman Empire and Persia were fully integrated into the European world market in the eighteenth century. This integration would mark the rise of the merchants as the true masters of the market. This is not to say that they did not have significant power, especially with regards to prices and goods sold, prior to this point (Hanna 1998). But these merchants existed within the confines of the governmental systems of the Islamic world, confines they would break, with the help of European powers, after 1750.

Retail Colonialism, 1750–1950

The solar organisation of the retail markets in the Middle East changed after 1750, when they were integrated into the European world economy (Kasaba 1988, pp. 11–35). The most significant development of this integration was that control of the markets moved from the hands of the government into the hands of the merchants. This transition, a defining feature of the period from 1750 to 1950 and one that was happening organically in America at roughly the same time, was the result of the free trade imperialism of the European powers, summarised by the phrase, 'trade with informal control if possible; trade with rule when necessary' (Gallagher and Robinson 1953, p. 13; Leach 1994; Howard 2015, pp. 1–51). Across the Middle East, European merchants, and the governments that backed them, sought cheaper sources of raw materials, new locales for investment and new markets for their goods. The keystone to these actions was securing favourable trade agreements between the governments. The clearest and most widespread example were the capitulations (*imtiyazat*) (Wansbrough *et al.* n.d.). These were trade agreements the Ottoman and Persian governments, in their early years, made with foreign merchants to ensure safe passage and trade. As their geopolitical position weakened in relation to Europe, these concessions (reduced taxes and tariffs, special legal status, etc.) grew to be more favourable for Europeans. They were then formalised in treaties, the Treaty of Balta Liman (1838, Ottoman) and the Treaty of Turkomānčāy (1828, Qajars). Part of this process was the expansion of the populations covered by this protection from just European merchants and ambassadors to protégés – residents who had acquired, sometime through purchase, the rights (*berat*) granted to Europeans (van den Boogert n.d.). Once these trade deals were signed, foreign merchants, those with foreign status, and even well-connected local merchants, became the real drivers of the markets in the Middle East.

The primacy of merchants significantly altered the reality of retail markets in the Middle East. Most importantly, it changed the rural-urban market structure. Where previously it consisted of small rural markets circled around entrepôts, which then circled major cities, it became dendritic. This meant that rural markets became bulking centres for raw material exports, which were then sent to one of the few major cities of the territory regardless of distance (Tunis, Algiers, Cairo, Oran, Istanbul, etc.). As for the small periodic markets, they became more interconnected with each other, but decoupled from these larger markets. They ultimately came only to serve the subsistence needs of the peasantry (Larson 1985, p. 516). This change in market connectivity was intertwined in the physical restructuring of the territories, a process funded by reforming Middle Eastern rulers and European powers, but directed by merchants. The transformation took the form of building infrastructure to better connect internal bulking centres to the major cities and the external markets and of reshaping, rebuilding or reorienting the major cities.

Infrastructure building, in this period, mainly concerned constructing roads, railroads, bridges and ports. For reforming rulers, especially the Ottomans, this infrastructure work was meant to "reformulate mechanisms of governance" (Çelik 2008, p. 69). They hoped to have better control of their provinces through a more mobile military, and better transport of goods inside and outside of the empire. Imperial powers, on the other hand, saw this infrastructure building as a method of enrichment, conquest, and colonisation (Çelik 2008, p. 69). As for the urban restructuring of this period, the European powers and reforming rulers were guided by Hausmanian ideals of cleanliness and sanitation and the hope of better movement through the city, especially for new technologies like the tram. They viewed the market areas as prime targets of "modernization". They hoped to replace the "traditional" *suq*, as they called it, with its narrow passageways and labyrinthine design, with wide boulevards and squares dotted with arcades (Çelik 2008, p. 72).

The difference in aims, plus technologic superiority, meant that European powers were more effective in their infrastructure projects. They were also playing with a stacked deck, as much of the reformers' infrastructure building was either financed by foreign powers, or carried out by companies that had little allegiance to the state. In fact, this "modernisation" work of Middle Eastern reformers often set the territory on the path of colonisation or total loss of fiscal autonomy, as it was underwritten by European powers and their merchants (Pamuk 1987). We see this pattern in the colonisation of Tunisia (France, 1881), Egypt (Britain, 1882) and Morocco (1884, Spain; and 1904, France).

When these territories came under European control, the odds were stacked even further in the favour of merchants. Thus we see the outflanking of the urban guilds, who they deemed an impediment to their work (Faroqhi 2009, p. 119). We also see a change in agricultural business, leading to the privatisation of land, the growth of large absentee landholders and merchants making profits as middlemen and landholders themselves (Shields 2008, pp. 48–54). Interestingly, the prominence of merchants also worked against the concept of the dual city, i.e. a city with a "modern" European centre cordoned off from a "backwards" native periphery, that framed much colonial architecture. The most severe example of the desire for a dual colonial structure is French colonialism in North Africa. In fact, this dual city was a distinctive feature of the French colonial experience in the Middle East (Reynolds 2012, pp. 18–19).

Nevertheless, the urban retail markets themselves contravened this duality and were characterised by the bleeding of the two together. Albert Camus noted, dismissively, that the shops of Oran combined 'all the bad taste of Europe and the Orient' (Horne 2006, pp. 47–48). With respect to the goods in the market, "foreign" goods would not be limited to the "foreign" sectors of town and would make their way in to the "traditional" markets of the city (Çelik 1986, p. 160). Thus you would find socks, shoes, buttons and tarbushes in the markets of the "medieval" city. Likewise, upscale and "European" shoppers, who were supposed to be segregated in their sections, would frequent the *suq* based on better prices and the presence of certain "authentic" and "traditional" goods.

However, it was not a one-way process. The foreign retail markets could also not keep out the elements of the native markets. Native-style markets would appear adjacent to European-style markets and serve a complementary role (Srougo 2011). In addition, flea markets and informal markets, supplied by smuggling or counterfeits, offered the latest styles, lower prices and the ability to create a modern look on a budget (Reynolds 2012, pp. 41–46). Even the assumed enclave of the Western residents and their imitators, the department store, was not exempt. With its location in the heart of the city, its doors were open to more than foreigners and the elite, but all residents. Residents who, if they had the money, could shop at these department stores for special occasions like weddings and the 'ids (Reynolds 2012, p. 71–72).

This mixing was also seen in the ownership of retail venues. While there were a few venues that were easily identifiable as either foreign or native, that is, exclusively owned and run by colonists or long-tenured Muslims, many more reflected a mixed transnational reality. It was particularly the migrants and non-Muslim populations that played with this boundary. The stereotype of this group was the retail merchant who used his foreign status (what at first was a *berat*, and came to be called protégé status) to amass a large fortune, and who participated in the colonisation of the country (Schreier 2012). Nevertheless, some of these merchants, especially the non-Muslim populations, felt strong attachment to their territories and were fully enmeshed in them (Miller 2011).

This period, termed the first globalisation, also brought a large working and lower-class foreign-born population to the Middle East (Kozma *et al.* 2015). This group joined the working and lower-class population of non-Muslims, who were more concerned with making a living than grand projects of colonisation. The retail venues they established or worked in reflected a hybrid identity. These were ventures that may have sold Western-style goods and may have been located in Western cordons of the city, but were ventures that had no real connection to foreign powers and carried markers (names, staff and products) that separated them from these powers. For example, the Circurel Department store in Cairo was founded by Sephardic Jews from Izmir, who, by 1947, considered themselves Egyptian citizens (Reynolds 2012, p. 58).

But beyond the passive resistance of cultural mixing and boundary crossing, retail markets also became venues of active resistance. There were hints of this change prior to World War I. Examples include the 1891 nationwide tobacco protest in Iran in the face of the government's concessions to the British and the 1908 boycott of Austrian goods in the Ottoman Empire to protest the annexation of Bosnia-Herzegovina (Keddie 2006, pp. 61–63; Reynolds 2012, p. 84). This trend grew as colonialism engulfed the region after the end of World War I. The end of the war brought the divvying up the Ottoman Empire and marked the appearance of the Wilsonian rhetoric of the self-determination of nations. This trend spurred on burgeoning nationalist movements across the Middle East and the world. A distinguishing feature of these anti-colonial movements was boycotts (Breen 2004, p. 20; Reynolds 2012, p. 82). They were, in fact, one of the only ways that colonial subjects could fight the power of colonial states. Boycotts could take the form of abstaining from foreign goods or buying local (Shoham 2013). These anti-consumerist actions popularised the idea that all products had a nationality and that this nationality should play a role in their purchase (Reynolds 2012, p. 83). Retail and retail choices were not value neutral, but could be part of a larger struggle to guarantee the future or identity of a country (Shoham 2013).

As a result, there appeared a new entrant into the retail typology of the colonial Middle East: the national retailer. This retailer and his success, in opposition to the foreign retailer, would help build the country and strike at foreign powers. These retailers also reflected a new assertion of national identity, as their consumers were not broad categories, but citizens of a country (Peter 2004). This push for nationalist retailers not only led to the establishment of new "national" venues, but led others to rebrand with a "national" name or some just to stock and promote national products as a way to capitalise on this new feeling. The result of these movements in the period from the 1920s until the 1950s was that wealthy locals (especially Muslims) entered into partnerships with foreign entrepreneurs or protégés to claim some of the profits of the retail market while attaching a national name to their product (Vitalis 1995). Likewise, many protégés shifted the identity of their establishments or the products that they sold towards the national. This especially comes through in their advertisements, which grew tremendously in this period (Shechter 2005). Thus we see advertisements for Egyptian socks, Syrian textiles and Jewish bananas (Reynolds 2011; Shoham 2013).

However, these actions did not represent a radical disjuncture with the preceding period. Yes, there was more space for local industry, "national" brands, and local entrepreneurs, but its effects were mainly limited to the upper classes. Thus it was men like Ahmed Farghaly Pasha, a scion of an Egyptian cotton family, or Fu'ad Saba, a Palestinian businessman who benefited tremendously (Seikaly 2016, pp. 28–29). There were also gains for the urban middle classes as native workers were given positions over the foreign (Shechter 2006, pp. 104–110). How much change this actually produced in the workforce is up for debate as the very definitions of "native" and "foreign" were being defined and redefined in this period (Foda 2014). Regardless, large swaths of the populations, especially the majority of the rural population were excluded from this uplift.

By the end of the colonial period, we are left with a retail market that reflected the economic reality of the colonial Middle East. In many urban areas there was a well-developed hybrid retail sector where consumers could produce a distinctively "native" style that was a mélange of the best of the boutiques and the *suq*. These consumers were likewise drawn from a developing middle class and well-established upper class. Nevertheless, there remained a large number of urban and rural poor.

Both middle and upper-class individuals recognised the economic inequity that colonialism had brought to the Middle East, and they both had solutions. The men of capital believed that the nation would be saved by the growth of an economy that they would lead, a free market economy guided by capital accumulation and consumer moderation (Seikaly 2016, p. 46). The middle class, who would come to control the governments of decolonisation, would see it another way. Governments would develop the economy, and the nation itself, by excising colonialists, predatory merchants and businessmen, and smashing the control of large landholders.

The retail of developmentalism, 1950–1990

The boycotts of the late colonial era transformed consumption, and thus retail, into a battlefield. It is no surprise then that in the decolonising Middle East, retail, among other things, would be a target of efforts to slough off the colonial yoke. One of the first and most violent examples is detailed by Nancy Reynolds in *A City Consumed*. As she describes it, some of the most prominent targets for the looting and fire-starting of the 1952 Cairo fire were retail shops (Reynolds 2011, pp. 186–187).

This ire represented the full enunciation of the ideologies that underlay the previous era's boycotts, that retailers, especially those carrying "foreign" names and "foreign" products were embodiments of the exploitation of the colonial powers. This feeling was especially powerful in the urban middle class, who would carry through much of the fight against colonisation in the Middle East and would take control of the seats of the power in many post-colonial governments (Eppel 2004, p. 152).

The policies of post-colonial governments charted a course of developmentalism. As Joel Beinin describes it, this was a World Bank and IMF-supported 'economic strategy based on import-substitution industrialization: replacing imported consumer goods with domestically manufactured products targeted to local markets and protecting uncompetitive "infant industries" with high tariff barriers' (Beinin 2016, p. 41). This strategy could also include 'government redistribution of large landholdings to increase the purchasing power of poor' and middling farmers, and state-led economic development through investment in key economic sectors, public utilities and industry (Beinin 2016, p. 41).

Developmentalism's most prominent example was Arab Socialism and its figurehead Gamal Abdel Nasser. Socialism, especially of the Arab kind, was very appealing to a region that looked to chart a third course in an increasingly bi-polar world. This appeal was only increased by Nasser's strong stance in the Suez crisis (Vandewalle 2006, p. 80). It is then not surprising that we saw some variety of this ideology in Algeria, Tunisia, Libya, Yemen, Sudan, Iraq and Syria (Issawi 1982, p. 180). However, developmentalism was not only limited to those countries that committed to Arab socialism. Many of its policies were features of the economic initiatives of Israel, Turkey, Iran, Jordan and the Gulf countries in the 1950s, 60s and 70s (Issawi 1982, p. 180). Iran deserves special notice, because its developmentalism, under Khomeini, was covered with an Islamic reformism and anti-western, anti-consumerist ideology (Webb *et al.* 2005)

In the eyes of post-colonial governments, retailers, especially those with the foreign taint, did little but extract precious resources from the native population in exchange for non-essential and "foreign" goods. It is then no surprise that these retailers were swept up in the government nationalisations that were a feature of this era (Addi 2006). Nevertheless, these post-colonial governments recognised that their plans of import substitution would only work with concomitant growth in the consumption of the goods that they were producing. From this realisation emerged a new retail entity in the Middle East, the government retailer.

In its most ideal form, this would be a retailer, which was part of a large government organisation or collective, that sold the consumer goods of another government industry. For example, in Egypt, the nationalised department store Sidnawi could sell *Ideal* brand washers, refrigerators, etc., whose producer was part of a larger economic organisation for consumer goods, which was under the control of the Egyptian government (Abaza 2006a, pp. 92–93). If there was not a large store to sell these goods, then the government would create one, like the Souk el-Fellah (Peasant's Market) in Algeria (Troin 1990, p. 90). This type of retailer was the full realisation of the "national" retailer from the colonial era.

There was also another government-controlled retailer, the state co-operative. They would draw their products from government-planned agriculture and industry. These, often in combination with rationing, were meant to make sure that the population, one that was primarily agrarian and poor, received the "essentials". What these essentials were varied, but would typically include foodstuffs and things like petrol, soap, sugar, etc. (Amuzegar 1993, p. 79; Abaza 2006a, pp. 153–154). Another aspect of this social net, which affected not only government co-operatives but small retailers more generally, was subsidies. These subsidies which set the prices of certain commodities were meant to ensure that all people received their "daily bread" (Amuzegar 1993, p. 79). Nevertheless, the small retailers who existed before developmentalism, persisted afterwards as they carried the badge of "authenticity" and were not big enough to draw the eye of the government. This meant that the small urban shops, peddlers, and rural periodic markets that existed before remained relatively unchanged. Nevertheless, government products replaced the foreign products that may have been present, and any staples sold were subsidised.

A problem with these government retailers, and one of the problems with import substitution, was that the success of a company was viewed through how much it produced, not how effectively it was able to meet the demands of a population (Shechter 2008, p. 576). Simultaneously, demand for products was growing globally as the US led the world into an era of mass consumption in the 1950s (Schayegh 2012).

It was the informal market that filled in for this demand. For example, in Egypt we have the appearance of a social institution called the *tujjar al-shunta* (bag merchants). These were primarily woman peddlers who sold smuggled fabrics, clothes, perfumes, crèmes, pullovers and underwear at affordable prices (Abaza 2006a, p. 123). However, it was not only in Egypt, as there were examples of strong informal markets in Algeria, Jordan, Turkey and several other countries (Doan 1992; Varcin 2000). Informal retail was part of the informal structures that appeared throughout the Middle East in response to another aspect of developmentalism in the region, the ruling party's domination of the state (Joffé 2002).

Informal markets and subsidies would continue, and be bolstered, as the region made a transition away from developmentalism. The first step away from this was the 1967 Arab defeat, which discredited Pan-Arab nationalism and Arab socialism. This defeat, however, was a massive boon for the Israeli economy, as they opened up new markets and cheap labour by occupying Gaza and the West Bank (Owen 1998, p. 181). They also saw a massive increase in defence spending and American aid, which both helped fuel the economy.

Nevertheless, Israel suffered, like European countries and America, in the 1973–5 recession and the subsequent period of stagflation (Beinin 2016, p. 60). This set of events would push the World Bank and the IMF, which were guided by America and Western Europe, away from developmentalism as a supportable strategy. They declared it a failure and moved towards the idea that reorienting towards foreign markets with a focus on exports would save the countries of the global south.

The countries in the Middle East and North Africa made some initial moves to the new world consensus, but they did not carry out any of the truly drastic measures of "structural readjustment" (massively reducing government budgets, privatising public institutions and removing trade exemptions and tariffs) as they were buttressed by the oil boom of the 1970s. The boom supported both the oil-rich countries (The Gulf Countries, Iraq, Algeria, etc.) and the oil-poor, who relied heavily on the remittances of workers in these oil-rich countries (Beinin 2016, pp. 58–60). The hallmarks of developmentalism would continue until, and sometimes after, the oil bust of the 1980s, which would force many of the countries of the region to turn to the world financial institutions (The World Bank and IMF) and accede to the "Washington Consensus" and its requisite Economic Reform and Structural Adjustment Program (ERSAP) (Beinin 2016, pp. 94–95).

It is at this point that the retail markets in the Middle East and North Africa started to move away from government retail towards neoliberal retail. This transition to neoliberalism meant a reintegration of retail markets into a global free-trade economy (Springer *et al.* 2016). It also entailed governments ceding control of the markets, over which they had just had gained control, back to merchants.

Neoliberal retail, 1990–present

The end of developmentalism and acceptance of the Washington Consensus was meant to "free" the markets of the Middle East and North Africa. It did, in the sense that it opened up the

Middle East to foreign direct investment, eased the process for the establishment of private businesses and lowered the trade barriers of the countries in the Middle East. But what did this mean for retail markets?

The changes are best encapsulated in three additions to the typology of the retail market. These were the retail chain, the hypermarket and the shopping centre, which were not present in the Middle East prior to the 1980s and 90s (Vignal 2007, p. 69). Retail chains were outposts of a typically foreign brand, i.e., McDonalds, Pizza Hut, Cinnabon. The hypermarket, on the other hand, was a large store that housed everything under one roof, a one-stop shop. Walmart was probably the most famous example of a hypermarket, but it was Carrefour, in conjunction with Majid al-Futaim (a Dubai-based holding company), that was probably the most famous in the region (Elsheshtawy 2006, p. 242).

The shopping centre was a structure that housed large stores, even department stores, selling a wide variety of goods and services. The shopping centre typically contained retail chains and hypermarkets. Each of these venues differentiated themselves from the "traditional" markets with their claims of cleanliness (tiled floors, glass windows), organisation (well-marked signage and directions), safety (video cameras and security) and ease of movement (wide thoroughfares, the presence of escalators and elevators) (al-Otaibi 1990; Markowitz and Uriely 2004, p. 28; Abaza 2006a, p. 274). In addition, these venues often would come as part of larger government projects of "beautification" (Singerman 2007).

Despite the fact that most of these venues were either western brands or Western-style venues, they typically functioned through license agreements and direct investment relationships between local and regional entrepreneurs and foreign investors (Vignal 2007, p. 69). In this respect, we see similarities with the pre-developmentalism era, especially when we consider that the group of local and regional entrepreneurs was comprised of the economic elite, governmental cronies and wealthy Gulf merchants. The other similarity is that these stores were aimed at urban and suburban middle and upper-class shoppers. These goals fit with the general economic trends of the post-developmental Middle East. Governments "freed" the markets, but at the expense of economic equality and the social support programs of the developmentalism era (Shechter 2009).

The results of this reality were starkly portrayed in the suburbs. Here shopping centres, filled with chains and hypermarkets, sat near exclusive suburban gated developments. They were only accessible through cars and thus presented one of the most exclusive retail locations in the Middle East (Abaza 2006b, p. 205). These venues were in sharp contrast to the periodic markets that existed on the peripheries of the city (Singerman 2007).

Bearing a striking similarity to the periodic markets that had been a feature of rural retail since pre-modern times, these markets served the low-income populations living in the informal housing on the edges of the city. Their resemblance to the rural market was not coincidental, but represented a distinct feature of urbanisation in the post-1980 Middle East. The majority entering the city and remaining in its periphery were rural people looking for greater opportunities in the face of the suffering agricultural sectors of the economy.

However, it would be incorrect to conclude that the introduction of these retail institutions created a new dual society. In a manner similar to what we saw prior to the 1950s, the retail market on the ground was both a site of cultural hybridisation and active resistance (Marr 2012, pp. 358–359). First, these shopping centres and hypermarkets did not replace the retail markets that existed before (Abdelghani 2013, p. 246). Rather, consumers incorporated them into their other retail habits. Each historical locus of retail, the *suq*, the colonial market, the subsidised government retailer, carried associations and identities that a consumer performed when he or she entered (Vicdan 2015).

Second, as these new shopping centres became part of the urban and suburban fabric, periodic markets grew up around them (Abaza 2006a, p. 258). Their product offerings were complementary or competitive with those offered in the mall – cellphones, entertainment devices and other electronics alongside clothes and other dry goods – but much more affordable (Ilahiane and Sherry 2008). The organisation of these informal markets resembled the rural retail markets, and contravened the government's "modernization" projects for their cities (Abaza 2006a, p. 258). They were part of the growth in the informal sector that neoliberalism brought to the Middle East (Doan 1992).

The ruralisation of the urban retail market was matched by the urbanisation of the rural markets (Troin 1990, p. 88). The periodic market remained the primary way that the rural populace acquired its consumer goods. However, these periodic markets grew to carry not only agricultural livestock and produce, but cheap imported dry goods (clothes, toys, appliances, etc.), arriving from urban centres (Troin 1990, p. 88). These markets also remained important points of local political organisation and social regulation (Mohieddin 1998, p. 309). In addition to the presence of imported goods in these rural markets, another significant change was that there were more permanent shops in rural towns and the in-between spaces between cities. These shops typically sold imported goods, but of a higher quality than those in the periodic markets (Mohieddin 1998, p. 308)

But it was not only on the outsides of the markets and cities, where the local population asserted themselves in the face of new retail realities. Since many of these shopping centres and supermarkets were urban they witnessed what Jillian Schwedler and Rodney Collins term transversals (Schwedler 2010). These shopping centres, as well as the periodic markets that formed around them, had porous boundaries between "foreign" and "native", which Middle Eastern residents of all social levels traversed. Their placement in the city centre meant that to keep the "wrong" people out was difficult, if not impossible.

Beyond population demographics, there was also the growing presence of Islam within these new shopping venues. As the region abandoned developmentalism for the neoliberal market orientation, it also suffered an identity crisis. The middle-class modernity that had been the dominant discourse since the late nineteenth century and saw its apotheosis in Arab socialism, was no longer workable in a post-developmental Middle East (Shechter 2008, p. 578). The policies that undergirded the middle class were slashed or under attack and its ideologues were impoverished, imprisoned or exiled. Although the governments pushed Middle Eastern countries towards a market orientation, this move was not typically met with the same ideological support that developmentalism was. Most governments after 1970 were ideologically very flexible and more concerned with their continued rule of the country, and profits from it, than articulating strong positions.

Into this void entered another take on modernity that had been simmering since the 1920s, but had been pushed aside by Arab nationalism and socialism – Islamic reformism (Starrett 1998). This Islamic modernity pushed Islamisation as the solution to the troubling realities of the Middle East after the 1980s: income disparities, the disassembling of the social safety net and repressive governments (Göle 2000). This Islamic modernity was not generally anti-capitalist, socialist or isolationist (Shechter 2011). Rather it meant to show how Islam could solve the ills of the new global market economy while also allowing countries to enjoy its benefits. It did not argue with the ends of market orientation, merely the means.

This ideology was helped in many ways by the success of Saudi Arabia in the 1970s. The Saudi ruling regime, which was heavily imbricated with the Wahhabi sect of Islam, one of the earliest and most severe reformist movements, did much to present a workable model of an Islamic capitalist economy. This ability to provide a template was especially clear in their early treatment of retail venues. Shopping centres, hypermarkets and other retail venues were at the vanguard of Saudi Arabian commercial evolution and urbanisation. However, they only entered under the terms of the government, who controlled the purse strings. This meant that they would be internationally structured and follow the latest trends in retail architecture, but also bear local – traditional names, match the local daily pace – shops closed for an afternoon break as well as prayer breaks – and facilitate state regulation of *halal* and price (Shechter 2011, p. 379). Although they would soon come to be one of the few public spaces Saudi women could inhabit, they were also the homes to the semi-official morality police and other community gatekeepers that kept them as places of enforcement of strict religious observance (Shechter 2011, p. 379).

Saudi Arabia provided a ready model for those who looked to reconcile the new global world and their desire for an Islamic life. It was a model that many would witness firsthand as Saudi Arabia served as the locus of internal Middle Eastern migrants profiting from the oil boom and sending home remittances. This group, and their Saudi-influenced ideologies, would come to replace the old middle class as the emergent middle section in Middle Eastern societies and would further bolster this Islamic modernity (Shechter 2009, pp. 34–35). But it was not only returning migrant workers who aided this movement, but the wealth of Saudi Arabia and the rest of the Gulf Countries. Their investment in other Middle Eastern countries, often times in the form of retail venues, was coupled with support of those local movements that would embrace their particular brand of Islamic reformism.

The result of this social movement is that Islam and retail became readily connected in the Middle East. Islamic retail took two forms in the markets in the Middle East. The first was the commodification of religious products. By that, I mean those products with 'direct association with acts of worship, as with prayer beads, or, more commonly, their bearing of sacred images or writing, often only the single word "Allah" or "Muhammad"' (Gregory Starrett 1995, p. 53). This group could include 'bumper stickers, keychains, posters, board games, jigsaw puzzles, colouring books, fans, clocks, framed Qur'anic verses, banners, greeting cards, decorative items in ceramic, brass, wood, cloth, and paper' (Gregory Starrett 1995, p. 53).

The second form is that of Islamized products, services and venues. In this mould, we see things like Islamic socks, Islamic ties, hijabi dolls, Islamic business associations, Islamic malls and Islamic banks (Abaza 2006a, pp. 198–204; Meneley 2007; Shirazi 2016, p. 23). Despite their names, all of these retail features are a messy mix of Islamic and neoliberal capitalist features and cannot be easily classified as products of either (Gökarıksel and Secor 2016). They are creations of the post-developmental Middle East and are thoroughly enmeshed in the retail venues discussed above. In these new shopping centres and hypermarkets, you can find stores selling Islamic goods, funded by Islamic banks and bearing Islamic names. You can even find shopping centres and hypermarkets that are "Islamic".

Finally, while governments may have abandoned developmentalism, the idea that consumption and the markets where it takes place are political battlegrounds did not disappear. The first and most famous example of this is the Bread Intifada in Egypt in 1977. When the Egyptian government tried to cut subsidies on sugar, tea, flour, rice and cooking oil, riots broke out in urban centres around the country. Clashes between security forces and demonstrators killed seventy-three, injured 800 and lead to arrest of 1,270 (Beinin 2016, pp. 96–97). It was not only Egypt, but Algeria, Tunisia, Jordan and Morocco that saw the manifestations of this return (Owen 1998, p. 191; Holden 2009, p. 215; Perkins 2013, p. 173). But it was not only riots over commodities that showed that the market was a battlefield. One particularly potent example was the bombing of the Dizengoff mall in Tel-Aviv on Purim in 1996. Malls, like cafes and discos, were potent targets for attack because they embodied the material privilege of the winners in the market (Carmeli and Applbaum 2004, p. 13).

The turn to neoliberalism was not solely an outside imposition, but an attempt to meet the demands of the population that no longer desired austerity, but demanded consumption. However, this came at the cost of the steps towards economic equality that developmentalist governments had taken. The clearest signal of this was the informal markets that grew in tandem with shopping centres and the Islamic ventures that featured in these places. The uniting factor between these two seemingly opposed retail features was that they both agreed that the system was broken and needed a different path. Soon mass movements, which concurred that the system was broken, would appear across the Middle East. Many of these movements would carry slogans and ideas that showed the continued political nature of retail in the Middle East. It is no surprise that one of the most well-known Egyptian slogans began with a demand for "Bread!"

Conclusion

The Arab Uprisings of 2011/2 were historic events, but did little to arrest the retail trends of the previous decades. In the years since, shopping centres and hypermarkets have been built, informal markets persist, and Islamic neoliberal institutions have grown. Nevertheless, they did mark a significant milestone in the social power of Internet technologies. Although they did not cause the movement, Internet technologies did have a well-observed impact (Kraidy 2016). The disbursement of these technologies has only grown since the uprisings, and this offers some interesting retail futures.

Most notably, online retail offers two powerful pathways. First, it empowers the informal retailers. As evidenced by a site like Etsy, one only needs an Internet connection and a camera to sell products directly to consumers. Online retail offers the ability to subvert the powered interests that necessitate the informal market (Ilahiane 2013). Second, the Internet provides connectivity to a global community. It not only offers larger world markets, but the ability to find like-minded individuals. In the case of retailers who prioritise the Islamic, the Internet offers the ability to tap into those within the Middle East and the world who are looking to assert their Islamic identity through their participation in the neoliberal world market (Abaza 2006a; Meneley 2007, pp. 198–204; Ilahiane 2013; Shirazi 2016, p. 23).

As I have shown, retail in the Middle East occurred on the ground in ways that defy or counter assumptions. There were "traditional" markets that showed significant dynamism, dual retail colonial scenes that in fact were a synthesis of foreign and native and Islamic retailers who were a mélange of Islamic and neoliberal ideas. Likewise, the arrival of one form of retail did not annihilate the previous model. Thus, while a fully developed online retail system in the Middle East may solve some problems, it will not be detached from the realities in place. But, regardless of the actual outcome, like the *suq*, the department store and shopping centre, this retail venue will be deeply imbricated in the politics of the day.

References

Abaza, M. (2006a), *The changing consumer cultures of modern Egypt: Cairo's urban reshaping* (Cairo: The American University in Cairo Press).

Abaza, M. (2006b), 'Egyptianizing the American dream: Nasr City's shopping malls, public order and the privatized military', in D. Singerman and P. Amar (eds.) *Cairo cosmopolitan: Politics culture, and urban space in the new globalized Middle East* (Cairo: American University in Cairo Press) 193–220.

Abdelghani, M. (2013), 'The impact of shopping malls on traditional retail stores in Muscat: Case study of Al-Seeb Wilayat', in S. Wippel (ed.) *Regionalizing Oman: Political, economic and social dynamics* (Dordrecht, The Netherlands: Springer) 227–247.

Addi, L. (2006), 'The political contradictions of Algerian economic reforms', *Review of African Political Economy*, 108, pp. 207–217.

al-Otaibi, O. (1990), 'The development of planned shopping centres in Kuwait', in A.M. Findlay, J.A. Dawson and R. Paddison (eds.) *Retailing environments in the developing world* (London: Routledge).

Amar, A.H. (2011), 'Hariq Ha'il fi 8 Tawabiq bi-Mawl Arkadia wa wafa 3 Askha', [online]. *AhramGate*. Available at: http://gate.ahram.org.eg/News/36728.aspx (Accessed 7 September 2016).

Amuzegar, J. (1993), *Iran's economy under the Islamic Republic* (New York: Distributed in the U.S. and Canada by St. Martin's Press).

Beinin, J. (2016), *Workers and thieves: Labor movements and popular uprisings in Tunisia and Egypt* (Stanford, CA: Stanford University Press).

Bianquis, Th., Guichard, P., Raymond, A., Atassi, S., Pascual, J.-P., David, J.-C., Gaube, H., Faroqhi, S. and Nizami, K. A. (n.d.), 'Sūḳ', in P. Bearman, T. Bianquis, C.E. Bosworth, E. van Donzel, and W.P. Heinrichs (eds.) *Encyclopaedia of Islam*, 2nd ed., http://dx.doi.org/10.1163/1573-3912_islam_COM_1109 (Accessed 1 August 2018).

Breen, T.H. (2004), *The marketplace of revolution: How consumer politics shaped American independence* (New York: Oxford University Press).

Bukhārī, M. ibn I., (1987), Ṣaḥīḥ *al-Bukhārī. Qasin Rifāʿī ed* (Bayrūt: Dār al-Qalam).

Cahen, C., Talbi, M., Mantra, R., Lambton, A.K. and Bazmee Ansari, A.S. (n.d.), 'Hisba', in P. Bearman, T. Bianquis, C.E. Bosworth, E. van Donzel, and W.P. Heinrichs (eds.) *Encyclopaedia of Islam*, 2nd ed., http://dx.doi.org/10.1163/1573-3912_islam_COM_0293 (Accessed 1 August 2018).

Carmeli, Y. and Applbaum, K. (2004), 'Introduction', in Y. Carmeli and K. Applbaum (eds.) *Consumption and market society in Israel* (Oxford: Berg).

Çelik, Z. (1986), *The remaking of Istanbul: Portrait of an Ottoman city in the nineteenth century* (Seattle, WA: University of Washington Press).

Çelik, Z. (2008), *Empire, architecture, and the city: French-Ottoman encounters, 1830–1914* (Seattle, WA: University of Washington Press).

Chmaytelli, M. (2015), 'Carrefour Franchisee to Pursue Egypt growth as retail recovers', *Bloomberg.com*, 24 Jan.

Clancy-Smith, J. (1994), *Rebel and saint: Muslim notables, populist protest, colonial encounters (Algeria and Tunisia, 1800–1914)* (Berkeley: University of California Press).

Cohen, L. (2004), *A consumers' republic: The politics of mass consumption in postwar America*, 1st ed. (New York: Vintage).

Constable, O.R. (1994), *Trade and traders in Muslim Spain: The commercial realignment of the Iberian peninsula, 900–1500* (New York: Cambridge University Press).

Doan, R.M. (1992), 'Class differentiation and the informal sector in Amman, Jordan', *International Journal of Middle East Studies*, 24 (1), pp. 27–38.

Elisséeff, N. (n.d.), 'Khān', in P. Bearman, T. Bianquis, C.E. Bosworth, E. van Donzel, and W.P. Heinrichs eds. *Encyclopaedia of Islam*, 2nd ed. http://dx.doi.org/10.1163/1573-3912_islam_COM_0492 (Accessed 05 August 2018).

Elsheshtawy, Y. (2006), 'From Dubai to Cairo competing global cities, models, and shifting centers of influence?', in D. Singerman and P. Amar (eds.) *Cairo cosmopolitan: Politics culture, and urban space in the new globalized Middle East* (Cairo: American University in Cairo Press) 235–250.

Eppel, M. (2004), *Iraq from monarchy to tyranny: From the Hashemites to the rise of Saddam* (Gainesville, FL: University Press of Florida).

Faroqhi, S. (2009), *Artisans of empire: Crafts and craftspeople under the Ottomans* (London: I.B. Tauris).

Floor, W. (1987), 'AṢNĀF', in *Encyclopaedia Iranica*, Vol. II/7, pp. 772–778. http://www.iranicaonline.org/articles/asnaf-guilds (Accessed 10 August 2018).

Foda, O. (2014), 'The pyramid and the crown: The Egyptian beer industry from 1897 to 1963', *International Journal of Middle East Studies*, 46 (1), pp. 139–158.

Gallagher, J. and Robinson, R. (1953), 'The imperialism of free trade', *The Economic History Review*, 6 (1), pp. 1–15.

Gökarıksel, B. and Secor, A.J. (2016), 'What makes a commodity Islamic: The case of veiling-fashion in Turkey', in A. Jafari and Ö. Sandıkçı (eds.), *Islam, marketing and consumption: Critical perspectives on the intersections* (London: Routledge).

Göle, N. (2000), 'Snapshots of Islamic modernities', *Dædalus*, 129 (1), pp. 91–117.

Hanna, N. (1998), *Making big money in 1600: The life and times of Isma'il Abu Taqiyya, Egyptian merchant*, 1st ed. (Syracuse, NY: Syracuse University Press).

Holden, S.E. (2009), *The politics of food in modern Morocco* (Gainesville, FL: University Press of Florida [online]).

Horne, A. (2006), *A savage war of peace: Algeria, 1954–1962* (New York: New York Review Books).

Howard, V. (2015), *From main street to mall: The rise and fall of the American department store* (Philadelphia, PA: University of Pennsylvania Press).

Ilahiane, H. (2013), 'Catenating the local and the global in Morocco: How mobile phone users have become producers and not consumers', *Journal of North African Studies*, 18 (5), pp. 652–667.

Ilahiane, H. and Sherry, J. (2008), 'Joutia: Street vendor entrepreneurship and the informal economy of information and communication technologies in Morocco', *Journal of North African Studies*, 13 (2), pp. 243–255.

Issawi, C.P. (1982), *An economic history of the Middle East and North Africa* (New York: Columbia University Press).

Joffé, G. (2002), 'The role of violence within the Algerian economy', *Journal of North African Studies*, 1 (1), pp. 29–52.

Kasaba, R. (1988), *The Ottoman empire and the world economy: The nineteenth century* (Albany, NY: State University of New York Press).

Keddie, N.R. (2006), *Modern Iran: Roots and results of revolution*. Updated ed. (New Haven, CT: Yale University Press).

Kozma, L., Schayegh, C. and Wishnitzer, A. (2015), *A global Middle East: Mobility, materiality and culture in the modern age, 1880–1940*, edited by L. Kozma, C. Schayegh and A. Wishnitzer (London: I.B. Tauris).

Kraidy, M.M. (2016), *The naked blogger of Cairo: Creative insurgency in the Arab world* (Cambridge, MA: Harvard University Press).

Larson, B.K. (1985), 'The rural marketing system of Egypt over the last three hundred years', *Comparative Studies in Society and History*, 27 (3), pp. 494–530.

Leach, W. (1994), *Land of desire: Merchants, power, and the rise of a new American culture*. 1st ed. (New York: Vintage).

Markowitz, F. and Uriely, N. (2004), 'Of thorns and flowers: Consuming identities in the Negev', in Y. Carmeli and K. Applbaum (eds.) *Consumption and market society in Israel* (Oxford: Berg) 19–37.

Marr, P. (2012), *The modern history of Iraq*. 3rd ed. (Boulder, CO: Westview Press).

Meneley, A. (2007), 'Fashions and fundamentalisms in fin-de-siècle Yemen: Chador Barbie and Islamic socks', *Cultural Anthropology*, 22 (2), pp. 214–243.

Miller, S.G. (2011), 'Making Tangier modern: Ethnicity and urban development, 1880–1930', In E.B. Gottreich and D.J. Schroeter (eds.) *Jewish culture and society in North Africa* (Bloomington, IN: Indiana University Press) 128–149.

Mohieddin, M.M. (1998), 'Rural periodic markets in Egypt', in N.S. Hopkins and K. Westergaard (eds.) *Directions of change in rural Egypt* (Cairo: American University in Cairo Press) 303–317.

O'Meara, S. (n.d.), 'Bazaar, Arab lands', in K. Fleet, G. Krämer, D. Matringe, J. Nawas and E. Rowson (eds.) *Encyclopaedia of Islam*, Three. http://dx.doi.org/10.1163/1573-3912_ei3_COM_24004. (Accessed 29 July 2018).

Owen, E.R.J. (1998), *A history of Middle East economies in the twentieth century* (Cambridge, MA: Harvard University Press).

Pamuk, Ş. (1987), *The Ottoman empire and European capitalism, 1820–1913: Trade, investment, and production* (New York: Cambridge University Press).

Perkins, K.J. (2013), *A history of modern Tunisia*. 2nd ed. (New York: Cambridge University Press).

Peter, F. (2004), 'Dismemberment of empire and reconstitution of regional space: The emergence of 'national' industries in Damascus between 1918 and 1946 Frank Peter', in N. Méouchy and P. Sluglett (eds.) *The British and French mandates in comparative perspectives* (Leiden/Boston, MA: Brill) 415–446.

Press, A. (2011), 'Cairo institute burned during clashes', *The Guardian*, 19 Dec.

Rafeq, A.-K. (2008), 'The economic organization of cities in Ottoman Syria', in P. Sluglett (ed.) *The urban social history of the Middle East, 1750–1950* (Syracuse, NY: Syracuse University Press) 104–140.

Reynolds, N.Y. (2011), 'National socks and the "nylon woman": Materiality, gender, and nationalism in textile marketing in semicolonial Egypt, 1930–56', *International Journal of Middle East Studies*, 43 (1), pp. 49–74.

Reynolds, N.Y. (2012), *A city consumed: Urban commerce, the Cairo fire, and the politics of decolonization in Egypt* (Stanford, CA: Stanford University Press).

Schayegh, C. (2012), 'Iran's Karaj Dam affair: Emerging mass consumerism, the politics of promise, and the Cold War in the Third World', *Comparative Studies in Society and History: An International Quarterly*, 54 (3), pp. 612–643.

Schreier, J. (2012), 'The creation of the "Israelite indigène": Jewish merchants in early colonial Oran', *Journal of North African Studies*, 17 (5), pp. 757–772.

Schwedler, J. (2010), 'Amman cosmopolitan: Spaces and practices of aspiration and consumption', *Comparative Studies of South Asia, Africa and the Middle East*, 30 (3), pp. 547–562.

Seikaly, S. (2016), *Men of capital: Scarcity and economy in mandate Palestine* (Stanford, CA: Stanford University Press).

Shechter, R. (2005), 'Reading advertisements in a colonial/development context: Cigarette advertising and identity politics in Egypt, c. 1919–1939', *Journal of Social History*, 39 (2), pp. 483–503.

Shechter, R. (2006), *Smoking, culture and economy in the Middle East: The Egyptian tobacco market 1850–2000* (New York: I.B. Tauris).

Shechter, R. (2009), 'From effendi to *infitāḥī*? Consumerism and its malcontents in the emergence of Egyptian market society', *British Journal of Middle Eastern Studies*, 36 (1), pp. 21–35.

Shechter, R. (2011), 'Glocal conservatism: How marketing articulated a neotraditional Saudi Arabian society during the First Oil Boom, c. 1974–1984', *Journal of Macromarketing*, 31 (4), pp. 376–386.

Shechter, R. (2008), 'The cultural economy of development in Egypt: Economic nationalism, hidden economy and the emergence of mass consumer society during Sadat's infitah', *Middle Eastern Studies*, 44 (4), pp. 571–583.

Shields, S.D. (2008), 'Interdependent spaces: Relations between the city and the countryside in the nineteenth century', in P. Sluglett (ed.) *The urban social history of the Middle East, 1750–1950* (Syracuse, NY: Syracuse University Press) 43–66.

Shirazi, F. (2016), *Brand Islam: The marketing and commodification of piety* (Austin, TX: University of Texas Press).

Shoham, H. (2013), '"Buy local" or "buy Jewish"? Separatist consumption in interwar Palestine', *International Journal of Middle East Studies*, 45 (3), pp. 469–489.

Singerman, D. (2007), 'Cairo cosmopolitan: Citizenship, urban space, publics and inequality', in B. Drieskens, F. Mermier and H. Wimmen (eds.), *Cities of the south: Citizenship and exclusion in the twenty-first century* (Berlin: Saqi, in Association with Heinrich Böll Foundation & Institut Français du Proche-Orient) 82–109.

Springer, S., Birch, K. and MacLeavy, J. (eds.) 2016. *The handbook of neoliberalism* (New York: Routledge, Taylor & Francis Group).

Srougo, S. (2011), 'The informal sector in a colonial regime: The Jewish economy of the lower classes in Casablanca between the two world wars', *Journal of North African Studies*, 16 (1), pp. 77–97.

Starrett, G. (1998), *Putting Islam to work: Education, politics, and religious transformation in Egypt* (Berkeley, CA: University of California Press).

Starrett, G, (1995), 'The political economy of religious commodities in Cairo', *American Anthropologist*, 97 (1), pp. 51–68.

Troin, J.-F. (1990), 'New trends in commercial locations in Morocco', in A.M. Findlay, R. Paddison and J.A. Dawson (eds.) *Retailing environments in developing countries* (London: Routledge).

van den Boogert, M.H. (n.d.), 'Beratlı', in K. Fleet, G. Krämer, D. Matringe, J. Nawas and E. Rowson (eds.) *Encyclopaedia of Islam*, Three. http://dx.doi.org/10.1163/1573-3912_ei3_COM_22696 (Accessed 2 August 2018).

Vandewalle, D.J. (2006), *A history of modern Libya* (New York: Cambridge University Press).

Varcin, R. (2000), 'Competition in the informal sector of the economy: The case of market traders in Turkey', *International Journal of Sociology and Social Policy*, pp. 5–33.

Vicdan, H. (2015), 'Evolving desire to experience the social "other": Insights from the high-society bazaar', *Journal of Consumer Culture*, 15 (2), pp. 248–276.

Vignal, L. (2007), 'The emergence of a consumer society in the Middle East: Evidence from Cairo, Damascus and Beirut', in B. Drieskens, F. Mermier and H. Wimmen (eds.) *Cities of the south: Citizenship and exclusion in the twenty-first century* (Berlin: Saqi), in Association with Heinrich Böll Foundation & Institut Français du Proche-Orient, 68–81.

Vitalis, R. (1995), *When capitalists collide: Business conflict and the end of empire in Egypt* (Berkeley, CA: University of California Press).

Wansbrough, J., İnalcık, H. and Lambton, A.K. (n.d.), 'Imtiyāzāt', in P. Bearman, T. Bianquis, C.E. Bosworth, E. van Donzel and W.P. Heinrichs (eds.) *Encyclopaedia of Islam*. 2nd ed. http://dx.doi.org/10.1163/1573-3912_islam_COM_0371 (Accessed 1 August 2018).

Webb, D., Khomeini, A., Khumaynī, R.A. and Ḫumaynī, R.A. (2005), 'On mosques and malls: Understanding Khomeinism as a source of counter-hegemonic resistance to the spread of global consumer culture', *Journal of Political Ideologies*, 10 (1), pp. 95–119.

27

MODERN RETAILING HISTORY IN JAPAN: FROM THE MEIJI RESTORATION OF 1868 TO THE BEGINNING OF THE TWENTY-FIRST CENTURY

Harada Masami

Introduction

After the Ansei Five-Power Treaties of 1858, Japan opened its country to the world and underwent a planned programme of economic and especially industrial development, orchestrated by the government of the Meiji Restoration. It was the first Asian country to be recognised by Europe and America as a modern, industrialised nation. However, the Meiji Government's policy for development did not specify how to modernise in the area of retailing. This chapter examines a range of modern retail formats which rose to prominence in the century or so after 1868: department stores, retail markets, supermarkets and convenience stores. After World War I, department stores and retail markets began to establish themselves in Japan as income levels rose and mass market began to grow. This growth was temporarily interrupted during World War II, but Japan once again achieved high economic growth in the postwar era. This was reflected in the growing number of supermarkets, which have been described as a "distribution revolution" in Japan. After the end of rapid economic growth in the 1980s, convenience stores became established as a new type of retailing business. Since the 1990s, it is these convenience stores that have become a leading retailing business style in Japan.

Japanese department stores, retail markets, supermarkets and convenience stores were all modelled after European and American retail models. After the Meiji Restoration, a few enterprising retailers actively sought to build a modern retailing sector, but many small and traditional retailing establishments, which existed in Japan long before the Meiji Restoration period, have survived despite programmes of industrialisation and modernisation. While some of these small retailing businesses attempted to keep up with change, many resisted modernisation and started a movement against the establishment of department stores. Their success can be seen in the Department Store Act of 1937, enacted to control the business activities of department stores. This developed into the Large Scale Store Act of 1973, which controlled the activities of department stores and supermarkets. The act as well as the Department Store Act of 1937 sought to mediate between the interests of traditional and modern retailers, although the former steadily declined in number, especially after the mid 1980s, due to the spread of supermarkets. The regulatory act was abolished in 2000.

The emergence of modern retailing

There are two major historical lineages of Japanese department stores in large cities. The first is the case whereby dry goods stores developed into department stores; the second pertains to the establishment of department stores by railway companies at their terminuses. With respect to the former, in many cases they had established their businesses in large castle towns such as Edo, Kyoto and Osaka in the pre-modern Edo era and evolved into department stores in the modern period. Mitsukoshi was the first, and typical, store that decided to convert from selling dry goods to the broader-based department store format.

Mitsui Echigoya, the name of Mitsukoshi in the Edo era, became a large dry goods store by introducing cash payments at the end of the seventeenth century. It also became a purveyor of dry goods to the Tokugawa Shogunate. After the Meiji Restoration, Echigoya changed its name to Mitsui Dry-Goods Store (Mitsui Gofuku-ten) in 1893. Two years later, Mitsui introduced a merchandise display on the second floor of the main store in Tokyo, replacing the traditional selling method of za-uri. By 1900, za-uri was completely abolished on all floors of the Tokyo store. Takahashi Yoshio, the director of Mitsui and the person in charge of the conversion, explained za-uri in his book published in 1936 as follows.

When a visitor finds his favourite clerk and tells him his order, the clerk shout in a loud voice 'errand boy, bring me the commodity'. In response to the clerk's voice the boy bring back the commodity on a square plate board from the warehouse to the sales floor, and the clerk receives it and shows it to his customer. This is the ordinary procedure for selling in a draper's shop. The reason why the deep blue curtain makes the inner shop dimly lit is for improving the appearance of commodities. It is said to be a secret skill of the clerk that he reduces opportunities to show commodities to and satisfy his customer (Takahashi, 1936; 253).

The switch from the traditional selling method of za-uri to a system of open display enabled customers to freely peruse the commodities (Sueta, 2010; 48). Its direct model of influence was the Wanamaker department store in Philadelphia, USA, and its origin might be found in the merchandise display of le Bon Marché in France, although there is undoubtedly a longer history of such practices (see Chapters 10 and 11). Mitsui Dry-Goods Store changed its name to Mitsukoshi Dry-Goods Store and became a stock company in 1904. In the following year, the store publicised "a department store declaration" in major newspapers. The declaration stated that Mitsui Dry-Goods Store would expand its scope of commodities in addition to dry goods and had sent a clerk to America to study a department store there.

Although the declaration made it clear that the business would become a department store, it was only the first step in the transition (Mitsukoshi, 1990; 42–43). After its announcement, Mitsukoshi increased the number of commodities it stocked, beginning to sell imported cosmetics, hats and caps made in Europe and America and accessories for infants in 1905; it established a Western clothing department, beginning to sell children's accessories in 1906. It also began to sell bags, footwear, umbrellas and hair care items (combs and ornamental hairpins) in 1907 and jewellery, tobacco and stationery in 1908. A year later, Mitsukoshi also established a restaurant and art gallery. This increasing range of goods and services led to the construction of a new wooden three-story building with 1,858m^2 of floor space in 1907. However, the building gradually became too crowded and Mitsukoshi built an alternative in 1914, which was constructed with reinforced concrete with one floor underground, five floors above ground and a total floor space of 13,210m^2. At the same time, Mitsukoshi added some provisioning departments stocking tea, dried bonito and flowers. Many scholars suggest that this outlet constituted the first true department store in Japan (Sueta, 2010; 55). However, there is no consensus on the precise timing of the transition from dry goods to department store retailing, partly because other dry goods stores quickly followed Mitsukoshi's example. By the mid-1910s, Shirokiya, Matsuzakaya, Daimaru, Takashimaya and Sogo had all introduced modern merchandise displays, increased the range of commodities for sale and became stock companies.

The second historical lineage for Japanese department stores occurred when railway companies established department stores at their terminuses. The first of these "terminal department stores", Hankyu Department Store, was established at the Osaka Umeda terminal station of the Hankyu Electric Railway Company in 1929. It consisted of a station concourse on the ground floor, a market selling fish and fruit and vegetables on the underground floor and five floors selling daily necessities and miscellaneous goods from the second floor to the sixth floor. It informed its customers in its newspaper advertisement that 'the department store would sell better commodities at lower prices than any other department store'. Subsequently, Hankyu completed enlargement of the building, then rapidly expanded its range of commodities. In 1931, it came to sell high-grade dry goods and kimonos. Moreover, in 1933, it established an out-of-store sales department, extending business to more customers. The total sales floor area of the store reached 56,200m^2 in 1936, becoming the largest department store in Osaka. By this time, it also seems to have established a departmental management system – a remarkable achievement for a store which was created from nothing.

Figure 27.1 New building of Mitsukoshi's main store, constructed in 1914

(Courtesy of Isetan Mitsukoshi Ltd)

The success of the Hankyu Department Store made it a pioneering example of terminal department stores in Japan. In Osaka, Takashimaya followed suit, although it had a longer history of retailing, having started a second-hand clothes dealership in 1831. In 1930, Takashimaya drew up plans for new store buildings in both Osaka and Tokyo to sell a large number of commodities to the masses. Nankai Store, which Takashimaya opened in Osaka in 1932 at the terminus of the Nankai Electric Railway, was the largest department store in the Kansai area. Building on this success, Takashimaya opened an eight-story outlet in Nihonbashi, Tokyo in 1933. In some ways, it was a pioneer, being the first dry goods store to build a terminal department store, but Takashimaya lagged behind Mitsukoshi and others in adopting the department store mode of selling.

After Takashimaya, other terminal department stores were opened: the Daitetsu Department Store and Daiki Department Store in Osaka, and the Toyoko Department Store and Keihin Department Store in Tokyo. These tended to be located at suburban railway terminuses, serving residents living along the railway (Sueta, 2010; 106). Keihan Department Store was one of the most interesting because it started as Keihan Market before evolving into a department store. The department store, which was established through equal investments from the Keihan Electric Railway Company and Shirokiya, sold mainly food and miscellaneous goods, and as such its sales area and sales volumes were not large. After the Department Store Act of 1937, this particular store, by reducing its sales area, escaped regulation – a reminder that expansion was not always the best option for a store (Taniuchi, 2014; 164, 170–171, 175). Japan's terminal department stores are sometimes said to be unique in the world. They were the product of railway companies identifying and pursuing business diversification opportunities (Ogawa, 2004; 210). Japanese terminal stations, in many cases, had connections with other railway stations (Terasaka, 2005; 28–29), undoubtedly an advantage for the terminal department stores vis-à-vis acquiring customers.

In 1928, when the popularisation of department stores was gathering speed, a magazine *Shotenkai* (the world of commerce) published the results of a questionnaire comparing department stores with traditional retail stores. The analysis was distributed across two articles. The first addressed the questions 'What makes you want to shop at a department store?' and 'What department store features appeal to you?'; the second considered 'What makes it difficult for you to shop at traditional retail stores?'. The respondents consisted of twenty-six people: a novelist, three professors, a lecturer, a beauty salon executive, an artist and nineteen untitled persons, many of whom seem to have belonged to the middle class. At the same time, judging from their addresses, titles and the contents of their answers, they seem to have lived in Tokyo. Among the answers, the following was typical of responses to the question concerning the attraction of department stores:

1 Free browsing; salespeople do not compel customers to buy things.
2 Since department stores display a very wide range of commodities, it is convenient for customers to buy other things beyond the target goods.
3 Free from deceit because fixed prices are displayed.

Overall, the answer showed that customers appreciated the new selling practices of department stores: merchandise displays, selling a variety of commodities and selling at fixed prices. By contrast, traditional retail stores lacked such benefits and were seen in a negative light when compared to department stores.

By the 1930s, Japanese department stores were supplying many of the commodities demanded by the general public, their main lines having changed from luxuries to utility goods. They made purchases of high cost durable goods easier by introducing monthly instalments, thus expanding their ability to attract customers from the ordinary population as well as the upper classes (Ooka, 2014; 226). This was important because the middle class was growing rapidly at this time, from 1.07 million in 1920, accounting for 4% of the total labour force, to 3.62 million in 1940, or 12% of the workforce (Hirano, 2005; 169). This increase in the size of the middle class promoted the expansion of department stores so that, by the end of 1937, there were fifty-three department stores in the six large cities and 110 in Japan overall (Sueta, 2010; 303–304).

This growth had deleterious consequences for traditional retailers, especially when the Showa Depression brought a prolonged slump to retailing in general. In response, department stores engaged travelling salesmen, established of branches in new places and extended store space. They also strengthened sales and the acquisition of new customers by holding bargain sales, promoting loss leaders and extending free delivery services. As a result, department store sales reached 32.3% of total retail sales in Tokyo in 1931–32, 15.6% in Nagoya in 1932 and 13.8% in Osaka in 1936 (Suzuki, 1980; 117–119). Such increasing market penetration drove traditional retailers into activities against department stores; they demanded that the Government should enact legislation to regulate the business of these burgeoning leviathans.

As a result, the Department Store Act was introduced in 1937. According to the act and the rules related to it, the department store was defined as a store where the sales floor area was more than 3,000m^2 in the six large cities (more than 1,500m^2 in other cities) and sold a variety of goods relating to food, clothing and housing. The act required department stores to obtain permission from the Ministry of Commerce and Industry regarding the opening of the store, establishment of branch stores, enlargement of sales floor area and so forth. The ministry was authorised to inspect department stores as necessary and to take action where required, including the suspension of business, dismissal of officers and rescindment of department stores' licenses. It is certain that the act, by regulating the activities of department stores, protected the activities of small and medium retailers; but it is also certain that, by regulating the opening of new department stores, it restrained competition among the existing department stores. The act was abolished in 1947 owing to the establishment of a broader Antimonopoly Act of 1947, but its key characteristics were enshrined in the 1956 variant of this act and in the Large Scale Retail Store Act of 1973, discussed below.

During the Edo era, retail markets ceased to exist and only wholesale markets operated in many castle towns (Toyoda, 1983; 388). The inhabitants of these towns bought daily necessaries from a small number of retail shops and a much greater number of pedlars. In the early twentieth century, drawing on the experiences of European cities, arguments for the establishment of municipal markets emerged in Japan. A rise in food prices after the Russo-Japanese War (1904–1905) fuelled such arguments and prompted a series of national inquiries into retail and wholesale organisations. Scholars such as Isoo Abe, a professor at Tokyo Technical College, Kaichi Toda, a professor at Kyoto Imperial University, and Susumu Kawatsu, a professor at Tokyo Imperial University, all insisted on the necessity of establishing municipal retail markets. The National Government's council reported that it was urgently necessary to establish municipal retail markets to improve the living standard of "the working poor". However, it took a several years for municipal corporations to establish their retail markets (Harada, 2016; 486–487).

World War I brought Japanese society both an economic boom and escalating prices. Although the former brought wealth to some people, many people suffered because of the latter. Newspapers and magazines reported the hard lives of *yofuku saimin* (poor people wearing suits), reflecting the difficulties faced by salaried men because their wages could not keep up with the rising prices. Prompted by such concerns, Osaka City Corporation established four municipal retail markets in April 1918 – the first municipal retail markets in Japan. After four months, the outbreak of the rice riots contributed to the spread of municipal retail markets through Japan. Many municipal corporations started to sell rice at low prices from their outlets and then established municipal markets. In Yokohama, Nagoya, Kyoto and Kobe, municipal retail markets were established immediately after the outbreak of the riots, although it took another year before Tokyo City followed suit. In each market, rice quickly becoming one of the most important commodities, constituting, for example, 51.3% of all commodities sold in the municipal retail market in Tokyo City in 1919, 46.4% in Osaka and 70.2% in Nagoya (Daitoshi, 1931; 62, 88, 102). Thereafter the percentage gradually diminished, but municipal markets continued to grow rapidly in number, reaching 409 in 1923 – just five years after the first was established. A certain amount of volatility ensued between 1925 and 1930, turning into a gradual fall to 304 markets in operation by 1931 and 257 in 1938. They remained primarily food markets. Fruit and vegetables, fish, meat and eggs as well as rice and other grains, accounted from between 74.2% to 93.2% of the total sales of the six large cities' municipal markets in 1932.

Osaka City's municipal retail markets were the most successful examples across the six large cities. It was, for example, the only municipal retail markets to remain in the black (Osaka, 1989; 36). It is important to remember that only Osaka City had established municipal retail markets before the outbreak of riots – as part of urban planning rather than a response to food crisis. This planning was introduced by Hajime Seki, a deputy mayor of Osaka City and a former professor at Tokyo Commercial High School who had experience of studying in European universities and was a specialist in Japanese urban policy. He was asked to take office as the deputy of Osaka City and later became the mayor of the City. The prosperity and success of Osaka City's municipal retail markets can in part be attributed to his knowledge and foresight. In contrast, Tokyo City's municipal retail markets were rather less successful. Before their establishment in Tokyo, existing retailers had united against the planning of municipal retail markets, delaying their establishment in the city. In the Tokyo City Assembly, it was even insisted that the municipal retail markets should not sell expensive goods such as high-quality fish, excellent rice cakes and so on, but should only sell low price goods such as low quality rice (Harada, 1991; 122). The result was that retail traders in Tokyo City's municipal retail markets were obliged to sell inferior goods, so they were said to resemble poor bargain markets. According to Nakamura, it is no exaggeration to say that Tokyo City's municipal retail markets became the retail organisation which reproduced the simple and poor eating habits of urban lower classes (Nakamura, 1989; 191).

Despite such problems, it should be emphasised that municipal retail markets played an important role. Fixed and marked prices, cash payments and personal collection were the operating principles of municipal retail markets – principles which are regarded as representing the modern characteristics of retail trade. Municipal retail markets, therefore, played an important role in the modernisation of the retail trade in Japan, because traditional retailers trade continued to sell commodities on credit and without price tags. In this sense, municipal retail markets developed a modern social relationship in which the retailer could sell commodities to anyone with the money to pay. However, it also needs to be pointed out that these modern characteristics of municipal retail markets had some limitations. One is that the majority of the daily necessities demanded by urban residents were supplied by small retail stores and private markets, not municipal retail markets. The sales volumes of municipal retail markets were therefore marginal relative to total retail sales across the city. For example, municipal retail markets accounted for only 0.4% of the total goods sold in Tokyo City in 1932 and 2.9% in Osaka City in the 1930s (Ishihara, 1989; 131). Therefore, the role of municipal retail markets was limited to checking and restraining general retail prices in private retail stores and private markets – important, but hardly revolutionary.

Even this limited role encountered a very difficult situation later on. A 1916 notice from the Vice-Minister of Agriculture and Commerce prohibited trade associations from any price agreement. In Tokyo, the Director of Bureau of Industry of Tokyo prefecture warned trade associations against establishing price agreements in 1921 and investigated retail trade associations on that basis. In response, the Federation of Tokyo Business Association, a network of retailers in Tokyo, determined to abolish price agreements in 1922. However, the global downturn of 1929 resulted in falling profits and business failures for many retailers; the Ministry of Commerce and Industry succumbed and in 1933 permitted price agreements within trade associations (Hirota, 2007; 242). The Government's acquiescence to price agreements resulted in the imposition of serious limitations on municipal retail markets over controlling general retail prices. The mayors of six large cities made futile efforts to petition the Ministries of Commerce and Industry, Health and Welfare, War and the Navy in 1938, requesting that municipal retail markets should be free from the restrictions imposed by trade associations' price agreements (Inoue and Tsuchiya, 1939; 366–368). The Government, however, chose to prioritise the interests of retailers rather than those of consumers, although following the end of World War II, trade association price agreements were again prohibited (Fujita, 1995; 269–270).

After World War II, municipal retail markets managed to maintain their social role until the end of the economic growth period, declining thereafter as price inflation eased. In sum, the municipal retail market as a retail type maintained its social and economic role only for fifty or sixty years in Japanese society. One of the reasons is that, whereas Europe's municipal retail markets were incorporated into their long histories of cities from the Middle Ages, Japan's municipal retail markets were not associated with such long history and thus were not institutionalised or embedded in the social fabric of the country to the same extent as their European counterparts.

Retailing in a mass consumption society

The first supermarket in Japan was Kinokuniya, established in 1953 in Aoyama, Tokyo, and based on a self-service format, rather than a face-to-face selling style. Kinokuniya's customers were mainly American soldiers in the Occupation Forces and their families. In 1956, Maruwa Food Center established in Kokura city was the first self-service style supermarket mainly for Japanese customers. It was on the recommendation of NCR Japan, an American overseas-company, that both supermarkets employed a self-service format. They were successful and profitable, suggesting that the self-service style improved labour productivity and contributed to increasing sales. Such an economic effect was not achieved in the Japanese retail trade more generally until the period of high economic growth after World War II (Yamaguchi, 2005; 157).

Table 27.1 shows the development of supermarkets in the period of high economic growth. The number of supermarkets grew more than threefold, store space nearly six-fold and sales nearly eleven-fold. The growth rate of turnover was even higher than the average economic growth rate. In this period, then, the number of supermarkets increased rapidly, the size of supermarkets became larger and supermarket sales increased more rapidly than the above two growth rates. Table 27.2 shows the percentage of consumers' expenditure by type of outlet in the same period. Traditional retail stores accounted for 48.0% of the total expenditure in 1964, decreasing to 37.4% in 1974, while supermarkets accounted for only 5.1% in 1964, increasing to 11.4% in 1974. Department stores' share of the market according to this metric decreased slightly over this 10-year period. With food expenditure, however, the market share enjoyed by traditional retail stores fell much more dramatically, from 78.4% to 56.4%, supermarkets growing from 9.2% to 23.6%. It is quite clear, then, that consumers rapidly changed where they shopped, especially for food.

Supermarkets were classified into one of four categories: food supermarket, clothing supermarket, general merchandising stores (GMSs) and others. Table 27.3 shows the percentage of sales by kind of supermarket in the period 1968–74. In 1968, food supermarkets and clothing

Table 27.1 Number of supermarkets in Japan, 1964–74

Year	*Number of supermarkets*
1964	3,620
1966	4,790
1968	7,062
1970	9,403
1972	10,635
1974	12,034

Source: Tsushosangyoshodaijinkanbo tokeichosabu (Research and Statistics Department of the Minister's Secretariat of the Ministry of International Trade and Industry), *Serufusabisuten ni kansuru tokeihyo* (Statistics of self-service stores), Tsushosangyoshodaijinkanbo tokeichosabu, Tokyo, each year.

Table 27.2 Expenditure by Japanese consumers by type of outlet, 1964–74 (%)

	Retail stores			*Supermarkets*			*Department stores*		
Year	*1964*	*1969*	*1974*	*1964*	*1969*	*1974*	*1964*	*1969*	*1974*
Total expenditure	48.0	43.8	37.4	5.1	7.7	11.4	5.9	5.4	5.5
Food	78.4	72.3	56.4	9.2	15.2	23.6	2.6	2.7	2.3
Household goods	34.6	38.0	34.6	1.7	3.5	5.9	6.7	6.0	6.0
Clothes	49.8	50.4	45.1	6.9	10.7	14.8	32.1	31.3	31.6

Source: Sorifu tokeikyoku (Bureau of Statistics of the Prime Minister's Office), Zenkoku shohi jittai chosa hokoku (*1974 National survey of family income and expenditures*), Vol. 11, 1977, Sorifu tokeikyoku, Tokyo, pp. 272, 275,276.

Table 27.3 Sale of different categories of goods by type of supermarket (%)

Year	*1968*	*1970*	*1972*	*1974*
Food supermarket	60.7	57.5	54.6	44.9
Clothing supermarket	20.8	16.9	16.5	9.8
GMS	11.6	21.9	24.5	42.4
Others	6.9	3.7	4.4	2.9
Total	100.0	100.0	100.0	100.0

Source: *Serufusabisuten ni kansuru tokeihyo* (Statistics of self-service stores), Tokyo, each year.

supermarket accounted for 81.5% of the total sales. However, afterwards GMSs, such as Daiei, Seiyu-Store, Jusco, Nichii and UNY, grew rapidly; their market share reached 42.4% by 1974. Japan's GMSs were different from those in America, as they dealt in perishable food as well as a wide variety of other goods. One reason for this is that Japan's GMSs had to accommodate a variety of goods because of poor growth in the mass consumption market (Tatsuki, 1995; 196). Another is that, because the profitability of perishable food in GMSs was low, these stores also had to sell a variety of goods, including clothing, in order to secure an adequate gross margin ratio (Yahagi, 1998; 128). Whatever the precise cause, GMSs grew particularly strongly. According to a survey of large-scale stores by Nihon Keizai Shimbunsha, in 1967, two supermarket companies reached the top ten retail companies by sales, four in 1969 and five in 1971. Daiei attained the top position in 1972.

Daiei is a typical Japanese GMS. Its founder, Isao Nakauchi, established his first supermarket store, Shufu no Mise Daiei (Daiei store for housewives) in 1957, dealing in pharmaceuticals, cosmetics, canned and bottled foods. Sandwiched by famous drugstores on both sides, Daiei soon suffered decreasing sales. To prevail against such difficulties, it pursued a broader diversity of goods. Clothing, meat, household articles, footwear and pesticides came into stock in 1959; fresh fish, fruit and vegetables, meats and household electric appliances such as televisions, transistor radios, refrigerators, electric rice cookers, washing machines, fluorescent lamps and electric lamps followed in 1960; and furniture, stationery and toys were added by 1961. The widening assortment necessarily required a massive and stable supply of goods. Nakauchi recognised that a management system for a chain store was necessary to improve his supermarkets when he visited supermarkets in Hawaii in 1962 (Mukoyama, 2009; 78–79). Daiei planned to introduce such a management system in 1962, establishing a chain store headquarters and a distribution centre in Kobe in 1963. In the same year, it opened five stores, one of which was a large store in a six-story building in Kobe with 5,672m^2 floor space. This was the first self-service discount department store (SSDDS) in Japan. Other supermarkets such as Seibu Store (later Seiyu) and Ito-Yokado also established SSDDS, laying down the management system in earnest (Mukoyama, 2009; 129–130).

In the early stage of their development, supermarkets introduced self-service systems and could manage only a single store. However, chain-store management systems became widespread

Figure 27.2 The first store of Daiei, Shufu no Mise Daiei, established in 1957

(Courtesy of Daiei, Inc)

in Japan in the later 1960s, shifting supermarkets towards bulk purchases, reducing management costs and enabling them to sell goods at low and thus highly competitive prices, not least because of labour productivity improvements (Takaoka, 1999; 12). Both the Pegasus Club established in 1962 and the Japan Chain Stores Association established in 1967 contributed to this diffusion. Their activities helped supermarkets to secure and benefit from economies of scale, make the best use of sales floor space, learn methods for managing merchandise, simplify operations, and rationalise facilities (Yamaguchi, 2005; 174). The Government, meanwhile, avoided regulating the growth of supermarkets in the period of high economic growth – another reason why they became widespread in Japan in this period. Although the Distribution Section of the Industrial Structure Council began to consider a "distribution policy" in late 1962, it determined not to regulate the growth of supermarkets by any law (Tateno, 1992; 121). Accordingly, it was not until 1973, the end of the period high economic growth, that the Government began to introduce regulations governing the growth of supermarkets.

The growth of supermarkets in the period of high economic growth brought an important change to Japanese society. Although only the department store was synonymous with the modern retail industry before the end of World War II, the supermarket appeared as a second example of this modernity in the period of high economic growth. The bi-polar structure of a few department stores and many more mom-and-pop retail stores that had existed until the end of World War II disappeared with the spread of supermarkets. That change brought a wider variety of retail suppliers to Japanese consumers (Yamaguchi, 2005; 179).

The Department Store Act of 1956 and the Law on Special Measures for Adjustment for Retail Businesses of 1959 were expected to restrict the growth of supermarkets. However, neither central government nor local governments applied these Acts to the case. In 1962, when medium and small retailers lobbied for restricting the growth of supermarkets, the Distribution Section of the Industrial Structure Council began to consider the role of distribution policy. After two years of discussion, the Council reached a conclusion that no legal restriction to the growth of supermarkets should be introduced because they considered that the government should not prevent supermarkets from promoting the distribution revolution (Ishihara, 2011; 31). A White Paper on Small and Medium Enterprises in Japan, published in 1964 by the Small and Medium Enterprise Agency, also appreciated that supermarkets improved the prevailing low labour productivity of retail businesses (Odaka, 2013; 380). From the late 1960s onwards, many supermarkets became increasingly large and were categorised as GMSs. Since these were similar in size and range of stock to department stores, they were called imitative department stores, yet they remained unregulated. Indeed, it is said that The Ministry of International Trade and Commerce even taught supermarkets how they could avoid the regulatory clutches of the Department Store Act (Ishihara, 2011; 30).

Small and medium retailers reacted against the growing and flourishing GMSs. In addition, department stores were also disconcerted by the growing GMSs which posed a threat to them, especially in smaller cities. Department stores made a request to the Government that GMSs and department stores should both be regulated by the same Act. Partly as a response to this, the Large Scale Retail Store Act of 1973 replaced the Department Store Act. It required that all large-scale stores, with a sales floor area over 1,500m^2 (3,000m^2 in government ordinance cities), should notify the Ministry of Trade and Industry of the location, sales floor area, business hours and business days of the store. The act also provided for the establishment of regional Large Scale Retail Stores Councils and Commercial Activities Adjustment Boards, the latter comprising representatives of local retailers, consumers and academics. Although the act was officially a notification system, it effectively operated as a licence system and it took a long time, often more than ten years, for Boards to provide consent for a new large-scale store.

Although there were 1,700 large-scale stores in Japan in 1973, when the act was enacted, the number of large-scale stores' notifications increased rapidly over the next five years. There were a total 1,991 notifications between 1974 to 1979, which would effectively have doubled the number of existing large-scale stores. Moreover, from the institution of the act onwards, many stores opened with sales floor areas of less than 1,500m² because there were no legal restrictions on stores of this size. These slightly smaller stores were a great threat to local small and medium stores, where the average sales floor area was only from 30–50m² at the time of the 1974 Census of Commerce by the Ministry of International Trade and Industry. To restrain such stores from opening, Toyonaka City in Osaka prefecture formed local regulations in 1976 and Kumamoto City enacted similar regulations with penalty provisions in the same year. Henceforth, many municipalities followed suit, and the number of such local regulations and guidelines reached seventy in September 1977 and 209 in September 1978 (Ishihara, 2011; 56; Tsushosangyosho 1985; 5). Furthermore, many local commercial organisations declared that any large-scale store project under development should be frozen (Ishihara, 2011; 84).

The result of this local action was that the act was amended in 1979. The most important amendment was that the sales floor area of large-scale stores was set at less than half of the previous standard. In other words, the amended act required that all large-scale stores, in cases where sales floor area exceeded 500m² (1,500m² in government ordinance cities), should notify the Ministry. With such strengthening of national regulation, local regulations by municipalities were supposed to be abolished, but in reality they survived because the amended act was regarded as the fruits of the traditional retailers' movement against large-scale stores. Affected by the second oil crisis and the impending implementation of the amended act, the number of notifications increased enormously. As a result, the problem of large-scale stores became extremely serious in the late 1970s and the early 1980s. Kyoto City announced in March 1981 that it would prohibit new large-scale store developments and many others followed: some twenty-eight prefectures and sixty-three commercial organisations in all. Some jurists who extolled the rights of small and medium retailers' even appeared. The Ministry determined to intervene further by strengthening its regulations, issuing a notice in January 1982 to restrain the opening of new large-scale stores. The political backdrop to this was that both the ruling party and the opposition claimed champion of the regulation of large-scale stores. The period from the late 1970s to the early 1980s is called 'the frozen era on opening large-scale stores' (Ishihara, 2011; 72–84).

While large-scale supermarkets, especially GMSs, grew rapidly in the period of high economic growth, food supermarkets dealing in perishable food could not grow in the same period. Most people bought perishable food in small amounts every day. Only specialists such as fishmongers, greengrocers and butchers had the requisite skills to process and maintain the quality of perishable food. Since most supermarkets, including GMSs, did not have such skills, supermarkets had to have those specialists enter as tenants or employ them directly. This caused supermarkets problems from a management perspective.

It was Kansai Supermarket that first innovated to mitigate such difficulties. Established in 1959 as a food supermarket in Itami, Hyogo, Kansai Supermarket had to accommodate a fishmonger and a butcher as tenants in the early stage. The tenants, especially the fishmonger, caused serious problems: management of fresh stock was poor; fish were not arranged on the sales counter by the opening time, and stock often sold out before closing time meaning that the fish department shut before the rest of the store. Those troubles, which suggest that the supermarket could not effectively control the business of the tenants, continued for several years and it was not until 1967 that Kansai Supermarket determined to directly manage the perishable food departments. While sending staff to America for training, the supermarket also began to independently seek a new sales system for perishable food. Its specific goal was to discover how the supermarket could scientifically manage the freshness of perishable food and sell it via self-service. To achieve its goal, it developed a new refrigerated display case suitable for Japan's humid climate; a set of new trays and film which covered the perishable food; a new manual by which anyone without bespoke skills could process perishable food, and a new cart by which the processed food could be efficiently carried to the sales floor. This series of largely technical innovations enabled the supermarket to manage the freshness of perishable food and to raise labour productivity in this area. Going further, Kansai Supermarket also determined to process perishable food in its backyard, which enabled it to always supply its customers with suitably fresh food. As a result, the supermarket could control intra-day fluctuations of perishable food, secure equality of access to food for all customers and reduce the loss of sales opportunities. It took the supermarket about ten years to achieve these innovations (Ishihara, 1998; 152–154).

Significantly, Kansai Supermarket published its innovations via the All Japan Supermarket Association (AJS) with the result that they were adopted all over Japan, often to the detriment of traditional retail stores. According to the Census of Commerce by the Ministry of International Trade and Industry, the number of traditional retail stores of perishable food started to decline 1979, reversing the trend of previous years (Nihon Keizai Shimbun, Inc., 1980; 8). It was not until 1985 that the number of traditional retail stores as a whole started to decline – a point at which it might be said that the distribution revolution had been accomplished in Japan.

The Marusho store established in Kobe in 1968 and My Shop in Toyonaka in 1969 were the first convenience stores in Japan. Both were independent stores. After 1973, companies in the large-scale supermarket business such as Seiyu, Ito-Yokado and Daiei, started to infiltrate this domain through establishing businesses such as Family Mart, 7-Eleven Japan and Daiei Lawson. Such entries caused rapid growth of the convenience store sector (Kim, 2001; 5). Table 27.4 shows that both the number and sales of convenience stores increased rapidly, although the growth of both slowed after the collapse of the bubble economy in 1991.

Japanese convenience store businesses considered various stores America as models, but important differences emerged between the stores in these two countries. One key difference was that Japanese supermarket companies played an important role in developing convenience store businesses, whereas American supermarkets did not. The reason was that the Large Scale Store Act of 1973, especially the amended act of 1979, restrained further expansion in the number of supermarkets. As a result, large-scale supermarket companies began to direct their funds to convenience store businesses (Kawabe, 2003; 139). According to a survey of Japanese retailing by Nihon Keizai Shinbunsha, it was in 1982 that convenience stores, including 7-Eleven Japan, San Chain and Daiei Lawson, first featured in the top 200 by sales (Kawabe, 2003; 139). Thereafter, these companies not only increased the number of their stores but also gradually raised their rankings. Major convenience store companies first strengthened their franchise systems and then

Table 27.4 The development of convenience stores in Japan

Year	*Number of stores*	*Sales (million yen)*
1982	23,235	2,177,609
1985	29,236	3,382,902
1988	34,550	5,012,549
1991	41,847	6,984,859
1994	48,405	8,335,279

Source: Tsushosangyoshodaijinkanbo tokeichosabu (Research and Statistics Department of the Minister's Secretariat of the Ministry of International Trade and Industry), *Shogyo tokeihyo* (*Census of Commerce*), Okurasho insatsukyoku, each year.

expanded the number of stores and their sales; in comparison, companies employing voluntary chain systems grew more slowly (Kawabe, 2003; 139–140). In 1986, the top ten companies accounted for 75% of the total number of convenience stores in Japan and 80% of the total sales in this sector (Kim, 2001; 80).

In the early stage, adopting a franchise system (the dominant strategy for opening convenience stores), introducing point of sale (POS) systems, and constructing physical distribution systems were regarded as important factors. With such strategies and systems, Japanese convenience stores successfully grew. 7-Eleven Japan, which began convenience store business under the license agreements with the Southland Corporation in America in 1973 (Seven-Eleven Japan, 1991; 14), was the most successful example in the country. Normal practice was for the convenience store head office to open a large number of stores in a specific area, a strategy that reduced distribution costs. Thus, as soon as 7-Eleven Japan opened the first store at Toyosu, Tokyo, it determined to open many stores around the first store. At the same time, it adopted a franchise system – common in Japanese convenience stores, but largely absent in America. The reason why a franchise system was selected by 7-Eleven Japan and became widespread in Japan was its favourable cost profile compared to the direct-management alternative. Accordingly, traditional retail shopkeepers who had their own shops and land became targets as franchisees of convenience stores. This was considered to be a good opportunity by many traditional shopkeepers because they had come to acknowledge the limits of their own business due to the quick growth of supermarkets, especially large-scale retail stores. Many shopkeepers, including those presiding over sake shops, which were the main target of 7-Eleven Japan, thus took up this opportunity.

7-Eleven Japan introduced joint delivery in 1976; this decreased the number of delivery operations and the overall cost of delivery to each store. The introduction of the POS system to every

Figure 27.3 The first store of 7-Eleven Japan, Toyosu store, established in 1974 (Courtesy of 7-Eleven Japan Ltd)

store in 1982 not only enabled the company to decrease stock quantities, but it also enabled every store to know which commodity was the best-selling. As a result, the company could achieve a great impact on its performance, with the result that other convenience store companies also introduced the similar systems in the following year (Kawabe, 2003; 158–159). It is said that the POS system was the secret to the success of Japanese convenience stores. In America, the system was introduced to reduce labour costs and to minimise human error, whereas in Japan it was developed to a high level of functionality so that it could contribute to commodity management, an ordering system and a supporting system to every store. With such high level POS, the company could create a business strategy for responding to the changing market environment (Sunaga, 2005; 259).

Retailing in the consumer recession

After the oil crisis in 1973, Japan's economy transitioned away from secondary industries, especially manufacturing that had driven the country's economic growth, to the tertiary sector. As a result, Japan transformed from an industrial into consumer society, where people could enjoy high consumption of commodities and services. The rise of bulk purchase, the expanding demand for cooked and semi-cooked food due to increasing female employment, and the widespread use of automobiles promoted consumers' purchasing in large-scale stores in suburbs. Through merging with or affiliating with different types of retail entities such as local department stores and discount stores, GMSs changed their previous business types and became diversified. The largest GMS, Daiei, for example, expanded beyond retail and into services, finance and development to such an extent that it regarded itself as a comprehensive information enterprise. The bubble economy in the late 1980s encouraged GMSs to diversity very quickly, but its subsequent collapse plunged many into difficulty or even bankruptcy (Sunaga, 2005; 209).

Real consumption expenditure declined after 1993, with the result that department store sales figures decreased year by year, while sales from GMSs remained lacklustre. In addition, bankruptcies of financial institutions, rising unemployment and a slump in incomes all served to amplify consumers' anxiety about the future and suppressed consumption. As a result, discount stores specialising in particular commodities such as clothing, food and home electric appliances – sometimes called category killers – grew in number. These discount stores, procured commodities at low prices from other Asian countries and sold them at low prices in Japan. To fight against such activities, GMSs also had to construct networks by which they too could acquire commodities at lower prices in the international market. However, this response by GMSs unfortunately backfired through deteriorating sales productivity and capital income rate (Sunaga, 2005; 239). Although some department stores opened new large-scale outlets, others reduced the number of employees, closed some existing stores and even filed for civil rehabilitation proceedings, which meant virtually going bankrupt. This was also true in the case of some GMSs. Yaohan, a GMS which aggressively developed stores overseas, went bankrupt in 1996, with Mycal also going under in 2001. It was Daiei that received the most attention due to its business slump. Since the company diversified by taking out large bank loans on the security of its real properties, the collapse of the bubble economy rapidly depressed the value of these properties, causing great damage to Daiei. It started to reconstruct its business with significant financial support from banks in 2002, but after two years had to seek support from a governmental institution, namely the Industrial Revitalization Corporation of Japan. Finally, in 2015, Daiei became a wholly owned subsidiary company of AEON.

In contrast, convenience stores enjoyed relatively good business performance during this period, with the overall number of convenience stores continuing to increase, from 39,614 in 1991 to 54,398 in 2000. 7-Eleven Japan, the largest convenience store company, secured the top position in retail industry sales in 2000. In 2005, the company merged the Southland Corporation of America, which had been the model of 7-Eleven Japan, and developed convenience store businesses in America, employing the franchise system. One reason for the uniquely strong performance of convenience stores this is that they won the trust and support of consumers by providing a variety of services such as collecting money for electricity bills, accepting home delivery requests and selling tickets. Another reason was that most convenience store companies adopted a method of gross profit share between the head office and the convenience stores (franchisees) as royalty payments. The economic effect of this method was that both the head office and the affiliated stores were motivated to pursue maximum gross profit (Ito, 2005; 212). To this day, the convenience store industry maintains the top position in the retail industry.

The global trend to economic liberalisation and expansion in exports from Japan to America affected Japanese distribution policy in the 1980s, especially the Large Scale Retail Store Act. The Federation of Economic Organizations proposed a document to the Government in 1985, suggesting that the act should be properly operated, indicating current failings in this respect. The chairperson of the Large Scale Retail Stores Council made a remark to the same effect in 1987. Two years later, the Prime Minister's investigative committee, called the Special Administrative Reform Promotion Council, also submitted a report asking the Government to improve the operation of the act. Accordingly in the same year, the Ministry of International Trade and Industry published 'A vision of distribution in the 1990s', in which they made it clear that operationalisation of the act would be improved. However, those domestic improvement plans could not foresee the subsequent pressures for abolishing the act.

It was the Structural Impediments Initiative (SII) convened by the Japanese and American Governments that pushed the act to abolishment. SII was established in 1989 through the American Government's proposal to inspect the Japan-United States mutual socio-economic systems to further open up Japanese markets. Although America demanded the abolition of the act in the negotiations, Japan declared its intention to loosen its application. These negotiations settled on a decision reflecting Japan's intentions and the act was amended in 1991. The key amendments were that the sales area of stores required for notification to the Minister was doubled compared to the previous level and that the Commercial Activities Adjustment Board was abolished so that only the Large Scale Retail Stores Council could discuss the notifications of large-scale stores. The abolition of the act meant that public policy which had existed to restrain retail industry activities for many years ceased to exist in Japan. The Joint Conference proposed that a Large Scale Retail Stores Location Act should be enacted, a recommendation adopted in 1998. The Large Scale Retail Stores Location Act replaced the Large Scale Retail Stores Act in 2000. The purpose of the act was to preserve the living environment of areas surrounding large-scale retail stores. Since large-scale retail stores were usually located in suburbs, many shoppers come to the stores by car. The noise and pollution from cars was regarded as a threat to the living environment of the surrounding area.

Conclusions

Department stores and retail markets established modern retail practices in Japan before the end of World War II. Department stores descended from dry goods stores in the Meiji era and established their business style in the early stage of mass market after World War I. They became more popular after widening their clientele to include the middle class, rather than just catering to the upper class, a shift that was both furthered and symbolised in the emergence of terminal department stores. Municipal corporations played a key role in establishing retail markets which employed a cash payment system and played a revolutionary role in Japanese retailing. Retail markets and department stores had at least one feature in common: the provision of a variety of goods under one roof. This made it easy for customers to buy whatever they needed in one location, a convenience aptly named "one-stop-shopping" and one not open to traditional and specialised retailers. Both department stores and municipal retail markets were part of a programme of conscious modernisation and westernisation of the Japanese retail sector. However, both developments caused unrest among traditional retailers. The Department Store Act of 1937 was the result; it mediated between the interests of traditional and modern retailers.

Supermarkets emerged as a major retail format in the postwar era and became a symbol of the mass market in Japan. They contributed to the widespread use of cash payment and a rise in the productivity of labour in retailing. The turnover of supermarkets surpassed that of department stores in the early 1970s, growth that again caused unrest among existing retailers, resulting in the Large Scale Store Act of 1973 and a plethora of local regulations. These restrained supermarkets from opening new stores, but gave way to a new retailing system: convenience stores. In Japan, these were franchises, a system different from that which existed in America, and one that enabled Japanese convenience stores to develop rapidly and to provide traditional retailers with opportunities to become convenience stores. After the collapse of the bubble economy in 1991, convenience stores maintained a high growth rate compared to other retail industries such as department stores and supermarkets. In 2005, 7-Eleven Japan, the largest company of convenience stores, purchased the American company which had provided its original inspiration – a remarkable symbol of the strength of this part of the Japanese retail sector.

References

Daitoshi (Daitoshi-chosatokeikyogikai) (The joint conference of investigation and statistics of large cities) (1931), *Daitoshi-kokigyo hikakuchosa* (Comparative investigation into the public utilities of large cities), Vol. 6, (Tokyo: Daitoshi-chosatokeikyogikai).

Fujita, T. (1995), *Kindai Nihon dogyokumiai shiron* (Historical study on modern Japanese trade associations), (Osaka: Seibundo Shuppan).

Harada, M. (1991), *Kindai Nihon shijoshi no kenkyu* (Research of Japanese modern market history), (Tokyo: Sosiete).

Harada, M. (2016), 'Japanese modern municipal retail and wholesale markets in comparison with European markets', *Urban History*, 43 (3).

Hirano, T. (2005), 'Nihon niokeru kourigyotai no hensen to shohishakai no henyo (The change of retail style and transformation of consumption society in Japan)', *Mita shogaku kenkyu* (Mita Business Review), 48 (5).

Hirota, M. (2007), *Kindai Nihon no kouriichiba* (Modern Japan's retail markets for daily necessities), (Osaka: Seibundo Shuppan).

Inoue, T. and Tsuchiya, S. (1939), *Senji sengo no chusho-shokogyo* (Small and medium retailers during the wartime and after the war), (Tokyo: Showa Tosho).

Ishihara, T. (1989), *Kosetsukouriichiba no seisei to tenkai* (Creation and development of municipal retail markets), (Tokyo: Chikura Shobou).

Ishihara, T. (1998), 'Singyotai toshiteno shokuhin-supa no kakuritsu (The establishment of food supermarket as a new type of retail)', in J. Ishii, et al. (eds.) *Eigyo ryutsu kakushin* (The innovation of business and distribution), (Tokyo: Yuhikaku).

Ishihara, T. (2011), *Tsushosangyoseisakushi* (History of trade and industry policy), Vol. 4, Keizaisangyochosakai (Tokyo: Research Institute of Economy, Trade and Industry).

Ito, M. (2005), 'Konbiniensusutoa no kakushin (Innovation of convenience stores)', in M. Ito (eds.) *Shinryutsusangyo* (New distribution industry) (Tokyo: NTT Shuppan).

Mitsukoshi (1990), *Kabushikigaisha Mitsukoshi hachijugonen no kiroku* (Stock company Mitsukoshi: eighty-five years' records), (Tokyo: Stock Company Mitstukoshi).

Mukoyama, M. (2009), 'Sogoryohanten no kakushin to henyo (Innovation and modification of mass sales stores', in J. Ishii and M. Mukoyama (eds.) *Kourigyo no gyotaikakushin* (Innovation of retail type) (Tokyo: Chuokeizaisha).

Kawabe, N. (2003), *Shinpan Seven-Eleven no keieishi* (New edition the business history of Seven-Eleven Japan), (Tokyo:Yuhikaku).

Kim Hyn Chol (2001), 'Konbiniensusutoa no nihontekitenkai to makethingu (Japanese development and marketing of convenience stores', in Markethingushi-kenkyukai (eds.) *Nihon ryutsusangyoshi* (History of Japanese distribution industry) (Tokyo: Dobunkan Shuppan).

Nakamura, M. (1989), *Ichiba no kataru Nihon no kindai* (Markets telling Japanese modern history), revised edition (Tokyo: Sosiete).

Nihon Keizai Shimbun, Inc. (1980), *Ryutsukeizai no tebiki* (Handbook of 1981 economy of distribution) (Tokyo: Nihon Keizai Shimbun, Inc.).

Odaka, K. (2013), *Tsushosangyoseisakushi* (History of trade and industry policy), Vol. 4, (Tokyo: Keizaisangyochosakai).

Ogawa, I. (2004), 'Dentetsugyo no takakuka (Business diversification of electric railway industry)', in Keiei-shi-gakkai (Business History Society of Japan) (eds.) *Nihonkeieishi no kisochisiki* (Basic knowledge of Japanese business history) (Tokyo:Yuhikaku).

Ooka, S. (2014), 'Taishushakai no tanchotekikeisei (The beginning of the formation of mass society)', in T. Otsu, et al. (eds.) *Iawanami koza Nihon rekishi*, Vol. 17, (Tokyo: Iwanamishoten).

Osaka (Osakashi-kosetsuichiba nanajunenshi hensaniinkai) (1989), 'Osakashi-kosetsuichiba nanajunenshi' (Seventy years' history of Osaka city's municipal retail markets) (Osaka: Federation of Osaka city's municipal retail markets).

Seven-Eleven Japan (1991), *Seven-Eleven Japan: 1973–1991*, (Tokyo: Seven-Eleven Japan).

Shotenkai (1928), 'Naze hyakkaten de kaimono suruka. Naze kouriten wa kirainanoka (Why do the customers buy commodities at the department store? Why do they hate the traditional retailers?)', *Sotenkai*, 8.

Sueta, T. (2010), *Nihon-hyakkatengyo seiritsushi* (History of the establishment of department stores), (Kyoto: Minervashobo).

Sunaga, N. (2005), 'Kodo-taishushohishakai no torai to ryutsugyo (The coming of the sophisticated consumer society and the distribution industry)', in K. Ishii (ed.), *Kindainihon ryutsushi* (Japanese modern distribution history), (Tokyo: Tokyodo Shuppan).

Suzuki, Y. (1980), *Showa-kyokoki no kourisho-mondai* (The problems of retailers during the Showa Depression), (Tokyo: Nihon Keizai Hyouronsha).

Takahashi, Y. (1936), *Hoki no ato* (Trace of broom), Vol. 1, (Tokyo: Shuhoen Shuppan).

Takaoka, M. (1999), 'Kodoseichoki no supamakketo no shigenhokanmekanizumu (The business practices of Japanese supermarkets during the period of high economic growth from the mid 1950s to the early 1970s)', *Shakaikeizaishigaku* (*Socio-Economic History*), 65 (1).

Taniuchi, M. (2014), *Senzen no Osaka no testudo to hyakkaten* (Railways and Department stores in Osaka before World War II), (Osaka: Toho Shuppan).

Terasaka, A. (2005), 'Toshi to hyakkaten (Cities and department stores)', *Ryutsukeizaidaigakuronshu* (The Journal of Ryutsu Keizai University), 39 (3).

Tateno, K. (1992), 'Wagakuni niokeru supa no seicho (The growth of supermarkets in Japan)', *Nagasakikenritsudaigakuronshu*, 25 (3 & 4).

Tatsuki, M. (1995), 'Ryohanten no keieisozo (Creation of business of mass retailers)', in T. Yui and H. Juro (eds.) *Kakushin no keieishi* (Business history of innovation), (Tokyo: Yuhikaku).

Toyoda, T. (1983), *Houken toshi* (Feudal town), (Tokyo: Yoshikawakobunkan).

Tsushosangyosho (Tsushosangyosho sangyoseisakukyoku) (The Industrial Policy Department of the Ministry of International Trade and Industry) (1985), *Daikibokouritenpoho no kaisetsu* (*Explanation of the Large-Scale Retail Store Act*), (Tokyo: Tsushosangyochosakai).

Yahagi, T. (1998), 'Sogosupa no seiritsu (Establishment of general merchandizing store)', in J. Ishii, et al. (eds.) *Eigyo ryutsu kakushin* (The innovation of business and distribution), (Tokyo: Yuhikaku).

Yamaguchi, Y. (2005), 'Kodoseichoka no taishushohishakai (Mass consumption society in the period of high growth)', in K. Ishii (ed.) *Kindainihon ryutsushi* (Modern Japanese distribution history), (Tokyo: Tokyodo Shuppan).

28

WESTERN MODELS AND EASTERN INFLUENCES

Japanese department stores in the early twentieth century

Rika Fujioka

Introduction

The development of Japanese department stores was influenced by Western department stores, which were established in the middle of the nineteenth century (see Chapter 11). Mitsukoshi, for example, was Japan's first leading department store and was strongly inspired by American and British department stores. Its first professional managing director, Yoshio Takahashi, visited Wanamaker in Philadelphia in 1888 and was keen to introduce Wanamaker's modern organisational structure, including its personnel management, into his own store. Indeed, in 1900 Mitsukoshi began to hire female employees, which was revolutionary in Japanese society at the time (Takahashi, 1933). The second professional managing director, Osuke Hibi, learned a great deal from Harrods in particular and studied the layout of the store, its interior and exterior design, its merchandise and the customer service of its sales assistants. He met Harrods' director, Richard Burbidge, and they discussed the department store's social mission as a modern retailer. After this insightful experience, Hibi aimed to use his newfound knowledge to transform his own Mitsukoshi store (Hibi, 1912). Following its great success, other Japanese stores soon followed suit.

This development of Japanese department stores had a great impact not only on retailing but also on the Japanese economy and on Japanese society. Department stores were the hub of many industries and innovations; this was largely due to the expansion of their merchandise to include brand new Western-style products, a strategy that was an important part of their transformation from traditional dry goods stores. Only department stores could encourage Japanese manufacturers to learn the advanced skills of Western companies and could use their trading companies to buy the necessary equipment from Western countries to create these new products; only they had the power to influence the manufacturing and distribution system in Japan. Department stores in Japan therefore acted as windows into the Western lifestyle, and Japanese consumers were encouraged to adopt this new lifestyle and buy the accompanying products. In this way, department stores led manufacturers and consumers in a process of Westernisation, and they consequently dominated the retail market in Japan in the early twentieth century.

This development in turn impacted on retailers and consumers in other Asian countries such as Korea and China. Japanese retailers began their international activities in the early twentieth century. Mitsukoshi started by launching a branch in Seoul in Korea in 1906 and many more overseas stores followed. These stores were a catalyst for the modernisation of retailing in Asia, as they included never-before-seen features such as point-of-sales displays, which changed the way that local consumers shopped. Mitsukoshi expanded its network of overseas stores to include Dalian, Beijing, and Shanghai (in China), Honolulu (US) and Singapore, before the outbreak of World War II. These modern, Western-style stores became symbols of the Westernisation of retailing. The original department stores therefore triggered a wave of Westernisation and modernisation that spread from the West to Japan, and then on to other Asian countries.

Despite the huge social and economic impact of this global phenomenon, many researches on department stores have focused on the development of Western department stores from the perspective of Western retailing and Western consumers: when innovative new methods were introduced, how these stores developed, and how they impacted on consumer habits. Many studies have also looked at the business history of leading department stores such as The Bon Marché (Zola, 1928; Miller, 1981; Kashima, 1991), Wanamaker (Gibbons, 1971; Zulker, 1993), Macy's (Hower, 1943) and Harrods (Dale, 1981). Although there are studies of Japanese department stores, these have also investigated how they developed and how they changed consumer habits within the Japanese context. Few studies have given any attention to why Japanese retailers decided to adopt the Western model of retailing and management in the first place, why they led and encouraged the westernisation of Japanese society and how they caused such dramatic changes in the retail industry and consumer habits across Asia. This chapter will therefore investigate how Japanese department stores not only caught up with Western department stores in terms of their development, but also carved out a path beyond the limits of the existing Western model, and by doing so charted the road ahead for the modernisation of Asian retailing in the early twentieth century.

From dry goods store to department store

The predecessors of Japanese department stores were dry goods stores, which dealt mainly in silk draperies in the Tokugawa era (1603–1868). Before their transformation into department stores, dry goods stores were always exclusive spaces and customers could purchase goods only under tightly regulated conditions. These practices are discussed in Chapter 29, but are usefully summarised here. Paying customers were the only people permitted to enter the store and these were mainly men. There were no window displays and no one would ever enter a store without a clear intention of making a purchase. Customers could never see the items available for sale inside the store; they would simply tell the sales assistants what they wanted to buy and some suitable goods would be brought out from the storeroom. The assistants were very knowledgeable and skilled at providing their customers with exactly what they were looking for. Mitsukoshi had used cash payment and a one-price policy since its business began in 1673 – innovations that came much later in most Western shops – but it did not begin to develop as a department store until around 1900.

Retail modernisation came about due to the difficult situation that Mitsukoshi found itself in, which forced it to change its business strategy in order to survive. After the Meiji Restoration, Mitsukoshi's sales sharply decreased due to the demise of its greatest patrons, the samurai class (Mitsukoshi, 2005). To recover its sales, in 1895 Mitsukoshi brought in a new director, Yoshio Takahashi, who was a manager of Mitsui Bank (a leading partner organisation) and had studied in the United States at Eastman Business College in Poughkeepsie, New York, in 1887. He introduced some sales innovations common to American department stores, specifically following Wanamaker's business model. He launched strategies such as point-of-sale displays and

Western-style double-entry bookkeeping (Takahashi, 1933). Mitsukoshi therefore broke out of the mould of the traditional retailer at the start of the twentieth century.

The prohibitive form of shopping that consumers experienced in the dry goods store was transformed forever when Mitsukoshi's anchor store, the Nihonbashi branch, was refurbished in 1895 and completely converted into a sales area with display cases in 1900. Sample patterns for new silk draperies were displayed in showcases and rotated regularly to attract all types of customers and encourage them to enter the store. For the first time in Japan, people were invited to enjoy browsing the store, completely at liberty to select products without being disturbed by sales assistants. In 1904, Mitsukoshi took the decision to completely transform itself into an American-style department store, and this was announced in newspapers in 1905. Mitsukoshi swiftly brought in the new retail format and embraced Western sales methods to become the first modern retailer in Japan. Soon afterwards, four other retail firms – Takashimaya, Matsuzakaya, Daimaru and Shirokiya – also set about adapting their stores into Western-style department stores, after the managers of these dry goods stores travelled to Belgium, France, Germany, the United Kingdom and the United States to learn from these Western retailers (see also Chapter 29). With this major initial overhaul, Japan began racing towards a genuinely modern retail industry. Department stores were the pioneers of modern retailing and only they succeeded in introducing Western sales techniques into their stores before World War II.

The Japanese government encouraged new industries to enable Japan to catch up with Western countries, and there was subsequently a large population shift from rural to urban areas to meet the huge demand for more factory workers. Tokyo's population tripled in fifty years from 671,000 in 1878 to 2.73 million in 1930, while the percentage of the Japanese population living in Tokyo increased from 1.9% in 1878 to 4% in 1903. The population of Osaka, the leading industrial city in Japan, increased even faster (Population Census, Statistics Japan). Within these growing cities, several dry goods stores transformed into department stores by around 1920, and then new department stores were also established. At the time, only traditional Japanese-style wooden buildings existed and so this process began with the construction of Western-style factories for several emerging modern industries that were needed; this then fed into the gradual industrialisation of Japan as a whole. Mitsukoshi was the first retailer to begin the process of building Western-style multi-storied buildings, but Japanese construction companies and architects had no experience of constructing a Western-style building for Mitsukoshi's new store. Mitsukoshi therefore asked Tamisuke Yokogawa, an architect in the Mitsui group who was planning a visit to the United States between 1896 and 1897, to inspect American department store buildings while he was there, so that he could bring back useful information about the skills they would need to develop and the materials they would need to acquire in order to construct such a building in Japan. Mitsukoshi went on to purchase the required materials, such as reinforced steel (Hatsuda, 1992).

Mitsukoshi's first modern, full-scale Western-style store was a six-story Renaissance-style building established in 1914, which introduced the escalator for the first time in Japan, along with lifts, air conditioning and heating – the latest facilities at the time. It had a stairwell in the centre of the store, similar to that of the Bon Marché, a garden on the roof terrace and a gorgeous lounge with lavishly designed interiors and Western furnishings modelled on Western department stores (Mitsukoshi, 2005). This store and other similar department stores became landmarks and symbols of the modern city in early twentieth-century Japan, which was characterised by greater industrialisation, urbanisation and Westernisation. In this sense, to understand the development of the Japanese retail industry is to also understand the Westernisation and modernisation of Japan.

Figure 28.1 Central Hall at Mitsukoshi Nihombashi store in 1914

(Courtesy of Isetan Mitsukoshi Ltd)

From the West to Japan

The new-style stores needed more space for customers to view the products and Mitsukoshi needed to provide a much wider range of merchandise to fill its sales floors. After Mitsukoshi had converted its format into the new display style, its sales area in 1905 was 1,260 square metres over two floors. In 1908 it expanded the building to 5,210 square metres over three floors before building its much larger store in 1914 – an imposing edifice with a sales area of 13,210 square metres (Mitsukoshi, 2005). From its initial focus on silk draperies, Mitsukoshi began diversifying its merchandise. Increasing the range of merchandise was crucial both in the definition and expansion of western department stores (Nystrom, 1919; Pasdermadjian, 1954); to do this, Japanese stores had to add Western products to their merchandise, so this was a doubly innovative process for them. Mitsukoshi first expanded its existing drapery lines and then introduced new product lines, including cosmetics, household goods, umbrellas, accessories and stationery. In order to meet the consumer's demand for Western products, Mitsukoshi and other leading department stores also started importing goods such as clothing, bags, shoes, cameras and blankets from Europe – replicating the product range found in many Western department stores. Adoption of western goods sparked a strong interest in Western goods and culture, but was not without its problems: with regard to clothing, the standard proportions of Westerners and Japanese people were very different, so many imported socks, shirts, shoes and jackets went unsold and became dead stock (Fujioka, 2006).

In order to expand their merchandise with new product lines, Japanese department stores therefore needed to develop hybrid products. They essentially had to create their own

Figure 28.2 Western-style umbrella, shoes and hair accessories department at Mitsukoshi Nihombashi store in 1914

(Courtesy of Isetan Mitsukoshi Ltd)

Western-style merchandise for Japanese consumers. This was a very challenging task and one that Western department stores did not need to consider at all. To establish its own production system, Mitsukoshi hired staff from London in 1906 to make clothing that would better fit Japanese customers. Another department store, Takashimaya, sent managers to Europe to inspect Western products and then developed hybrid products such as clothing, carpets and furniture. The stores also introduced point-of-sale advertisements to help sell their products by suggesting how they could be used to help Japanese consumers adapt their existing lifestyle into something more Westernised.

The carpet is a good example of a Western product that was introduced in Japan during this time. When the government decided to build its imperial palace in 1888 with a Western style of design and decoration for public spaces and traditional Japanese style for the façade and residential spaces, the government also decided to use mostly domestic products rather than imported ones in order to encourage and support the development of its domestic industry (Nakamura, 2000). Takashimaya became one of the suppliers of these Western-style products and also received another order to supply Western-style carpets to the Diet Building in 1889. However, it had never dealt with high-quality Western ornamentation and had little technical knowledge about how to produce carpets, so this was a huge challenge for Takashimaya. The company began by making a thorough study of Western interior design. Then, its associated manufacturer, Suminoe, performed reverse engineering on the textiles in order to examine how they were manufactured. Takashimaya eventually succeeded in training its Japanese workforce to sufficiently high standards to be able to reproduce authentic Western carpets together with Suminoe in 1890, but then needed to buy Western power looms through its trading company in 1901 so that it could maintain a consistent standard of quality for carpets (Takashimaya, 1941; Suminoe, 1975). Takashimaya also began promoting carpets to its upper-class customers. Takashimaya introduced point-of-sale advertisements to increase the marketability of carpets, which included information about carpets and suggestions of how they could be used to adopt a more westernised lifestyle. In 1920 Takashimaya held an event that showed a mock-up room with Western furniture and interior products at its store, and looked at how Japanese rooms could be modified with Western products. With the actual products in front of them, customers could easily visualise this new lifestyle and identify how these new products were used, and this event successfully increased the sales of Takashimaya's Western-style products. Furthermore, if customers accepted one Western-style product, they would then quickly accept other products, making it possible for Takashimaya to succeed in its goal of diversification (Fujioka, 2006).

The creation of new products was simply not possible without extensive cooperation between manufacturers and retailers; neither one could do it alone. While department stores depended on manufacturers for their merchandise, budding manufacturers relied completely on retailers buying and selling huge quantities of products in order for them to succeed in their new enterprise. During this time, some manufacturers began to introduce similar Western-style production systems and to obtain detailed knowledge of Western products through governmental support. However, if these products suffered poor sales, then they inevitably collapsed under the new production system. Takashimaya endeavoured to secure the market for these manufacturers and then transferred their knowledge into its own associated manufacturers. By doing this, Takashimaya and other Japanese department stores were able to offer their customers a very wide range of Western merchandise. Takashimaya's new Osaka branch benefited from a more modern framework after achieving its goal of diversification and by 1931 the sales in non-drapery departments – of goods such as accessories, bags, cosmetics, shoes and household goods – had grown to 32% compared with the sales of silk draperies, which stood at 42.3% (Fujioka, 2006).

While dry goods stores introduced retail innovations and diversified their merchandise, they also needed to reform their management and organisational structure. Mitsukoshi, for example, reformed its traditional business organisational structure and introduced a new form of personnel management. Mitsukoshi's first professional managing director, Takahashi, recruited highly educated graduates from universities and business schools and gave them leadership positions. He clarified the specific tasks and roles of each unit and each staff member and established clear rules of employment and a wage structure (Mitsukoshi, 2005). Before this restructure, Mitsukoshi and other retailers had used traditional, patriarchal personnel management, originating in the Tokugawa era (Yui, 2012; Kikkawa, 2012). Under this system, a boy aged around 13 would be employed as an apprentice and would then climb the career ladder until he became a senior manager at around the age of 30. During this time, employees would generally be obliged to live in an in-house dormitory at the store where they worked. The company treated all employees like members of a family, providing them with food, clothing and education. Employees were educated in good manners, social consideration, reading, writing and arithmetic, in addition to the knowledge and skills needed for their jobs. Although their salary was quite low, the traditional Japanese perception was that companies were not just a means of earning money, but a way of life. Employees lived and grew up together harmoniously as a company family in a feudatory culture.

Takahashi, however, did not have any experience of living with his co-workers. He received a large salary from the beginning for his professional work to reform Mitsukoshi. When he arrived, he felt that the traditional apprenticeship system was too old to transform. He therefore introduced a completely new personnel system, which was a very modern idea in Japan at the time. The new system was met with resistance from some of the older employees, who were subsequently dismissed. Soon afterwards in 1900, Mitsukoshi began to hire female employees in addition to university graduates. A total of twenty-six female sales assistants were employed by 1903 and their training was very strict. Recruiting female staff was revolutionary in Japanese retailers at the time as women had not traditionally been part of the workforce in Japan. From 1910, employees' dormitories were moved off-site, and they began commuting to the store each day. For the first time, they could separate their home life from their work life (Mitsukoshi, 2005). This revolution of personnel management proved to be very successful at Mitsukoshi. The new professional staff members then introduced further retail innovations at the department store. Soon afterwards Mitsukoshi became a joint stock company and so was able to raise huge amounts of investment capital with which Mitsukoshi constructed its new Western-style building that become a showcase for the latest Western technology. With this reform of organisation and management, Mitsukoshi successfully transformed its business model from a traditional dry goods store to a modern department store (Fujioka, 2014).

Another large store, Takashimaya, also had a conflict between old and young generations among board members and so had to restructure the organisation. Takashimaya introduced some new sales methods that had been used by Mitsukoshi before its transformation to a department store. Indeed, this transition was by no means inevitable. While Mitsukoshi had suffered from falling sales and had no other option but to restructure, Takashimaya's business was doing well. It was responsible for creating a boom in European admiration for Japanese products and culture due to its presence at world expositions in Europe where the company displayed kimonos and silk tapestries of Japanese art work. It was difficult, therefore, to make the decision to transform into a department store (Takashimaya, 1968). In time, however, Takashimaya found itself competing with Mitsukoshi's increasingly successful new department stores in Osaka and it became clear that Takashimaya would need to follow suit to remain competitive. In 1919, it transformed into a modern-style department store, becoming a public company to gain the funds to build a new eight-story Gothic-style anchor store in Osaka with a sales area of about 10,000 square metres in 1922. Takashimaya furthermore changed its personnel system at its Kyoto branch in 1909, its Osaka branch in 1914, and its Tokyo branch in 1916: building off-site dormitories for its employees to commute from. The department store then reformed its standard corporate structure from a family-owned business to a modern organisation to develop even further.

The penetration of department stores across Japan

Japanese economic growth supported the development of department stores. In 1912, the gross national product (GNP) was 4.77 billion yen, which increased to 15.45 billion yen in 1919. With Japan's industrial development, real wages and income increased; with the development of the Japanese economy, sales in department stores grew dramatically. Also, as total personal consumption expenditures (PCE) increased from 3.66 billion yen in 1912 to 11.3 billion yen in 1919, consumers had more opportunity to enjoy shopping (Okawa et al., 1974). Consumer demand grew hugely during this time and only department stores were able to respond quickly enough to meet this increase. Mitsukoshi increased its sales and expanded its workforce (Mitsukoshi, 2005). When it announced its intention to transform into a department store in 1905, its gross profit was 537,000 yen. This increased to 1.7 million yen in 1910, then 2.4 million yen in 1915, then 9.6 million yen in 1920 and to 14 million yen in 1930. Mitsukoshi's number of employees also increased from 323 in 1905 to 1,407 in 1910, 5,101 in 1925 and 8,464 in 1935. The main reason for this steady increase in sales and employees was the great success of its new retail format, especially in its 1914 building established in Nihonbashi, Tokyo. Mitsukoshi went on to establish more new stores in other big cities across greater Tokyo and the country as a whole, including Kobe in 1926, Kanazawa in 1930, Takamatsu in 1931, Sapporo in 1932 and Sendai in 1933.

At the time, Mitsukoshi's main customers were upper-class and upper-middle-class people who lived in urban areas, because most products on sale were expensive and the stores were located only in big cities such as Tokyo and Osaka. When the Great Kanto Earthquake struck in 1923, however, the business model of Japanese department stores began to change. The earthquake and subsequent large-scale fires inflicted catastrophic damage on department stores in Tokyo: those of Mitsukoshi, Matsuzakaya and Takashimaya mostly burned down. They began selling essentials such as soap, basic clothing, dishes, cans of food and rice at temporary stores. Next, stores expanded their scope to cater for a wider and lower economic class of consumers than before. The incomes of these new middle-class consumers also steadily increased, a combination of factors that prompted the popularisation of department stores and the beginning of mass consumption in Japan (Suzuki, 1980). It was an exciting experience for shoppers to visit such a store and walk around buying new products that they had never seen before. As a result, the department stores became important attractions for both visitors and residents.

Focusing on this wider target market, new department stores soon spread to many cities in Japan. In addition to the department store format that evolved from dry goods stores, there were various other routes to becoming a department store. For example, Jyuichiya, a store that sold hair accessories, bags and shoes in Nagoya, transformed into the department store Maruei in 1922; Daiwa used to specialise in selling imported products in Kanazawa, becoming a department store in 1923; and Tenmaya started out as a dealer in building materials in Okayama, but established itself as a department store in 1925 (Hida, 1998). Some railway companies also created a uniquely Japanese type of department store (see Chapter 29). The Hankyu department store was firmly established in 1929 in Osaka. While other department stores were located on main streets in city centres, it was located at a major train station terminal and its target customers were urban commuters travelling to and from work between the city centre and suburban areas. The founder of Hankyu had shrewdly anticipated that locating stores at a train terminal would eliminate the need for advertising of any kind, since the potential customers were already there (Kobayashi, 1970). The store mainly sold food, toys, books, household goods, cosmetics, stationery, shoes and silk draperies, all of which were slightly cheaper and more practical than the more fashionable products sold at Mitsukoshi and Takashimaya. Keen to take advantage of this newly discovered market, other department stores soon began to open at train station terminals: Takashimaya launched a new store in Osaka in 1930, Toyoko opened its first store in Shibuya, Tokyo, in 1934 and Iwataya established its store in Fukuoka in 1936. In this way, the number of department store companies began to increase from the late 1920s.

Department store companies expanded the size of each store's sales area and increased the number of their stores, and more and more companies entered the market. With their expanded target market, they spread throughout Japan, although they were almost always found in large cities. In order to reach out to consumers in smaller cities, sales staff from leading department stores travelled to these neighbouring centres to sell the store's products. For example, Wakayama was one of the twenty largest cities near Osaka, yet there were no department stores there; big city stores therefore rented public or private venues to use as temporary sales spaces for a few days, so that consumers in the city could browse their products and enjoy shopping. There was a big demand from wealthy people in these cities and they looked forward to buying new products from these temporary stores. Any department store that had a temporary presence in these areas each month therefore had a huge impact on local stores in terms of sales (Fujioka, 2014). In addition, department stores started a mail order service so that everyone could order products, even if they had no access to a nearby department store and were unable to visit a temporary store. Mitsukoshi, for example, launched its mail order magazine in 1912 and expanded its business (Mitsuzono, 2014). Then, customers of department stores spread across Japan, and the latest fashions and Western products also reached wealthy people in smaller cities in Japan.

The dramatic growth of department stores, with their huge sales, completely overwhelmed all other Japanese retailers and adversely affected smaller retailers in particular. While there were only 36 department stores in Tokyo in 1932, which was only 0.027% of all retailers, the sales of department stores amounted to almost 25% of total retail sales and 55% of total clothing sales. The fifth largest city in Japan, Nagoya, had five department stores, which were 0.016% of all retailers, yet they enjoyed 15.6% of total sales and 44.4% of total clothing sales in 1932 (Nakanishi, 1938). Japanese department stores therefore became very powerful and dominated the retail market in Japan.

From Japan to other Asian countries

Before the Meiji Restoration in 1868, Japan was closed to foreign commerce except Korea, China and the Netherlands, and Japanese people were banned from travelling to and from foreign countries. Even in the early Meiji era, there was little information on Western countries, so Japanese politicians and bureaucrats needed to study Western systems in order to restructure Japanese society and economy in the Meiji era. Department stores were exceptional retailers in Japan and, as we have seen, were a driving force for the modernisation of Japanese business and the Westernisation of the Japanese lifestyle, in part because they initially catered for the wealthy ruling class. Leading modern companies such as the Mitsui trading company and Mitsui Bank grew from the largest retailer, Mitsukoshi. There were also other department stores that had a big effect on other industries: Shirokiya first started producing Western-style clothing when its politician customers introduced a policy of wearing Western clothing at the Western-style guest house for visiting overseas politicians, and Matsuzakaya established a modern-style bank in Nagoya at almost exactly the same time as it transformed into a department store. Their customers were also powerful and influenced others, such as imperial families, politicians (including prime ministers), directors of big business, wealthy entrepreneurs, venerable Buddhist monks and highly educated people. With this influential position in Japanese society, these stores could effectively modernise retailing and catch up with Western department stores within a short period of time. Their positioning was therefore very different from Western department stores, and they were able to have a huge impact not only on Japanese consumption but also on the entire economy of their country.

These powerful retailers also launched overseas branches in Korea, mainland China, Taiwan, Hong Kong, Singapore and Malaysia, largely in order to meet the demand of existing Japanese clients in the early twentieth century. The Japanese army and the South Manchuria Railway Company, which was established by the Japanese government and private companies in 1906 and formed the major military base of occupied Manchuria, were looking for suppliers and importers of goods such as food, military and civilian clothing, and camping gear – especially as things moved onto a war footing. They sounded out several department stores for this logistic support, some of which were able to meet this demand through their long history and strong relationship with the government and other leading companies (Shirokiya, 1957; Daimaru, 1967; Takashimaya, 1982; Matsuzakaya, 2010). Japanese department stores that had originated as dry goods stores were ideal partners in this case, since they had two established divisions that were ideally suited to the task. These divisions did not exist in Western department stores or in other Japanese department stores that had grown from railway companies. The first division was the Gaisho department, which was literally a sales department for external customers; Gaisho sales assistants would visit the homes of loyal customers or the offices of loyal companies to take their orders, building a special one-to-one relationship. The other division was the Trading department, which traded with other companies – purchasing materials and using associated manufacturers from Western countries – to make its own products such as Western clothing and furnishings; in other cases, it set up its own supply chains with associated and outsourcing manufacturers to produce specified goods on demand for a client company.

At that time, the Japanese government was a loyal Gaisho client of Mitsukoshi, Takashimaya, Matsuzakaya, Shirokiya and Daimaru. Due to the government's national policy concerns, these department stores expanded their market towards Asia during the difficult wartime conditions in Japan, and the government loosely assigned a trading area to each of them (Shirokiya, 1957). For example, as a loyal Gaisho client of Takashimaya, the South Manchuria Railway Company asked the department store to supply bench seats for its trains (Fujioka, 2006). Takashimaya was able to manufacture bench seats with Suminoe, its associated company that produced carpets (as described above). The Gaisho department in Japan received its orders from the South Manchuria Railway Company and Takashimaya's branch office in Manchuria was established in 1933[1] to communicate with the railway company; the trading department then purchased the materials and controlled the manufacturing at Suminoe's Manchurian factory, established in 1939. The local branch in Dalian, which had a trading division and a store, also played a crucial role as a hub to expedite the handling of orders. In this way, Takashimaya expanded its overseas stores in the 1930s; it opened a store in Tianjin in 1937, in Nanjing and in Shanghai in 1938 and in Tsingtao in 1939, and a total of twenty-seven branches and stores in Korea and China before World War II. Crucial here was its ability to make deals with military companies, which further expanded its business in East Asia (Takashimaya, 1941).

There were a lot of uncertainties and risks in these markets and they required serious investment; but the department stores had no other option but to comply with the government's requirements under these conditions if they wanted to keep their business from this particular loyal client. Shirokiya established 38 local offices in China catering for the Japanese military (Shirokiya, 1957). Matsuzakaya launched a branch in Tianjin in 1939 and had a total of twenty-five local offices in China, Java and Sumatra (Indonesia) by 1942, Kuala Lumpur (Malaysia) and Singapore in 1943. These branches imported industrial products from Japan, produced furniture on site, sourced military supplies and ran a restaurant for Japanese residents, in addition to managing stores (Matsuzakaya, 2010). Daimaru established its local office in Tianjin in 1938, which supplied food, oil and wool for the Japanese military. The Tianjin office then opened a full-scale store in 1940 to cater for Japanese residents, with 1,300 square metres for its sales floor and restaurant. This was its largest overseas store and had over 150 employees in 1943: thirty Japanese men and ten Japanese women were sent from Japanese stores to teach their sales techniques to locals; a dozen highly educated Japanese-speaking Chinese men were sent to Daimaru's anchor store in Osaka to learn the Japanese way of retailing; and a hundred Chinese women worked as sales assistants. Daimaru also had stores in Singapore and Malaysia and branch offices in Vietnam, Thailand, Indonesia and Myanmar for military supplies (Daimaru, 1967).

The outbreak of war between China and Japan and subsequently World War II brought a worsening economic situation in Japan. There was little merchandise in department stores because manufacturers only produced essential products in the newly controlled economy, many of the stores' staff had been conscripted into the military, and the stores' exhibition spaces were exploited for military use by the government. However, their overseas stores did well during this time, contrasting strongly with decreasing domestic sales. The total sales from all Japanese department stores began to decline, from 886 million yen in 1941 to 462 million yen in 1945, but the decline was uneven (Japan Department Stores Association, 2013). For example, sales in Mitsukoshi's Seoul branch amounted to 11 million yen in 1943 and its Dalian branch generated 6.8 million yen; this compared favourably with 2.9 million yen at the Sapporo branch in Japan, despite the similar sales areas (approximately 7,500 square metres) in each store. In 1945 Mitsukoshi's largest store in terms of sales remained its flagship store at Nihonbashi in Tokyo, but the second largest store was its overseas store in Seoul, which had overtaken the Osaka branch, established for as long as the Nihonbashi branch and formerly its other flagship store (Mitsukoshi, 2005). Takashimaya had a workforce overseas of 141 Japanese employees in 1938, which grew to 417 in 1944 across all its overseas branches; in addition it hired local sales assistants. Sales in its overseas branches amounted to 5 million yen in 1938 and increased to 15.8 million yen in 1941, remaining at this level for three years. Sales in the overseas branches accounted for 67.1% of its total sales in the second half of 1944, and so these overseas branches became vital stores during World War II (Takashimaya, 1982).

This expansion of Japanese department stores in East Asia influenced the local communities not only politically but also culturally. As Fujioka (2013) has observed, the overseas branches of Japanese department stores were ethnic enclaves; internationalisation was purely aimed at spatial expansion, as the Japanese government intended. Their launch of overseas stores and their engagement was simply a response to the requirements of their loyal customers behind the colonial power; these stores opened mainly to cater for Japanese residents and tourists in these countries. However, it is hard to ignore the impact these stores had on the host countries, in terms of the modernisation of retailing. In Seoul, for example, there were four Japanese department stores, Mitsukoshi, Minakai, Chojiya and Hirata, and one Korean department store, Hwasin, in the 1920s. While Mitsukoshi had only one store in Seoul, which was the biggest department store by sales in Korea, Chojiya had three stores in Korea and three stores in Manchuria, and Minakai had twelve stores across Korea and three stores in Manchuria. These stores' main target customers were Japanese residents, but Korean people also visited them. Mitsukoshi targeted the

Figure 28.3 New-built Seoul store in Korea in 1916
(Courtesy of Isetan Mitsukoshi Ltd)

wealthy, whereas Hwasin expanded its customer base to the middle class and even lower classes after the mid-1930s. With an increasingly intense competition among stores, 60% of Chojiya customers were Korean, while 90% of Minakai customers were Japanese (Hayashi, 2004).

Mitsukoshi's store in Seoul was designed in a Renaissance-style, with the very same design and structure as Mitsukoshi's flagship store in Nihonbashi, Tokyo; its interior was also similar, with a central hall, a stairwell, lifts, lounges, restaurants, a roof garden, an art gallery, a theatre, a tea room and even a small Shintō shrine. It was impressive and highly distinctive Western architecture in Korea at that time. Mitsukoshi also had an outdoor rooftop café with a balcony, which had by the 1930s become a popular meeting place for local Koreans, as it was seen as a new landmark of colonial Seoul and, perhaps ironically, a symbol of Westernisation (Kal, 2008). Minakai opened a seven-storey Renaissance-style flagship store in Seoul in 1933 and introduced the first escalator in Korea (Hayashi, 2004). Wealthy and highly educated Korean people prefered to shop at the Japanese department stores, especially Mitsukoshi, rather than Korean department store, Hwasin, and some of them disdained its offerings. They were called 'modern girl' and 'modern boy' and Japanese department stores were in the heart of modern culture (Oh and Kahm, 2018).

In addition, their merchandise and Western-style sales practices were entirely new to Korean customers. Japanese department stores sold mainly Japanese and Japanised Western products that were imported from Japan (Hirano, 1999). With this Western-style retailing, wealthy Korean customers enjoyed browsing new products from Japan and modern retailing therefore penetrated into the Korean market through these Japanese department stores. Furthermore, Japanese intermediaries collaborated with Korean manufacturers to reinvigorate traditional goods (Oh, 2016). Japanese tourists were looking for authentic Korean products as luxury souvenirs, and Mitsukoshi's "Chosŏn Product Showroom" was a well-known place to get reliable, high-quality

Figure 28.4 New-built Dalian store in China in 1937

(Courtesy of Isetan Mitsukoshi Ltd)

Korean Chosŏn products. The most popular items sold in this showroom were Koryŏ celadon and lacquerware inlaid with mother-of-pearl. The Koryŏ celadon products were not original antiques, because these had virtually disappeared before the 1880s. However, the Japanese colonial elite endorsed this as the best of Korean art, and affluent Japanese expatriates and tourists (as well as those from other countries) were eager to purchase Koryŏ celadon products either for their own collections or as gifts; as a direct result, the price of genuine Koryŏ celadon inflated. When this happened, a Japanese entrepreneur began a business that produced modern replicas as an affordable substitute for overpriced genuine ones. These replicas were produced at local workshops run by skilled Japanese artisans, who had professional knowledge of ceramic materials and techniques and, as Korean workers were employed to undertake this work, this in turn developed the revival of Koryŏ celadon production in Korea. These items became some of the best-selling Korean products at Mitsukoshi. Therefore, while Mitsukoshi developed as a leading modern retailer in Korea, it also influenced both Korean consumer culture and Korean manufacturing.

The modernisation of retailing in China was mainly brought about by overseas Chinese entrepreneurs, who had gained their business experience in Australia and Hong Kong in the late nineteenth century, before returning home in the early twentieth century. In Shanghai, there were four leading department stores run by these Chinese directors: Sincere opened a store in 1917, Wing On in 1918, Sun Sun in 1926 and The Sun in 1936. They built traditional English-style buildings and each store included a hotel, a tea room and a restaurant (Shima, 1995; Chan, 1998; Ching-hwang, 1998; Young, 1998, Shimanaga, 2007). Their target market consisted of wealthy local customers and foreign expatriates living in China; they used modern sales methods and their main merchandise consisted of imported products from the West and Japan, as well as luxury domestic products. These stores were considered to be a symbol of Chinese modernity (Shima, 1995; MacPherson, 1998). The first Chinese store to be named a "department store", following the Japanese usage, was in Shanghai in 1921. The term first appeared in a Chinese dictionary in 1923, where it was defined as a business that is engaged in large-scale retailing that is divided into individually managed departments, is highly profitable and has very good facilities for customers; it also implied a modern organisation that included foreign goods in its merchandise (MacPherson, 1998).

Chinese art had strong historical links with Japanese art and Japan had the role of being China's window on the West (Wong, 2006). The Mitsui Trading Company, for example, distributed advertisements promoting Western-style wedding fashion with Japanese captions that constructed an exotic image, encouraging customers to transform their lives (Zhao and Belk, 2008). Japanese products, including cosmetics, fabrics and food, were widely accepted by Chinese customers. In the 1930s, however, Chinese department stores became the target of criticism when the Chinese government began promoting the purchase of Chinese products following the 1932 Shanghai Incident. An increasingly strong nationalist movement grew, which campaigned fiercely against the sale of Japanese products (Lien, 2016). The women's magazine *Linglong*, for example, endorsed this government-led campaign; at the time, 90% of toys were imported, mostly from Japan and readers were encouraged to buy Chinese toys for Christmas, the headlines reading: 'Let's buy a Chinese Christmas gift'.[2] When Chinese department stores promoted Christmas gifts, they circulated their promotional catalogue and leaflets, and offered luxury imported products from Japan with lower prices. Japanese products were therefore very common as good quality and less expensive options than Chinese products at that time. Following these nationalist campaigns, Chinese department stores subsequently changed their merchandise to comprise mainly domestic products. For example, Wing On's domestic products formed 25% of its merchandise during the 1920s, but 65% in 1937 (Shima, 1995). Despite the movement against Japanese products, Japanese department stores in China continued to develop in the 1930s. First, these department stores expanded their target market to include a much broader range of Chinese customers, selling low-cost, high-quality products (Zhōngxíng, 1933). Second, the number of Japanese stores increased along with the requirement of the Japanese government to supply goods both to its military institutions and to consumers in China. The impact of Japanese products and stores was therefore huge on both the retail industry and consumer culture in China.

From a global perspective, the birth of department stores began in the West, with modern retailing established in the late nineteenth century. Around fifty years of Western innovation gave Japanese retailers a direction to follow for their own development. Japan then created its own unique type of department store, which was a hybrid model between East and West. Japanese department stores learned to adapt their merchandise in a Western style and thereby produced their own original products to better fit with the existing Japanese lifestyle. Setting a good example to follow, this new Japanese model then expanded throughout East Asia, bringing modern retailing to a global market in a different way from Western department stores. This movement from Japan to East Asia continued in the period of economic development after World War II. For example, the Singaporean Apollo Hotel invited the Japanese department store Isetan to open a branch next to its new modern-style hotel in 1970. This joint venture was supported by Singapore's government in order to attract foreign investment and modern Japanese retailers to the country. Isetan seized the opportunity to launch its first overseas store, which opened in 1972. At that time, customers in Singapore had never encountered Isetan's modern fixed-price policy and were daunted by it, so the store was not an immediate success; but as customers gradually became accustomed to fixed prices the store began to increase its sales, and both Isetan and the Apollo Hotel enjoyed widespread popularity (Isetan, 1990).

In addition, Taiwanese department stores began partnerships with Japanese department stores from the late 1970s; Taiwan's Evergreen department became affiliated with Japan's Tokyu department store in 1977 and Taiwan's Pacific and Japan's Sogo began a joint venture in 1987 (Chang and Sternquist, 1993). When Japanese department stores entered the Hong Kong market to meet the demand of Japanese tourists, they had a big advantage because local department stores had comparably little experience and little money to invest. The first Japanese department store to open branches in Hong Kong was Daimaru in 1960, and during the 1970s Isetan and Matsuzakaya also launched into this market. By the 1980s, there were fourteen Japanese department stores in Hong Kong, with a market share over 30%. These stores attracted younger, fashion-conscious shoppers and were symbols of high technology, modernity and efficiency (McGoldrick and Ho, 1992).

Conclusion

The development of department stores had a great impact on the Japanese economy, Japanese society and on the wider Asian market. First, Japanese department stores made a major contribution to the Westernisation of Japanese society and the modernisation of Japanese companies, as a direct result of their radical transformation from traditional Japanese dry goods stores. In contrast, Western department stores simply underwent a process of modernising their existing retail format (Shaw, 1992). Japanese department stores were the hubs of modern industry relating to the Western-style products they sold. Although they did not manufacture all of their products themselves, they managed the development of new Western products with their associated factories and trading companies to fit the Japanese lifestyle. They forged a supply chain with manufacturers, who often gained advanced skills through working with department stores;

this partnership bridged the gap between supply and demand, and created new Western-style products using Western machinery and materials that were imported by department stores. With these new products, department stores not only boosted their sales but also encouraged new industries to emerge. Therefore, department stores developed in tandem with the industrialisation of Japan.

The modernisation of Japanese retailers was a process of continuous innovation, including new sales methods, new management and organisational structures and the Westernisation of Japanese society through the promotion of Western products. This led to the creation of an entirely new form of consumer culture in Japan, similar to that created by Western department stores; the Bon Marché and the Louvre in Paris were described as cathedrals of modern commerce (Crossick and Jaumain, 1999) and dream worlds (Williams, 1982), and American department stores embodied a new culture of consumer capitalism (Leach, 1994). With a modern display of products and new sales methods in place, Japanese customers – in particular women and children, who had not been able to enter dry goods stores – were able to enjoy shopping for the first time, which quickly became a leisure activity. In these new "cathedrals of consumption" in Japan, the new products boosted consumer demand and created an entirely new shopping experience. Mitsukoshi's second professional managing director, Osuke Hibi, said that stores should present their displays to be appealing to children and their families, because if children enjoyed coming to the stores, then they would grow to become loyal customers in the near future; this was part of his marketing strategy for further development (Hamada, 1948).

The development of Japanese department stores also impacted on retailers in other Asian countries. Japanese department stores expanded their new stores in Korea and China in the early twentieth century. This expansion had more far-reaching consequences than simply increased sales for Japanese department stores: the new Western-style buildings that had been built to house the stores in Seoul and Shanghai visibly impacted on local consumers with their striking presentation of Western culture. Wealthy locals, and eventually a broader range of customers, enjoyed experiencing Western-style shopping for the first time at these stores, alongside the Japanese community living abroad, which was originally the main target market. The extent of this impact has yet to be fully assessed, due to the lack of statistical data. However, when local retailers in South Korea, Hong Kong and Taiwan wanted to modernise their own stores after World War II, it is apparent that they were keen to work with Japanese department stores so that they could model their new stores on the Japanese format. Japanese department stores were therefore not simple imitations of Western department stores and they developed along their own original path. This chapter has shown the unique path of the modernisation of Asian retailing and the role of Japanese department stores as an intermediate between West and East.

Notes

1 Takashimaya first established its local office in Dalian, Manchuria in 1924, then closed it in 1925. In 1929 it opened a liaison office for its staff to communicate with its clients (Takashimaya, 1941).
2 Anonymous, 'Let's buy a Chinese Christmas gift', *Linglong (Lin Loon Magazine)* (1931). 1(41).

References

Chan, W. (1998), 'Personal styles, cultural values, and management: The sincere and wing on companies in Shanghai and Hong Kong 1900–1941', in K. L. MacPherson (ed.) *Asian department stores* (Honolulu, HI: University of Hawaii Press) 66–89.

Chang, L. D. and Sternquist, B. (1993), 'Taiwanese department store industry: An overview', *International Journal of Retail & Distribution Management*, 21 (1), pp. 26–34.

Ching-hwang, Y. (1998), 'Wing on and the Kwok brothers: A case study of pre-war Chinese entrepreneurs', in K. L. MacPherson (ed.) *Asian department stores* (Honolulu, HI: University of Hawaii Press) 47–65.
Crossick, G. and Jaumain, S. (1999), 'The world of the department store: Distribution, culture and social change', in G. Crossick and S. Jaumain (eds.) *Cathedrals of consumption: The European department store, 1850–1939* (Aldershot: Ashgate).
Daimaru (1967), *Daimaru 250-nenshi (A 250-year history of Daimaru)* (Osaka: Daimaru).
Dale, T. (1981), *Harrods: The store and the legend* (London: Pan Books).
Fujioka, R. (2006), *Hyakkaten no seisei katei (The development of department stores)* (Tokyo: Yuhikaku).
Fujioka, R. (2013), 'The pressures of globalization in retail: The path of Japanese department stores, 1930s–1980s', in M. Umemura and R. Fujioka (eds.) *Comparative responses to globalization: Experiences of British and Japanese enterprises* (Basingstoke: Palgrave Macmillan) 181–203.
Fujioka, R. (2014), 'The development of department stores in Japan, 1900s–1930s', *Japanese Research in Business History*, 31, pp. 11–27.
Gibbons, H.A. (1971), *John Wanamaker*, Vol. 1 (New York: Kennikat Press).
Hamada, S. (1948), *Hyakkaten isseki banashi (A short story of department stores)* (Tokyo: Nihon Denpo Tsushinsha).
Hatsuda, T. (1992), 'Study on the report of American commercial architecture in 1896 by Tamisuke Yokogawa' (in Japanese), *Nihon Kenchiku Gakkai Taikai Gakujyutsu Kouen Kitsugaishu*, pp. 1109–1110.
Hayashi, H. (2004), *Maboroshi no Minakai hyakkaten (Phantasmal department store, Minakai)*, (Tokyo: Banseisha).
Hibi, O. (1912), *Shobai hanjo no hiketsu (The key to prosperous business)* (Tokyo: Daigakukan).
Hida, T. (1998), *Hyakkaten monogatari (The story of department stores)* (Tokyo: Kokusho Kankokai).
Hirano, T. (1999), 'Retailing in Urban Japan, 1868–1945', *Urban History*, 26 (3), pp. 373–392.
Hower, M.R. (1943), *History of Macy's of New York 1858–1919: Chapters in the evolution of the department store* (Cambirdge, MA: Harvard University Press).
Isetan (1990), *Isetan 100-nenshi (A 100-year history of Isetan)* (Tokyo: Isetan).
Japan Department Stores Association (2013), *Nihon hyakkaten kyokai toukei nenpo (Annual Report of Japan Department Stores Association)* (Tokyo: Japan Department Stores Association).
Kal, H. (2008), 'Seoul and the time in motion: Urban form and political consciousness', *Inter-Asia Cultural Studies*, 9 (3), pp. 359–374.
Kashima, S. (1991), *Depart wo hatsumei shita fufu (The couple who invented the department store)* (Tokyo: Kodansha).
Kikkawa, Y. (2012), 'From Kimono store to department store: The change of Mitsukoshi in the late 19th century to the early 20th century', in P. Fridenson and T. Yui (eds.) *Beyond mass distribution: Distribution, market and consumers (Proceedings of the Japan and French Business History Conference)* (Tokyo: Japan Business History Institute).
Kobayashi, I. (1970), 'Watashi no kigyo senjyutsu (My cooperate strategies)', in K. Nakagawa and T. Yui (eds.) *Keiei tetsugaku/ keiei rinen (Management philosophy/ corporate identity)* (Tokyo: Diamondsha).
Leach, W. (1994), *Land of desire: Merchants, power, and the rise of a new American culture* (New York: Vintage).
Lien, L. (2016), 'Promoting foreign products while being patriotic: Chinese department stores and the native goods movement in the interwar period (1918–1939)', *Proceedings of the 75th Annual Conference of the Association for Asian Studies*, pp. 1–6.
MacPherson, K.L. (1998), 'Introduction: Asia's universal providers', in K.L. MacPherson (ed.) *Asian department stores* (Honolulu, HI: University of Hawaii Press) 1–30.
Matsuzakaya (2010), *Matsuzakaya 100-nenshi (A 100-year history of Matsuzakaya)* (Nagoya: Matsuzakaya).
McGoldrick, P.J. and Ho, S.S.L. (1992), 'International positioning: Japanese department stores in Hong Kong', *European Journal of Marketing*, 26 (8/9), pp. 61–73.
Miller, M. (1981), *The Bon Marché: Bourgeois culture and the department store, 1869–1920* (Princeton, NJ: Princeton University Press).
Mitsukoshi (2005), *Kabushikikaisha Mitsukoshi 100-nen no kiroku (A 100-year history of Mitsukoshi)* (Tokyo: Mitsukoshi).
Mitsuzono, I. (2014), 'Expansion of Japanese department stores and mail-order retailing catering to the affluent rural classes', *Japanese Research in Business History*, 31, pp. 29–45.
Nakamura, K. (2000), *Bunmei kaika to Meiji no sumai (Civilization and enlightenment in Meiji era and habitation)* (Tokyo: Rikogakusha).
Nakanishi, T. (1938), 'Hyakkaten tai chusho kourigyo mondai (Issues on department stores vs. small and medium-sized retailer)', in T. Nakanishi (ed.), *Hyakkatenho ni kansuru kenkyu (Investigation on the Department Stores Law)* (Tokyo: Dobunkan).

Nystrom, P. (1919), *The economics of retailing* (New York: The Ronald Press).

Oh, Y. (2016), 'Made in Korea, made for Japan: The Korean product showroom of Mitsukoshi department store in colonial Seoul', *Proceedings of the 75th Annual Conference of the Association for Asian Studies,* pp. 1–7.

Oh, J, and Kahm, H. (2018), 'Selling smiles: Emotional labor and labor-management relations in 1930s Colonial Korean department stores', *Jounal of Korean Studies*, 23 (1), pp. 3–24.

Okawa, K., Takamatsu, N. and Yamamoto, Y. (1974), *Choki keizai tokei: Kokumin shotoku (Historical statistics: National income)* (Tokyo: Toyo Keizai Shinpousha).

Pasdermadjian, H. (1954), *The department store: Its origins, evolution and economics* (London: Newman Books).

Population Census, Statistics Japan. Statistics Bureau, The Ministry of Internal Affairs and Communications, Available at: www.e-stat.go.jp/SG1/estat/List.do?bid=000000090004&cycode=0 (Accessed 9 November 2016).

Shaw, G. (1992), 'The evolution and impact of large-scale retailing in Britain', in J. Benson and G. Shaw (eds.) *The evolution of retail systems, c. 1800–1914* (Leicester: Leicester University Press) 135–165.

Shima, I. (1995), 'Kindai Shanhai ni okeru departgyo no tenkai (The development of department stores in modern Shanghai)', *Keizaigaku Ronso*, 47 (1), pp. 1–61.

Shimanaga, T. (2007), 'Chugoku no hyakkaten niokeru bunkateki kinou no keisei: Seiseiki niokeru Shanhai no hyakkaten ni shoten wo atete (Aspect of Culture of Chinese department stores: Focusing on Initial Stage of the Development in Shanghai)', *Kobe Gakuin Daigaku Keieigaku Ronshu*, 4 (1), pp. 55–66.

Shirokiya (1957), *Shirokiya 300-nenshi (A 300-year history of Shirokiya)* (Tokyo: Shirokiya).

Suzuki, Y. (1980), *Showa shoki no kourisho mondai (Retailers' agenda in early Showa era)* (Tokyo: Nihon Keizai Shinbunsha).

Suminoe (1975), *Suminoe Orimono 60-nenshi (A 60-year history of Suminoe Orimono)* (Osaka: Suminoe Orimono).

Takahashi, Y. (1933), *Hoki no ato (After the sweeping)* (Tokyo: Shuhoen).

Takashimaya (1941), *Takashimaya 100-nenshi (A 100-year history of Takashimaya)* (Kyoto: Takashimaya).

Takashimaya (1968), *Takashimaya 135-nenshi (A 135-year history of Takashimaya)* (Osaka: Takashimaya).

Takashimaya (1982), *Takashimaya 150-nenshi (A 150-year history of Takashimaya)* (Osaka: Takashimaya).

Williams, R. (1982), *Dream worlds: Mass consumption in late nineteenth-century France* (Berkeley/Los Angeles, CA: University of California Press).

Wong, A.Y. (2006), *Parting the mists: Discovering Japan and the rise of national – Style painting in modern China* (Honolulu, HI: Association for Asian Studies and University of Hawaii Press)

Young, J. D. (1998), 'Sun Yatsen and the department store: An aspect of national reconstruction', in K.L. MacPherson (ed.), *Asian department stores* (Honolulu, HI: University of Hawaii Press) 33–46.

Yui, T. (2012), 'Introduction: Traditional commercial business to modern distribution system in Japan', in P. Fridenson and T. Yui (eds.) *Beyond mass distribution: Distribution, market, and consumers (Proceedings of the Japan and French Business History Conference)* (Tokyo: Japan Business History Institute).

Zhao, X. and Belk, R. (2008), 'Advertising consumer culture in 1930s Shanghai: Globalization and localization in Yuefenpan', *Journal of Advertising*, 37 (2), pp. 45–56.

Zhōngxíng (1993), 'Rising Japanese Department Stores in Shanghai' (in Chinese), *Zhonghangyuekan (Bank of China Monthly Review)*, 7 (2), p. 128.

Zola, E. (1928), *Au Bonheur des Dames* (Paris: F. Bernouard).

Zulker, W.A. (1993), *John Wanamaker: King of merchants* (Wayne, PA: Eaglecrest Press).

29
RETAILING IN INDIA
Strategic overview

Nitin Sanghavi

Retailing in India is about capturing the opportunities of a complex consumer class – either you will swim or you will sink

—*(Jawaharlal Nehru, 1st Prime Minister of India, 1948)*

Introduction

India has been a leading nation in International trade since the fourth century B.C., when the Mauryan Emperors unified the subcontinent, building and maintaining roads and transportation hubs for most of the country, forming trade routes and minting coins for trade. During the first to eleventh centuries A.C., India had nearly 33% of world GDP, making it world's largest economy (Menon, 2009). This also attracted various traders from Europe, including the Portuguese, Dutch, French and English, who sought to establish trade status in India, especially from the sixteenth century onwards. Most notable were the English traders, who arrived during the seventeenth century and established various trading missions, starting with the first one in Calcutta (Kolkata) in eastern India and then on to norther and southern parts of India, and finally all the way to up to Cochin (Kochin) – a major centre for spice manufacturing and trading. From the late seventeenth century, the East India Company monopolised English trade with India, waging economic and military warfare to drive out and/or reduce the presence of various other traders and their trading missions, and generating huge flows of trade between India and England. It also exerted political influence over several Kings and Princes throughout India in order to maintain and enhance this trade. This led to massive unrest in several regions of the country, eventually resulting in the British Government taking over The East India Company in 1858 and ruling until 1947. However, during this period, Indian economic performance was mediocre at best: its share of world GDP plummeted from 24.4% in 1700 to 3.6% in 1947 and it has been estimated that the yearly agricultural wage was higher in 1810 than in 1946 in real terms (Nehru, 1948). Although economic performance picked up in the latter part of the nineteenth century, India was still desperately poor in 1946. After India won independence in 1947, it embarked on gradual reforms to rebuild its economy and infrastructure.

Retailing in India has a huge impact on its economy, accounting for over 10% of GDP and around 8% of all employment. According to the latest research (India Retail Report, BCG,

2015), the Indian retail market at present is estimated to be over US$600 billion and one of the top five retail markets in the world by economic value. It is also one of the fastest growing markets in the world with a market size of 1.2 billion people. The Indian retail sector is likely to grow at a compound annual growth rate (CAGR) of 23% to reach US$1 trillion by 2020–1. Modern retailing is expected to grow three times from its present share of 11% at US$66 billion to 21% of the overall retail market reaching US$210 billion by 2020–1, with traditional retailing also growing at 10% per annum. India is also expected to become the world's fastest growing e-commerce market, driven by a rapid increase in the number of Internet users and smart phone owners as well as the arrival of major foreign e-tailors. Indian e-commerce sales are expected to reach US$5 billion by 2020. India's direct selling industry is also expected reach US$3.6 billion by 2020. All these developments are and will continue to make Indian retailing dynamic, exciting and challenging for domestic as well as foreign players.

This chapter aims to set this recent and future growth into a longer historical context, beginning with the early history of Indian retailing, then charting the emergence of modern retail in India and discussing the various factors shaping current and future developments.

The history of Indian retailing

Early years

The origin of retailing in India is as old as the trade itself. Barter was the oldest form of trade. The Indian retailing of lifestyle goods dates back to prehistoric period (Nehru, 1948). Evidence of ornaments, apparel, foot ware, handicrafts, paintings and sculptures were found in the excavations at Mohenjo-Daro and Harappa. In the ancient period, the diversity in clothing and food habits was largely dependent upon the climate, physical features and traditions in respective regions; variables which continue to shape consumption even today. For centuries, most merchandise was sold in the marketplace or by travelling merchants and sales persons. Medieval markets relied on local farmers for supplies of perishable food as the journey time would be too long to bring these goods from greater distances. Customers also travelled regularly to particular places for specialty items traded at market places comprising haats, melas and mandis.

Haats are locations which witness a public gathering of buyers and sellers of perishable and household items at fixed times and fixed locations. These periodic markets remain a major part of the rural market system in India, with an estimated 42,000 haats spread across India. Melas are fairs (sometimes selling commodities and sometimes associated with religious festivals) and almost all states in India have melas for which they are known e.g. Madhya Pradesh for Kumbh Mela. It is estimated that more than 2,500 melas are held commonly in the country lasting between three to seven days, each one having over 600 stalls selling a variety of products. Mandis are permanent markets set up and regulated by state government for the sale of mainly agricultural produce sourced directly from farmers and other food consumables. There are currently around 7,500 mandis spread across India that play a key role in both supplying local communities and providing better prices to farmers. In earlier times, most trade at these locations was through barter, but this gradually moved to exchange of gold and silver coins and then to local currency. The most popular village locations saw their trade increase and exchange became more permanent, allowing them to grow into Mandis or Haats.

It is important to understand Indian geo-demographic as well as consumer segmentation aspects and their impact on the growth and diversity of the retail landscape over the centuries. From earlier times, Indian society was segmented into main and sub religions, casts and sub casts; clothing, food habits and purchasing decisions were largely governed by the prevailing customs and traditions shaped by these structures. Culture was thus the major influence on the purchase decision (Nehru, 1948). Occupation was the basis of casts and sub casts, and birth was the base for religion and sub religion. Society was segmented into four classes: *Kshatriyas* (fighter, warrior), *Brahmin* (teacher, preacher, religious leader), *Vaisyas* (traders, merchants) and *Shudras* (servants, peasants, artisans, landless labourers). Retail activities were mainly carried out by Vaisyas, who then opened small shops to stock them with products customers needed and wanted with the vision of providing convenience at the doorstep of the consumers. Much later, in the nineteenth century, the shops became "mom-and-pop" or *kirana* stores and formed the hub of their local community. These form the basis of the traditional retail sector today. With a small area averaging at around 300 sq. ft., stocking food, packaged grocery and household goods, customised to the needs of the target customers in their catchment area, they are usually operated by the owner and family members and in many cases have been owned by successive generations.

One of the key features of the evolution of retailing in India is how it has been underpinned by huge variations across regions and communities, discussed more fully below. These variations in culture, traditions and customs have been reflected over the centuries in the different retail propositions found across the country. Indeed, significant differences in the taste, preferences and buying habits between consumers and the corresponding retail propositions between the North and the South of India exist even today. The South of India is more traditional and conservative, so there is a large number of shops selling sarees, jewellery and ethnic ware. The North, with its rich heritage of artisans, dating back to Mughal Empire times, has large numbers of retail shops decorative art, home furnishings, furniture and carvings. The colder regions of North India have also developed domestic crafts such as carpet weaving and embroidery work, some of which have grown into very large industries.

Over the last 150 years, Indian retailing has grown significantly, mainly at a local and regional level catering to significant local/regional differences and preferences. This growth was largely driven by trading families which had been going over several generations. Many of them had either a product and/or category specialisation; coupled with a good location, this allowed them to create their own unique selling proposition (USP), image and positioning with personal customer service. The key areas of differentiation were based on range, choice, colour and design, price, quality and service or some combination of these. Some of the notable examples of these trading families are the Nallis and Kumarans of Chennai, specialising in *sarees* and ethnic ware; Sighania with Raymond, the textile brand, and Wadia with Bombay Dying for textile furnishing.

Other important retailers in late nineteenth and early twentieth century India included the Canteen stores, mainly supplying the army and certain classes of government employees and their families with a limited range of food and household items, and the Post Office, which transported huge quantities of the consumer goods across India between 1890 and 1920. During the British Raj in India, several famous specialist British and later European retailers established their stores in larger cities in India. Retailers such as Spencers, the Army and Navy Stores, Trufitt & Hill and Lawrence and Mayo catered mainly to the expatriate community, rulers and wealthy Indians. Some of them have survived and even prospered into the twenty-first century, maintaining their appeal to an elite customer base.

During early 1940s, immediately before independence from Britain, the Public Distribution System (PDS) was established by the government and was run by local government bodies and their appointed agents in several cities and towns. These sold a very limited range of product categories, comprising mainly food, grains, sugar and other essential commodities such as fuel. The idea was to achieve "fair" distribution of these essential items to the masses across India and at "fair" price – a price which was highly subsidised and heavily regulated by the government. The intention was to deal with frequent droughts and shortages, and the scheme was subsequently extended to other cities and towns in the late 1940s. By the year 1946, nearly 780 cities/towns were covered by this system, making it one of the largest retail chains in India. Even after independence, this continued for several decades, only gradually shrinking with the emergence of modern retail stores. Even today, there are still a few hundred of these stores remaining, though most face an uncertain future.

Taking a different approach to supporting local economies, the Khadi and Village Industries Company (KVIC) was set up post-independence to promote hand spun and hand woven cotton textiles (known as Khadi) and thus support hundreds of thousands of farmers/ workers in villages across India. Today, there are more than 7,000 KVIC stores spread all over the country. The co-operative movement was also championed, post-independence, by the government, resulting in the establishment of several stores, known either as Sahakari Bhandar or Apna Bazar, selling a range of food, household and other essential home/family related items. To date, there are over 200 of these stores in existence across India, many of them averaging in size between 1,000 and 5,000 square feet.

Emergence of organised (modern) retail in India

The emergence of the first wave of modern retailing in India can be traced back to when a shopping centre came into existence in the year 1861 in Bombay (Mumbai). Known as The Crawford Market, after the then Municipal Commissioner of Bombay Sir Crawford, it took nearly 7 years to build having a unique design which blended Indian and British architectural elements. In 1874, The Hogg Market (popularly known as New Market) was established in Calcutta (Kolkata). The shopping centre was designed by an East India Railways Company architect R R Banga and was named after the then Municipal Commissioner of Calcutta Sir Stuart Hogg. These markets mainly catered to the expatriate community as well as rich and discerning Indians, stocking specialty items such as imported food items, fruits and vegetables, specialty teas and spices and household items. Even today, the Crawford Market and the New Market continue to be premier shopping areas in Mumbai and Kolkata respectively, frequented by upper and middle class Indian consumers. In early 1900, a similar development was also initiated in Delhi, called Connaught Circle, which again remains an important shopping area, selling imported clothing and household items as well as specialty ethnic ware. These developments were similar to developments in various "colonial cities" around the globe, e.g. Singapore and Santiago, mimicking largely prevalent European styles with a touch of local architecture.

During 1920s, in Madras (Chennai), a lake known as "Long Tank" was drained to create the first "planned" shopping/residential town. It was named Thiagaraya Nagar, popularly known as T-Nagar (city). Many specialty retailers such as Nalli, Kumaran Silk and GRT Jewellers opened their stores in T-Nagar between the late 1920s and the 1940s, selling upmarket sarees, jewellery, occasion ware and accessories to the rich and famous including a small number of expatriates. Today, T-Nagar, a stretch of around 2 kilometres, popularly known as "The Golden Mile", has become India's largest high street by revenue, home to more than fifty large regional and Indian brands. It attracts more than 50,000 shoppers and 75,000 vehicles on a daily basis, swelling to 500,000 shoppers and 150,000 vehicles each weekend. During festivals such as Diwali and Pongal, it draws as many as two million shoppers in a single day.

The second wave of organised retailing can be traced back to the year 1931, when the Bata Shoe Company opened chain stores (mixture of company owned and franchised outlets) in various cities and towns across India. This was quickly followed by DCM and Raymonds, which sold clothing and textiles from their shops across India. The 1940s and 1950s also saw the establishment of a few department stores in metropolitan cities, including "Akbarally" in Mumbai, and Nilgiris and Spencer in Chennai. These were often created by local entrepreneurs based on the inspiration of their visits to European cities (see also Chapter 28). During the late 1970s and 1980s, multi-product, multi-brand retailing also emerged in the largest cities, with key retailers including The Heritage Emporium in Delhi, Benzer and Amarsons in Mumbai and Pantaloons in Chennai. They enjoyed similar success to the department stores and many of them are still in business today.

Useful parallels can be drawn here between the emergence of "modern" retailing in India and the West. The High Street came into existence in Europe between the twelfth and fourteenth centuries, comprising of specialty and variety stores; the department store concept was launched in Europe and the US around 1880 and quickly spread to provincial towns, and chain stores established national coverage within a few short years. In contrast with what can often seem like revolutionary changes, the emergence and spread of modern retailing in twentieth-century India was regionally diverse, with a clear focus on longevity and slow but sustainable growth.

The wind of change

In 1991, the government headed by then Prime Minister P V Narsimha Rao and the finance minister Dr Manmohan Singh, liberalised the country with sweeping changes that formed a catalyst for the emergence of "New India". Most restrictions and archaic laws were done away with. Many entrepreneurs and businesses saw this as a huge opportunity to invest in existing and new businesses/sectors. The Indian IT sector, telecom sector and service sector started growing rapidly. Indian professionals also saw a huge opportunity in various sectors for career development and career enhancement. Increasing urbanisation also resulted in large job growth in metropolitan centres and large cities. All this created a significant opportunity for Indian retailing to grow and modernise since this liberalisation and rapid economic growth has fundamentally changed the country's consumers at all levels. The average household income is rapidly growing and large middle and professional, educated classes have emerged with increased spending power, sophisticated tastes and shopping habits.

In response to this increase in demand, the supply side also started to witness significant growth in retail real estate development in all metropolitan centres and several large urban centres. A number of private and multi-brand outlets also opened in 1990s and in the first decades of the millennium. Notable among these was Shoppers Stop – a department store founded in Mumbai in 1991 by the property company K. Raheja Corporation (see Figure 29.1). This was the first modern department store in India with the selling area of around 30,000 square feet, stocking clothing, textile, foot ware and accessories. Today, Shoppers Stop has become the largest department store chain in India with over eighty stores across India, with a combined retail floor space of nearly 4 million square feet. The company also owns a national chain of hypermarkets called Hypercity. Big Bazar – a multi category retailer, part of the Future group, opened its first store in Mumbai in 2003 selling food and non-food items to lower and middle class citizens. Today, it has become one of the largest retail chains in India with multiple formats selling food and non-food items in nearly 800 stores located not just in the metropolitan centres and big cities, but also in towns across the country. One of the largest businesses conglomerates in India, TATA Sons also entered retailing in 1999 with the creation of the Trent retail group and launched the store brand called Westside. Subsequently, Trent also brought Zara, Tesco and Starbucks into India through a variety of partnership arrangements. At the same

Figure 29.1 Shoppers Stop, Andheri, Mumbai 1991 and 2017

time Landmark – the multibillion-dollar retail group from Dubai – also entered India with its Lifestyle brand.

In the last 10 years, many of India's biggest business conglomerates have entered retailing either as branded/multi branded/supermarkets/hypermarkets or combination of these and spread their operations across India. These include Reliance, one of the largest companies in India with a focus on petroleum refining and distribution as well as telecoms, and Birlas, another very large conglomerate with wide-ranging business interests in textiles and construction. Such organisations have clearly recognised retailing as an important growth area, as have overseas retailers: the first millennium decade saw arrival of several foreign brands such as LVMH, Nike, Tommy Hilfiger, Jack-n-Jones, Diesel and other specialty stores such as Body shop and MAC cosmetics. Shopping malls also started mushrooming all over India during this period. The first, Inorbit Mall, was opened in Mumbai in 2005 with around 250,000 square feet of selling space. Consciously copying western patterns, this was quickly followed by many others, built in a similar style but varying hugely in size, from 30,000 and 300,000 square feet, depending on their location and competitive intensity. By 2008, India had 225 operational malls; 5 years later this had mushroomed to over 600 malls in metropolitan centres and in Tier 1–1 and 2 cities with a total area of over 200 million square feet (RAI, 2013). With the possible exception of China, no other country has seen this type of huge growth and interest in retailing nationally and internationally within the last two decades. Indeed India ranked as one of the most attractive markets to invest in between 2008 and 2011, according to A.T. Kearny Global Retailing Index.

Indian retailing today

Today, India is the world's largest democracy, with a population of more than 1.2 billion and the tenth largest economy in the world, amounting to GDP of US$2 trillion. With an average growth rate of 6–7% per annum in the last 5 years, it is likely to become the third largest economy in the world by 2030 (World Economy – 2012). Indeed, in terms of Purchasing Power Parity (PPP), it has already reached this milestone (World Economic Outlook, 2012). The median age of the population is 25 years, making India one of the youngest countries in the world (RAI, 2013). These young and increasingly educated consumers, with their numbers increasing year on year as more of them join the workforce, like to spend money on shopping and services. Coupled with the easy availability of credit, this has allowed retail spending to grow 8–9% year-on-year in the first decade of this century. Moreover, according to forecasts, Indian consumers are likely to grow four times from their present numbers by 2025 (Gadkari, 2009) with average consumption set to increase threefold between 2010 and 2020, the highest growth being in clothing, fashion, footwear, housing and consumer durables. The key drivers of this growth are income growth (which showed a threefold increase between 2010 and 2020), urbanisation (40% of population living in urban areas by 2020), nuclearisation of households (180 million nuclear households growing at 4% CAGR compared to 2% growth in total population) and a growing workforce (137 million people will be added to the workforce by 2020 bringing the total to 752 million).

With all these attributes, India has emerged as a very attractive market for retail investment. However, political decisions such as recent overnight demonetisation of large currency notes can create significant adverse short-term impacts on retailing. In addition, the level of bureaucracy at central and state government can also make India a complex and a tough country in which to do retail business. Despite recent improvements, India still ranks 130th in the world in terms of ease of doing business (Ease of Doing Business Ranking, World Bank, 2017).

India has the largest number of retail outlets in the world, with more than 12 million outlets compared to around 3.8 million in USA and 300,000 in the UK. Retail is one of the most important sectors of the Indian economy, contributing to 35% of GDP and employing 40 million people directly or indirectly (Rao, 2006). However, neither retail employment nor retail businesses are evenly distributed. Economists categorise Indian cities into four tiers, as Tier 1, Tier 1–1, Tier 2 and Tier 3 cities/towns, based on factors such as infrastructure, skill availability, concentration of population and quality of life (Deloitte, 2013). Whilst these are objective measures, they are the product of centuries of urban development and often reflect the hierarchies established by earlier rulers, including the British Raj, despite refinements put in place following independence.

The Tier 1 cities, sometime called Metro cities, are major metropolitan areas with superior infrastructure, skill availability, concentration of population and the quality of life. Generally, these cities have the biggest modern and luxury retail markets – a position which they have enjoyed since the nineteenth century or earlier. These cities, which include Mumbai, Chennai, New Delhi and Kolkata, have the largest segment of upper middle, upper and rich consumers; they account for around 60% of the total retail real estate space and global consumers. However, as these cities have become saturated with modern retail formats, retailers have started to move to Tier 1–1 cities, which share many of the same characteristics but are smaller and a little behind in the above four parameters. Cities like Hyderabad, Pune, Bangalore, Navi Mumbai, Ahmadabad and Gurgaon have therefore become increasingly important for retailers in terms of driving the growth of their business. Tier 2 and 3 cities are also becoming more important: their collective numbers are significant, they are growing at a faster pace, and their increasingly affluent populations are spending more on goods and services. Places such as Ludhiana, Coimbatore, Nasik and Rajkot are set to become important for the growth of retail businesses over the next 5 years. Below this, there are estimated to be around 400,000 villages across India, many of them with populations of less than 800 inhabitants. Many of the people living in these villages are poor, with very limited spending power. Most of their spending goes on basic essentials such as food and fuel. Yet it is important to remember that, despite significant growth in modern (organised) sector in the last 10 years,

Indian retailing is still dominated by traditional (unorganised) retail. As indicated earlier, there are over 12 million retail outlets operating across India, most of which are Kirana (mom-and-pop) stores and small stores in market towns and villages, with only 4% of them being larger than 500 sq. ft. (RAI, 2012).

As the modern retail sector slowly starts to mature, different players are adopting different strategies in the battle for a share of the consumer's mind and wallet, focusing on key sectors and target customers. Many of these strategies are underpinned by the history of the company, their origins and their owners' vision, underlining the importance of the past for the present. Some players like The Future Group sought the lower and middle-income groups from the beginning. Founded in South India in the late 1990s by the entrepreneur, Kishore Biyani, The Future Group became the largest retailer by value. Biyani first opened a retail store named Pantaloon selling men's clothing at very competitive prices and has continued to focus predominantly on middle and lower income groups with clear value driven propositions, selling fashion, housewares and food through different formats. On the other hand, from its origins, Shoppers Stop Group has targeted rich, upper middle and middle segments with a focus on differentiation, service, choice and ambience. Other players such as Trent are focusing more on fashion and affordability. The Lifestyle Group has chosen a "middle of the road" positioning with something for everyone; the Aditya Birla group is developing and leveraging specialty retailing brand/formats; and the Reliance Group continues to target high future growth and market share potential sectors such as food and groceries, apparel, electronics, footwear and jewellery. There are echoes here of the market differentiation of British department stores in the early twentieth century. However, markets and consumers continue to fragment at a faster pace than previously, due to the arrival of several domestic as well as foreign players with varied and, in many cases, superior propositions targeted at many of the customers of the established retailers. This has resulted in a much higher level of competitive intensity during the last 3 years. In response, many of these established retailers are beginning to refine their positioning as well as exploring unmet wants and desires of their "core" customers in adjoining spaces for future growth and survivals.

Going forward, it is very evident that traditional retailing in India is here to stay, at least for now. It will start to lose market share to modern retail in many sub-sectors, but this will be a slow process, especially in food and grocery. In the foreseeable future, both modern and traditional retail sectors will continue to grow, albeit at different speeds.

Digital revolution – e-commerce

The Indian e-commerce sector commenced around 2010 and is still in its developmental stages, especially when compared with China and the US. E-commerce, at present, accounts for only 4% of the organised retail sector in India compared to 7% in USA and 30% in China. However, the e-commerce market in India is expected to quadruple to US$60–70 billion over the next 5 years, representing CAGR of 50% in goods and 23% in services (Retail Report, BCG, 2016). Current Indian and foreign off-line/online players are making substantial investments in marketing, customer acquisition and infrastructure development/enhancement to retain or build customer numbers and market share. E-commerce and M-Commerce propositions and channels are becoming increasingly attractive to customers because of the superior value, broader choice and selection, and the greater convenience offered by the operators. In this sense, they appeal to the same values and priorities that have long driven consumer choice. In India, the leading categories in e-commerce, measured by transaction share, are devices (35% – mobile, tablet, accessories); fashion (28% – fashion, footwear and accessories); electronics (18% – computers, cameras, electronics and appliances) and books (7%). The online grocery market in India is still undeveloped and has a market share of less than 0.1%, but this is likely to grow as big players such as Amazon (India), Reliance Retail and Future Group have all recently announced ambitious plans to invest and grow their market share faster. This responds both to the position of rival businesses and the huge growth in Internet use expected in India – to 600 million by 2020. This is driven by: increased ownership of smart phones, reaching between 600 and 700 million by 2020; the lower cost of connectivity; and the expanded coverage in Tier 2 and 3 cities and rural areas as a result of significant investment by the key operators (BCG, 2016).

Structure of the Indian retail sector

Indian consumers – a complex and constantly changing picture

> Sometimes, we, a nation of over one billion people, think like a nation of one million people.
>
> —*(A.P.J. Abdul Kalam, former President of India)*

It is important to highlight that every one of India's twenty-eight states is different in terms of climate, language or dialect (there are estimated to be over 2,000 dialects in India) as well as in term of clothing, fashion, style, colour choices, jewellery ornaments, food and eating habits – all developed over several centuries. However, over the last 10 years, with the onset of 'National localisation', some common themes have emerged which are starting to reduce these regional distinctions all over India in terms of food and fashion. For example, North Indian foods are becoming popular in South and vice-a-versa; Southern sarees with their unique designs and strong colour themes are gaining high acceptance across India, and Northern male styles and designs of Kurta (Top) and Salwar (Bottom) have become very popular across western, eastern and middle India. These changes have affected all consumer classes, with varying degree of sophistication in terms of either quality of the material and/or designs. In addition, the Indian film industry has also acted as a catalyst to bring about these common themes, as Bollywood movies are increasingly becoming popular all over India and more and more consumers throughout India are following the fashion trends set by these movies. All these make India an incredible and extraordinarily diverse country in term of culture.

Retailers have also had to consider India's weather related and seasonal variation, e.g. severe winters in parts of North India versus an almost tropical climate in South India, and very hot summers in north and west of India versus heavy summer rain fall in the east and south of India. These variations are not new and it has long been important for retailers to buy and stock appropriate merchandise in their stores, aligning them appropriately with these climatic and seasonal variations. There is a famous example of Zara, the international fashion brand, launching autumn/winter ranges in their Delhi and Mumbai stores simultaneously in 2015. The merchandise sold well in Delhi with its severe winter weather, while it hardly moved in Mumbai's subtropical climate. Domestic as well as foreign retailers in India need to be very mindful of major as well as subtle but significant differences in the shopping attitudes and buying behaviour patterns of Indian consumers in their chosen locations to ensure that the store layout, colour scheme and décor are also suitable to attract or retain their target customers. They also need to be sensitive to cultural perspectives, including the style, length and colour of clothing, pink being less popular in Southern India than in middle India. Brand names can have different meanings in Northern and Southern India, e.g. Hariyali means "pleasant greenness" in several Northern Indian languages but is a personal name in some Southern languages. They also need to take into account family and household structural differences between various casts, religions and types of settlement in urban and rural areas. It remains important for retailers to understand areas of convergences and divergence here to ensure that the right product is offered in the right place, in the right way at the right time.

With economic and demographic growth, as well as a cascading of income to the "bottom of the pyramid" and, more particularly, a growing middle class with a rising household income, the Indian consumer market represents a huge opportunity over the next decade and beyond. There will be an opportunity (and challenges) in every segment of the market from the bottom to the apex of the pyramid. With the increasing penetration of new media, Bollywood films and television series, huge aspirations are building up in consumers for better living conditions and quality of life, leading to increased quantity and quality of consumptions of goods and services. The number of households in the middle will expand, resulting in a threefold increase in the average household income by 2020 from its 2010 level (E&Y retail report 2013). This increase will be seen not just in urban but also in semi-rural areas. This is evident from recent report by E-commerce companies such as Amazon (India) and Flip kart etc. that nearly 45% of their sales growth comes from Tier 2 and 3 cities and towns. These consumers are shopping the same way for similar brands online as the metro and Tier 1–1 cities consumers. However, one consumer behaviour that is cutting across all classes, from luxury to malls, is the search for "value" by looking for lower prices and an overall better value for money. Indian consumers have always been value conscious, but – as in other emerging markets such as China, Brazil and South Africa – consumers are becoming more conscious of this priority, not least because of slowing economic growth and slower job and income growth. This trend is evident in most of the product categories. Indian consumers are increasingly using smart "mixing and matching" of brands and retailers to create a "superior value proposition" for themselves.

Over the last several centuries, as was the case in the West, women in India traditionally took the role of a home maker, looking after and taking care of the family and the elders who were part of the family. There were women entrepreneurs such as Mrs Scindia, who, after the death of her husband in early 1950, took over the reins of the vast business empire and made a great success of it, but this was exceptional. This situation changed significantly in the West during the early twentieth century. In India, over the last 30 years, more and more women have been emerging from their traditional roles and are taking on the dual role of working as well as home-making – a transition which is much more evident in large urban centres than rural areas. The emergence of educated, working women has also fuelled the growth of convenience goods and services. This trend is likely to continue, having a significant impact on types of products, packages, delivery and services consumed by these women and their families. Examples here are the growth of home related services in areas such as meal deliveries, cleaning, personal shoppers, personal life-organisers and wedding planners. At the same time, children are having a growing influence in household and personal decisions as the traditional power-distance between various generations is diminishing. Children (and especially teens and tweens) are increasingly demanding and having their say in shopping, eating out, choice of brands and retailers, holidays, electronics and automobile purchases.

It should be remembered, however, that in India there are multi-tiered consuming classes segmented by socio/economic cultural, religious and location aspects. These traditional divisions in Indian society and consumer practice are being blended with these recent trends noted above to create a complex consumer market. Many of the successful retailers, such as Shoppers Stop, Pantaloon and Westside, have understood these subtle but significant differences and have adjusted their propositions relating to styles, colours, fashionability, etc., and have communicated effectively with customers in the right language using the right phrases. In summary, India has a complex retail market in many different ways. Its multicultural, multilingual and multi-ethnic consumers, with significant geo-demographic differences, make it a unique, interesting and challenging emerging market for all retailers.

Retail channel structure

It is also important to look at the channel structure of Indian retailing. Like Western countries in the nineteenth and early twentieth centuries, the traditional channel structure comprising of manufacturer, distributor/wholesaler and retailer has been the norm in India. However, in common with all emerging economies, this structure is also changing and evolving in India with the blending of modern and traditional retailing. At present, the retail and wholesale channel structure is divided into six key areas (E &Y, 2012): traditional retail, modern retail, online retail, direct retail, cash and carry and wholesaler. There is also a growing franchise sector, but at present it is too small to be classed as a separate sector and is merged into modern retailing.

As discussed earlier, traditional retail is made up of the Kirana (mom-and-pop) stores and small stores. Modern retail has emerged as the most important channel in Metro, Tier 1–1 and Tier 2 cities, the top ten cities contributing around 70% of the organised market. These and other cities from Tier 1–1 and 2 represent significant growth opportunities for both domestic and international retailers now and in the future. Online retail is also a new channel, growing significantly and is typically available in the top seventy-five cities in India. This is now widening to include smaller cities and towns as Internet and smart phones penetration increases. As noted earlier, Indian online retail sales are expected to reach around US$6 billion by 2020 (Retail Report, BCG, 2016), but the development of online retailing requires capital, time and infrastructure investment. Here, major foreign players such as Amazon and Alibaba have entered India and are making substantial investments in infrastructure development and marketing areas with the aim of grabbing greater market share from traditional and modern retailers going forward. Direct retail is an alternative retail channel which uses agents who contact customers directly, either in their homes or via social gatherings such as Kitty Parties to bring customers to their homes to display various items with the intention of making sales. This channel is becoming popular especially in semi-urban and rural areas of India, where the social bonds are much higher than in Metros, where many women are working. It is estimated that this channel has a total distribution base (agents) of around four million people, with total customer numbers at approximately 20 million, focusing mainly on health, well-being, beauty and household categories across India. Another emerging channel is cash and carry, located mainly in the Metros and certain Tier 1–1 cities. This is not strictly retailing as cash and carry outlets are only allowed to serve only trade customers at present, but Walmart of the United States and Metro of Germany are currently using this channel to establish their foothold in the Indian market. It is anticipated that the government may relax rules in the next few years to allow these retailers to sell direct to customers who via membership, as it is the current practice in Europe and the US. Distributors and wholesalers, such as Gokuldas and DCM Shriram, established themselves between the 1930s and the 1950s as the consumer markets started to develop and now dominate the channel structure with an intricate network of main, regional and local distributors and wholesalers. They played a vital role in creating the essential infrastructure, connecting manufacturers and consumers and in the continuity of supplies to small "traditional" retailers throughout India. Even today, these distributors and wholesalers dominate many sub-sectors such as FMCG products and small electrical appliances at regional and local levels. However, their dominance is diminishing with the growth of modern retailers, many of whom are bypassing them and going direct to the manufacturers; but their decline will be a slow and geographically uneven process.

There are four major categories in the Indian retail sector. *Food and grocery*, including fresh and packaged products, is the largest category which accounted for over 80% of the retail market between the 1940s and the 1960s. However, today it accounts for around 60% of the retail market, is dominated by the traditional sector and is very fragmented. The modern sector, especially supermarkets, food stores and hypermarkets are expanding their footprint and gaining greater market share in this category; but most of these are located in Metros and Tier 1–1 cities and account for less than 5% of this category. Although this is likely to increase to around 10% by 2020, the traditional sector will still dominate this category for some years to come. *Apparel and accessories*, including clothes, apparel, textile, footwear and jewellery is the second largest category. Dominated by the wholesalers and independent traditional retailers over the last 70 years, this category has witnessed significant changes within the last 10 years in terms of moving from unorganised to organised sector with modern trade share ranging from 40% for footwear, through 35% for clothing and apparel to 11% for jewellery. *Consumer durables* is the third largest category and include electronics, mobile and telecom, home interior and household items. This category was also dominated by wholesalers, distributors and independent retailers over the last 40 years. It too has witnessed significant changes and also growth over the last 5 years, especially in electronics and electrical products, where modern retailing accounts for 20% of sales. The category is still dominated by independent stores, especially for mobile and telecom segments, but several regional and national chains are slowly increasing their market share. *Health and beauty aids* is the fourth largest category and includes beauty and personal care, eyewear and pharmacy. This category, dominated by distributors, wholesalers and retailers over the last 50 years, has witnessed the most dramatic changes in the channel structures and has also achieved substantial growth within the last 5 years with a five-fold increase in sales (RAI 2016). Although still dominated by independent operators, this category has witnessed the rise of several regional and national chains, many with highly ambitious growth plans for the next 5 years. The other categories are leisure, alcohol, beverages, tobacco and food services, and are still mainly dominated by independent retailers.

Explaining change: the impact of PESTEL factors

A combination of political, economical, social/cultural, technological, environmental and legal (PESTEL) factors have impacted retailers in developed as well as developing countries and continues to do so in terms of retail strategy in terms of opening of the stores; expansion plans, and resource, customer and distribution decisions. In India, government policies and area priority for economical and societal development during both the pre- and post-independence periods have led to many challenges and uncertainties facing domestic as well as foreign retailers at central, state and local levels, with myriad rules and regulations to deal with. One of the most notable of these policies was The Agricultural Produce Marketing Committee Act (APMC), which was brought in during the 1940s and 1950s to safeguard the interests of poor farmers and prevent their exploitation by providing them with fair prices for their goods. However, today the 75-year-old laws are seen by many as stifling the growth of an effective and efficient supply chain from farm to fork, depriving all stakeholders (farmers, manufacturers, retailers and consumers) of cheaper prices, improved quality and continuity of supply of agricultural products, including pulses, grains and fresh produce. At present, a farmer can sell vegetables, fruits, grains, cereals, milk and so on only in specified mandis. They cannot sell directly to a retailer or in far off cities or in another state; nor can they export to foreign countries. Recently, central government has relaxed some of these rules, allowing farmers direct access to the city markets and modern retailers. So far, however, this has proved very inefficient in practice, as state governments are allowed their own interpretation and policing of these revised rules.

During the last decade, environmental regulations have become the biggest cause of delays in the approval of developing malls and retail sites. The regulators at both the central and the state level have been neither able to build capacity nor develop the capability to clear quickly enough several retail project proposals which are either in the pipeline or being put together. Even when approved, the implementation of most of the regulations is patchy and they are not well monitored or policed. There are no restrictions on domestic retail companies in their choice of location for opening any type of retail outlet in any part of the country, as long as the retailer has obtained all necessary permissions and licenses. In contrast, the current Foreign Direct Investment (FDI) rules prevent foreign retailers from entering towns with a population of less than one million. There are also restrictions in opening stores in locations where the state government does not support FDI in retail. This has led to significant challenges for several foreign retailers with their plans to create a pan-India presence. However, the central government recently changed the law to allow foreign retailers to hold a majority stake in single brand retail, thus freeing up the market a little. During the 2017 Spring Budget Session, the government also indicated its willingness to allow majority shareholding by a foreign retailer in multibrand retail in the near future, though with several restrictions. It is important to note that, at present, there is no specific policy that governs the relationship between retailer and supplier and no forum to address any grievances. Therefore, most of these disputes are settled out-of-court rather than going through civil courts, which can take up to 10 years for the judgement.

Retailers all over the world need to get four key areas right for survival and success. They were relevant to retailers one hundred years ago, are relevant today and will remain so for the next thirty years at least. They are popularly referred to as 4Ps of retailing: Proposition, People, Property (Location) and Processes. Examining these 4Ps in the context of Indian retailing, the past and the present, highlights the following issues. *Proposition* includes the merchandise, merchandising, price, service, brand image and positioning. Early Indian entrepreneurs during the nineteenth and twentieth centuries such as Mr Nalli, Mr Kumaran and Mr Wadia knew the importance of this and were able to develop their special blend of these factors to create their own USP and successful retail business. They also understood that, as consumer's needs, wants and desires change, they also need to change accordingly. With the right adaptations at the right time over the years, many of these businesses are thriving today.

People includes all employees: frontline, back-office and management, and all other related key stakeholders such as suppliers and local communities. Again, Indian retail pioneers knew the importance of getting this right; they understood clearly that without people with the right and relevant skills, knowledge, capabilities and competencies at all levels in the retail business, it would not survive and prosper. Many of them developed innovative methods of employee training to ensure that they all created customer empathy and loyalty. They also knew how to initiate, manage and lead when and where it was required. As a result of this, many of these retailers have developed long-lasting and successful businesses. As the impact of technology on retailing intensifies, the people aspect will become even more important for both modern and traditional retailers.

Property. All over the world, retailers know the importance of having the right store in the right place of the right size at the right price. Within the Indian context, during the nineteenth and twentieth centuries, successful retail entrepreneurs understood the critical importance of this aspect and used their intuition in most cases, as today's sophisticated retail location technology was not available, to get this right. Inevitably, mistakes were made. For example, Mr Nalli built a large store in a in a Southern city which had to be shut few years later because it was too far removed from the main retail locus. Relocated just 500m away and on the "right" street, it proved a great success. But the right location comes at a price. The absence of a suitable retail zone policy and with a lack of appropriate infrastructure development since independence by successive central/state governments across cities and towns, has led to very high land prices for the "prime" retail locations and overcrowded high streets not just in Metros, but also in Tier 1–1 and 2 cities and towns.

Processes. One of the key factors for success in retailing is to have appropriate and timely processes and systems in the right places. During first decade of the millennium, this was a major issue for many Indian retailers such as Big Bazar of Future group and More superstores of the Birla retail group, which led to a lot of duplication, the overrun of costs, stock mismanagement and eventually to customer dissatisfaction, as happened with some Western retailers. However, huge advances were made on this front in the west within the last 40 years or so with the help of technology, especially within the last decade. As the modern retailing sector is still evolving in India, many retailers lack the proper and appropriate process map within their organisation. Retailers such as Shoppers Stop, Trent and Lifestyle group are working on these issues by using global benchmarks as standards. In some ways this is helpful because they are starting with "what good looks like" but the reality is that some of these processes and benchmarks need to be adapted to emerging market and country specific scenarios, with their special and unique features. Currently there is a lot of development work going on within the modern retail sector in terms of establishing relevant process maps and accompanying KPI's as well as setting up measurement criteria for these KPI's with the right feedback loops. It is anticipated that this will make Indian retailing more robust and efficient in the medium to long term.

Conclusion

India has been a leading nation in international trade since the fourth century B.C. As a result, retailing in India has a very long and colourful history going back over 2,000 years. During this period it has gone through many changes, mainly as a result of external changes such as PESTEL factors, as well as internal aspects such as resource, distribution, consumer, channel, competitive, people and capability, along with the rise of modern (organised) retailing. The Indian retail market at present is estimated to be over US$600 billion and one of the top five retail markets in the world by economic value. The Indian retail sector is likely to grow at CAGR of over 20% to reach US$1 trillion by 2020–1. Modern retailing is anticipated to grow three times from its present share of 11% at US$66 billion to 21% of the overall retail market, reaching US$210 billion by 2020–1 with traditional retailing also growing at 10% per annum. It is anticipated that in the foreseeable future, both traditional and modern retailing, will co-exist as has been the case in several Asian countries such as Thailand, Malaysia and South Korea. Retailing in India is exciting yet challenging. This is a country where the customer habits change every 100 kilometres and, with citizens speaking more than 2000 dialects, it is not easy to build a successful retail business across the whole of India. The potential on the other hand is huge, with rapidly growing middle class consuming population. Just remember this: retailing in India is like driving a car in India – you need loads of patience, excellent judgement and lots of luck.

References

BCG, *India Retail Report*, 2015.
BCG, *India Retail Report*, 2016.
Deloitte, *India Retail Report*, 2013.

Earnst and Young, *Economic Survey*, 2012.
Earnst and Young, *Road to India's Consumer Markets*, 2013.
Gadkari, Saurabh, *Indian Retail Industry*, 2009.
Menon, Prakash, *Indian Retailing – the Future*, 2009.
Nehru, J., *Personal Essays, American Retail Stores*, 1948.
RAI (Retail Assoication of India), *Trade Briefing Reports*, 2013.
RAI (Retail Assoication of India), *Trade Briefing Reports*, 2016.
Rao, N.C., *Organised Retailing in India*, 2006.
Retailers Association of India (RAI), *Trade Briefing Reports*, 2012.
World Bank, *World Economic Outlook*, 2012.
World Bank, *Ease of Doing Business Ranking*, 2017.

INDEX

Printed in the United States
by Baker & Taylor Publisher Services